Transcultural Nursing
Concepts, Theories, Research & Practices
Second Edition

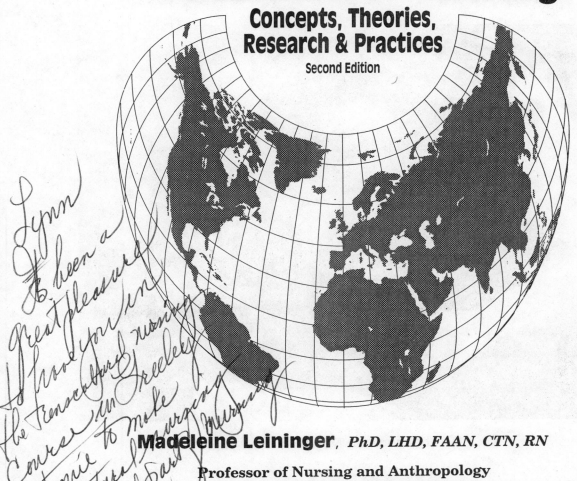

Madeleine Leininger, *PhD, LHD, FAAN, CTN, RN*

Professor of Nursing and Anthropology
Colleges of Nursing and Liberal Arts
Wayne State University, Detroit, MI

Dr. Leininger is the founder of Transcultural
Nursing and leader in Human Care Research.

McGraw-Hill, Inc.
College Custom Series

New York St. Louis San Francisco Auckland Bogotá
Caracas Lisbon London Madrid Mexico Milan Montreal
New Delhi Paris San Juan Singapore Sydney Tokyo Toronto

[Handwritten inscription:] Lynn, It's been a great pleasure to have you in the Transcultural nursing course in Greeley. Continue to make Transcultural Nursing an integral part of nursing. Dr. M. Leininger, July 23, 1998

McGraw-Hill's College Custom Series consists of products that are produced from camera-ready copy. Peer review, class testing, and accuracy are primarily the responsibility of the author(s).

Dr. Leininger in New Guinea

TRANSCULTURAL NURSING
Concepts, Theories, Research & Practices

567890 BKM BKM 909807

ISBN 0-07-037660-3

Editor: Jan Scipio

Printer/Binder: Book-mart Press, Inc.

Transcultural Nursing: Concepts, Theories, Research and Practices

Contents

Foreword

As the world becomes smaller through rapid transportation and communication and increasingly depersonalized through high technology, human beings have come to cherish their cultural identities and cultural differences, and the importance of transcultural nursing has increased. Since the landmark publication of Leininger's original *Transcultural Nursing* book in 1978, some issues have changed, but in a world of increasing complexity one factor remains constant: humankind is made up of cultural beings. Today, more than ever, transcultural knowledge is critical to meeting health needs by understanding the cultural beliefs, values, and norms of individuals and groups. Leininger's textbook continues to be the major source used in preparing nurses in the field of transcultural nursing and in helping nurses and other health professionals use human understanding to work with the culturally different.

As early as 1955, Dr. Leininger began her pioneering efforts to help the nursing profession become aware of the need to consider caring within transcultural contexts. Since that time, a small cadre of nurse-anthropologists and transcultural nurses, in large part educated and guided by Dr. Leininger, has grown to a powerful force. Now her futuristic urgings are at the forefront of clinical and curricular changes in nursing as well as other health fields. In part, these changes are occurring in response to a heightened social awareness of cultural diversity and the implications of health care practice within a cultural context.

Leininger's scholarly work is based on nearly forty years of systematic study and research in nursing and anthropology and it provides a sound conceptual framework for understanding cultural diversity and humanistic nursing care. Leininger thoughtfully presents the rationale, theories, and issues of the emerging field. Having developed a critical theoretical and conceptual base, she illustrates by examples and research findings how her theory can be applied in a caring process. This book contains creative and original research and field studies in transcultural nursing by nurse anthropologists and other nurses to illustrate the scope and the theoretical and practical basis of transcultural nursing. And since nursing has both pure and applied dimension, her work provides the basis for a scientific and humanistic foundation to nursing.

Leininger has provided curricular direction in transcultural nursing for nearly three decades and has given faculty suggested content for teaching and curricular work. The content-curricular and teaching approaches used in this volume should be an asset to schools of nursing as well as to other health and social science disciplines as they develop similar transcultural health programs or courses. She has also provided innovative and enthusiastic ways to teach and mentor undergraduate and graduate students studying transcultural nursing.

As a nurse anthropologist, Leininger presents her own field research beginning with her first study in New Guinea, which is an example of excellent anthropological and nursing research. Transcultural nursing researchers use cultural anthropology and other appropriate research methods including ethnonursing, case studies, ethnographies, participant observation, ethnoscience, and controlled comparison. This book provides a number of original transcultural ethnonursing research studies conducted in the United States and in other cultures. They provide rich illustrative materials to help the reader understand a variety of transcultural nursing problems or conditions as well as the methods and theories used. Much can be gained by studying the research findings to provide new modes of caring for clients or to improve existing practices. Much new content has been added to this second edition. Leininger's theory of Culture Care Diversity and Universality has been further explicated, revealing its usefulness for generating transcultural nursing knowledge and practice modalities worldwide.

Nursing, a scientific and humanistic profession, cannot be ignorant of nor complacent about the urgency of comprehending the cultural needs of humans. Cultural needs are just as real and important as biological and psychological needs. Transcultural nursing built on a scientifically sound and humanistic base is essential to nursing. It provides direction today and in the coming years to meet people's holistic cultural needs. This timely book provides substantial content to help nurses learn about transcultural nursing as an essential and legitimate area of formal study and practice in nursing.

Coincident with the first publication of *Transcultural Nursing* in 1978, the Alma Ata World Health Organization's Declaration of Health for All by the Year 2000 was signed by 150 member states. This declaration promotes health care that is culturally relative to each society. Thus the application of the concepts and theories of transcultural nursing are essential to meet the local as well as global health care needs of human beings worldwide. Nurses and other health care providers are increasingly seeking resources to help them understand cultural diversity within a nursing perspective. This textbook continues to be an essential and outstanding resource to help achieve this goal.

JoAnn Glittenberg, PhD, FAAN, CTN, RN
Professor of Nursing
University of Arizona
Tucson, Arizona
United States of America

Preface

Since the 1950s Madeleine Leininger, a visionary nursing leader, has consistently and persistently predicted that cultural competence in human relationships should be a major concern in nursing and other health related disciplines because societies throughout the world will become increasingly multicultural. As the twenty-first century approaches, it is commonplace to read articles such as, "Multiculturalism may Prove to be the Key Issue of our Epoch", in the November 4, 1992, issue of *The Chronicle of Higher Education*. Media information abounds on cultural diversity. Both lay and professional publications have recently emphasized cultural influences on health and health care. Yet no authors have provided scholars and practitioners with such a sustained and substantive contribution on transcultural theory and research related to health, care, nursing practice, and education, as has Leininger.

The first edition of this book has become an acknowledged classic in the field of transcultural nursing. It is generally cited by nursing authors as an authoritative text even though more recent articles by Leininger are available. This is probably due to the fact that Leininger expertly presented in this text some of the major concepts of transcultural nursing theory, research, practice, and education, separately and in relation to each other, in a way that has been useful to many nurses. This book has been distinguished by the attention Leininger has given to theoretical formulations and research findings related to practice and education. It is comprehensive, futuristic, and accessible to a wide readership.

One of the assets of this second edition is the update and explication of Leininger's Culture Care theory with research findings. The articulation of her theory and research program undergirds all aspects of the book. Culture-specific care related to various cultures is generally presented from a research perspective by authors many of whom have been Leininger's colleagues or students, thus conceptually linking the data from the specific cultures. As nurses and health care institutions become more aware of the need for transcultural approaches to the delivery of health care services, the conceptual linkages that undergird culture-specific care will gain in importance. Leininger's emphasis on learning principles about culture care, gaining skills in doing culturological assessments, and expanding the knowledge base of culture care diversity and universality provides a valuable and essential direction for nurses and other health care providers.

Another clarion call from Leininger relates to ethical and moral issues. Clients should expect that there will be a fit between their health and care values and available health care services. In addition, professionals who believe that people's health care practices are culturally determined, are ethically bound to understand themselves first and then their clients as culture bearers, to learn how to do culturological assessments, and then to provide culturally congruent care.Leininger emphasizes that all people are cultural beings and that health and illness beliefs and values are culturally constituted. Therefore, all nursing contexts need to be understood from the cultural perspectives of the client (as part of a family, group, or community), of the nurse and of the health care institutions involved. Ethical and moral issues in these nursing and health care situations have both universal and culture-specific dimensions that will become more complex as communities become increasingly multicultural.Finally, Leininger calls for nursing to be practiced from a global perspective. That is, nursing and health care situations are influenced by societal factors, i.e., global economics, political affairs, material and human resources, as well as individual factors related to the experience of care givers and recipients, including people who have lived and worked in many parts of the world. Therefore, the integration of transcultural concepts into nursing education, practice and administration is essential. In addition, transcultural nursing specialists are needed to deal with complex issues and proactively help to create culturally competent nursing contexts. Leininger is to be commended for her provocative leadership and for the revision of this most valuable textbook.

Anna Frances Wenger, PhD,FAAN, CTN, RN.
Associate Professor and Director
Transcultural and International Nursing Center
Nell Hodgson Woodruff School of Nursing
Emory University
Atlanta, Georgia
United States of America

Introduction

Since the mid 1950s when transcultural nursing was envisioned as a legitimate and imperative formal area of study and practice for nurses, a major cultural care movement occurred in the United States and in other places in the world. Nursing has gradually changed as nurses take responsibility for developing a body of transcultural nursing knowledge for all aspects of nursing education, research, and practice. This cultural movement is continuing to influence nursing education and practice in significant ways because transcultural nursing provides a comprehensive holistic perspective of individual, family, and community lifeways.

Transcultural nursing has become imperative to know and understand nursing practice. It is the new and challenging frontier of the importance of transcultural nursing not only to provide quality-based nursing practice but also meaningful nursing education. It is important to realize that only four decades ago, transcultural nursing was virtually unknown and of limited interest as a formal area of study and practice. But today it is recognized as essential for nursing to function in an intensely multicultural world. As the founder of the field and the first doctorally prepared professional nurse anthropologist, it has been most encouraging for the author to see transcultural nursing slowly transforming nursing. This transformation process, however, is in process and it will take until nearly the year 2020 to see the benefits in nursing education and practice.

The idea of globalization of transcultural nursing in all areas of the world remains a major challenge in nursing education, research, and practice. This goal can best be realized as more nurses are prepared in transcultural nursing. When this occurs, one can anticipate that nursing practices and education will be reshaped and transformed into different ways of knowing and practicing nursing. Amid this encouraging cultural movement to bring transcultural nursing concepts, principles, and research findings into education, practice and administration, there are still many nurses who have not had the opportunity to learn about transcultural nursing. Without transcultural nursing knowledge and skills, many problems related to cultural conflicts, stresses, and unfavorable imposition practices will occur as nurses assist immigrants, refugees, and other people from many different countries in the world. These nurses will learn how to use transcultural nursing concepts and research-based knowledge to work with individuals and families in different community and institutional contexts. They will discover that people can be misdiagnosed, mismanaged, and misunderstood without transcultural nursing insights. Thus these opportunities and discoveries await nurses who are eager to learn about transcultural nursing and practice it in different contexts.In the future worldwide consumers of health care will expect nurses to be transculturally sensitive and competent to meet their human needs. Nurses with transcultural preparation are in a unique position to achieve this goal and to support quality nursing care practices. For indeed, the quality and excellence of care will be contingent upon how nurses use transcultural knowledge with full awareness of the clients' worldview, social structure factors, environmental context, language, and knowledge of their cultural values and beliefs. So as the profession and discipline of nursing moves into the twenty-first century, nurses prepared in transcultural nursing will be able to serve people with quality nursing care if they are grounded in transcultural nursing knowledge and skills.

The age of transculturalism and the trend of globalization of nursing is essential today. It is, however, one of the most difficult and challenging goals because it requires considerable understanding of cultural patterns and of comparative care and health practices in different environmental living contexts. Globalization necessitates a comparative perspective with the maintenance of holistic care and the prevention of illnesses. From the beginning, transcultural nursing has always emphasized a comparative and holistic perspective. Holism has been a cardinal perspective of anthropology and of transcultural nursing. This comparative holistic view has been important to move nursing beyond the medical model to that of a holistic nursing caring perspective. This holistic perspective must continue to be maintained in nursing with fresh insights and skills from transcultural nursing in order to assist people of diverse cultures in the world. Most importantly, nurses must move beyond an international focus of studying the relationships between two cultures to that of considering several cultures from a transcultural comparative focus. This means expanding one's views and using critical analysis by contrasting insights and knowledge from several Western and non-Western cultures.

The purpose of this second edition of *Transcultural Nursing: Concepts, Theories, and Practices* is to assist nurses to expand significantly their knowledge base about people of different and similar cultures in the world and to discover new ways to assist people by using transcultural nursing concepts, principles, theories, and research knowledge. The book is written for nursing students, staff nurses, and others interested in increasing their knowledge of diverse cultures in the world from a transcultural nursing care perspective. From the study of different cultures, nurses will discover appropriate ways to provide sensitive, competent, and responsible care to individuals, families, and community groups. Nurses will realize the nature, scope, and significance of transcultural nursing as they enter the world of each culture and as they make comparative reflections to guide their actions and decisions in care services.

This book offers a comparative knowledge of about thirty different Western and non-Western cultures. From these comparative data should come a deep appreciation by nurses that nursing care must be flexible and accommodate the needs, values, beliefs, and lifeways of people. Such comparative data will help nurses gain many new insights and approaches to care for people of diverse cultures in meaningful, congruent, and compassionate ways. An open mind and a willingness to learn about different cultures is essential to discovering such new knowledge and to making a meaningful journey through this book. In keeping with one of the major transcultural nursing principles, an open learning attitude and a willingness to be an active learner about new lifeways is essential.

In this book, the author's theory of Culture Care Diversity and Universality, the major theory of transcultural nursing, has served as the framework for studying many of the Western and Eastern cultures. The ethnonursing method has also been used to help nurses discover some of the most subtle, covert, or embedded ideas related to human caring, health, and transcultural values and beliefs. Both the theory and the method provide a major new approach to knowledge discovery and to identify modes of action and decision in providing culture-specific nursing care. Hence a wealth of transcultural nursing knowledge is offered for nurses to reflect upon in their work with people from different places in with world.

The book is organized into five major sections. In Section I the importance and focus of transcultural nursing is presented along with its history, basic concepts and principles. Of particular interest is the evolution of transcultural nursing over the past three decades. An overview of the theory of Culture Care Diversity and Universality is presented with the Sunrise Model to study and guide nursing decisions and actions and how to do culturalogical health care assessments. The role of the transcultural nurse specialist and generalist as important practitioners of nursing worldwide is discussed. In this section the nurse learns about cultural imposition, cultural blindness, ethnocentrism, cultural conflicts and stresses.

In Section II the reader learns about different types of health practices and especially about cultural imposition. Since food is closely linked to care and culture, the reader can discover how foods are used for healing, nurturance, and for special lifecycle ritual ceremonies in different cultures. Most importantly, this section presents ideas on the culture of nursing and hospitals as essential knowledge to guide nursing practices and to understand the dominant features of health institutions. Contrasts with the cultures of nursing and medicine are presented in this section to learn about the particular and comparative features of each health care tribe. Since pain is a pervasive phenomenon of particular interest to nurses, the reader learns about cultural factors influencing pain expressions. Other special topics in this section include transcultural mental health nursing and some ethical, moral, and legal dimensions of transcultural nursing.

In Section III the reader has the opportunity to learn about a number of specific Western and non-Western cultures. The purpose is to increase the nurse's knowledge about ways to provide culture-specific and general nursing care practices. Some of the cultures in this section are the Anglo-Americans, Arab, Philippine, Mexican, Lithuanian, Jewish, Japanese, Polish, Native Americans, New Guineans, Southeastern Asians, and South African. In studying these cultures, the reader discovers the importance of nursing theory to guide nurse's thinking and actions. The importance of the comparative focus is also important to gain a deep appreciation for *why* cultures can be similar or different.

Section IV is focused on teaching transcultural nursing in undergraduate and graduate programs. Suggested objectives, content domains, and learning experiences are offered to assist faculty who are developing courses in transcultural nursing. This section is extremely important as faculty develop meaningful and appropriate courses in transcultural nursing. This is a welcome addition because many faculty are often at a loss to know what might be included in transcultural nursing undergraduate and graduate courses. The author shares here knowledge about the *what*, *how*, and *ways* to teach transcultural nursing in undergraduate and graduate programs drawing upon her three decades of experience in teaching and curriculum leadership endeavors. References and suggested films are provided to guide faculty in curriculum development and in the teaching of transcultural nursing.

In the last section the author focuses on the future of transcultural nursing. The theme of globalization of transcultural nursing is emphasized to move nurses into the twenty-first century to meet worldwide changes in a shrinking world with many different cultures in diverse community contexts. This section is extremely important to planning and preparing for the future with different cultural expectations in education and practice. In sum, this second edition provides a vast wealth of new and important content for the beginner or the nurse experienced in transcultural nursing.

The book builds upon the first edition but takes the readers much further demonstrating the use of theory and research findings to guide nursing practice and education. The author's vast experiences and sustained leadership in establishing and developing transcultural nursing contributes to the credibility of this book. Indeed this book reflects a lifelong career of the author in developing transcultural nursing through active teaching, research, consultation, and practice. This book has been especially prepared to help nurses make transcultural nursing an integral part of all aspects of nursing in order to prevent cultural care problems, frustrations and conflicts in the different arenas in which nurses work. Newcomers and strangers to the health professions will also benefit from this book in their efforts to provide sensitive and therapeutic care practices.

This book is of special significance as it includes the theoretical thinking, research, and professional experiences of transcultural nurse specialists who have been prepared in transcultural nursing and who have been active leaders to make transcultural nursing a reality. These experienced nurse leaders demonstrate the importance of transcultural nursing in all areas of nursing and with cultural care issues and future directions. Thus the book provides authoritative and substantive knowledge to help the reader learn about the growing field of transcultural nursing. It is important for the reader to realize that the first edition of *Transcultural Nursing*, published in 1978, was the first major book focused on the subject of transcultural nursing. This first book has been viewed by many nurses as a publication way ahead of its time, this second edition builds upon some dimensions of the first book, but takes the reader further with new insights of today and into the future to demonstrate the knowledge areas that have been developed since the mid 1970s. The reader will be excited and pleased to note the tremendous growth and major developments in transcultural nursing the past two decades. Those who are just beginning to discover transcultural nursing will find the book, *Nursing and Anthropology*, extremely helpful to see the linkages and differences between nursing and anthropology. Fortunately these publications, (the latter originally published in 1970), and the first edition of *Transcultural Nursing: Concepts, Theory and Practices*, (originally published in 1978), have been reprinted by Greyden Press because they remain of importance as classic knowledge in the field.

Finally, this book signals the author's unique and sustained contribution to the discipline and profession of nursing over the past four decades. Although it has been a great challenge to establish transcultural nursing research, education and practice, it has also been rewarding to see transcultural nursing becoming a reality. It is the author's sincere hope and expectation that future generations of nurses will continue to discover, refine, and advance the important body of transcultural nursing knowledge in all aspects of nursing education and practice. It is also her hope that nurses themselves will grow in their personal insights and professional knowledge as they study transcultural nursing of people and cultures worldwide. With these wishes and expectations the author feels that her lifelong work and dream of 1960 has become a reality. That the culture care needs of *all* people will be met by nurses prepared in transcultural nursing will then have a significant meaning and relevance.

Madeleine Leininger, PhD, LHD, FAAN, CTN, RN.
Author and Founder of Transcultural Nursing
and Leader of Human Care Research and Theory

Dedication and Acknowledgments

This book is dedicated to the many nurse clinicians, scholars, and researchers who have become aware of the importance of transcultural nursing as a legitimate and essential formal area of study and practice to improve people care. It is especially dedicated to the growing cadre of transcultural nursing students and specialists who are the risk-takers, creative thinkers, and innovators who establish and maintain transcultural nursing in clinical, educational, and community contexts. This book is particularly dedicated to transcultural nurse leaders who are doing remarkable work to provide culturally congruent, sensitive, and responsible culturally-based nursing. I am most grateful to these leaders and their many followers.

This book is also dedicated to my brothers and sisters and their families who have always been patient and understanding of me as I pursued and fulfilled my many academic and professional activities.

My special thanks goes to Rebecca Ensign, Dennis Geraghty, Jan Scipio, and Andrea Fritz of McGraw Hill and Greyden Press who recognized the significance of this book and of my lifelong work in transcultural nursing to share ideas with many nurses worldwide. These people have worked in a diligent, conscientious, and relentless way to bring this book to publication, and I am most grateful to all of them. I also appreciate the secretarial support and assistance in preparing this book provided by Delores Jones and Stephanie Purcell, employees of Wayne State University, College of Nursing.

Contributors

Annette Bodnar, MSN, RN.
Doctoral Student
College of Nursing
Wayne State University
Detroit, Michigan
United States of America

Rauda Gelazis, PhD, CTN, RN.
Associate Professor of Nursing
Ursuline College
Pepper Pike, Ohio
United States of America

Beverly Horn, PhD, CTN, RN.
Associate Professor of Nursing
School of Nursing
University of Washington
Seattle, Washington
United States of America

Madeleine Leininger, PhD, LHD, DS, FAAN, CTN, RN.
Professor of Nursing and Anthropology
Colleges of Nursing and Liberal Arts
Wayne State University
Detroit, Michigan
United States of America

Sandra Lobar, PhD, ARNP, RN.
Assistant Professor of Nursing
Child-Rearing Nursing
Undergraduate Program
School of Nursing College of Nursing
Florida International University
North Miami, Florida
United States of America

Linda Luna, PhD, CTN, RN.
Director, Nursing Education and Research
King Faisal Specialist Hospital and Research Center
Riyadh
Kingdom of Saudi Arabia

Grace Mashaba, D. Litt. et Phil, RN.
Professor of Nursing
Department of Nursing Science
University of Zululand
Republic of South Africa

Marilyn McFarland, PhD, CTN, RN.
Former Doctoral Student
College of Nursing
Wayne State University
Detroit, Michigan
United States of America

Marjorie Morgan, PhD, CNM, CTN, RN.
Nurse Practitioner and Instructor
Department of Health and Environmental Control
Myrtle Beach, South Carolina
United States of America

Suzanne Phillips, EdD, ARNP, RN.
Associate Professor of Nursing
Child-Rearing Nursing
Undergraduate Program
School of Nursing
Florida International University
North Miami, Florida
United States of America

Antonia Villarruel, PhD, RN.
Assistant Professor of Nursing
University of Michigan
Ann Arbor, Michigan
United States of America

Canadian Transcultural Nurses learning from West Africans in their environment.

Burnei nursing students with Dr. Leininger.

Gadsup children with Dr. Leininger in their New Guinea village.

Section I:

Transcultural Nursing: Importance, History, Concepts, Theory, and Research

Chapter 1
Transcultural Nursing: Development, Focus, Importance, and Historical Development

Madeleine Leininger, PhD, LHD, FAAN, CTN, RN

Our world continues to change and is bringing people close together in one world with many diverse cultural values, beliefs, and lifeways. With these global cultural changes have come new expectations and challenges in nursing to prepare nurses through transcultural nursing education to become competent, sensitive, and responsible to care for people of diverse cultures in the world.

This statement sets the purpose and focus of this chapter which is to discuss the nature, definition, characteristics, and importance of transcultural nursing and to provide information on the historical development of transcultural nursing. Such content is important to understand the focus of transcultural nursing and how this major field was established and continues to transform nursing education and practice.

During the past three decades, transcultural nursing has become an imperative area of study and practice in nursing which is offering nurses many new insights about human beings, cultures, and new ways to care for people of different cultures. With rapid migration and movement of people worldwide, transcultural nursing has become of central importance to nurses and all health care providers. Providing health care to immigrants, refugees, minorities (or underrepresented groups) from virtually every place in the world challenges health personnel in ways never before experienced. Moreover, with current emphasis on health care reform and new configurations of health care services, cultures and subcultures require special attention as they will be driving the health care systems and practices of tomorrow. Transcultural nursing has become the area of study and practice concerned with human conditions, lifestyle patterns, wellness modes, health prevention, health maintenance, and how to provide sensitive, holistic, and competent nursing care to cultural groups. Most importantly, transcultural nursing must become the arching framework for all areas of nursing in order to provide culturally relevant, responsible, and meaningful care to people of different cultures.

In the twenty-first century all nurses will need to be prepared in transcultural nursing with substantive knowledge and skills to function in an intense multicultural world. Nurses will be expected to understand the purpose, knowledge domains, essential skills, and the historical evolution of transcultural nursing. These trends are already becoming evident, but the process of educating nurses in transcultural nursing will need to be markedly increased to meet multicultural clients' needs worldwide. It is indeed most encouraging today that many nursing students are aware of these needs and are shaping the future of nursing by taking courses and developing skills in transcultural nursing. It is this new generation of nurses who will make transcultural nursing a reality through their education, research, and practice. There are a number of transcultural nursing generalists and specialists who are exemplars practicing in hospitals, homes, agencies, and in special community health services. The nurses are transforming nursing education into culturally responsible and competent care practices. Many of these nurses are demonstrating how to meet consumer needs and expectations in line with clients' culture care values, beliefs, and lifeways. These nurses are advocates to change nursing practices and to make transcultural nursing one of the most stimulating, relevant, and imperative areas of study and practice. They also recognize that all areas of nursing are essentially transcultural in nature, as nurses work with clients, staff, and people of many different cultures. But let us turn to understanding the full nature, characteristics, and importance of transcultural nursing in a rapidly changing world.

Definition, Nature, Rationale, and Importance of Transcultural Nursing

Transcultural nursing is a formal area of study and practice in nursing focused upon comparative holistic cultural care, health, and illness patterns of individuals and groups with respect to differences and similarities in cultural values, beliefs, and practices with the goal to provide culturally congruent, sensitive, and competent nursing care to people of diverse cultures.[1,2] Several important ideas which need to be considered are included in this definition. *First*, transcultural nursing is a legitimate and important societal need requiring nurses to respond appropriately to the needs of people who have different cultural values and lifeways. The legitimacy of transcultural nursing comes from the fact that people have a human right and expectation to have their cultural values, beliefs, and needs met by nurses as professional caregivers.

Culture is an integral and essential aspect of being human, and the culture care aspects cannot be overlooked or neglected. More and more nurses are realizing that they must be knowledgeable about cultures and ready to assist people of different cultures in meaningful and beneficial ways. Transcultural nursing has, therefore, become the area of study to learn about different cultures and subcultures and to develop competencies to meet the cultural lifeways, beliefs, and values of those they serve. In the early history of modern nursing, the cultural care dimensions of nursing were not recognized, studied, or emphasized, largely because of the lack of specific educational programs, and research-specific practices in transcultural nursing.[3] But since the early 1960s, transcultural nursing has been established as an essential and legitimate area of study and practice with the goal of preparing professional nurses to be competent and knowledgeable in ways to assist people whose cultural lifeways, beliefs, and practices are different or similar.

Second, transcultural nursing as a formal area of study and practice in nursing means that in order for nurses to know, understand, and practice transcultural nursing, they need to be educated by taking courses and/or completing programs of study focused specifically on transcultural nursing. The need for educational preparation is evident because both cultures and care are complex phenomena. Nurses need to acquire in-depth knowledge about cultures and care so that they understand and are taught specific needs of individuals and groups. Most importantly, nursing students need to learn from faculty who themselves have been educationally prepared in this area. These faculty can today draw upon a body of knowledge that has been established by transcultural nurse researchers, theorists, and practitioners. This development in nursing has occurred only in the last three decades but has now become imperative knowledge for professional practices. The teaching with thoughtful transmission of transcultural nursing continues to occur and supports the idea that all nurses must study transcultural nursing to insure nursing competencies with many clients of strange or unknown cultures.

Today a new generation of nursing students is practicing transcultural nursing care. They are helping others to see that transcultural nursing is knowledge that is providing new insights and some entirely different approaches to caring for people. Thus, formal courses with qualified faculty are essential to understand and feel reasonably confident to help people.

Today nurses can no longer remain ignorant of culture care factors. Nor should they rely on their common sense, prejudices, or "being kind" to assure competencies with the culturally different. Moreover, biases and prejudices about different cultures usually lead to serious problems, many frustrations, and non-therapeutic nursing care practices. Transcultural nursing faculty are expected to help students examine their cultural biases, myths, and inaccurate knowledge about cultures. But the faculty must also help nursing students to value the strengths and assets of cultures and to use the knowledge as they serve people. Learning about the ways cultures mainstream health, humanistic care, and healing modes is essential to advance nursing.

Transcultural faculty are responsible for helping students develop creative ways to make appropriate decisions and actions so that clients of specific cultures will benefit from nursing care services. Currently, many nursing students in transcultural nursing courses discover that transcultural knowledge and understandings of people can greatly change the client's recovery and treatment outcomes. Learning how to care for people whom they may have never heard about, or known vaguely in their lives requires a lot of thought and guidance from faculty. Moreover, as nursing students reexamine their own family beliefs and prejudices they often realize the cultural biases in their family.

It is always encouraging to hear nursing students tell faculty how much transcultural nursing has expanded their worldview to a much larger perspective. It is most rewarding to see nursing students discover some such entirely new ideas about nursing, about themselves and their own culture, and the world in which they live.

Transcultural nursing education and concomitant practices generally provide a deep appreciation of human cultures, their histories, and how cultural values and beliefs can be so powerful and meaningful to people. As nursing students learn about different cultures, their shared excitement is communicated to others as one of the most interesting, complex, challenging, and meaningful aspects of nursing. Students often ask nursing faculty *why* the nursing profession failed to develop formal courses and programs in transcultural nursing until very recently, as these courses and experiences are equally as important as anatomy, physiobiology, microbiology, chemistry, and other courses students take in nursing. When students discover the power and pervasiveness of transcultural nursing they become alarmed at how much there is to learn, and yet there is usually still too limited time to study transcultural nursing. Moreover, students realize that a little cultural knowledge can be dangerous, and so they must learn through qualified faculty to gain as much accurate holding knowledge as possible about a culture in order to be sensitive and responsible to clients.

Being prepared in transcultural nursing means not only learning about diverse cultures that have lived and survived in many different environments over time, but also studying one's own cultural values, beliefs and needs. Learning about one's own culture and other cultures generally gives an entirely new perspective. It also helps to appreciate diverse human cultures and the importance of nurses incorporating such culture care knowledge into their many practices. Courses in anthropology can be valuable to gain in-depth knowledge of a specific culture, but transcultural nursing faculty are responsible for making the nursing viewpoint come forth. Moreover, as students learn transcultural nursing, they are daily and nightly challenged as they work in hospitals, clinics, and alternative community health programs or services to demonstrate cultures that are similar to or different from others. They learn how to do holistic culturological assessments so that nursing care values and needs are known and used. Lastly, the students assess their own cultural values and beliefs about the people as they learn about complex, diverse, and similar aspects of cultures and their environmental settings.

In the process of studying transcultural nursing, one often discovers many different views about caring, health, and well-being, as well as what may lead to illnesses, disabilities, and death in a culture. How specific cultures have maintained health or prevented illnesses is often knowledge new to nursing students. In addition, students often discover there are many hidden "cultural secrets" about human care and health in cultures. Many of these secrets are embedded in their religion, kinship, politics, language expressions, and other areas which require faculty mentors to discover these secrets with student and cultural representatives. Uncovering these embedded ideas and largely unknown areas in nursing from a comparative viewpoint is a major reason why transcultural nursing is a formal area of study for nurses.

Today there are many nurses who have visited, observed, or worked in a "foreign" culture but often without transcultural nursing or anthropology preparation. As a consequence, one often finds that these nurses fail to understand *why* cultures believe what they do and *why* certain values are upheld. Many of these nurses have had an interesting or terrible experience depending largely upon what they know about a culture before going into the "foreign" group. Some nurses have many misinterpretations and need to examine their prejudices, biases, or misinformation about a culture. Nurses conducting tours or professional seminars in countries generally have not had a preparation course in transcultural nursing or anthropology and these well-intentioned tour nurses may pose problems and generate knowledge deficits and biases that hinder accurate knowledge of a culture. *Being in a culture does not necessarily mean one knows or understands the culture.* Transcultural nursing, therefore, remains an essential and major area of formal and legitimate study in nursing. It will continue to grow in importance to nurses worldwide as we live and function in an intense multicultural world.

A *third* aspect of the definition of transcultural nursing is a focus on comparative differences (diversities) and similarities (commonalities) among cultures in relation to humanistic care, health, wellness, and illness patterns, beliefs, and values. Transcultural nursing uses a *comparative focus* to study patterns, expressions, values, and lifeways within and between cultures. Understanding how and why cultures are alike or different with respect to care, health, and illness can provide new insights to improve or advance nursing care practices. Discovering *why* cultures have different patterns of caring and different ways they keep well or become ill is central to transcultural nursing. Comparative cultural interpretations and explanations of human care expressions and meanings usually give new perspectives to traditional nursing or medical views.

In studying transcultural nursing, students learn how to do comparative culture care assessments with individuals, families, groups, institutions, and communities. From these assessments, come cultural variations, identifying similarities and differences within and between cultures. Both subtle and gross differences among Western and non-Western peoples in beliefs, values, and lifeways are important to identify. Such findings help nurses to realize that while one must treat individuals or groups as human beings, still there are differences to respond to in nursing. Indeed, the tendency to treat "all just alike" is challenged with comparative cultural data. This concept, which I call the *all alike syndrome*, gradually becomes understanding *cultural variations*. For example, children from Russia tend to respond quite differently to pain compared to most Anglo-American children or adults. Different cultures such as Russia have taught their children to view pain differently than Americans. The Russian children have learned to accept in a stoic way rather than crying or taking a lot of attention to get pain relief. Different cultural learnings are often persistent over time, and are not forgotten when children or adults seek health care services from nurses and other health care providers.

Using a comparative focus as a dominant feature of transcultural nursing keeps the nurse alert to the idea of cultural variations and helps the nurse recognize different expressions and needs of people. It is the comparative cultural knowledge that helps nurses to become sensitive, compassionate, and competent care practitioners as they promote healing and well-being or help clients face death. The transcultural comparative focus challenges nursing students, staff nurses, educators, researchers, consultants, and administrators to value and respond appropriately to subtle and gross cultural differences or similarities in their practices. Moreover, it is an awareness of these comparative features that leads many clients to want quality human care services in which their special cultural meanings, body gestures, symbols, values, use of space, perceptions of events, and historical or current life experiences are recognized and responded to in transcultural nursing. Learning how to use comparative transcultural knowledge, values, and beliefs in skillful and sensitive ways with individuals and groups becomes a major challenge for nurses. Discovering ways to respect commonalities as shared human attributes and differences as unique features of people becomes paramount in transcultural nursing practices. Transcultural nurses learn ways to remain constantly alert to comparative expressions and to make appropriate decisions relative to differences and similarities.

The idea of culture-specific care comes from identifying comparative care practices that need to fit or are tailor-made to help clients. For example, many cultures will vary in the United States by their daily life expectations regarding what they like to eat, their daily life routines, and how they wish to be cared for when they become ill or disabled. The sensitive and knowledgeable nurse identifies these subtleties and provides culture-specific care to these clients. It was in the early 1960s that I coined the term "*culture specific care*" which is now being used rather extensively in nursing. The idea is to make nursing care practices and decisions fit closely to the client's needs or lifeways so that the client benefits from the outcome as helpful and meaningful care. Culture-specific care is tailor-making the client's specific needs to be congruent with daily lifeways, so that recovery and health maintenance will be sustained over time, especially when the client returns home. For without culture-specific care, clients often show signs of slow recovery, non-compliance, uncooperative behavior, and other unfavorable signs. Often negative client views of nursing care can be identified when the nursing care fails to fit with the client's lifeways, needs, and expectations. Hence, the concept of culture-specific care makes a great difference in client outcomes and is a central to the author's theory of Culture Care in which the goal is to provide culturally congruent and beneficial nursing care. The theory will be discussed in another chapter.

The *fourth* major feature in the definition of transcultural nursing is that culture is central to know, understand, and serve people. The concept of culture comes from the discipline of anthropology and has long been studied by anthropologists.[4] Although there are many definitions of *culture*, I have defined *culture as the learned and shared beliefs, values, and lifeways of a designated or particular group which are generally transmitted intergenerationally and influence one's thinking and action modes*. Culture is, indeed, a powerful influence on the way people view the world, make decisions, and determine their actions. Culture is known as the blueprint to guide human lifeways and to predict patterns of behavior. Culture is so much an integral part of one's ways of living, doing, and making decisions that one seldom pauses to recognize it as culture. Many hidden or built-in directives for rules of behavior, beliefs, and moral-ethical decisions are related to culture. Such cultural influences not only guide, for example, what one chooses to eat, but also the way one prepares and eats the food. Culture influences how one lives, talks, and one's daily and nightly patterns of behavior in different life situations. Culture pervades one's way of being in the world and how one lives and survives in the world. I deliberately chose culture to be a central aspect of transcultural nursing to understand nursing care lifeways, actions, and decision modes. Transcultural nurses are therefore studying the cultural lifeways, values, and beliefs of human groups in order to understand ways to care for or with people, but also to find ways to help people keep well, avoid illnesses and accidents, and live in lifeways as healthy as possible.

In further consideration of the phenomenon of culture, transcultural nurses realize that all *human beings are born, live, marry (or remain single), stay well, become ill, and die within a cultural frame of reference which embodies one's specific and common shared values, beliefs, and action modes*. The pervasiveness of culture as a learned way of living is often difficult to understand fully unless one studies particular cultures over time, for such practices require nurses to identify specific cultural values, beliefs, and patterns of living. Verbal and non-verbal communication are part of cultural patterns, as are ways of doing or not doing something. Discovering and becoming fully aware of the patterns of culture care communication and of different patterns of being in the world are central to transcultural nursing. Becoming aware of the *why* of cultural actions and decisions of self and others and understanding why certain choices are made and others rejected are part of becoming transculturally astute in nursing care practices. Most individuals or groups are free to choose and act in desired ways, but still there are powerful cultural values and beliefs that influence such choices and actions. For example, if a client or family is non-compliant with the expectations of health personnel, negative feedback occurs. Moreover, individuals deviant of cultural practices in a community context are often viewed as "problem," "peculiar," "strange," and sometimes "mentally or physically ill" persons. In transcultural nursing, one recognizes that such variations in cultural expressions and values frequently occur and may be viewed as expected rules of behavior. Identifying and understanding aspects of culture and their influences on human expressions are essential learning in transcultural nursing and in developing appropriate nursing action modes. These cultural dimensions can be learned in transcultural nursing under the guidance of experts who have been prepared in the field.

The *fifth* major theme in the definition of transcultural nursing is the focus upon human care and caring expressions, values, patterns, symbols, and practices of cultures. In establishing transcultural nursing, and as the founder (the first graduate professional nurse anthropologist) I held that human care was central to nursing and needed to be rigorously studied to advance nursing knowledge.[5,6,7] This was in the late 1940s when I, as a direct caregiver to clients, realized the importance of care and that care, like culture, had been greatly neglected in nursing education, research and practice. However, nurses would speak of care and of giving nursing care without an awareness or meaning to the clients.[8] The systematic study of care had not been forthcoming nor was care recognized as central to nursing outcome practices. I began to study care and made it central to transcultural nursing.

In spearheading the movement to get nurses to study *care* and *caring* as the central and dominant features of nursing, I defined *care as the learned and transmitted cultural ways of assisting, supporting, enabling, and helping people whether ill, well, or dying, with compassion and respect in order to improve a human condition or help an individual face death or disability*.[9] Moreover, I declared that *caring is nursing, caring is the heart and soul of nursing, caring is power, caring is healing, and caring is the distinctive feature which makes nursing what it is or should be as a profession and discipline*.[10,11] I contended that caring decisions, actions, and ethical behavior would make a major difference as to whether individuals stay well, become ill, or die, and that cultural factors influence caring attitudes and practices. How cultures express human care when well or ill was largely unknown until a cadre of transcultural nurses began to study human care in the early 1960s. Studying care differences and similarities between caregivers and care receivers in different cultures was an intriguing idea and an untapped area of knowledge in the 1950s and 1960s. But to establish *care as the central, dominant, and unique aspect of nursing* and to do so from a transcultural nursing perspective were the major developments required to advance nursing as a discipline and profession. This focus was a great challenge for all nurses, but especially transcultural nurses, in making care essential and central to nursing. Indeed, the nursing profession had failed to study human care systematically let alone transcultural nursing care phenomena until a cadre of scholars led this challenge nearly four decades ago.

In an effort to make culture care the dominant and central focus of transcultural nursing, the theory of Culture Care Diversity and Universality was established.[12] This brought care and culture together as a new construct and direction in nursing. For with the discovery of culture care knowledge and understandings, new insights and meaningful nursing decisions and actions were forthcoming. Such culturally-based nursing care was held as essential to guide nurses in working with people of many different cultures. The Culture Care theory was, therefore, established to encourage nurses to ascertain what was universal (or common) and what was diverse about human care in wellness, illness, disability, and other human conditions. Culture care knowledge became central to transcultural nursing and the substantive base explain, interpret, and predict nursing care practices. Other aspects and outcomes in the use of the theory are explained in later chapters.

The above definition of transcultural nursing, therefore, had many important dimensions to establish an entirely new direction for the discipline and profession of nursing. The definition of transcultural nursing has guided many nurses since the 1960s and is leading nurses to many new discoveries with different ways to help people of different cultures. Transcultural nursing has become a formal and essential area of study and practice and is continuing to transform nursing as nurses function in a highly multicultural world.

Purpose and Goal of Transcultural Nursing

The *purpose* of *transcultural nursing remains to discover and establish a body of knowledge and skills focused on transcultural care, health (or well-being), and illness in order to assist nurses giving culturally competent, safe, and congruent care to people of diverse cultures worldwide.*[13] Transcultural nursing continues to meet a critical and long-standing need in nursing to care for people of diverse or similar cultures worldwide. This formal area of study and practice is generating culture-specific knowledge for different ways of knowing, understanding, and assisting people whose lifeways are culturally known and expressed. The *goal* of transcultural nursing, however, is ultimately to provide *nursing care that fits with or has beneficial meanings* and health outcomes to people of different or similar cultural backgrounds. Hence, both the *purpose* of discovering new knowledge and the *goal* of using the transcultural nursing knowledge are important to understand.

Transcultural nursing will continue to transform nursing as it shifts nurses' ways of practicing from a largely monocultural focus to a transcultural focus. Helping nurses to value this major shift in focus has been difficult because of past cultural values in nursing. However, many clients seeking nursing and health services are eager to see their values, beliefs, and lifeways understood and acted upon by nurses prepared in transcultural nursing. This major new breakthrough in nursing began in the mid 1950s and continues to be a goal of transcultural nursing. Stimulating nurses to learn about different cultures and care practices and to use this knowledge in all aspects and areas of nursing remains a goal yet to be fully realized. Shifting nurses from uniculturalism to multiculturalism was frightening to many nurses, largely because they had no previous knowledge to make the shift in perspective. Nurses also had to understand people from beyond their physical and psychological needs to the cultural aspects.

Transcultural nurse researchers, however, had the greatest challenge in establishing a body of transcultural nursing knowledge so that nurses could use such knowledge in teaching, research, and clinical practices. From the beginning I held that an explicit body of transcultural nursing research-based knowledge was essential to support the new are of study and practice. This position seemed logical and essential to support an entirely new area in nursing. Nursing desperately needed a much broader or holistic perspective and to reconsider its members' firm dependency on medical symptoms, diseases, and treatment modes that characterized mid twentieth century nursing.

In those early days, I envisioned that many nurses in the future would need transcultural knowledge. Nurses working in foreign cultures now and in the future should not impose their practices and beliefs onto people of other cultures. This could only lead to major transcultural conflicts and clashes that would not be beneficial to clients and staff. I called this practice *cultural imposition* which I viewed as one of the most serious problems in nursing. For one culture to impose its cultural values, beliefs, standards, techniques, and practices on another culture seemed unethical. However, such practices could be observed in any nursing context and were limitedly questioned or indeed unrecognized. How to reduce or avoid cultural imposition practices and establish client-family centered nursing practices had yet to be realized in the mid 1950s and 1960s. Transforming nursing in these areas and in other aspects was critical to make nursing a relevant profession and sound discipline. Unquestionably, the day had arrived for transcultural nursing to be the arching and central focus of all areas of nursing.

The Scope, Rationale of, and Factors Influencing Transcultural Nursing

Several worldwide factors gave rise to establishing transcultural nursing as a specialty and general area for research, education, and practice. These influencing factors of transcultural nursing will be identified first and then briefly discussed.

1. A marked increase in the migration of people worldwide with the need for differential health care services.
2. A rise in multicultural identities with people expecting that their cultural beliefs, values, and lifeways would be respected and understood.
3. An increase in high technology with diverse impact on people whose health values and beliefs were different from mainstream cultures.
4. A predicted increase in signs of cultural conflicts, clashes, and violence impacting on health care as more cultures interacted with each other.
5. An increase of people traveling and working in many different places in the world.
6. An increase in legal suits due to cultural conflict, negligence, ignorance, and imposition practices in health care.
7. A rise in feminism and gender issues with new demands on health care systems to meet women's and children's needs and concerns.
8. An increased demand for community and culturally based health care services in diverse environmental living contexts.

The *first* and major factor that had a great influence on the establishment of *transcultural nursing was the current and projected marked increase in the migration of people within and between countries worldwide.* Never before in the history of humankind had there been so many people moving about in virtually every place in the world. While migrations have always been characteristic of human beings, the number and frequency of migrations have increased considerably since World War II.[14] This trend was largely related to new technologies in air and ground transportation and in electronic modes of communication as well as a strong desire of people to see or work in other places in the world. The major forces of wars, feuds, political oppression, famine with severe economic conditions, and other factors led people to migrate to different countries. For example, the collapse of the Iron Curtain in Eastern Europe and the fall of Communism in the Soviet Union around 1989, the Persian Gulf War in the Middle East, and political oppression in China and South Africa greatly influenced worldwide migrations. For many years, refugees have also been a major part of migrations due mainly to war and political/economic oppression. The United States has been a country of many immigrants with Europeans, Vietnamese, Old Order Amish, Russians, Jews, Chinese, Japanese, and many others. The tremendous diversity of cultures that *never "melted"* but retained their cultural identities was ground for transcultural nursing and transcultural health services.

Also contributing to the many waves of immigrants were climatic factors such as droughts, floods, earthquakes and hurricanes. Terrorists and drug distributors also influenced worldwide migrations. Such migrations have largely occurred for protection, economic gains, freedom, justice, and new opportunities. With such large and small migrations, nurses and health care providers have encountered strangers from many different cultures and geographic places in the world. Many nurses have experienced cultural shock and have been overwhelmed at how best to communicate with, help, and understand these strangers in therapeutic ways. These nurses have reported how helpless, frustrated, and concerned they were about working with cultural strangers who failed to comply or cooperate with them. The need for transcultural nursing has been apparent since the beginning of nursing, but the idea of preparing nurses through formal education was never developed until I took steps in this direction in the mid 1950s.

The *second* influencing factor on transcultural nursing was a *marked rise in multicultural identities with an expectation that nurses and other health personnel would respect and respond appropriately to people of different cultures or subcultures*. This trend had also been clearly evident in nursing worldwide as people increased their multicultural identities. With multicultural identities came the need to study and understand diverse cultures. This was a need in nursing as nurses had a societal mandate to give care to people in one's country. Nurses as direct caregivers needed to understand, respect, and provide culturally sensitive and competent care.

Unquestionably, most clients of different cultures expected to be respected, valued, and understood as a cultural and basic human right. For example, in the United States, there has been a rise in demands for cultural identity and human rights with Mexican Americans, African Americans, Native Americans, Amish, and many other cultures. Both minorities or underrepresented cultures expect nurses to respect them and especially their cultural beliefs and values and not to suppress such cultural identity factors. Some cultures have struggled for years to gain full cultural identity and respect, such as those in post-communistic countries or in many countries where political oppression has occurred. Respecting the rights of all humans as cultural beings has led to the increased demand for all health personnel to learn and practice transcultural health care. There has, however, been a greater demand for professional nurses because of their first contact with clients in clinics, hospitals, nursing homes, health services, or other agencies and their continuous care services. Indeed, nurses are usually the first to talk with clients when the latter enter a health care service, and they remain with them often for an extended time span. If nurses fail to understand these cultural representatives, they also have difficulty caring for them. If the nurse cannot communicate with clients due to language barriers, one finds that nurses tend to avoid these clients, which is usually interpreted as a non-caring behavior and action mode. Transcultural nursing was clearly needed to relate effectively to clients of diverse cultures and to work in therapeutic and ongoing professional relationships with them.

The *third* factor and *rationale for transcultural nursing has been the marked increase in high technology with its impact on clients' health care.* Since World War II, there was a significant increase in the use of high technologies in many Western health care systems, such as in the United States, Japan, Korea, Canada, Europe, and other countries. This trend has led to new diagnostics and different ways to serve people. But with this trend have come conflicts with clients of different cultures, because some of these high technologies have been very frightening and counter to their beliefs. Some cultural representatives have never been in a hospital and others have never been exposed to high technology tests and treatments and to largely electronically run environments. For example, high-tech diagnostic tools, high powered x-ray machines, CAT scans, and ultrasound equipment can be frightening to Native Americans, Eskimos, Old Order Amish, and many others. Accordingly, some clients have refused treatments, been non-compliant, or have left the hospital because they fear such modern equipment even with the best of explanations. Some view such powerful equipment and treatments as evil forces or spirits that can cause more harm than benefits. Nurses and other health personnel with a unicultural focus realize that holding to one's own ethnocentric cultural beliefs, experiences and values can greatly influence negative outcomes. Moreover the diagnosis, treatment and nursing care practices may not fit the client's beliefs or expectations. Clients from diverse cultures have had significant problems with some high technologies in the hospital, home, and clinics. The day has come for health personnel to be knowledgeable and sensitive to differences among cultures to gain client and family cooperation and to prevent depersonalization, cultural conflicts, and negative client outcomes.

Today some of our high-tech centered environments with noisy equipment or with flashing lights and monitors can be disturbing to clients who expect a quiet and restful hospital setting. The continuous clicking of machines at the bedside and use of a variety of mechanical measurement instruments by staff can make some clients anxious. Some clients feel at times like another machine or object in the bed to be measured and observed. Hence feelings of being devalued, depersonalized, or disrespected can occur with cultural groups. High-tech procedures and treatment modes may be counter-indicated with some cultures due to religious beliefs, such as the Old Order Amish who generally avoid high technologies. Jehovah's Witnesses, as well as many traditional Koreans, may refuse blood transfusions and high-tech treatments because of their religious beliefs. In contrast, many middle and upper class Euro-Americans, Japanese, Canadians, and Australians and other cultural groups may greatly value high-tech equipment as essential in care and treatments. High technology treatments can also interfere with daily cultural practices. For example, Islamic Muslim clients are expected to say prayers five times a day and they become concerned when treatments and nursing care practices interfere with their expected prayer times. In general with the increase in the use of high technologies, different cultures continue to have diverse responses to them which has necessitated that all health personnel, but especially nurses, know and understand the transcultural health practices of different cultures in the world.

The *fourth* reason why transcultural nursing has been greatly needed is in *relation to worldwide signs of cultural conflicts, clashes, and violence among many cultures in a rapidly changing world in which nurses need to understand these matters in client care practices.* Cultural clashes, violence, and the killing of hundreds of people in the world call for greater understanding among and between cultures and especially emergency care practices. The terrible violence in Rwanda, South Africa, Bosnia, the Middle East and many other places has been some of the worst in the history of humankind. Such international conflicts and killings have increased and call for a greater understanding of the ethnohistorical reasons for such violence. Nurses and other health personnel who are expected to care for the victims of violence toward women, children, and other groups need to understand some of the clients' views of such violence and how best to help them in a compassionate and understanding way.

Cultural factors related to family, urban, and rural violence are still limitedly understood among health personnel, and yet nurses are called upon to serve those in distress. A holistic transcultural approach is needed which includes kinship, ties, religious values, political conflicts, and many other factors along with the biophysical factors related to violence. How violence and intercultural conflicts become expressed is often based on intergenerational breaking of normative cultural values and practices. An understanding of transcultural patterns of potential violence within and between cultural groups could help nurses to work with cultures to prevent serious acts of violence and to promote health caring behaviors.[15] With nurses caring for victims of violence, one needs to consider using positive cultural taboos, values, and strategies to facilitate non-violent culture care patterns. Moreover, nurses need in-depth study of specific cultures to develop prevention modes, understand cultural violence and to protect themselves. How nurses handle open violence is usually culturally defined and expressed, and this is of interest to transcultural nurses.

The *fifth* factor influencing *transcultural nursing has been a marked increase in the number of nurses traveling and working in different places in the world.* Today and even more in the future, nurses will continue to travel and be employed in many different countries. Transcultural *holding knowledge* becomes essential as one moves into and remains in a culture. For without even basic holding or reflective knowledge of a culture, serious problems can occur with the people and with the stranger nurse. Nurses need to know and understand some of the basic characteristics of a culture *before* moving or taking a position in these countries. While many nurses are traveling to different geographical locations out of curiosity, today more nurses are seeking employment in other countries. As nurses work and live in these countries, they need to understand the cultural groups they are serving. They need to be ready to demonstrate the use of transcultural knowledge and competency skills with clients to improve care. Being able to assess care patterns and health values of families and groups requires substantive knowledge by the nurse of different cultures in order to ensure accurate appraisals. Biophysical and emotional assessments also need to be culturally grounded in order to be accurate and understood.

If the nurse is employed in a foreign country, major language problems can occur. These language problems often result in misdiagnosis and misunderstanding of the individual, family, institution, or community. In addition, nurses often experience cultural conflicts and stresses with many differences between nursing and health personnel of a different culture in the hospital or health agency context. Transcultural nursing knowledge is imperative to prepare nurses to work in unknown or foreign countries. Nurses with holding knowledge can reflect on what they observe and can often make sense with such holding cultural knowledge. Moreover, the nurse can identify patterns of behavior as well as ways to prevent negative consequences with clients and staff. With the use of transcultural nursing concepts, principles, and skills, the nurse in a foreign culture will have more confidence and ways to deal with cultural differences.

If nurses are working in one's home culture, they can be handicapped as there usually are many cultural groups living in a local community. And since most cultures are very complex, the nurse will need not only holding knowledge, but help from expert mentors and teachers in transcultural nursing. Short orientation or on the job sessions will usually be inadequate and superficial. For example, it is difficult for Western nurses to function in the Kingdom of Saudi Arabia if only short orientations are provided before they leave the country. Transcultural nursing knowledge of the Arab culture is much needed when Western nurses work in Saudi Arabia. They also need to speak the Arabic language if they are to be employed or remain in the country over a span of time to insure their own protection and professional effectiveness. This principle needs to be recognized in other cultures for, indeed, a host of problems can occur when nurses do not understand the culture, language, and ethnohistory. This is especially true if values are in sharp contrast with the foreign culture. Understanding sex role differences, religious beliefs, daily dress expectations, and kinship expectations are most difficult for nurses unless they are prepared in transcultural nursing. Some nurses may be returned to their homeland when cultural rules are violated or when political circumstances arise.

The *sixth* factor influencing the need for *transcultural nursing is related to a growing number of legal suits against nurses and other health personnel because of cultural negligence, ignorance, and imposition practices in health care practices.* While this factor may be difficult for some nurses to realize who have never studied cultures or transcultural nursing, it is a major and growing problem that will be more evident in the twenty-first century.

We are living in a litigious world and the cultural rights, values, and norms of people must be upheld by nurses and other health personnel or legal action will occur. As cultures use their legal and political standards, they know when their rights are violated. For example, in the United States, lawyers are being called to assist in legal suits when members of specific cultures contend their rights have been violated, neglected, or misused. Different cultures use different legal sanctions and often they have different ways to interpret and resolve cultural conflicts. More and more immigrants are suing health personnel and institutions if their rights are violated. For example, a Laotian family found their cultural values were violated in the United States when a nurse reported a child with a small cleft palate, and insisted that the parents have the child undergo surgery to correct the defect. The Laotian family, however, strongly refused the surgery for cultural-religious reasons. The large extended Laotian family raised funds to sue the hospital for doing the surgery "for the sake of the child" according to Western norms. The Laotians held that the hospital violated their cultural beliefs because the cleft palate was viewed as a sign of a blessing and gift from God and was a minor defect which the family was handling well. Similarly, a Jehovah's Witness family refused blood transfusions for their child and challenged legal forces. Other cultures with similar expectations have become assertive of their cultural rights. They may sue the nurse and other health personnel when they find their cultural norms have been violated.

In the next century, one can predict there will be many legal suits due to transcultural conflicts, cultural negligence practices or cultural ignorance, and cultural conflicts between clients and health care providers from different cultures. Professional nurses will need transcultural nursing knowledge and skills to function competently with many different cultures and to understand what constitutes legal offense or negligence with different cultures. Cultural defense cases will increase and nurses will also be called to testify regarding their observations, experiences, and practices regarding cultural negligence and other violations. Accordingly, lawyers, physicians, social workers, and others will need to be prepared in transcultural Western and non-Western cultural and legal knowledge to function and survive in an increasingly legal-oriented society.

A *seventh* factor influencing *transcultural nursing is the rise in feminism with women taking active leadership roles and monitoring their health care rights and needs and those of their children.* In recent decades the feminist cultural movement has markedly increased with women asserting their rights and taking leadership positions. Moreover, women are empowering themselves and expressing their intuitive and valuable healing insights gained from years of experience.[16] Today, women constitute more than fifty percent of the work force outside of the home in most Western cultures.[17] As a consequence, women's societal roles are becoming recognized and many feminists' rights, values, interests, and beliefs in the health care arena are asserted in culturally specific ways. Cultural conflicts between health personnel, especially with male physicians, are evident as women express their personal, family, and other needs. Nurses need to be especially cognizant of these trends and listen to women and children as they often know what is best and what works for them in their home and other cultural settings. Moreover, changes in traditional female work roles in different cultures in relation to child and health care, domestic health work roles, employment, economic situations, and other factors greatly influence the health and well-being of women and children. Nurses are in a unique position to observe these changes and desires and to support women and children in their health care needs.

Transcultural nursing and anthropological knowledge is also greatly needed to understand and help women and children deal with cultural stresses, violence, and gender role problems. Nurses will need to understand cultural differences in women and men's roles in non-Western and Western cultures in order to work therapeutically with them in different cultural contexts. Indeed, women have always been healers and carers in diverse cultures, but their role has not always been understood as well as men's roles. Wenger's research with the Old Order Amish and Leininger's work with the Gadsup are good examples to recognize gender role differences in cultures.[18,19] Differences in cultural values of what women believe constitutes good and acceptable family lifeways and what roles men are expected to take in home care, religious services, public offices, and other roles are areas for nurses to study as they change over time. And since nurses are expected to help in family counseling, psychiatric therapies, infant and elder care, and in many other aspects of the life span, nurses are extremely handicapped without transcultural knowledge to guide their actions and decisions with clients. Nurses with *cultural holding knowledge* are in the best position to reflect upon and understand men and women and how to respond appropriately to life span needs. Moreover, *cultural holding knowledge* is essential to prevent unnecessary cultural clashes and conflicts between nurse and family members or individuals. Such knowledge is also essential to understand traditional and changing roles of genders in different cultures, especially with women and children as they move forward to assume new and different leadership roles in health care and their well-being maintenance goals. Likewise, nurses need to understand their own gender roles, cultural values, beliefs, and lifestyle changes in order to avoid cultural imposition and conflicts with clients. Hence, transcultural gender knowledge with competency skills is a significant and important reason for establishing transcultural nursing. For without the knowledge area, women and children will be thwarted in their health care goals.

The *eighth* factor giving rise to the *importance of transcultural nursing is the growing trend in the Western world to care for clients in diverse community-based health care contexts.* With the current health care reform movement today and well into the twenty-first century, health care will be *community-based and driven by consumers of diverse and similar cultures*. Cultures and subcultures living in different community contexts will drive or greatly influence professional health care reforms and services. This is difficult to envision, but it is already occurring in some places. These cultures will seek new alternative kinds of health care services that are in accord with their cultural needs and values.

Of equal importance will be a major shift from hospital care services to home or community health services worldwide. Only special acute and long-term health care specialty services will remain principally in hospitals or special health institutions. Some of these health care changes are already occurring in the United States, Canada, Japan, Australia, Europe, and in other countries with the health transformation and reform movement.[20,21] Health care services must become more accessible and less costly to people worldwide.[22] And since clients are being sent home early from Western hospitals due largely to cost factors, nurses will be serving people in their home environment, on their "turf", and will be required to know the client's cultural rules and practices. This is a significant shift in who controls and what will be culturally acceptable in the home or community. Diverse rural and urban communities will challenge the most astute health personnel as new services evolve.

Unquestionably, community based cultural care practices will markedly increase, which will require nurses and other health personnel to understand cultural lifeways and practices. Home health care with many new kinds of culturally-based alternative health services will be established in Western cultures and some of those established in non-Western cultures will be reaffirmed. Caring for many people in these kinds of services will require nurses to be knowledgeable about different cultures and the different communities in which the people live in order to provide effective services. As cultural consumers take charge of their values and lifeways on their home turf, they will expect nurses to anticipate and understand their home care needs, language, and cultural beliefs and practices. Transcultural nursing knowledge will be in great demand as health personnel scurry to learn about specific cultures and as cultural consumers regulate what they want and how they want the services provided, especially in Western cultures. Already with the influx of immigrants almost overnight in some communities, health personnel are seeking transcultural nurse experts as consultants to help with cultural shock experiences. Co-participant health care is emerging as nurses learn from cultures how best to develop community health care programs.

In many non-Western cultures such as rural Africa, Asia, and Papua New Guinea, it is important for nurses to realize that most nursing care has already been grounded and maintained in the village, home, or community for many years. Nurses in these countries generally know how to work with large extended families for home deliveries, emergency care, and for family care practices. Many members of non-Western cultures generally go to a Western-like hospital or clinic if it is available, if they can afford the services and are treated with respect. Western nurses who have always functioned in large urban hospitals often experience culture shock when they visit in non-Western rural community contexts. These Western primary care practitioners, public health nurses, and midwives tend to feel handicapped about village or rural lifeways as the values and practices are quite different from urban Western ones. The need for transcultural nursing knowledge becomes essential for these Western nurses to provide appropriate rural care that fits with the people's lifeways.

For the above reasons, transcultural nursing is currently in great demand, and the demand will steadily increase for nursing and all health professions by the year 2000. Granted, there are other factors that will impact on the need for transcultural nursing knowledge and competencies, but the pendulum has swung to transculturalism health care based on cultures as consumers. In considering other reasons for transcultural nursing worldwide, these questions are relevant:

1. What factors are limiting nurses from getting to know the cultural health care needs of people in different communities and ways to change health services for them?
2. Why are clients from different cultures relying so much on their generic or folk health care practices, especially when professional services are accessible to them?

3. How can cultures best communicate their health care needs or conditions to health personnel?
4. Why are some health problems, illnesses, or deaths more prevalent in some cultures and environments than others?
5. How can nurses in the future be effective and successful with rural and urban clients' needs?
6. How can nurses enter and remain in a culture to learn from the people how they deal with their own concerns?
7. How can nurses shift to study the assets of cultures rather than negative or illness accounts?

Most importantly, nurses will need transcultural nursing knowledge to understand their own cultural values, beliefs, and behavior patterns in order to become a competent and effective nurse in rural and urban contexts, but especially in non-Western cultures. Understanding one's own cultural heritage becomes the critical basis for working with cultures in different environmental contexts. For unless nurses understand their own culture, there will be a tendency for cultural biases, prejudices, and inappropriate actions to occur as they assist others in the community or hospital. Today more than ever before, nurses are realizing why transcultural nursing has become imperative and will be in even greater demand in the next century.

Scope of Transcultural Nursing

In developing transcultural nursing as a new are of study and practice, it is important to grasp the scope of the field. Transcultural nursing is worldwide in scope both in study and in practice, for the field explicitly includes *all* cultures and subcultures in the world. This global scope was perceived early by the founder as essential because professional nurses are expected to serve people wherever they exist and wherever nurses function. This broad scope of transcultural nursing helps nurses realize the scope of nursing focused on many cultures and subcultures in the world. The scope of transcultural nursing goes beyond local, regional, and national views to that of worldwide nursing or the global view of nursing.

In conceptualizing the scope of transcultural nursing in the mid 1950s, I held that the nursing profession must maintain a global perspective so that nurses could be prepared to serve individuals, families, groups, institutions, communities, cultures, subcultures, and societies worldwide. Figure 1.1 depicts the broad perspective of transcultural nursing from the individual to global societies.

Scope of Transcultural Nursing: Individual to Global Focus

Transcultural nursing is broad in scope and yet it can be particularistic as nurses function with individuals, families, institutions, and communities in different world societies. Often nurses will be working with individuals and groups, but within institutions and in rural or urban communities. For example, a Canadian nurse often works with Cree Native American families in a large rural geographic area. This nurse has to remain aware of the larger community in which the Cree natives live, which is sometimes near other cultures such as the Mennonites. Nurses may be working with Southeast Asians which includes Vietnamese, Cambodians, Laotians, and others in the geographic area. These Asian cultures have both similar and different cultural values and lifeways. Sometimes nurses will be functioning in a major country or in regions or provinces and are responsible for overseeing the nursing care practices in the region or whole country such as the Chief Ministers of Nursing in Canada, Japan, England, Ireland, Sweden, Finland, Australia, Africa, South America, the Caribbean, or Oceania. Thus the scope of transcultural nursing may vary from individual culture care to large regions or nations in which the nurse is held responsible for understanding and planning for the cultural needs of the people. In the United States, the Indian Health Service is a national focus for services to Native Americans. Some transcultural nurses have been functioning with Middle Eastern cultures of which there may be twenty-two different Arabic speaking cultures in the geographic area. Wherever nurses function, transcultural nursing becomes important because nursing is a service to provide the best care possible to people.

Transcultural nursing has become recognized by many nurses as global nursing and as the arching framework for all areas of nursing. This idea will become even more recognized in the future as nurses become prepared in transcultural nursing

Figure 1.1: Scope of Transcultural Nursing: Individual to Global Focus

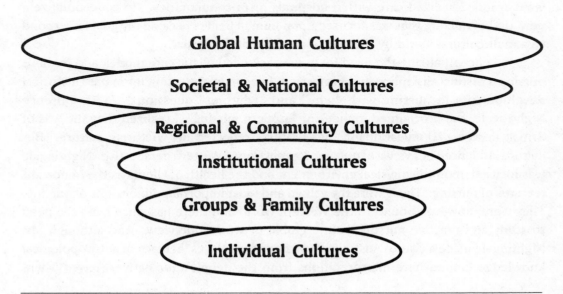

and realize that all aspects of nursing must be transculturally based in practice, education, research, and consultation. Indeed every situation, experience, and activity is a transcultural experience between individuals, groups, family members, nations, communities, and institutions. This is why I contend that transcultural nursing is the arching framework for nursing and in the *future nursing* should be *called transcultural nursing to accurately depict its scope and responsibilities.* This global perspective with new commitments is only gradually being recognized because of the past focus on individual and group care and because of nursing's narrow educational perspective that failed to teach about different and similar cultures in the world. When transcultural nursing becomes globally conceptualized, then transcultural nursing as nursing will be realized and proclaimed.

Conceptualization of Transcultural Nursing

In the late 1950s, as I conceptualized transcultural nursing as an entirely new and distinct area of study and practice, my anthropological insights made me realize that the world was becoming one in which all humans would soon be known to one another by the end of this century. Anthropologists had this global perspective from their broad interest in humans and their research over the past century. Nursing had a much narrower and restricted view of the world and its people, hence the need to expand nursing's view and value the anthropological perspective with transcultural nursing. Moreover nursing was far too centered on medical values and practices. To change nursing's image of its scope and nature was problematic and seemed impossible initially. The world was rapidly changing and yet nurses were focused on a narrow view of individualized care within hospitals or in communities. To conceptualize a new kind of nursing that was focused upon human beings became my goal to respond to a multicultural world by the end of the twentieth century.

In conceptualizing the need for a new vision, a holistic care model, and to make nursing a distinct discipline and profession, I began by reflecting upon past historical developments in nursing with "why" and "why not" questions. With Florence Nightingale, the proclaimed founder of "modern nursing", I realized that she was of British descent. Unquestionably, her writings reflected her Victorian culture. Her culture influenced her views of nursing, largely from a Western perspective. Nightingale was focused upon the physical environment and the health of clients as the important features of nursing. These were the valued and most important dimensions of nursing. They were, however, bound to the Western world and there has since been the need to study and practice nursing from a global or worldwide view. And although Ms. Nightingale made a visit to Australia and a few other places, her lack of anthropological knowledge limited here interpretations from the people's (or native) views. There were a few other early nurses who traveled abroad, such as Linda Richards, before and after the war. Those nurses were eager to share their ideas but often by imposing their values, beliefs, and standards on the host cultures. This often occurs between stronger and dominant cultures. Clearly the comparative knowledge base through research and education about different cultures was the missing dimension. None of these early leaders had conceptualized or envisioned transcultural nursing as a distinct and future area of importance to advance the nursing profession or discipline worldwide. Moreover, the term transcultural nursing was not coined until I brought it forth in the mid 1950s. So while some today are proclaiming that Ms. Nightingale started transcultural nursing, this point cannot be substantiated as the field and ideas were not known and established until I launched the area in the early 1960s. Moreover there were no concepts, principles, models, or specific practices, and the term transcultural nursing was unknown in the early days of nursing. It was, however, encouraging that the International Council of Nursing (ICN) had been established as a nursing organization in the late nineteenth century with the goal of improving professional nursing standards and practices among nurse leaders largely in Western countries. This organization gave no emphasis to the formal preparation of nurses to serve in different cultures.

At the same time I had begun to demonstrate the need for transcultural nursing, a few anthropologists such as Brown, Saunder, and McGregor began to share their views with nurses and nursing organizations in order to incorporate social science ideas into nursing education.[23,24,25] I never had discussions with Brown or McGregor, so they did *not* influence my independent work to establish the field of transcultural nursing. Their focus was primarily on social organizations and general anthropological ideas. Later I found many of their ideas were largely medically oriented and dealt with medical diseases, illnesses, and dysfunctional social institutions, thus Brown and McGregor did not influence my thinking to develop the field of transcultural nursing. I had met Saunders and he was concerned about ways to help nurses communicate with Mexican Americans. I saw the need for transcultural nursing through his research and experiences. Most of these anthropologists' ideas fit with medical anthropology which was developed as a subfield of anthropology in the late 1960s, nearly a decade after transcultural nursing was conceptualized and launched.

One of the important groups that made me fully aware of the need for transcultural nursing were nurses in overseas military and mission work. When these nurses heard about transcultural nursing as an area of studying and practice in nursing, they were extremely pleased and encouraged me to proceed quickly as they felt extremely handicapped in working with people of different cultures without understanding them. Their many stories of difficult nursing situations hastened my efforts considerably.

None of these mission and military nurses I visited with in the 1950s had any preparation in anthropology in their nursing program. Later nurses in the service and in missionary work wrote to me about how pleased they were about transcultural nursing. They wrote, "This is what we desperately needed to understand clients and staff from many places in the world." They shared many stories about how baffled they were about the patient's beliefs, behaviors, and practices while in service. They also spoke of their feelings of frustration, anger, and helplessness as they tried to work with patients and staff in different cultures. These letters and accounts were reassuring to support the urgent need for transcultural nursing to help nurses functioning in important service roles.

In further envisioning the new field, I chose the term "transcultural nursing" rather than "medical anthropology" or "cross-cultural nursing" because I wanted to differentiate this area of study that had different foci from anthropology, and yet there were useful ideas from anthropology.[26] It was clear to me that anthropology was a discipline in its own right with a focus on the study of people in diverse geographic places and over a very long time span. In contrast, I envisioned transcultural nursing as different from anthropology in that the focus was on *comparative human care, health, and well-being in different environmental contexts and cultures*. Moreover, I did not want transcultural nursing to focus primarily on medical symptoms, diseases, and illnesses as anthropologists tended to be emphasizing in the late 1960s. Hence, *transcultural nursing was not the same as anthropology nor the same as applied or medical anthropology*.

The term "transcultural nursing" was, therefore, chosen to refer to the development and use of a *distinct body of transcultural nursing care and health knowledge generated through theories, research, and clinical practices*. While the term "cross-cultural" had been used by anthropology, the term "transcultural" had not been used to convey nursing knowledge. I wanted nurses to develop transcultural nursing knowledge that could be distinct from anthropology, medicine, and other disciplines because nursing needed an identifiable and distinct discipline focus in the 1950s and 1960s. I further held that transcultural nursing was *not* the same as international nursing because inter (Latin prefix) refers to "between some thing or place"; whereas transcultural nursing was viewed as a much broader concept in scope and purpose as it cut across many cultures with a comparative perspective. It was this comparative viewpoint focused on human care and health that I postulated would advance nursing's knowledge and bring forth some entirely new or distinct perspectives to guide nurses' thinking and actions. International nursing, which denoted between two cultures, has a limited view and still today is viewed as exchanges between two nations in which some nations are not cultures. Hence the importance of the term "transcultural nursing" as a means to bring forth a distinct body of nursing knowledge, which has been occurring in the last four decades.

In developing transcultural nursing, I envisioned that all nurses would need to be prepared with comparative knowledge so they could function effectively with many people of different cultures who would pervade our nursing and health care world. I wanted nurses to move away from the dominant and traditional medical model emphases that had long been held by nursing to a different cultural health maintenance, illness prevention, and to draw upon the caring modes of different cultures in order to practice nursing in *culturally specific ways*. I, therefore, coined the terms "culture-specific care" and ":" in the 1960s to be future goals of nursing and transcultural nursing. These concepts are already conveying different goals and approaches to nurse practitioners. Nurses in the twenty-first century will be deeply involved in providing competent, sensitive, and responsible care to individuals, families, and cultures from different communities and institutions. If this goal were not realized, then one would predict many serious cultural care and health problems because cultures would expect health practices to be culturally relevant to them. These ideas were important as I envisioned and spearheaded a new area of study and practice. However, major problems were recognized related to shifting nursing from a largely unicultural to a transcultural perspective and changing nursing to focus more on comparative care than the traditional pathology models of medicine. I had no specific solutions but I held that with a rapidly changing world, nursing could benefit from and be at the forefront with knowledge and skills in transcultural nursing.

Discovering and Using Transcultural Nursing Knowledge: Model and Process

In developing transcultural nursing knowledge, it was important to envision how nurses could discover and use such knowledge. In Figure 1.2, three phases are presented to show the process in developing and using transcultural nursing as a dynamic process.

Phases of Transcultural Nursing Knowledge and Uses

In Figure 1.2, there are three phases to consider as nurses become aware of transcultural nursing, develop knowledge, and use it. In Phase I, nurses become aware of and sensitive to the idea of cultural differences and similarities among people of diverse cultures. They identify overt and subtle cues related to cultural behavior and want to understand what they see, hear, or experience. Cultural awareness is an important first step, but nurses must try to explain and know more about what they have observed or experienced. Generally awareness precedes sensitivity to the meanings of expressions.

In Phase II, nurses use theories to explain, interpret, and predict the phenomena they observe or have become aware of in clinical or diverse settings. Nurses choose a theory such as Culture Care Diversity and Universality and examine the theory using appropriate research methods. In this process, nurses can use existing transcultural knowledge to study transcultural nursing phenomena. Discovering cultural and health expressions, patterns, and meanings of clients through theory and research with detailed observations and participant experiences with clients can lead to new knowledge to guide nursing practices.

Figure 1.2: Phases of Transcultural Nursing Knowledge and Uses

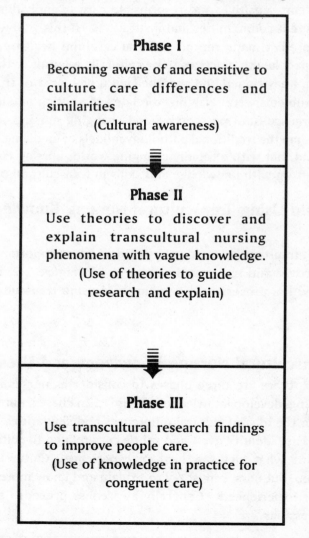

Phase I

Becoming aware of and sensitive to culture care differences and similarities
(Cultural awareness)

Phase II

Use theories to discover and explain transcultural nursing phenomena with vague knowledge.
(Use of theories to guide research and explain)

Phase III

Use transcultural research findings to improve people care.
(Use of knowledge in practice for congruent care)

In Phase III, nurses discover new knowledge or reaffirm existing knowledge and are ready to use this transcultural knowledge to improve client care. This phase requires the creative application of findings to different situations, documenting and observing what difference the knowledge makes in people care. The creative thinking and action to apply knowledge discovered or to use existing knowledge is highly rewarding, for it gives confidence to nurses. It also starts nurses on another cycle of going from Phase I through Phase III as an ongoing process in transcultural nursing. It is these three phases that help nurses to advance transcultural knowledge from a beginning awareness to use of theories, and then, the use of the research findings to people care situations or needs.

Overview of Transcultural Nursing Practice

In this section, a general overview of transcultural nursing practice is presented primarily with a focus on the United State of America, but with a few glimpses from other countries. In the last chapters further information on this topic is offered.

During the past two decades, it has been encouraging to see transcultural nurse specialists and generalists functioning in hospitals, clinics, and community health agencies within and outside the United States. The need for transcultural nurses has been keenly felt primarily with many new immigrants and refugees seeking health services in addition to the presence of "cultural strangers" in health settings. The transcultural generalist has been able to identify common needs and concerns of cultural strangers while the transcultural specialist offers in-depth guidance to nursing staff working with clients of particular cultures such as the Vietnamese client. The roles of these transcultural nurses are presented in more detail in Chapter 5. The transcultural nurse specialists and generalists have been extremely valuable in dealing with strange client behaviors toward the staff in hospital and community nursing settings. This nurse also deals with interstaff tensions, conflicts, and problems related to cultural differences. There are still far too few of these transculturally prepared nurses, so that the full impact has yet to be realized in health services. Far more transcultural nurses are needed to deal with many intercultural clashes and conflicts between client and staff in most places in the world. In fact, transcultural nurses are essentially new or unknown in some countries despite obvious needs. Unquestionably the demand exists for transcultural nurses, but there are still too few prepared for this important and complex role.

During the past three decades, transcultural nurse researchers have been studying nursing problems and client stresses in hospitals, nursing homes, health agencies, and in communities. These research studies have revealed a number of transcultural nurse-client-staff areas of conflict or stresses which have influenced the quality of nursing care to clients. For example, Spangler's research on intercultural conflicts and value differences between Philippine and Anglo-Americans is an excellent example of a transcultural nursing research in a general hospital in the United States.[27] A number of other transcultural nursing studies have identified cultural conflicts between nurse-client and other staff in hospitals and other settings. Transcultural problems related to client-staff misunderstandings, non-compliance, and resistive behaviors that have influenced client satisfaction and recovery have also been identified. Several community-based studies of specific cultures have lead to new insights to provide culturally congruent care. Most of these research studies of different cultures are presented in subsequent chapters for the reader to study.

Unquestionably, one can identify an increase in transcultural health problems with increased migration and mobility of people in all countries. Already these problems are influencing client recovery as well as staff satisfaction in the work situation. One of the greatest problems is the language barrier with nurses unable to communicate adequately with clients who speak a different language than the nurse. In Europe and Canada, more nurses can speak several languages than in the United States. Some hospitals and agencies have translators, but problems remain with many of these lay translators.

Still another area of major concern is the avoidance of clients who speak, dress, and act differently in health care systems. Many avoidance problems are related to uncomfortableness in talking to and helping cultural strangers. Some nurses actually fear clients who act strangely or do not respond immediately to the nurse's own cultural ways of relating to strangers. It is clear that most nursing staff in hospitals and other institutions need transcultural nursing concepts, principles, and practices to work effectively and comfortably with cultural strangers. In some countries, such as West Germany, there is considerable antipathy for immigrants entering or remaining in the country. These negative feelings carry over to health settings, making it difficult to work with cultural strangers.

Currently worldwide, most health institutions have a limited number of nurses prepared in transcultural nursing, and yet nurses are expected to care for clients from many different cultures. But nursing is not alone, as there are similar educational deficits among health disciplines and especially in cities like New York, Miami, Seattle, and along most coasts and big cities where there are hundreds of different cultures and very few health personnel prepared to work with the cultures. Granted, some nursing staff are being exposed to one-day crash workshops and conferences on transcultural nursing, but this is insufficient preparation to handle effectively very complex cultural care issues and problems.

In Canada nurse administrators, staff nurses, and physicians have been fairly active to prepare many of their hospital staff with multicultural mental health education since the Multiculturalism Policy of Canada Act was passed in July of 1988.[28] The Constitution of Canada has provided that its citizens will be protected to preserve and enhance the multicultural heritage of Canadians, which refers to *all* cultures in Canada. The government recognizes the diversity of Canadians and is committed to a policy of multiculturalism to achieve equality of all Canadians in the economic, cultural, social, and political life of Canada. This policy is reinforced and supported as a law by the constitution, is unique in the world, and is a model to consider in other countries. In the United States and in many other countries, there still are no explicit policies buttressed by law to support and reinforce multicultural or transcultural education and practices. Hence the cultural health care needs of people often get limited consideration until major conflicts, acts of violence or sometimes killings related to multicultural stresses and problems occur.

As a transcultural consultant in many of the Canadian provinces since the early 1960s, it has been most encouraging to see changes occur in Canada due to the commitment to multiculturalism. Moreover, Canadian nurses were among the first to recognize and value transcultural nursing. Several Canadian nurse leaders held that transcultural nursing and the focus on human care were the most significant development in nursing in the twentieth century. In contrast, nurses in the United States have been slow and reluctant to recognize the importance of transcultural nursing or multicultural education until recently. This fact seems difficult to understand with so many immigrants in the country and because transcultural nursing was launched in the United States. The reluctance of Americans appears largely due to the melting pot myth, ethnocentrism, fear of dealing with intercultural racial concerns, and women leadership jealousies. The slowness to focus on the idea of culturally competent nursing care was recognized only in 1992 by the American Academy of Nursing, and then it failed to recognize the parent field and its significant leaders.

In many other health agencies and hospitals in the world, the idea of transcultural nursing is recognized, but considerable education is needed as these countries make transcultural health care a reality. Many countries are beginning to establish clinical practices and to encourage nurses to become prepared in transcultural nursing as witnessed in the Republic of South Africa, Australia, Scandinavia, Middle East, Brazil, and areas in the Pacific Islands. Many of the nurse leaders in these countries recognize the need for transcultural nursing and are learning ways to use transcultural nursing concepts, principles, and research findings to improve client health care.

It is of interest that after nearly three decades of promoting native healers, curers, and carers in health care systems, a few native healers are now active participants in selected hospitals and community clinics in Canada and the United States. Where the native folk healers have been involved as carers, diagnosticians, curanderos, spiritualists, and other folk practitioners, the benefits toward client healing have been evident. There are, however, physicians and other health personnel who do not understand the important role of native healers, and so they have been restricted to enter hospitals and health agencies. As an advocate in the early 1960s of blending professional health care practices with native healing modes so that the client benefits, this trend is gradually occurring amid great reluctance over the years by professional practitioners. We shall, however, see a significant increase in this direction in most health settings worldwide in the twenty-first century and as a major goal of transcultural nursing practices. Transcultural nurses have remained the leaders with anthropologists to blend indigenous healers as care and cure providers in health care services.

In most hospitals worldwide nurses and other health personnel struggle to provide holistic care that incorporates cultural values, religious, kinship, and ethnohistorical factors, and educational modes into client services. Western hospitals tend to focus on the biophysical and some emotional needs of clients within a high-tech and medically dominated system. The transcultural nursing approach of holistic care that recognizes and incorporates family care with religious values and other cultural imperatives has yet to be fully achieved in hospital services. Hence health care remains fragmented rather than culturally based holistic care. Nursing staff conduct primarily physical and emotional assessments with very limited holistic or culturalogical nursing care assessments. Most encouraging, however, is the fact that professional nurses are generally listening to clients' stories as they give care, and these stories help nurses to discover some cultural lifeways, values, and beliefs. Today, more hospitals worldwide have begun to recognize the importance of client cultural food preferences and that food with eating modes are closely related to spiritual, cultural values, and beneficial healing. Transcultural nurses have been active advocates to support the importance of using and valuing food preferences of clients. Considerably more work lies ahead to sensitize health personnel about the fears and beliefs of clients from diverse cultures and their reluctancy to use powerful technologies related to x-rays and uranium scans.

In my consultation visits in many different countries, I have discovered some innovations in providing transcultural nursing care. For example, in Australia, a group of nurses are providing Cluster Group Cultural Care practices by having Greek, Portuguese, and Anglo-Australians functioning together in group care in order to have elderly clients learn from each other as well as to promote well-being.[29] In Finland, nurses have developed transcultural, community-based, nursing projects to meet the culture-specific needs of recent immigrants. In the United States two certified transcultural nurse clinicians in California have effectively demonstrated how they have incorporated transcultural nursing concepts and practices into clinical nursing practices in a large general hospital, and they have developed a videotape which was given recognition by the Sigma Theta Tau organization in 1992.[30] Nurses in the Republic of South Africa have been innovative in using transcultural nursing concepts, principles, and research findings to care for diverse tribal groups. In Detroit, we have developed in the past decade two large, urban transcultural research and care maintenance-based, community-centered projects with Arab-Muslims, Italian, Asian, and other Americans which have led to many positive outcomes.[31] The Detroit projects have also provided valuable educational and research centers for many nursing students to study transcultural nursing care. Other innovative transcultural nursing care projects continue to be developed showing positive signs of ways to provide culturally congruent, compassionate, and responsible care.

Another important trend to support clinical nursing practices has been the certification of transcultural nurses through the Transcultural Nursing Society. In 1987 the Society began to certify transcultural nurses in order to ensure that clients received culturally competent and safe care. Currently there are approximately 80 nurses who have been certified as transcultural nurses, and some are seeking recertification after five years. Transcultural nurses and the public are recognizing the importance of being certified through written and oral examinations with evidence of formal courses and field experiences in transcultural nursing. Certification has become essential to protect clients of diverse cultures and to increase nurses' clinical skills in transcultural nursing. The development of worldwide certification by members of the Transcultural Nursing Society has been a new and highly innovative approach to global nursing. I predict that similar global certification in other fields will prevail in the twenty-first century to ensure safe, quality cultural care to clients of many different cultures. Currently, the Transcultural Nursing Society remains the only organization with a cadre of master and doctorally prepared transcultural nurses who are certifying transcultural nurse specialists and generalists. Certification will help to protect nurses from legal suits and gives status and recognition to nurses' achievements. While there are other developments and trends in transcultural clinical health services, the above offer an overview of some encouraging ones.

Glimpse of Transcultural Nursing Education Worldwide

Increasingly transcultural nursing education is being recognized as essential content with field experiences in many schools of nursing worldwide. In some places, progress has been slow and uneven due to many factors such as:

1. The lack of sufficient numbers of qualified transcultural nursing faculty in schools of nursing.

2. The failure of academic nurse leaders to value, recognize, and promote transcultural nursing in schools.
3. The dominance of unicultural and traditional nursing curricula.
4. The serious lack of funds to support transcultural nursing education, research, and curricular changes.
5. The dominance of biomedical and psychological content in nursing education.
6. The fear of moving to use transcultural content.
7. Cultural ignorance, prejudices, and biases among faculty and administrators.[32]

Despite these major hurdles and barriers, transcultural nurse leaders have been innovative and persistent in finding ways to teach and incorporate transcultural nursing into nursing curricula and into clinical practices. They have drawn upon existing concepts, principles, and research practices to enrich and change traditional nursing curricula amid incredible hurdles. As one of the many persistent leaders for nearly four decades, I helped almost single-handedly to establish undergraduate and graduate transcultural nursing in four schools of nursing in the United States, and have worked as a consultant to many schools within and outside the United States. Since the early 1960s, I estimate that I have taught transcultural nursing to approximately 10,000 undergraduate and graduate students within and outside the United States through workshops, conferences, and short-term nursing courses. Each summer since 1975, generally, a three-week intensive transcultural nursing course has been offered to nurses from many places in the world at several major universities. These efforts and others by transcultural nurses have paved the way for making transcultural nursing a reality. Transcultural nursing conferences have been held in South America, The Republic of South Africa, The Netherlands, Finland, Sweden, Yugoslavia, Japan, Australia, Papua New Guinea, New Zealand, Jordan, Saudi Arabia, Iran, Canada, Alaska, Mexico, and Prince Edward Island. The outreach efforts by myself and others have been extremely important to learn about transcultural nursing and to establish courses and different ways to teach and bring the ideas into nursing curricula. Where nurses have been participants in transcultural nursing, they have been quick to recognize the importance of transcultural nursing and have enthusiastically viewed transcultural nursing as a new and relevant area of study and practice in nursing. Their eagerness to push transcultural nursing forward into all aspects of nursing education and practice has been most encouraging.

Although progress has been made in some areas in several countries, there still remains a great need to educate more fully the nearly 4.5 million nurses in the world about transcultural nursing. This will require persistent work with nurses with qualified faculty, money, and active faculty participation. Transcultural nursing must become fully an integral part of nursing education and clinical services to ensure quality based nursing care that reflects competencies and an in-depth understanding of cultures. The current generation of nurses who have been prepared in transcultural nursing will be core leaders to facilitate this important goal in nursing. With the critical shortage of prepared faculty and programs in transcultural nursing, progress will be slow in meeting societal demands for culturally-based care. Moreover, if nurses are not well prepared in transcultural nursing, one can predict many problems, as this is an area which requires highly knowledgeable, sensitive, and competent faculty in the classroom and as skilled mentors in clinical or field areas. And since some national nursing organizations have been slow to recognize and support transcultural nursing, this will limit progress even as cultural consumers make more urgent demands on nurses. With the serious lack of faculty prepared in transcultural nursing, we are already finding nurses representing a culture but not prepared in the field attempting to teach transcultural nursing. This trend is posing serious problems and leading to inadequately prepared students. In the United States, we have taken leadership in transcultural nursing to provide quality education since the early 1970s. There are presently four graduate programs and one international exchange program. The major and largest graduate program has been at Wayne State University in Detroit with master, doctoral, and post-doctoral courses and programs in transcultural nursing. At this institution students can pursue a master's degree (M.S.N.) in transcultural nursing with several courses and mentored field experiences, or students may pursue a doctoral (Ph.D.) degree in nursing with a focus on transcultural nursing and human care research. In addition, the College of Nursing offers a Liberal Arts course entitled ":" to fulfill general education, foreign culture, and language requirements for multidisciplinary students. The latter course is unique and the only one in the world to fulfill general education requirements. The course was developed and has been taught since 1987 by the author with a growing current student demand of 100 to 125 students each year.

The second transcultural nursing program is located at the University of Washington (Seattle) which offers selected courses and research in this area through the Community Nursing Systems Department. While serving as Dean in the School of Nursing at this university in the early 1970s, I initiated and taught the first course (1973) which was "Comparative Transcultural Nursing Systems" however, this offering was later called "Cross-Cultural Nursing" and taught by Dr. Noel Chrisman, an anthropologist. Nurses use anthropological and transcultural nursing in community and clinical settings through a masters degree program. Dr. Beverly Horn was the first nurse prepared in transcultural nursing at this university. The University of California in San Francisco offers a master and doctoral (Ph.D. or D.N.S.) focused on community health and administration in international nursing. The University of California in Los Angeles offers a D.N.S. with research focus in mental health and sociocultural diversity. The University of Miami in Florida offers master (M.S.N.) and doctoral (Ph.D.) preparation in transcultural nursing.

While the above are the major graduate degree programs with special education to support transcultural and international nursing, there are other schools of nursing offering one or two courses in transcultural nursing, such as Emory University in Atlanta. This university has established a Center for Transcultural and International Nursing under Dr. Anna Frances Wenger, who was prepared through doctoral (Ph.D.) education in transcultural nursing. There are also similar transcultural nursing courses at the Medical College of Georgia and Florida Atlantic University under Drs. Joyceen Boyle and Marilyn Ray. The latter were also prepared through doctoral (Ph.D.) program in transcultural nursing faculty. At the University of Toronto, a transcultural nursing course is offered, as well as at the University of Sydney and Cumberland College in Australia. In Australia, O. Kansaki, A. Omeri, and F. Jones have been pioneer leaders to make transcultural nursing a reality in that country. These graduate programs of study and courses on transcultural nursing remain extremely important to prepare the new generation of nurses to be knowledgeable and competent to teach, conduct research, and mentor students in this area. Because of the complexity of culture and care phenomena, graduate programs without prepared and competent transcultural nursing faculty, one will find faculty teaching anthropology and failing to bring in transcultural care dimensions. Such practices undermine the major focus of transcultural nursing and lead to mainly teaching anthropological courses in schools of nursing—a trend relinquished in the mid 1960s. The preparation of graduate nursing students in transcultural nursing remains very important to demonstrate transcultural nursing specialty practices. Undergraduate transcultural nursing education provides nurses with new approaches to nursing and lays the foundation for graduate education in this specialty.

In general, transcultural nursing education and practice has become recognized as extremely important to nurses who serve people in a multicultural world. Considerable variability exists in the extent of educational offerings, but there is a growing commitment to make this knowledge an integral part of nursing as a fundamental base of nursing and as an advanced specialty knowledge. The demand for courses and programs in transcultural nursing continues to increase with nursing students and graduate nurses who are keenly aware of this important need of clients who want culturally competent care. While there remains far too few faculty qualified to develop, teach, and do research in transcultural nursing, still the standards for transcultural nursing education remain essential to ensure quality programs and practices. Far more graduate transcultural nursing programs are in demand, as well as funds to support transcultural nursing education and research in most countries in the world. Transcultural nursing courses continue to be requested by students almost daily along with faculty to mentor their field experiences. In the United States, it is estimated that in 1993 only thirty-four percent of National League for Nursing (NLN) accredited baccalaureate nursing degree graduates and fifteen percent of master degree programs had substantive courses to prepare students in transcultural nursing, and two percent of nurses in doctoral nursing programs.[33] These factors attest to the critical need to move transcultural nursing quickly forward to meet transcultural care needs in the twenty-first century.

General Transcultural Nursing Research

Since the first transcultural nursing research began with the author's study of the Gadsup of Papua New Guinea in the early 1960s, a new pathway was established with great potential to advance nursing's knowledge transculturally. The idea of comparative in-depth transcultural nursing studies worldwide was difficult for many nurses to comprehend, except for nurses who were prepared in this area or anthropology. Moreover, the idea of diverse qualitative methods was unknown to most nurses in 1960. Qualitative ethnonursing and ethnography research methods were especially chosen by the author in order to establish substantive and in-depth transcultural nursing knowledge. It was this knowledge base that would guide nurses to practice nursing with a cultural care and health focus, shifting nurses' views from the dominant medical disease emphasis and from a heavy reliance on quantitative research methods. Most importantly, the author was convinced researchers were needed *to learn from the people about their particular lifeways, values, beliefs, and practices with a focus on human caring, health, and well-being.* As the first doctorally prepared, qualitative ethnonursing researcher, the author encouraged other nurses to use qualitative methods to obtain the people's views, as they know their lifeways, in order to develop credible and accurate transcultural nursing care meanings and practices. Accordingly, the author initially encouraged many nurses to be prepared in qualitative ethno-research methods mainly from anthropology and later from the author's courses in order to document the world of the people being studied. The outcome of the past three decades has been significant, especially in making qualitative research methods an important area of study which has been pursued mainly by transcultural nurses and now taught by them.

Today, many transcultural nurses have been leaders in developing the substantive body of transcultural nursing knowledge through the study of nearly seventy-five Western and non-Western cultures.[34] Research findings from these major cultures as reported mainly in the *Journal of Transcultural Nursing* have become the major sources of knowledge for teaching, clinical work, and research. There are a number of transcultural nurse researchers who are continuing to study these cultures within a transcultural nursing perspective. For example, Horn continues to study the Muckleshoot natives; Boyle and Glittenberg maintain their research interests in Guatemalan villages; Muecke in Thailand; Roessler, Leininger, and Cameron in China and Southeast Asia; Edmunds with Mennonites in Mexico and Canada; Spangler with Anglo-American and Philippine nurses within hospitals and communities; Rosenbaum with Canadian Greek widows; McKenna with Northwest Native Americans and Southeast Asians; Spielman and Scott on the homeless subculture; Luna, Kulwicki, and Leininger with Arab cultures; McFarland and Leininger with Polish and African American elderly in nursing homes; Gates with hospice and hospital culture; Gelazis with Lithuanians; Morgan with urban and rural prenatal care of African American women; DeSantis with the Haitians; and Leininger with the New Guineans; MacNeil with AIDS families in Africa; Finn with Euro-Americans, and many other cultures. These are a few examples of transcultural nursing research by doctorally prepared nurses which continue to grow each year. There are also several anthropological research studies done by nurses, but some of these support anthropologic knowledge with only a few focused on transcultural nursing knowledge.

Many of the above cited research studies are published in several transcultural nursing books, journals, and chapters, but especially in the *Journal of Transcultural Nursing*, which is the official publication of the Transcultural Nursing Society. It is of special interest that the journal was conceived in early 1980s but did not get launched until 1989 due to lack of funds. Currently, there are only two publications with this journal, and so many articles are evident and valued by transcultural nurses to teach nursing students. Many nurses inform the author, as the editor and initiator of this journal, how much they value and use the journal because of the theoretical focus and research findings which help to advance the reader's transcultural nursing knowledge. Currently, transcultural nursing research articles are published in approximately forty books, 800 articles, and many book chapters. Prior to the *Journal of Transcultural Nursing* much of the research in this field was published in yearly proceedings beginning around 1970, or in any nursing journal that would accept transcultural nursing articles. These sources were very few until 1988.

Transcultural Nursing Institutes and Centers in the United States and in other countries are much needed to help the growing numbers of nurses learn about transcultural nursing and to conduct worldwide comparative research studies. While this goal has not been realized, it remains an important one to advance transcultural nursing worldwide. In the United States federal funds for transcultural nursing and qualitative research have been exceedingly minuscule for research and education. This has been a major barrier to advancing transcultural nursing knowledge, education, and practices. There have been some funds limited to "cultural minority education" of the four USA federal groups, and unfortunately most of the nurses doing research and education have not been prepared in transcultural nursing. Hence, there is a need for research and curriculum funds to study *all* cultures and subcultures throughout the world and not a few specified ones.

Transcultural Nursing and Related Organizations

In order to further the development of transcultural nursing, several organizations were established. In 1968 the author established the Council on Nursing and Anthropology Association (CONAA) with the goal of promoting interdisciplinary research exchanges between nurses prepared in anthropology and non-nurse anthropologists at the annual meetings of the American Anthropological Association and at the Society for Applied Anthropology. Initially, this organization grew in membership with much interest from 1968 to 1975, but since then, membership has decreased as well as interest for many reasons. It is apparent that CONAA served its early purposes, and now that the transcultural nursing field is well established and growing, CONAA is no longer needed.

In 1974 the Transcultural Nursing Society was established as the official organization of transcultural nursing worldwide. It continues to grow in membership with the purpose of advancing transcultural nursing knowledge and competencies worldwide through education, research, consultation, and clinical services. From the beginning, the Transcultural Nursing Society was envisioned and organized for nurses worldwide who would be interested in sharing their ideas, theories, research, and clinical experiences with nurses committed to advancing transcultural nursing. Currently, there are approximately 900 members worldwide who are helping to support the purposes and goals of the organization. Annual meetings are held in the United States and in other countries. The meetings are highly informative with transcultural experts and with master and doctoral students sharing their research, theoretical ideas, and practices with many nurses worldwide. For example, the nineteenth annual Transcultural Nursing Society meeting was held in 1993 at Flagstaff, Arizona, with the theme focused on North American natives and transcultural nursing practices. Many nurses attended the convention, including nurses from the Indian Health Services and from other countries, sharing their research in stimulating and informative ways. Scholarships, research support, certificates of recognition, and the Leininger Award (for outstanding leadership in the field) are but a few of the activities and offerings of the society. Past and current presidents and board members of the society have been exceptional leaders and exemplary role models to promote and maintain the philosophy and goals of the Transcultural Nursing Society.

In 1978, the Council on Cultural Diversity of the American Nurses Association was established to focus primarily on diversity clinical issues. This council has limited membership and very few transcultural nurses. It is supported mainly by African American nurses not prepared in this specialty. It is of historical interest that in 1972 the author encouraged the executive Director of the American Nurses Association (ANA) to initiate a Council on Transcultural Nursing, but the idea was rejected as its director was frightened to deal with nurses and clients of different cultures. This council never developed a transcultural perspective and is currently considering disbanding. The American Academy of Nursing of the ANA established a committee on Cultural Diversity in 1991 to develop "culturally competent nursing" knowledge and practices, but this group failed to draw upon the substantive theoretical and research work of many transcultural nursing's leaders and experts since the early 1960s.[35] As a consequence, several members of the Transcultural Nursing Society shared their concerns about participating in and relying on non-scholarly work.[36,37] Since around 1985, Australia, with several nurse leaders, developed a transcultural council which is growing in membership and goal attainments. Likewise, Canada has been active in developing successful international nursing projects and work activities in many places in the world, e.g. China, West Africa, and South America. Thus, considerable variability exists in organizations to support transcultural nursing.

From the beginning, comparative cultural care was a major focus of transcultural nursing, and some nurses felt there should be a separate organization to advance human care knowledge. In 1978, the National Research Conference was established by the author, and the Transcultural Nursing Society continued its pioneering work, but also kept care central to research. In 1987, the National Research group changed their names to the International Association of Human Caring. Currently, many transcultural nurses continue to participate in both organizations with mutual interests and benefits.

Other organizations with similar transcultural nursing interests are the National Philippine Nurses Association, the American Indian and Alaskan Native Nurse Association, the National Black Nurses Association, the Hispanic Nurses Association, Arabic Nurses Group, and the Ukrainian Nurses Group. In addition, many countries, such as Finland, The Republic of South Africa, have now established their own local and national transcultural nursing chapters for ongoing dialogue and to support annual worldwide conferences. The above organizations and others reveal the active and growing interest of transcultural nurses to be organized worldwide. From the above glimpses of transcultural nursing practice, education, and research, one can see many exciting and continuous developments in a highly relevant field. The reader is encouraged to learn more about transcultural nursing in subsequent chapters and in other publications such as the works of Dobson, Boyle and Andrews, Kavanaugh, Kennedy, and others.[38,39,40]

A Historical Perspective of Transcultural Nursing

As the founder and a leader of transcultural nursing, I am frequently asked:

1. What factors led you to establish transcultural nursing as an area of study and practice?
2. How did you envision that transcultural nursing could improve and advance nursing as a discipline and profession?
3. What enabled you to persevere over time and almost single-handedly develop the field of transcultural nursing?
4. What are your dreams and vision for transcultural nursing in the future?

In this section I will respond to these queries and give an overview of related developments in establishing the field of transcultural nursing from a historical perspective. The narrative will be given in the first person, to make clear the founder's views.

In the mid 1950s while working as the first graduate child psychiatric clinical specialist in nursing in a psychiatric unit in the Midwest, I experienced cultural shock at not being able to respond appropriately to the children's needs and behavior.[41] It was then that I discovered the many different cultures. There were Appalachian, African, Mexican, Jewish, German, and Euro-Americans in this child psychiatric guidance home. These children spoke different languages and they would only eat certain foods, accept certain medications and treatments, and would respond differently to daily nursing practices. Some children played alone and others always wanted to be with others. I observed that the Appalachian children always wanted to go to bed at night with a wooden stick and string, whereas the Euro-American children sucked their thumbs or the corner of a soft blanket. When the parents came to visit, the Jewish child clung to his mother and wanted chicken soup, while the German child remained "brave" and the mother commented about how clean the child was in dress and body appearance. These differences and others demonstrated that cultural differences clearly existed and influenced my nursing care. Unfortunately, I felt helpless as I did not understand these children's behavior even though I had recently completed a graduate program in psychiatric nursing and worked in nursing for several years.

Soon after a series of these cultural difference encounters, I realized that the major and critical feature of nursing was the absence of cultural aspects of nursing care. I soon discovered that the discipline of anthropology was a major source of cultural knowledge, which I had never realized previously in my professional endeavors. This led me to pursue a graduate degree in anthropology. While in the rigorous program at the University of Washington, I gained a wealth o knowledge about different cultures which I had never heard or learned before. I became excited about what I was learning and what all nurses should know about different cultures. It was then that I envisioned establishing a new field or area of study in nursing which I called transcultural nursing. The more I studied, the more I could see ways to develop transcultural knowledge and experiences in nursing to help nurses in the future give a new kind of nursing care. I saw the *close relationship of nursing and anthropology as alike yet different.* I became aware that *nursing should not be anthropology* and that *anthropology was not nursing,* for these disciplines were different but had some important shared features. Both disciplines were interested in people over time and in different places; both valued to know and understand human beings throughout the life cycle and at critical times in life. Both disciplines need a broad holistic view to know human beings.

The awareness of commonalities and differences between nursing and anthropology led to writing my first transcultural nursing book in 1970 entitled *Nursing and Anthropology: Two Worlds to Blend*.[42] In this book I identified areas of commonalities and differences between nursing and anthropology, recognizing that anthropology was a social science field focused on a broad range of material and nonmaterial culture. In contrast, nursing was a caring science with a humanistic care focus. I held that anthropological courses were equally important or more important than courses in microbiology, chemistry, anatomy and physiology, and psychology, which were required courses for nurses in the 1950s and 1960s and still are today in many schools of nursing. Most of these courses offered little to help nurses understand and care for people as cultural beings. Getting transcultural care content and experiences into nursing in the mid 1950s was virtually impossible as there simply were no faculty prepared in anthropology let alone considering transcultural caring. Nonetheless, I held that culture care was important if nurses were to be helpful to clients.

Near the completion of my doctoral program in anthropology, I was expected to conduct a major field research study. I chose the Gadsup of the Eastern Highlands and New Guinea. I did an ethnographic and ethnonursing study of these people in the early 1960s, living alone with them for nearly two years. This anthropological approach to entering the Gadsup world and learning directly from the people was invaluable to me and to establishing transcultural nursing. As I lived in the village with the dark-skinned non-Western Gadsups for nearly two years, I experienced the very different lifeways, beliefs, and values of the people. The Gadsup world was in sharp contrast to my Anglo-American life with high technology, modern equipment, and other features of the American culture. My rural farm life in earlier days helped me to stay with and endure hardships and the lack of Western conveniences such as running water and electricity. Gadsup lifeways, beliefs, values, and language in two villages was very different from my previous ways of living. In fact, I experienced culture shock as virtually none of my American ways of communication, eating, and living were like the Gadsup lifeways. This convinced me that Western nursing needed transcultural knowledge in order to function with people from any culture but especially very different cultures. This New Guinea experience convinced me that nursing had to change and soon in order for nurses to be responsive and effective care providers with diverse cultures. Indeed, nurses would be greatly handicapped in living and functioning with Gadsup—their success and failure would rest on understanding the people they were serving. Most assuredly, there were many more cultures like the Gadsup and even in one's homeland which would require knowledge and skills to work with them. Thus, the Gadsup taught me convincingly that cultural differences necessitated that nurses must learn about diverse cultures in the world and they needed courses and programs to achieve this goal.

After my New Guinea field research, I was more committed than ever to establish the field of transcultural nursing. I began to develop concepts and principles and do research in order using some different approaches to people care. While I was excited about developing and practicing transcultural nursing, I realized other nurses did not share my enthusiasm. One nurse leader told me, "What a strange idea. It will never be realized in nursing, as nurses are wed to medical, physical, and mental diseases with their symptoms and treatments. Culture is unknown to them." Other nurse leaders said, "Nurses will never change their practices to include cultural factors, as they have never had to in the past, so why now?"; and "Your ideas are totally strange to nurses. It will take years before they see and value your ideas about transcultural nursing." Nonetheless, I kept pursuing my goal and dream to develop a new area of nursing education and practice. I dealt daily with nonbelievers, skeptics, and resistant nurses. Establishing a new field was extremely difficult as the patterns of nursing and the views of nursing leaders and organizations in the United States in the 1960s were largely wed to medicine's views and survived under medicine.

It seemed that transcultural nursing was an idea too distant and strange to nurses who were deeply entrenched in medical model ideas and following the clinical areas of medical, surgical, pediatric, obstetric, psychiatric, and many other medical model names and areas for nursing. Nurses in the 1960s and 1970s were truly dependent upon biopsychophysical and psychological ideas as well as carrying out physicians' medical orders. High technologies with many different medical treatments had to be carried out by nurses. Cultural factors were unknown and not included in most nursing and medical books. The idea of transculturalism was not used or knowingly practiced in nursing. The idea of culture-specific care and culturally congruent care were harshly challenged when I talked about them. Culture care "would never go" was the common feedback statement from my colleagues.

With my persistence, determination, and enthusiasm for what I believed in, I pushed forward and gradually got a few nurses to join me. I also held that if one truly *believed in something and had a goal, one should never relinquish it, for someday and somehow it could become a reality.* My mother's Irish sense of humor and my father's German determination became active forces to sustain me in the development of transcultural nursing. In addition, Margaret Mead challenged me to do something to deal with the absence of cultural knowledge in the health field.

One major question dominated my thinking, how could I ever change nurses to become interested in transcultural nursing when they had *no* interest, *no* preparation in anthropology, and were satisfied with the status of nursing within a biomedical viewpoint? I decided to share, with enthusiastic talks, my ideas as well as my experiences in New Guinea and with other cultures I had been studying as a post-doctoral teacher and practitioner. I went ahead and developed a few undergraduate and graduate transcultural nursing courses and encouraged students to enroll in them. The first courses were at the University of Colorado in the mid 1960s and were highly successful and valued by nursing students. I then gave satellite lectures across the United States and in the Pacific Islands, as the first in nursing and these were well received. Community health nurses also saw the need for transcultural nursing knowledge and skills in their work with cultural groups in different communities. Gradually nurses in pediatric and obstetric nursing became interested. Psychiatric and medical/surgical nurses were the most resistant to the idea of transcultural nursing and could see virtually no role for culture in their thinking and work.

Another important strategy was to encourage nurses to read anthropology books and transcultural nursing literature such as *Nursing and Anthropology: Two Worlds to Blend.* This was most helpful to nurses to extend their ideas and to link nursing with anthropology with transcultural nursing. I also encouraged some nurses to enroll in anthropology courses, pursue a minor in the field and to consider theoretical ideas about culture and care linkage areas to they could be prepared to help with transcultural nursing. Anthropology faculty frequently asked me why nurses would be interested in anthropology. They wanted these nurses to become full-fledged anthropologists, not nurses. As the first graduate prepared (M.S.N.) nurse to earn a Ph.D. in anthropology, other nurses thought this was the answer. However, my goal was to gain in-depth knowledge and research skills in anthropology as a beginning step to develop graduate degrees (the M.S.N. and Ph.D.) in transcultural nursing. At that time, medical anthropology had not been developed as a specialty until late in the 1960s and early 1970s so transcultural nursing preceded this subspecialty. Moreover, this specialty when developed was much too medically based for transcultural nursing.

As I continued to teach undergraduate and graduate students and encourage them to take anthropology courses as electives, more nurses became interested in transcultural nursing. By the mid 1960s and early 1970s approximately thirty nurses had pursued doctoral study in anthropology. Some of the nurses remained in anthropology and have never linked their research and teaching to nursing. However, some sought faculty appointments and good salaries in schools of nursing without teaching or doing research focused on transcultural nursing. This was disappointing to me, however, there were other nurses who quickly perceived the relevance to transcultural nursing and became most helpful in the field.

While serving as Dean of the School of Nursing at the University of Washington (Seattle), administrative steps were taken to establish the first departmental unit and a course focused on transcultural nursing in 1973. In addition, the first individualized Ph.D. in nursing with a focus on transcultural nursing was initiated. Later in 1978 while at the University of Utah, I established the first master (M.S.N.) and doctoral (Ph.D.) programs in transcultural nursing in the world. Similar master (M.S.N.) and doctoral (Ph.D.) programs with a focus on transcultural nursing were developed at Wayne State University in Detroit around 1982–84. These formal courses and program offerings were significant breakthroughs to institutionalize transcultural nursing and to prepare a cadre of specialists in this area. Many of these transcultural nursing graduates continue to promote and demonstrate transcultural nursing in their teaching, research, and practice.

The concept of cultural diversity began to take on relevance by the mid 1970s, but sometimes without an in-depth focus on transcultural nursing. A recent book by Kavanagh and Kennedy on the subject has helped to clarify some of the many issues related to cultural diversity.[43] Likewise, Spector's book on *Cultural Diversity in Health and Illness*, since 1985, has been most helpful to study diverse aspects of traditional healing and curing.[44] The terms people of color and ethnic nurses of color became popular with minority nurses, not prepared in transcultural nursing. This led to some misconceptions about skin color and divided perspectives. It also led to minority nurses being cast into teaching positions of nursing often without any formal preparation or mentorship in transcultural nursing or anthropology. As a consequence, many problems occurred that limited the full development of minority nurses in becoming experts in transcultural nursing. Likewise, the social movement of affirmative action in schools of nursing and clinical areas became evident based on the idea of compensatory justice and equal opportunities for minorities. This well-intended approach has led to a number of ethical dilemmas for some cultural groups.

Despite increased numbers of immigrants, refugees, and a growing multicultural world in the 1970s and into the 1990s, it remained difficult to get basic and graduate transcultural nursing courses into nursing curricula in schools of nursing in the United

States and in other places. The common saying was "no room for any new courses" while increasing medical-surgical courses and clinical hospital experiences. Many transcultural nursing curricula remain full of medical-surgical (often adult primary medical care), maternal-child, mental health, community health, oncological, and other medically-based courses. Most recently is an earlier trend to establish physician assistant and primary care nurses prepared in medical and nursing diagnoses as assessment skills. Courses such as chemistry, microbiology, biophysics, anatomy and physiology, and psychology are found in undergraduate nursing programs often with very little on transcultural nursing care, or anthropology as cognate courses. In some nursing curricula, the concept of *culture* and other transcultural concepts may appear in course outlines, but may be limitedly discussed unless taught by transcultural nursing faculty. In some schools, uniculturally-based content exists because faculty are unprepared to teach about other cultures. Some faculty fear "racial discrimination" if they teach cultural concepts. Thus transcultural nursing varies if it is incorporated into nursing curricula despite many students' please for such content because these students realize they need cultural preparation to work with clients of diverse cultures. Of course, there are some schools of nursing that are exemplars in teaching and curricular work in transcultural nursing which is most encouraging to see.

In the clinical settings in the United States such as hospitals, clinics, and public health agencies, nursing service administrators and staff nurses were often unfamiliar with concepts and practices related to transcultural nursing until the early 1980s. These staff nurses tended to treat all clients alike to prevent cultural conflicts and related problems. As transcultural nurse specialists (master and doctorally prepared) and some transcultural generalists (largely baccalaureate) began to function in clinical settings, they have been extremely important to change nursing practices by accommodating the culturally different. Today transcultural nursing ideas are becoming better known in nursing service and education practice, but much work remains to make transcultural nursing an integral part of nursing.

Another important development to promote transcultural nursing has been the certification of nurses. This was an important means to protect the public from unsafe cultural care practices. In the early 1980s, it was clear that cultural consumers needed to be protected from cultural negligence, cultural imposition practices, and other unethical or harmful practices. By 1989, certification in transcultural nursing was established with written and oral examinations and portfolios of the clinical experiences and educational preparation of the applicants. Certification protects the public from unsafe practitioners dealing with diverse cultural care needs and issues. Currently more nurses are being certified in transcultural nursing worldwide. Applicants are reviewed every six years by transcultural nurse experts through the Transcultural

Nursing Society to keep nurses knowledgeable and competent in culture care. A great sense of pride, confidence, and commitment has been evident with nurses certified in transcultural nursing a they demonstrate their ability to provide culturally safe, appropriate, and competent transcultural nursing care.

Although there have been many more interesting and significant developments in establishing and maintaining transcultural nursing since the mid 1950s, this brief history provides a general overview to understand some aspects. Today, transcultural nursing has been well conceptualized and soundly established and is a major area of study and practice that is growing worldwide because of a rapidly changing world. And as global images and practices occur, there will be more demands for transculturalism in every aspect of business, health, and all aspects of living and working. Launching the new field has necessitated a great deal of strategic planning, political wisdom, and a lot of perseverance. But it is encouraging that more nurses are now valuing and recognizing the significance of transcultural nursing than even a decade ago. In fact, some nurses are now proclaiming that they have been doing transcultural nursing because of a few intercultural contacts. This stance or myth, however, cannot be supported, as transcultural nursing is more than casual contacts. As transcultural nursing continues to advance nursing as a discipline and profession, it is bringing forth some entirely new and different perspectives to nursing. The field has helped to expand nurses' worldviews, and challenged them to modify nursing care practices with clients and families of different lifeways. It is challenging nurses to learn and practice nursing in different ways—ways that bring satisfactions when clients acknowledge the nurses sensitivity to them. Most assuredly, transcultural nursing is transforming nursing in some encouraging and futuristic directions.[45]

My original statement and logo for transcultural nursing still remains a central goal and challenge for all nurses, namely, *"That the cultural care needs of people in the world will be met by nurses prepared in transcultural nursing."* Indeed, the challenge goes out for all professional nurses to study cultures and their care and health or well being in all places in the world. It is also the theory of Culture Care that will remain a significant theory to discover what is common and what is different among cultures. And as the reader will see in subsequent chapters, a growing body of transcultural nursing knowledge is now available to help nurses to become culturally competent practitioners. In this chapter, some major characteristic and an interpretive definition of transcultural nursing were presented. Several significant forces influencing the need for transcultural nursing as a formal area of study and practice were discussed. Several historical and philosophical ideas were explained to understand the development of transcultural nursing over thirty-five years. In this last section, some summary statements will be offered to help the student grasp some of the significant points covered in this chapter.

Summary Review Points on Transcultural Nursing

1. Transcultural nursing was envisioned in the mid 1950s and developed as a formal area of study and practice by its founder, Madeleine Leininger, in the early 1960s. An awareness of the need for transculturalism occurred as Leininger was studying and practicing the clinical role of the child psychiatric nurse specialist. Leininger identified the two major missing dimensions in nursing as cultural factors and human care/caring phenomena. This led Leininger to pursue a doctoral degree (P.D.) in cultural and social anthropology and to become the first nurse graduate (M.S.N.) to have a Ph.D. in anthropology.

2. Transcultural nursing is a formal area of study and practice focused on comparative culture care/caring differences and similarities among individuals and groups i order to use this knowledge to provide culturally congruent and beneficial care to clients. Transcultural nursing is different from anthropology and from cross-cultural nursing, as well as from medical anthropology.

3. The first transcultural nursing research study was done by Leininger in early 1960 which focused on comparative ethnonursing care and an ethnography of the Gadsup of the eastern highlands of Papua New Guinea. Since then, many significant transcultural nursing research studies have been conducted to develop a body of knowledge to support transcultural nursing. The ethnonursing method developed by Leininger was the first research method in nursing to study specific nursing phenomena with her theory of Culture Care. She also conducted the first ethnographic research study focused on nursing phenomena. The founder's early and prolonged experiences in New Guinea supported the development of the field of transcultural nursing and encouraged nurses to use qualitative research methods to study complex and covert nursing phenomena.

4. The theory of Culture Care Diversity and Universality became the first nursing theory to explicate transcultural nursing focused on human care and health. Although the theory was developed in the late 1950s, it has been only in recent decades that the theory has taken on meaning and relevance due to major cultural gaps in nurses' knowledge of culture and care from both a nursing and anthropological perspective.

5. The first formal transcultural nursing courses and telelectures were initiated by Leininger in 1965–69 at the School of Nursing at the University of Colorado. It was at this university that she also initiated the first Ph.D. Nurse-Scientist program with a focus on anthropology with transcultural nursing perspectives.

6. Leininger was the first master's prepared nurse to complete a Ph.D. in cultural anthropology which occurred at the University of Washington. In 1973, the first academic department of transcultural nursing (later called "Cross-Cultural Community Nursing Systems" around 1975) was initiated by Dean Leininger. Beverly Horn was the first nurse to complete an individualized Ph.D. program

with a focus on transcultural nursing at this university in 1974. Then in 1978 at the University of Utah, Leininger initiated the first master (M.S.N.) and doctoral (Ph.D.) programs in transcultural nursing. The first nurses to complete the Ph.D. in transcultural nursing were Marilyn Ray, Joyceen Boyle, and Janice Morse. Since then, a number of nurse leaders have completed Ph.D.'s in nursing with a research focus on transcultural nursing. To date, there are approximately seventy nurses who have completed a Ph.D. in nursing with a transcultural nursing focus. There are some nurses who have completed a Ph.D. in anthropology, but not all of these nurses have been active in helping build a body of transcultural nursing knowledge. Many of their contributions are largely to the discipline of anthropology.

7. Of historical interest, undergraduate and graduate programs (or graduate courses) in the United States are as follows:

    a. First courses (undergraduate and graduate courses) at the School of Nursing, University of Colorado (Denver), in 1965–69 initiated by the author.

    b. First graduate courses and the establishment of a department of Comparative Transcultural Nursing in 1973 at the University of Washington (Seattle) was accomplished under Leininger's deanship and changed later to Cross-Cultural Community Nursing.

    c. In 1978, the first doctoral (Ph.D.) program in transcultural nursing was established at the University of Utah and the first master's degree (M.S.N.) program in transcultural nursing established and approved in 1978–9 under the author's leadership. Unfortunately, neither of these master or doctoral degrees of specialized programs in transcultural nursing are available today.

    d. The Department of Human Services at the Pennsylvania State University (Hershey, Pennsylvania) offered a course, which is no longer available, in transcultural nursing and the elderly in 1978 under Laurie Gunter.

    e. Since 1982, Wayne State University College of Nursing (Detroit), under Leininger, has initiated undergraduate, master, doctoral, and post-doctoral courses and programs in transcultural nursing. A master's degree (M.S.N.) in transcultural nursing is offered at Wayne State University as well as doctoral and post-doctoral research mentorship. Currently, this university has the largest number (worldwide) of transcultural nursing students and academic offerings in the specialized program areas. Transcultural research and educational exchange programs have been established.

    f. The University of California (Los Angeles) initiated courses focused on sociocultural aspects of mental health in a master's degree (M.S.N.) program beginning in 1984 under Julian Lipson.

    g. Since the mid 1980s, the University of California (San Francisco) has offered master's and doctoral (Ph.D. or D.N.S.) degrees in International Nursing under Dr. Afaf Meleis.

   h. Since the early 1990s, the University of Florida (Miami) initiated master's level nursing courses in "Culture, Care, and Health" through a research institute under Lydia DeSantis.

   i. Other courses in transcultural nursing are continuing to be developed and offered at other universities, but many more graduate programs in transcultural nursing are urgently needed.

8. The first book in transcultural nursing was *Nursing and Anthropology: Two Worlds to Blend*, written in 1967 and published in 1970. The second definitive transcultural nursing book, prepared in the mid 1970s and published in 1978 was entitled *Transcultural Nursing: Concepts, Theories, and Practices*. A book of anthropology readings for nurses was prepared by P. Brink entitled *Readings in Transcultural Nursing* and published in 1977. Another book *Transcultural Nursing* (1979) was a collection of proceedings from the three major conferences of the Transcultural Nursing Society. There were no articles or books on the subject of transcultural nursing until the mid 1960s, and since then there are now about twenty-five books and about 700 published articles on the subject. Many book chapters and films have been developed largely by transcultural nurse specialists on the general subject.

9. As of 1994, it is estimated that 900 nurses are prepared as transcultural nursing generalists, approximately 200 master and doctorally prepared transcultural nurse specialists, and approximately ninety certified transcultural nurses (C.T.N.). It is estimated that nearly 10,000 nurses (of 4.5 million nurses in the world) have had at least *one* substantive course in transcultural nursing or a course focused on culture, health, and nursing.

10. The Committee on Nursing and Anthropology (CONAA) was spearheaded in 1968 by Leininger for an exchange between nurse anthropologists and non-nurse anthropologists to share common interests, theories, research findings, and application of knowledge to people care.

11. In 1974, the Transcultural Nursing Society was established as the official worldwide organization for transcultural nursing. It was developed to serve nurses worldwide and to contribute to transcultural nursing knowledge through research, using such knowledge in teaching, consultation, and in clinical and community health care practices. Certification in transcultural nursing began in 1988 to protect the public.

12. A critical shortage of transcultural nursing faculty as well as clinical experts in transcultural nursing exists in schools of nursing and in nursing services in most countries. There is an urgent need to prepare faculty in transcultural nursing and to establish graduate programs in this field.

13. Transcultural nurse specialists with graduate preparation are taking leadership in many countries to facilitate education, research, and clinical practices. Their leadership has been essential to assist nurses and others to deal effectively with many cultural stresses and conflicts of clients, students, faculty, and administrators of multicultural orientations and values in the workplace.

14. Nurses completing the transcultural nursing education and graduate degrees have been employed in a variety of roles, different settings, and in diverse kinds of leadership positions in education, research, and clinical practices. Transcultural nurses frequently have defined their employment roles in settings where the role is unfamiliar to the staff. Transcultural generalist and specialist roles are gradually being established in a variety of new kinds of alternative health and education services as well as in traditional institutions. Health care is undergoing a major transformation, with consumers of different cultures making their needs and demands known. Likewise, nurses and other health professionals are being expected to alter their practices and to participate in the health care reform from a transcultural nursing perspective. Successful health care transformation and reform will be largely contingent upon prepared transcultural nurse practitioners, consultants, and researchers. Immigrants will increase, and with the transmobilization of people will come major problems of handling large numbers of multicultural people in nursing education and service. Without skilled transcultural staff, one can anticipate violence and many difficult and destructive problems. The continued focus on uniculturalism and the medicalization poses serious problems in being responsible for culturally based nursing care.

15. Research funds and money for several transcultural institutes and centers remain critical as well as for master, doctoral, and post-doctoral programs in transcultural nursing.

References

1. Leininger, M., "Transcultural Nursing Theories and Research Approaches," *Transcultural Nursing Concepts, Theories, and Practices*, M. Leininger ed., New York: John Wiley & Sons, 1978, pp. 32–33, reprint, Columbus, Ohio: Greyden Press, 1994.

2. Leininger, M., *Nursing and Anthropology: Two Worlds to Blend*, New York: John Wiley & Sons, 1970.

3. Ibid.

4. Ibid.

5. Leininger, M., "Caring: The Essence and Central Focus of Nursing," *American Nurses Foundation*, Nursing Research Report, v. 12, no. 1, February, 1976, pp. 2, 14.

6. Leininger, M., *Care: An Essential Human Need*, Detroit: Wayne State University Press, 1988a. (Originally published by C. Slack, Inc., 1981).

7. Leininger, M., *Care: The Essence of Nursing and Health*, Detroit: Wayne State University Press, 1988b. (Originally published by C. Slack, Inc., 1984).

8. Leininger, op. cit., 1988a.

9. Ibid.

10. Leininger, op. cit., 1988b.

11. Leininger, M., "The Theory of Culture Care Diversity and Universality," *Culture Care Diversity and Universality: A Theory of Nursing*, M. Leininger ed., New York: National League for Nursing Press, 1991, pp. 5–68.

12. Ibid.

13. Leininger, M., *Transcultural Nursing, Concepts, Theories, and Practices*, New York: John Wiley & Sons, 1978.

14. Spector, R., *Cultural Diversity in Health & Illness*, Norwalk, Connecticut: Appleton & Lange, 1991.

15. Leininger, M., "*Cultural Variation of Violence with Relationship to Caring and Non-Caring*," (in press) Detroit: Wayne State University Project, 1994.

16. Achterberg, J., *Women as Healer*, Boston: Shambhala, 1991.

17. Ibid.

18. Wenger, A. F., "The Culture Care Theory and the Old-Order Amish," *Culture Care Diversity and Universality: A Theory of Nursing*, M. Leininger, ed., New York: National League for Nursing Press, 1991, pp. 147–178.

19. Leininger, M., "The Gadsup of New Guinea and Early Child-Caring Behaviors with Nursing Care Implications," *Transcultural Nursing: Concepts, Theories, and Practices*, New York: John Wiley & Sons, 1978, pp. 375–397, reprint, Columbus, Ohio: Greyden Press, 1994.

20. Leininger, M., "Transcultural Nursing: A Worldwide Imperative for Nurses Today and in the 21st Century," *Nursing and Health Care*, v. 15, no. 2, May 1994.

21. Porter-O'Grady, T., "Building Partnerships in Health Care: Creating Whole System Changes," *Nursing and Health Care*, v. 15, no. 1, January 1994, pp. 34–38.

22. Altman, S., "Health Care in the Nineties: No More of the Same," *Hospitals*, v. 64, no. 64, April 5, 1990, p. 64.

23. Brown, E., *Nursing for the Future*, New York: Russell Sage Publishers, 1948.

24. Saunders, L., *Cultural Difference and Medical Care: The Case of Spanish-Speaking People of the Southwest*, New York: Russell Sage Foundation, 1954.

25. MacGregor, F., *Social Science in Nursing*, New York: Russell Sage Publishers, 1960.

26. Leininger, op. cit., 1970.

27. Spangler, Z., "Culture Care of Philippine and Anglo-American Nurses in a Hospital Context," *Culture Care Diversity and Universality: A Theory of Nursing*, M. Leininger ed., New York: National League for Nursing Press, 1991, pp. 119–146.

28. Multiculturalism Policy of Canada Act, Ministry of Health, Ontario, Canada, 1987.

29. Paech, S., "Cluster Group Cultural Care Project," (unpublished manuscript) Prince Albert Hospital, Sydney, Australia: 1991.

30. Bloch, C. and C. Bloch, "Transcultural Nursing in Hospital Practices," (videotape), Los Angeles: 1991.

31. Leininger, M., "Culturally Specific Action-Research Projects in Two Urban Communities," (unpublished manuscript) Detroit: Wayne State University, 1987.

32. Leininger, M., "Survey of Schools of Nursing Incorporating Transcultural Nursing in Undergraduate and Graduate Programs in USA," (unpublished manuscript) Detroit: Wayne State University, 1981.

33. Ibid.

34. Leininger, op. cit., 1991.

35. Anderson, P., "AAN Expert Panel Report: Culturally Competent Health Care," *Nursing Outlook*, November/December 1992, pp. 277–283.

36. Leininger, M. ed. "Rebuttal Excerpts on the American Academy of Nursing Panel Report on Culturally Competent Health Care," *Journal of Transcultural Nursing*, v. 4, no. 2, 1993, pp. 44–47.

37. Anderson, C. ed. "Letters to the Editor," *Nursing Outlook*, November/December 1993, pp. 281–283.

38. Dobson, S., *Transcultural Nursing*, London: Scutari Press, 1991.

39. Boyle, J. and M. Andrews, *Transcultural Concepts in Nursing Care*, Glenview, Il.: Scott & Foresman, 1989.

40. Kavanagh, K. and P. Kennedy, *Promoting Cultural Diversity: Strategies for Health Care Professionals*, Newbury Park: Sage Publications, 1992.

41. Leininger, op. cit., 1978.

42. Leininger, op. cit., 1970.

43. Kavanagh and Kennedy, op. cit., 1992.

44. Spector, op. cit., 1991.

45. Leininger, M., "Transcultural Nursing: An Essential Knowledge and Practice Field for Today," *Canadian Nurse*, v. 80, no. 11, 1985, pp. 41–45.

Bridging Reflections to Chapter 2

In chapter one, the nature, definition, and factors influencing transcultural nursing were discussed. The significance and historical evaluation of transcultural nursing were presented showing three decades of work to establish this field of study and practice. Several basic facts were highlighted as well as general experiences of the founder of transcultural nursing. It is clear that transcultural nursing is a growing and essential area for nurses and other health care providers today and in the future. Transcultural nursing has a different focus than many traditional and current areas in nursing. The reader is encouraged to reflect upon transcultural nursing and place oneself in this world with consumers from many different places to get health care.

In this chapter several important transcultural nursing concepts are defined with practical clinical and community examples to help nurses envision the nature and practice of transcultural nursing concepts are defined with practical clinical and community examples to help nurses envision the nature and practice of transcultural nursing. Using specific concepts and principles with clinical experiences should help the reader understand their practical uses in nursing situations. For the newcomer to transcultural nursing, many of the clinical incidents will stimulate the nurse to recognize cultural conflicts and ways to consider dealing with serious intercultural difficulties. Use of the concepts and principles becomes an important means to alleviate cultural care stresses and to provide culturally sensitive and congruent care. This chapter also encourages the nurse to reflect upon one's own cultural beliefs and life experiences in order to be effective with clients and others.

Chapter 2
Transcultural Nursing Perspectives: Basic Concepts, Principles, and Culture Care Incidents

Madeleine Leininger, PhD, LHD, FAAN, CTN, RN

Transcultural nursing is a highly relevant and stimulating area of study and practice today which has great relevance for nurses living and functioning in a multicultural world. This area of study and practice often leads to some entirely different ways of knowing and helping people of diverse cultures. With a transcultural focus, nurses think about differences and similarities among people and their beliefs, practices and lifeways. Nurses learn to value understanding people regarding their special needs and concerns and to develop different ways to assist clients. As nurses discover the client's particular cultural orientation, they learn from the client ways to provide sensitive, compassionate, and competent care that is beneficial and satisfying to the client. Gaining a deep appreciation for cultures with their commonalties and differences is one of several goals of transcultural nursing. At the same time, the nurse discovers many nursing insights about her own cultural background and how to use such knowledge appropriately with clients with clients whether in a particular community, hospital, or other kinds of health care services. Transcultural nursing is the knowledge and competency area that generally opens many new windows of knowledge that have usually been closed to nurses before.

In this chapter several major transcultural nursing concepts will be defined and discussed along with specific knowledge to guide nursing practices as used in transcultural nursing. In addition, generic and professional nursing care are defined and explained as major concepts to discover differences and similarities to guide nurses in practicing transcultural nursing. In the last section several recurrent clinical transcultural nursing incidents with interpretations are presented to help nurses envision the nature of transcultural nursing. Several questions are raised so the reader can reflect upon ideas bearing upon transcultural nursing in order to provide nursing care that is culturally competent, safe and congruent. Discovering the whys of each transcultural incident with the concepts helps the nurse to gain in-depth knowledge of culture care situations.

In this chapter you may consider that you are functioning or living in part of the country largely unknown to you. You might envision yourself in a hospital assigned to care for a client who spoke a different language, was dressed differently, and acted in strange ways. You are baffled by what you see and hear, and are wondering how you could possibly give good nursing care. How would you feel? What would you do? This is a transcultural nursing, situation which many nurses face today in most hospitals, homes, and health services. This situation and others in this chapter challenge one to realize the critical need for transcultural nursing knowledge, principles and skills to work with cultural strangers in therapeutic ways.

Major Concepts to Understand in Transcultural Nursing

In the evolution and development of a field of study and practice, it is essential for nurses to understand the major concepts, theories, and principles of transcultural nursing. Transcultural nursing leaders have identified, defined, and explicated a number of concepts in order for nurses to use the ideas in meaningful and appropriate ways. Such fundamental knowledge assists nurses to communicate effectively with others and to avoid unfavorable conflicts or troublesome interactions. It is, therefore, essential that nursing students study the concepts and apply the ideas to real life situations.

In chapter one a definition of transcultural nursing was presented. Let us reflect upon its essential feature. *Transcultural nursing is a substantive area of study and practice focused on comparative cultural care (caring) values, beliefs, and practices of individuals or groups of similar or different cultures with the goal of providing culture-specific and universal nursing care practices in promoting health or well-being or to help people to face unfavorable human conditions, illness, or death in culturally meaningful ways.*[1] This definition of transcultural nursing contains many important ideas such as the emphasis on discovering culture care values, beliefs, and practices of specific cultures or subcultures in order to assist people with their daily health care needs. A comparative viewpoint is maintained in order to identify differences and similarities among or between cultures. It is this comparative viewpoint that enables the nurse to identify culture-specific and what constitutes universal care to clients or groups. Thus the ultimate goal of transcultural nursing it to tailor-make nursing care to fit reasonably the client's cultural specific expectations and care needs for beneficial health care outcomes and to identify universal nursing care practices.

As one ponders transcultural nursing further, the idea of human care (caring) values, beliefs, and practices becomes a central focus for nurses in learning about and practicing transcultural nursing. The author has declared since the late 1940s that care *is the essence of nursing and what the profession should be* focusing on. *Nursing is a caring professional and discipline* which directs nurses to discover and to provide knowledgeable and skilled care to clients. I defined *nursing as a learned humanistic and scientific profession and discipline focused on human care phenomena and caring activities in order to assist, support, facilitate, or enable individuals or groups to maintain or regain their health or well-being in culturally meaningful and beneficial ways, or to help individuals face handicaps or death.*[2] This definition reinforces the idea of *care as the essence and fundamental focus of nursing and transcultural nursing.*

In considering nursing as a caring profession and discipline, it is important to remember that nursing as a profession has a societal mandate to serve people. The professional nurse is challenged to serve others who need the assistance of a person prepared to respond to or who can anticipate the actual or covert needs of people. Nurses are professional persons who are ultimately held responsible for and accountable to people in a particular society or culture to give care that will help them to regain and maintain their health and to prevent illness.

Nurses function best as professional persons when they know and understand people are different cultures in relation to their life experiences, human conditions, and cultural values and beliefs. Today *all* professionals practices need to be culturally based and maintained to be effective and sustaining over time. Nursing is a culture and should have culturally defined modes of functioning and being which may change over time with societal changes. As a discipline, nursing is expected to discover and use knowledge that is distinctive and which explains and interprets nursing within and outside nursing. Most importantly, nursing as a discipline implies that there is a substantive body of knowledge to guide its members' thinking and actions. The discipline of nursing needs to focus on care/caring to explain health and well-being in different or similar cultures. Care, health, and well-being as nursing's discipline knowledge are central to what nursing is or should be. Transcultural nursing contributes some of the most significant knowledge to nursing as a discipline with its comparative care focus and with ways to use this knowledge to serve members of a given society but also to serve people worldwide.

In a number of publications I have discussed *human care and caring as the central distinct, and dominant foci to explain, interpret and predict nursing as a discipline and profession.*[3,4,5] *Human care*, a noun, refers to a specific phenomenon that is characterized to assist, support, or enable another human being or group to achieve one's desired goals, or to get help toward certain human needs. In contrast, *human caring* is focused on the *action aspect* or activities to provide service to other human beings. Differences in the meanings of care (noun) and caring (an action mode) are extremely important to advance the discipline of transcultural nursing and to practice caring as a professional art. More explicitly, I have defined care and caring as follows.[6]

Care *(noun) refers to an abstract or concrete phenomenon related to assisting, supporting, or enabling experiences or behaviors toward or for others with evidence for anticipated needs to ameliorate or improve a human condition or lifeway.*

Caring *(gerund) refers to actions and activities directed toward assisting, supporting, or enabling another individual or group with evident or anticipated needs to ameliorate or improve a human condition or lifeway, or to face death.*

These two definitions of care and caring are used in transcultural nursing and more recently in all areas of nursing as fundamental ways to guide nurses in discovering culture care knowledge and providing direct care. But since care is embedded in culture and is an integral part of all aspects of a culture, one needs to understand fully culture and its linkage to care/caring.

Culture comes from the discipline of anthropology. Culture has been defined and used by anthropologists and other social scientists for over 100 years. The term culture, however, was not used and did not have significance within nursing until I raised awareness that it was a crucial and major dimension of nursing in the early 1950s. Gradually, by 1990, culture began to be recognized by nurses and today the term is being used in a variety of ways with some questionable definitions. Because definitions are important, these definitions have slight modifications have been used in transcultural nursing for some time are provided:

Culture *refers to the learned shared, and transmitted knowledge of values, beliefs, norms and lifeways of a particular group that guides an individual or group in their thinking, decisions, and actions in patterned ways.*[7]

Subculture *is closely related to culture and refers to a group that deviates in certain areas from the dominant culture in values, beliefs, norms, moral codes, and ways of living with some distinctive features of its own.*[8]

Cultures and subcultures are developed by groups of people or population aggregates who have different values, beliefs, and lifeways that are preserved and usually transmitted intergenerationally. Subcultures are a smaller population group that establishes certain rules of behavior, values, and living ways that are different from dominant or mainstream cultures. Subcultures have some distinctive patterns of living with sets of rules, special values, and practices that are different from the dominant cultures. For example, there are subcultures of the homeless, substance abusers, elderly, abused women and children, chronically disabled, mentally retarded, deaf, AIDS victims, and often some religious sects and cults, political and social groups. These subcultures closely identify with their own group and see themselves as different from dominant or larger culture such as Anglo-Americans, African Americans, British, or Hispanic cultures. Transcultural nurses study and give attention to these subcultures for they, too, have culture caring needs, special health practices, and care problems.

Since culture is of central and importance to understand in transcultural nursing, several major features are identified. At the outset, the nurse should keep in mind that culture is as powerful a construct to anthropology as care is to nursing, and bringing them together in a new perspective makes culture care so relevant and powerful. Culture was first conceived and studied by anthropologists beginning in the nineteenth century, and continues to be central to anthropology. Culture, as simply defined refers, to learned and shared values, beliefs, and rules of behavior or standards of living that are valued and passed on intergenerationally. In transcultural nursing, culture becomes the critical and foundational base to understand people and to nursing as a culture with the many people nurses serve from different cultures. Culture is the broad yet specific context and concept to understand care and other aspects of nursing. It was, indeed, the missing element that was not recognized, studied, or drawn upon in nursing until the start of transcultural nursing. But we need to go further to understand the complex features of cultures.

First, *a culture reflects shared values, ideals, and meanings that are learned and guide human behavior, decisions, and actions.* With shared cultural values and norms, individuals and groups tend to value and uphold the rules for living in a culture because doing so brings security, order, and regulates behavior. Cultural values usually transcend individual values and have more influence to control and regulate group behavior. Cultural beliefs, values and behaviors are learned and are usually not genetically or biologically transmitted or determined phenomena. Cultures can have a powerful influence on people's behavior because they are learned and shared values, rules, and practices over time. They tend to become ethical and moral standards to guide behavior as expected obligations and responsibilities.

Second, *cultures have manifest (readily recognized) and implicit (covert and ideal) rules of behavior and expectations. Manifest cultural norms* or rules of behavior are the obvious and known beliefs and practices that are usually adhered to by people. *Implicit and ideal values* are usually covert cultural rules which are difficult for outsiders to discover and understand, but they exist and are important influences in making culture care decisions and actions. Ideal values must be reinforced in order to benefit the cultures or subcultures.

Third, *cultures have material items or concrete goods such as artifacts that give meaning and are special symbols of the culture.* Coke and Pepsi cans in the United States or bows an arrows in Papua New Guinea are example of cultural materials. *Cultures also have nonmaterial expressions and symbols that characterize the culture.* Beliefs in good and bad spirits by the Native American, the Vietnamese, Cambodian and other cultures are examples of nonmaterial culture. Nonmaterial cultural symbols, values, and beliefs are usually powerful influences that are often used to protect and reassure people. Human beings have unique abilities for symbolic thought and for making and using symbols in special ways. In transcultural nursing, nurses are expected to learn about material and nonmaterial cultural forms and their functions and roles in different cultures.

Fourth, *cultures have cultural traditional ceremonial practices such as religious rites and social feasts that are transmitted from one generation to another increasing the solidarity and unity of cultures.* Cultural rituals also pervade health care practices with nurses, physicians and others practicing rituals and ceremonies. For example, nurses have morning bathing rituals for clients and these rituals are learned by observing patterned behaviors as well as listening and talking to others involved in ritual activities. Rituals and ceremonies tend to reinforce healing and feelings of social group and cultural unity.

Fifth, *cultures have their local or emic (insider's) views and knowledge about their culture that are extremely important to discover and understand.* Emic ideas and beliefs are usually not openly expressed to or shared with cultural strangers until they observe signs of trust between themselves and outside strangers. Transcultural nurses are challenged to build trusting relationships to discover the people's emic "secret" knowledge world, because it is from this knowledge that they can learn so much about people. Emic information is usually the crucial knowledge to guide people behaviors. The nurse, however, must also learn about etic or outsider's knowledge. Etic data often contrasts sharply from the local emic cultural views or values. *Both emic and etic knowledge are studies to guide transcultural nursing practices.* I first discovered Pike's emic and etic terms in the late 1950s and have transformed these linguistic ideas into transcultural nursing.[9] Today these terms are now used as important ways to discover different world cultures.

Sixth, *all human cultures have intercultural variations between two or more cultures as well as intercultural variations within a particular culture.* Cultural variation is an essential anthropological concept to keep in mind when studying cultures. For example, African Americans in the United States and Italians from the northern and southern parts of Italy show intercultural variations in daily lifeways, food preparation, response to illnesses, death and in other areas. Intercultural variations exist in the values, beliefs and lifestyles between Greeks, Finnish, British, Latin Americans, Iris, and Germans. Transcultural nurses are taught about such intercultural and intercultural variations with thought to past traditions and contemporary patterns of living. Cultural variation becomes an imperative concept in nursing to accept and know in order to prevent stereotyping or making everyone exactly alike or to fit one defined mold of behavior.[10,11] In general, cultures are patterned, learned, and show small or great variabilities between and within cultures with respect to values, symbols, beliefs, rituals and other features.

Ethnicity is another term that needs to be clarified. *It refers to the social identity and past origins of a social group due largely to a language, religion and national origins.* This concept tends to be used more frequently by sociologists and psychologists than by anthropologists or transcultural nurses. "Ethnicity" often becomes vague with so many different uses especially by the lay public that it has become a catch all term with limited explanatory value. In transcultural nursing the term "culture" is used because it has more definitive characteristics, is more inclusive and has specific indicators. Culture also refers to the holistic patterned lifeways of a culture rather than to selected ethnic features or origin aspects.

Western and non-Western are terms used in transcultural nursing for general comparative purposes. *Western* refers to those cultures that are usually *highly industrialized and tend to be dependent on modern technologies with their lifeway practices.* Western cultures are also known for their emphasis on being efficient, using scientific or measurable factors, and of viewing themselves as progressive and modern. Modern cultures are, however, more recent in cultural history in the origin of human civilization compared to non-Western ones. Western cultures might include the United States of America, Canada, Europe, Japan and Australia. *Non-Western* (sometimes called Eastern) refers to *those cultures that have existed for thousands of years and have generally strong philosophical ideologies and usually rely less on modern technologies and other Western values.* Non-Western cultures tend to value their traditional philosophical beliefs, life experiences, and symbols. They may resist Western lifeways as counter to their values. Non-Western cultures might include countries such as China, South Africa, Indonesia, Vietnam, Papua New Guinea, Brunei, and areas within South America. These non-Western cultures have been slow to adopt modern Western ways of living with industrialization and other Western features. Instead, they tend to let their religious beliefs, kinship and cultural values and social-political ties guide them. Transcultural nurses are expected to assess signs of Western and non-Western cultural values in order to grasp the culture's orientation and caring modalities.

Culture values are generally viewed as *critical elements to understand in transcultural nursing because they greatly influence human behavior and action modes. Cultural value refers to the powerful internal and external directive forces that give meaning and order to an individual's group's thinking, decisions, and actions.* Discovering and understanding the cultural values of a culture becomes extremely essential in transcultural nursing because it is the values of an individual or group that greatly influence what clients do, how they react to strangers, and what they refuse to do or will do to cooperate with the nurse. Identifying and understanding specific cultural values of clients becomes the means to develop sound and reliable nursing care plans an decisions to provide therapeutic nursing care practices. Unfortunately, cultural values are not readily identified or shared by clients or other strangers. Instead many clients may not reveal their values and yet they may demonstrate them in subtle and critical situations. For example, Anglo-Americans value independence, freedom of speech, privacy, physical appearance, and desire to achieve as dominant in their lives. If these values are taken away, such as when Anglo-American men were hostages in Iran, these American men were reported to be very depressed, frustrated, and became ill. The Malawi people of Africa greatly value their extended family and children, and feel lost when they are not near them. Amish people value community living and praying together. Other cultures have their cultural values to guide their lives. Cultural values are therefore essential to know as they are powerful forces on everyday people's behavior in what one does and thinks each day. Some values are ideal and difficult to know compared to manifested values, such as Muslims praying five times a day. *Observing and identifying cultural values is one of the key skills of transcultural nurses.* Fortunately, many cultures have been studied with their cultural values by anthropologists and transcultural nurses, but the nurse must study any changes that may have occurred. *Cultural core values refer to those major and dominant values that are promoted and upheld by a particular culture, generally over time.* Several examples are given in this book with each culture because transcultural nurses have studied these core values and cultural care values in nursing practices. Values such as individualism and freedom to think and act are examples of cultural core values with Anglo-Americans, and these values dominate their way of living.

Culture shock is another key concept used in transcultural nursing that has been derived from anthropology. It *refers to an individual feeling disoriented or unable to respond appropriately to another person or situation because the lifeways are so strange and unfamiliar that one feels helpless, hopeless and confused.* Nurses, clients, families and researchers experience cultural shock in a variety of ways, usually with feeling of being unable to act in a given situation. There are many examples of nurses and other health personnel who experience culture shock in hospitals and clinics. For example, the nurse may be shocked to find a mother failing to respond to a crying child until the child throws something at the mother. I experience culture shock when I went to New Guinea and found no Western living conveniences such as running water and electricity in the homes and many children surrounding me each day. An Old Order Amish client may experience culture shock because he has never been in a hospital and is suddenly in an emergency room with many staff, electronic equipment, bright lights, and masked faces looking at him and his injured and uncovered body. Amish clients often experience culture shock and feel unable to respond to unfamiliar people and situations. Nurses who go overseas to work with people about whom they have never heard before usually experience culture shock. Culture shock limits one's ability to function in the strange culture and may leave one with continued feelings of helplessness.

Uniculturalism and multiculturalism are two concepts that need to be understood to guide one's thinking and actions in transcultural nursing. *Uniculturalism (or monoculturalism) refers to the belief that one's universe is largely constituted, centered upon and functions from a one-culture perspective and reflecting some cultural ethnocentric views. Multiculturalism* refers to *a perspective and reality that there are many different cultures and subcultures in the world which need to be recognized, valued, and understood for their differences and similarities.* Multiculturalism can enhance and help people to appreciate others and live together in a changing world, but it may be extremely difficult for nurses and health staff to develop flexibility and become more multiculturally-oriented.

Ethnocentrism is *a central concept in transcultural nursing* because it, too, is a strong influence on human behavior and action modes. *Ethnocentrism refers to the belief that one's own ways are the best, most superior, or preferred ways to act, believe, or behave. Ethnocentrism is a universal phenomena* in that most people tend to believe that their ways of living, believing, and acting are right proper, and even morally correct. However, a strong ethnocentric attitude can become a serious problem when one holds to firmly to one's own beliefs and standards and does not accommodate or even listen to someone else's views. Learning to value, appreciate, and understand the *why* of other cultures and their particular viewpoints is essential in transcultural nursing. For it is this knowledge and awareness of other's views that leads to creative ways to serve people. Indeed, differences which seem bizarre or strange may be common and important to a person from a specific culture. Strong ethnocentric views are usually related to strong uniculturalism and a lack of knowledge about other cultures. Sometime ethnocentrism is related to resistance to learn and change. Fear of changing one's own beliefs and values can greatly hinder professional relationships with clients, staff, and systems. It also limits nurses' professional growth and is a major concern for nurses who practice transcultural nursing. In general, ethnocentrism can lead to a host of cultural problems, tensions, and professional stresses.

Ethnocentrism often becomes apparent in different clinical practices and contexts. For example, if the nurse believes that there is only one way to make a hospital bed or to feed a child or adult. Clients will tell nurses that such views are questionable and problematic. Clients from different cultures make their beds differently according to their lifeways, and can be most unhappy when a bed is made that is too tight at the foot or and does not accommodate sufficient room for one's feet and moving about. Or take the example of the nurse who is so ethnocentric that she experiences culture shock with a client who eats snakes, bugs, kidneys, and opossum meat as delicacies. The nurse may be ethnocentric that she misinterprets the offerings and tries to impose her beliefs as to these people's eating habits without realizing the client's values or preferences. Rigid ethnocentric practices and attitudes by nurses usually lead to nurse-client stress, non-compliance, and many nurse-staff clashes. Professional ethnocentrism in nursing is not always recognized and discussed in educational and clinical settings, and so the problem may continue for some time. Client and nurse dissatisfactions will also be noted where strong ethnocentric attitudes and practices prevail.

Cultural bias is closely related to ethnocentrism. It refers to *a firm position or stance that one's own values and beliefs must govern the situation or decision.* A culturally biased person usually fails to recognize their biases and are difficult to work with in multicultural situations as they are too rigid in their thinking. Strong ethnocentrism is usually buttressed by cultural biases and leads to major difficulties in client care and staff relationships.

Cultural relativism has become a popular concept in anthropology and transcultural nursing. It refers to *the position that cultures are unique and must be evaluated according to their own values and standards.*[12] Cultural relativism may be a desired ethnocentric position for security and political reasons. True cultural relativists argue for an extreme position that a culture should not be judged by the values and lifeways of another culture and that all cultures are particular and nothing is universal about culture. A cultural relativist will uphold a practice of a particular culture and take steps to protect the culture. For example, letting a deformed child die because the culture abhors children that are not able to function in the society later in life, may be difficult to accept by professional staff but is a position upheld without judgment or decisions by outsiders. Transcultural nurses learn to become aware of their rigid cultural relativistic positions and avoid such stances. They learn to suspend judgment about a culture until one understands the meaning of cultural relativity and that cultures may change and one must respond to lifestyle and value changes. Transcultural nurses learn to respect cultural differences and consider ways to help cultural changes. Most cultures show variabilities and may wish to maintain some old and new ways of living.

Cultural imposition refers to the tendency of an individual or group to impose their beliefs, values, and patterns of behavior upon another culture for varied reasons.[13] In the mid 1950s, I coined this concept for transcultural nursing practices as I could see in clinical and in educational situations that it was a major problem for clients and students. Unfortunately, most nurses and health care providers were unaware of the way they were imposing their values onto others in clinical practices, teaching and administration. Cultural imposition remains a major and largely unrecognized problem in nursing due to cultural ignorance, blindness, ethnocentric tendencies, biases, and other factors. Cultural imposition practices exist between professional staff and clients, especially when clients find the staff hold considerably more power, influence and authority over their decisions and actions. Clients of some cultures perceive they have virtually no power or influence because of the strong authoritative action of the staff. Hence cultural imposition practices prevail and are a serious problem in health care. It is interesting to see how nursing and medical personnel often use their ethnocentric views in order to get clients to conform to their expectations and "to get the task done".

One can observe cultural imposition practices between nurses and clients in which the nurse believes her (his) views are the right, best, and most therapeutic professional ways and that the client's views are strange, bizarre, and non-desirable for their health. For example, a nurse imposed her stance that a Vietnamese client must eat hamburger and drink milk to be healthy despite the client's lactose intolerance problem and dislike for hamburger meat. A host of additional examples can be found in the daily practice of nursing service and in nursing educational institutions. Cultural imposition is not unique to nursing as other professional staff also practice it in similar and different ways. It remains a very serious problem because it is often used when the client is most vulnerable. This concept is demonstrated and discussed in other sections of this book.

Cultural blindness refers to the inability of an individual to recognize one's own lifestyle, values, and modes of behavior and those of another individual because of strong attitude to make them invisible due to ethnocentric tendencies. This is another term I coined and have used in transcultural nursing since the early 1962. It may seem strange to think that people are so blind that they cannot see other ways of living, doing things, or to learn from another's beliefs and values. For example, an Anglo-American nurse was caring for an Arab-Muslim who told the nurse several times that he would be gone from his room to say his prayers at certain times in the day and evening. The nurse came to give this client his medication at noon and became very upset because the client was not in his room. The nurse refused to recognize and accept what the client had told her and could not see or understand the importance or the Arab-Muslim's prayer expectations. Or consider the American nurse who believes every baby should be "bonded with his mother," and then finds a mother from a particular culture not upholding this belief. Moreover, the Anglo-American nurse had cultural blindness and could not understand the father's behavior and practice of protecting and holding the baby at a later age. In this situation, the nurse had cultural blindness and could not really "see" or understand the father's behavior or wishes. Many additional examples of cultural blindness can be identified as nurses work with clients, families and groups of different or similar cultures, and strong ethnocentrism is often at the root of the blindness.

Cultural pain refers to the suffering, discomfort, or unfavorable responses of an individual group towards an individual who has different beliefs or lifeways, usually reflecting the insensitivity of those inflicting the discomfort. This concept was coined by the author while observing such behavior between and among individuals or groups who were culturally or physically different. While nurses are aware of psychophysical pain expressions, they often are unaware that cultural pain exists and may be more hurtful than other kinds of pain. Cultural pain is a relatively new concept that has come to nurses studying transcultural nursing. Nurses prepared in transcultural aspects of pain are quick to identify such expressions and sources. For example, breaking a cultural taboo may be extremely painful as may culturally offensive comments from outsiders who do not know and understand the culture. Some clients of a particular culture feel they cannot respond to insults or demeaning comments but talk about experiencing cultural pain. Member of different cultures with different body sizes such as the tall Masai or the small pygmies of Africa may experience cultural pain from those who make offensive comments about their body build or movements.

There is also wide variability in how people respond to physical and emotional pain stimuli based on cultural values and beliefs. Some cultures are very expressive about pain and make loud verbal cries or other signs such as Jewish and Italians; whereas Russian, Lithuanian, German and Slovenian people seldom express pain in a noisy or overt way. The latter tend to be stoic or remain silent even when physical pain seems so evident as with injections or surgery without analgesic. Cultures learn to value stoicism and children are taught ways to ignore or not complain about pain. Enduring major pain often is linked with religious beliefs, whereby one gains grace and favor wit God or higher beings. In contrast, other cultures learn to respond to even the slightest pin prick, injury, or bodily offense. Nurses who have studied different cultures become aware of culture variabilities with pain for children and adults and respond appropriately to client pain differences in therapeutic and sensitive ways. Cultural pain as a new area of study in nursing will provide many insights previously unknown and unexplained in the health fields. The important *principle* is that what *constitutes pain for an individual or group is largely culturally learned and patterned from an early time in the life cycle.*

Bioculturalism refers to how biological, physical, and different physical environments of diverse and similar cultures relate to care, health, illness, and disabilities.[14] The human being is a person living within a holistic context with cultural, biological, physical, and emotional factors influencing one's lifeways, health and well-being. The holistic or total human perspective and lifeways is an essential principle to keep in mind in practicing transcultural nursing. How genetic, biocultural and other cultural aspects fit together in different ecological environments is important to consider in the assessment and care of people. For example, the Gadsup of Papua New Guinea like their ecology that blends with their total lifeways as they use the forest, grassland, gardens, and available rivers. And since Gadsup adults are small in body size compared to Anglo-Americans or Scandinavian people, one finds their physical stature works well in their environmental activities. It is of interest that one seldom finds a fat

Gadsup man or woman, due largely to cultural, biogenetic and environmental influences. Currently, the biocultural linkages and environmental aspects in transcultural nursing have only been limitedly explored except for work by J. Glittenberg and her associates.[15] Glittenberg is a nurse-anthropologist who has been especially interested in the biocultural aspects of human beings over time and in different ecological settings. Students in transcultural nursing are strongly encouraged to study *biophysical and genetic* research from the subfield of physical and cultural anthropology.

Culture-bound refers to specific care, health, illness, and disease conditions that are particular, highly unique, and usually specific to a designated culture or geographical area. For example, in the Highlands of Papua New Guinea, *kuru* was discovered in the early 1960s while the author was conducting field study in the area. It is a condition in which adult females died within approximately nine months. The illness response patterns were unique to the highland cultures and largely related to biocultural factors in transmission and frequency. Many theories and observations were made about *kuru*, which occurred mainly in the Highlands of New Guinea.[16] In Malaysia, one finds the culture-bound phenomenon of *running amok* in which males have violent running sprees and attacks animals, people, or objects. *Voodoo death* is another culture-bound condition largely found in the Caribbean in which death follows a curse from a powerful sorcerer. Anthropologist have studied these culture-bound conditions for many decades and their findings often reveal specific cultural areas and influencing factors until discovered elsewhere in the world. Transcultural nurses need to study culture-bound expressions and conditions in order to identify the nursing care needs of the people which seem to be unique or culture-bound within some cultures. This area of special interest could well open a major area of research in transcultural nursing.

Cultural diversity refers to the variations and differences among and between cultural groups due to differences in lifeways, language, values, norms, and other cultural aspects. Cultural diversity was one of the first central concepts in transcultural nursing because nurses tended to see all peoples and cultures as alike. Transcultural nursing takes into account general cultural differences and variabilities among cultures in order to prevent stereotyping or viewing all people alike. Identifying cultural diversities and the reasons for the variabilities is a major area continuing in transcultural nursing. Cultural diversity helped nurses to realize the differences but also how to provide culture specific and universal (common) care practices. Currently, cultural diversity is overemployed and often a meaningless cliche as nurses without preparation in transcultural nursing use the ideas. This book offers examples of cultural diversity which needs always to be examined along with cultural similarities among cultures.

Cultural universals refers to the commonalties among human groups in different contexts and among or between cultures. Cultural universals are the opposite of cultural diversity.

With the former, one seeks to discover and understand what is common or similar among cultures with respect to human care, health and well-being or illness states. Transcultural nursing focuses on both cultural diversities and universals (commonalties), and the ideas are supported by the major theory in the book, Culture Care Diversity and Universality. *The goal of this theory is to discover similarities and differences about care and its impact on the health and well-being of groups.*[17] Granted, it is difficult to find absolute universals, because cultures tend to vary in some aspects and would never be identically the same. However, *commonalties in lifeways, values and rules among cultures can be found.* The discipline of nursing needs to value culture care universals in order to know and understand millions of people it serve, worldwide. *For it is the commonalties among cultures that will help nursing to develop broad principles and care practices.* While most nurses without transcultural nursing tend to view most clients as *more alike*, more effort must be given to subtle diversities too. Keeping the view of all clients being alike is largely due to the absence of transcultural nursing knowledge and to avoid fear of the unknown or to make changes in nursing practice.

Racism is a term frequently used in the popular culture and media, but it is a term that is often misunderstood. *Racism is derived from the concept of race, and it is usually defined as a biological feature of a discrete group, whose members share distinctive genetic traits inherited from a common acestor.*[18] Race has become a popular and often negative term in the United States, Germany, Great Britain and many Western cultures with diverse usage linked to angry feelings about some cultures entering a country or taking positions they deserve. Other ideas about race need to be considered. For example, Anglo-Americans believe that as a race, they are "white" or "caucasian" skinned people. "Blacks" and others view African Americans as skin colored determinants. These color referents are only a part of the understanding of a culture. Moreover, there are often many shades of "black" that range from tan to brown, and to dark black. For example, Fijians in the Pacific Islands belong to the Polynesian culture and they have dark skin color, but they are not "black" and they dislike being called "black." These skin colors are referring to *phenotypes* which are external appearances of people by which people tend to be classified and labeled based largely on physical features.[19] These physical features are generally crude indicators and often develop over a long-term interaction between genes and environment. Understand race is with the concept of genotype. *Genotype* refers to a group with certain gene frequencies or cluster of genes that appear to be a more stable biologically or genetically based on common ancestry over time.[20] Genetic features are markers to change and are held to be important features to study.

Kottak discusses the idea that people are often talking about social races rather than genetic or biological races in public discourse, which nurses need to understand.[21] Social attitudes and perceived differences based on prejudices, discriminations, or different lifestyles enter into the use of race and racism. Still another way to understand *racism* is to refer to *it as the subordination and use of power and preconceived ideas and beliefs toward individuals, groups, or institutions for various reasons, due largely to a lack of understanding or prejudices about an individual or group.* The term *"ethnic people of color"* is also quite misleading and tends to be used by some "minority" nurses. The use of this term is not recommended in transcultural nursing because of its ambiguity, impreciseness and several misleading ideas. Unfortunately, racism can become vicious labeling with unsupported accusations, especially between "whites" and "blacks" and others. It can and does lead to anger, violence and prolonged alienation of human groups from others. In nursing, "racist" practices often lead to avoidance and to interpersonal tension, isolation, discrimination and covert anger. Nurses prepared in transcultural nursing can be helpful to explain cultural differences among nurses in values, beliefs, patterns and lifeways and to understand the *why* of these differences. A lack of understanding of cultural values and beliefs can be at the root of institutional racial labeling, disruptive behavior and prolonged animosity between nurses of different cultures. Racial problems do exist in nursing, but how they are interpreted and responded to merits the expertise of transcultural nurses and other experts in this area.

These terms prejudice, discrimination, and stereotyping are other concepts closely related to racism. The following definitions have been formulated by the author from anthropological and other sources, and are used in transcultural nursing. *Prejudice* refers to *preconceived ideas, beliefs, or opinions about an individual, group, or culture that limit a full and accurate understanding of the individual, culture, gender, race, event, or situation. Discrimination generally refers to the limiting of opportunities, choices, or life experiences because of prejudices about individuals, cultures, or social groups. Stereotyping refers to placing people and institutions, mentally or by attitudes, into a narrow, fixed trait, rigid pattern, or with inflexible "boxlike" characteristics.* I call stereotyping "boxing-in" people into a rigid picture or narrow view of people with no variability or differences. When nurses stereotype individuals or groups, they *fail* to recognize individual and *group cultural variations and cultural changes.* Stereotyping is one of the most common concerns of nurses when they being to study different cultures and learn about transcultural nursing. Nurses who make hasty pronouncements or generalizations without looking at the importance of cultural variability and patterns of diverse thinking and acting are usually limiting an understanding or people, which leads to stereotyping. In general, transcultural nursing knowledge can increase the nurse's awareness of prejudice, discrimination, and stereotyping, and especially help the nurse avoid rigid stereotyping or labeling a client or staff member with these terms without carefully assessing and understanding them from a transcultural perspective.

Culture encounter or contact occurs when a person from one culture meets or interacts briefly with a person from another culture. With casual encounters and brief normative exchanges of ideas, a person does not become acculturated or encultureated to another lifeway. Nor does a nurse with limited knowledge and study of the people automatically become an expert or an authority about a culture. All too frequently, nurses giving tours or on brief visits to a foreign area who encounter or interact with people of different cultures proclaim themselves to be experts about the culture. This leads to serious problems for the tour participants and also when tour leaders are published in nursing literature as if they were accurate. Often the leaders do not know and understand the culture. Brief encounters in a culture are superficial experiences and usually lead to major misinterpretations about the culture unless grounded in and mentored by transcultural nurse experts. As nurses continue to visit different countries one can predict the problem of superficial knowledge and inaccurate reports in journals and book publications will continue. Such practices can lead to "cultural backlash" and ethical problems which means that local cultures become negative to a tour experience. It is an ethical responsibility to know and report cultures as accurately as possible to avoid some of the transcultural problems cited above.

Enculturation is a very important concept in transcultural nursing and anthropology. It refers to *in-depth learning about a culture with its specific values, beliefs, and practices in order to prepare children and adults to function or to live effective in a particular culture.* For example, one speaks of a child becoming enculturated in a particular culture. When he (she) learns what is acceptable or unacceptable of the local values, beliefs, and actions within the culture in which raised. Accordingly, nurses can become enculturated within the nursing profession by learning the normative rules of behavior, values, and other features of the nursing culture. Much more attention needs to be given to how nursing students become fully enculturated into professional nursing values, norms, and lifeways in order to practice desired professional nursing norms. Transcultural nurses can greatly facilitate understandings related to enculturation practice with its strengths and limitations in nursing education and practice.

Acculturation is closely related to the concepts of enculturation and socialization, but different. *Acculturation refers to the process by which an individual or group from culture A learns how to take on many of the behaviors, values, and lifeways of culture B.* We speak of an acculturated individual when a culture A person adopts almost fully the lifeways and functions of people with norms and values of culture B. While an individual from culture A may sill retain and use some traditional values and practices, this individual has largely taken on a different way of living and valuing culture B lifeways. Diverse reasons for becoming attracted to another culture exist and are of interest to discover and understand. For example, a Vietnamese family which came as refugees to the United States initially retained its own values, but after ten years became acculturated to Anglo-American lifeways, largely for economic, political, and educational reasons. Many Vietnamese families, however, tend to retain their major religious beliefs and kinship values and do not give them up for Anglo-American lifeways. *Actually, few cultures become 100 percent acculturated to another cultural lifeway.* Cultures tend to be *selective* in what they choose to change and retain. Through culturalogical care assessments, the nurse identifies the areas of acculturation and ways they have taken on a different lifeway or patterns of another culture.

Socialization is another key concept important in transcultural nursing. It refers to the *social process where by an individual or group from a particular culture learns how to become a part of and function within the larger society in order to know how to interact with others, vote, work, and live in a society.* When Japanese people come to the United States to live or work, they need to learn how to become socialized into the American society by learning how to live, shop, buy goods, and interact and communicate with Americans and others in the American culture. Socialization is different from acculturation because the goal of socialization is to learn how to become a part of a larger society with its dominant values, ethons or national lifeways. *Socialization is learning to be an acceptable member of society.* Becoming a social being able to function in a society is an important aspect of socialization.

Assimilation refers to the *way an individual or group from one culture selectively takes on and chooses certain features of another culture without necessarily taking on the total attributes of a particular culture.* Assimilation is different from becoming fully acculturated or enculturated to another culture. With assimilation, the individual generally is attracted to certain features, techniques, material goods, or lifeways of a culture. Often with assimilation the individual does *not* adopt the total characteristics of another culture. For example, a Navaho nurse liked the specific ways that Anglo-American nurses feed newborn infants and so she adopted these particular attributes in her practice. She did not like the way Anglo-American nurses handled the Navaho mother's placenta after delivery, and she rejected that idea and did not assimilate this aspect of nursing care as it was counter to her cultural beliefs and practices. This Navaho nurse also encouraged American nurses to use the traditional infant cradle board in maternal care with Navaho women for several cultural reasons, such as the infant feeling secure and the advantages to the mother when working in her home (hogan) or in the field. The nurse remains attentive to what not be chosen due to cultural clashes and incongruities with the culture. The above concepts of culture contact (encounters), acculturation, enculturation, socialization, and assimilation are all major concepts to understand and use to assess and provide culturally congruent nursing care practices with cultures. Understanding these and can prevent serious culture clashes, conflicts, stresses and other care problems. Such knowledge and concomitant practices are an integral part of transcultural nursing knowledge and skills.

Culture Care

In the early 1960s I developed the construct of *Culture Care* to be used as central to transcultural nursing knowledge and practices. It *refers to the cognitively learned and transmitted professional and indigenous folk values, beliefs, and patterned lifeways that can be used to assist, facilitate, or enable another individual or group to maintain their well-being or health or to improve their human condition and lifeway.*[22] This construct is extremely important and will be discussed more fully in the theory chapter with examples of its use appearing throughout this book.

Configurative culture care has become a use full idea in transcultural nursing because it brings together larger patterns of behavior or rules of conduct of individual or groups. This term is defined as *pattern expectations of a culture (or subculture) and of the way these patterns fit together in meaningful clusters or characteristics.* It was developed by the author to help transcultural nurses look at large *gestalts* or *patterns of care* focused on ways the lifeways of an individual, group, or institution fit together. Establishing culture care configurations or different sets of patterns of care are extremely helpful to synthesize diverse and common care needs for clients. For example, configurative care as *a pattern of protective care* may closely fits several staff and client's patterns of care-giving and care-receiving. Another configurative care patterns would be *comfort care* and *supportive care* showing *sets of care fitting together in meaningful ways to clients.* There are preventive configurative care patterns that bring together local and professional care patterns in meaningful, holistic and practical ways. Another example would be American Gypsies who value protective group care as an integral part of the care patterns and this pattern is linked with watchful care and maintenance care in their daily lifeways.[23] The Gypsies also expect *maritime* (pure and impure) care patterns to be linked with protective care. Hence configurative culture care patterns are valuable to merge together interrelated features or components of care in a culture in configurative care patterns will be linked with protective care. Hence configurative culture care patterns are in order to provide culturally congruent and meaningful care practices. In the future, configurative care patterns will be sought to practice transcultural nursing as they provide *larger pattern sets to guide nursing care.*

Culture-specific care/caring refers to the particularized or tailorized modes of care practices that are identified or abstracted from an individual or group of a particular culture in order to plan and implement care that fits the client's specific care needs and lifeways. This term, culture-specific care, was conceived and used by the author in the mid 1960s in order to assist nurses to realize that culture care could be *specific or tailor-made to fit client and group needs.* The intent was to identify the construct as used by nurses to provide *culturally congruent care* and is discussed throughout this book.

The construct of *generalized culture* care was also coined and developed at the same time as *culture specific* are. It *refers to common professional nursing care techniques, principles, and practices that are useful to many clients as common or general human care needs.* *General culture care* concepts and practices are applied to *several cultures* and are used as beginning humanistic ways to relate to clients of several different cultures. They are sometimes known as the "common sense," "intuitive feelings," or as traditional ideas in nursing until the nurse has more in-depth and *differential knowledge* about the clients' culture care needs. *Generalized culture care* contributes to culture care universals or commonalties. It has led to the need for culture-specific care when clients fail to respond to general common needs. With more research worldwide of different cultures, nurses can anticipate a wealth of general knowledge and specific care knowledge and practices.

Culturally congruent nursing care refers to those cognitively based assistive, supportive facilitative, or enabling acts or decision that are mostly tailor-made to fit with an individual's, group's, or institution's cultural values, beliefs, and lifeways in order to provide meaningful, beneficial, satisfying care that leads to health and well-being.[24] This construct was conceived as a central idea and goal of the theory of Culture Care. It is explained with many examples in other chapters of this book as well as in the theory chapter.

Culture care conflict refers to the *areas of distress, concern or incompatibility when nursing care practices do not fit with a client's expectations, beliefs, values, or normative expectations.* It is closely related to culture care clashes, except that with culture care conflicts, the client generally refuses to comply with a nurse's requests or expectations with comments such as "I do not think it is good for me;" "My family does not approve of this treatment," or similar statements. The client may also show signs of being uncooperative or non-compliant when client culture conflicts are evident.

Culture care clashes refer to *sharp differences between the nurse and the client which occur because nursing practices are clearly incompatible, incongruent, or are perceived to be unacceptable with the client's values and expectations.* This concept was again identified as an essential one for transcultural nursing because cultural clashes in care giving practices were readily observed and heard between clients and nurses. The concept was noted in clinical units, for example, when a client refused nursing and medical treatments and became resistant, angry, and uncooperative because the taking of blood was a clash with the client's values. Cultural clashes can be observed non-verbally such as when a Vietnamese mother refused to breast-feed her newborn as her "real milk had not come through in her breast." Some clients remain silent and use a *"conspiracy of silence"* to show their dislike for nursing or medical care when it clashes with their cultural values and beliefs. To prevent such potential cultural clashes, the nurse carefully assesses the client's cultural needs, history of care, past hospitalization, and home care patterns and some current or past ways about the client's resistances with the nurse or others. For example, and *Arab-Muslim mother was told by the nurse in a large children's hospital that she could not remain with her child.* The mother responded, "But I must stay with my child." Immediately, a major culture clash was evident, and the Arab-Muslim mother took her child home and did not return. In this incident, the child was acutely ill, and it was the Arab-Muslim mother's cultural responsibility and obligation to remain with her child when ill and to care for her in the hospital. The Arab mother handled this cultural clash by taking her child home even though the child might have benefited from nursing and medical services. Such cultural norm expectations cannot be tossed aside, but must be understood and dealt with by the nursing staff.

Culture time refers to the *dominant orientation of an individual or group to different time periods related to past, present, and future which guides one's activities and thinking.* Interestingly, *cultures* tend to have their own *concept* of time which may differ considerably among cultures and from the time orientation of health professionals. Most *Anglo-Americans* tend to focus on the *present and future* times. In contrast, Africans, Hispanics, Latin Americans, and Southeast Asians tend to focus on the *present* time. African Americans often refer to *"BCT" (black colored time)* which means it is their own culture time and it is usually later than Anglo-American's exact clock time. Hence African Americans may be late for appointments and will gauge their activities within their time orientation. Anglo-Americans tend to live and function by nearly precise clock time in which appointments are made by specified clock time. They usually expect other cultures to conform to this clock time and get quite annoyed with lateness or "no show" appointments. Chinese, Vietnamese, British, and Koreans especially value past traditional time periods, but in more recent years, the Chinese, Japanese, and Koreans are valuing present time and Western oriented time efficient business schedules.

In many Western cultures precise clock time prevails, in which time is exactly measured by the minutes or hour of each day with activities that fit often with thought time schedules for the busy executive or professional person. Keeping exact clock time is often associated with money gains (or losses) and with production and product outputs.

But there is another kind of *time*, called *social time* in several cultures. *Social time refers to time for leisurely interactions and activities, with exact clock time as unimportant or of lesser significance. Cycle activity time* is important to know in transcultural nursing. This refers to *when certain activities occur each day, night, month, or during the year and cultures regulate their activities as a cyclic rhythm of life.* For example, the Gadsups of New Guinea value cyclic time as they regulate their daily and nightly activities by cycles of doing and living. They have had no watches or clocks, except for a few men in the government or "big business" affairs. The villagers regulate their concept of time by garden activities, picking coffee, eating and hunting which are all regulated by the sun, day-night activities, and sequential rhythm village and community activities. Transcultural nurses working in different cultures learn about different time orientations in order to function and live in the cultural world working or studying people. Clients in hospitals and homes use the time orientation they know, and so the nurse in culturalogical assignments discovers the clients' time and may negotiate time with clients or families to reduce anger, frustration, and breaking of appointments. Awareness of differential time also facilitates establishing and maintaining favorable relationships with individuals and groups in different cultural worlds.

Cultural space is another important idea to understand in transcultural nursing to prevent cultural conflicts and classes. *Cultural space refers to the variation of cultures in the use of body, visual, territorial, and interpersonal distance to others.* Understanding cultural spaces enables the nurse to anticipate, recognize, and respond to people in the space variations. Most nurses are unaware of cultural space variations or implicit or explicit space requirements of cultures. Without such awareness, the nurse will have difficulty with clients as they will violate another's space. This often leads to interpersonal stress, anger and a host of communication problems. Hall found in Western cultures that there were three primary space dimensions, namely: 1) the *intimate zone* (zero to eighteen inches), the *personal zone* (eighteen inches to three feet), and *social or public zone* (three to six feet).[25] The use of personal space was also studied by Watson who found that Canadians, Americans, and British require the most personal space, whereas Japanese, Arab Muslims, Latin Americans, and Africans needed less personal space.[26] Africans seemed to tolerate crowding in public spaces, but Japanese like more open living spaces. Germans and Scandinavians like lots of personal and environmental space. Further ideas about time and space are presented in early and insightful publications.[27,28]

Body touching between cultures also varies and is often gender related. Arab, South Vietnamese, and Papua New Guinea men touch in public arenas more frequently than women. Generally, *no-Western, traditionally oriented women* seldom *touch men in public places*, but are comfortable to touch appropriately other social friends, relatives, and familiars in their homes and non-public places. *Anglo-Americans generally touch* when they meet new and old friends and relatives. Often gender touching may be viewed as associated with homosexual behavior, but in many non-Western cultures such as Indonesia, Africa, and New Guinea, touching and holding hands is usually not interpreted or viewed as homosexual behavior. *Age grade companionship touch* is also accepted in Africa and other cultures. There is much to be learned about cultural space an touching as major areas of significance to transcultural nurses in discovering the meanings, forms, patterns, and changes over time. *Body touching* and human caring are largely *culturally defined and maintained as important modes of communication, human expression and for healing and well-being.*[29] The therapeutic value of touching as healing is often known to nurses, but more precise studies with specific outcomes need to be conducted transculturally.

Cultural context, refers to *the totality of shared meanings and life experiences in a particular social, cultural and physical environment that influence attitudes, thinking, and patterns of behavior.* Cultural context has long been neglected in nursing and yet it is a powerful concept to understand human behavior. Cultural context provides information on *shared meanings and responses* associated with particular events, cultural values and social situations. Cultural context is closely related to cultural values, social structure, and environmental factors viewed within the totality of a situation or ecological setting. Context often alerts people to recurrent life experiences to quickly grasp a situation and understand what is occurring in diverse situations.

Hall, an anthropologist, *identified high and low cultural contexts. High context culture refers to being deeply involved, knowing each other and the situation, and respecting shared values and beliefs almost instantly with less variability and with a desire to maintain these values.* In contrast, *low context culture refers to fewer shared meanings of life experiences or values with a tendency to change or allow situations to be altered.*[30] Since my 1970 use of *cultural context (the first in nursing)*[31] and Wenger's 1991 study of the phenomenon with Old Order Amish, nurses are using the idea more in nursing.[32] Wenger's research continues to be actively pursued as cultural context has many implications to understand clients and to respond to high or low contexts with implications to understand clients and to respond to high or low contexts with meaningful nursing responses. As transcultural nurses seek information about cultural context, they learn to include factors such as the home environment, cultural values, family relationships, education, worldview, political forces, and other holistic total needs of people. If nurses focus primarily on diseases, physical symptoms or individual behavior, they will miss valuable information related to cultural context. The Sunrise Model, with the theory of Culture Care, can be used as a guide to assess and arrive at the total cultural context for individuals and groups (see chapter four). The Sunrise Model helps the nurse focus on worldview, social structure, and ethnohistorical factors and related areas that influence high and low cultural contexts. In general, it is the cultural context of people that provides the nurse with a truly holistic picture to understand fully clients' behavior and their cultural group.

Culture comforts refers to the *diverse ways the nurse uses culture care patterns, specific information, and previous client life experiences to ease or relieve the clients' distresses, strains, or concerns.* Comforting clients, families, and others in crisis and non-crisis situations is a knowledge and skill area that needs far more attention from a transcultural perspective. And since comfort care expressions are largely culturally based, they can be observed and studied in a variety of contexts such as in the home, hospital and clinic, but especially in hospice settings and homes for the elderly and foster children. Different cultures have many subtle and explicit ways to provide culture comforts.

Generic (Lay and Folk) and Professional Care/Caring

There are two very important concepts in transcultural nursing that provide new insights and directions to nurse practitioners, researchers, and educators. They are generic care and professional nursing care. It is important to differentiate these concepts with definitions to advance nursing knowledge transculturally and to become competent in transcultural nursing.

Generic care (caring) refers to culturally learned and transmitted lay, indigenous (traditional) or folk (home care) knowledge and skills used to provide assistive, supportive, enabling, and/or facilitative acts (or phenomena) toward or for another individual, group, or institution with evident or anticipated needs to ameliorate or improve a human health condition (or well-being), disability, lifeway, or to face death.[33]

Professional nursing care (caring) refers to formal and cognitively learned professional care knowledge and practice skills, obtained through educational institutions, that are expected to provide assistive, supportive, enabling or facilitative acts to or for another individual or group in order to improve a human health condition (or well-being), disability, lifeway, or to work with dying clients.[34]

These two definitions of care are now being used and studied by nurses in different nursing contexts. These concepts were coined and developed by the author to differentiate transculturally two important dimensions of human care. They have become central to the study of transcultural nursing and especially in relation to the Culture Care theory. Examples of many differences in generic and professional care findings are discussed in several chapters in this book.

The author has studied a number of Western and non-Western cultures with respect to comparative generic (folk) and professional care characteristics and discovered contrasts between these two kinds of care systems. These dominant contrasts of findings are presented in Table 2.1 and can be used as reflective or "holding knowledge" for the nurse to reflect upon as one cares for clients, families, and groups of different cultures. Granted, some cultural variability prevails, but the patterns and general features were substantiated with many key and general informants in qualitative ethno care research over three decades. These characteristics can assist the nurse in the hospital or in home-based communities.

Table 2.1

Dominant (Emic) Comparative Features of Generic (Folk) and Professional Health Care from the Consumer's Views[1]

Generic Folk, Lay Care/Caring	Professional Health Care
1. Is humanistically-oriented and people-centered.	1. Is scientifically-oriented and patient-illness centered.
2. Uses practical knowledge in familiar ways to care for others.	2. Uses strange or unfamiliar terms and approaches to treat patients.
3. Focuses on broad holistic lifeways, beliefs, values, and life experiences and worldviews of people.	3. Seems fragmented and uses on symptoms, body-mind parts, specific diagnoses, and curative medical treatments with many diverse staff.
4. Has as its focus caring and curing modes with the use of home, community, or familiar resources.	4. Has as its major focus body-mind curing modes in unfamiliar medical or hospital settings.
5. Relies on lay practices and understanding cultural factors to help people regain health and for doing daily functions.	5. Relies on biophysical and emotional factors of patients with pathologies and treatment regimes.
6. Focuses on preventing illnesses and deaths by maintaining cultural rules, practices and taboos known and tested in the culture over time.	6. Focuses on repairing body or mind conditions based on medical specialists in the profession and some care givers.
7. Focuses on how to use folk home remedies and carers or healers as they know what is best for the client. A client goes to professional staff and hospitals at last resort.	7. Cost for services are very high and often beyond ability for many poor or minority cultures to use. Consumers tend to avoid using unless have they have lots of money.
8. Reflects high cultural context modes of communication.	8. Reflects low cultural context modes of communication.
9. Limits use of high tech tools and instruments, uses more cultural rituals.	9. Uses many high tech tools and machines in hospital with rituals.

[1]These emic or local characteristics were obtained from Leininger's in-depth qualitative ethnonursing study with many different cultural informants over nearly two decades (1973-1990). The characteristics reflect the people's emic views of differences between the generic folk or lay system with those of professional care systems in fifteen non-Western cultures.

The concepts of generic folk care remain largely unknown to most health personnel, and yet the concepts are critical to health care outcomes and to provide culturally congruent care. Interfacing generic and professional care into creative and meaningful nursing may well unlock the essential ingredients for quality health care. Other health disciplines are finding generic and professional care of great interest in professional practices.

Overview of Transcultural Nursing's Phases of Development (1955-1994)

Undoubtedly, the reader must be wondering how transcultural nursing came to be. Table 2.2 provides an overview showing the major phases and foci from the mid 1950s to 1994. One can see in table 2.2 that Phase I focused on the dominant transcultural constructs of interest in the 1960s which were: 1) culture care/caring; 2) health; 3) environmental contexts; and 4) illness experiences. Humanistic care and caring from a generic and professional stance were a central focus of transcultural nursing. Knowledge from nursing, anthropology, and other disciplines was selectively used, but largely reformulated to fit the philosophy and goals of transcultural nursing. The theory of Culture Care was developed to provide a conceptual and theoretical framework to discover transcultural nursing knowledge. In Phase II knowledge was generated from transcultural nursing and ideas from a few other disciplines according to the interests of transcultural nurses. In Phase III transcultural nurses used transcultural nursing knowledge and evaluating how the practices improved client care services to diverse consumers worldwide.

From table 2.2 one can see the evolutionary developmental phases of transcultural nursing over four decades. Transcultural nursing was planned with an orderly transition to establish the field on a sound basis. Moreover, this development was based on envisioning and predicting nursing constructs, domains of inquiry with theories and research methods to explicate a body of transcultural nursing knowledge. The use of theories to guide nurses continues to be used in a variety of cultural contexts. The knowledge generated is used to benefit clients health care of many diverse cultures. Today these phases are diffusing into different schools of nursing and health settings in different ways world wide. Phases II and III need far more attention, but a considerable body of knowledge in transcultural nursing is now available to help guide students, teachers and practitioners. More studies are needed to show the short and long term benefits of transcultural nursing on people's health and well-being.

Table 2.2

Phases of Transcultural Nursing (1955-1994)

Phase I (Constructs, Theories and Research)		Phase II (Uses)	Phase III (Benefits)
Major Transcultural Nursing Constructs:	Major Theories and Methods to Develop Transcultural Research-Based Knowledge:	Use of Transcultural Nursing Knowledge in Education and People Services:	Assessing Benefits of Transcultural Nursing to:
1. Culture Care/ Caring	1. Culture Care Theory (Leininger)	1. Educational Settings	Consumers/Clients Health Providers
2. Health (Well-being)	2. Explanatory Theory (Kleinman)	2. Hospital/Clinics	Nursing Services
3. Environmental Contexts	3. Structural-Functional	3. Home and Community Agencies	Nursing Education Researchers
4. Illness Experiences	4. Others	4. New and Alternative Services	Consultants Health Professionals
Contributions from Other Disciplines	Research Methods	5. Diverse Context Settings	
Anthropology and other Social Sciences	Ethnonursing Ethnography Ethnoscience	6. Consultation	
Humanities, Liberal Arts and Philosophy	Life histories Narratives		
Health and Medical Sciences	Phenomenology Audiovisuals		
	Other qualitative and quantitative methods		

Basic Transcultural Nursing Care Principles

In this section some basic transcultural nursing principles are presented which incorporate a number of concepts, principles, and ideas discussed earlier in this chapter. The principles stated below are offered as guides in transcultural nursing practices. They have been used by faculty, students, and practitioners over time. Some of the principles reflect some of the general assumptions supporting the Culture Care theory to advance transcultural nursing knowledge. As transcultural nursing moves to become the central and arching framework for all areas of nursing, these principles will have even greater meaning and uses in health care reforms and in providing some distinct directions for health care. They are important principles to help beginning and advanced nursing students in classroom and clinical field settings.

As you study each principle, its important to let your mind form creative ways to apply these examples to people care in different cultural contexts. One needs to consider both similarities and differences with individuals, families, and groups seeking health care. The nurse draws up professional nursing knowledge, but always with generic nursing care knowledge of different cultures. The client's own natural and familiar caring life experiences need always to be included.

The transcultural nursing principles are as follows:

1. Human caring with a transcultural focus is essential for the health and well-being of individuals, families, groups and institutions.
2. Every culture has specific beliefs, values, patterns of caring and healing which nurses need to discover and use in the care of people of different and similar cultures.
3. Comparative cultural expressions, meanings and patterns of culture care and health are fundamental sources of knowledge to guide nursing care practices.
4. Cultures have the right to have their cultural care values, beliefs and practices respected and appropriately used in nursing and other health services.
5. Culture care and health practices vary in Western and non-Western cultures and may change over time.
6. Understanding and using the language of the people is extremely important in culture care.
7. Transcultural nursing knowledge and skills provide valuable data to develop meaningful, competent, congruent, safe, and beneficial nursing care practices.
8. Understanding culture care differences and similarities from the people's emic worldview, language, ethnohistory, history, and social structure features (including religion, kinship, education, economics, politics, and cultural values), and from particular wellness and illness patterns, communication modes, and space concepts are essential reflective knowledge to know, understand, and practice transcultural nursing.

9. Generic (folk lay) and professional care knowledge and practices are generally different knowledge and experience bases which need to be assessed and compared before using the information in client care.

10. Through time, human cultures learned different patterns of communication and different culturally-based ways to obtain caring or healing practices.

11. Different modes of learning and transmitting culture caring and health through the lifecycle are major foci of transcultural nursing education and practice.

12. Transcultural nursing begins by understanding one's own culture and then reflecting how one's own culture might influence another culture in behavior, actions, and decisions.

13. Transcultural nursing goes beyond cultural diversities and includes cultural similarities to provide beneficial client care practices.

14. Transcultural nursing that is built upon culture care patterns and life experiences as the central focus of transcultural nursing brings distinct and different knowledge and skills to nursing and to client services.

15. Transcultural caring actions or decisions should reflect the creative use of research-based knowledge to assist people from a holistic people-centered perspective that is rooted in the cultural context of human behavior.

16. Transcultural nursing necessitates co-participation of client and nurse for the nurse to be an effective transcultural nurse practitioner, using Leininger's three modes of nursing action and decisions generated from the theory goals.

17. Transcultural nursing is focused more on other-care than self-care in order to meet more universal human cultural needs of people worldwide.

18. Active observations, participation and reflection constitute the desired transcultural nursing mode to discover and respond to client family needs.

19. Transcultural nursing involves attention to verbal and non-verbal language in cultural context with meanings and symbols in order to have beneficial and therapeutic culture care outcomes.

20. Understanding the cultural context of the client is a powerful means to assess and understand nurse-client relationships and ways to respond to cultures of diverse contexts.

21. Transcultural nursing is directed toward the goal that someday all nurses will provide culturally congruent nursing care to all peoples in the world.

Incidents to Learn about Transcultural Nursing

In this last section several actual nursing incidents between nurse and clients, and between nurses and other health personnel are presented to help the reader learn about and understand the importance of transcultural nursing. Reflection questions are offered to help the nurse center-in or focus upon important concepts and principles already presented in this chapter. These transcultural nursing incidents have been taken from real life experiences, observations, stories, life events and narrative epics with nurses and clients in different cultural settings. Let us first consider these following reflective questions before focusing on the transcultural nursing incidents:

1. What do you believe is occurring in this incident?
2. What makes this a transcultural nursing incident?
3. What transcultural nursing understandings are needed for the nurse to respond to this incident in a culturally sensitive, responsible, and competent way?
4. What signs are evident that the nurse(s) and other health personnel responded or failed to respond effectively to this transcultural situation?
5. What transcultural nursing concepts, principles and influencing factors were evident in this incident or situation?
6. With your current insights about transcultural nursing, how would you have responded to this situation?
7. What did you learn from this incident about the nature and importance of transcultural nursing?
8. How do you believe this incident should have been responded to differently to provide culturally nursing care?

Transcultural Nursing Clinical Incidents

1. Clinical Incident: Vietnamese Child

A Vietnamese child was hit by a car on the street and was brought to a general hospital emergency unit. Six family members rushed into the emergency unit and hovered over the child's head. The Vietnamese elders quickly placed a white cloth on the child's head. The family members cried loudly and were very upset. The emergency room nurse and physician were stunned with the extended family's behavior, and could not understand why so many family member came and why they were persistent to be with the child and covered the child's head immediately. The child died and the family members began to grieve loudly, keeping their hands on the child. The nurses experienced culture shock and felt helpless. Later a transcultural nurse specialist explained the parent's behavior to the staff with two major ideas: 1) the extended family were expected to be present and to cover the child's head with a white cloth because the head is sacred, 2) the white cloth was to protect the spirits which are power forces for healing. Other cultural factors were also evident and call for reflection by the reader.

2. Clinical Incident: African American Woman

An African American woman from the southern United States wanted to wear a cord with knots around her waist during the delivery of her child. A head nurse said, "I need to remove this string. It is too dirty and unnecessary." She took the cord without the client's consent and was going to destroy it. The client, however, held firmly to the cord and would not let the nurse have it. The client kept saying, "I need this (cord) to have a safe delivery." After the mother was given the anesthesia, the staff nurse removed the knotted cord and destroyed it. Unfortunately, the infant died during the delivery and the grieved woman attributed the death of her child to the fact that the staff "took her cord away." When the woman left the hospital, she was very upset and kept saying, "I want my baby and my cord." The nursing staff did not understand why the cord with knots was so important to this African American woman. What would explain this transcultural incident?

3. Clinical Incident: Chinese Man

A recent Chinese immigrant had major bladder surgery. He was told by the nursing staff to "force fluids." The client did not understand the "forced fluid" expectation. He refused to drink the glasses of cold water from the big pitcher left on his bedside table. Each time the nursing staff entered the client's room, they reminded him that he needed to force fluids and drink many glasses of water. They threatened that his physician would order intravenous fluids if he did not drink more water. He refused to drink the water on his bedside. The staff said he was "uncooperative," "strange," and a "non-compliant" person. When the client's daughter came to see him, she told the nursing staff that he would drink hot herbal tea but not cold water. Finally, the nurses gave him the hot tea, and he drank several cups. The nurses did not understand why the hot tea was culturally acceptable as it was not what the nurses would drink. Later, a transcultural nurse explained the "hot and cold" theory of the Chinese people and its importance in nursing care. Additional cultural factors evident in this nursing situation need to be examined.

4. Clinical Incident: Navaho Mother

A Navaho mother gave birth to a baby girl in a large urban hospital. The nurses assisting with the delivery put the placenta and umbilical cord in a delivery pan and had the nursing assistant dispose of it. When the Navaho mother got ready to leave the hospital, she asked for her placenta and umbilical cord. She learned that the staff had destroyed it. The Navaho mother and her family were very upset as they thought the nursing staff understood the significance of the umbilical cord and that it would be saved for the mother. The nursing staff did not like the Navaho woman's request. To the nurses, this woman's request was a very strange one, as "No other patients would want a bloody placenta and cord, and none had ever requested them before." The Navaho mother and her kinsmen cried as they left the hospital and said, "We have no hope for our child. We must not return to this hospital."

5. Clinical Incident: Chinese, Italian, and Philippine Clients

An evening nurse was caring for Chinese, Italian, and Philippine clients who had surgery. She observed that only the Italian client requested pain medication, which she gave to him. The Philippine and Chinese clients remained silent. The nurse asked if they were having pain and needed medication which the physician had ordered "per the request of the patient." The Chinese client, who had major surgery, firmly refused the medication. The nurse "knew he had pain" and again offered him some pain medication. The Chinese client refused pain medication and became angry saying, "I don't need anything." The nurse acknowledged his wishes. When the physician came, he noticed the client had minimum pain medication. He ordered that the client have a morphine injection immediately. The client again firmly refused the physician's order and said, I don't take pain medicines, as I know how to handle pain." The physician told the nurse to give a small dose to the client despite the client's stance. What are the ethical aspects of this situation?

Interestingly, the Italian client frequently called for pain medication and never seemed to be relieved of pain. The Philippine client did not ask the nurse for pain medication, but he explained to the nurse, "It is Bahala no (God's will), and I can bear the pain Jesus give me." The nurse talked to the Philippine client and said, "I hear you, but God wants you to have some medication to ease your pain." The Philippine client reluctantly accepted the nurse's expectation because nurses are professional authorities. The nursing staff did not understand why there were so many differences with the Italian, Philippine, and Chinese clients. Later, they learned that "God's will" and stoicism were cultural values that guided the Philippine and Chinese clients' beliefs and decision. Interestingly, the Italian client cried for pain medication and got medication immediately from the nurse. The cultural variabilities among the clients of different cultures were baffling to nurses on the critical care unit.

6. Clinical Incident: Mexican American Woman

A Mexican American client had an appointment at 2:00 p.m. with a nurse and a physician for a "big lump in her abdomen and complaints of pain." At 2:00 p.m., the client did not appear at the office. The nurse and physician were upset and said, "If she comes, she will have to make another appointment as we can not see her later or whenever she arrives." At 4:00 p.m., the client came to the office but was told, "You missed your appointment time. We can not take you and you will need to make another appointment." She was upset. She attempted to explain that she could not find a relative to care for her three small children and she had to wait for a relative to bring her to the clinic. She told how their car did not run well and was out of gas, and that she had also lost the address. These explanations did not help, and she had to get another appointment. The client became upset about it and said, "I am in pain and I hope I will still be alive when I return next time. I knew I should have gone to our local healer - they understand me." The physician appeared and gave the client a lecture saying, "Money is time for us and you need to be on time." She went home, but was upset and crying. Later that evening she said, Those people do not understand our lifeways."

7. Clinical Incident: Fijian Man

A client from the Fiji Islands was admitted to an American hospital in Hawaii for diagnostic testing and a CAT scan. This Fijian man had never been in a large modern hospital nor in Hawaii. He was apprehensive about the many new things he and his family saw as they entered the city and the large public hospital. Nevertheless, he was urged to get the tests and CAT scan done quickly because of a possible brain tumor. As his extended family members remained in the waiting room, the client went into a room for tests without any family members with him. The family members in the waiting room were very anxious and requested to be with him. A hospital nurse told the family members, "It is against hospital rules that you can be with the client when tests are given. We cannot change the rules for you." They were told to read the magazines on the table in the reception room. They were too anxious to read, and they also found the magazines were in English, not written in their language.

In the meantime, the client entered to have a CAT scan with two technologists and a nurse. They explained the machine to the client in scientific terms pointing to parts of the huge machine. However, he was obviously anxious and his English was inadequate to share his feelings. He said, "It looks too big for me." He was told that the staff would put him inside the CAT scan and close the lid. Then they told him that they would "take slicing pictures or sections of different parts of your brain. The machine does everything. Just remain quiet and cooperate." The client placed in the chamber, but he was terrified. He remained stoic and tried to show that he was a brave man with a fighting spirit. Inside he believed the machine would kill him. He envisioned that they would "slice" his brain and that it was a "death machine." After a few minutes, he called for his family members, but they were gone. The nurse kept saying to him, "It will take a few more minutes and you will be finished." The words did not satisfy him, and he interpreted this to mean that he would soon be killed. He insisted on getting out of the machine. The work "CAT scan" made him worried and it frightened him for a "cat" to have such power, as it was a negative symbol in his culture. The whole experience was terrifying for him. He and the family left the hospital. He went back to Fiji and returned to his folk healers. Interestingly, he was healed by the folk healers in his familiar environment, and with his family present. He often tells others about his experience of going to "a strange country, a strange big city, and being with strange people who almost killed me."

8. Clinical Incident: Arab Muslim Man

An Anglo-American senior baccalaureate nursing student was assigned to care for an acutely ill and apparently dying client who recently had come from the Middle East. Unfortunately, the student had no course or preparation in transcultural nursing, but was told by the head nurse to "care for a newly admitted client who spoke another language." When the student entered the client's room, she found eight people around the male client's bed. She asked all of the visitors to leave the room as she was to give "morning care to him." The visitors refused to leave the room and continued to talk to the client. The nursing student returned to the head nurse expressing her frustration at not being able "to get those visitors who speak a strange language to leave the room." The head nurse told her to return to the room and "to be firm." But this time when she came into the room, the visitors moved the bed so it faced an east window. The visitors, whom she realized later were close relatives, were praying loudly and calling for "Allah." She became more upset and felt it was impossible to care for the client. She firmly told the relative that, "That this bed has to be returned to its proper place as it is a hospital regulation." One relative who spoke some English said, "It must be in this place so Allah can take care of him." The nursing student did not know who Allah was and tried to clarify this with the male relative, but she though the explanation was strange. The student then returned to the head nurse and emphatically refused to give any care. She said, "It is impossible to give (him) care." Later in the day, the student learned that the client had died and that he was an Arab Muslim. This incident baffled her because the situation was so bizarre, and the client with all the family was so different from Anglo-American clients she had cared for in the past. She felt so ineffective and unsuccessful in her nursing care. The why of the Arab Muslim behavior was never fully understood by the nurses and other health personnel. Later, when this critical incident was discussed in a transcultural nursing course, the student surprised at how the others would have handled it. "Now I care for this client I did not understand before." And to the faculty she said, "Why was I cheated in my nursing program without knowledge of these different cultures we are expected to care for in nursing?" The faculty explained they never had transcultural nursing and never though students would need it today. This statement annoyed the student.

Summary

In this chapter a number of fundamental and essential transcultural nursing definitions, concepts and principles were presented along with several clinical transcultural nursing incidents. The ideas in this chapter provide an important foundation for understanding and working with clients of different or similar cultures.

The evaluation of transcultural nursing in phases was also presented to demonstrate development of a new field of study and practice in nursing. Indeed, transcultural nursing knowledge has become essential today to understand and work with people in order for nurses to provide competent, responsible and appropriate nursing care. Understanding these different concepts, principles, and incidents can prepare the nurse to enter the world of the individual, family and community to give transcultural nursing. It is the use of transcultural nursing knowledge and practices that is transforming nursing to meet our rapidly changing multicultural world. Moreover, with transcultural nursing insights one can see from the eight clinical transcultural incident how important and essential such knowledge is to understand and help the nurse, client and other staff members. This chapter challenges nurses to study available knowledge in transcultural nursing in order to prevent cultural imposition practices, cultural clashes and conflicts. Most importantly, the use of transcultural nursing concepts and principles can lead to effective and satisfying nursing care to clients - the true purpose of nursing as a professional and humanistic service.

References

1. Leininger, M. M. "Transcultural Nursing: A New and Scientific Subfield of Study, in Nursing, *Transcultural Nursing: Concepts, Theories, and Practices,* M. Leininger, ed., New York: John Wiley & Sons, 1978, pp. 8-12.

2. Ibid. pp. 32-33.

3. Leininger, M. M. "The Phenomenon of Caring: Importance, Research Questions, and Theoretical Considerations," *Care: An Essential Human Need,* M. Leininger, ed., Detroit: Wayne State University Press, 1988, Thoroughfare, New Jersey: C. Slack, Inc., 1981, p. 9.

4. Ibid.

5. Ibid.

6. Ibid.

7. Leininger, M. M. "Some Basic Curricular Teaching - Learning concepts," *Transcultural Nursing: Concepts, Theories, and Practices,* M. Leininger, ed., New York: John Wiley & Sons, 1978, p. 491.

8. Ibid. p. 493.

9. Pike, K. *Language in Relation to a Unified Theory of the Structure of Human Behavior*, v. 1, Glendale, California: Summer Institute of Linguistics, 1954.

10. Leininger, M. M. "The Significance of Cultural Concepts in Nursing," *Journal of Transcultural Nursing,* v. 2, no. 1, Summer, 1990, pp. 52-59.

11. Haviland, W. *Cultural Anthropology,* 7th ed., Orlando: Harcourt Brace Jovanovich College Publishers, 1993, pp. 30-35.

12. Ibid, p. 49.

13. Leininger, M. M. "Becoming Aware of Types of Health Practitioners and Cultural Imposition," *Journal of Transcultural Nursing,* v.2, no. 2, Winter, 1991a, pp. 32-39.

14. Moore, L. P. Van Arsdale, J. Glittenberg, and R. Aldrich. *The Biocultural Bases of Health,* Prospect Heights: Waveland Press, 1980.

15. Ibid.

16. Haviland op. cit., p. 10.

17. Leininger, M. M. *Culture Care Diversity and Universality: A Theory of Nursing,* New York: National League for Nursing Press, 1991b.

18. Kottak, P. *Anthropology: The Exploration of Human Diversity,* New York: McGraw Hill, Inc., 1991, p. 68.

19. Ibid. pp. 64, 69.

20. Ibid. p. 68.

21. Ibid.

22. Leininger, M. M. "The Theory of Culture Care Diversity and Universality," *Culture Care Diversity and Universality: A Theory of Nursing,* M. Leininger, ed., New York: National League for Nursing Press, 1991b, p. 47.

23. Bodner, A. and M. Leininger, "Transcultural Nursing Care, Values, Beliefs and Practices of American (USA) Gypsies." Journal of Transcultural Nursing. vol. 4, no. 1, Summer, 1992, pp. 17-29.

24. Leininger, M. op. cit., 1991b p. 49.

25. Hall, E. T. *The Silent Language,* Westport, Connecticut: Greenwood Press, 1966.

26. Watson, O. M. *Proxemic Behavior: A Cross-cultural Study,* The Hague: Mouton de Gruyter, 1980.

27. Hall, E. T. Op. cit.

28. Hall, E. T. *The Hidden Dimension,* New York: Doubleday, 1966.

29. Leininger, M. M. "Selected Culture Care Findings of Diverse Cultures Using Culture Care Theory and Ethnomethods," M. Leininger, ed., *Culture Care Diversity and Universality: A Theory of Nursing,* New York: National League for Nursing Press, 1991b, pp. 355-357.

30. Hall, E. T. *Beyond Culture.* Garden City, New York: Anchor Press, 1976.

31. Leininger, M. M. *Nursing and Anthropology: Two Worlds to Blend,* New York: John Wiley & Sons, 1970, pp. 111-113.

32. Wenger, A.F. "The Culture Care Theory and the Old Order Amish," *Culture Care Diversity and Universality: A Theory of Nursing.* M. Leininger, New York, National League of Nursing Press 1991, pp. 147-173.

33. Leininger, M. op. cit., 1991a, p. 38.

34. Leininger, M. op. cit., 1991c, pp. 355-375.

Chapter 3
Overview of Leininger's Culture Care Theory
Madeleine Leininger, PhD, LHD, FAAN, CTN, RN

Theories are creative ways to discover new "truths," refute inadequate explanations, and gain in-depth insights about a phenomenon in order to advance discipline knowledge and improve human conditions.

During the past four decades a number of nurse theorists have been active in developing and disseminating knowledge for the profession and discipline of nursing. These theorists have been eager to use the theory-based knowledge to establish new practices or to improve or change existing conditions. The pursuit and use of theoretical knowledge is similar to other scholars' work in the discovery of new findings or to refute established ideas in the history of human beings.

Theory construction and the use of findings from different nurse theorists have been some of the most encouraging and important developments in nursing. Several nurse theorists have stimulated nurses to explore diverse theoretical ideas in order to improve people care and advance nursing knowledge. The use of nursing theories has challenged nurses to be creative thinkers, to discover the nature and essence of nursing as a discipline and to use findings in ways to improve nursing practice, education and in other human services. Most importantly, nursing theories continue to reshape and transform nursing into a scholarly discipline and show the value of theory findings in different societies. Nursing theories have helped to explain nursing and change the public image of nurses as scholars with great intellectual and practice abilities to make significant contributions to humanity. Accordingly, the public is recognizing that nurses are capable of developing and guiding their own discipline and professional practices. In several places, the public knows that nursing is no longer and extension of physicians or mini-physician practitioners. Nurse theorists have stimulated nurses to study phenomena that characterizes the unique and distinct features of the discipline. These developments in the use of theories are some of the most encouraging and rewarding trends in nursing.

Taking a lead in theory development with the use of theory findings, some transcultural nurses have been active since the early 1960s to develop theories and research methods to study the trancultural care phenomena. Since cultures have different values and lifeways, they need to be studied in theory development and uses. This reality was central to the development of transcultural nursing, and lead to the theory of Culture Care Diversity and Universality. The search for transcultural nursing theories has been imperative for the generation of transcultural knowledge, but especially to discover the essence and nature of nursing and humanistic health care in diverse environmental and cultural contexts. The theory of Culture Care was developed and continues to grow worldwide in importance, providing many new insights about culture care variations within and between cultures.

In this chapter and overview of the theory of Culture Care Diversity and Universality is presented with the basic assumptive premises of the theory and the use of the Sunrise Model. The theory of Culture Care has become one of the central and most important theories in the development of transcultural nursing knowledge in all areas of nursing. Moreover this theory is used by many nurses worldwide because it is so timely, meaningful, and relevant to guide nurses to thinking and to work with people of diverse cultures. While the Culture Care theory was one of the first theories in nursing being established in the mid 1950s, it has only been in recent decades that theory has become meaningful and of major significance to many nurses worldwide. As a consequence, research studies and publications on the theory of Culture Care are increasing and leading to many new insights into nursing.[1,2,3,4,5] The reader is encouraged to study the theory and use it in different cultures worldwide as a guide to nursing practice and to discover largely unknown nursing care phenomenon.

Development of the Theory

The initial ideas for the theory of Culture Care Diversity and Universality came to the theorist while caring for patients on a medical-surgical unit in a general hospital in the late 1940s. Patients on these units frequently affirmed that it was nursing care practices that help them to get well, stay well or adjust to another state of well-being. These patients often told me and several nurses that it was the nurses' "good care" and "effective caring ways" that made them well to return home and function again. As a recent graduate, I greatly valued the patient's comments, but I could not explain what helped these patients get well through caring actions and attitudes. While I felt that I had given "good care" and was persistent in helping patients, I did not understand what actually made them well. Moreover, I was frequently giving nursing care to German, Italian and Irish patients and their families in this homes in the 1940s and 1950s. I recognized some of the differences in the needs of these families, but I could not explain the differences in care and cultural needs. I believed that "good care" was important to patients and seemed to be the essence and secret of successful nursing practices.

These early experiences lead me to declare that *care was the essence* of nursing, care makes nursing what it is. I also held that *care was the dominant, central, and major characteristic of nursing.*[6,7,8,9] Moreover, nurses needed to give knowledgeable, compassionate, and humanistic care to people through caring actions, attitudes, and decisions. These caring modes were the powerful means to prevent illness, promote healing and help in recovery processes. The basic ideas about nursing and human care remained central to my thinking not only in clinical practice, but in education, research and in any service to human kind. The cultural factors were very important and they needed to be considered in all aspects of nursing. The idea of *culture came from anthropology* and *care from nursing.* They were two major concepts brought together to develop the theory of Culture Care. And in the mid 1950s, my experiences in a child guidance center firmly convinced me that culture care factors were critical and could not be ignored. Most importantly, culture and care needed to be conceptualized and synthesized as a dominant feature to discover, interpret and establish transcultural nursing knowledge and practices.[10]

In the 1940s and 1950s, it is important that the reader realize that there were no formal, explicit, or specific theories of nursing. There were, however, general ideas by nurse leaders that were held to be extremely important to guide nursing practices. The work of Peplau on nurse-patient relationships in psychiatric nursing in the early 1950s was important. However, her ideas were not a theory per se.[11] There were lists of functions, activities and problems by nurses, but these were not theories. After World War II, many nurses in the United States were deeply involved in medical ideas and in supporting physicians' work in curing diseases by giving many medical treatments and medications of a great variety. Most assuredly, many nurses were following the medical model with ideas and practices focused on treating patients' pathological diseases, physical and emotional conditions using ideas largely from physicians. There was virtually no emphasis on developing nursing knowledge with nursing theories and using findings to improve or advance nursing care practices. In fact, the word theory was usually viewed as useless and a negative word by nurses, but especially by physicians who feared they would lose nurses if they went to college and learned such "ivory tower stuff." Theories were held to be irrelevant and not practical for nurses in their day-to-day practices.

With respect to caring as a central concept of nursing, many nurses openly denied and refused to view caring as important in nursing in the 1950s and 1960s. Instead nurses valued and believed in the magic of the physicians' medical treatments and their curing modes. Accordingly, nurses were deeply involved in giving many kinds of medications and treatments to clients to meet physicians' orders with their authoritative male expectations of female nurses. So while I was eager to advance culture care knowledge with my theory in the early 1960s, I found virtually no support or interest in this idea. Instead, I was discouraged from studying culture care because "care was too vague, too soft, non-measurable (hence unscientific) and too feminine." Moreover, many nurses declared that the concept of culture would never take hold in nursing as no one understood it and it was unimportant to nursing. To be a "good nurse" in the 1960s (and in some places today) was to know a host of medical diseases, symptoms, different techniques and activities to help patients get well or recover.

Another problem was evident in the early days in that most nurse scientists who had been largely prepared in other disciplines valued measuring everything through quantitative experimental research methods. This posed tremendous problems to discover human care with a transcultural perspective. As one of the first nurses prepared in qualitative methods, developing the ethnonursing method and other methods to discover culture care in the late 1950s, was a lone venturer in this pursuit. I was, however, determined to pursue my interests in developing the Culture Care theory and wanted to use an inductive, naturalistic, and emic interpretive approach to discover the largely covert, invisible, and unknown aspects of transcultural care and other nursing features.

Around 1978 I encountered still another major hurdle with a small group of "Eastern" USA nurse researchers who declared in nursing publications that nursing's major foci or "metaparadigm" for the discipline and metaparadigm of nursing would be *health, nursing, person,* and *environment.*[12] It was quite clear to me that these nurses blatantly failed to recognize human care, caring, and cultural factors were important phenomena of nursing. It appeared to me and other care scholars that this small elite group were lobbying against the rapidly growing interest in care and transcultural nursing. Prior to this time, a core of transcultural nurses and care scholars were establishing a significant body of care knowledge in the literature as the central domain of nursing. Care scholars such as Gaut, Watson, Ray, Leininger, and others had explicitly focused on care and transcultural nursing.[13,14,15,16,17] These care scholars were excited and committed to care as the central phenomenon of nursing and of transcultural care. Moreover, it was obvious than, and still is today, that nurses could not explain nursing per se as it would be redundant to use the same term to explain nursing. Furthermore, to use the term "person" was inaccurate and inadequate as a metaparadigm concept because some cultures never focus on person because they do not have a linguistic term for person. I also held that Western nurses needed to go beyond the concept of persons and consider Eastern focus on families, groups, cultures, institutions, communities, and world societies. These ideas were often more important than the individual. Today nurses are reconsidering the above four concepts largely due to transcultural and anthropological insights about diverse cultures and nursing worlds.[18] With transcultural nurse knowledge and consumer demands, many nurses are recognizing that *human care, health,* and *environmental cultural context* must become the *central focus, essence, and dominant domains of nursing knowledge* to replace the "Eastern four concept metaparadigm in question.

Purpose and Goal of the Culture Care Theory with the Ethnonursing Method

The purpose of the Culture Care theory is to discover human care diversities (differences) and universalities (similarities) in order to generate new knowledge to guide nursing care practices. How cultural values, beliefs and other cultural aspects could ultimately provide or improve nursing care through the use of knowledge generated by the theory was important. *The goal of the theory was to provide culturally congruent and competent nursing care that would lead to client or group health and well-being.*[19] *The purpose of the theory was directed toward describing, explaining, interpreting and predicting phenomena related to human care and culture* in order to identify and document specified care knowledge that would fit with and be acceptable to people nurses served. Discovering new lines of thinking, or refuting ideas that are no longer tenable is always a function of theories. Although there are many definitions of a theory, I defined *theory in a direct and an open-discovery was as a domain of inquiry, and question, or something to be explained, interpreted, understood, and predicted to gain knowledge.*[20] This definition also fits with the purpose of the qualitative research paradigm, which is to gain a full understanding and meanings of an phenomena under study in naturalistic contexts or familiar ways of those being studied. This definition is in marked contrast to the quantitative paradigm such as Polit and Hungler's definition of theory as "a set of interrelated concepts, definitions, propositions, or hypotheses with specific and measurable relationships to predict and control phenomena under study."[21] The qualitative theoretical definition was most congruent to nursing and especially transcultural nursing because so little knowledge had been identified regarding specific culture care expressions, meanings, and needs. Still today there are many cultures and subcultures that await discovery by nurse researchers. Hence, the qualitative research approach, the theory assumptions, and many other aspects were bold new steps to discover a largely unknown body of nursing.

In developing the theory of Culture Care, I saw the need for the ethnonursing research method in order to enter into the people's world and let the people tell me first hand their ideas and experiences related to culturally based care.[22,23] I wanted people to teach me about culture care meanings, symbols and practices in their cultures. A broad theory and an open research method were held to be essential to discover the largely hidden and unknown facts about culture and caring within the people's perspectives and environmental settings. The ethnonursing qualitative research method was therefore developed by the researcher to obtain the people's ideas, values, beliefs, and practices of care and to contrast them later with nurses' knowledge. This ethnonursing research approach was new and entirely different from the established quantitative logical positivistic methods with *a priori* preconceived variables, hypotheses, and other ideas about some specific phenomenon that was studied under tightly controlled, measured and experimental ways by a researcher.[24] The latter approach was troublesome to me as it would restrict and exclude some of the most important knowledge about people and culture care. Moreover, some cultural informants would probably show a great dislike for tightly controlled or manipulated ways of collecting data. Probing tools and instruments characteristic of quantitative research would be unnatural, frightening and strange to many cultural informants, and especially non-Western peoples. Thus the ethnonursing research method was essential to discover knowledge from cultures or subcultures about their ideas in a naturalistic, familiar and people-centered method.

Theorizing and Developing Culture Care Theory

As the theory of Culture Care began to be developed in the mid 1940s and 1950s I posed these critical questions: Is human care and nursing universal? If not, what would explain the diversities among cultures? Is human care essential for the growth and survival of people through the life cycle and over time in different places in the world? If care were universal, how would this help nurses to function? If care were diverse in all human cultures, how would this limit nurses' functioning? I also wondered how nurses would be able to function in a predicted rapidly changing multicultural world by the twenty-first century without transcultural care knowledge and skills. I foresaw that nursing would need to make major changes to work with clients who came from different cultures in the world. Rapid transportation, electronic communication modes, wars, and political economic shifts in the world were already moving nursing to know and understand transcultural nursing. The nursing profession needed a theory to explain, understand, interpret, and predict cultural care practices with people they were already caring for or with in health settings. The theory of Culture Care would become more and more important to nursing if it were to survive and grow as a discipline and profession in a rapidly changing multicultural world.

The following perplexing questions have continued to challenge my thinking and that of others in the past three decades:

1. How have human beings in different cultures (or subcultures) remained well or recovered from illnesses through caring practices?
2. What specific care/caring values, beliefs, and practices have contributed to the health and well-being of individuals, groups, families or communities of diverse cultures?
3. How does the environmental context of different cultures contribute to the well-being and health of people, or lead to illness patterns and death of the human species?
4. In what ways do the worldview, language, religion, kinship, cultural values, technology, political, economic and educational factors influence the health and well-being of people from different cultures?
5. If nurses are knowledgeable about the cultural lifeways of people, how can they prevent illnesses and preserve the healthy lifeways of cultures?
6. Can nurses provide culture-specific and congruent care that would be beneficial and satisfying to clients and contribute to their health and well-being, or to help people face death?

These questions of the 1950s and 1960s pushed forward my work in the development of the theory of Culture Care Diversity and Universality.

In constructing the Culture Care theory, I wanted it to be holistic rather than a fragmented way of viewing people as cells, diseased organs, body parts or symptoms. I wanted to discover people from their cultural background and lifeways of clients rather than disease entities. The theory would need to help identify the assets and strengths of a culture rather an all its problems and medical diseases. The concept of culture as *holistic lifeways of people with their values, beliefs, lifeways and assets was highly desirable philosophy and goal of the theory*. I wanted nurses to relinquish the emphasis on mind-body split entities, or of separate physical and emotional diseased conditions. Nurses needed to know and understand people with their worldview, religious (or spiritual) beliefs, family relationships, home remedies, social ties and many cultural values and beliefs. The ethnohistory and language of people was also important to having a holistic view of people. These cultural care dimensions of knowing people were much broader than nurses' previous conceptualizations of people as sick and diseased.

It was these philosophical ideas and viewpoints that led me to make the theory different. It was broad in scope and comprehensive so that nurses would see individuals and groups in a much bigger picture and with many factors influencing their caring and health needs. The theory, therefore, had to reflect the following features: 1) It needed to be culturally broad (worldwide) and comprehensive to be meaningful and holistic; 2) It needed to be developed so that nurses could use the theory worldwide; 3) It needed to be centered on human care as the essence of nursing, and culture as a significant force to guide nursing actions in a multicultural world; 4) It needed new research ways to obtain knowledge about the worldview, social structure, cultural values, language and ethnohistory from the people in order to discover and accurately interpret cultural care expressions, meanings, symbols, rituals, and other dimensions; and 6) It needed to be developed so that culture care universals (commonalities) and diversities could be identified among and between many different cultures in the world to develop ultimately worldwide nursing knowledge. If these theory features were evident then I predicted nursing would have a distinct meaningful, and relevant new body of transcultural nursing knowledge for the discipline and profession of nursing. This was ambitious, very broad, and different goal for most nurses in the 1960s who were far more interested in learning about highly specific, fragmented and narrow pieces of medical symptoms and treatment regiments of patients.

One of the most difficult yet promising features of the theory was to bring the concept of care from nursing and the concept of culture from anthropology into a very close synthesis or integrated linkage. This was difficult because so few nurses in the 1950s were prepared in anthropology or were interested in discovering the relationship between nursing and anthropology. There was, however, a good possibility of some shared commonalties with the two disciplines as well as some differences, as discussed in my first book, *Nursing and Anthropology: Two Worlds to Blend*.[25] To many nurses, culture was viewed largely as fossils, or as form of art, music, or archaeological artifacts. The idea of culture as the lifeways of people today or in the past was not a prevailing view among nurses in the pre-1960s. And since human care was not fully known or valued by many nurses, it was difficult to conceptualize care and culture together. The idea of promoting wellness, preventing illnesses and maintaining health through in-depth knowledge and exquisite cultural caring skills was predicted to have many benefits and outcomes in nursing. To shift nurses to consider knowing and using culture-specific care constructs such as presence, connecting with, enabling, and involvement with a new nursing focus looked almost impossible, yet it was a new direction for nursing science. Far too many nurses were still performing physicians' tasks and often taking care of physicians' needs rather than clients'. Nonetheless, it was exciting to think nursing could change and rely on nursing knowledge based on culture care constructs such as comfort care, protective care, compassionate care, and many other undiscovered care modalities as the art and science of nursing and as the distinct and guiding focus of nursing. Culture Care nursing theory was much needed to discover these largely unknown "golden nuggets" about human caring and to use them skillfully as powerful and effective healing modes.

Helping nurses enter, learn from and act upon people's cultural care meanings and experiences was another perplexing challenge. Late in 1959 I discovered in Pike's work the concepts of *emic* and *etic* and reformulated them so they would be they would be useful to nursing.[26] I linked these ideas with *generic* and *professional* care/ caring phenomena and practices and predicted that generic care would be largely emic based and would provide highly valuable knowledge about culture care. In contrast, I held that professional care would be largely the etic or outsider's views to clients, as most nurses were initially strangers to clients. Generic and professional care could contrast with each other and lead to cultural clashes, conflicts, and misunderstandings. There could, however, be some knowledge and practice areas in which generic and professional care would be shared or common rather than diverse. I defined generic (folk or lay) and professional care as important components of and speculations within the theory of Culture Care to be studied in-depth and transculturally to generate new or distinct knowledge in nursing. I defined generic and professional care as follows:

> *Generic (folk or lay) care refers to those largely emically learned and transmitted indigenous (or traditional) folk (home-based) cultural knowledge and skills used to provide assistive, supportive, enabling or facilitative acts toward or for another individual or group with evident or anticipated needs, to ameliorate or improve a human lifeway, health condition, or to deal with handicaps and death.*[27]

> *Professional care (including nursing) refers to congnitively learned knowledge and skills (largely etic to cultural groups) that have been obtained through formal professional programs of study in special educational institutions in order to assist, support, and help clients seeking professional services.*[28]

These two major definitions were theoretical perspectives to be discovered with the theory and crucial to establishing culturally congruent care knowledge and skills.

Interestingly, generic (folk) care had not been of interest to nurses when the theory was conceived, and yet it seemed so important if nurses were to provide meaningful and beneficial nursing care to people. Granted, anthropologists had identified and studied folk practices for many years. They showed that cultures which used folk practices such as caring ways, herbal materials, oils and local medicines often healed the local people. But the largely unknown invisible generic care practices such as comfort care, facilitatory care, and others had not been tapped. I called these folk or indigenous practices generic care, as they were the oldest forms of helping or healing people's ills, concerns or general needs. Such generic or folk care when brought into nursing and medicine in the 1950s was largely viewed as culturally taboo. To many nurses, physicians, and other health disciplines, folk medicines and care were primitive, non-therapeutic, potentially destructive and contradictory to modern medical practices. However, the generic or folk healing practices and practitioners of particular cultures were largely unknown, or if known, physicians and nurses thought they had strange and non-therapeutic practices.

I theorized that knowledge of generic care practices could revolutionize nursing and health care practices if combined thoughtfully and responsibly with professional care knowledge. I also predicted in the theory that clients of diverse cultures would show signs of faster recovers from illness, less cultural stress and conflict with professional services, and a great potential to remain well when the best of both generic and professional care practices were skillfully integrated and used by nurses. I also predicted that if generic care meanings and practices were not effectively integrated into professional nursing practices, one would find unfavorable client outcomes and the absence of culturally congruent care. Helping nurses and other health professionals discover, value and combine the use of generic and professional care was exciting. However, with the heavy medicalization of professionals, imbued with an mainly etic perspective of health services as the best and only therapeutic mode of good professional work, ethnocentric bias was evident and difficult to overcome.

Still other ideas were developed with the theory of Culture Care. I held and predicted that human care was culturally constituted or rooted epistemically in the people's emic lifeways, but that there were diverse forms, expressions, patterns, meanings, structures and attributes of culture care worldwide. Accordingly, I predicted there would be some universalities (or commonalities) in human care among cultures along with the diversities. The *purpose* of the Culture Care theory was, therefore, to discover human care diversities and universalities and to use this knowledge to provide *culturally congruent nursing* care as a pathway *to health and well-being or to help people face disabilities and death.* Nurses needed to accommodate cultural diversities with the commonalities. The assumption with the diversities and universalities was that all cultures have culturally-based or patterned ways that help people remain reasonably well, but if illness or death occurred, these phenomena could be largely explained within the culture. And since most humans want to remain healthy and to function in their daily lives, culturally-based care knowledge would be essential to understand and use in professional work. The holistic or total cultural lifeways of people would be invaluable to discover what comes naturally and what occurs as a diverse or different expression. Both diversities and universalities were important and an essential feature of the theory.

Another theoretical hunch was that if care were culturally based, this had undoubtedly influenced the human species' survival over millions of years. It would support the reality that *homo sapiens* exist today and due largely to human care modalities, did not become extinct. From an anthropological perspective the power of culturally-based care as a means to save the human species was a revolutionary thought. Anthropologists had not considered the power of care, it awaited nurses' attention. I contended that transcultural nurses could contribute to this riddle about the power of culture care with its diverse forms, patterns, and expressions through time and in different places in the world. Indeed, transcultural care research would be a major discipline and professional contribution to expand knowledge about human beings worldwide. Discovering the unknown culture care secrets of how cultures cared for others throughout the life cycle, in crisis situations, and many critical and unexpected human conditions could bring forth new and distinct comparative knowledge for nursing and humankind. Transculturally prepared nurses could ultimately make this knowledge known, recognized, and valued by people worldwide.

Finally, I speculated that since nursing is a profession with the primary goal serving people, culture care research data were needed to provide culturally specific nursing care decisions and action. I, therefore, envisioned three major modes of action and decision that could be used to provide culturally congruent care. They were: 1) *culture care preservation and/or maintenance;* 2) *culture care accommodation and/or negotiation;* and 3) *culture care restructuring and/or repatterning.* I predicted that if nurses studied these three modes systematically in the relation to the worldview, generic and professional care, ethnohistorical factors and the environmental context, they could creatively and appropriately make responsible decisions and take actions that could lead to culturally congruent nursing care promoting health or well-being. These action and decision modes could be specific and could lead to major transformations in the provision of nursing care to clients of diverse or similar cultures. Such caring science knowledge and concomitant practices were already becoming imperative to care for people of diverse cultures; and yet there was no explicit knowledge or practices to support this goal in nursing.

Assumptive Premises of the Theory

With any theory, the theorist formulates assumptions to guide the researcher as a basis for the theory and draws upon the theorist's conceptual and philosophical perspectives. Assumptions are the fundamental premises or givens upon which the theory is conceived and which can be systematically studied for their credibility or general truth over time. They are the major premises upon which the theorist made the above theoretical tenets of hunches as predictions about culture care. The theoretical assumptive premises of the theory of Culture Care Diversity and Universality are the following:[29,30]

1. Care is the essence of nursing and a distinct, dominant, central and unifying focus.
2. Care (caring) is essential for well-being, health, healing, growth, survival and facing handicaps or death.

3. Culture care is the broadest holistic means to know, explain, interpret and predict nursing care phenomena to guide nursing care practices.

4. Nursing is a transcultural humanistic and scientific care discipline and profession with the central purpose of serving human beings worldwide.

5. Care (caring) is essential to curing and healing, for there can be no curing without caring.

6. Culture care concepts, meanings, expressions, patterns, processes, and structural forms of care have differences (diversities) and similarities (toward commonalities or universalities) among all cultures of the world.

7. Every human culture has generic (lay, folk or indigenous) care knowledge and practices and usually professional care knowledge and practices which vary transculturally.

8. Culture care values, beliefs, and practices are influenced by and tend to be embedded in the worldview, language, religious (or spiritual), kinship (social), political (or legal), educational, economic, technological, ethnohistorical and environmental context of a particular culture.

9. Beneficial, healthy, and satisfying culturally-based nursing care contributes to the well-being of individuals, families, groups and communities within their environmental context.

10. Culturally congruent or beneficial nursing care occurs only when the individual, group, family, community, or culture care values, expressions or patterns are know and used appropriately and in meaningful ways by the nurse.

11. Culture care differences and similarities between professional caregivers and generic (folk or lay) caregivers exist in human culture worldwide.

12. A client who experiences nursing care that fails to be reasonably congruent with the client's beliefs, values, and caring lifeways will show signs of cultural conflicts, noncompliance, stresses and ethical or moral concerns.

13. The qualitative paradigm provides new ways of knowing and different ways of discovering epistemic and ontological dimensions of human care transculturally.

The above theoretical assumptive statements are purposefully broad in order to guide researchers in discovering largely unknown phenomena especially through qualitative enthnonursing studies. If the theory were tested from the quantitative perspective, the researcher would develop specific hypotheses in relation to the theory tenets and the above assumptive premises. This theory with its assumptive premises has been largely studied with the ethnonursing qualitative method, which was designed to obtain largely undiscovered knowledge. Thus, specific hypotheses and relational statements were not developed as they fit with the quantitative paradigm which limits the full discovery of detailed, explicit and largely unknown qualitative data.[31] The theory can, however, be studied or tested within either the qualitative or quantitative paradigm, but one should not mix paradigms as they have different purposes, goals and outcomes.

Orientational Definitions

In keeping with the open-discovery approach of the qualitative enthnonursing method, orientational definitions were formulated. These definitions are deliberately broad and not operational statements in order to study the people's global emic ideas, focusing on the concepts and predictions of the theory. The following orientational definitions serve as a guide to users of the theory:[32]

1. *Care* (noun) refers to abstract and concrete phenomena related to assisting, supporting, or enabling experiences or behaviors toward or for others with evident or anticipated needs to ameliorate or improve a human condition or lifeway.

2. *Caring* (gerund) refers to actions and activities directed toward assisting, supporting, or enabling another individual or group with evident or anticipated needs to ameliorate or improve a human condition or lifeway, or to face death.

3. *Culture* refers to the learned, shared, and transmitted values, beliefs, norms, and lifeways of a particular group that guide their thinking, decisions, and actions in patterned ways.

4. *Culture care* refers to the subjectively and objectively learned and transmitted values, beliefs, and patterned lifeways that assist, support, facilitate, or enable another individual or group to maintain well-being and health, to improve the human condition and lifeway, or to deal with illness, handicaps, or death.

5. *Culture care diversity* refers to the variabilities and/or differences in meanings, patterns, values, lifeways or symbols of care within or between collectivities that are related to assistive, supportive or enabling human care expressions.

6. *Culture care universality* refers to the common, similar, or dominant uniform care meanings, patterns, values, lifeways or symbols that are manifest among many cultures and reflect assistive, supportive, facilitative or enabling ways to help people. (The term "universality" is not used in an absolute way or as a significant statistical finding.)

7. *Nursing* refers to a *learned humanistic and scientific profession and discipline focused on human care phenomena and activities in order to assist, support, facilitate or enable individuals in order to maintain or regain their well-being (or health) in culturally meaningful and beneficial ways, or to help people face handicaps.*

8. *Worldview* refers to the way people tend to look out on the world or on their universe to form a picture or a value stance about their life or world around them.

9. *Cultural and social structure dimensions* refers to the dynamic patterns and features or interrelated structural and organizational factors of a particular culture (subculture or society) which includes religious, kinship (social), political (and legal), economic, educational, technologic and cultural values, ethnohistorical factors, and how these factors may be interrelated and function to influence human behavior in different environmental contexts.

10. *Environmental context* refers to the totality of an event, situation or particular experiences that give meaning to human expressions, interpretations and social interactions in particular physical, ecological, sociopolitical and/or cultural settings.

11. *Ethnohistory* refers to those past facts, events, instances and experiences of individuals, groups, cultures and institutions that are primarily people-centered (ethno) and which describe, explain, and interpret human lifeways within particular cultural contexts over short or long periods of time.

12. *Generic (folk or lay) care systems* refers to culturally learned and transmitted, indigenous (or traditional), folk (home-based) knowledge and skills used to provide assistive, supportive, enabling or facilitative acts toward or for another individual, group or institution with evident or anticipated needs to ameliorate or improve a human lifeway, health condition (or well-being), or to deal with handicaps and death situations.

13. *Professional care system(s)* refers to formally taught, learned and transmitted professional care, health, illness, wellness and related knowledge and practice skills that prevail in professional institutions, usually with multidisciplinary personnel to serve consumers.

14. *Health* refers to a state of well-being that is culturally defined, valued, and practiced, and which reflects the ability of individuals (or groups) to perform their daily role activities in culturally expressed, beneficial and patterned lifeways.

15. *Culture care preservation or maintenance* refers to those assistive, supporting, facilitative or enabling professional actions and decisions that help people of a particular culture to retain and/or preserve relevant care values so that they can maintain their well-being, recover from illness or face handicaps and/or death.

16. *Culture care accommodation or negotiation* refers to those assistive, supporting, facilitative, or enabling creative professional actions and decisions that help people of a designated culture adapt to or negotiate with others for a beneficial or satisfying health outcome with professional care providers.

17. *Culture care repatterning or restructuring* refers to those assistive, supporting, facilitative or enabling professional actions and decisions that help clients reorder, change or greatly modify their lifeways for new, different and beneficial health care patterns while respecting clients' cultural values and beliefs and providing a lifeway more beneficial or healthier than before the changes were coestablished with the clients.

18. *Culturally congruent (nursing) care* refers to those cognitive based assistive, supportive, facilitative or enabling acts or decisions that are tailor-made to fit with individual, group or institutional cultural values, beliefs and lifeways in order to provide or support meaningful, beneficial and satisfying health care or well-being services.

Sunrise Model: A Guide to Discovering Culture Care

The *Sunrise Model* (figure 3.1) was designed early in the theory to provide nurses with a visual image to aid in conceptualizing the components of the theory. The idea of a "rising sun" was used to symbolize the hopeful goal of the theory in discovering new or distinctive knowledge that could markedly raise nursing to a bright sunrise of knowing, as fully as possible cultures worldwide. To show the multiple and diverse influences on culture care required several revisions of the model which are found in writings since 1960. The model, therefore, serves as visual guide or a cognitive map to help users envision a holistic perspective of many influences on culture care with individuals, families, groups, institutions and communities and different health care systems. The model is often used as a visual guide to help the researcher consider multiple potential aspects influencing nursing care. Using the model, the nurse becomes cognizant that different cultural forces influence care which in turn influences the health or well-being of people. This model should not be viewed as a theory per se, but rather as a depiction of the multiple components of the theory and ways to study the major tenets of the theory being systematically examined as influencers of culturally congruent nursing care.

In using the Sunrise Model, the researcher can start studying the theory from different areas in the model. Often the researcher begins with a focus on the middle section, studying the individual, group, family, institution or community, but only *after identifying the researcher's special area of interest or domain of focus.* For example, a *domain of inquiry* might be African American meanings, patterns and expressions of culture care within an urban environmental context. This domain is intentionally broad in order that the researcher can discover some of the broadest and yet detailed aspects of the theory in relation to a stated domain of culture care. Another example of a domain of inquiry might be culture care grief expressions, meanings and symbols on the loss of a Mexican American family member. This domain permits the research to move with the people to discover culture care aspects of grief with Mexican American families. The ethnonursing domains contrast with hypotheses and research problems used in quantitative studies that are narrowly defined to a few variables and hypotheses, and limits an open emic discovery from the people. The ethnonursing researcher uses a few broad questions related to the above domains of inquiry to guide further their own predictive hunches related to the general theory of Culture Care.

The ethnonursing researcher often starts with the Sunrise Model by studying the worldview, social structure factors, and ethnohistory of the people or one may start with the generic (folk) and professional care part of the model to discover ideas related to the domain of inquiry, but later reflects on social structure and other factors. Whether one

Figure 3.1
Leninger's Sunrise Model to Depict the Theory of
Culture Care Diversity and Universality

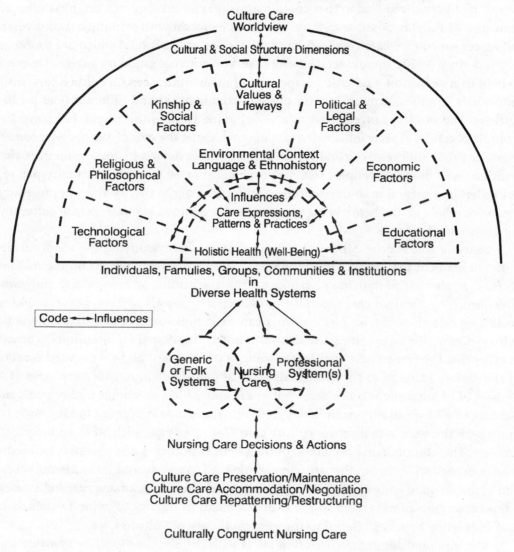

From *Culture Care Diversity and Universality: A Theory for Nursing* by M. Leininger, 1991
New York: National League for Nursing. Reprinted by permission.

focuses on the central, top or bottom part of the model, the researcher is free to explore ideas in any area that influences care and health. The researcher is free to explore ideas in any area of interest as the informants identify influencers on their care and health. As one uses this model, one soon discovers how quickly the different components or elements of the model become imprinted on one's thinking. These component areas are usually and readily identified by most informants to give a true holistic view of the people and their lifeways. The whole model with the different components are studied to discover their culture care diversity and universality patterns and to provide information related to culturally congruent care.

The worldview and social structure factors are often new areas to many nurses unless they are grounded in the social sciences, and yet these factors are usually critical to identify and understand culture care. The nurse will find that some components of the social structure may be more dominant in some cultures than others. For examples, religion and kinship is very important with Arab Muslims, whereas technology and economics are important to Euro-Americans. Such in-depth study of these aspects often reveals care values that have to be teased out of the social structure, such as spiritual care or protective care in their religious or spiritual beliefs. Each component in the model needs to be studied in-depth to identify care aspects and understand the people and their environment. The Sunrise Model should not be viewed as a casual, linear or logical model with controlling variables or people responses. Instead, and open, naturalistic inquiry approach is used in ethnonursing to discover subjective and objective information about culture care. The researcher also moves with informants in different situations to *learn from the people*, and their experiences in their familiar work or home environment. Covert and hidden dimensions of care are often embedded in language and social structure factors, so researchers need ethnonursing enablers (not instruments which are often too impersonal and frightening to most lay informants) to discover knowledge and understand the people under study.

The researcher will find that preparation in transcultural nursing and in anthropology can be valuable to obtain what I call "holding and reflective knowledge." Such holding knowledge is the available knowledge about a culture which can guide the researcher to see and hear what specific culture informants are saying in their environmental context. Informants are encouraged to share their ideas and to help nurses know fully what they see, hear, feel or observe. Holding knowledge is important to grasping the meanings and explanations of behavior and to reflecting upon what has been heard or experienced. Without transcultural nursing holding knowledge the researcher often misinterprets what they hear and see, or uses their own ethnocentric cultural interpretations and explanations which may be inaccurate. Thus transcultural nursing, anthropological and other social science basic knowledge helps researchers to discover new ideas and to be reflective of existing knowledge already available.

But, *open learning from the people and within the people's context is imperative.* Reflective knowledge should not lead to stereotyping or rigid views but can prevent stereotyping and to look further for culture variation and in-depth understandings. It is the narrow or "boxed-in" views that lead to stereotyping and often inaccurate date. Researchers must document with verbatim comments and observations the informants' emic and/or explanations or interpretations to insure accurate information to the researcher.

After exploring the worldview, social structure factors and generic and professional care, the researcher examines the interviews, observations and participant experience data to support and guide the three predicted theoretical modes of nursing care decisions and actions which are: 1) culture care preservation and/or maintenance; 2) culture care accommodation and/or negotiation; and 3) culture care restructuring and/or repatterning. These three modes require the researcher to discuss with informants their ideas of ways to reach and maintain culturally congruent nursing care. Creative thinking and drawing upon the data already collected and studied provide a sound basis for providing culturally congruent care that will be beneficial to those being served. Sometimes action and decision data can be identified for all three modes, but sometimes only one or two modes are important to informants for nursing practices. The researcher is encouraged to use the theorist's Four Phases of Ethnonursing Analysis Qualitative Data to generate specific data for the three modes of analysis.[33] The publication *Culture Care Diversity and Universality: A Theory of Nursing* provides valuable and additional information about the theory, the ethnonursing method and specific studies using the theory with several different cultures.[34] The reader is encouraged to study specific cultures in relation to the use of the theory in the many publications now available, including the *Journal of Transcultural Nursing*.[35] In the past six years this journal has provided research studies with excellent examples of the use of the theory with research findings in approximately 60 cultures.

During the past three decades it has been most encouraging to see a new generation of baccalaureate and graduate nursing students valuing and using the theory of Culture Care in addition to nurse clinicians and research scholars. Nurses are seeing the many benefits of using the theory to develop and provide culture-specific care and care that is meaningful to clients who are culturally different. Since we are living in a new age of discovery with many new aspects to consider, nursing students, faculty, clinicians and administrators are seeing the critical need for transcultural nursing. As a consequence, nurses are discovering some entirely different ways to help people and to prevent culturally unfavorable conditions, such as casting an evil eye on infants or inappropriately bonding parents to their child. Many nursing students have become powerful promoters and advocates of the Culture Care theory to provide culturally congruent, competent and sensitive nursing practices. A growing number of master and doctoral students prepared in transcultural nursing have been the real pioneers to use the Culture Care theory within transcultural nursing. For example, research studies are available such as the research by Luna on the culture care of Arab Americans;[36] Bohay on Ukranians;[37] Stasiak on Mexican Americans;[38] Cameron on the Canadian elderly;[39] Rosenbaum on Canadian Greek Widows;[40] Wenger on Old-Order Amish;[41] Gelazis on Lithuanians;[42] Morgan on African Americans;[43] and McFarland on Euro- and African Americans in Nursing Residences.[44] These research studies and many others demonstrate the use and importance of the Culture Care theory to improving client care and changing practices in nursing education, research, consultation and interdisciplinary work.

In this chapter some of the essential and major features of the theory of Culture Care Diversity and Universality have been presented to stimulate and guide nurses in the use of the theory. This chapter provides information to understand subsequent chapters in this book in which the theory is applied to specific cultures in familar and naturalistic ways. The reader first needs to study the theory with the research studies presented in this book. This will make the theory come alive and show how relevant and meaningful it is to different cultures and the ways to provide transcultural nursing care. Moreover, I have found through the years that many nurses become attached to the theory because it is truly holistic, comprehensive and fits knowing different cultures in familiar and naturalistic ways. The theory supports respecting and understanding the cultural rights and lifeways of people. The theory is also becoming useful and relevant with other disciplines as they too need to become knowledgeable, sensitive and responsible to people of diverse cultures. Most importantly, the knowledge generated from the theory of Culture Care has been a powerful and significant force to establish and advance transcultural nursing knowledge and practice skills that are gradually influencing nursing education and practice in our multicultural world. This development is significant in light of the theorist's prediction that *all* areas of nursing will and must become transculturally-based by the year 2010 or sooner.

References

1. Leininger, M. *Culture Care Diversity and Universality: A Theory of Nursing,* New York: National League for Nursing Press, 1991a.

2. Leininger, M. "Theory of Nursing: Cultural Care Diversity and Universality," *Nursing Science Quarterly,* R. Parse ed., Baltimore: Williams & Wilkin Press, v. 1, no. 4, 1988, pp. 152-160.

3. Leininger, M. "Culture Care Theory: The Relevant Theory to Guide Functioning in a Multicultural World," M. Parker, ed., *Patterns of Nursing Theories in Practice,* New York: National League for Nursing Press, 1993a, pp. 103-122.

4. Reynolds, C. and M. Leininger, *Leininger's Culture Care Diversity and Universality Theory,* Newbury Park: Sage Publications, Inc., 1993.

5. Leininger, M. "Culture Care Theory: The Comparative Global Theory to Advance Human Care Nursing Knowledge and Practice," D. Gaut, ed., *A Global Agenda for Caring,* New York: National League for Nursing Press, 1993b, pp. 3-19.

6. Leininger, M. "Caring: The Essence and Central Focus of Nursing," *American Nurses Foundation,* Nursing Research Report, v. 12, no. 1, February 1976, pp. 2, 14.

7. Leininger, M. *Nursing and Anthropology: Two Worlds to Blend,* New York: John Wiley & Sons, 1970. (Reprint, Columbus: 1994, Greyden Press).

8. Leininger, M. *Care: An Essential Human Need,* Thorofare, New Jersey: C. Slack, Inc. 1981. (Reprint, Detroit: Wayne State University Press, 1988b.)

9. Leininger, M. *Care: The Essence of Nursing and Health.* Thorofare, New Jersey: C. Slack, Inc. 1981. (Reprint, Detroit: Wayne State University Press, 1988b.)

10. Leininger, M. *Transcultural Nursing, Theories, concepts, and Practices,* New York: John Wiley & Sons, 1978, pp. 1-36.

11. Peplau, H. *Interpersonal Relations in Nursing: A Conceptual Frame of Reference for Psychiatric Nursing,* New York: G. P. Putnam & Sons. 1952.

12. Fawcett, J. "The Metaparadigm in Nursing: Present Status and Future Refinements." *Image: The Journal of Nursing Scholarship,* v. 16, no. 3, 1984, pp. 84-87.

13. Gaut, D. "Conceptual Analysis of Caring," *Caring: An Essential Human Need,* M. Leininger, ed., Thorofare, New Jersey, C. Slack, Inc., 1981, pp. 17-24.

14. Watson, J. *Nursing: The Philosophy of Science Care,* Boston: Little, Brown, & Co., 1979.

15. Ray, M. "Philosophical Analysis of Caring," *Caring: An Essential Human Need,* M. Leininger, ed., Thorofare, New Jersey: C. Slack, Inc., 19881, pp. 25-36. (Reprint, Detroit: Wayne State University Press, 1988.)

16. Leininger, op. cit., 1991a.
17. Ibid.
18. Fawcett, J. "Leininger's Theory of Culture Care Diversity and Universality," *Analysis and Evaluation of Nursing Theories,* Philadelphia: F. A. Davis. 1993, pp. 49-88.
19. Leininger, op. cit., 1991a, p. 39.
20. Ibid.
21. Polit, D. and B. Hungler, *Nursing Research: Principles and Methods,* Philadelphia: J. B. Lippincott, 1983.
22. Leininger, M. "Ethnonursing: A research method with enablers to study the theory of culture care," *Culture Care Diversity and Universality: A Theory of Nursing,* M. Leininger, ed., New York: National League for Nursing Press, 1991b, pp. 73-118.
23. Reynolds, C. and M. Leininger, op. cit. 1993. Leininger's *Cultural Care Diversity and Universality Theory,* Newbury Park: Sage Publications, Inc., 1993.
24. Polit and Hungler, op. cit.
25. Leininger, op. cit., 1970. (Reprint, Columbus: Greyden Press, 1994.
26. Pike, K. *Language in Relation to a Unified Theory of the Structure of Human Behavior,* v. 1, Glendale: Summer Institute of Linguistics, 1954.
27. Leininger, op. cit. 1991a, p. 48.
28. Ibid.
29. Leininger, op. cit. 1991a, pp. 44-45.
30. Leininger, op. cit. 1988a, pp. 154-155.
31. Leininger, op. cit. 1991a, pp. 78-118.
32. Ibid, pp. 46-48
33. Ibid, p. 95.
34. Leininger, op. cit. 1991a.
35. *Journal of Transcultural Nursing,* Dearborn: Desktoppers USA, 1989-1994.
36. Luna, L. "Transcultural Nursing Care of Arab-Muslims," *Journal of Transcultural Nursing,* Memphis: University of Tennessee Press, v. 1, no. 1, Summer, 1989, pp. 22-26.
37. Bohay, I. "Culture Care Meanings and Experiences of Pregnancy and Childbirth of Ukranians," *Culture Care Diversity and Universality: A Theory of Nursing,* M. Leininger, ed., New York: National League for Nursing Press, 1991, pp. 203-230.
38. Stasiak, D. "Culture Care Theory with Mexican-Americans in an Urban Context," *Culture Care Diversity and Universality: A Theory of Nursing,* M. Leininger, ed., New York: National League for Nursing Press, 1991, pp. 179-202.
39. Cameron, C. "An Ethnonursing Study of Health Status of Elderly Anglo-Canadian

Wives Providing Extended Caregiving to their Disabled Husbands," doctoral disseration, Detroit: Wayne State University, 1990.

40. Rosenbaum, M. "Cultural Care of Older Greek Canadian Widows Within Leininger's Theory of Culture Care," *Journal of Transcultural Nursing,* Memphis: University of Tennessee Press, v. 2, no. 1, Summer, 1990, pp. 37-47.

41. Wenger, A. F. "The Culture Care Theory and the Old-Order Amish," *Culture Care Diversity and Universality: A Theory of Nursing,* m. Leininger, ed., New York: National League for Nursing Press, pp. 147-178.

42. Gelazis, R. "Lithuanian Care Meanings and Experience with Humor Using Leininger's Cultural Care Theory," Doctoral dissertation, Detroit: Wayne State University, 1992.

43. Morgan, M. "Prenatal Care of African American Women in Slected USA Urgan and Rural Cultural Contexts Conceptualized within Leininger's Cultural Care Theory," doctoral disseration, Detroit: Wayne State University, 1994.

44. McFarland, M. "Ethnonursing and Ethnocare and the Culture of a Nursing Home with Leininger's Culture Care Theory," Detroit: Wayne State University Press. (In press, 1995.)

Chapter 4
Culture Care Assessment to Guide Nursing Practices

Madeleine Leininger, PhD, LHD, DS, FAAN, CTN, RN.

The roots of culture care are deep and widespread. It requires that health personnel discover the similarities and differences in a sensitive and competent way in order to provide meaningful health care services.

Leininger, 1978

One of the greatest challenges in nursing is to discover how culture care factors can make a difference in understanding others and in providing meaningful and satisfying nursing care to those served. To achieve this goal, nurses need to develop knowledge and skill in doing culturalogical health care assessments. This means learning from people about their cultural values, beliefs, and lifeways in order to grasp their world, their needs and values in relation to professional nursing beliefs and practices. From culturalogical care assessments nurses can greatly expand their understanding of people and discover different approaches to assist them.

The purpose of this chapter is to identify and discuss cultural health care assessments with the goal of enhancing or providing a new, specialized nursing care practice for those of different cultures. The author draws upon some of the transcultural nursing concepts and principles presented in chapter two and the theory of Culture Care Diversity and Universality with the Sunrise Model (chapter three) to provide a foundation of knowledge to do a culture care assessment. The Sunrise Model (Figure 4.1) is most valuable to guide nurses in providing a truly holistic approach to know and understand clients. The reader will realize that the central goal of doing a culture care assessment is to provide culturally congruent, specific, and meaningful care to individuals, families, special groups or subcultures. The reader will be guided in ways to establish trusting relationships in order to enter the client's world and discover cultural secrets often concealed within family values, religious beliefs, economic factors or in other areas depicted in the Sunrise Model. Nursing students who study and master doing a culturalogical care assessment often express their deep appreciation for learning about broad cultural life values and experiences of people seen through the people's lens so that nurses can provide professional care. Accordingly, the nursing student learns to appreciate that life experiences and cultural values are extremely important and can make a difference in whether the nurse provides competent care practices. Only a practitioner skilled in culturalogical care assessments can demonstrate comparative care differences with beneficial client outcomes.

Rationale, Definitions, and Characteristics of Culture Care Assessments

Since cultures are different and human care expressions tend to vary transculturally, the professional nurse first seeks to discover what factors tend to influence cultural differences in lifeways, values, and care needs of clients. The nurse keeps in mind discovering what care values and other life activities are similar or common features with a client and those of other cultures. As the nurse becomes involved in doing care assessment, one soon realizes that the historical roots of culture are deep and are not readily relinquished when sick or well. To discover such knowledge requires time, patience, and some holding knowledge to explore and affirm what clients say and do. Moreover, social structure factors, such as the client's religious beliefs and kinship ties, are often deeply embedded and it requires skill, creativity, and patience to have the client share their knowledge. Similarly, cultural values and beliefs are especially strong influences on the care, health, and illness of human beings.

Synthesizing sizable amounts of shared information from clients necessitates that nurses develop active listening and reflecting skills in order to bring together many ideas from clients. It takes time to reflect upon what clients say and do as they share their world with the nurse. The nurse links ideas related to different dimensions of the Sunrise Model. The assessment process varies to accommodate the client's mode of being and expressing ideas to the nurse. As the nurse does a culturalogical assessment, some clients such as the Old Order Amish may talk about their fears of hospital technologies because they do not value or generally use technologies in their daily life. Identifying such diverse culture care factors and their relationships to care and social structure factors are important and central to nursing assessments. During the assessment process the nurse remains alert to special language statements, to the client's expressions and to the meanings the client gives to an idea. Nonverbal communication, use of space and patterns of action or non-action become important areas of observation and reflection, as these factors influence care, health, illness, and patterns of being. These aspects of culture care assessments are important as are the very elusive, covert or invisible areas that often make a difference in helping people such as religious beliefs of healing and

Figure 4.1
Leninger's Sunrise Model to Depict the Theory of Culture Care Diversity and Universality

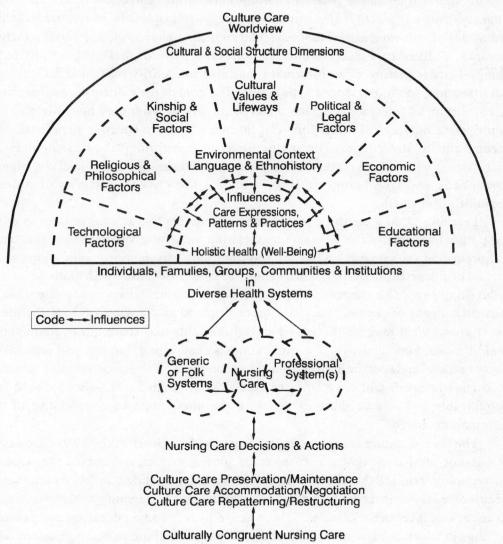

From *Culture Care Diversity and Universality: A Theory for Nursing* by M. Leininger, 1991
New York: National League for Nursing. Reprinted by permission.

caring. These covert or invisible ideas of care are generally not shared readily with strangers such as the nurse.

Before proceeding further, a definition of culture care assessment is needed. *Culture care assessment refers to the systematic identification of the culture care beliefs, meanings, values, symbols, and practices of individuals or groups within a holistic perspective including the worldview, life experiences, environmental context, ethnohistory, and social structure factors.*[1] Culture care assessments are directed toward obtaining a holistic or comprehensive picture of an informant, but also to identify particular factors that have meaning and importance to the client. The goal of the culture care assessment is to obtain as full and accurate an account of the client as possible so that appropriate nursing care decisions can be made that are specific, beneficial, and meaningful to the client. The major focus of culturalogical assessment is on ascertaining culture care patterns, expressions, and meanings that reflect the client's care needs and well-being, or that influence the client's patterns of illness, disabilities, or death.

Learning to do a culture care assessment requires that the nurse keep in mind the purpose and goal of the assessment in relation to nursing care needs and practices. Culturalogical assessments go beyond the traditional psychomotor, physiological, or mental health assessments to the broad holistic aspects of culture with multiple factors influencing people's behavior. Culturalogical assessments, however, pay attention to particular needs of clients. They are interesting and challenging because the nurse never knows what may be discovered and what clients may share or not share about their life values and lifeways. The uncertainty is challenging, but the goal remains to obtain general and specific information about the client. If the nurse remains sensitive to client's behavior and open to learn much can be gained. The client should feel comfortable and safe to share ideas which the nurse must be appreciative of the information shared.

The idea of culture care assessments began with my work in the 1960s. However, it was not until later that a core of transcultural nurses and nurses prepared in anthropology realized the value of these assessments in nursing.[2] Today, culturalogical health care assessments are viewed as an essential part of nursing practice in our care to client's of diverse background. There are, however, some education and practice settings in which the traditional biomedical aspects continue to be emphasized with cultural dimensions avoided or not recognized in client assessments. However, nurses who are prepared in transcultural nursing and in the use of the theory of Culture Care with the Sunrise Model are generally quite skilled in doing holistic culturalogical assessments. These nurses work to grasp an accurate and reliable view of the client and the family or significant others and can demonstrate use of knowledge in client care.

Since culturalogical assessments came into nursing, several different principles, models, guidelines, and techniques have been presented in the literature. Dobson provides a summary of some of these different models and guidelines which the reader may wish to review.[3] Some models are no longer available in published sources. There are some that offer a limited guide to cultural factors, but instead direct the nurse back to traditional biomedical-nursing perspectives. Some assessment models focus on community nursing but fail to include specific cultural dimensions. Orque's comparative assessment provides another approach to culturalogical assessments, but several aspects of my assessment model were presented inaccurately.[4] Currently, the author's culturalogical assessment model remains one of the broadest, most holistic, most comprehensive statements and yet is quite specific to assess the individual, family, group, and communities.[5] This statement becomes meaningful as one use the Culture Care Theory with the Sunrise Model and studies the use of data with clients.

During the past three decades the author has identified several purposes of a culture care assessment; they are: 1) to discover the client's culture care and health patterns and meanings in relation to the client's worldview, lifeways, cultural values, beliefs, patterns, and social structure factors; 2) to obtain holistic culture care information as a basis in providing nursing care decisions and actions; 3) to discover specific culture care patterns, meanings, and values, that can be used to make differential nursing decisions that fit the client's lifeways and aspects of professional knowledge; 4) to identify potential areas of culture care conflicts or clashes due to emic and etic value differences between clients and professional health personnel; 5) to identify general and specific dominant themes or patterns that need to be understood in context to develop and implement congruent care practices; 6) to identify comparative culture care information among clients of different cultures, so that information can be shared and used appropriately by nurses in clinical, teaching, and research practices; 7) to identify similarities and differences in human needs that require nurses to think and make critical judgments in order to provide quality care; and 8) to demonstrate the importance of theoretical ideas and research approaches that can be readily used to improve client care practices and to advance the body of transcultural nursing knowledge.

Some nurses believe that the major purpose of a cultural assessment is to serve as a culture broker. The concept of *culture broker* is derived from anthropology and refers to how the nurse serves as a mediator or broker between the client and health professionals in order to support the client's cultural beliefs and values.[6] This concept has merit, however the nurse cannot be an effective culture broker or cultural mediator unless the nurse is truly knowledgeable about the client's culture and the potentially multiple factors influencing the client's lifeways. Nurses with superficial, biased, or narrow views of a client's culture could not function as a culture broker and would encounter many difficulties. For example, a Hispanic nurse tried to serve as a culture broker for an Arab Muslim but failed because she was unaware of the client's cultural background values and orientation. She also had many biases and a narrow view of the Arab Muslim client. To be an effective culture broker requires that the nurse understand almost fully the client's culture and especially the political, legal, ethnohistorical other social structure factors as depicted in the Sunrise Model. The culture broker functions best when prepared in transcultural nursing with appropriate skills and sensitivity to cultural factors. In general, it is very difficult to be a culture broker unless one first understands the culture before doing a culturalogical assessment and then uses the culture-based assessment knowledge in a sensitive way avoiding ethical problems and cultural imposition practices.

Another consideration in doing and using culture care assessment data is related to the current trend that nurses are expected to arrive at a nursing diagnosis such as those proposed by the North American Nursing Diagnoses Association (NANDA) and discover that clients' lifeways generally fail to fit the NANDA classification scheme.[7,8,9] Currently, nursing diagnostic labels have been derived from Western nursing cultures and most fail to fit non-Western or underrepresented cultures such as minorities or subcultures. To label a client's behavior and needs in ways that are inaccurate creates ethical problems and leads to a host of other serious problems. Most nursing diagnostic taxonomies are still too biomedically focused, culture bound, and do not reflect theory-based knowledge. They fail to include cultural language terms and specific emic cultural data. Many cultural knowledge deficits exist with the NANDA or modified nursing diagnoses. Such diagnostic rituals greatly limit the nurse obtaining an accurate assessment of clients of a specific culture. In any assessment, specific cultural terms and conditions must be identified, understood and correctly used to prevent misunderstandings and to avoid cultural imposition practices. Moreover, some cultures do not have some Western medical diseases, symptoms, or explanations. Instead they may have other kinds of human conditions that need to be assessed in their cultural context, such as *susto* (magical fright), evil eye, and other conditions. Many of these transcultural nursing problems and ethical issues have been discussed by the author in other sources.[10] More transcultural nursing research based knowledge of Western and non-Western cultures is needed before Western nursing diagnostic labels can be used in other cultures. Nurses who are unprepared in transcultural nursing usually fail to recognize such problems and issues of diagnostic labeling, and one finds a host of ethical, legal, and other problems such as gross misdiagnosis and inappropriate treatment and care of clients. Hence, the use of nursing diagnoses without knowledge of the culture and use of culturalogical assessments must be used with great caution and reluctance. The author predicts that the nursing diagnoses era will cease in the near future because of the above reasons stated.

Use of the Sunrise Model and Principles for a Culture Care Assessment

During the past several decades the Sunrise Model has been most valuable and appropriate to use for culture care assessments (see Figure 4.1). This model helps nurses to envision a total or holistic picture of the client being assessed. Pharmacists, physicians, social workers, anthropologists, and others in the health field have also found the Sunrise Model offers a complete assessment of client's health and care needs. The model can be used with slight modifications by other disciplines according to their particular areas of interest. As the nurse uses the Sunrise Model for assessment of individuals, families, groups, cultures, communities, and/or institutions, it is important to keep in mind the central focus of nursing, namely human care and its influence on the health or well-being of the client. The nurse can begin anywhere in the model according to the domain of inquiry being assessed or the special interests of the nurse. For example, the nurse may be specially interested in assessing kinship and religious factors influencing the care needs of African mothers during pregnancy. This nurse would start with a focus on this part of the model and assess other factors later in keeping with the theoretical focus of activity and client expressions.

The Sunrise Model serves as a guide to insure that different factors that can influence the clients' care and health during pregnancy are assessed. The major areas of assessment are worldview and social structure factors, which include a) cultural values, beliefs, and practices; b) religious, philosophical or spiritual beliefs; c) economic factors; d) educational beliefs; e) technology views; f) kinship and social ties; and g) political and legal factors. In addition, the nurse assesses generic folk and professional beliefs, practices and experiences, searching for the client's cultural interpretations or explanations in relation to generic and professional nursing care. Ethnohistorical and environmental context factors are also kept in mind.

The environmental context in which the client lives is important, as well as food resources, home conditions, and other resources. The nurse draws upon any biophysical and mental factors in relation to culturally based information bearing upon client care needs and ways to promote and maintain wellness. Material and nonmaterial cultural resources such as housing, living and social environment, technologies used, and other factors are always assessed in order to get a comprehensive picture of the client. The worldview and social factors are often some of the richest areas to help the nurse understand the client. These dimensions of the Sunrise Model were defined and explained in chapter three and will not be restated here. The reader is encouraged to study the suggested guide (Appendix A) to understand what ideas could be explored with social structure factors. The domains of inquiry and suggested inquiry modes are offered to gain understanding of each dimension for a meaningful assessment of clients.

As the nurse uses the Sunrise Model for a culturalogical assessment, the *first principle is to give attention to gender differences, communication modes, special language terms, interpersonal relationships, use of space and foods,* and many additional aspects which the client may share. Attention to the physical and dress appearance of the client are as important to document as attitudes. The nurse remains attentive to these areas throughout the assessment. The *second principle is to show a genuine interest in the client and to learn from and to maintain respect for the client.* The nurse must be honest and tell the client that she (he) is interested to learn from him (her) about cultural values, beliefs, and lifeways through visiting with the client.

The *third principle is to study the Sunrise Model before doing the assessment in order to draw upon these factors.* Understanding the different components of the Sunrise Model provides a guide with holding or reflective knowledge to understand and respond appropriately to the client, family, or community group being assessed. The model can be used like a road map to ensure that the major paths and signs are considered when doing the assessment. The nurse keeps alert to whatever the client shares about culture care values, religion, kinship relationships, and other factors. The nurse's preparation in transcultural nursing about cultures, care, and health serves as holding or reflective knowledge as the nurse explores social structure and other areas.

A *fourth principle for an effective culture care assessment is for nurses to discover and remain aware of their own cultural biases and prejudices.*[11] Nurses' biases, prejudgments, and narrow views can greatly limit an accurate assessment. Some nurses may have strong lifetime or negative views and prejudices about a culture which can greatly influence and distort what they see, hear, and interpret from clients. Nurses who come from a culture very different than the client may have negative views about the culture which then become evident in talking with the client or in discussing cultural factors. Negative family and community biases are often related to cultural ignorance and blindness and limit a reliable and accurate assessment of the client. Hence, the nurse's attitudes and viewpoints need to be assessed by self or a mentor before conducting a client assessment. Currently, there is a belief that nurses of a culture are the best nurses to assess their own people. This is a myth because some nurses may have cultural blindness or strong ethnocentric tendencies and may be acculturated to a culture entirely different than the nurses'.

Cultural blindness is one of the most serious factors limiting effective nursing assessments and care practices. *Cultural blindness refers to the fact that one is unable to see one's own cultural values and lifeways due to cultural biases, attitudes, and prejudices.* Cultural blindness is generally related to strong ethnocentrism, cultural ignorance and the lack of transcultural knowledge experiences with cultures. Often a person may be so acculturated to another culture that they cannot "see" their own traditional culture. Or the person dislikes his (her) own culture and does not want to be identified with the culture. The professional nurses need to assess themselves and their own cultural biases, prejudices, and other factors to prevent or limit cultural blindness. In traditional nursing courses and field experiences, the faculty mentor helps the student to become aware of cultural blindness, biases and prejudices about other cultures. Most importantly, students in transcultural nursing have the opportunity to learn how to do culture assessments and to appraise their own cultural biases with a mentor. The dictum "know thyself" in relation to knowing people of other cultures remains an important principle and professional goal.

The *fifth principle to guide the nurse in doing a culturalogical assessment is to be aware that clients may belong to subcultures or special groups such as the homeless, AIDS and HIV infected, drug users, lesbians, gays, the deaf, mentally retarded, and many other particular groups.* These groups are often subcultures with some particular cultural patterns, values, norms, and practices that fit with the criteria of a subculture. *Subcultures are small or large groups of a dominant culture who maintain certain values and beliefs, but who differ in certain areas from the dominant culture.* These subcultures show differences in their special norms, values, and lifeways that make them different in certain respects from the dominant culture. The nurse observes and documents the special lifeways, dress, and identifies differences from the dominant culture. Sometimes subcultures may be called odd, unacceptable, or questionable by members of dominant cultures. Subcultures such as gays, lesbians, the homeless, the retarded, and others may be openly devalued and discriminated against because they show patterns deviant from the dominant culture. Nurses must be aware of these subcultures in any society and how they differ from "social" groups. Subcultures must be respected for their rights to be understood, heard, and lived.

Stereotyping cultures is another concern in doing an assessment. The nurse needs to avoid stereotyping or seeing people in rigid, fixed, or "cookbook" ways. Cultural variability helps nurses to avoid stereotyping. Nurses need to look at group cultural patterns but also individual variations within and between groups. The author often uses a triad role-playing method to help nurses avoid stereotyping clients and to prevent biases, prejudices, and prejudging people before knowing them. The triad role includes the nurse, client, and an observer or mentor. The observer-mentor is a skilled transcultural nurse who can identify cultural patterns and values between nurse and client. The mentor provides feedback to the nurse to improve assessment skills and avoid prejudices and stereotyping. The use of such reflective role playing appraisals often helps the nurse to change unfavorable attitudes and to modify negative judgmental tendencies. Transcultural nurse mentors are, therefore, essential to help students overcome or deal with long-standing family or group prejudices. Doing cultural assessments in the classroom before doing an assessment of clients in clinical areas is important to develop new skills and insights. In clinical settings transcultural nurse specialists have been most helpful to staff nurses and interdisciplinary colleagues in changing biases and prejudices of people through assessments.

The *sixth principle is for nurses to know their own culture with its variabilities, strengths, and assets.* All too frequently, the nurse is unaware of her (his) own cultural roots, values, and behavior. If the nurse is unaware of her (his) own culture or subculture this may lead to problems in doing an assessment, as the nurse's values can influence the assessment outcomes. This principle became evident to the author when I first went to New Guinea. While I had some general ideas about my Irish and German American cultural values and roots, I discovered them more fully as I observed the Gadsup. Assessing a totally strange culture makes one keenly aware of cultural differences and how one's cultural tendencies can influence cultures. Sometimes nurses want to make another culture like theirs in order to become comfortable with the people or because of ethnocentric biases. Choosing a culture very different from one's own to study often prevents the tendency to make them like oneself, because of great difference between the cultures. It may also help to reduce cultural blindness and biases because the culture is so totally different that one cannot force the culture to fit one's image. At the same time, such major cultural differences can lead to culture shock, avoidance tendencies, or to spending less time with the people. The idea of beginning with a very different or strange culture was advocated by Margaret Mead in the 1950s because she held one learned more about a "new" culture and could not rely on traditional responses, as they usually did not fit the new culture. This advice to me supported my studies in the Eastern Highlands of New Guinea as my first and major attempt to learn cultural differences and similarities. The shockingly different lifeways of the Gadsup made me think anew and become a learner from the people. The people stimulated me to discover many unknowns. Learning how to value and respect cultural differences and to look for reasons why cultures are different or similar can be enormously valuable for new breakthrough knowledge areas in nursing.

The *seventh principle guiding the nurse in doing a culture care assessment is to clarify and explain at the outset to the individual, family, or group the focus of a culturalogical or lifeway assessment is to help clients*. Cultural assessments are quite different from "hands on" medical or physical assessments and cannot be conducted like physical or mental assessments in a short span of time. Culturalogical assessments often take two or three twenty–thirty minute sessions with informants to obtain a holistic perspective. In the hospital setting, this assessment often has to fit the busy hospital norms by not staying too long with a client. Spacing time to be with the client provides reflective time between talk sessions. The nurse tries to find a reasonably quiet place to do the assessment so that disruptions will be minimal and to enable the client and nurse to focus on different areas of the Sunrise Model. Moreover, a cultural assessment may be a very new experience for some clients, and so the nurse will need to clarify what is being done, often to physicians and other interdisciplinary staff in the hospital setting who are unfamiliar with this kind of assessment. In-service staff programs are becoming essential to learn about culturalogical assessments. The client's family may also need to understand the purposes and goals of culturalogical assessments and how the information will be used. Sometimes the client's family members are invited to participate directly in the assessment to obtain shared family perspectives or to reaffirm certain ideas. If a family assessment is done, the nurse usually meets two or three times in the home to assess different aspects of the Sunrise Model. Most cultural assessments are viewed as beneficial and therapeutic to clients.

The *eighth principle is to maintain a holistic or total view of the informant's world and environmental context by focusing on the multiple components as depicted in the Sunrise Model*. The nurse remains alert to biophysical or emotional aspects, but usually does not begin with these aspects as it often makes the client respond in the traditional medical model way. Instead cultural factors such as family values, beliefs, and care aspects related to health and well-being are explored. It may take some time for clients to focus on cultural aspects because they are often oriented to the dominant medical disease-and-symptom questions. Shifting the client's thinking to reflect on cultural beliefs and lifeways often stimulates the client to have a new and meaningful experience. For example, an Arab Muslim woman was experiencing severe cultural pain because she was very restless in the labor and delivery room due to a male physician attempting to deliver her baby. The client's values were counter to the male physician seeing or touching her vagina. This Arab Muslim woman told how she became so culturally upset that she screamed and got off the delivery table for she could not accept a strange male physician looking at her female organs. She desperately expected a female physician or female nurse to do the delivery. As a consequence of this cultural pain and shock, the woman's blood pressure increased and she became acutely ill. Today clients are often pleased to have transcultural nurses do a cultural assessment in order to prevent such happenings and to anticipate care that will fit the client's expectations and not be an insult or offensive. With the advent of transcultural nursing, non-Westerners, minorities, and subcultures are becoming aware that their cultural taboos, pain, conflicts, and imposition practices may be respected and dealt with. An Armenian woman said to the author "I have long waited for this day, as I have been in this country for twenty years and no nurses and physicians ever talked to me about my cultural background, values, interests, and needs. This is the first time that someone has assessed my cultural needs, beliefs, and interests and how it has influenced my health. It makes me feel good and hopeful." Such statements reaffirm the great benefits of culturalogical assessments and having clients tell their stories to the nurse.

Throughout the cultural assessment the nurse listens to clients, learning from the clients' information about their lifeways, beliefs, and values that can be helpful to nurses in caring for them. Focusing the assessment interview on clients' beliefs and lifeways and less on medical symptoms and problems tends to free clients to share their special lifeways and interests and what the clients believe is important for the nurse to know. Some clients are more eager than others to share. The nurse, however, needs to maintain a genuine interest in clients and encourage them to share ideas about their expectations of care and of their lifeways in order to stay well and to prevent illness conditions. Granted, most Western clients are oriented to discussing medical symptoms and procedures and it often takes them a while to shift to broader lifeways and cultural values and beliefs. The nurse uses the transcultural nursing principle of remaining an active learner and listener to facilitate the clients telling their stories or sharing their narrative experiences related to different areas of the Sunrise Model. Story telling has been a valuable means to learn about cultural values, caring, and health with narrative accounts to document client views. The nurse encourages clients to be active participants in the assessment. The nurse remains an astute observer of non-verbal communications, body language, and cultural expressions in the particular setting or context in which the assessment occurs.

During the culturalogical assessment the nurse reflects upon what I call "transcultural holding knowledge" about the client's particular culture, but does not openly use this knowledge with the client except to reflect upon or to clarify cultural ideas such as evil eye, good spirits, *susto* (fright), and other cultural terms expressed by the client. The nurse always reflects upon what the client says or shares about the culture. The nurse uses mainly broad and open inquiry statements such as "Tell me about your family lifeways," or, "I would like to learn about your experience with your children or what you value in caring for your family." Throughout the culturalogical assessment the nurse uses the client's language terms rather than the nurse's in order to enter and remain in the client's emic or local, familiar world. Very few direct questions are used, but rather indirect and inquiry comments such as "Could you tell me about your experiences at home?" The nurse also remains alert to intergenerational ideas of differences and similarities within or between generations to discover any changes in cultural values and practices over time influencing care practices. Male and female differences are noted as well as acceptable or non-acceptable gender expressions and values in human caring and health, with respect to social structure factors, daily and nightly living patterns, ceremonies, and other client-centered experiences.

Throughout the assessment the nurse maintains a flexible and open attitude with a willingness to *listen and move with the client.* There is no rigidly prescribed or fixed technique to do a culture assessment. Instead, a cultural assessment reflects a dynamic process in which the nurse seeks to understand the client, gain insights about the meanings of care, health, and well-being. The nurse always moves with the client in thinking and actions in clarifying and understanding the person. If the above practices are maintained, the nurse will usually find that the client's interest in sharing markedly increases, and the nurse obtains many valuable insights and data to make care decisions and actions appropriate for the client's well-being.

The nurse is not expected to cover fully all domains depicted in the Sunrise Model in one session. Instead, the nurse takes cues from the client and returns to talk with the client in subsequent sessions according to the client's available time and other considerations. Initially, the nurse usually begins the assessment with comments such as "What would you like to share with me today about your experiences or beliefs to help you keep well? Are there some special ideas or ways you would like nurses to care for you?" Generally, the first session in a hospital or clinic is about twenty minutes, and subsequent ones may be longer. Allowing time between sessions during the day or night helps the client to think about cultural beliefs and values to share with the nurse at the next visit. During the early sessions, some clients may wonder if the nurse can be trusted and if the nurse is genuinely interested in the client's sharing cultural secrets. Testing between nurse and client may occur if the client wants to be reassured to tell folk practices and other secrets to the nurse. The nurse remembers to focus on the domains of interest to the client, and does not pursue her (his) agenda, especially if the topic makes the client uncomfortable. From the author's experience over many years, clients from non-Western cultures like to talk initially about their family and some of their values and beliefs. In contrast, Western (particularly Anglo-Americans) like to talk initially about treatments, tests, technologies, and personal health story experiences. Before closing the sessions, the nurse always asks if clients want to share other thoughts, experiences, or ideas they have not had an opportunity to talk about. They are also free to call the nurse later and share ideas they had difficulty recalling. The nurse always thanks the client or family in a sincere way after each session. If the client refuses a culturalogical assessment, the nurse respects such wishes. However, most clients find many benefits and like the opportunity to share about their lifeways and care needs.

The real secret of an effective cultural assessment is the nurse's ability to remain an active learner and reflector of what the client has shared and of areas that the client deems important. If the assessment is done in the client's home, the nurse often has an opportunity to see the client's environment and material culture and to meet others in the family or group. Seeing the cultural context of the client is extremely important. For example, when doing a home cultural assessment the client often wants the nurse to meet his family and to talk with them at their favorite visiting or naturalistic setting. For example, a Mexican American woman wanted to visit at the kitchen table and also to see her plants (herbs) in the backyard. She showed me generic folk herbs "that heal" and introduced me to traditional healers and their roles. Her garden was filled with folk herbs to ease many different health concerns, and they were also available at home to all the family members. Sometimes clients in the community may want to show the nurse where they work, where the children go to school, or which hospital they have used in crisis situations—all part of sharing their lifeways.

Sometimes the most negative experiences or stories are told at the end of the sessions along with cultural secrets, such as revealing generic healers and local cultural practitioners they rely on for health care. The reason for this is often that trust has been established and cultural secrets can now be safely revealed to the nurse as a trusted friend. If the session is done in the clinic or hospital, the sessions usually take more time, and there are always more interruptions by other health personnel than in the home. Sometimes cultural secrets are not shared in the hospital, as trust may not be fully established on stranger's turf. Finally, it is important for the nurse to realize that culturalogical assessments can be extremely valuable to learn from clients, but they can be enjoyable experiences for both clients and nurses. The author has found over the past three decades that culturalogical assessments have been informative and most helpful to get close to, understand, and to grasp the meaning of the lived experiences of clients. Much rich data can be forthcoming about care, caring, health, well-being, and illness consequences if the components of the Sunrise Model and the Culture Care theory are used. However, these aspects are often embedded in many social structure factors such as family relationships, religion, politics, and philosophy of life. Cultural assessments are generally quite congruent with the client's lifeways. Assessments tend to be refreshing to clients, and they provide a different way to tell nurses their stories rather than talking mainly about medical diseases and illnesses.

Cultural assessments acknowledge clients' lifeways, self-esteem and ability to express their interests and viewpoints rather than those of the medical establishment. Moreover, culturalogical assessments put the client in a central position to share and give them a sense of control, power, and having their ideas about caring and health shared. The benefits of the assessments to the client, family, or friends are often stated as most beneficial and important to the client's well-being. For the nurse, grasping the meaning of care and health from the client's viewpoint often provides very new or different kinds of knowledge for culture-specific care.

Summary Points and Principles for an Effective Assessment

In doing a culturalogical care assessment, the following summary points can guide the nurse to an effective assessment:

1. The Culture Care Theory with the Sunrise Model can serve as an excellent guide to obtain a holistic view of the individual, family or group, and for institutional assessments. The worldview, social structure factors, ethnohistory, language uses, and environmental context are the elements essential to getting comprehensive yet specific information. Some components will be of more interest than others with specific cultures. For example, Mexicans, Africans, Italians, and Arabs generally will emphasize the importance of care to their extended families. Anglo-Americans want to talk about the economic, technological, and legal aspects of health care. The nurse listens to the client to guide the assessment, but seeks always to get a holistic picture.

2. Throughout the assessment the nurse maintains a role as an active listener, learner, and reflector rather than being a teacher or in a "know it all" role. The nurse refrains from using a lot of professional jargon or medical terms, as this tends to suppress informants from sharing their ideas in their emic ways. If the informant inquires about professional knowledge, the nurse shares and is obligated to inform the client, but does not make professional nursing or medical ideas the major focus of the assessment.

3. The nurse always keeps the assessment focused on the clients internal world of knowing (the emic focus) rather than the nurse's etic (or outsider's) ideas about care, health, and lifeways. The nurse's professional ideas on health and care should be viewed as secondary to that of the client's. If nurses are prone to and eager to sell their ideas to clients, this often leads to cultural conflicts, clashes, or latent backlash responses.

4. The nurse encourages the client or family to think about some of their cultural values, beliefs, and lifeways and how they think these areas influence their health care lifeways. Clients may wish to share their values and lifeways through stories, special life experiences, photographs, letters, or material

cultural symbols such as talking about a "blue stone" or the "medicine bag" that promotes or hinders healing and well-being in their culture. Clients like to share material items and nonmaterial ideas that have meaning for them in their life. Maintaining the meaning of the clients' ideas to him or her during the assessment is extremely important. Accordingly, some family members may like to use a videotape to share their meanings and special experiences during a home assessment with the nurse, e.g., Philippine families with their dancing, music, eating, and praying as caring modalities.

5. The nurse usually asks very few direct questions but instead focuses on areas of inquiry with open ended comments such as "Tell me about yourself and your family. I would like to learn more about they way you care for your children. Could you tell me about your experiences the last time you sought health care? I am trying to understand what you meant by the word 'comfort' care. Tell me more about this idea as it will be helpful to nurses as care facilitators." The nurse uses the client's words and frame of reference rather than the nurse's in order to keep in the client's world of knowing and understanding. This strategy is of vital importance throughout the assessment.

6. The nurse explores not only present experiences and values but also past and future views related to the general domains of nursing, i.e., culture care/caring, health, well-being and environmental context—the central and major domains of nursing from subjective and objective data.

7. The nurse recognizes that most clients are capable of explaining and interpreting their experiences related to care, health, and maintaining wellness. Often narratives, poems, cultural taboos, songs, pictures, and symbols have cultural meanings that the client can explain and interpret. Thus the nurse may not always be the expert interpreter and analyzer, but instead the client is capable of playing this role. The nurse's etic (outsider's) views often differ greatly from the client's emic interpretations, and so it is the responsibility of the nurse to be fully cognizant of this assessment approach focus.

8. The client's cultural secrets are generally not shared unless the client believes the nurse can be trusted, is genuinely interested in him (her) and can protect cultural secrets and viewpoints. Individuals fear that their cultural ideas and experiences might be demeaned or devalued by outsiders. Hence, respect for all cultural ideas as well as protecting cultural secrets shared with the nurse is imperative, especially spiritual ideas.

9. If the client wants to wear traditional dress, adornments or symbols for the assessment, the nurse respects and encourages this practice. Seeing the client in familiar or treasured dress and decor modes can help the nurse learn much about the culture, health, caring, and healing modes.

10. Throughout the cultural care assessment the nurse tries to make the client or family comfortable and enjoy sharing ideas with the nurse. Confidential matters may be presented, and, if so, ethical considerations with the client must be respected.

11. The nurse remains appreciative of the client's sharing his (her) ideas or material cultural. The nurse expresses a "thank you" after each session and values the client's information to improve client care.

12. Throughout the assessment the nurse seeks to assess if the information is accurate or credible to the client's lifeways, the family, or as representatives in the community.

In general a culturalogical assessment is a creative and dynamic discovery and learning process that is often packed with surprises of information generally unknown to most nurses and health care providers. The Culture Care Theory and the Sunrise Model help to make the journey an exciting and meaningful discovery process and one of benefit to the client.

Caring Rituals as Important Areas to Assess

In doing a culturalogical care assessment there may be additional areas to consider such as special and healing rituals. Practically all cultures have caring rituals that reflect sequenced activities or strategies people use to maintain wellness, prevent illness, and to regain health. Generic caring rituals are learned and used in the home. They may be transferred to health or hospital situations because they are held to be essential to life. Caring rituals serve specific functions and are usually held to be beneficial and therapeutic in the home setting. Nurses also have rituals of practice which may not be congruent with the client's. Ritual care expectations such as care to the hair and skin or doing exercises may differ greatly between the client's (generic) and the nurse's (professional) practices. Such major differences can lead to cultural clashes and conflicts and to non-compliance or uncooperative behavior. Rituals have cultural functions such as giving people security of what to expect, when, and where. Rituals can provide a sense of well-being through activities that need to be carried out daily. Some generic (folk or home) and professional care rituals may blend together and can be creatively used in professional caring practices with the client. Since caring rituals are often important to assess with clients, some different examples are offered next.

A. Eating Rituals: Individuals, groups, and families generally have established patterns of eating with special ritual activities. For example, individuals may always wash their hands and put on clean clothes before eating. Some persons may dress in special attire because "Our family has always done this." The way a client eats his (her) food and what is done during the sequence of eating is important to observe. There may be certain foods that are avoided and specific times of eating. Culturally taboo foods, observance of the cold-hot theory about foods, gender uses, and what foods are eaten at certain times of the day or night are all important to observe and assess. The environmental setting for eating may be extremely important to the client. Some clients like to be alone while others like someone to talk with. Children often have special cultural rituals they have been taught such as ways to eat an egg or fruit. They may become upset if not permitted to carry out these cultural rituals. Transcultural differences exist in all aspects of food selection, consumption, and disposal of the remaining uneaten foods.

B. Daily and Nightly Ritual Care Activities: It is always fascinating to observe the client's patterns of daily and nightly care rituals. What daily personal exercises are done each morning or evening are important to know. For example, Japanese people wherever they live maintain their early morning health group exercises with their kinsmen with religious meanings. Americans have many morning and evening running and walking rituals which they do alone or with others. Some cultures have praying rituals, such as those of Arab-Muslims. The latter pray five times a day using prayer rugs, beads, and washing hands and body parts before praying. These religious ritual activities are extremely important and need to be understood as they contribute the client feeling spiritually cared for and remaining well. The nurse needs to accommodate these ritual activities largely by respecting and facilitating the activities. Roman Catholics have rituals for the sick and dying which need to be respected and supported by priests and family members.

C. Sleep and Rest Ritual Patterns: Every culture has patterns of sleep and rest that are usually established early in life and often reinforced throughout the life cycle. Children and the elderly especially like and expect rituals of eating and sleeping. What are these rituals in different cultures and how are they used in nursing care practices? When adults or children become ill, do they alter these rituals? If so, how do changes influence their well-being or lead to unfavorable outcomes? Sleep and rest patterns are largely culturally-based and need to be assessed by the nurse to provide culturally congruent care.

There are some other cultural rituals related to folk healing and caring that need to be learned from clients and studied for their uses in professional caring. Integrating generic and professional rituals is an extremely important transcultural nursing challenge. Generic folk healing rituals are usually traditional with specific activities for each culture or subculture. These rituals and others need to be studied for the beneficial or less beneficial outcomes. Spector's and Leininger's writings on this subject will be helpful, as will many sources from anthropology.[12,13]

Life Cycle Rituals of Clients and Nurses

Transcultural nurses and anthropologists have been studying life cycle rituals in diverse cultures for many years to discover commonalties and differences related to healing and health. *Life cycle rituals* are especially important because they provide a sense of *cultural identify, self-esteem, and often reflect new roles or status for people in the culture*. Life span rituals can make one feel cared for or about as they occur in different times throughout life and as they become meaningful experiences of groups when well or ill. Students in transcultural nursing are learning about life cycle rituals at birth, marriage, death, and in relation to developmental periods, i.e., becoming a child, adolescent, and adult.

Occasionally life cycle rituals can be stressful, but usually they are beneficial. One of the oldest theories about rituals comes from van Gennep in his classic study, *The Rites of Passage*, which was originally published in 1908.[14] Van Gennep hypothesized that there were major phases which accompanied the rites of passage which were *a phase of separation, a phase of transition*, and *a phase of incorporation*. Individuals undergoing a change in position or status generally become separated from their old role as they take on a new role. When individuals move into the second phase, it is known as a transitional phase, often with uncertain role expectations. In the last phase, individuals learn to take on and incorporate a new role or position in society or the cultural group. Rites of passage and rituals are useful ways to understand the changing role and status of a person in any culture.

Nurse Caring Rituals

Nurses have many rituals that are often not recognized, and yet they occur daily in hospitals and other settings where nurses function or are employed. There are nursing rituals of administering medications, giving baths, checking clients, etc. Clients learn to observe nurses' rituals and when they can call upon them. Some clients are quick to know rituals such as morning reports and time with physicians and so they regulate the time when they can expect to receive care. Many immigrants may not know these rituals and are especially dependent upon the nurse to help them learn these rituals to get food, shelter, and basic needs.

Some nurses fail to recognize their own personal and professional rituals in the hospital or in community health agencies with the functional or dysfunctional outcomes. Such rituals need to be assessed periodically for their benefits and uses. Some nurses are reluctant to speak about rituals, as they have a negative view about rituals as being too rigid, too conforming, and non-flexible rules or laws. Most rituals have favorable or less favorable features in caring for clients. For several decades transcultural nursing students have identified and assessed nursing rituals and what purposes they may serve in caring for clients or in working with other nurses in hospital systems. Interestingly, these nurses have identified many care and medical rituals in client care. For example, staff nurses have routine morning and evening care rituals at certain times to make morning rounds or to give staff reports at changing shift times. Nurses have ritual activities or procedures for giving treatments and in charting. Many of these sequenced ritualized activities may be done without the staff knowing them as rituals. However, they are rituals of nursing that may or may not benefit clients and staff. Some rituals lose their caring when they become efficiency tasks and procedures to get done or out of one's way. Wolf's work is an example of a systematic study of hospital rituals.[15] Spector's work gives several examples of folk rituals that nurses could use to prevent illnesses such as how to handle the evil eye casting due to nurses' praise of the child.[16] In the literature, there are numerous examples regarding how nursing service maintains and changes rituals in nursing service, and of new rituals over time.

In schools of nursing there are many nursing rituals related to how students enter, remain in, or complete nursing programs. Faculty and administrators have rituals in preparing for the day, for classes and research activities. These different rituals of sequenced activities may likewise have more or less caring value to students and faculty. There are many curriculum and teaching rituals which faculty carry out in academic settings which are interesting for faculty and students to assess and know.

Returning to nursing rituals related to caring and healing, the nurse observes and often participates in these rituals with clients. Reflection about these rituals provides important data in caring practices. For example, a client experiences ritual activities when admitted to the hospital or an emergency unit. The nurse can help clients to understand these rituals from their viewpoint, but the client's experiences with such rituals are even more important to assess and understand. For example, some clients see admission rituals as punishing, demeaning, detrimental to self-esteem, and as non-caring rituals. The nurse needs to be aware of how clients see or view certain hospital experiences.

Sometimes nurses may give little attention and time to being with and knowing the client but spends more time doing paper work and getting unit tasks done. Van Gennep's theory of the client separating from their family, and entering a new transitional role as a client, and then trying to become incorporated as a part of the hospital culture may be difficult to assess but is often identified in nursing. Do clients ever feel a part of the hospital culture? Do they see themselves in a marginal or transitional phase? Can clients benefit from care in a marginal or not fully accepted role in the hospital? Do the nursing staff really care about or for them from entry to the time the client leaves the hospital? We hope they do, but this question needs to be assessed from the client and family views.

Cultural factors related to rituals enter and take on meaning for clients in different cultural contexts such as the hospital. For example, in some cultures when individuals are separated from their extended family, they may feel abandoned at the hospital, for the hospital is a place to die or become ill. In several cultures the ritual of admission often communicates to children and elderly clients that it is a place where they will die and be abandoned, unless handled in different ways by the staff. The family and client may be most reluctant to go to the hospital and only as a last resort. If the client dies in the hospital, the family usually goes into immediate mourning or dying rituals. A relative may wail loudly for several days as this is an expected ritual upon the loss of a loved one. Mourning rituals are held to be beneficial to Arab Muslims, Mexicans, and Vietnamese, and so the nurse needs to let them grieve in their own way and with their cultural symbols and people. Transcultural nurses since 1970 have helped to establish "mourning rooms" in hospitals for such cultural expressions. This has made the family feel that nurses do care for and about them. This ritual grieving may mean the nurse should provide the family with a private room or place to grieve. Sometimes hospital visiting rules and rituals limit family caring rituals and grief times.

Individual clients and families from non-Western societies often rely heavily upon healing rituals to help them adapt to hospital changes and maintain their rituals in the hospital. In the home, family rituals are carried out without interference from professional health personnel. In the hospital, Jewish clients and clients of other cultures want certain ritual food practices maintained. Several cultures in the Pacific Ocean have special birth, child, and adolescent rituals at each stage of development such as menstrual celebrations to show how pleased they are that the daughter will be ready for marriage, motherhood, and childbearing. There are often birth and early child rituals for other cultures which need to be assessed, understood, and planned for in the hospital.

In general, caring rituals of clients and nurses are powerful forces to know and understand. Clients expect nurses to have their rituals but also want their care rituals to be respected and upheld. Comparative caring rituals of different cultures have been studied in several cultures for nearly three decades and provide data of care diversities and universalities in caring means, expressions, and rituals.[17,18,19] Most of these transcultural caring constructs which are often associated with caring rituals are meaningful to clients to maintain their health. Nurses need to discover more about client care rituals and special care activities to guide nurses in providing culturally congruent care. Nurses also need to be aware of their rituals regarding nursing rounds, morning visits, and staff coffee or beverage breaks for their positive and less positive ritual functions. In the operating room, there are many nurse rituals of a stressful nature which Chrisman has assessed and analyzed.[20] Thus, transcultural nurses and others are studying and learning ways to assess and evaluate selected caring rituals in nursing practices to advance transcultural nursing knowledge and improve care practices.

Stranger-Friend Enabler as a Guide for Assessment

The *Stranger-Friend Enabler* was developed and has been used by the author for nearly three decades. It has been an extremely useful guide in doing culturalogical assessments and caring for clients.[21] (See Figure 4.2.) The purpose of this enabler is to guide the nurse and other health professional users to assess one's own behavior in relation to that of the client as one begins as a stranger (to most clients) and moves to become a friend of the client. This enabler was built upon the philosophical belief that nurses *can become friends* of clients, and in so doing the nurse will be more effective in care practices. The author holds that *friendship is a caring mode of being with clients* and an important means *to assist clients in a trusting relationship.*

The Stranger-Friend Enabler is like a sensitive barometer to help the nurse assess her (his) own behavior as one moves from a stranger to friend relationship with the client or group. It was based upon many years of experience doing research and working with people in Western and non-Western cultures. This enabler was based on the belief that when nurses or others begin to work with people, they are usually strangers and it takes time and sensitivity to become a trusted friend. Indeed, there were several basic premises in developing this enabler. *First*, nurses and people being assessed or studied are generally viewed initially as strangers to each other. Signs of distrust, doubt, suspiciousness, and other expressions often occur between two strangers. If the nurse happens to know the client, still there are some signs of strangeness that need to be tested and dealt with as the friend moves into a relationship. *Second*, in order to be helpful and get accurate and reliable data from the client, the nurse needs to change from a distrusted stranger to a trusted friend. *Third*, the Stranger-Friend Enabler helps the nurse to avoid earlier rejection or an unfavorable response because the nurse knows she (he) has to develop and work to become a trusted nurse. *Fourth*, the professional nurse can develop knowledge and skills to become a trusted friend and to work with clients in special caring ways that are mutually satisfying and beneficial. Some nurses may have to get comfortable with the goal of being a friend, especially if enculturated in nursing schools to maintain distance and not get involved in therapeutic caring ways. *Fifth*, as the nurse becomes a trusted friend, she (he) will discover that accurate, reliable, and very meaningful data will come forth because of being a trusted friend who knows and understands the client. Nurses who remain in the stranger or non-involved role often get less accurate data as the client will not trust a controlling or suspicious nurse who cannot enter the emic ways of knowing. The nurse needs to study the specific indicators on the Stranger-Friend Enabler before beginning a culturalogical assessment.

Figure 4.2
Leininger's Stranger to Trusted Friend Enabler Guide*

The purpose of this enabler is to facilitate the researcher (or clinician) to move from mainly a distrusted stranger to a trusted friend in order to obtain authentic, credible and dependable data (or establish favorable relationships as a clinician). The user assesses him or herself by reflecting on the indicators as he/she moves from stranger to friend.

Indicators of Stranger (Largely etic or outsider's views)	Date Noted	Indicators as a Trusted Friend (Largely emic or insider's views)	Date Noted
Informant(s) or people are: 1. Active to protect self and others. They are "gate keepers" and guard against outside intrusions. Suspicious and questioning. 2. Actively watch and are attentive to what the researcher does and says. Limited signs of trusting the researcher or stranger. 3. Skeptical about the researcher's motives and work. May question how findings will be used by the researcher or stranger. 4. Reluctant to share cultural secrets and views as private knowledge. Protective of local lifeways, values and beliefs. Dislikes probing by the researcher or stranger. 5. Uncomfortable with becoming a friend or confiding in a stranger. May come late, be absent and withdraw at times from the researcher. 6. Tends to offer inaccurate data. Modifies "truths" to protect self, family, community, and cultural lifeways. Emic values, beliefs, and practices are not shared spontaneously.		**Informant(s) or people are:** 1. Less active to protect self. More trusting of researchers with "gate keeping" down or less. Less suspicious and less questioning of researcher. 2. Less watchful of the researcher's words and actions. More signs of trusting and accepting a new friend. 3. Less questioning of the researcher's motives, work and behavior. Signs of working with and helping the researcher as a friend. 4. Willing to share cultural secrets and private world information and experiences. Offers most local views, values and interpretations spontaneously or without probes. 5. Signs of being comfortable and enjoying friends and a sharing relationship. Gives presence, on time, and gives evidence of being a genuine friend. 6. Wants research "truths" to be accurate regarding beliefs, people, values and lifeways. Explains and interprets emic ideas so the researcher has accurate data.	

* Developed and used since 1959 by author.

Adapted from *Culture Care Diversity and Universality: A Theory for Nursing* by M. Leininger, 1991. New York: National League for Nursing. Reprinted by permission.

The indicators can help the nurse assess her (his) behavior in relation to the client. At the same time, the nurse assesses the client's behavior in relation to each indicator and at different times in the relationship or encounter. Nurses who are afraid to become professional friends to clients will find differences in the quality of nursing care and in being effective in transcultural nursing. The nurse will find the Stranger Friend Enabler Guide one of the most valuable transcultural nursing guides for effective and accurate culturalogical assessments and in developing therapeutic caring relationships.

Acculturation Enabler to Assess Culture Care and Health Patterns

Another enabling guide which the author developed in the early 1960s was the *Acculturation Health Care Assessment Guide for Cultural Patterns in Traditional and Nontraditional Lifeways* as shown in Figure 4.3.[22] This Acculturation enabling guide can assist the user in assessing clients, whether in a more traditional or nontraditional lifeway. Since acculturation is focused upon how a client takes on the lifeways of another culture, this dimension of assessment is important to obtain the dominant patterns of living with respect to several indicators or criteria. Although this Acculturation Enabler was developed to obtain data for the ethnonursing method and the theory of Culture Care, it has been used by other disciplines and health care providers to get credible, reliable, and meaningful data about informants. This enabler is another facilitator to help the nurse obtain a holistic assessment, especially when using the Culture Care Theory and Sunrise Model by providing a systematic assessment of a client or family from a particular culture with respect to the worldview, social structure, language, environmental context, and generic and professional care practices. The nurse assessor makes notations on Part I and uses this information in Part II to make a summary profile of the client as to whether the person or family is more traditionally or non-traditionally oriented in cultural values, beliefs, and lifeways. The data can be used to develop guidelines in nursing's actions and decisions from the three modes of the theory, namely: 1) culture care maintenance/preservation; 2) culture care accommodation/negotiation; and 3) culture care repatterning/restructuring. It is important to document and describe the place of the assessment, such as the home, hospital, or alternative health settings, as the context greatly influences the responses and meanings. The enabler is not intended to be used by the client, but rather by the nurse who is responsible for the assessment and is closely linked to the tenet and components of Culture Care Theory and the Sunrise Model. It is also used as a research guide for information to substantiate or refute theories related to the degree of acculturation.

Figure 4.3
Leininger's Acculturation Health Care Assessment Guide for Cultural Patterns Traditional and Non-Traditional Lifeways*

Name of Assessor_____ Date _____

Informants or Code No._____ Sex_____ Age _____

Place or Context of Assessment _____

Directions: This guide provides a general qualitative profile or assessment of the traditional or nontraditional orientation of informants and their patterned lifeways. Health care influencers are assessed with respect to worldview, language, cultural values, kinship, religion, politics, technology, education, environment and related areas. This profile is primarily focused on emic (local) information to assess and guide health personnel in working with individuals and groups. The etic (or more universal view) may also be evident. In Part I, the user observes, records and rates behavior on the scale below from 1 to 5 with respect to traditionally or non-traditionally oriented lifeways. Numbers are plotted on the summary Part II to obtain a qualitative profile to guide decisions and actions. The user's brief guide is *not* designed to be a quantitative measurement guide, but rather a qualitative guide of information with respect to the above areas of informant knowledge as direction of interest or lifeways.

....

Part I: Rating Criteria to Assess Traditionally and Non-Traditionally Patterned Cultural Lifeways or Orientations

	Mainly Traditional	Moderate	Average	Moderate	Mainly Non-Traditional	Rater Value No.
Rating Indicators:	1	2	3	4	5	

Culture Dimensions to Assess Traditional or Non-Traditional Orientations

1. Language, communications and gestures native or nonnative). Notations: _____
   _____

2. General environmental living context (symbols, material and nonmaterial signs). Specify: _
   _____

3. Wearing apparel and physical appearance. Notations: _____
   _____

4. Technology being used in living environment. Notations: _____
   _____

5. Worldview (how person looks out upon the world). Notations: _____
   _____
   _____

continued

6. Family lifeways (values, beliefs and norms). Notations: _____

7. General social interactions and kinship ties. Notations: _____

8. Patterned daily activities. Notations: _____
    _____

9. Religious and spiritual beliefs and values. Notations: _____

10. Economic factors (rough cost of living estimates and income). Notations: _____
    _____

11. Educational values or belief factors. Notations: _____
    _____

12. Political or legal influencers. Notations: _____
    _____

13. Food uses and nutritional values, beliefs, and taboos. Specify: _____
    _____

14. Folk (generic, lay or indigenous) health care-cure values, beliefs and practices. Specify: _
    _____

15. Professional health care-cure values, beliefs and practices. Specify: _____
    _____

16. Care concepts or patterns that guide actions, i.e., concern for, support, presence, etc.: __
    _____

17. Caring patterns and expressions: _____
    _____

18. Informants ways to:
    a) prevent illnesses: _____
    b) preserve or maintain wellness or health: _____
    c) care for self or others: _____
    _____
    _____

19. Other indicators to support more traditional or non-traditional lifeways including
    ethnohistorical and other factors. _____
    _____
    _____

Part II: Acculturation Profile from Assessment Factors

Directions: Plot an X with the value numbers placed on this profile to discover the orientation or acculturation lifeways of the informant. The clustering of numbers will give information of traditional or non-traditional patterns with respect to the criteria assessed.

Criteria:	Mainly Traditional 1	Moderate 2	Average 3	Moderate 4	Mainly Non-Traditional 5
1. Language and communication modes					
2. Physical-social environment (and ecology)					
3. Physical apparel appearance					
4. Technologic factors					
5. Worldview					
6. Family lifeways					
7. Social ties/kinship					
8. Daily/nightly lifeways					
9. Religious/spiritual orientation					
10. Economic factors					
11. Educational factors					
12. Political and legal factors					
13. Food uses/abuses					
14. Folk (generic) care-cure					
15. Professional care-cure expressions					
16. Caring patterns					
17. Curing patterns					
18. Prevention/maintenance factors					
19. Other indicators, i.e. ethnohistorical					

Note: The assessor may total numbers to get a summary orientation profile. Use of these ratings with written notations provide a holistic qualitative profile. Detailed notations are important to substantiate the ratings in these areas.

* **Note:** This guide has been developed, refined, and used for three decades (since early 1960s) by Dr. Madeleine Leininger. It has been frequently in demand by anthropologists, transcultural nurses and others. It has been useful to obtain an informant's orientation to traditional or non-traditional lifeways. It provides qualitative indicators to meet credibility, confirmability, recurrency and reliability criteria for qualitative studies. This copyright guide may be used if the *full title* of the guide, recognition of *source* (M. Leininger), and *publication outlet* (*Journal of Transcultural Nursing*) are cited.[22] The author would also appreciate a letter to know who has used the guide, the focus and summary outcomes. Permission originally granted from Leininger, M., "Leininger's Acculturation Health Care Assessment Tool for Cultural Patterns in Traditional and Non-Traditional Lifeways, *Journal of Transcultural Nursing*, v. 2, no. 2, Winter, 1991, pp. 40–42.

An Alternative Short Assessment Guide

Another alternative assessment guide which has been used with undergraduate and graduate students since 1985 and with nursing staff in short term, emergency, and acute care centers has been a *Short Culturalogical Assessment Guide* (Figure 4.4). This guide provides a brief and general assessment of the client, but does not usually provide in-depth holistic features as found with the Sunrise Model. This guide, however, has been very helpful to nurses functioning in an acute care or emergency setting where time and space constraints are very limiting. The assessment data offers information to develop a nursing care plan or to make decisions about a client from a particular culture. The author often refers to this assessment guide as Model B to contrast it with the Sunrise model as A. The nurse begins with Phase I and proceeds to Phase V to get an overall assessment of the client.

Figure 4.4
Leininger's Short Culturalogic Assessment Guide (Model B)

Phase V   Develop a culturally-based client-nurse care plan as a co-participant for decisions and actions for culturally congruent care.
⇧

Phase IV   Sythesize themes and patterns of care derived from the information obtained in phases I, II and III.
⇧

Phase III   Identify and document recurrent client patterns and narratives (stories) with client meanings of what has been seen, heard or experienced.
⇧

Phase II   Listen to and learn from the client about cultural values, beliefs, and daily (nightly) practices related to care and health in the client's environmental context. Give attention to generic (home or folk) practices and professional nursing practices.
⇧

Phase I   Record observations of what you see, hear or experience with clients (includes dress and appearance, body condition features, language, mannerisms and general behavior, attitudes, and cultural features).
⇧

Start Here

Note: Nurses indicate at the outset whether assessing an individual, small group, family or culture.

Summary

In this chapter the reader has been presented with several principles, guidelines, models, and strategies to do a culturalogical assessment. The purpose of this assessment is to obtain information in order to guide the nurse to provide culturally congruent care or care that fits reasonably with the client's values, beliefs, and lifeways. Such assessments are essential to assure quality care and to promote the health and well-being of the individual family or group. The Sunrise Model (A), derived the theory of Cultural Care and an Alternate Short Culturalogical Assessment Guide (B) were offered to assess the client. In addition, an Acculturation Enabler was presented to assess indicators of the client or family being more traditionally or non-traditionally oriented. Nurses with transcultural nursing preparation will find these forms most useful, but other health disciplines find them helpful in making assessments. The information obtained can be used in client care and also for educational and research purposes. Nurses using this information can greatly increase their ways of knowing clients and new kinds of information to be used in client care. Culturalogical skills can become one of the nurse's most rewarding experiences in nursing because they generally provide new insights about people and help one to see a broader yet very specific and practical way to help people. Most importantly, the nurse learns much about herself (himself) and diverse cultures and greatly expands her (his) worldview of people when doing culturalogical assessments.

References

1. Leininger, M., "Culturalogical Assessment Domains for Nursing Practice," *Transcultural Nursing Concepts, Theories, and Practices*, M. Leininger, ed., New York: John Wiley and Sons, 1978a, pp. 85–106.

2. Leininger, M., *Nursing and Anthropology: Two Worlds to Blend*, New York: John Wiley and Sons, 1970.

3. Dobson, S., *Transcultural Nursing*, London: Scutari Press, 1991, pp. 116–124.

4. Orque, M., B. Black and L. Monroy, *Ethnic Nursing Care*, St. Louis: The C.V. Mosby Co., 1983, pp. 55–74.

5. Leininger, M., *Culture Care Diversity and Universality: A Theory of Nursing*, New York: National League for Nursing Press, 1991a, pp. 1–64, 98–104.

6. Tripp-Reimer, T., "Expanding Four Essential Concepts in Nursing Theory: The Contribution of Anthropology," *Current Issues in Nursing*, J. McCloskey and H. Grace, eds., Boston: Blackwell, 1985, pp. 91–103.

7. Kim, M., G. McFarland and A. McLane, *Pocket Guide to Nursing Diagnosis*, 2nd ed., St. Louis: The C.V. Mosby Co., 1987.

8. McFarland, G. and E. McFarlane, *Nursing Diagnosis and Intervention: Planning for Patient Care*, St. Louis: The C.V. Mosby Co., 1989.

9. Leininger, M., "Issues, Questions, and Concerns Related to the Nursing Diagnosis Cultural Movement from a Transcultural Nursing Perspective," *Journal of Transcultural Nursing*, Memphis: University of Tennessee, v. 2, no. 1, Summer, 1990a, pp. 23–32.

10. Ibid.

11. Leininger, op. cit., 1978, pp. 87–97.

12. Spector, R., *Cultural Diversity in Health and Illness*, 3rd ed., Norwalk, Connecticut: Appleton & Lange, 1991, pp. 122–149.

13. Leininger, M., *Transcultural Nursing: Concepts, Theories, and Practices*, New York: John Wiley and Sons, 1978b, pp. 100–102, 199, 455.

14. Van Gennep, A., *The Rites of Passage*, London: Routledge & Kegan Paul, 1960.

15. Wolf, Z. R., *Nurse's Work: The Sacred and Profane*, Philadelphia: University of Pennsylvania Press, 1990.

16. Spector, op. cit.

17. Leininger, M., "Selected Culture Care Findings of Diverse Cultures Using Culture Care Theory and Ethnomethods," *Culture Care Diversity and Universality: A Theory of Nursing*, New York: National League for Nursing Press, 1991b, pp. 355–375.

18. Leininger, M., *Care: Discovery and Uses in Clinical Community Nursing*, Detroit: Wayne State University Press, 1988.

19. Leininger, M., "The Phenomenon of Caring: The Essence and Central Focus of Nursing," *Nursing Research Report*, American Nurse's Foundation, v. 12, no. 1, 1977, pp. 2–14.

20. Chrisman, N., "Cultural Shock in the Operating Room: Cultural Analysis in Transcultural Nursing," *Journal of Transcultural Nursing*, Memphis: University of Tennessee, v. 1, no. 2, Winter, 1990b, pp. 33–39.

21. Leininger, op. cit., 1991a, p. 82.

22. Leininger, M., "Leininger's Acculturation Health Care Assessment Tool for Cultural Patterns in Traditional and Non-Traditional Lifeways, *Journal of Transcultural Nursing*, v. 2, no. 2, Winter, 1991, pp. 40–42.

Appendix A

Leininger's Suggested Inquiry Guide for Use with the Sunrise Model to Assess Culture Care and Health

Instructions: The purpose of this ethnonursing guide is to enter the world of the client and discover information to provide holistic, culture-specific care. Use broad and open inquiry modes rather than direct confrontational questions. Move with the client (or informant) to make the inquiry natural and familiar. These inquiry areas are examples for the inquiry and not exhaustive. Identify at the outset if assessing an individual, family, group, institution or community. (This inquiry guide focuses on the individual). Identify yourself and the purpose of the inquiry to the client, i.e., to learn from the client about his/her lifeway to provide nursing care that will be helpful or meaningful.

Domains of Inquiry: Suggested Inquiry Modes

1. Worldview

I would like to know how you see the world around you. Could you share with me your views of how you see things are for you?

2. Ethnohistory

In nursing we can benefit from learning about the client's cultural heritage, e.g., Korean, Philippine, etc. Could you tell me something about your cultural background? Where were you born and where have you been living in the recent past? Tell me about your parents and their origins. Have you and your parents lived in different geographic or environmental places? If so, tell me about your relocations and any special life events or experiences you recall that could be helpful to understand you and your needs. What languages do you speak? How would you like to be referred to by friends or strangers?

3. Kinship and Social Factors

I would like to hear about your family and/or close social friends and what they mean to you. How have your kin (relatives) or social friends influenced your life and especially your caring or healthy lifeways? Who are the caring or non-caring persons in your life? How has your family (or group) helped you to stay well or become ill? Do you view your family as a caring family? If not, what would make them more caring? Are there key family responsibilities to care for you or others when ill or well? (Explain.) In what ways would you like family members (or social friends) to care for you? How would you like nurses to care for you?

4. Cultural Values, Beliefs and Lifeways

In providing nursing care, your cultural values, beliefs, and lifeways are important for nurses to understand. Could you share with me what values and beliefs you would like nurses to know to help you regain or maintain your health? What specific beliefs or practices do you find most important for others to know to care for you? Give me some examples of "good caring" ways based on your care values and beliefs.

5. Religious/Spiritual/ Philosophical Factors

When people become ill or anticipate problems, they often pray or use their religion or spiritual beliefs. In nursing we like to learn about how your religion has helped you in the past and can help you today. How do you think your beliefs and practices have helped you to care for yourself or others in keeping well or to regain health? How does religion help you heal or to face crisis, disabilities or even death? In what ways can religious healers and nurses care for you, your family or friends? What spiritual factors do we need to incorporate into your care?

6. Technological Factors

In your daily life are you greatly dependent upon "high-tech" modern appliances or equipment? What about in the hospital to examine or care for you? (Explain.) In what ways do you think technological factors help or hinder keeping you well? Do you consider yourself dependent upon modern technologies to remain healthy or get access to care? (Give some examples.)

7. Economic Factors

Today, one often hears "money means health or survival." What do you think of that statement? In what ways do you believe money influences your health and access to care or to obtain professional services? Do you find money is necessary to keep you well? If not, explain. How do you see the cost of hospital care versus home care cost practices? Optional: who are the wage earners in your family? Do they earn enough to keep you well or help you if sick?

8. Political and Legal Factors

Our world seems full of ideas about politics and political actions that can influence your health. What are some of your views about politics and how you and others maintain your well-being? In your community or home what political or legal problems tend to influence your well-being or handicap your lifeways in being cared for by yourself or others? (Explain.)

9. Educational Factors	I would like to hear in what ways you believe education contributes to your staying well or becoming ill. What educational information, values or practices do you believe are important for nurses or others to care for you? Give examples. How has your education influenced you to stay well or become ill? How far did you go with formal education? Do you value education and health instruction? (Explain.)
10. Language and Communication	Communicating with and understanding clients is important to meet care needs. How would you like to communicate your needs to nurses? What language(s) do you speak or understand? What barriers in language or communication influence receiving care or help from others. What verbal or nonverbal problems have you seen or experienced that influences caring patterns between you and the nursing staff? In what ways would you like people to communicate with you and why? Have you experienced any prejudice or racial problems through communication that nurses need to understand? What else would you like to tell me that would lead to good or effective communication practices with you?
11. Professional and Generic (folk or lay) Care beliefs and Practices	What professional nursing care practices or attitudes do you believe have been or would be most helpful to your well-being within the hospital or at home? What home remedies, care practices or treatments do you value or expect from a cultural viewpoint? I would like to learn about your home healers or special healers in your community and how they help you. What does health, illness or wellness mean to you and your family or culture? What professional and/or folk practices make sense to you or are most helpful? Could you give some examples of healing or caring practices that come from you cultural group? What folk or professional practices and food preferences have contributed to your wellness? What foods are taboo or prohibited in your life or in your culture? In what ways have your past or current experiences in the hospital influenced your recovery or health? What other ideas should I know about what makes you well through good caring practices?
12. General and Specific Nursing Care	In what ways would you like to be cared for in the hospital or home by nurses? What is the meaning of care to you or your culture? What do you see as the link between good nursing care and regaining or maintaining your health? Tell me about some of the barriers or facilitators to good nursing care? What values, beliefs or practices influence the ways you want nursing care? What stresses in the

hospital or home need to be considered in your recovery or in staying well? What else would you like to tell me about ways to care for you? What community resources have helped you get well and stay well? Give some examples of non-helpful care nursing practices? What environmental or home community factors should nurses be especially aware of to give care to you and your family? What cultural illnesses tend to occur in your culture? How do you manage pain and stress? (Clarify.) What else would you like to tell me so that you can receive what you believe is good nursing care? Give specific and general examples.

Chapter 5

Transcultural Nurse Specialists and Generalists: New Practitioners in Nursing*

Madeleine Leininger, PhD, LHD, FAAN, CTN, RN

A significant new direction in nursing occurred nearly three decades ago when the field of transcultural nursing was established as an essential and legitimate area of study and practice.[1,2] It has been a major breakthrough in the field of nursing by advancing nursing knowledge and establishing a new way to practice nursing. The development and use of transcultural knowledge as a basis to provide care to peoples of different cultural values, beliefs and lifeways has been a major challenge to nurses who have practiced nursing with a dominant unicultural perspective. Transcultural nursing has become a new field of knowledge and practice with new kinds of generalists and specialists. It is a field of great relevance as nurses learn how to function in a multicultural world in which people want and expect their cultural values and lifeways to be respected and understood. This new field in nursing reflects the use of a body of transcultural knowledge to guide nursing decisions and actions so that clients from different cultures receive congruent care that takes into account slight or marked differences in their cultural lifeways.

The purpose of this article is to present the nature, characteristics, educational preparation and practice role of the transcultural nurse specialist and generalist with focus on the actual and evolving role of these new practitioners in nursing in a rapidly growing pluralistic world. It is intended to help nurses become knowledgeable about the existence of transcultural nurse specialists and generalists in nursing and to understand why these nurses are needed not only in clinical practice, but also in education, research and as competent consultants handling complex and sensitive intercultural policies. The article supports the author's position that transcultural nursing has not only become a refreshing and major new breakthrough in nursing, but that the field will continue to grow as a specialized area of education and practice the knowledge and skills of which will be used in all areas of nursing by the year 2010. Moreover, transcultural nursing insights, theoretical perspectives, and research findings will continue to revolutionize nursing education and nursing practices in significant ways. [3,4,5]

Transcultural Nursing: Focus and Rationale

Since there may be nurses who are unfamiliar with the concept and field of transcultural nursing, the founder's definition of transcultural nursing is in order at the outset. Transcultural nursing refers to a formal area of study and practice of diverse cultures in the world with respect to their care, health and illness values, beliefs and practices in order to provide culture specific or universal nursing care that is congruent with the client, family or community's cultural values and lifeways.[6] As one notes from this definition, transcultural nursing is a major area of study and practice which requires in-depth study of different cultures in any local, national or international setting, so that the nurse can be knowledgeable about the client's cultural background in order to provide culture-specific care or some universal (common human) care needs.[7]

The idea of transcultural nursing as an essential, formal, and legitimate area of study and practice in nursing was recognized as a critical need by the author in the mid 1950s. At that time it was clear that the important dimension of culture was blatantly missing in nursing education and practice. Instead, clients were receiving from nurses mainly physical and some emotional care for many medical or biophysical conditions. It also became clear to the author that clients came to hospitals from diverse cultures with different health needs and needed to be understood and helped in accord with their cultural values, needs and expectations. As the founder and leader of the field, the author envisioned that the nurses needed to be prepared to function in a multicultural world that was becoming more complex each day. The author predicted that cultural conflicts in health care would be a major problem, especially in providing quality nursing car to clients, by the end of this century unless nurses were prepared in transcultural nursing. This prediction made in 1960 has become a reality.[8] Transcultural nursing knowledge and skills have now become essential to all areas of nursing, and also as a specialized field of practice.[9]

The central goal of transcultural nursing is to provide knowledgeable, sensitive and skilled nursing care to people of diverse cultures. The field has no geographic boundary but includes the study and practice of transcultural nursing worldwide. And although the birthplace of transcultural nursing was the United States, the field has become relevant and essential to nurses in all countries and it will be even more relevant in the next century.

Transcultural nursing is based on the premise that all humans are cultural being who are born and live within a cultural frame of reference, and that cultural factors greatly influence a person's state of well-being, health or illness. The field was established on the basis that cultures (or subcultures) are complex and diverse and requires that nurses study the total lifeways of a cultural group and develop transcultural nursing knowledge and related skills from the people's perspective. Moreover, one could not "integrate knowledge" unless there was first an established body of knowledge to integrate. Hence, knowledge development through research was essential, as was establishing formal programs of study under faculty who were knowledgeable and skilled in transcultural nursing. As the founder of the field and the first graduate nurse with doctoral preparation in anthropology, I was fully aware that knowledge from the disciplines of anthropology, comparative sciences and the humanities would be essential to develop a body of transcultural nursing knowledge. Building such knowledge and skills to care for people of different cultures was a major challenge and goal. It required in-depth systematic study of many cultures in order to help nurses become aware of and knowledgeable about transcultural caring in different cultures. Superficial knowledge or "bits and pieces" of ideas about culture could have serious consequences. Understanding different cultures, their values and patterns of care, health and illness was essential for hospital and community nurses. The author also discovered that culture care values were largely vague, elusive and embedded in a social structure which was difficult for most nurses to discover. Transcultural nursing had to become an area of formal study and a major focus of nursing if nursing was to serve multicultural groups and function effectively in a transitional world. Moreover, as in any discipline, transcultural nurse generalists and specialists would be essential in advancing knowledge and skills in the new domain of nursing. This was a major challenge for the future.

Developing Transcultural Nurse Specialists and Generalists

Since the rationale for developing the field of transcultural nursing with specialists and generalists became apparent to the founder by the mid 1960s, it was evident that nurses had no body of transcultural knowledge to guide their thinking and decisions to provide care to clients of different cultures. Cultural ignorance prevailed and nurses functioned with their own largely unicultural personal and professional knowledge. How culture influenced the individual's family's or cultural group's well-being was unkown and unrecognized in the early 1950s.[10,11,12] That nurses ought to morally or ethically attend to and provide care that fit the client's values and lifeways was, indeed, a strange idea then. Moreover, it was difficult to imagine that cultural differences could play a significant role in the client's recovery or maintenance of health. A more serious problem was that most faculty in schools of nursing had no formal preparation about cultures or interest in culture in nursing curricula. Nursing curricula in the 1950s were heavily weighted in biophysical medical content, in technical skills, tasks and practices, and were devoid of cultural perspectives.[13,14,15] Virtually no faculty saw the critical and long-standing need to incorporate cultural values, beliefs and lifeways (or folk healing) practices into the nursing curricula. Nursing needed to change its narrow Western and local views to a broader multicultural view. But how could this be done in a profession with virtually no faculty interested in or knowledgeable about cultures? The relationship of culture to nursing and of nursing to anthropology needed to be discovered.[16]

To develop the new field, a cadre of nurse leaders and followers had to be developed. Most importantly, transcultural nursing knowledge had to be developed by nurses prepared in anthropology and nursing in order to derive a sound knowledge base relevant to nursing practice. Transcultural nurse specialists and generalists were needed to develop knowledge, disseminate and build the new field. Interesting a new generation of students in learning about transcultural nursing and seeing the need for the future, was, indeed, a major challenge. Moreover, nursing faculty had to become aware of their biases and prejudices about different cultures in order to learn about and work with students of diverse cultures. Money and faculty were desperately needed but were not available. Such considerations and others challenged the author to develop the field despite many hurdles and limited professional awareness and support.[17,18]

Because of the undeveloped field, transcultural nurse specialists and generalists had to prepared in institutions of higher education with a research focus. Transcultural nurses needed basic anthropologic knowledge as well as specialized clinical knowledge to evolve soundly this area of nursing. Graduate education with a strong theory and research focus was essential for broad and in-depth knowledge of cultures. Nurses had to develop transcultural nursing concepts, principles and theories relevant to caring for clients of diverse cultures. Students had to learn about culturally-based care of clients in hospitals, clinics, homes and special institutions and societies.

From the outset, the author realized that transcultural nurses would be different from nurses prepared in medical-surgical, maternal-child, psychiatry or other areas of nursing because the knowledge base was very different as well as practice focused. This was strange for most faculty to perceive because of their strong medical model and traditional views.

From an anthropological perspective, cultures were many and had great variability. This point became clear to the author in the 1952 while attempting to develop the role of the first clinical specialist in child psychiatric nursing.[19,20] With no cultural knowledge to guide my actions or to interpret the children's cultural behavior, I experienced transcultural shock. This stimulated me to study in the field of anthropology. With such knowledge, I gradually became aware of many critical care conflicts between the nurse client, and other health providers due to cultural ignorance and gross ethnocentrism among health care personnel.[21] In order to deal with these clinical problems, nurses had to be educated at the graduate level. This was essential as cultural care problems were complex and needed rigorous study. The new knowledge base of transcultural nursing became essential to preparing transcultural nurse specialists and generalists and to providing knowledge to be integrated into other areas of nursing. Hence, graduate education was the first step and a wise decision to develop the field of transcultural nursing and its experts. There were, however, other reasons why transcultural nurse generalists and specialists are needed not only not, but also in the future in the United States and worldwide.

Reasons for Transcultural Nursing

Today, the world of nursing has become clearly multicultural. Nurses and others are aware of cultural variabilities as they travel to many places within or outside their country. Nursing's view is shifting from an isolated and unicultural viewpoint to a multicultural one. Our societies have rapidly and noticeably changed the past two decades due to modern technology, communication and transportation modes. Living in most local communities and countries are people from many different cultures. Likewise, out health facilities have clients from virtually every place in the world. Unfortunately, many health personnel have not moved with these realities to communicate and work effectively with clients from many different cultures. There has been a major cultural knowledge deficit with health personnel which prevents them from working well with clients and to understand cultural differences among clients. Still today, many nurses and physicians seldom consider the cultural background of their clients, let alone that cultural factors could lead to illness, disabilities or death.

But with new modes of transportation, communication and technology, nurses are being rapidly brought into a multicultural world reality and must appropriately respond to cultural factors of clients. Many nurses today experience transcultural shock making them feel stunned, disoriented and unable to help cultural strangers. Of course, some nurses proceed as if cultural differences do not exist and they impose whatever they have to offer clients from their personal viewpoints and without sensitivity to cultural differences.[22,23] As a consequence, serious problems often arise with the clients feeling frustrated, demeaned and sometimes insulted by gross cultural imposition practices. Some critical questions are: How can a nurse be considered professionally competent and knowledgeable without effectively dealing with clients' cultural needs and expectations? How can quality of nursing care be assured when multicultural factors are noticeably over looked by staff? What are the ethical and moral consequences of nurses who are not aware of or knowledgeable about culture care? What consciousness raising steps need to be made to help nurses become aware of transcultural nursing concepts and practices? These questions have been some of the major reasons to establish formal transcultural nursing programs.[24,25,26]

Prior to preparing nurses in the field of transcultural nursing, it was interesting to hear some nurses talk about trying to understand and help clients from different cultures. There were many stories, myths and some cultural biases about people they "heard about" or "those strangers they never did understand." One male nurse said, "It was a shocking experience for me to care for an Arab woman with a black scarf on her head, and one who refused to accept care from me." Another nurse said, "Why don't those Mexican fathers want to bond with the infant they - they need a lot of teaching." Another nurse said, "I never did understand that foreigner from the South - they talk and act differently...Why can't they be like us Yankees?" Still other nurses said, "Those foreigners are uncooperative and resistant. I do not like to care for them." These candid comments reflected distrust and a lack of cultural understanding. Problems of noncompliance, frustration and anger toward the culturally different prevailed. Nurses often labeled, avoided or talked down to the cultural strangers when they did not understand their behavior and needs. Transcultural nurse generalists and specialists were needed to help with these clinical problems and conflicts.[27,28]

Another major reason for developing transcultural nurse specialists and generalists was because of the growing problem of cultural imposition and ethnocentrism between nurses and clients and with other health personnel. Cultural imposition was evident in many ways as nurses inadvertently or intentionally imposed their values, beliefs and lifeways onto the client, family or community groups.[29,30] This serious problem denied the client's cultural and ethical rights, and often made the client feel helpless, angry, frustrated and sometimes ready to leave the hospital. Cultural imposition is related to ethnocentrism, in which a person holds that one's own values, beliefs and practices are superior to or more desired than another person's. Cultural imposition and ethnocentrism have ethical and moral implications for nurses, which can seriously limit the nurse's effectiveness with the client's recovery or healing processes.

Still another major reason for the new field was that many nurses were working in different places in the world and with many different cultures. Unfortunately, most of them had no substantive educational preparation about cultures or in transcultural nursing. A few nurses often got a brief "orientation" a few days before they left the country, or at most a week before, with nurses who had likewise been inadequately prepared to work in a strange culture. Past experiences and tales from other nurses proved less helpful to nurses if they had any different cultural and role experiences. Thus, transcultural shock, cultural anxieties and many other problems were evident with overseas nurses and limited the nurse's effectiveness and success in the new culture.[31,32]

Since the 1950s, the author had received many calls and letters form nurses in foreign countries wanting help to understand "foreigners." They were frustrated by "trying to change foreigners to be like Americans." Many of these nurses became strong supporters of transcultural nursing education to reduce cultural clashes and misunderstandings as nurses work with people of different cultures. Several nurses have said, "We all need to be transcultural nurses and even more so in the future, so hurry and prepare us." These overseas nurses have seen problems with physicians and other staff from unknown countries whom they have had to work with under life-or-death situations. Many intercultural communication problems, ethical dilemmas and interprofessional conflicts have been identified as nurses work with cultural strangers overseas or in this country. Unquestionably, transcultural nurse specialists were needed to deal with many of these tough and complex intercultural problems, and especially as they affected clients' well-being or health. Specialists were also needed to ease conflicts and tensions among nurses, physicians and clients of different cultures, and especially when clients refused to comply with health professionals' expectations.

Another reason for the field was that many nurses did not realize that there are actually no universal standards for nursing practices due to marked cultural diversity among the clients they serve; and yet, nurses tend to function as if there were universals. This is related to cultural ignorance and the faulty assumption that all people are alike. This "all alike syndrome" limited nurses' ability to accommodate clients' diverse expressions and needs. It made it extremely difficult to make accurate judgments and take actions when cultural variabilities were not recognized, assessed and accommodated in client practices. Granted, some nurses had uncanny ways to detect cultural problems that were largely learned by "trial and error" past experiences. The author has predicted that by the next decade clients will be more demanding of nurses to know and understand these problems in order to meet their cultural needs. No longer will clients be willing to hide their identities or concerns from health personnel in the future. Accordingly, one can expect that clients will legally demand that their cultural rights be respected by health personnel. For these reasons, transcultural specialists and generalists are a critical need now and in the future of nursing education and practice.

Last, but no least, another major reason to develop transcultural nurse specialists and generalists was related to the growing need for expert cultural consultants in this country and overseas to deal with interstaff and nurse-client culturally-based problems. Transcultural nurse specialists are being requested more and more to deal with the "strange behavior" of clients from different cultures in hospitals and clinics, and where "cults of efficiency and high productivity" failed to understand clients. This latter has been especially evident with rapid ways to move clients in and out of health institutions. When patients, especially "foreigners," do not comply, this leads health personnel to become frustrated. Nurses become distraught, angry and impatient with these clients and those who talk and act differently. Helping nurses to discover why clients from different cultures are uncooperative and non-compliant has been a major task for transcultural nurse specialists. Transcultural nurse specialists are prepared to help staff understand such behavior, facilitate cooperation and improve relationships among health personnel by using specific cultural knowledge and skills. It has also been most rewarding to see clients and families relax when their cultural values, beliefs and lifeways have been given consideration. Assisting staff and clients of different cultures in hospitals and other health settings has been a critical need for this new specialist.

In general, the demands for a new kind of practitioner in nursing have been clearly apparent and a reason to prepare transcultural nurse specialists and generalists. The author's visits during recent years to many countries such as Saudi Arabia, Australia, New Zealand, Europe, South America, Africa and Fiji attest to the critical, worldwide, need and importance of transcultural nurses for education, research and practice. Many nurses in these countries are requesting transcultural generalists and specialists to help them with education and services. Several nurses told the author, "Transcultural nursing truly makes sense today as we have so many client migrants and nurses from many different cultures that we never had even one decade ago." A nurse form Australia said, "We really recognize our educational programs are not quite adequate to meet today's nursing world of transnationalism." These nurse and others are recognizing that past education has not prepared nurses to function with cultural strangers of foreign lands, except to be "nice and friendly to them." They also recognize that most nursing curricula still have virtually no content to understand people who have different beliefs and lifeways, and that nursing education must drastically change in many areas to meet multiculturalism.

Nurses need to realize that a lecture or a one-day workshop is most inadequate for nurses to learn about complex cultures and hoe best to work with intercultural care issues. Today, are concerned about nurses who proclaim they are international nurse consultants but have not been prepared in transcultural nursing. Trying to be an "expert" in a foreign country for which one has meager or no knowledge of the cultural history, values and life forces influencing a culture's health services and education is highly problematic. Unquestionably, inadequately prepared consultants can often lead to more problems for a host country. Nursing consultants need to be prepared today to analyze, know and understand the specific cultures they are purporting to help. Host leaders are fully aware of this need and of the need for transcultural nurse consultants who fully know the host country before introducing new models, ideas or changes. In the future, there will be transcultural nurse specialists in cultural areas who will be sought to serve as consultants. New policies and guidelines for transcultural consultants are being developed to help to reduce transcultural shock, cultural imposition practices and cultural conflict problems as nurses function as nurse consultants.[33] These current realities and past long-standing problems give further support and justification for preparing transcultural nurse generalists and specialists as expert consultants in one's own country and overseas in order to reduce cultural ignorance of nurses to prevent unnecessary nursing problems or conflicts.

Preparation of Transcultural Nurses

With the above reasons, state of affairs and critical issues, the preparation of transcultural nurse specialists and generalists became obvious to the author, and steps were taken to meet this growing worldwide critical need. The preparation of these new practitioners in nursing has been a major undertaking because of limited human and financial resources. A few nurses who were eager to help in the 1960s began to realize they would be functioning in a different way than nurses prepared in previous generations. These nurses were eager to study transcultural nursing and to be "traveling transcultural nurses," living and working in several countries in their career. This generation of nurses saw many new opportunities before them worldwide, and they wanted to be prepared for such career goals. These nurses became another major impetus to initiate graduate programs in transcultural nursing like other clinical specialist programs. Nursing was truly at the crossroads to prepare a new generation of nurses to serve people of diverse cultures with special preparation in transcultural nursing. Many students realized they could no longer ignore this reality or assume they could get by with largely unicultural education practices in a growing multicultural world. Thus, transcultural nurse specialist and generalist programs were initiated in the mid 1960s with different educational expectations and roles than those found in the past history of nursing.

Preparation of Transcultural Nurse Specialists

In the field of transcultural nursing, it was important to develop transcultural nurse specialists through master and doctoral programs in nursing. It was also important to focus first on specialist preparation rather than generalist preparation. Special transcultural nursing knowledge that reflected the explicit purposes and goals of the program had to be developed. Since there were a few graduate specialist programs in mental health in the 1960s, the author drew upon this evolving philosophical perspective. Specialization in graduate programs was wisely supported by many nurse leaders. Interestingly, theory and research had more limited emphasis than clinical skill development. The author stressed, however, the importance of research and theory through graduate study to identify and develop a body of transcultural nursing knowledge.

Sources of derived transcultural nursing knowledge were selectively considered from anthropology and other social sciences, and the humanities bearing upon transcultural nursing knowledge. Gradually, derived knowledge domains were systematically examined, transformed or reconstructed to fit evolving specialist or generalist knowledge in transcultural nursing. This was a most exciting and stimulating approach for faculty and students, as it encouraged them to develop knowledge anew without the constraints of previously held nursing ideologies, medical science content and past practices. As a consequence, the field of transcultural nursing began with an explicit focus on theory and research to develop a sound knowledge base and to guide nursing practices. This was significantly different approach than found with other clinical expert programs.

The first transcultural nursing student, Beverly Horn, was prepared through a specialized Ph.D. (individualized) program (1972-74) under the author's mentorship while at the University of Washington with the above focuses to examine content potentially relevant to the field of transcultural nursing. A number of other students were later prepared as specialists through a master and doctoral transcultural nursing programs which the author spearheaded and developed at four other universities from 1972 to the present. The faculty worked conscientiously to derive from anthropology, but with thought to current nursing care knowledge for this new specialist in nursing. Creating specialized transcultural nursing content and the projected role of the nurse had exciting, but also some uncertain and speculative dimensions. Transcultural nursing faculty held that specialists had to be highly knowledgeable and demonstrate skills in handling complex culture care situations. Moreover, the specialists had to be good researchers, theorists, teachers, consultants and expert clinicians. This was a tremendous challenge, but essential, as there would be a critical shortage of transcultural nursing specialists for several decades and they would have to serve in multiple roles. Transcultural nursing specialists would be new practitioners in nursing, with a different base of knowledge and ways to practice nursing. Much of the comparative transcultural content was outside the mainstream perspectives of nursing and somewhat strange to its parent-derived discipline of anthropology. Nonetheless, with tenacity and persistence in studying and communicating the project goals and purposes of the new field, a small cadre of transcultural nurse specialists was prepared in graduate programs by the mid 1970s. At times, it seemed to be a single-handed effort of the founder because there were so few nurses who could envision this new area of study and practice, and who were willing to risk and support a new area of commitment. The laborers were indeed few in number. Moreover, there were no national nursing organization interested or willing to support the ideas or filed. It was difficult to launch the new field, but with tenacity of purpose transcultural nurses became a reality and were prepared as essential and legitimate practitioners, and nursing organizations are now valuing the importance of transcultural nursing.

In considering further the educational preparation of transcultural nurse specialists, it was imperative that the specialist have in-depth knowledge and culture-specific skills to help clients. Transcultural specialists focused on human care, health (well-being) and environmental context as the major domains of nursing to generate transcultural nursing knowledge.[35,36,37,38,39] It was encouraging to see students' interests grow as they took undergraduate and graduate courses in anthropology, the humanities and other comparative fields in developing transcultural nursing knowledge. There were many potential concepts and theories that seemed to be so fertile and rich to develop transcultural nursing content. Graduate faculty and students could not be wholesale borrowers of ideas and research findings from anthropology, but were challenged to transform and reconceptualize ideas into transcultural nursing knowledge. At the same time, students studied different nursing and non-nursing theorists' views as they developed their own theoretical perspectives about transcultural nursing. These theoretical and philosophical views led students to their research interest and to examine systematically theories by the use of mainly qualitative research methods. Qualitative methods were appropriate due to the nature of the undiscovered phenomena such as culture care and health with a theoretical perspective.[41]

Students in the transcultural nursing specialists program focused on knowledge developed by systematically collecting, documenting, and analyzing largely unknown phenomena. Qualitative methods were mainly used because of the need to discover previously unknown knowledge in the field. Unfortunately, qualitative methods are still limitedly known, valued or understood in nursing, except by a few nurse anthropologists and sociologists.[42] Rigorous field studies have been a major focus of specific cultural areas using transcultural nursing theories and qualitative methods to study transcultural nursing phenomena. Ethnography, ethnonursing, and ethnoscience methods have been invaluable methods to explicate transcultural nursing phenomena. Graduate students learn how to use these and other research methods while doing field studies. Students are expected to study at least two cultures in-depth with focus on the comparative aspects of care, health and environmental context - the major distinctive concepts of nursing. Using research findings in nursing contexts as generalists or specialists, or as a consultant and teacher of transcultural nursing are also emphasized.

Students in the master and doctoral programs learn how to do culturological care and health assessments of clients with traditional and non-traditional lifeways. They discover ways to develop culture-specific care and differential transcultural policies for people of diverse cultures. Learning how to be an effective consultant and teacher in local and foreign cultures is emphasized as the transcultural nurse practitioner works in diverse community contexts. Studying culture care variabilities and identifying similarities and differences between or within different cultures are major learning experiences to prepare a competent transcultural specialist for worldwide practices.

One of the richest learning experiences for transcultural nurse specialists has been the study of specific phenomena with a comparative focus using emic and etic modes of data collection and analysis. Discovering the informant's inside worldview and lifeways (the emic perspective) provides insights to help students see comparative views and new knowledge about human beings. It requires time to discover such insights and to redirect the learner's past, traditional tendencies of focusing mainly on professional (etic) views, biases and ethnocentrism in nursing. Reexamining past tendencies of nurses with their etic professional views tends to limit the nurse knowing the client's emic views. Nursing students who have been wed to study medical symptoms, diseases and treatments rather than discovering human care and health often require considerable time to refocus on nursing phenomena. Skilled faculty mentoring has been necessary to redirect graduate students' thinking to a transcultural, comparative viewpoint and to get into the world of the people or clients under study. Direct field guidance and graduate seminars on cultural nursing care phenomena have been essential in developing transcultural nurse specialists who are much different practitioners than students prepared in the traditional clinical fields of nursing.

Teaching, direct practice and consultation experiences are integrated into the students' clinical and community-based experiences. Again, these experiences are usually new kinds of experiences as students use transcultural care knowledge. Students also learn how to change traditional nursing practices into transcultural ones as they use research findings, concepts and principles from the field. These experiences are naturally most meaningful, but difficult due to their past enculturation experiences of relying on medical ideologies and practices. Faculty mentorship has been extremely important for the learners to establish new norms and practices and new modes of care.

In general, the purpose of transcultural nursing specialist programs has been to prepare highly knowledgeable and skilled specialists of selected cultural areas who have in-depth cultural knowledge and are prepared to work with people in an understanding and competent way. Transcultural nurse specialists are prepared with culture knowledge and field research experiences in selected cultural areas such as Africa, the Middle East, North and South America, Oceania or Southeast Asian cultures. These specialists know the body of health care literature in these cultural areas and how to be a competent practitioner, consultant and teach related to one or two of these cultural areas. The specialists' specific areas of research and practice become evident and are supported by their clinical skills. Transcultural nursing programs are designed to accommodate students' past experiences and to help them function in new roles.

Doctoral and post-doctoral students who have not had any transcultural nursing or anthropological foundation knowledge are expected to acquire basic knowledge in these areas before entering the graduate program or conducting a research study. These students are given special attention regarding their specific program interests and goals. Many doctoral and post-doctoral students are expected to take graduate seminars in transcultural nursing as the majority have no foundation in their new field, and it would be difficult for them to succeed in their research without this knowledge. Their program of study may be slightly longer due to the factor of field research. Students are expected to do original field research in communities and clinical agencies under skilled transcultural nursing faculty. Many new insights about transcultural nursing are usually discovered, and this makes students value the importance of field research. Cultural imposition and ethnocentric nursing practices and their consequences are often studied with client cultural needs. The specialist learns how to develop new research skills and to use transcultural nursing theories in clinical and community settings through these experiences. The faculty mentor takes an active role to help students develop their specialist skills and to gain special comparative insights. The faculty mentor challenges the students to discover new insights of transcultural nursing and to develop different role performances with self-evaluation skills. The development of transcultural knowledge and the use of this knowledge in culture specific ways is the hallmark of the doctorally prepared transcultural nurse specialist.

During the past two decades, the number of students pursuing transcultural nursing specialization has markedly increased. To date, the author has prepared the majority of nurse specialists in transcultural nursing. Some nursing faculty in other institutions prepared nurses to apply anthropological concepts and research findings rather than to develop and use transcultural nursing knowledge. These programs are generally referred to as applied anthropology or cross-cultural nursing programs with an anthropologist focus. They are quite different from advanced transcultural nursing programs.[44]

Transcultural nurse specialists are increasingly in consumer demand. Schools of nursing need to develop transcultural nursing courses and establish new roles of practice to incorporate transcultural nursing into different areas. Several specialists are functioning in hospitals, clinics and satellite agencies to deal with a large number of "foreign" cultural clients. In schools of nursing, some transcultural nursing experts are misused when administrators or department heads assign them to teach traditional nursing courses such as medical-surgical nursing, maternal-child nursing and other areas. These well-prepared transcultural nurse specialists are often put through such *rites* of passage to gain entry into the system to fill faculty vacancies, or to resist or demean the talents of a specialist in a new practice field in nursing. Such practices leave the specialist frustrated and deprive clients of knowledge and skills they desperately need to function in our multicultural world. After about two years, some transcultural nurse specialists leave the school and either establish entrepreneurial work, or find a school that values their expertise. Considerably more education is needed to help faculty in schools of nursing to understand the role and contribution of the transcultural nurse specialist. The conservative and traditional norms of schools of nursing can greatly limit the specialist's functioning in schools of nursing. The transcultural nurse specialist, however, is much needed in schools of nursing to prepare students with new and different knowledge and practice skills, and to function in clinical settings.

Transcultural Nurse Generalists

The purpose of the transcultural nurse generalist program is to prepare nurses to function with a broad and comparative perspective about many different cultures in the world. The generalist learns how to use transcultural nursing principles, concepts, theories and research findings to care for clients of diverse cultures. Unlike the specialist, the generalist has been prepared to function with people in a very generalized manner and without in-depth knowledge of specific cultures and their variabilities. The generalist is usually prepared through baccalaureate nursing programs, and occasionally in master degree programs. The students has typically had two or three courses in transcultural nursing and cognate courses in anthropology or related social sciences. Generalists learn to appreciate transcultural care factors that influence and explain wellness, health or illness patterns. They study people from several cultures and the general care problems they encounter in hospitals, clinics and community health agencies. Generalists learn about cultural values and their importance in nursing and how to do culturological care assessments. They learn how to identify the client's specific and general culture care needs by the use of the transcultural nurse specialists' knowledge and theories. Generalists can develop and implement nursing care plans and practices for individuals and families. They learn about cultural differences and similarities among clients with their particular cultural lifestyle and needs. Generalists learn about cultural care and health needs of people in selected communities and use transcultural nursing concepts, principles and research findings to improve care to community groups. The program is designed to help the nurse function in a very generalized way to help clients of diverse cultural backgrounds. Their knowledge is general, and limited in depth and specificity.

It is important that the transcultural nurse learn how to do a mini-ethnonursing study to obtain current data to practice transcultural nursing. This is usually a new experience for baccalaureate and master degree students, as their research courses do not include ethnonursing and other ethno research methods to study families and communities of different cultural backgrounds. The comparative viewpoint is taught to generalists so that they keep an open learning and discovering perspective. Most importantly, they learn ways to examine their ethnocentric and cultural biases or prejudices and how these factors can influence cultural imposition practices in nursing.

Discovering their ethnocentric biases is usually a new and disturbing revelation, but one that brings invaluable learning to students. They also learn how illness and well-being may be due to conflicts with cultural values and beliefs and that there are culture-bound conditions limitedly known in medicine and nursing. The most difficult task of faculty is to redirect the students from culture-bound models such as Maslow's hierarchy of needs to a transcultural and comparative view that does not always follow the Maslow dictum. Learning about social structure factors and world view are other new areas for generalists in transcultural nursing.[45,46,47,48]

Most importantly, generalists learn about folk and professional health practices and emic and etic knowledge areas. This is the first time undergraduate nursing students have become aware of folk and professional knowledge systems. They learn about folk healing modes and preventive cultural health practices. Unfortunately, some students learn about these areas at the end of their baccalaureate or master degree programs. As a consequence, students are often angry and disappointed because it is so late to apply and master the concepts in clinical practices. Teaching transcultural nursing late in the program deprives students of knowledge they need that is highly relevant to their clinical work. As students say, "It's too little too late and still limitedly valued by most faculty in baccalaureate nursing programs." Some schools emphasize cultural diversity but without a transcultural nursing focus. Illustrations of transcultural nursing content and learning experiences can be found in several publications which the reader is encouraged to study relative to undergraduate and graduate nursing programs (Leininger [49,50,51,52] Boyle and Andrews).

In sum, the transcultural nurse generalist: 1) knows general transcultural nursing concepts, principles and practices and can apply the ideas to clients of several different cultures; 2) can develop nursing care plans that reflect a sensitivity to and awareness of differences among clients and their general cultural needs; 3) recognized signs and problems related to ethnocentrism, cultural clashes, cultural biases, and cultural imposition conflicts or stresses; 4) recognizes some ethical dilemmas, culturally-based care dilemmas and related intercultural nurse-client concerns; 5) identifies transcultural nursing care practices that reflect the client's general cultural values, beliefs and lifeways; and 6) can do a cultural care assessment and a mini-ethnonursing field study. To become a competent certified generalist in transcultural nursing, nurses need approximately eight to twelve semester credits in transcultural nursing under qualified transcultural nurse faculty instructor and field mentor. Generally, this nurse realizes the need for more preparation in transcultural nursing and returns to pursue doctoral preparation in transcultural nursing. The complexity and knowledge required to function well often become apparent to the generalist over time.

Today, approximately 36% of undergraduate and 20% of graduate nursing programs in the United States have specific transcultural nursing courses to prepare a nurse sensitive to and reasonably capable to care for clients of a few cultures.[53] Some generalists may have had limited transcultural nursing content; and are using mainly anthropological concepts rather than transcultural nursing principles, concepts, and theories in their work. Anthropology cognate courses are valuable to transcultural nursing and should be viewed as equally essential to nursing education as the traditionally required cognates of psychology, sociology, microbiology and many anatomy and physiology courses. Students often tell the author how extremely meaningful, essential, and relevant transcultural nursing courses are to them and how they use selected anthropological ideas relevant to nursing. But still today, far too many nursing students get limited transcultural nursing courses and can not always get anthropology courses as cognates because "there is no room for such courses" in nursing programs. The stark reality is that nursing students must care for clients of diverse cultures in all aspects of nursing and they need no preparation to do so. There is also myth that transcultural nursing is "integrated into all areas of nursing." The reality is that most faculty are unable to "integrate" such knowledge because they have limited knowledge about transcultural nursing. The author contends it is an ethical and moral responsibility for faculty of schools of nursing to establish transcultural nursing course into undergraduate and graduate nursing curricula. All professional nurses should have at least generalist preparation to help them function in our multicultural world. But we also need to prepare transcultural specialist in graduate programs. Faculty and administrators need to make this a moral imperative in schools of nursing today.

Status of Transcultural Nursing to Prepare Generalists and Specialists

In 1988, there were about five or six graduate programs to prepare transcultural nurse specialists or generalists in the United States. Most of these programs have been initiated and developed by the author, beginning with the first transcultural nursing courses at the University of Colorado in 1966 and the first doctoral courses at the University of Washington in 1972-73. Since then, transcultural nursing courses or similar programs (sometimes by different names) have been developed such as those at Wayne State University, the University of Washington, the University of Miami, Emory University, the University of San Francisco and the University of Los Angeles. Some Universities offer "nursing and anthropology," "culture and health" or similar graduate courses, but no transcultural nursing programs per se. Presently, Wayne State University has the largest graduate program with students enrolled in master, doctoral and post-doctoral study in transcultural nursing. Schools of nursing in Canada, Australia and other countries are developing transcultural nursing courses with clinical field experiences similar to those in the United States. To date, there are no established graduate degree programs in transcultural nursing in other countries; but, several countries are planning to initiate such programs in the near future.[54]

With the growing interest and worldwide need for nurses to be prepared through formal programs of study in transcultural nursing, there remains a critical shortage of transcultural nursing programs and faculty. Each year, more nursing students are requesting study in this field which increases the demand for more transcultural nursing faculty. Transcultural nurse specialists and generalists are much needed in many places, but only a few are available for hospitals, clinics, and public health agencies in this country and overseas. Some transcultural nurses are employed in schools of nursing and in a few international health centers. These new practitioners of nursing usually have to create and establish their role wherever they are employed. Some have to take traditional nursing positions such as medical-surgical, psychiatric, community and maternal-child nursing, and then find ways to incorporate transcultural nursing content into these existing fields. The expertise of these nurses are still limitedly recognized and use din most education and practice settings.

In hospital settings, the transcultural nurse specialist and generalist often have to cover several units, serve as resource persons or consultants, and be skilled to work with staff and clients having a number of unicultural concerns. While this gives the specialist an opportunity to help where clients and staff need her/his expertise, it does stretch the time and skill of the specialist to cover work expectations in a large general hospital. For example, one transcultural specialist was employed to be "on call" on all hospital and clinic units, and so she moved from one place to another in a typical work day. Still other specialists have been employed on a specific unit such as prenatal, oncology or medical-surgical units to facilitate culture care practices. These nurses had a good opportunity to identify and deal directly with clinical nurse-client cultural problems and to work toward a resolution of them.

Still other examples can be cited of role expectations of this nurse. For example, one transcultural nurse specialist (an expert in Arab Americans) worked in a large Arab community hospital helping the nursing staff to understand why an Arab client refused treatment for cancer because of cultural beliefs that "Allah would take care of her." She also worked with a mother who refused prenatal tests because the mother feared the tests might kill her baby. Another transcultural nurse specialist worked with African Americans and helped Anglo nurses understand why the client was terrified to have kidney dialysis treatment because of cultural beliefs about maintaining "good dark blood in the body." Many additional problems have been addressed as transcultural nurses deal with complaints about clients from "strange lands" who are "uncooperative," noncompliant," or "resistive" to professional treatments and general nursing care. The specialist helps staff nurses to provide culture care of clients with using their native food, providing privacy and other specific or important cultural expectations. As a consequence, client satisfactions are evident as culture care practices are experienced. Client costs and staff frustrations have been eased with the use of transcultural nurses. Family satisfactions of care and more rapid recovery are other benefits from the use of transcultural nursing experts in hospitals, clinics and community health settings.

It has been most encouraging to find some nursing service administrators recognizing the role of transcultural nurses, especially in large multicultural hospitals or community agencies. These administrators are beginning to realize that hospitals are corporate cultures which are organized and rely on specific cultural values, norms and practices. More than ever before, these nurse administrators, managers and head nurses need transcultural nursing knowledge to be successful and effective, not only with multicultural staff, but to work effectively with minority cultures, immigrants, refugees and other cultural clients and their families.

Marketing and employing transcultural nurses with their consistency skills is occurring in some hospitals, community health agencies, and new health centers. Many transcultural staff and client problems exist in these places and transcultural nurses are sought to advise staff in supportive ways. In some hospital settings, transcultural nurses are desperately needed. For example, one hospital had many Japanese clients from Japan with a new car factory in the community. Health personnel had never known or worked with Japanese people before, and so they requested a transcultural nurse specialist through a marketing firm. Likewise, a large group of Vietnamese refugees came to one community almost overnight and public health nurses knew nothing about the Vietnamese; again, transcultural nurses were requested to orient nurses to these people. Transcultural nurses have worked with several nurses to take care of the Vietnamese, and they encourage community nurses to take courses in transcultural nursing at nearby universities. These are but a few examples where transcultural nurses have been desperately needed and have had to function on an emergency basis.

Another major area requesting more transcultural nurse specialists has been in overseas positions. During the past decade, there have been several request for nurses prepared in transcultural nursing to work in the Middle East, Europe, Africa, Australia, South America and other places in the world. Nurses unprepared in transcultural nursing often take position in these foreign lands and experience transcultural shock. For example, American and other Western nurses experienced transcultural shock when they entered an Arab Muslim culture with major differences in dress codes, language, male and female relationships and different religious values. Some nurses gradually adjusted to this new culture, but others did not. Some worked until they had enough money to return home as the culture was too difficult and strange for them. Similar experiences occur as nurses go to Africa, China and other largely unknown cultures. However, nurses who prepared themselves prior to entering the "new" cultures can anticipate and value the experience as anew kind of professional nursing. Moreover, it can greatly expand nurses' views about a global nursing profession.

Requests for transcultural nurse educators continue to increase in schools of nursing in the United States, Canada and other countries. More transcultural nurses are needed to conduct transcultural nursing research, and to develop and implement sound transcultural nursing educational programs. Western schools of nursing are just beginning to shift to a multicultural focus and to develop new curricular approaches. Transcultural nurse experts are also needed to help with transitional curricular and other teaching and research changes to help nurses enter the next century and understand differences and similarities between Western and on-Western nursing programs, and reduce cultural imposition practices. Recently a nurse from Jordan came to an American university. She wanted courses and faulty to help her develop a nursing curriculum that would be "multicultural" and not necessarily American. The American nursing faculty were surprised, for they though she came to America mainly to learn how to export our nursing programs and ideas. A transcultural nurse faculty member helped the faculty to realize this nurse's request and to initiate plans for a multicultural curriculum. One can anticipate similar requests from faculty and also requests from students who may not want to be educated with limited uni- or bicultural nursing perspectives. Transcultural nursing has become a powerful impetus to recruit applicants to nursing programs because of these trends and worldwide needs. Transcultural nursing may well ease the critical shortage of nurses worldwide, and more importantly, improve nursing education and practices to become multicultural.

Transcultural nurses are much in demand to give yearly workshops, conferences and short-term summer courses on transcultural nursing. During the past two decades, this demand has steadily increased not only with nurses, but also with physicians and social workers who want transcultural knowledge in order to deal with recurrent client problems. These requests usually are for "instant learning" to meet crisis situations, to reduce non-compliance problems, or to prevent legal action and discrimination threats. For others, it reflects a sincere desire to learn about transcultural health care and how to work with different cultures. Each year, the author receives about sixty requests from nurses and non-nurses which cannot be met. This is an encouraging but demanding trend. The author's "hot line" phone services have helped many nurses. Unquestionably, transcultural nursing requests for workshops will increase as long as consumers make demands for culturally based nursing care and medical services.

Early in 1980 some initial plans were made to certify nurses to insure safe and effective nursing care of people of diverse cultures. The certification process has been implemented and the first group of transcultural nurses was certified in 1988 by the Transcultural Nursing Society. The latter is a worldwide organization open to all nurses practicing or interested in transcultural nursing. Competency examinations, portfolio documents, and other certification requirements have been established. Transcultural nurses are encouraged to meet certification expectations. This has been a significant step to increase the visibility and legitimacy of competent and safe transcultural nursing practices.

In sum, the early work of the author who anticipated and envisioned the field of transcultural nursing in the mid 1952 has now become a reality in the United States and in many other place in the world. As a consequence, formal programs of study to prepare transcultural nurse specialists and generalists have been developed. These new roles are essential to improve nursing practice, education and research. Transcultural nursing has not only become a legitimate and important formal area of study and practice, but is now recognized as a societal imperative for the future. More nurses are realizing that they need to be well prepared to work effectively and knowingly with people of different cultures. Nurses are realizing that cultures are complex and multifaceted and so one cannot use superficial knowledge or rely on "common sense" to help specific cultures. Transcultural research-based nursing knowledge generalists and specialists in this field indeed, transcultural nursing has become one of the most significant breakthroughs in nursing and it will continue to grow with new insights and practices in nursing. Most importantly, transcultural nurse specialists and generalists will continue to influent transnational nursing policies and practices. While considerable progress has been made, much work lies ahead to prepare nearly five million professional nurses in the world to be culturally sensitive, knowledgeable and competent skilled as transcultural nurse generalists and specialists. In time, this will be a reality and the author's dream as the founder and leader of the field will be realized.

References

1. Leininger, M. *Nursing and Anthropology: Two Worlds to Blend.* New York: John Wiley & Sons, 1970.

2. Leininger, M. *Transcultural Nursing: A New and Scientific Subfield of Transcultural Nursing: Concepts, Theories and Practices,* New York: John Wily & Sons, 1978.

3. Leininger, M. "Transcultural Nursing: An Essential Knowledge and Practice Field for Today," *The Canadian Nurse,* v.80, no. 1, 1984a, pp. 41-45.

4. Leininger, M. "Leininger's Theory of Transcultural Care Diversity and Universality," *Nursing Science Quarterly,* v. 1, no. 4, 1988a, pp. 152-160.

5. Leininger, M., op. cit., 1978.

6. Ibid. pp. 8-10.

7. Leininger, M., op. cit., 1988a.

8. Leininger, M., op. cit., 1984a.

9. Ibid.

10. Leininger, M. "Clinical Specialist in Child Psychiatric Nursing," Cincinnati, Ohio: University of Cincinnati Press, 1955.

11. Leininger, M., op. cit., 1970.

12. Leininger, M., op. cit., 1978.

13. Leininger, M., op. cit., 1955.

14. Leininger, M., op. cit., 1970.

15. Leininger, M., op. cit., 1978.

16. Leininger, M., op. cit., 1970.

17. Leininger, M. "Transcultural Nursing: Developments and Issues," McCloskey, ed., *Current Issues in Nursing,* Boston: Blackwell Scientific Publications, 1985a.

18. Leininger, M. Critical Cultural Incidents Limiting Quality Care, 1960-1988, Unpublished Study, Wayne State University, Detroit: 1988b.

19. Leininger, M., op. cit., 1955.

20. Leininger, M., op. cit., 1978.

21. Leininger, M., op. cit., 1988b.

22. Leininger, M. "Transcultural Nursing," *Proceedings from the Fourth Transcultural Nursing Conference,* New York: Masson Publisher, 1979, pp. 1-30.

23. Leininger, M. *Care: Discovery and Uses in Clinical and Community Nursing.* Detroit: Wayne State University Press, 1988c.

24. Leininger, M., op. cit., 1970.

25. Leininger, M., op. cit., 1978.

26. Leininger, M., op. cit., 1985a.

27. Leininger, M. "The Transcultural Nurse Specialist: Imperative in Today's World," *Nursing and Health Care,* v. 10, no. 5, 1989. pp. 251-256.

28. Leininger, M., "Conflict and Conflict Resolutions: Theories and Processes Relevant to the Health Professionals." M. Leininger, ed., *Transcultural Health Care Issues and Conditions, Health Care Dimensions,* 3rd ed., Philadelphia: F. A. Davis & Co., 1976, pp. 165-180.

29. Leininger, M., op. cit., 1978.

30. Leininger, M., op. cit., 1988b.

31. Leininger, M. "Survey of Transcultural Nurse Generalists and Specialists Prepared in the United States" unpublished paper, Detroit: Wayne State University, 1987.

32. Leininger, M., op. cit., 1984a.

33. Leininger, M., op. cit., 1988b.

34. Leininger, M., op. cit., 1985a.

35. Leininger, M. *Caring: An Essential Human Need.* Detroit: Wayne State University Press, 1981.

36. Leininger, M. *Care: The Essence of Nursing and Health.* Detroit: Wayne State University Press, 1984.

37. Leininger, M., op. cit., 1979.

38. Leininger, M. *Qualitative Research Methods in Nursing.* Orlando, Florida. Grune & Stratton, 1985a.

39. Leininger, M., op. cit., 1988a.

40. Leininger, M., op. cit., 1985b.

41. Pike, K. *Language in Relation to a Unified Theory of the Structures of Human Behavior,* 2nd ed., The Hague: Mouton, 1967.

42. Leininger, M., op. cit., 1985b.

43. Leininger, M., op. cit., 1985a.

44. Leininger, M., op. cit., 1987.

45. Leininger, M., op. cit., 1978.

46. Leininger, M., op. cit., 1989.

47. Leininger, M., op. cit., 1979.

48. Leininger, M., op. cit., 1985b.

49. Leininger, M., op. cit., 1978.

50. Leininger, M., op. cit., 1979.

51. Leininger, M., op. cit., 1984a.

52. Boyle, J. and Andrews, M. *Transcultural Concepts in Nursing Care.* Boston: Scott, Foresman/Little Brown College Division, 1989.

53. Leininger, M., op. cit., 1988c.

54. Ibid.

Footnote: An edited version of this article was published in the *Journal of Transcultural Nursing,* v. 1, no. 1., Summer 1989, pp. 4-16.

Section II:

General Transcultural Nursing Domains

Chapter 6

Types of Health Practitioners and Cultural Imposition*

Madeleine Leininger, PhD, LHD, FAAN, CTN, RN

People would not be people if they were not alike or different from one another. Human differences and similarities have existed since humanity's earliest beginnings, and they will undoubtedly continue to exist. Differences among people stimulate our thinking and curiosity, although differences may also produce tensions, conflicts, fears, and critical problems. Becoming aware of cultural differences and similarities is one of the greatest challenges today for health professionals to become effective providers of health services.

Currently, health practitioners in the United States have achieved many profound and important accomplishments. They can prolong life or take it away. They can replace diseased organs with non-diseased ones. They can eradicate many known communicable diseases. They can monitor physiological conditions using technological equipment with considerable efficiency and accuracy. They can alleviate distress of individuals who have different kinds of emotional or mental health problems. These achievements and many others positively reflect the capabilities of our health practitioners and scientists.

Interestingly, a major dimension remains which has not received active attention by the health professions, and this is understanding and developing effective skills to work with people of diverse cultural backgrounds. This remains a major worldwide goal for health practitioners. In earlier writings I identified some of the needs, problems, and the critical importance of focusing upon transcultural phenomena in order to provide a new kind of health care service to people.[1,2,3,4,5,6] Likewise a few anthropologists and other social scientists in early 1950 and 1960s shared their viewpoints to support this need in the health field.[7,8,9,10] It has been my stance that cultural factors are an integral part of health care, and they are essential to providing effective, satisfying, meaningful and beneficial health care to clients. Without the inclusion of cultural factors in health services, health personnel can only provide partial or incomplete health services.

Cultures are as different today as they have been in the past because most human groups tend to vary along several dimensions through time and different places in the world. Accordingly, our health care practices should vary to meet these cultural variations with respect to health needs and concerns. Health practitioners should be cautious in making broad generalizations about the health needs of all people, for they can completely miss what specific cultures need most in health care services. Nurses working with people of different cultural and subcultural orientations (whether in the United States or in other countries) need to become increasingly sensitive to and knowledgeable about the subtleties of cultural differences in direct client care, and not assume that "all clients are alike." The *error of similarities* can lead to some very unfavorable consequences and problems. However, some cultural similarities in the areas of basic human needs, concerns, and aspirations exist and need to be recognized. Health practitioners are expected to identify and use both similarities and differences in health care values, beliefs and practices when working with individuals or groups of a particular culture. Similarities help to establish humanistic care attributes, while the diversities stimulate one to new discoveries and approaches. Whether cultural differences are of a major or minor magnitude, it is the responsibility of the health practitioner to assess these differences, and determine ways in which the practitioner can appropriately respond to them within a cultural context and with use of current professional knowledge.

Cultural identity and pride are important indicators of the strength of cultural values and life experiences of any cultural group. Cultural pride provides the "life thrust" for meeting daily stresses, problems, and difficulties, and it greatly influences actions and decisions. Cultural identity is an integral component of cultural pride which makes one attentive to such recurrent and important questions as: who am I?; what do I live for?; why do I do what I do?; what am I becoming?; and who do I identify with most often?

Another dominant feature of a culture is that its people can experience considerable pressure for changes coming from both within and outside a culture group. These forces of change are often influenced by economic, technologic, social, political, cultural and environmental factors. Such forces of change can subtly or grossly change the lifeways of a culture. The amount of change, however, varies with the degree of cultural pride, identity, and the strength of cultural values and social structure factors. With any cultural group, seldom care cultural changes occurring at the same rate and in the same manner, for there are cultural barriers and facilitators that influence the degree and kinds of changes that may occur.

With these thoughts in mind, I will first present some types of health practitioners which the author has observed and studied in different settings within and outside the

United States. These types of practitioners are presented to help health practitioners understand that they exist and can greatly influence health care services to people in different cultures. Health practitioners need to be aware of these types and to reexamine their own interests, tendencies, and patterns of working with cultures. Becoming aware of these types of practitioners can aid in becoming an effective transcultural health care practitioner whether in this country or overseas. I will also present and discuss the concepts of *cultural imposition* (which I coined in the mid 1950s) and *ethnocentrism*, as both greatly influence types of health practitioners. These ideas are important to prevent cultural conflicts, stresses, imposition practices, and other problems in caring for people of different cultures.

Types of Health Practitioners

Type one: The Genuinely Interested Practitioner

The genuinely interested practitioner can be viewed as the ideal prototype for transcultural nursing practices and for all professional health practitioners. This health care worker manifests a positive, healthy, and genuine interest in a cultural group, thereby giving evidence of a sincere desire to know and serve the people in the best possible way. This practitioner maintains an open and willing attitude to learn from the people about their beliefs, values, and ways of living. It is a type of practitioner who gives evidence of a genuine interest in cultural health practices, the why of behavior, what the people believe will help them most to have an effective health program in light of their local resources, cultural values, environment, and social structure factors.

By taking a *learner* and *facilitator* role with people, this practitioner learns about local folk cultural roles and lifeways, and tries to combine professional knowledge with that of the local culture. Most importantly, this health worker reveals a pattern of being able to *learn from others* and to *become involved in the lifeways of the people* as wall as to respond constructively to cultural patterns in light of the people's cultural health care values, beliefs, and practices. Accommodating and adjusting to the people's lifeways rather than imposing or forcing the practitioner's lifeways upon the cultural groups is a noteworthy characteristic of this type of practitioner. Flexibility, intellectual astuteness, patience, tolerance, and willingness to learn from others are major features of this practitioner's pattern of helping people of different cultural backgrounds. This practitioner blends in skilled and appropriate ways professional knowledge of the health world with that of the cultural group's health beliefs and values.

Cultural groups usually respond in a positive manner to this type of health practitioner. The practitioner show evidence of greatly expanding one's professional insights and skills while working with cultures. This genuinely interested practitioner is always stimulated by cultural experiences and usually wants to remain with the cultural group over an extended period of time. The cultural group often speaks about this practitioner as "our good helper," or says "he (she) is one of us." Likewise, the health practitioner often speaks of the cultural group as "my people," "my cultural group," or my special people." Trust, confidence and comfortableness can be found between the health practitioner and the cultural client when this ideal type of practitioner is functioning in the community, hospital, home, or in other settings.

Type Two: The Isolated and Non-Involved Practitioners

This practitioner does not become fully involved in the lives, values, and beliefs of a cultural group, but instead remains aloof and isolated from the people. This type of practitioner performs expected professional tasks in a routine and regularized manner remaining emotionally detached and removed from a full awareness of the people. Interestingly, this practitioner follows and lives in his (her) own cultural world showing limited interest in the client's culture or world. The practitioner's style of working is to perform physical or routine expected tasks in an efficient way, but not become involved in the psychocultural and social interests of clients a different culture.

A prevailing attitude of this non-involved practitioner is that clients from X culture should be *glad* to receive anything being offered as it is "better than nothing" or better than "what the client has now." Clients from minority cultures are especially expected to appreciate whatever health professionals are doing for them. Seldom does this type of practitioner pause to consider *how* his (her) services are meeting the people's cultural health needs, or *how* the people are accepting the practitioner.

It is fascinating to observe how this type of practitioner tends to isolate and avoid direct involvement with people for a period of time by doing many mechanical tasks or keeping busy. Moreover, this type of practitioner tends to get rewards from professionals for performing technical tasks and "being different" in routine ways. There is a belief that this practitioner is doing something and getting tasks done well. Clients of different cultures are usually quick to recognize that this practitioner knows how to isolate himself (herself) or avoid getting involved with them. Clients observe that this practitioner is skilled in ways to withdraw from people or situations and is not responsive to the cultural, social, or emotional needs of clients. Cultural groups in the community or hospital often refer to this practitioner as "the person who really does not care for us or like us," or state that "this practitioner does not understand...." While it may be difficult for some to imagine this type of health practitioner, they still exist and can be identified in the field, hospital, and other settings.

Type Three: The Practitioner Who is Curious About Others

The "curious about others" practitioner show a strong interest and desire to work with people who are different than those in one's usual surroundings or life experiences. This practitioner shows a high motivation to learn about and live with cultural strangers, and will talk about wanting to work with people who are "exotic," "very interesting," "primitive," or "very different." This practitioner is willing to travel to remote places in the world and discover the exotic or culturally different people in the world.

After the practitioner enters the new culture, there is a high initial interest in the people. Gradually this practitioner often becomes disillusioned or disappointed about the cultural group and finds reasons for wanting to remain only a short time with them. Interestingly, this practitioner discovers that the "exotic people" once imagined to be so different from the practitioner's lifeways have some common human expressions and needs. This realization is often subjective but frightening and disappointing to the nurse practitioner as the client was perceived to be very different. This practitioner often experiences cultural shock with this discovery and does not know how to cope with cultural similarities and at the same time keep one's own cultural identity and be fascinating to identify this health practitioner in foreign countries with anxiety and restlessly of behavior. Usually this practitioner returns home early from a field placement, town or visit. One of the major problems with this practitioner is the need for a transcultural mentor to help him (her) deal with cultural similarities and differences.

Type Four: The Practitioner with a Hopeless Image

The practitioner with a hopeless attitude or image can be identified as a person who interacts with a cultural group but views them as a "hopeless group." This type tends to view cultures as inferior or believes that the culture will never become successful, achieve anything, or "get on its feet to succeed." The practitioner stereotypes the culture and expresses biases, prejudices, and hopeless views about the people while working with them.

Unquestionably, this health practitioner is uncomfortable working with people and is viewed as unable to succeed, and so the practitioner struggles with the people daily. The practitioner's nonverbal modes of communication, gestures, and lack of interest in the people reveals a hopeless and negative view of the people. Comments are frequently heard such as , "No matter what I do for these people, they will never be successful." Or the comment is made, "It is hopeless to change these folks, as it will never work in the long run." These silent or spoken comments often reflect long-standing biases, racial prejudices, or way the person has been socialized by parents or influential peers at an early age. Their attitudes and beliefs are deeply embedded in the culture. The practitioner's hopeless attitudes and image gets communicated to others and perpetuates negative views of a culture. Hopefully, a perceptive health colleague will become aware of this type of health care provided and offer counsel or advice. If this negative image prevails, it may be reason for the practitioner to be counseled away from serving people directly in fields such as nursing. Sometimes, however, effective counseling with transcultural nursing can change this practitioner and make him (her) effective.

Type Five: The Exploiter

The exploiter type of health practitioner focuses primarily upon his (her) own self-interests, self-gains, or self-needs at the mercy of other individuals or groups. This practitioner uses cultures for one's own self interests, needs and gains. Materialistic, financial, and self-interest desires of the practitioner become clearly apparent as well as a lack of caring attitude for others and non-altruism. Usually this practitioner spends time trying to figure ways of working with a culture primarily for self-benefits such as financial gains, notoriety, publicity, or to get publications for promotion, status, and other reasons.

Exploiting any cultural group has serious ethical concerns and violates ethical principles as beneficence. It poses ethical questions about "using" a culture or individual for self-interest, profits, or exploiting human interests. Research practitioners who fail to consider human subject consent requirements or who violate cultural norms are of great concern. These researchers much make clear to cultures or clients their purposes, goals, and how research findings will be used. Otherwise they violate human subjects' rights and are deceptive to those being studied. Sometimes this type of health practitioner is not discovered as employers are too busy and fail to ask about their reasons or purposes of being a health care provider. Inquiries of how health practitioners ought or should behave or make decisions in caring for clients are crucial to discover ethical behaviors and to function in health care. When these practitioners are discovered they are often asked to leave or are confronted with their motives.

Type Six: The Escapist

The escapist practitioner is one who has left his (her) homeland or familiar environment to live and work in another culture or context. Although the reasons for the practitioner's escape to another place may not be fully known, it is often done to avoid great stresses, personal conflicts, feeling depressed or for legal reasons. Sometimes the escapist seeks another place because of personal problems that are unbearable or because of the lack of success in the home situation. These practitioners desire to start life anew in a different place. The escapist practitioner often states, "I just need to get away from it all and live elsewhere. I need a change and to get away from this place and these people."

As this practitioner escapes to another culture, cultural shock may be experienced because the practitioner tends to choose a culture that is strikingly different or exotic. Cultural shock occurs more frequently because the escapist is so absorbed in his (her) own personal problems and concerns that he (she) has not prepared himself or the new culture often in a very different geographic location. The escapist in the new culture usually has no one to help reduce cultural shock, and adjustment to a foreign country or area is very difficult. As a consequence this practitioner does not fare well in the new place and may become more depressed and eager to return home. Generally, this person needs psychocultural counseling to deal with unfavorable personal problems. Occasionally the excapist is successful in another place, which speaks well of their goals and cultural adaptation abilities.

Type Seven: The Over-Protector

Still another health practitioner can be identified in working with clients of another culture, and this the cultural over-protector. This practitioner takes a strong protective role for a cultural group and becomes an active cultural protector or too much of a cultural advocate. This practitioner actively protects and defends the people from many outside stressors, changes, or threatening external influences perceived as detrimental to the cultural group or individual. They are highly empathic to what the culture needs or wants, and tend to protect anything a culture desires or values. The over-protector practitioner tends even to act before the client requests help and does not listen carefully to the client's views and needs because this practitioner feels the culture has been oppressed or denied basic needs and rights. The over-protector intervenes on the basis that he (she) knows what is "best for them." Such an overprotecting attitude and practice tends to thwart the cultural group's or individual's growth and discovery of what might be best for them. As a consequence, cultural imposition practices are evident and not helpful to the people. This practitioner greatly limits opportunities for cultures to make decisions, adopt, test or try what may be important to it. Granted, some cultures have been oppressed with great needs, but seldom do they value an overprotective practitioner who limits their self-growth, choices, and ability to make meaningful decisions that are congruent to them.

Undoubtedly, there are other types of health practitioners found in hospitals, clinics, and community agencies working with clients of different cultures, but these types are the most common ones that merit awareness. Employers need to be aware of these types of health practitioners and especially of health personnel going into foreign cultures or entering different lines of health institutions. Most importantly, health practitioners need to understand themselves, i.e., their motives, attitudes, and interests in working with cultural groups or going to foreign culture. Many positive satisfactions can occur when the practitioner's interest, actions, and motives are understood and fit with the culture and its interests and goal. The important principle is to know and understand oneself and to learn about other cultures in order to provide beneficial care practices.

Health practitioners need to be aware that there are often many assets of a culture with positive values, lifeways, and practices that need to be recognized, respected, and appreciated.[10] Health professionals who are conscious of the general principle and try to understand their own personal and professional tendencies can generally be helpful to clients of different cultures. Understanding oneself and the importance of a caring attitude is essential. If one assumes that one knows all about oneself or about another culture, great problems can occur. In general, working with people who have cultural values and practices from markedly different from those of the practitioner often leads to major conflicts, stresses, or feelings of helplessness, frustration, and uncomfortableness. Cultures are indeed sensitive to their values and to the attitudes and behavior of health practitioners. They often assess and can label those who are least or most helpful to them. Moreover, most cultures test whether outsiders will fit their culture. Anthropologists and transcultural nurses, knowledgeable and skilled in working with people of different cultures, can be most helpful to health personnel who are not prepared in transcultural work. It is also important to realize that there are a few health personnel who, by their life experiences, are "naturals" to work effectively with cultural strangers. There are many others who need and must be prepared in transcultural nursing to function effectively with the culturally different.

The Cultural Imposition Phenomenon

Cultural imposition remains one of the most serious problems in the health field, and a problem limitedly recognized by many health practitioners. The *tendency for health personnel to impose their beliefs, practices, and values upon another culture because they believe that their ideas are superior to those of another person or group,* is a prevalent and largely unrecognized phenomenon in the health field.[11] The phenomenon of cultural imposition is probably more universal than realized because health professionals assume they have the best answers or decisions for nonprofessional clients.

In the past, cultural imposition has been clearly evident in colonial contracts when dominant cultures took over less dominate ones, often in an oppressive or militaristic way. Some cultural groups experience cultural imposition in highly forceful and deliberate ways so that there was limited recourse to rebound from such experiences. Dominant cultures such as the British and American often had a powerful influence on cultures without fully realizing the impact and consequences upon another culture. Minority cultures often responded to such imposition practices by becoming passive, or showing signs of being resistive, angry, noncompliant, or unable to change the situation. These tendencies have also been evident in the history of humankind between health care providers and indigenous clients.

Cultural imposition phenomenon have been especially evident as Western health practitioners work in developing countries or in non-Western cultures.[12] Western health practitioners may not realize the potential impact of their beliefs and practices upon non-Western indigenous or local cultures, and especially on traditional health care practices. While Western practitioners are providing new ideas and services to people to improve their health, they may not realize that indigenous health care values and norms are culturally embedded and often do not change readily. Western health practitioners' ideas are often quite difficult to accept because the values and practices are not congruent with a non-Western culture. In the so-called "underdeveloped" or "third world countries," Western health practitioners may not be fully aware that the health practices they are trying to get adopted may be very strange and frightening to the people. In such situations, cultural imposition practices may be evident with signs of conflicts and stresses as Western health personnel impose their ideas and practices upon the people. Our Anglo-American middle and upper-class health practices may have little meaning to non-Western cultures whose health values and practices are markedly different in their environment. As Western health practitioners gain knowledge of a local culture's health systems, they are able to identify areas of cultural conflict and imposition.

In general, as health practitioners become genuinely involved with and learn from different cultures, they will realize that there are often many cultural differences in ways to address and study questions about the therapeutic benefits of Western practices upon non-Western cultures. Moreover, our Western scientific theories and findings may be of limited help to some cultures because the theories and research measurement tools are often culture-bound and do not take into account the particular values and practices of a culture. There may also be limits to the extent that Western theories can be used as universal theories, as often a theory may not fit a culture, and yet the theory and findings may be imposed upon the people to explain universal findings.

Cultural imposition is closely related to *ethnocentrism*. The latter refers to *the belief that one's own ideas, beliefs and practices are the best, superior, or preferred to other lifeways.*[13] The lack of awareness that other cultures may have better answers or know best how to live and survive in their environment may often be overlooked by an ethnocentric health practitioner. To overcome such ethnocentric biases, health personnel must take an honest and critical look at their beliefs, knowledge, and values. By reducing one's strong ethnocentric tendencies, health practitioners can generally reduce cultural imposition practices and improve health care practices to people of different cultures.

From an anthropological perspective, health and illness are largely culturally defined, constituted and maintained over time, and so local health systems tend to fit with their values and practices.[14,15,16,17] The challenge for health practitioners is to identify the dominate values of a culture, work *within* this particular culture context, and avoid strong ethnocentrism and cultural imposition practices. In transcultural health care, the practitioner needs to use the local frame of reference or value system to provide meaningful, congruent and beneficial health services to the cultural group. Thus, to provide culturally congruent health care, health practitioners need to understand health and illness from the culture being served and to pay attention to social structure factors such as the economic, political, educational, religious, and kinship systems of the culture.

Understanding the way health care values and practices are related to the total culture, history, and social structure is a major and central challenge to health practitioners today and in the future. In cultural imposition situations, the "imposed upon culture" may be greatly troubled by health practitioners when they fail to take into account the total cultural context. This tends to occur when European Americans isolate health and illness from social structure and worldview factors. Although European Americans think they use a holistic perspective about health and illness, the latter are often separated from religion, kinship, cultural values, and other factors which non-Western cultures hold as important reasons for illnesses and wellness states. Western health assessments and practices may seem questionable and inconsistent to non-Western cultures because they do not fit with diverse and important social structure factors influencing human well-being. Moreover, our Western health systems tend to reverse health practices over time such as encouraging bottle-feeding and then shifting to discourage bottle-feeding and then go back to breast-feeding. Or, we have valued and promoted smallpox vaccination, and then suddenly such practices are discouraged for small children. Still another example is the past emphasis upon having yearly tuberculosis x-rays and physical examinations as an "essential" health requirement. Today, these practices are being questioned or not valued as routine practices or expectations. Such imposed values, practices, and expectations by Western cultures upon non-Western cultures communicate that Western cultures do not seem to know what is best for health care and that their "scientific facts" change rather quickly.

Currently, Western cultures are promoting a smoking taboo, holding that smoking is a health hazard which endangers human lives or causes cancer. However, some non-Western cultures may question this practice as they have been smoking tobacco for hundreds of years and there is no evidence of death due to tobacco usage. A case in point is Gadsup people of New Guinea who have smoked and chewed tobacco for almost three centuries.[18] These examples and others lead non-Western cultures to question Western health practices, and why Westerners impose their beliefs and practices upon them.

In general, health practitioners who impose their beliefs, values, and practices upon another culture may lead to inappropriate and unethical practices. Cultural imposition practices can lead to some serious cultural conflicts and stresses due to marked differences between cultural values and beliefs. American and European Western health professionals need to study and understand cultures before attempting to sell or impose their ideas on non-Western cultures. They need to be cognizant of ethnocentric tendencies and social structure factors which can greatly influence health behaviors and practices.

Conflict Areas with Cultural Imposition

In the United States the dominant cultural value of egalitarianism, which stresses equal rights and opportunities for all people, may be questioned by many cultures and subculture groups that believe in stratification of cultural values or unequal rights due to social class and gender role differences. In our American culture there are indications that no all cultures receive or have equal opportunities because of historical, economic, political, social and cultural factors. Hence equal rights and privileges in our American democratic society may be more of an ideal value than a manifest reality as well as the American cultural value of uniformity in treating all people alike.

The related and important American values of democracy and freedom are deeply valued and expressed. Rugged competition, individual rights, open capitalistic enterprises, freedom of speech and diverse ways of living are manifestations of democracy and freedom. Interestingly, democracy is not always congruent with the values of egalitarianism, and so Americans find themselves explaining democracy in qualifying ways in order to reduce conflicts or to support our democratic values and expressions to strangers. Likewise, professional health personnel may be confused about the use of democracy and egalitarianism when working with diverse cultural groups within the united states. Transcultural nurses often wonder how they can practice egalitarianism and democracy when different cultures have very different values, expectations and needs. Although the federal government, religious groups, and other groups may stress that health personnel must provide equal care and treatment to all American, still cultural differences prevail and need to be accommodated in nursing care practices. Moreover, to treat everyone in the same or in a similar manner is unrealistic and violates the belief of individualism, cultural differences and democratic beliefs.

Health practitioners need to be able to accommodate diverse patterns and needs of people because of diverse cultural health values and needs of different cultural groups. Nurses are especially expected to accommodate and respect differences of cultures while respecting common shared values. Cultural diversity is important to support intercultural variability and survival. From an anthropological viewpoint, human beings have survived through time because of their cultural differences which have helped people to deal with their changing environments, life situations, and available resources. So while the values of democracy, egalitarianism, and cultural diversity may lead to cultural conflicts and cultural imposition practices, these values are important but need to be explained or interpreted in light of cultural variability and cultural diversity factors. Nurses and other health practitioners need to be flexible, respect cultural differences and avoid unfavorable cultural imposition practices that may stifle the development, survival, and growth of a culture. Keeping in mind the strengths and capabilities of cultures in imperative to preserve the favorable aspects of cultures and to value practices that maintain cultural well-being. Promoting structural and attitudinal flexibility in thinking and action patterns can help cultures to maintain positive and meaningful health practices.

Finally, to reduce cultural conflicts and cultural imposition practices, health personnel need to recognize that different health care systems and practices exist among cultures in the world, and that these differences serve cultures in different ways. So rather than imposing a dominant health system on another culture, it is important to study carefully a health system of a culture before introducing changes. It is also possible that much can be learned from an anthropological study of different health systems for comparative purposes to gain new insights about health care. Culturally diverse health systems may well be the order of the future rather than making cultures fit a few dominant Western health systems.

In this paper different types of health practitioners were discussed to help health practitioners become alert to their own tendencies, motivations, or interest in working with people of different cultures. Becoming aware of these different types of practitioners can help prevent unnecessary and stressful cultural conflicts, problems, and imposition practices. Such an awareness of one's own dominant cultural values and ethnocentric tendencies is essential for effective and successful professional work. Most importantly, practitioners need to respect and value cultural differences in health beliefs and practices, and to avoid "heavy-handed" cultural imposition practices. There is much yet to be discovered about the impact of cultural imposition and ethnocentrism upon developing or less politically powerful cultures. Nurses are in a good position to study such practices if grounded in transcultural health and anthropological knowledge. And since nursing is the profession expected to give intimate, individualized, and personalized services to individuals and groups, cultural care practices are essential for our multicultural world.

---

* Note: This is a revised and edited version from the article originally published in the first edition of *Transcultural Nursing: Concepts, Theories, and Practices,* New York: John Wiley & Sons, Inc., 1978, and recently published in the *Journal of Transcultural Nursing,* Memphis: University of Tennessee Press, v. 2, Winter, 1991, pp. 32-39.

References

1. Leininger, M. "The Culture Concept and its Relevance to Nursing," *The Journal of Nursing Education*, v. 6 1967, pp. 27-39.

2. Leininger, M. "The significance of Cultural Concepts in Nursing," *Minnesota League for Nursing Bulletin*, v. 16 1968a, pp. 3-12.

3. Leininger, M. "Cultural Differences among Staff Members and the Impact on Patient Care," *Minnesota League for Nursing Bulletin*, v. 16 1968, pp. 5-9.

4. Leininger, M. *Transcultural Health Care Differences and Similarities among Western and Non-Western Cultures.* Denver: 1979. (Unpublished manuscript.)

5. Leininger, M. *Nursing and Anthropology: Two Worlds to Blend.* New York: John Wiley & Sons, Inc., 1970.

6. Leininger, M. *Transcultural Nursing: Concepts, Theories and Practices.* New York: John Wiley & Sons, Inc., 1978.

7. Paul B. *Health, Culture and Community: Case Studies of Public Relations to Health Programs,* New York: Russell Sage Foundation, 1955.

8. Saunders, L. *Cultural Differences and Medical Care,* New York: Russell Sage Foundation, 1954.

9. Spicer, E. H. *Human Problems in Technological Change.* New York: Russell Sage Foundation, 1952.

10. Leininger, M., Op.cit., 1969.

11. Leininger, M., Op.cit., 1970.

12. Leininger, M., Op.cit., 1969.

13. Leininger, M., Op.cit., 1970.

14. Leininger, M., Op.cit., 1967.

15. Leininger, M., Op.cit., 1968a.

16. Paul, B., Op.cit., 1955.

17. Saunders, L., Op.cit., 1954.

18. Leininger, M., Op.cit., 1969.

Chapter 7
Transcultural Food Functions, Beliefs, and Uses to Guide Nursing Practice*

Madeleine Leininger, PhD, LHD, FAAN, CTN, RN

Probably no topic has intrigued human beings more universally and persistently over time and in different geographic places than food. It is a subject which our early ancestors must have talked about in their daily search for food in order to survive in different environments. Today the topic of food is popular and pervades our lives at home, in social gatherings and in virtually every place where people live and work. From an anthropological perspective food is more than a source of nutrition, for it has social, economic, political, religious, and cultural meanings and uses. From a transcultural nursing view, food remains essential for human growth, health, and survival. Food has long been used as a powerful means to establish and maintain relationships with individuals and groups. It can make people feel physically better and psychologically good, but food also has many cultural and social functions. In general, food has always had multiple functions and uses with special symbols and meanings in different cultures. Such knowledge is extremely important for nurses to learn in order to provide culturally acceptable, congruent, and beneficial nursing care to those served.

This chapter discusses the importance of nurses' understanding food beliefs, functions, symbols, and practices from a transcultural nursing perspective. Some differences and similarities related to functions and uses of food among selected Western and non-Western cultures are discussed. The relevance of food meanings, uses, and functions is emphasized to help nurses understand the role of food in keeping people well and in aiding recovery from illness or disabilities. And since culture strongly influences the beliefs and uses foods in health and wellness, nurses need to realize the significant part cultural factors can play in the care of clients' health. Gaining an understanding of specific transcultural food beliefs, functions, and practices, can lead the nurse to provide for culture-specific care practices.

At the outset, several universal and diverse food questions need to be considered by nurses, nutritionists, physical anthropologists, ecologists, social scientists, health personnel and others interested in transcultural comparative foods and their uses. They are: (1) What are the basic nutritional needs of people transculturally?; (2) How do religious, worldview, emotional, educational, kinship, and ecological factors influence food uses and consumption transculturally?; (3) Are there common foods that tend to be eaten or avoided in different cultures when well or sick?; (4) What foods tend to support wellness patterns over time in different cultures?; (5) What factors often lead to changes in patterns of food production, consumption, and usage?; (6) What foods tend to be most beneficial throughout the life cycle for infants, children, and adults transculturally?; and (7) What is the role of nurses and other health personnel in helping clients to remain well or through appropriate food uses preventing illness?

Nurses Have an Important Role in Nutrition Uses

One of the most important functions of the nurse is to take an active role in helping clients maintain a favorable nutritional status. The client's daily well-being and nutritional needs in illness depend considerably upon the nurse's knowledge, decisions, and actions to provide appropriate nutrients to clients. Helping the client recover from illnesses, diseases, and disabilities through appropriate food uses is an important part of nursing care. The nurse as a primary care provider is in a unique position to help the client and the family establish and maintain good health through food uses throughout the life cycle.

But, to be effective in maintaining the health of clients, the nurse needs to be knowledgeable about different cultural foods, the client's food likes and dislikes, and the cultural context in which food is prepared, served, and eaten. It is essential and important to become knowledgeable about food nutrients and what foods are generally preferred by clients throughout the life cycle. In addition, the nurse should understand the uses of foods for ceremonial purposes at birth, marriage, religious events, and death, as this can make a difference in communicating with and helping individuals and groups of specific cultures. Transcultural nursing also requires that nurses learn about cultural explanations such as the "hot-cold" theory in order to provide effective ways to combine generic (folk) with professional health care practices. In general, the nurse needs to realize that cultural foods are a powerful means to facilitate family relationships, communication, and well-being. The transcultural nurse, therefore, remains alert to different foods in diverse cultures, the eating patterns of cultures, and the ways foods are used to help individuals stay well or become ill. Let us turn to some transcultural universal (common) and diverse food functions in selected cultures worldwide.

Universal Functions and Uses of Foods

First, food has been used universally since the beginning of *homo sapiens* to *provide essential nutritional needs to help people maintain body functions and energy and survive.*[1] Food provides energy for humans to keep well, grow, work, communicate with others, and socialize. Transculturally, there still exists considerable variability among different cultures regarding what constitutes the essential or basic nutritional needs of human beings in different ecological settings. Bogan has identified some essential nutrients for human evolution, but considerable intercultural and intercultural variability still exists.[2] How nutrients are used depends upon the quality of the nutrients and how they were produced, processed, and prepared for the consumption. How food nutrients are metabolized in the body and the extent of activities of people also influence their uses. In addition, the way foods are prepared and served can greatly influence food consumption. The nurse considers these factors in working with clients of different cultures whether at home, in the hospital, or other contexts.

Nutritionists and physical and cultural anthropologists have discovered that cultures tend to require different amounts of food depending upon biological, genetic, social, cultural, and ecological factors. If infants and adults do not get sufficient basic food nutrients, signs of nutritional deficiencies, illnesses, inability to function and death occur. For example, *kwashiorkor* is a nutritional disorder seen in children due primarily to a protein-scarce diet.[3] This condition was first described in West Africa and has been frequently found in some non-Western tropic countries where the diet consists largely of starchy foods such as cassava, yams, and taro. This condition has also been seen in the United States and other Western countries. With *kwashiorkor*, the child's legs and body are edematous as fluid is retained and the child becomes withdrawn and whiny largely due to low protein intake. Children with *marasmus* have slightly different symptoms than children with *kwashiorkor*, but they too show signs of low protein and calorie intake and reflect a failure to grow.[4] Every culture over time has developed what they believe are essential and preferred foods in their diet and also have patterned ways to prepare foods for children and adults. Sometimes cultural groups may not have balanced or highly nutritional diets as we know them in the Western world. Nevertheless, certain foods are desired and many may have important nutrients that we may not know about. For further study on the physical nutrient needs of cultures, the reader is encouraged to read McElroy and Townsend[5] and Bogan's[6] comprehensive and insightful publications on this subject, including the evolution of food nutrients with preferred foods in different cultures.

A *second,* universal function of *food transculturally is to establish and maintain social and cultural relationships with friends, kinfolks, strangers, and others.* Many social friendships have been initiated with the sharing of food, and personal and professional ties have been maintained. Food is a way of expressing relationships and communicating ideas between individuals, family members, groups, and human organizations. It has become a symbol to indicate special social and cultural patterns with individuals and groups, and to test and maintain relationships. Rituals are frequently associated with food uses to bring people together or to initiate and maintain positive relationships. Relationships with strangers that are tense and questionable are often tendered through food rituals and social uses. For example, in the United States, coffee or beverage breaks have become a significant work and social ritual; at certain times in the work situation individuals or groups come together over a cup of coffee or tea to talk or gossip about their work, friends or those that please or annoy them. The morning, afternoon, or evening beverage breaks have become well institutionalized in the United States, Canada, Europe, and Scandinavia with a variety of ritual practices in each work institution. Originally, these beverage breaks in the United States served to give employees a brief recess from their intense and routine work during the early industrial era in America. Today these beverage breaks have different functions beside a rest break, as they tend to serve to renew and maintain work friendships, communicate, gossip about work happenings, and plan work strategies for survival or promotion. Thus the "ritual beverage break" serves as more than a nourishment or rest break, and has many important social and cultural functions for employees.

Procuring and distributing foods are often closely linked with cultural status and prestige functions related to work, marriage, achievements, and with birth and death ceremonies. In our industrialized Western world, if an individual gets an award, a new job, or is promoted, dinner celebrations or cocktail parties often occur. At these dinners, special, prestigious foods are often served in fancy ways with special titles. Tables are often decorated with a special tablecloth and flowers. Special foods are usually served, such as steak for Anglo-Americans, lamb for Britians, veal for Greeks, and a special bean and rice dinner for Mexicans and other Hispanics. For North American Indians a potluck feast with native food exchanges would occur. At these social gatherings, the honored guest is toasted with special cultural beverages or foods to acknowledge achievements or change in status. These food feasts reinforce social and group cohesion, recognize the person being honored, and strengthen cultural identities with preferred cultural foods.

Cultural foods are especially evident at wedding feasts, religious holidays, and at particular life cycle events (rites of passage). The Jewish bar mitzvah and bat mitzvah are important life cycle religious events for young boys and girls as they become adults. These celebrations have great symbolic religious significance which is actually more important than the nutritional aspects of the food. Christmas, Easter, and other religious and nonreligious holidays reflect the preparation and use of special food dishes to celebrate such occasions. The time, place, guests, and context for the celebrations are important to foster a desired social milieu and special cultural experience.[7]

Food has general universal functions in all ceremonies for people to display prestige, exchange wealth, and renew bonds of friendship and solidarity. These functions in food ceremonies are evident in Western cultures, but are often more impressive in non-Western food ceremonies. For example, in many non-Western cultures people gather large amounts of food that they have produced to honor supernatural spirits or gods and express their gratitude for the foods and for the good harvest. Harvest food festivals are often annual occasions in non-Western cultures and they are very colorful, happy, and often spiritual occasions with people wearing bright, festive costumes. At these food festivals people like to dance, perform certain rituals, or show their talents and appreciation for the food.

Birth ceremonies are special, big occasions in most non-Western cultures. Special foods are prepared and used to symbolize a child's entry into the family, community, and world. Family and friends gather to celebrate the infant's arrival and to see the child as a future active participant in their lives. In some cultures there are much greater birth celebrations by gender with food and local activities than in other cultures. This is especially true in Iran and other Middle Eastern cultures. For the Gadsup of Papua New Guinea, both boy and girl infants are warmly welcomed into the world with a special birth ceremony after two months. During the Gadsup birth ceremony the infant's father's brother holds the female infant and places small, soft particles of garden food in her mouth.[8] In this female birth ceremony, food is highly symbolic of future work role and anticipated pleasures. As the father's brother places the food on the infant's tongue, he says, "We give you these Gadsup foods from our female gardens so that you will want to grow them like other women in the village have done in the past." This beautiful but simple birth ceremony uses food to signify that the female infant is special and has a special future role when she become an adult. Interestingly, male Gadsup children are given foods to taste that are related to their gender, so that when the child becomes an adult, he will want to hunt and gather foods with other men; females are associated with the garden foods and family caring.

Universally, foods for ceremonial feasts vary in quantity and quality, but also in how rare, exotic, expensive, and highly preferred they are by the people. The preparation and selection of ceremonial foods make the ceremony a special day to remember and to maintain through time. Food ceremonies require considerable time for people to collect, prepare, and ritualize the foods for ceremonial purposes. In most cultures ceremonial food must also be prepared and served or distributed properly, with attention to cultural food taboos and preferences, especially those associated with invited guests and special occasions. For example, the Gadsup would spend several weeks collecting food that they had grown, store it, and then display it in piles at the large group ceremonies. Displaying these foods increased the village's status and prestige and brought great honor to the villagers, tribe, and community. Food ceremonial competition existed between villages especially for harvest and life cycle events. One can think of many similar preparations of special foods and saving money to collect and prepare food for wedding ceremonies in North and South American, European, and Southeastern cultures of the world.

Recognition of food taboos associated with ceremonies is extremely important. Many cultural groups may abstain from eating foods that are generally choice, highly desired foods. Some foods cannot be eaten by males or females at ceremonies because they are believed to bring harm, illness, or reduce one's importance. Religious groups often have strong food taboos and strict ritual observances in which the "sacred" (of religious significance) and the profane (worldly and often unclean, or viewed as dangerous) are observed. For example, at Yom Kippur, Jews observe a twenty-four hour fast. And in keeping with their religious beliefs, all pig products are taboo as are fish without fins and scales. Only animals with hooves and that chew a cud and have been ritually slaughtered may be eaten. Milk and meat dishes must never be mixed at the same meal. Some similar food taboos are practiced by Muslims in that pork or pig products are taboo and they can only eat food from animals that chew a cud and that are ritually slaughtered (*halal*). The Muslim fast of Ramadan is observed during the ninth month of the lunar year. During this fast food and drink are taboo between sunset and dawn for Muslims who are of the "age of responsibility" (twelve years for girls and about fifteen years for boys). Strict food taboos are often associated with religious beliefs and yearly ritualized ceremonies.[9,10]

Life cycle initiation rites remain fairly universal in using food for symbolic purposes. There are, however, cultural variations with life cycle rites and some cultures have reduced their importance for a variety of reasons. Where they prevail, the ceremonies are used to recognized that an individual has moved from one life cycle period to another with changes in social status. For example, in many Papua New Guinea villages in the past, these life cycle rituals were extremely important for transition from a young boy to becoming a man.[11] Before the initiation ceremony, the boy initiates were expected to observe strict food taboos by not eating eel and cassowary meat. But at the end of the intense, long male ritual ceremony, the boys had become men they were now strong enough to eat these "powerful male foods." Today these initiation ceremonies have been simplified but special foods and activities are still used to impress male initiates of their changing role, status, and new privileges as a man. Becoming a man means that a Gadsup boy may marry and have children.

Although many Western cultures do not have such definitive life cycle initiation rites as the Gadsup, still one can find different forms, expressions, and interpretations. For example, in Western cultures when a boy or girl reaches adolescence, or is twenty-one years of age, parents help celebrate this occasion by preparing a special dinner with favorite cultural foods, i.e., meats, cakes, and vegetables. They may also honor them with gifts and sometimes a social gathering with their peers or friends. The life cycle event is also acknowledged by the adolescent usually obtaining a driver's license or other cultural symbols. Our Western life cycles are not generally as elaborate, prolonged, and ritualized as those of non-Western cultures, but special foods are used.

A *third* function of *food is to assess social relationships or interpersonal closeness or distance between people.* Universally, foods are often used to determine the extent of friendship or distrust between individuals, families, or groups. An example of this function comes to mind from my ethnographic and ethnonursing field study in the early 1960s with the Gadsup of New Guinea.[12] I began my field research as a complete stranger to the Gadsup and entered their world as a white, single woman. Initially, the people perceived me as a potential sorceress—or a stranger who could harm them. They distrusted me and watched me carefully until I became a friend. During the first six weeks, a few village men and women brought me small amounts of withered, small, and scrubby–looking sweet potatoes, fruit, and greens. They would cautiously give me the food and quickly leave. The food was of poor quality and reflected that they feared me, and therefore, did not want to give their best foods to such an unknown stranger or sorceress. Later, as the villagers got to know me (about the second month), they began to bring me better quality fruits and vegetables, and occasionally fresh foods from distant places. By the end of the first year the Gadsup were bringing me lots of fresh pineapple, vegetables, and even rare foods that they had obtained by walking nearly twenty miles. Thus, I became their friend, the quality of food markedly improved and the quantity increased. This example shows how food was used to reflect cultural stranger-to-friend interpersonal relationships.

Transculturally and universally, food use often reflects the social stratification of society and indicates which people are to be respected or hold positions of higher authority or status. The way a culture may be stratified, such as by castes, classes, or clans, determines who gets what foods and how the foods can be used by people of particular classes or castes. In some stratified societies such as India, certain foods are highly restricted for certain castes, and food is regulated by the rules of the caste system. People in higher castes, such as the Brahmins, often are given high quality food. Food also becomes a powerful means for regulating social and political controls and maintaining cultural norms and rules of behavior. In stratified societies, cultural diversity exists because of economics, politics, and the way a society is organized and controlled by cultural norms.

A *fourth universal function and symbolic use of food is to cope with emotional stresses, conflicts, and traumatic life events.* In many cultures in the world, foods and diet patterns are used to relieve anxiety, tensions, and interpersonal conflicts or frustrations related to work at home, at the office, or in daily living. The way cultures deal with emotional stresses and conflicts varies considerably in Western and non-Western cultures. Western cultures such as Anglo-Americans, Europeans, Canadians, and Australians generally rely on eating to relieve their daily stresses, in ways they may not be fully aware of until weight gain occurs. Some people tend to almost constantly eat or nibble on food or drink to relieve their anger, frustrations or anxieties. Some individuals hoard food to have it readily available when they get upset. Compulsive eating and hoarding of food to relieve tensions or anxieties are largely learned and patterned from cultural practices. Compulsive eating to relieve tension tends to occur more frequently in Western cultures where food is more readily available and conspicuous than in non-Western cultures. In the latter cultures where food is often scarce, seasonal, and cannot be stored in refrigerators, people relieve their anxieties by activities such as running, hunting, fighting or being aggressive at political and social gatherings. In these cultures one seldom finds obesity problems and depression because they have other ways to deal with stresses.

In some Western American and European cultures, individuals may handle their anxieties and tensions by avoiding eating. These individuals under stress who will not eat food are often depressed, have low self-esteem, and are not interested to eat anything, or do not feel worthy to eat or receive foods. They may, instead, take drugs, drink alcohol, become very active or withdraw. In Western cultures, the mental health conditions of anorexia nervosa and bulimia exist, especially in teenagers. Individuals with anorexia nervosa usually refuse to eat anything and have no appetite. As a consequence, they become very thin and underweight. The individual with bulimia will often gorge large amounts of food and soon after vomit and not retain the nutrient values of the food consumed. These conditions are well known in Western cultures, but may be limitedly found in non-Western cultures.

Nurses with preparation in transcultural mental health are alert to cultural variations related to cultural patterns of overeating or undereating, and can observe, listen to, and counsel the client. The nurse can help the individual, group or family work toward resolving their problems within their cultural lifeways and values. Most cultures have prescribed ways to relieve feelings of boredom, disappointments, and dissatisfactions and the nurse can discuss these with clients. Foods such as sweets and drinks are commonly used in the United States by adults and children to handle their emotional frustrations, whereas vegetables and daily outside activities are generally used in non-Western cultures.

A *fifth universal function of food transculturally, with some cultural variations, is the use of food to reward, punish, and influence the behavior of others.* In most cultures in the world there are norms and practices of the ways children and adults are rewarded, punished, or receive positive or negative sanctions with food. Foods have long been used by humans to regulate cultural behaviors that they want rewarded, maintained, or curtailed. Moreover, cultures know what foods have highly favorable rewards and which ones communicate dislikes or negative rewards. For example, Anglo-American children are often reward for good behavior with all kinds of sweets, i.e., candy, sugared cereals, drinks, and cookies. In contrast, the Gadsup children were rewarded for desired cultural behavior with non-refined foods such as vegetables, nuts, taro, fruits, fish, or forest meats. Sweet foods consumed in America often have led to dental and other health problems over time. Most importantly, infants and children are quick to learn how parents and adults use foods for rewards and punishment, and so food-giving becomes symbols of children's "likes and dislikes" in a culture. Children may also try to control and test parents by the uses of foods in their culture. Moreover, if food is eaten in a culturally and socially unacceptable way, parents become embarrassed with their child and maybe view themselves as inadequate parents. Parents or surrogates are often expected in most cultures to reprimand children with foods in order to conform to culturally appropriate ways. For example, an eight-year-old boy was eating food with his fingers at a formal dinner. The parents reprimanded him gently at the table for this cultural offense. Later the child was harshly reprimanded at home because the parents were extremely embarrassed by the child's unacceptable cultural behavior: it reflected "poor upbringing" by the parents.

A *sixth universal function of food is to influence the political and economic status of an individual or a group.* Transculturally, food has great economic importance and political uses and these two aspects are closely interrelated. Food has been used to build political alliances with people and for economic gains. Politically and economically, food can reaffirm and sustain traditional ties and help establish new alliances. Sometimes food has been used to test political relationships and to test the strength of alliances. Serving food before, during, and after political meetings often leads to friendly and congenial outcomes as food tends to "soften" political group behavior or ease questionable relationships. In some cultures, political leaders are offered rare or very choice foods or drinks before political meetings to ease a strong leader's potential aggressive or polemic disposition. Generally, food has been a means to build and maintain smooth relationships, gain votes, and to foster desired political alliances and support. Some examples to support this general function will be offered.

The Gadsup for example, carefully select foods given to one's political friends and to enemies at political gatherings. The Gadsup spend a lot of time getting some of their choicest foods for their political friends to maintain good ties. They will, however, also get choice foods for enemies in order to prevent further hostilities, accusations of sorcery, or to reestablish favorable political relationships. If the Gadsup did not give the best quality food to their friends or enemies, they could be accused of sorcery which might lead to illnesses and deaths in a village. Traditional enemies are usually strong in political power, and so foods offered and eaten at the public gatherings impress the politically oriented "big men" of different villages. Foods which are not fresh or look of questionable quality are always suspected by enemies as potentially harmful, and will be avoided. Political uses of foods exist in other cultures, but often with different meanings, forms, purposes, and ritual giving.

In many European countries and in the United States, gift-giving occurs regularly and in different ways among political and social interest groups to promote positive relationships and to win over new political and social friends. Presidents and prime ministers of countries often receive lavish or expensive gifts which reaffirm their political, economic and social status, and relationships with the public. Such gifts to special people are usually displayed in visible places but always under protected security.

Economically, the food is important in exchanges to maintain basic food supplies and to provide diversity in the people's diets. The economics of food is of great concern worldwide and so the production, accumulation, and distribution of goods and services are given due consideration. Farmers and peasants of different cultures often know the best ways to maintain their economic lifeways, however, they have limited political and economic power with bureaucrats. Cultures learn what food other groups need or desire. They try to increase trade exchange patterns for economic benefits. For hundreds of years people have made food exchanges to support political ties, provide essential foods, and to strengthen one's economic position. Good food imports and exports, whether of small or large amounts, are central to the development, maintenance, and survival of cultures worldwide. An imbalance in the production and distribution of foods can cause serious problems in any society and can ultimately influence the health status of people. As frequently seen in Africa, thousands of people have died of hunger due to war, political feuds, economic greed, and poor distribution of foods. Food taken to international food distribution points may never reach its goal due to political groups taking the food, such as was the case in Somalia, Africa in 1993 and 1994. Hungry and dying people may never receive the food. Hence charitable organizations that try to help starving people may never see their food received by those who so desperately need it.

Periods of drought, floods, earthquakes, and other environmental conditions continue to have a devastating impact on the production and distribution of foods in many countries. Farmers in the United States, Canada, and other countries often fail to get their surplus foods exported to "have not" countries due to government politics and poor marketing policies and practices. Moreover, farmers struggle to get fair or adequate prices for their food products to meet their farm production costs. There is a very close relationship between politics and economics in most cultures which transculturally oriented nurses need to realize when working in foreign countries or in rural or urban communities. These factors influence health care practices worldwide.

A *seventh and major universal function of food is to assess, treat, and prevent illnesses or disabilities of people transculturally.* Anthropologists have long observed and studied how food is used as a means to diagnose, treat, and deal with illnesses and stresses in different cultures.[13] Practically all cultures today still rely on both folk and professional caring and curing of illnesses. Some cultures have skilled folk diagnosticians (or diviners) who assess the health and illness states of their people before considering professional services. Folk practitioners often use symbolic figures and foods to assess the health or illness status of their people. They know what foods people should eat, and why some foods should be eaten or rejected because of certain physical illnesses and sociocultural conditions. In most non-Western cultures folk diagnosticians look for cultural reasons for illnesses; whereas in Western cultures professional diagnosticians often seek physical or emotional rather than cultural causes. Such insights are important as nurses work with many different cultures worldwide.

Transculturally, food is used to explain why certain illnesses occur or conditions exist. Food is used to predict possible illnesses, reasons, and consequences for both professional Western diagnosticians and non-Western folk diviners and healers. For example, if a client drinks milk and complains of intestinal discomfort (e.g., abdominal pain, cramping, diarrhea, and vomiting), Western health personnel will identify this as a sign of lactose intolerance.[14] This condition has been found in nearly two thirds of the world's population after early childhood, and is due to problems with the production of the enzyme lactase.[15,16] In contrast, folk healers will often diagnose this condition in relation to disturbances in social ties and breaking cultural rules.[17] Food is the medium to diagnose factors that can initiate or aggravate biophysical and cultural illnesses. Lactose intolerance is important for the nurse to know about, as it is found in many cultures and can aggravate a client's health status markedly.

Food products are often used by folk diagnosticians to warn people of potentially unfavorable sociocultural relations with friends or strangers in a culture. It is believed that favorable or malevolent behaviors can lead to illnesses which most health personnel fail to see or understand due to the lack of knowledge and the disbelief that cultural factors can lead to illnesses. Western scientific medical practitioners are quite determined to view all illnesses as due to genetic, biophysical or emotional causes, or due to cell, organ, and body dysfunctions. Until physicians, pharmacists, and other medically oriented personnel become knowledgeable about comparative health and illness, they will continue to use such explanations exclusively.

In many cultures food remains important to prevent and cure certain illnesses such as hypertension, diabetes mellitus, peptic ulcers, coronary diseases, and other disorders which nurses need to be alert to in their nursing practices. In the United States, Canada, Europe, Japan, Australia, and other Western cultures, large sums of money are spent on radio and television advertisements to promote optimal health through eating "the right kinds of foods" and avoiding others. Food tends to dominate the Western mass media so that people are almost obsessed with food interests and ways to live by what is being advertised, promoted, marketed, and studied. Some of these food values change over time, leaving some cultures baffled about scientific "food facts." The critical emphases remain in Western cultures eating the right foods, exercising, and regulating one's own food intake. In contrast, non-Western cultures are more concerned about procuring and distributing food among their kin, social, political groups, and getting enough food for daily survival.

There are a number of non-Western cultures such as Southeast Asians, Mexicans, Caribbean, and related Latin Americans that are attentive to assessing and using "hot and cold" foods, beverages, and medicines. The *hot and cold theory* is a very old belief, which originated in these countries and in ancient Greece with the desire to balance body fluids or humors between perceived hot and cold substances.[18] If an imbalance of hot and cold body fluids occurs, this is believed to cause illnesses and even death. Foods, beverages, and medicines remain classified as hot and cold by many people in these cultures to prevent and treat illnesses. In general, hot or warm foods are believed to be easier to digest than cold or cool foods. To treat human conditions, it is important to assess the substance taken or to be used in order to provide usually the opposite effect, i.e., one counters too much exposure to cold substances with hot foods and beverages or medicines, but cultural variations remain on uses. For example, an upset stomach condition may be caused by eating too many cold foods, and so warm foods are needed to correct the imbalanced state. In general, foods and medicines are classified and used by cultures in different ways. Nurses need to study the cultural classifications and their meanings as they vary transculturally.[19,20,21]

Interestingly, the Chinese according to the ancient philosophy of Taoism have, for nearly 3,000 years, been attentive to the *yin* and *yang* elements to maintain harmony and balance in the universe.[22] *Yin* signifies the cold, female, and darkness element, whereas *yang* signifies the hot, male, and light element. Accordingly, when foods are digested, they can lead to either *yin* or *yang* conditions. The important principle is to balance *yin* and *yang* components of foods in order to maintain good health. Excesses or imbalances of either *yin* or *yang* can lead to illnesses, diseases, or unfavorable conditions. To provide culturally congruent and competent care, nurses need to be knowledgeable about hot and cold (*yin/yang*) theories and others related to food, drinks, and medicines in healing, caring, and curing.

It is also especially important to realize that many professional medications, surgical operations, or medical treatments such as chemotherapy, are usually considered to be "hot" and powerful. Clients of different cultures are sometimes baffled as how best to counteract such "hot" professional treatments or avoid them. Clients may be non-compliant or refuse medicines and treatments because they are too hot or cold. Noncompliance and uncooperative behavior of clients, with their refusal of nursing care, medicines, and treatments can be related to cultural fears, clashes, or uncertainties which some health personnel need to understand or know about. Nurses and other health professionals may demean and offend clients who hold beliefs about foods and their favorable or less favorable uses.

Most importantly, the nurse who has studies transcultural differences in the uses of foods will be attentive to the food preferences of cultures in order to promote health and prevent unfavorable responses of individuals and families to foods. Since cultures have specific food preferences and dislikes which can make a difference in caring for clients of different cultures in the hospital or at home, the nurse considers these foods and their nutritional values within the client's health needs to provide culturally appropriate counseling. It is extremely important to ask the client and family to tell about these foods rather than guessing or using an inaccurate source. To facilitate recovery from illness, maintain health status, and prevent illness, cultural knowledge within a holistic perspective is imperative. For example, the nurse should understand that Vietnamese people like fish, rice, fresh vegetables, and herbal teas. Unless fully acculturated, they may consistently refuse hamburgers, potatoes, carbonated beverages and other Western foods. When Vietnamese are served their cultural foods, it is wonderful to see them smile and eat "their foods." Eating culturally desired foods can lead to a quicker recovery from illness and greater client satisfaction than when these clients are expected to eat strange or taboo foods. Most nurses realize that when one is ill or under stress, there is a longing for foods that one knows about and likes. Indeed, American hospitals waste far too much good food because clients from other cultures dislike the food as it is strange or cannot be eaten for cultural reasons. Such hospital food wastes are difficult to accept, however, they occur because the food was culturally taboo or inappropriate. Transcultural nurses learn what cultural foods should be served and what clients need. They need to help other nurses and staff to make clients' culture-specific food needs known in the dietary department. Moreover, hospital staff need to be prepared about culture food likes and dislikes through in-service education and academic courses on transculturalism.

Although considerable variability exists with African Americans due to acculturation factors and whether they are from the North or South, many African Americans enjoy and prefer green vegetables of many kinds, pork, legumes, chicken, cornbread, and soul foods. Hot breads and fried or boiled foods are popular. The author has found these preferences remain strong from her fourteen years of study with African Americans living in urban and rural areas of the United States.[23] With the current and serious African American health problems related to stroke, hypertension, and general cardiovascular conditions, nurses and other health professionals need to be aware of food uses by African Americans and especially by those who have limited income and are living in poor areas. Bailey's study of African Americans in a large urban context, in which he used both anthropological and transcultural nursing principles and theories, provides valuable insight about these problems.[24]

Although Mexican Americans' and Puerto Ricans' preferred foods vary, they tend to like foods such as beans, chicken, chili peppers, tomatoes, onions, squash, and herbal teas, especially chamomile tea when ill or experiencing cultural pain or stresses. Hispanics in the Southwestern area of the United States enjoy enchiladas, tostadas, tamales, chili con carne, chicken, and chili dishes. Nurses need to provide these common foods that will be acceptable and beneficial to clients.

Native Americans in Canada and the United States were the first to introduce foods such as maize, beans, and squash into Anglo-American diets. The many different Native Americans of different tribes have different food choices due to their ethnohistory, environmental context, and traditional food and spiritual rituals. Generally, though, Native Americans like fresh fish, fruits, berries, corn, beans, squash, wild greens, root foods, and game meats. Since more are moving to urban areas, they often miss their traditional and highly valued foods because they are closely related to their religious or spiritual beliefs and to their natural environment. As the nurse becomes knowledgeable about the close interrelationship of the Native Americans in Canada and the United States, they will discover that foods are extremely important. Food uses and consumption must be harmonious with mankind and the environment. Their environment for the food practices bears upon this reality, as well as the close relationship of foods to their sacred beliefs and life cycle rituals.

As nurses become more knowledgeable, sensitive, and competent to learn about transculturalism, their ability to provide culturally congruent care will increase. Knowledge about the people's environment with an understanding of what foods are available is also important as one counsels clients about food resources and intake. How foods are produced and used largely depends upon the agricultural resources and the urban distribution of foods at markets and other places for costly and less costly prices. Geographic environments and climates generally determine what foods will be raised and available, and which products can be relied upon for health care maintenance or restorative processes. The climate, soil, amount of rainfall, seasonal plants and animals, available technologies and human resources in any ecosystem, greatly influence food values and uses over time in cultures. Some cultures live on day-to-day gardening and hunting foods, or have limited daily subsistence food supplies. Other cultures may live on American foods obtained from supermarkets. Western cultures tend to rely largely on frozen foods and meats, fish, fruits, and vegetables as they become seasonally available to them. As nurses work with clients, these transcultural factors are assessed and worked into nursing care practices. Holistic transcultural care incorporates not only food factors, but social structure and environmental factors influencing food uses and functions.

Another fascinating factor which needs to be mentioned is that the genetic, constitutional, and metabolic processes of human beings may differ considerably with different cultures, and have different consequences. Nutritional anthropologists, geneticists, and biochemists continue to study these factors. Some cultural groups have found that some imported foods brought into their areas can aggravate and/or threaten the health of the people. Sometimes missionaries, health personnel, and lay people who have good intentions may not turn out to be so good for the health of the people. The reasons may be related to metabolic, genetic, and cultural intolerance. For example, Brunce reported about a metabolic disturbance found in northeast Brazil in which the population was predisposed to any aggravation of Vitamin A deficiency.[25] Dried milk was introduced into the community which caused the people to experience sudden growth. However, this led to a rapid depletion of the existing meager supply of Vitamin A. As a consequence, an outbreak of night blindness, xerophthalmia, keratomalacia, and irreversible blindness occurred. Brunce offered a warning to people who have the good intention of improving dietary inputs in undernourished countries because the foods may be highly disruptive to the normal metabolic functions of the people. Other studies are needed to evaluate and predict the consequences of introducing new foods into a new or different cultural area.

Considering the above facts, principles, and research studies related to food universals and non-universals, the nurse prepared in transcultural knowledge can be a great care facilitator to help clients with their food needs and appropriate uses. Nurses of tomorrow, however, must increase their knowledge of cultural uses and abuses of foods in diverse cultures. Transcultural nursing insights about general aspects of the client's food culture is essential to making appropriate culture-specific and culturally congruent care.

In the process of doing a culturalogical care assessment (see Chapter Four), the nurse identifies food preferences, beliefs, and practices within the different areas of the Sunrise Model, i.e., kinship, cultural values, etc., as they relate to care and well-being. As mentioned above, the transcultural nurse may need to help other nurses and health personnel to use the model appropriately with clients, families, or groups.

In the future, one can anticipate more demands for culture-specific foods to reduce illnesses, improve health care, and avoid food wastes. More attention in hospitals needs to be given to the way clients want their foods served, i.e., hot or cold, and to give serious attention to client and family ideas of what helps them to keep well and become ill. The nurse should be sensitive not to force clients to eat certain foods just because of professional beliefs that they are good for the client because professionals know this. There is much yet to learn about cultural food uses and their nutritional benefits. The color, form, shape, and nutritional value of the food often determine if a client will eat and retain the food. For example, the color red may be a taboo color in a culture, and so red foods are not acceptable. How foods are prepared and served influences acceptance or rejection of the food. Cultural ethnocentrism with imposition by the nurse can lead to psychophysical illnesses and cultural pain such as vomiting, gastrointestinal upsets, high anxiety, and passive-resistive behaviors. An important transcultural nursing principle is always to talk with the client and family about food likes and dislikes and how they prefer to eat the foods, i.e., raw, cooked, fried, etc. It is also wise to talk about foods that keep them well or tend to make them ill (or uncomfortable), especially when they return home from a hospital experience or have had outpatient treatments. In order to provide appropriate advice or direct services in an acceptable way, the transculturally oriented nurse tries to enter the food world of the client and understand how they view and use foods. Remaining sensitive to client's food interests and needs is an extremely important means to effective and therapeutic nursing care practices and to promote the well-being of those whom nurses serve. The nurse with transcultural caring knowledge about food uses and functions and flexible caring skills is invaluable to promote client or family well-being, recovery from illnesses, and to maintain daily functioning in our changing multicultural world. In sum, the nurse should keep this message in mind: *Culture defines food uses, functions, and benefits over time and in different places in the world. The nurse's challenge is to discover this reality and to use foods congruently with cultures.*

---

*This chapter is a revised and updated version from the earlier article published in the first edition of *Transcultural Nursing: Concepts, Theories, and Practices*, 1978, pp. 203–219.

References

1. Kottak, C., *Anthropology: The Exploration of Human Diversity*, New York: McGraw-Hill Co., 1991, p. 176.
2. Bogan, B., "The Evolution of Human Nutrition," *The Anthropology of Medicine*, *2nd ed.*, L. Romanucci-Ross, D. E. Moerman, and L. R. Tancrei, eds., New York: Bergin and Garvey, 1991, pp. 158–195.
3. McElroy, A., and P. K. Townsend, "Nutrition Throughout the Life Cycle," *Medical Anthropology in Ecological Perspective*, *2nd ed.*, Boulder: Westview Press, Inc., 1989a, pp. 207–216.
4. Ibid.
5. McElroy, A., and P. K. Townsend, "The Ecology and Economics of Nutrition," *Medical Anthropology in Ecological Perspective*, *2nd ed.*, Boulder: Westview Press, Inc., 1989b, pp. 166–202.
6. Bogan, op. cit.
7. Helman, C., "Diet and Nutrition," *Culture, Health, and Illness*, Bristol: John Wright PSG, Inc., 1990, pp. 31–54.
8. Leininger, M., "Culture Care of the Gadsup Akuna of the Eastern Highlands of New Guinea," *Culture Care Diversity and Universality: A Theory of Nursing*, M. Leininger, ed., New York: National League for Nursing, 1991, p. 231–280.
9. Leininger, M., "Transcultural Eating Patterns and Nutrition: Transcultural Nursing and Anthropological Perspectives," *Holistic Nursing Practice*, Rosse, ed., Md, Aspen Publishing, v. 3, no. 1, 1988a, pp. 12–26.
10. Helman, op. cit., pp. 32–36.
11. Leininger, op. cit., 1988a, pp. 18–24.
12. Leininger, op. cit., 1991, pp. 231–280.
13. McElroy and Townsend, op. cit., 1989, pp. 243–289.
14. Bunce, G. E., "Milk and Blindness in Brazil," *Natural History*, v. 78, no. 2, February 1969, p. 44.
15. McElroy and Townsend, op. cit., 1989b, pp. 180–181.
16. Davis, A. E., and T. D. Bolin, "Milk Intolerance in Southeast Asia," *Natural History*, v. 78, no. 2, February 1969, pp. 53–55.
17. Leininger, op. cit., 1991.
18. Manderson, L., "Hot-Cold Food and Medical Theories: Cross Cultural Perspectives," *Introduction to Social Science and Medicine*, v. 25, no. 4, 1987, pp. 329–420.
19. Boyle, J., and M. Andrews, *Transcultural Concepts in Nursing Care*, Boston: Scott, Foresman, and Co., 1989, pp. 335–337.
20. Leininger, op. cit., 1988a.

21. Spector, R., *Cultural Diversity in Health and Illness*, Norwalk, Connecticut: Appleton and Lang, 1991, pp. 126–130.
22. Manderson, op. cit., 1987.
23. Leininger, M., "Southern Rural Black and White American Lifeways with Focus on Care and Health Phenomena," *Care: The Essence of Nursing and Health*, Detroit: Wayne State University Press, 1988b, pp. 195–217.
24. Bailey, E., *Urban African American Health Care*, Lanham, Maryland: University Press of America, Inc., 1991.
25. Bunce, op. cit., 1969.

Chapter 8

Culture of Nursing: Focus on American Nursing and Hospital Culture

Madeleine Leininger, PhD, LHD, DS, FAAN, CTN, RN.

In the early 1960s the author wrote about the culture of American (United States)* nursing to help nurses discover and understand some of the dominant professional norms, values, and lifeways of professional nurses and their potential influence on others.[1] The author was interested in establishing comparative transcultural data about the American nursing culture and other nursing cultures in the world. In the early 1960s the idea of identifying, describing, and analyzing nursing as a culture or subculture was new for nurses. In fact, when the author first discussed the idea of a culture of nursing, it was quickly rejected as being a waste of time and a useless venture. To consider an abstraction of collective patterned behavior was strange because professional nurses were interested in individuation, specific work activities, patients' illnesses, and medical viewpoints. Hence collective and abstracted patterned expressions and lifeways were viewed as irrelevant to nurses. But as a nurse anthropologist with keen interests in understanding people and possessing ethno research skills, the author believed the time was ripe to study and analyze nursing cultures. This was an important focus in order to help nurses understand their own personal and professional cultural values, norms, and lifeways. It was also important to guide human interactions and establish effective actions and decisions with people of many different cultures. Moreover, knowledge of the culture of nursing could advance nursing knowledge and practices, for in the 1960s nurses were unaware of a culture of nursing in the United States or elsewhere.

From *anthropological* and transcultural nursing experiences, the author had observed, listened to, and talked to many nurses about the major features and characteristics of nursing and nurses. It soon became clear that nursing was a culture with identifiable norms, values, and lifeways. Hence some beginning descriptions and abstractions of the subculture of nursing were made in the mid 1960s which became the first work in nursing to reflect the values, attributes, and norms of the American culture of nursing.[2] Identifying a culture of nursing seemed long overdue as the nursing profession was nearly 100 years old, and yet there had been no depiction of nursing as a culture. Such research findings soon became useful to nursing students who were eager to learn about the nature and general features of the nursing profession. This anthropological and nursing perspective of the American nursing culture led to the author's interest in studying nursing cultures worldwide for diverse and universal knowledge about the nursing profession.

In the 1960s the author recalls that when she began to talk with other nurses about a subculture or culture of nursing, typical comments were: "How could nursing be a culture, as every nurse is highly individualistic and there are no common or specific nursing patterns?" "Nurses will resist this idea as it is too far fetched to be useful;" "It is an interesting idea, but I never thought of nursing as a culture, as nurses are a collection of individuals who think and act differently in all situations." In general, most nurses thought it was impossible to identify or abstract dominant patterns of nursing behavior, especially particular collective values, symbols, norms, beliefs, and practices. These comments, however, stimulated the author to study the culture of nursing in the United States from an anthropological, ethnographic, and ethnonursing perspective and to pursue the approach in other countries in order to expand nursing knowledge.

Accordingly, over several years the author observed, interviewed, and documented the dominant cultural lifeways, patterns, values, and norms of nurses within the United States, looking for any regional and transcultural differences. This work led to the identification of the "Tribes of Nursing in the United States" and to the "Gnisrun and Enicidem," (nursing and medicine) tribes as descriptive and analytical features of the culture of nursing.[3,4] The later study contrasted the cultures of nursing and medicine within the hospital context where the largest numbers of nurses have been employed over the past century. From this study it was evident that the hospital culture and medicine had greatly influenced nurse's values, beliefs, and practices for many decades. Moreover, the medical and nursing cultures have greatly shaped the American hospital culture for many years. The author's forty years of direct experience of studying nurses in hospitals, schools of nursing, and other contexts using largely qualitative research methods and criteria such as recurrent patterning, saturation, and confirmability were important to establish the findings presented in this chapter. But why is it so important to study the culture of nursing?

Why Learn About the Culture of Nursing?

Why should nurses be interested in and learn about the culture of nursing? This question is important to consider at the outset. There are several major reasons why nurses need to focus on the culture of nursing. First, knowledge of the culture of nursing can assist newcomers to the nursing profession in understanding some of the dominant, recurrent, and patterned features of nursing. It can help experienced nurses reflect upon their behavior and gain new insights or perspectives about the beliefs and practices of the nursing profession.

Second, an awareness of the culture of nursing serves as a valuable historical guide to reflect upon changes in the nursing profession over time and speculate about possible reasons for any changes. Anthropologically speaking, nurses need to realize that nursing as a culture can change over time in varying ways.

Third, knowledge of the nature, beliefs, and characteristics of diverse and similar cultural features of nursing is essential to provide sensitive and understanding nursing care practices. Nurses' cultural behavior can influence the clients. Gaining knowledge about the culture of nursing can be enormously helpful to guide nurses in their interactions with clients and health personnel whose personal culture values may be quite different from those of the nurses. In fact, the cultural values, beliefs, and practices of medicine, social work, pharmacy, physical therapy, and other health professions generally are different from those of the nursing profession and often different from the client's.

A fourth major reason for the nurse to understand the culture of nursing is to appreciate differences and similarities among nursing cultures regionally, nationally, and worldwide. Such knowledge is invaluable to help nurses realize that not all nursing cultures are alike. Such transcultural nursing knowledge has been helpful to nurses traveling and working in many different places in the world such as in Europe, Korea, China, Japan, Australia, the Middle East, and Papua New Guinea. Nurses often experience cultural shock when they discover that their own values, norms, and standards may be very different from those of other nursing groups in the world. From current transcultural nursing findings, there is evidence of more diversity than similarities among nurses and nursing cultures worldwide.[5] Yet amid these diversities are always some commonalties. Hence, it is imperative for nurses to learn about differences and similarities among nursing cultures in the world in order to serve clients effectively and to work well with other nurses. Tolerance and flexibility is essential today for nurses to meet such cultural differences. An appreciation of the cultural history and diverse factors influencing nursing cultures helps the nurse to understand specific differences and similarities among professional nurses. Therefore, knowledge of cultures has become essential today for nurses to function with people in any culture and society in order to become and remain effective. For without such knowledge and awareness, nurses can encounter a host of intercultural problems and stresses without understanding why these stresses occur and how to take appropriate actions.

Fifth, knowledge of one's own nursing culture along with others in the world, can stimulate nurses to pursue comparative research on diverse cultures transculturally. Discovering comparative features and speculating about the reasons for differences and similarities often leads to many new insights to guide professional nursing practices and thinking.

Amid the transcultural diversities, the author holds there is a globally shared culture of nursing values with features that characterize the nature, essence, and dominant attributes of the nursing profession and discipline. The global or universal culture of nursing, however, has yet to be fully discovered, but some transcultural nurses are pursuing this goal. If such knowledge of a universal culture of nursing is established, this could provide valuable knowledge to nurse scholars and students, but also to others interested in the nursing profession. The author predicts this goal will not be reached until well into the twenty-first century after studying specific nursing cultures worldwide.

Definition of Culture and Subculture of Nursing

Culture of nursing refers to the *learned and transmitted lifeways, values, symbols, patterns, and normative practices of members of the nursing profession of a particular society.* In contrast, a *subculture of nursing* refers to a *subgroup of nurses who show distinctive values and lifeways that differ from the dominant or mainstream culture of nursing.*[6,7] Cultures and subcultures are dynamic and abstracted entities that tend to change over time in different ways, however, they also have patterns and general characteristics that provide distinct features over time. However, cultures and subcultures have some stability and constancy over time and place which help nurses to know and understand them.

Cultures also have ideal and manifest features that are usually recognizable and can be studied and transmitted to others. An *ideal culture* refers to *attributes that are the most desired, preferred, or the wished for values and norms of a group; whereas manifest culture refers to what actually exists and is identifiable in the day-to-day world as patterns, values, lifestyle patterns, and expressions.*[8] For example, nurses may ideally say that they value and respect elderly people in a nursing home and that the elderly get "good nursing care." This ideal philosophy and image of "good nursing care," may not always be manifest or what actually exists as a reality. The manifest cultural reality is that elderly clients may receive rather inadequate or even negligent nursing care and may not always be respected by nurses. Noticeable differences may exist between the ideal and the manifest culture of any group and especially within the culture of nursing. Furthermore, the emic or the inside expressions and patterns of a culture may be limitedly known by its members; whereas the etic or outsider's views or public knowledge about a culture may be well known and described by others. These definitions are important to guide nurses in their pursuit of identifying and understanding the culture of nursing, especially regional or national subcultural differences or similarities.

Identifying the Culture(s) of Nursing

In the process of studying the culture of nursing in the United States, the author recalls several experiences which helped her to learn about the culture. For example, in the early 1960s the author was attending a national nursing convention in Chicago. As she entered the hotel, she said to the hotel receptionist, "Could you tell me where the nurses are meeting?" The two female receptionists quickly replied, "Yes, there are nurses here." They gave the author directions to the convention room. As the author walked to the convention room with the receptionist, the latter kept talking about nurses and how well she knew them. The author asked, "Could you describe more about how you know nurses and how they differ from other professional groups that come here for conventions?" She replied, "Well, nurses are quite different in that they tend to stay together in a group, talk about hospital, school work, and physicians. They always wear similarly styled clothes." She continued, "They are friendly and eager to help others, but they are not too assertive or politically astute. Nurses are generally quiet, passive, kind, and tend to do what is expected of them as nurses. They do not seem to have any power to deal with doctors in the hospital." She then told about her hospital experiences with nurses and said, "When I was hospitalized, nurses were very busy persons and hard workers. They always seemed to be doing things for the doctor and sometimes less for some patients and other nurses." She told how in 1964 nurses were attentive to fulfill physicians requests and that nurses "strictly follow doctors' orders." This American lay citizen's views indicated that she knew about the culture of nursing as an outsider to the profession. The author was amazed how well this non-nurse knew and described the culture of nursing and her image of nursing. These factors and others reinforced the author's goals of discovering the culture of nurses nationally as well as of any regional groups of nurses across the United States.

In identifying the culture(s) of nursing, the researcher searched for the patterns, rules (norms), and values of nurses within the general culture and society, such as the American culture with its dominant features. The culture or subculture groups of nursing live within the larger society but have some special features that make them different from those of the rest of society. Most assuredly, the norms, values, and action modes of the society and the world culture influence the culture of nursing. The culture of nursing may deviate from the dominant culture in certain values and lifeways that are identifiable and provide specific data to understand it. There are generally some commonly shared values and beliefs among nurses that help to support the broadest features of a culture of nursing within a society and worldwide.

An important consideration in identifying a culture of nursing, is to study the past and present history of nursing in which patterns and values of nursing can be identified and abstracted with specific examples. The cultural history of nursing is extremely important because it provides specific facts and patterns of behavior that help to establish the credibility of the culture of nursing over time. The study of images of nursing is another way to discover aspects of nursing culture.

Historical Images of Nursing from Kalischs' Research

During the past several decades two American historians have systematically and extensively studied American nursing using historical documents, audiovisual media, and other data. These outstanding scholarly leaders are Philip and Beatrice Kalisch who have devoted almost a lifetime to studying images of American nurses. They are well known for their detailed and rigorous work on the past and changing image of nursing from the days of Florence Nightingale until the present.[9] Their mass media image data have included "the printed media (200 novels, 143 magazine short stories, poems, and articles, and 20,000 newspaper clippings), as well as newer non-print media (204 motion pictures, 122 radio programs, and 320 television episodes).[10] Since this research work they have continued to study general changes in the image of nursing. The author has known these scholars over several decades and has seen their creative, detailed, and systematic work on nursing images. Indeed, the Kalischs' many publications have provided some of the most substantive, scholarly, and rigorous documentation we have on the images of American nurses and the nursing profession.[11,12]

In the Kalischs' historical research on the image of nursing, they identified six images of nursing. While these images are *not* the culture of nursing per se, they provide meaningful data to support some features of the American culture of nursing. They are presented to provide knowledge and special insights about the images of nursing as another perspective of the author's focus on the culture of nursing from transcultural nursing and anthropological viewpoints. The research is viewed by the author as scholarly and valuable for nurses to understand and appreciate the evolutionary image of nursing over time.

The first image identified by the Kalischs is the *Angel of Nursing*, in which the nurse is portrayed "as noble, moral, religious, virginal, ritualistic, and self-sacrificing."[13] This image prevailed from 1914 to 1919 and concluded with World War I when nurses were viewed as heroic and noble. While it was held the Florence Nightingale reflected this image, she also showed other features such as her noteworthy leadership, altruism, and direct efforts to make nursing a respected profession.

The Kalischs' second image called *Girl Friday*, prevailed as an image from 1920 to 1929. The nurse was portrayed as "subservient, cooperative, methodological, dedicated, modest, and loyal."[14] This image showed the nurse as a handmaiden and revealed some decline in nursing educational standards due to the proliferation of hospitals with nursing students being exploited to staff hospitals under poor working conditions and receiving no salary.

The third media image was called *The Heroine*, which covered 1930 to 1945. This image portrayed the nurse as "brave, rational, dedicated, decisive, humanistic, and autonomous."[15] The Kalischs' drew heavily upon the biographies of Edith Cavell, Florence Nightingale, and Sister Kenney to reveal this image.

The fourth image portrayed the nurse as a maternal, sympathetic, passive, and domestic person, called the *Mother Image*, from 1945 to 1965. In this period it was believed that married women nurses should be in the home and function as dutiful and conscientious lay mothers rather than as professional working persons.

The fifth image was the most negative, in which the nurse was viewed as a *Sex Object*, who was "a sensual romantic, hedonistic, frivolous, irresponsible, promiscuous individual."[16] This sexy image was seen recently as in television programs such as *M*A*S*H* and *Trapper John*. This image failed to portray nurses as professionals or intellectually self-directed persons.

The Kalischs' sixth image was *The Careerist*, which they described as "an intelligent, logical, progressive, sophisticated, empathic, and assertive woman who is committed to attaining higher and higher standards of health care."[17] These six images discovered by the Kalischs' have provided some valuable image characteristics of nurses obtained largely through the mass media in specific historical periods from 1920 to the mid 1980s.

The American Culture of Nursing: Early (1940–1974) and Recent (1975–1994) Eras

Having realized that the nursing profession had not been studied nor the culture(s) of nursing identified, the author saw this as an essential area necessary to understand the profession of nursing. Being specially prepared to study human cultures from a transcultural nursing and anthropological perspective, the author conducted research by examining major past and recent periods in nursing from ethnonursing and ethnographic methods. The author identified two major contemporary periods of nursing, namely the Early (1940–1974) and the Recent (1975–1994) Eras of the nursing culture (see Figure 8.1). Data for the findings drew upon the author's continuous lived through personal and professional experiences in these two eras along with the two research methods cited. With the ethnonursing method, extensive observations and participant experiences along with interviews of many key and general informants provided many data to identify and substantiate the dominant features of the culture of American nursing.[18,19,20] The data analysis went beyond nursing images to broad perspectives and abstractions about the culture of American nurses over the past fifty years. The ethnonursing method, drawing upon emic (insider's) and an etic (outsider's) data, was especially rich to abstract and substantiate comparative data of differences in nurses' values, beliefs, and practices over the two periods presented in Figure 8.1.

Dominant Comparative Core Features of the American Culture of Nursing

The past and present cultural eras were identified to show mainly dominant themes and contrasts in values, beliefs, and practices from an earlier to the recent day culture. In fact, nurse informants used the terms "early" and "recent" to describe the periods in nursing. For example, one nurse said, "In the earlier days we would never do that but recently we do." Figure 8.1 provides a comparison of dominant themes to capture the culture of nursing over the two eras of nursing. By studying these dominant features, the nurse can learn about general features that characterize the culture of nursing. These themes can be most helpful as the nurse works with nurses who represent different eras in nursing. Such comparative data gives general features of the professional nurse in a changing profession over four decades. There is no intent to provide evaluative judgment of what is "good" or "bad" within each era, but rather it is a means to assist nurses to grasp the past and present eras of American nursing as a part of the culture of nursing. Most importantly, there is no intent to stereotype but rather to identify common themes or patterns in each cultural era. Of course, not all possible individual themes have been identified, but instead abstracted patterns and general features reflecting consistent patterns over time are given.

In the Early Era the culture of nursing showed a commitment in common and recurrent sayings, i.e., "I gave good care, total care, and comprehensive care whether in the home or in the hospital." Nurses had a deep sense of pride and commitment to provide comprehensive and total care to patients. In the early 1940s to the 1960s private duty nursing was widespread, and nurses were frequently employed to give private duty care to patients in a home context, and a few nurses were on private duty while caring for patients in the hospital. The author remembers that in 1948 she was often called to do private duty nursing in home and hospital settings. She developed a close relationship with the family and was often referred to by the family as "our

Figure 8.1
Dominant Comparative Core Features of the American Culture of Nursing

Early Era (1940-1974)	Recent Era (1975-1994)
1. Caring for patients with interpersonal skills and commitment.	1. Serving clients by relying mainly on high-tech skills and efficiency acts.
2. Other-care practices based on altruism, self-sacrifice and vocation calling with professional responsbilities.	2. Self-care practices of clients to alleviate mainly psychophysical stresses.
3. Professional dedication to work (overworked, underpaid long working hours), and being responsible.	3. Professional self-gains and interests, (better pay, shorter hours and financial gains) professionalism valued.
4. Limited supplies and equipment (improvisation to provide care).	4. Modern, high-tech equipment and supplies (limited improvisation).
5. Interdependence among nurses for comprehensive or total care.	5. Independence and autonomy of nurses for managed and primary care.
6. Deferent and compliant to authority except for strong leaders.	6. Competition with authority and limited deference and compliance.
7. Politically passive, but strong leaders used diverse management strategies.	7. Polically active with open and direct confrontation and female empowerment.
8. Male dominance and patriarchal systems (nurses as handmaidens to physicians).	8. Pursuit of equal sex rights with rise in feminism and women's issues.
9. Limited competition among nurses (get along and work together).	9. Increased nurse competition with female status seekers, assertiveness and jealousy.
10. Relationship ties tested over time.	10. Sociopolitical ties and alliances.
11. Innovative leadership ideas with practice breakthroughs.	11. "Bandwagon" leadership patterns with sociopolitical and self-gains.
12. Recognition of a few well-respected, outstanding leaders and scholars.	12. Recognition of sociopolitical leaders, pseudo-scholars and some real scholars.

family nurse." Private duty brought nurses into a close and intimate relationship with the patient and the family in their familiar home environment and community. The nurse was often viewed as part of the community and knew it.

In the Early Era, nurses had limited modern equipment and high technologies to give patient care. Nurses were known for their interpersonal caring skills and for using whatever material culture items were available for patient care. The concept of *improvisation* was much valued in the Early Era, as it signaled that a nurse could give care without lots of gadgets and that the nurse knew how to handle many uncertain situations and unexpected consequences. Most nurses were frugal, flexible, and open to making the best of any situation. They also valued and respected those in authority. Nurses interviewed said, "We seemed to know how to take hold of nursing situations and get the job done no matter what was needed and no matter how long it took to do what was expected of us." Many nurses in this era were strong leaders and could function in many different situations because they were risk-takers and felt responsible to achieve the supervisor's expectations or role assignments. Commitment to nursing was clearly evident as a vocational calling and to serve others, i.e., the patients, families, communities, or whomever needed them. Nurses were responsible, adaptable and could improvise with whatever was available to them.

In the Early Era of the 1950s and 60s nurses viewed themselves as *altruistic*, dedicated, and ready to serve others, for nursing was viewed as a vocational calling and professional responsibility. Nurses repeatedly said, "We knew how to care for patients with compassion, dedication, and empathy." They believed that their caring acts of giving comfort measures to patients, touching them, listening to their stories and providing physical and emotional support were important. Accordingly, many patients who were acutely or chronically ill often spoke of the "good nursing care and the hard-working nurses with dedication to nursing." Some patients referred to nurses in this era as "Angels of Mercy" and "responsible nurses." Spiritual aspects of care were practiced by many nurses as patients expressed their needs.

Nurses told about their almost complete dedication to "their patients" and "their work." They often worked many hours beyond the eight hour shift in order to "be sure the patient was taken care of." They also saw such behavior as part of their commitment to nursing and patients' needs. Nurses in the Early Era were loyal to their profession and did whatever was expected of them, especially by their superiors. Nurses in authority roles as head nurses or supervisors gave nurses assignments and expected nurses to complete the work. Many nurses functioned as private duty nurses in the home or community, which made them fully responsible and accountable for their nursing care practices. Usually there was no one to mentor or supervise nursing students in the home. Students and graduate nurses were always pleased to receive positive feedback from the client's family members about their nursing care practices. Nurse informants offered many stories and narratives about their direct nursing care experiences with patients and how satisfied they were when patients were fully cared for. Nurses knew "their patients" and spent time with them.

Nurses in this era showed many signs of being self-sacrificing for others. They would often sacrifice personal gains or interest for the good of the patient or for the good of nursing. Such behavior fit with the concepts of nursing as a vocational calling and a professional commitment to serve others. Some viewed self-sacrificing behavior as a part of their religious beliefs and motives; others as a part of duties, responsibilities, and expectations of caring for others as one should as a professional nurse. Nurses showed self-sacrificing behavior by being committed to patients and giving the best care possible as an expectation of being a competent, dedicated, and responsible professional nurse. Unquestionably, nurses were underpaid and overworked.

In the Early Era, some very outstanding nurse leaders showed autonomy in their decision-making, leadership, and being responsible for professional actions and decisions. A number of these leaders were clear about what should or ought to be done as a professional nurse. These leaders were exemplars to help nurses see a strong and active leader in action. Many of these nurse leaders held key positions in nursing service and in schools of nursing. Leaders of this era valued primarily care of the patient, but also education to enable nurses to become professional nurses. Young initiates were inspired by strong nursing leaders who could handle difficult situations. Many of these leaders were quite effective in handling male physicians and their oppressive dominance and authoritative manners. There were many physicians who were unreasonable and assumed power and authority over patients and staff, and who even tried to run schools of nursing. However, strong and responsible nursing leaders maintained their roles and seldom let physicians rule over them. Such nursing leaders were role models who served to demonstrate how nurses could maintain their rights with male administrators and outsmart them in female-male situations. A few male nursing administrators were among these nurse leaders, but they were usually readily accepted by male physicians as being "like one of them." There were, however, female nurses in the Early Era who were passive, dependent, and subservient to males. Being assertive and autonomous were not universal features in the Early Era of the culture of nursing.

In contrasting the Early Era with the Recent Era, one finds that nurses since 1975 have been known as active doers to and with clients. Since 1975 nurses have been known as "high-tech" and "low-touch". Nurses since this time have been technologically competent and confident of their technical skills especially in acute care settings. These nurses still keep busy administering many medications and giving high-tech treatments, fulfilling physicians' orders and meeting normative hospital expectations. It is in the hospital where nearly eighty percent of all American nurses work today.[21] Amid many nursing assistants are some clinical specialists who have been prepared through graduate nursing (master degree) programs. These nurses are generally known for their clinical competencies and capable leadership to manage client care needs. These specialists are generally knowledgeable about the use of diverse electronic or computerized equipment that pervades modern hospitals and emergency clinics in the United States. Most of these clinical nurse specialists are grounded in physiological nursing and are intrigued with high technologies and their efficacious uses in different treatment modalities. Many of these nurses are working in critical care nursing units where there are opportunities to learn about high-tech skills and to do managed care. Their ability to function in high-tech emergency and critical care units with a focus on mainly the physiological and medical treatment regimes is clearly evident today.

Most recently, there is a trend to move these nurses into "managed" primary care in community settings because their physiological assessment skills and competencies in handling high-tech equipment are valuable in homes where clients are dependent on technologies for their survival. While these nurses are competent in medical-technological areas, few are prepared to work in community nursing and very few have had preparation in transcultural nursing. To focus on assessing the holistic and the multiple social structure and cultural factors influencing people care, needs, and concerns is not evident. This current trend in primary community care will fail unless nurses become knowledgeable about the culturalogical care needs of the diverse cultures in the community. Clinical specialists with high-tech skills are known for their efficiency and ability to manage very complex and intensive hospital care situations. The "cult of efficiency" and high-tech competencies are known to characterize the acute care settings in which many of these specialists work. Monitor machines and the necessity of being skilled in the handling of emergency situations is clearly evident. The era of high-technology prevails in the present cultures of nursing with nurses being expected to handle diverse technologies and new equipment in some of the most modern technological hospitals in the world. Life and death situations are often contingent upon the competencies of critical care high-tech nurses. A number of these high-tech nurses experience "burned out" in hospitals due to such intense monitoring of acutely ill clients and the constant monitoring of high-tech, complex equipment. Transcultural holistic assessment skills and knowledge of how to provide culturally competent care are not areas of competence for most of these nurse specialists.

During the 1960s an emphasis on discovering human caring knowledge and action modes was initiated by the author and gradually captured the interest of a cadre of care scholars. Care was held as the essence and central and dominant domain of nursing.[22,23] The author held that the discipline of nursing needed a substantive knowledge domain to explain nursing and as a basis for actions and decisions. The absence of care scholars in academia and clinical areas was evident, as was the need to redirect nursing's dependency on medical ideologies, symptoms, and diseases. After the author and a small cadre of nurse scholars took a definitive stand to study human care as the central knowledge base of nursing, nurses slowly began to value human caring and to study the phenomenon.[24,25,26] The Transcultural Nursing Society, the National Care Conference Group, and the International Association of Caring have been the major organizations to support actively the study of humanistic and scientific care in nursing since the late 1960s. Only since the mid 1980s have other nurses begun to study systematically caring phenomena in different areas of nursing. There still remains far too limited evidence of the use of caring research knowledge in clinical practices, especially with technology-oriented nurses grounded heavily in the physical aspects of nursing practices. The words of care and caring are being used in physiological and primary care nursing practices but with limited explication and use of transcultural care-specific constructs such as comfort, compassion, presence, nurturance, and others into their practices. Until these caring constructs are explicitly used in high-tech clinical specialists' practices, one can anticipate that only partial or fragmented nursing care practices will occur.

Another trend characterizing the culture of nursing in the Recent Era has been an emphasis on self-care ideology, theory, and practices. This trend began in the mid 1970s with Dorothea Orem's Self Care Theory.[27] Self-care is largely an Anglo-American middle and upper class practice which is quickly adopted by nurses of similar cultural values and life experiences who value self-reliance. Initially, the theory emphasized nurses providing care where "self-care deficits" with patients could be identified. This deficit need was largely of a psychophysical nature, and the nurse was to encourage the client to meet this deficit in diverse ways. Nurses relying on high-technologies in patient care are adept at encouraging clients to take an active role in self-care. The lack of knowledge by many self-care nurse advocates using transcultural nursing perspectives of cultural differences is limited. The absence of such culture care knowledge has raised questions about the use of self-care practices with cultural groups and individuals transculturally.[28] The author's research and that of others in transcultural nursing reveals nursing problems with the use of the self-care theory and practices when other-care expectations and beliefs are dominant in some cultures.[29] Resistance from non-Anglo-American clients has been identified by transcultural nurses because self-care ideology may be in conflict with the cultural norms and values of people who rely upon *other-care* practices based on their cultural value expectations.

Still another area of contrast between the Early and Recent Eras in the culture of nursing is that nurses of the latter era tend to be centered more on their self-interests and economic gains than on the professional values of dedication, commitment, and care for or with others. The seeking of self-interests and gains by today's nurse is often expressed by nurses as an important means to improve the professional image and status of nursing. Better salaries and more favorable working conditions are firmly upheld by many nurses today. Self-interests, status, and gains have led some female nurses to pursue top executive positions in order to advance their personal and professional interests. Most importantly, female nurses are seeking comparable pay for comparable worth positions that have been traditionally held by males in American society. It is encouraging to see female and male nurses advancing themselves with advanced master and doctoral nursing education and certification. They are seeking new positions in nursing as well as honors and recognition. Thus a focus on autonomy, self-gains, assertive behavior, empowerment of women, and achieving top professional and corporate positions are helping to make American nurses visible and publicly recognized. This trend has been a major pattern in the new era of American nursing especially during the past two decades. Struggles remain, however, for female nurses to get and retain top positions due to budget cuts, recessions, and competition with males for such positions. The current catchwords or metaphors of "cut backs," "economic crunches," "the bottom line is cost reduction," and an emphasis on "managed care" all have symbolic meaning of continued struggles and of changing economic and sociocultural conditions for nurses in the present decade. The critical issue is for nurses to include care into nursing practices with a transcultural focus.

Currently, interprofessional competition is evident with nurse leaders and consultants being removed from some of the high-salaried positions. Often nurses with master and doctoral degrees are dismissed due to budget cut backs and other reasons related to cost reductions. This recent trend of dismissing or laying off female nurses remains of concern, as their expertise is much needed in all health systems, but especially in corporate organizational cultures. Only a few American nurses have broken the glass ceiling amid some valiant efforts. Thus, the self-gain, self-interest, and seeking top positions to regulate or control practices in nursing contrasts with nurses of the past era whose interests were different. In fact, self-interests and gains were largely a cultural taboo or viewed almost as counter to being a professional nurse in the early culture of American nursing. Let us look next at the specific culture of nursing values, beliefs, and practices in the two eras.

Authority Relationships and Female Rights

In the Early Era of nursing most nurses were socialized to be deferent to and respectful of those in authority. Nurses were generally taught to yield to male physicians, hospital administrators, presidents, religious leaders, and others in authority roles.[30,31] Males were in authority roles. Male physicians were viewed as knowing what was best for women, especially nurses. Physicians held almost complete power to enforce their authoritarian roles in hospitals, clinics, and university medical systems. They controlled the clinical and hospital settings and wanted to control nurses and nursing education. However, the strong female nurse leaders referred to earlier knew how to handle most of these hegemonic male leaders. In fact, these nurse leaders were quite clever in getting what they needed, often indirectly so as to not threaten or make male physicians and hospital administrators too defensive. Some nurses listened to males, but remained firm and authoritative at the appropriate times. Leadership successes included holding male leaders in their places in hospitals and preventing physicians from taking over schools of nursing, quite a feat in the Early Era. The author and many other nurses witnessed these attempted power and control takeovers by male physicians in many situations, but especially during the Early Era of nursing culture.[32,33]

Political nursing was not a topic for discussion in the Early Era, nor was the idea recognized until the author introduced one of the first articles in nursing written in the mid 1960s and published in the 1970s.[34] Since then, political aspects of nursing are now a dominant and frequent topic in hospitals and schools of nursing. Unquestionably, female political strategies were clearly needed for survival and for the full development of nursing as a profession and discipline amid male medical dominance. Interestingly, most of the strong and successful political administrative nurse leaders who made pathways for future nursing leaders never relinquished their goals to achieve what was believed best for the profession. These female leaders of the Early Era could be viewed as exemplary role models, as many were quite skilled at assessing male leadership behaviors and retaining their administrative positions and keeping schools of nursing going despite difficult hurdles. Creative management strategies and uncanny leadership skills were important to establish a number of significant directions in nursing education and service. Some of the strong nurse leaders of this era should be studied with oral and written histories to discover more fully how female leaders succeeded in highly patriarchal systems since the 1940s in the United States, but also in other places in the world.

The feminist movement in nursing was an outgrowth of biases, discriminatory acts, and oppression by male leaders in health care systems and other organizations.

Female leaders made their concerns known and took steps to alleviate problems that had greatly limited nursing achievements and progress. Most assuredly, cultural values, norms, and organizational practices had to be changed in most situations to help nurse leaders to be heard, recognized, valued, and respected in health care systems. The author, then dean of the School of Nursing at the University of Washington in the late 1960s and early 1970s, recalls how it was very difficult to raise the salaries of nursing faculty and female deans, and to establish the first departmental structures in nursing schools in the United States because male physicians and administrative leaders believed nursing did not have the same market value as medicine and wanted to control nursing. It was clear, however, that female professions and schools had lower salaries, and yet some nurses had more education and expertise than their male counterparts. Slowly, such salary and power inequities were changed, but often only after legal suits and persistent actions. It was not until 1975 that nursing salaries began to increase in the United States.

Today equal rights and respect for women nurse is gradually being respected and acknowledged in health disciplines and in the public sector. Valuing nurses' experiences, skills, and creative contributions are important and frequent topics for discussion by nurses not only in the United States but in many places in the world where nurses' rights and concerns merit equal attention as males'. There are, however, female nurses who continue to struggle to obtain favorable salaries, working conditions, employment benefits, and basic institutional needs. There are also come cultures in the world where women are well-respected, have equal rights, and can make decisions in domestic and public arenas. Transcultural nursing research has helped nurses expand their awareness of these realities and pursue comparative cultural knowledge and experiences, especially related to gender roles in Western and non-Western cultures.

In the Early Era in the United States there was no question that nurses were overworked and underpaid. The author remembers that her beginning staff nurse salary in 1948 was $5,000 per year. Through the active political and economic leadership of the American Nurses Association, the National League for Nursing, and other organizations, better salaries and other benefits have been forthcoming to staff nurses, administrators, faculty, and others in nursing. This active stance has also contributed to a better working environment for nurses. In 1994 the beginning staff nurse salary in large urban hospitals was reported to be near $40,000, and clinical specialists and primary nurse practitioners with masters and doctoral degrees in nursing may be earning $55,000 to $75,000 in the United States, especially if connected with major university research and health science centers.[35] These are noteworthy changes which have significantly changed the image, worth, respect, and status of professional nurses in the United States. These cultural changes sharply contrast with nursing in the Early Era in which nurses seldom complained about their salaries, took limited political action to change their economic status, and accepted what they were given. Nurses are taught today in schools of nursing how to become politically active and use empowerment strategies to negotiate and bargain for ways to improve their salaries, employment rights, and work environment.

One would be remiss not to identify that in the Early Era many American hospitals and schools of nursing had working conditions for nurses that were often undesirable. Nurses usually had very limited or undesirable space to do their work in clinical and academic facilities. They not only had limited space to prepare medications but also had no space for staff conferences and in-service meetings within the hospital. Schools of nursing often had to use buildings undesired by medicine or other disciplines, until federal monies were obtained by the courageous nurse leaders of the era. By the mid 1970s in the United States hospitals and several schools of nursing had comfortable modern conference rooms, well-equipped and well-lighted nurses stations, and other conveniences such as conference rooms, lounges, dining areas obtained with federal funds. Working conditions and salaries have steadily improved in the American culture of nursing due largely to the American Nurses Association and the American Colleges of Dean's political and economic actions. This has also led to an improvement in faculty and staff morale and the self-esteem of nurses.

Still another feature of the culture of nursing in the Early Era was that hospital staff nurses were often exploited by working many additional hours with low salaries. Likewise, nursing students were also exploited as they were used to provide major nursing services to hospitals with no or very limited pay and sometimes with limited faculty guidance. Hospitals were largely maintained by nursing students (three year non-degree programs) in which students provided most of the direct patient care services without pay for their clinical work. This exploitation of hospital nursing students continued in the United States until nursing education programs moved into institutions of higher education, i.e., colleges and universities. When this occurred, nursing students became learners with educational opportunities comparable to other university students on campus. Today the apprenticeship role of nursing students in hospitals has nearly disappeared in the United States except for a few hospitals that still control and exploit nursing students primarily from diploma nursing programs. Moreover, nursing students are often employed in hospitals and other health agencies today after they become registered nurses. These students can receive salaries commensurate with other staff nurses roles and preparation, role responsibilities, and areas of expertise.

Political Power and Politics

As indicated earlier, one of the major contrasts between the Early Era and today is that many nurses today have become politically active and informed about diverse nursing, but national and some international health care issues. Some professional nurses have become politicians and are astute about political aspects of nursing and how to confront political leaders, legislators, and other politicians about their health platforms and policies. Nursing students are socialized today to be politically active and to achieve specific goals through nursing organizations such as the Student Nurses Association, the Transcultural Nursing Society, the American Nurses Association, the National League for Nursing, the American Association of Colleges of Nursing, political action groups, and other organizations. As a consequence, young nurses are active in local, state, national, and international organizations and some are holding key paid political positions. While registered nurses have not gained presidential positions worldwide, there are nurses holding legislative and key government positions in the United States and elsewhere. These are noteworthy cultural changes from the Early Era, when most nurses were politically inactive or it was viewed as improper for a professional nurse to be politically active or to take public political positions on nursing matters.

Politics, religion, and sex were generally known as the three cultural taboo areas in nursing in the Early Era. Granted there were some politically successful nurse leaders in the Early Era who handled the dominance and authority of male physicians, hospital administrators, and university officials, but such political leaders were seldom discussed or promoted in nursing in the pre-1970 era. The author recalls that as the first full-time President of the American Association of Deans of Colleges of Nursing from 1970 to 1972 she led a group of deans to the Office of Budget Management in Washington, D.C. to let government officials know of nursing's critical need for capitation funds for schools of nursing. This became known as the first "March of Deans on Capital Hill" which was successful and led to schools of nursing receiving capitation funds to advance nursing education. At that landmark meeting with government leaders in 1971, the deans learned about the politicians' image of nurses primarily as "pillow fluffers" without awareness that nurses were the direct care giver and managers of client care. Such shocking gaps of knowledge by top governmental officials about nurses in service and education awakened deans and faculty of schools of nursing to the importance of political strategies and action modalities. Since the early 1970s nurses have markedly increased their political activities on practically anything that can impact nursing. But it is interesting that one of the popular terms used in nursing circles today is to "empower" nurses.

Faculty are teaching about empowering nurses, and taking action related to empowerment modes for political action in nursing service and education. This linguistic term still reflects the culture of nursing to get and retain power for changes and needs in nursing. While no nurse can really empower another nurse, still the image and message is like contagious magic to have nurses gain power from diverse sources to achieve goals for self or the nursing profession.

In the Early Era patriarchalism reigned in hospitals, community agencies, universities, and key executive and political positions were usually held by men. Moreover, these men often received salaries three to four times higher than women in similar roles and with similar responsibilities. Such salary differentials were evident with nursing deans and faculty who were doctorally prepared in two disciplines. As noted earlier, several strong nursing leaders of the Early Era had vision and knew what needed to be changed to move nursing forward. Several female leaders began slowly to break "glass ceilings" to get new positions as president or vice president and to receive salaries comparable to those of their male counterparts. In the mid 1960s the author also encouraged several nurses to study law and politics through the Nurse Scientist Program. Today there are a number of nurse lawyers functioning in top leadership positions in nursing associations and educational systems especially in the NLN, ANA, AACN, and NLA. These developments have helped change the culture of nursing to advance political, economic, and legal skills in nursing. However, transcultural comparative political and legal knowledge in Western and non-Western cultures remains a virtually untapped knowledge and skill area.

Still today there are far too few males in nursing, even though one of the first schools of nursing in the United States was for men on the East Coast. Male nurses also have their struggles in nursing because of negative views held by some female nurses and a fear that male nurses will ultimately dominate the nursing profession. Male nurses are reexamining their roles and rights with female nurses and within many general American gender role changes in nursing in the care of people from birth to death. There are male nurses who share power and equal rights with female nurses. Recently, male nurses have become organized with a national associations that encourages discussion of "male concerns including males abuses" and other political and professional issues threatening their status within nursing. It is reasonable to predict that cultural backlash and legal suits from male nurses in the future will occur and that male nurses will seek ways to protect their rights within the profession. Thus the gender battle in nursing is open with unresolved issues to be addressed in the American culture of nursing.

Competition and the Culture of Nursing

Another comparative features noted in Figure 8.1 has been the cultural value of competition. While competition for human and physical resources has always existed among nurses in service and education arenas, today there is more open and higher competition among American nurses and colleagues for scarce resources in relation to perceived needs. Competitive behavior among nurse administrators and educators is expressed through direct confrontation, managing resources, and group alignments. Negative gossip and putting nurses out of favor in order to get control or to be recognized generally requires competitive moves and social alliances. There is presently a strong desire for nurses to be socially recognized among female colleagues in order to gain prestigious awards, or to gain access to top positions within and outside of nursing. Granted, some degree of competition is usually healthy and expected among human beings, but sometimes female nursing competition becomes destructive, demeaning, humiliating, and unethical. This concern has been limitedly discussed among American nurses but statements are made such as, "Nurses are their own worst enemies;" "You can never trust your best nurse friend when it comes to what some nurses will do to get what they want;" "You scratch my back and I'll scratch yours;" and "You got to fight for your rights to survive among female nurses." Female jealousy and the need for recognition, the author holds, are major professional problems that need far more attention. It is of deep concern that some of our most outstanding and true nurse scholars, leaders, educators, clinicians, and administrators do not get recognized due to female jealousies, or not being in the right social nurse group to get recognized or promoted. There is still a strange norm in American nursing to give often recognition to unqualified and less capable nurses, including minorities, when they have less competence and are less qualified. This trend appears related to female competition, female jealousies, and close sociopolitical ties of female nurses with those they wish to recognize to maintain social relationships. In the culture of nursing in the United States more attention needs to be given to outstanding and true leaders in nursing who have made substantial contributions to nursing and society.

Competition among nurses in the present era appears related to nurses establishing strong sociopolitical ties with women whom they view as influential, powerful, or in the know to gain status and recognition or to be placed in highly desired professional roles or positions. Nurses already in a key position often bring their next closest friend into a related position within the same agency, hospital, or academic institution. Many social and political alliances can be found in the culture of nursing such as with nurses who get into the perceived prestigious American Academy of Nursing. From the perspective of the author and other observers in the

Academy, nurses are often sponsored by and voted in through their social friends who have done favors or promoted them in the past. Strong political and friendship ties in the Academy exist among the members which further increases social and political alliances. It also tends to decrease getting members who are among the most outstanding nurses in nursing. As a consequence, some of the most scholarly and talented nurse leaders are not in the Academy nor in the sociopolitical Institute of Medicine. Some nurses may not be chosen for Sigma Theta Tau awards because of not having social or political nurses to sponsor them. It is interesting that when some outstanding nurse scholars have discovered the growing social and political aspects of these Associations they refuse to show interest or to join the sociopolitical clan. As a consequence, pseudo leaders, non-distinguished scholars, and sociopolitical competitive leaders become evident in these nursing organizations. While minorities are sought to increase the numbers or visibility of the nursing associations, some of these nurses may not be outstanding but become token members to increase the representation of minorities in the nursing organizations. Thus, current concerns exist about nursing organizations and how true scholars and distinguished nurse leaders are recognized and honored to advance nursing and to promote a favorable public image of the American culture of nursing.

In the Early Era of nursing there were a number of outstanding and distinctive nurse leaders who had achieved their status as unique leaders with patterned and established contributions over time. These leaders were recognized and respected for having advanced nursing in unique ways such as Lillian Wald, Lavinia Dock, Isabel Hampton Robb, and Mary Brewster. These leaders were well known because of their unique leadership ability to make substantive, cutting edge contributions to nursing. In the culture of nursing and from an anthropological perspective, these were the achieved leaders, whereas today there are many leaders who are proclaimed or ascribed leaders by virtue of sociopolitical and friendship ties. Without promoting and reaffirming some of the most outstanding breakthrough scholars and leaders in nursing, much which could advance the discipline and profession of nursing is being lost. Hopefully, with awareness of these cultural patterns and trends, nursing organizations and nurses will reexamine these tendencies and others.

There is also a tendency of American nurses and others worldwide not to recognize outstanding leaders or scholars until they are dead. This appears related to a tendency to avoid controversies that may be related to female jealousy to avoid open problems surrounding outstanding or controversial leaders. Controversial and dynamic leaders are often some of the most outstanding, successful, and provocative leaders in nursing. In fact these leaders are usually great risk-takers and willing to uphold their convictions and goals. Mediocrity and dependency are seldom these leaders' aspirations. The author holds it is time to recognize these cultural issues and to study the culture of nursing in local, regional, and national arenas for areas of change.

Unquestionably, American nurses have long valued higher education as a means to help nurses gain knowledge and skills and become competent in their profession. There are some highly innovative, talented, and creative American nurses who have been innovators in nursing education and services for many decades. Many of these nurses are known by their colleagues, graduate student nurses, and non-nurse leaders, and scholars. Again, some of these outstanding leaders may not be recognized in their homelands due to political reasons, friendship times, and female jealousies. Interestingly, these outstanding nurse leaders are often held in high esteem by nurses in other countries, but may not be recognized as a "prophet in one's homeland" within the American culture of nursing. Becoming aware of such cultural norm tendencies can help nurses deal with less desirable features and change images of the profession.

Glimpses from Other Cultures of Nursing

It has been of great interest to be a participant-observer with nurses in other countries as they share their emic local views and knowledge about nursing cultures. Some overseas nurses are quick to compare American nursing with their own cultural values and action modes. In the author's extensive travels, there is the perception that American nurses are friendly and the innovative leaders in the world of nursing. But some nurses contend that American nurses are a bit too ethnocentric and fail to value nurses' contributions in other countries. Generally, nurses from other countries are highly laudatory of American nurses because of their willingness to educate, share information, and of their generosity and willingness to help nurses in other countries. Nurses from other countries expect American nurses to be prepared in transcultural nursing in their homeland, before trying to establish educational contracts, visits, or exchanges. They also hope American nurses will learn to speak different languages especially that of the culture in which they will be visiting or working, so that they can better understand local cultures. Most overseas nurses have been quick to see the importance of transcultural nursing and culture care, and are eager to have shared experiences.

Probably the greatest challenge for American nurses and other nurses worldwide is to realize that there are cultural differences and some similarities among nurses in the world that must be studied and fully recognized. It is the cultural diversities that can stimulate our thinking, and it is the commonalties that help to link nurses together in areas of mutual interest. At the present time, the diversities appear more evident worldwide.[36] For example, the author has discovered in her several visits to Australia, that Australian nurses tend to act independently and speak frankly about outsiders.

They seem to feel confident about what is best, or right about certain issues after studying the matter. Australian nurses are comfortable speaking out, confronting, and challenging other nurse leaders, generally without personal grievances. It is of special interest that Australian nurses tend to cut down figuratively what they call a "tall poppy" or a nurse leader who moves too fast in leadership or becomes too pompous in attempting to move into certain prestigious positions or roles.[37] Australian nurses know how to "cut off the stem of the tall and wild poppy" in order to symbolically curtail the growth of a "wild nurse." There is a covert cultural practice in Australia to reduce the nurse's pompous leadership when it appears to be getting out of hand. In so doing, it puts the nurse back into an egalitarian status with other Australian nurses. It also controls nurses who might exert too much intense leadership and controls nurses before they are professionally ready for top leadership roles. Such a phenomenon was fascinating for the author to discover in talking with Australian nurses and in observing aspects of this cultural norm.

Many other cultures of nursing await discovery to enable nurses to know some of the distinct and common features of their nursing cultures. One would be remiss not to give a glimpse of the British nursing culture, which the author has had the opportunity to observe, experience, and read about with British nursing associates over time. The British culture of nursing reflects great pride and respect for their strong, early leaders in nursing who helped to shape the profession. Florence Nightingale's leadership set the pace and pride for British nurses. As a consequence, they have great difficulty and reluctance to recognize other significant and outstanding transcultural leaders such as Jeanne Mance of Canada, whose significant work preceded Nightingale's by more than 200 years.[38] Florence Nightingale's image reigns pervasively among nurses in Britain. British nursing ethnocentrism is evident, which has made some nurses reluctant to learn about other nurses in the world who have made contributions to nursing equal or sometimes greater than those of some of their own nurses. Besides Nightingale, British nurses are also proud of other nurse leaders and extol their work.

With the British nursing culture highly valuing their historical legacy, there are signs of attempts to maintain the status quo in nursing and accommodate only urgent or imperative changes or changes which are mandated or fully justified. Several British nurses told the author, "If changes are being promoted, one finds traditional nurse leaders remaining as the powerful conservative in-group to control what exists and not to make any major changes." These nurses held that, "Older British nurses are quite conservative and very guarded about making any new, drastic, or sudden changes in nursing or in the existing health care systems." As these key British nurse informants said, "We do not want to upset the British apple cart or to lose our treasured, traditional ways." There are however, young British nurses and nurses from other countries who are eager for changes in British nursing. These nurses say it is difficult to change outdated British nursing practices or to implement modern values due to strong historical and traditional values of older nurses. They contend that outdated and dysfunctional practices have been used for years but need to be changed to fit the modern world. Younger nurses with counterculture ideas are trying to modernize British nursing and to be more like modern American nursing, "but they feel they have limited authority and power to do so." Maintaining order, normative standards, and preserving the past are valued and important in the British nursing culture. British nurses value controversy and intellectual arguments. They are willing to discuss matters that are worthy of debate and discussion. British nursing with *colonialization* has had a great influence on nursing in many places where people were under their rule. The current European unification plans are a recent development. There are nurses in Europe who have different views about the unification of Europe with some nurses fearing that British nurses will dominate nursing in all areas of Europe as the country did in the earlier colonial times. The diversity of nursing in many North, South, East, and West countries in Europe greatly challenges the idea of unification within nursing. Nurses from Russia and Eastern countries are just rebounding after the Communist fall and have different needs and goals.

In considering the culture of Canadian nurses, there are some similarities to the American nursing culture, but there are more differences than similarities. Since her first consultation visit and keynote addresses in Canada in the early 1960s, the author has found that Canadian nurses are realists but also visionaries who forge ahead and take action when necessary. Jeanne Mance's mid seventeenth century pioneering hospital work in Montreal along with the Grey Nuns of the mid eighteenth century served well as role models for many Canadian nurses.[39] These great leaders held to the spirit of preserving human life, practicing, caring, and nourishing the spiritual needs of those serviced. Throughout the history of Canadian nursing, nurses have been resourceful and adventuresome in establishing important directions. Canadian nurses have had strong nursing leaders who have served well their profession and country. While Canadian nurses have been influenced by British and American nursing, still they have developed some unique ways to help people in their homelands and overseas. In recent decades, Canadians have become more intensely transculturally oriented and helpful with nursing care practices in West Africa, South America, China, and other places in the world. Professionalism permeates the Canadian nursing culture in lifeways, standards, values, and actions. Their organized nursing groups such as the Canadian Nurses Association, the provincial nursing associations, and nursing unions adhere rather firmly to professional roles and responsibilities as they continue to shape Canada's nursing destiny and future.[40] There are many signs of assertive thinking and acting in their culture.

In recent years, Canadian nurse leaders have struggled with provincial legislation in their efforts to move master and doctoral nursing programs forward. For example, it has taken several years to get master of nursing degrees (M.S.N.) and doctoral nursing programs (Ph.D.) established in Canada.[41] Canadian nurses have also struggled with provincial governments to get funds and to maintain their self-regulatory profession amid diverse leaders. They have had to function in large professional bureaucracies, as most Canadian nurses work in public sector institutions rather than private ones. As Canadian nurses function within their national health program, they have learned to value transcultural nursing because many diverse Native Canadian, English, Scottish, and other cultural heritage groups settled in their vast territory over a long time span. Native Canadian nurses, like others in the country, remain restless as they seek ways to reduce the cost of living, increasing self-governance, and putting more political controls in the people's hands. While these challenges are for all Canadians, Canadian nurses providing health care to many transcultural population groups in remote places within and outside Canada continue to seek financial resources to support their work. In general, the culture of nursing in Canada reflects nurses who are strong foragers, capable, and persistent leaders, and who are providing quality care to many diverse cultures in their vast land. The cultural values of commitment, vision, hard work, and strong determination characterize the culture of Canadian nurses. Canadian nurses are keenly aware of multiculturalism and urgently need to establish graduate transcultural nursing programs to improve the health of their people and the many immigrants in their country. While other cultures of nursing could be identified and discussed, the above examples illustrate how important it is for nurses to have some knowledge of nursing cultures in the world and the ways they may be similar or different.

The American Tribes of Nursing

Since the author first wrote about the tribes of nursing in the United States in the late 1960s, nursing students and others have frequently requested this information. The idea of "tribes of nursing" came to the author during her frequent consultations, visits, work, and interactions with nurses in different regions of the United States.[42] The anthropological concept of tribe seemed appropriate to describe cultural variations among nursing groups within the national American culture of nursing. A tribe refers to a large number of people who claim common group identity, are generally loosely organized, but remain an identifiable large group with shared values and lifeways. Accordingly, since the early 1970s, the author has identified four major nursing tribes in different regions in the United States.[43,44,45,46]

The first tribe identified by the author was found in the southern region of the United States. The author appropriately called these nurses the "Friendly Tribe" because they were friendly to outsiders and maintained an open and hospitable attitude toward strangers. Nurses of this tribe had a positive view about people, life, and what they were doing in nursing. They showed an easy going and conservative pace of living and working. They welcomed and wanted other nurses to join them in their nursing culture with its Southern lifeways. Most of these tribal members were Southern women who had been born and lived most of their lives in the southern region of the United States. Besides being exceptionally polite to strangers, they tried not to offend, confront, or make trouble with anyone. They would use Southern jokes, stories, and expressions of humor to ease any tensions or controversies and to maintain positive relationships with others.

While serving as a visiting professor at one of the major southern universities, the author also learned that deans of schools of nursing knew the best ways to get what they needed from their male university colleagues. Their approach was interesting as they used a warm and friendly greeting with common Southern courtesies and chit-chat. They would remain polite and interested in male viewpoints. They avoided any open confrontation with male leaders, as they held such behaviors to be inappropriate to their cultural practices. These nurse leaders knew that aggressive female behavior often turns Southern males off resulting in negative outcomes. Interestingly, these female nursing deans were quite successful in getting what they most desired from their male academic and most hospital leaders.

Nurses from the Southern tribe were closely attached to their families and to home life values, which they firmly upheld. The tribal members seemed relaxed about domestic, political, and economic nursing issues in their conversation even though there were a number of serious political and economic matters to address. The Southern tribe was quick to state and reinforce their cultural values and lifeways when working with nurses from other places in the United States. They would speak of "how they did things in the South and how they differed from the Yankee nurses in the North." A nurse from New York spoke about such cultural differences. She said, "I sure see a lot of differences between Northern and Southern nursing practitioners, especially the way we practice nursing in New York City. I have lived in this Southern area for two years and I find the nurses are very different. They are too passive, kind, relaxed, and conservative for me. They are also too deferent to males." Another nurse from Minnesota said, "These nurses are friendly and good nurses, but we live and act differently in the North. We live a faster and more competitive and assertive pace of life than these Southern nurses." She continued, "We Northerners are far more work-oriented and get more done in one nursing shift than most of these easy-going Southern nurses do in three days." These non-Southern nurses were also concerned about losing their clinical skills and returned to their Northern homelands within a short span of time. Such comments and other similar ones commonly heard by non-Southern nurses provided some important comparative insights about differences in cultural lifeways, values, and practices of the Southern nursing tribe.

The second nursing tribe identified in the United States by the author was called the "Novel Tribe." This tribe has many members dispersed along the west coast of the United States, with the largest numbers found in California. This tribe is distinct in that they tend to view themselves as establishing and promoting new ideas and novel approaches to old issues or problems in nursing. Although there was variability among these tribal members, still a dominant feature of the nurses was to do something quite different from what most nurses were doing in other places in the United States. Their tribal leaders wanted to make their ideas known publicly as novel ones and to market and sell them to nurses across the United States and overseas. In fact, some nurses from the Midwest Tribe often said to the author, "Whatever these Western nurses develop, it tends to get lots of written and oral publicity as something entirely new or novel, but some ideas are not really that new." The concern was that their ideas diffused rapidly across the country and tended to be adopted in a short span of time. The Novel Tribe members are competitive in making their ideas known to many nurse leaders so that their ideas would be used widely by many nurses. These tribal members believed their ideas to be some of the most exciting to advance the nursing profession and to deal with national problems. Other nurses held that the Novel Tribe needed to give further thought to their ideas and refine them before selling the, as the ideas were often viewed as premature and needing further research or documentation. Nonetheless, the Novel Tribe usually received national recognition for their innovations or special contributions. These nurses often proclaimed, "We were the first in the United States with that idea, theory, or practice mode and want other nurses to use our ideas in order to move nursing forward." Some Western tribal members are not only highly competitive, maintain elitism, but can be destructive and non-supportive to one another.

Amid the innovative Novel Tribe members, there are some very conservative nurses who dislike their progressive, liberal, or novel advocates. These nurses can still be found in small rural communities in Oregon, Washington, and California. Their conservative views are known to the Novel members, but they seldom win on the innovative ideas. Interestingly, many of the conservative nurses are immigrant nurses from overseas who have been living in small rural communities and working in nearby general hospitals.

Still another distinctive feature of the Novel Tribe has been the tendency to dress in the latest fashions, wear bright colors, and present some of the latest fashions such as "exotic" earrings, belts, head pieces, and dresses. Many of these nurses are from large cosmopolitan cities such as San Francisco and Los Angeles. They readily identified with other nurses when they attended conferences in other regions of the United States because of their dress and mannerisms.

The author called the third tribe the "Historic Tribe." This tribe was firmly committed to preserving their nursing heritage as well as their regional artifacts at all costs. Most of the members mainly lived on the East Coast particularly in the northeastern and eastern coastal areas of the United States such as in Maine, Connecticut, New York, New Hampshire, and Massachusetts. These tribal members make firm claims about, "Holding the history of American nursing." They greatly treasure ways to preserve the traditional features of the nursing profession. Most of these nurses were born and had lived in the area most of their lives. These nurses are eager to tell or show strangers about their rich cultural history affecting nursing leaders with their practices and material artifacts. They were proud to say, "We are true Bostonians, Connecticut, or New York nurses who have preserved the American nursing culture for years." They also said, "This is the best place to live and practice nursing, as we have the rich American history of nursing here." While these tribal nurses may leave the area for various reasons, they prefer not to be gone very long and are always eager to return to their tribal area. The Historic Tribe not only cherished what they held as true American nursing values and practices, but they are eager to preserve, and to make future contributions. They remain alert and sensitive to transmitting their cultural heritage features to succeeding generations of nursing students and to outsiders. They have a deep historical, respect for most nursing leaders. They value archival materials, places and symbols of past nurses and nursing practices in their historic settings.

Nurses who have been born and reared in the Historic Tribe often have some difficulty with the idea of transculturalism and adopting other cultural lifeways, beliefs, and norms because of their ethnocentrism. For example, several nurses from Connecticut, West Virginia, Massachusetts, and New Jersey told the author, "We have always had lots of strangers coming to this area. They are very different from us and yet they are like us." Another key informant said, "Why would anyone want to come here if they failed to value and appreciate our great historical roots and places." They are aware that many European immigrants and nurses came to their region early in American history. These tribal nurses believe that anything and everything worthwhile in nursing really began in this region of the United States. They are very proud of their cultural heritage.

The Historical Tribal members have many old nursing documents and artifacts that reaffirm nursing's cultural identity. When nurses from other tribal areas come to visit or to work with members of this tribe, they are quick to present cultural artifacts, but also to share stories and special events of nurses. For example, a nurse from the Novel Tribe was employed in a very historical hospital for three years. She told the author, "I am ready to go back to California as these nurses are far too conservative, ethnocentric, and too protective of their traditional ideas and historical nursing practices." She found that nothing pleased these tribal nurses more than to talk about their cultural heritage, historic artifacts, and the places to visit in the area. In general, the Historic Tribe emphasized that nurses need to be active to preserve historic places and to value nursing's early, pioneering work in America and many noteworthy contributions. Within this Tribe there were some younger generation nurses with different values who were eager for major changes from the preoccupation with historical views and perspectives. Interestingly, the true Historic Tribal members prefer not to make major changes in nursing or to relinquish their values in preserving nursing's historical legacy in the region. Doing what was historically proper, acceptable, and valued characterized this Historic Tribe. Many of these nurses remain powerful political leaders and advocates of nursing today.

The fourth major nursing group the author called the "Blue Collar Tribe." These nurses reside in the Midwest or the midlands of the United States in largely rural agricultural areas and in cities such as Chicago, Detroit, Minneapolis, Pierre, Omaha, Iowa City, and Kansas City. The term "Blue Collar Tribe" reflects that these nurses are hard, common and practical nurses who were employed in industrial, urban, or rural health care centers in the region. Besides being oriented to agricultural and industrial lifeways, they are known for their ability "to pitch in and get things done soon," rather than delaying to get tasks started. These nurses are capable of handling a great variety of different nursing roles, tasks, and jobs. They are known for their ability to improvise, adapt to new tasks, and achieve specific desire goals. These tribal nurses are frequently referred to by outsiders as the "down to earth nursing folks who know who to get work done and can make a difference in nursing practices."

The Blue Collar Tribe are economically and politically astute because of their long history of dealing with strong labor unions or politically motivated urban and rural groups. Most of these nurses are knowledgeable about collective bargaining and negotiating modes with labor groups and organizations. These nurses are generally united by a strong work ethic, know how to deal with unions, and complex bureaucratic organizations. They have learned how to strategize with competitive rural-urban groups. They know how to adapt to terrible agricultural and industrial losses due to many factors such as natural disasters, industrial crises, lay offs, and the use of many new and different technologies. Generally the Blue Collar nurses know "their people" in the rural communities and those residing in small communities outside urban areas. They often have to deal with low and high context expectations. Rural nurses are usually challenged by urban nurses on professional issues and trends, and offer valuable solutions to urban concerns.

Having lived for fourteen years in Michigan, the author found Blue Collar tribal members tend to give far more medications under physicians' standing orders and rely more on high-tech modes in caring for clients than nurses in other United States regional areas. The administration of many medications and using many different kinds of high-tech equipment was often explained as our nursing care practices in an industrial and union area. Nurses' strikes and boycotts were also viewed as essential to prevent economic losses to nurses and to improve employment practices. Most nurses prefer to fight rather than acquiesce to standard of practices that were not favorable or desirable to nursing. Such practices and values were explained to the author as part of their long term physician-nurse relationships in industrial urban settings, union philosophy, and available high technologies in their hospital.

The Blue Collar Tribe, with many female nurse executive administrators and supervisors, distinguishes themselves today by wearing two-piece business suits as they work in hospitals, academic settings, and top administrative positions. The business suits are often similar to male executive styles. These suits symbolize nurses' desire for power, businesslike endeavors, and to deal with patriarchal norms. Staff nurses tend to wear white or blue two-piece pant suits while working in hospitals and community agencies. Several tribal nurses told the author, "If someone wears bright colored dresses, suits, or uniforms (except in children's units), we generally know these nurses are probably outsiders or from the West Coast as this is not our usual fashion.

The Blue Collar tribal members generally have local group or union nurses as their friends and co-workers who can be relied upon in times of need. This is also evident among rural nurses because interdependence and group work is valued in professional role expectations. Rural nurses are generally viewed as practical and are less aggressive than urban nurses. Rural nurses are the exceptionally hard workers who know how to improve and deal with rural situations. The Blue Collar Tribe are known for being practical and getting things done quickly and effectively. Although cultural variation exists among the rural and urban tribal members, still there are common bonds that make them feel connected to and supportive of one another.

In general, the Blue Collar Tribe has not been an especially showy tribe and does not push for publicity or to make their achievements known quickly and in dramatic ways. They are moderately conservative in their viewpoints and actions. They are also known for their persistent attitude, diligent work ethic, and their ethical and moral viewpoints. Blue Collar nurses have only recently begun to market their unique skills and contributions in a comparable way to the Novel Tribe of the West Coast. The sharing of ideas among the Blue Collar Tribe occurs when friendship and professional ties are well established, trusted, and respected. These tribal members have been recently advocating and encouraging nurses to seek power, empower female nurses and active in political-legislative affairs. They are also becoming interested in transcultural nursing, managed care, and entrepreneurial practices.

The above four American Tribes of Nursing, namely the Friendly, Novel, Historic, and Blue Collar Tribes, have been presented in this chapter as another way of learning about and knowing subcultures within the dominant American culture of nursing. All of these tribes share with each other some common values and practices within the dominant American nursing culture particularly with respect to valuing independence, autonomy, self-reliance, depending upon high technologies, empowerment of women, and their desire for power and to be professional nurses.

The identification of similarities and differences among the four tribes within the American culture of nursing remains of great importance in order to assist nurses who frequently travel or move from one place of employment to another. Nurses need to be alert to cultural differences and similarities in order to understand factors that can facilitate or hinder their entry into the new nursing communities, institutions, and diverse employment arenas. Many nurses have told the author their cultural shock stories regarding their experiences as they sought employment or worked in unfamiliar settings in the United States. Different cultural values, beliefs, and nursing practices greatly impacted upon their personal and professional lifeways. Nurses today continue to experience cultural shock, cultural conflicts, and cultural clashes along with a host of other problems as they work with nurses, clients, and health personnel of different cultures. Nurses who are culturally knowledgeable and understand nurses and people in other cultural areas through advanced study in transcultural nursing can experience a significant difference in their job satisfaction, employment goals, and professional achievements.

Some nurses may choose a particular job but are unaware of cultural area differences in values and practices. As nurses continue to relocate at a more rapid pace than in the past fifty years, they will need to have far more holding knowledge about diverse cultures within American nursing and in other places in the world. Dealing with transcultural differences and similarities can lead to better nurse images, better role performance, and more satisfying and congruent professional experiences. While there are more particular features of the above four tribes of nursing, these general features can help nurses to become alert to cultural variations among American nurses. And as nurses from foreign countries increase in the United States, American nurses need to realize that cultural variability exists among them and that not all nurses in the world are alike. Transcultural nursing research is much needed to ascertain further changes and commonalties among nurses within the United States and in many worldwide nursing cultures.

American Hospital Culture

In this section some general features of hospital culture in the United States will be highlighted. Today nurses realize that hospitals are cultures and that the culture of the hospital influences the way nurses, clients, and staff function, make decision, and share viewpoints. Urban and rural hospitals are cultures that become known to the public for what they value, believe, and contribute to society. Urban hospitals and medical health science centers are usually largely cultural bureaucracies that tend to function like businesses and corporate industrial organizations. These organizational structures and cultures powerfully influence the work of nurses and all employees, but especially clients' health and well-being.

Currently American health care practices in hospitals and other health services are undergoing changes to make health care more accessible, acceptable, and less costly to Americans.[47] Universal health care along with other changes was proposed by President Clinton as part of health care reform. American hospitals do not serve all people nor are they accessible and affordable to many people, especially cultural minorities and people without health insurance. Modern technologies, medical specialists, and costly medical and surgical services have driven the cost of health care high in America.

Nurses remain the largest health professional group who are employed in American hospitals. There are a great variety of workers who are called "nurses," such as practical nurses, registered nurses, clinical nurse specialists, nursing case managers, primary and tertiary nurses, nurse researchers, and many more nurse employees in the hospital culture. The wide diversity of educational preparation of so-called nurses and how they dress and perform makes it difficult for the average health consumer to know who is the professionally prepared nurse and who can be relied upon for competent care practices. Clients from different cultures who have never been in the hospital are often confused and feel uncertain about nurses and their roles because there are some many different kinds of nurses.

Many changes are already occurring in hospitals largely due to actual and anticipated health care reforms or ways health providers want their practices to occur. As a consequence, structural reorganization, economic cutbacks, new management schemes, and other practices occurred in 1994. Professional nurses are losing or changing positions and some are being replaced by aides and practical nurses to obtain cheaper services without corporate managers congruent with the impact on quality-based professional nursing care services. These are unsettling times for professional nurses, clinical experts, and top nursing administrators in hospitals and innovative nursing agencies. It is also unsettling as a major shift is expected to occur with nurses and other health care providers working in homes, community centers, and in new kinds of alternative health care services.

American urban hospitals have evolved into very complex organizational structures with a wide variety of health services which have changed since the early 1950s. Many urban hospitals are acute medical-surgical places with very short term stays for clients. High costs of hospital services, health care specialists, technologists, therapists, and many nonprofessional staff have increased the cost and complexity of health care. Health professionals are expected to be highly competent employees and work within constricted budgets and use cost-saving managed care providers.[48] Accordingly, clients who enter urban hospitals find the hospitals to be not only a highly complex and technologically driven system from admission to dismissal, but they often feel helpless and uncertain about being in the institution. Some clients are frightened by seeing so many different nurses, employees and high-tech equipment.

Large health science hospitals are busy places that can make new clients and their family feel less important and less involved unless the professional nurse is present to help them feel safe, respected, and wanted. After admission, clients are often sent to many different departments, clinics, or different places for tests and treatments. Some get lost going from their room to another service despite instructions, signs, and directional color line markers in the hallways. Clients are also aware of many different personnel coming to do something to them, such as getting blood samples, obtaining information, and taking vital signs. Sometimes, different kinds of high-tech equipment come into the rooms with several technicians and nurses. Staff enter and leave the clients' rooms day and night, sometimes not saying anything to the clients as the staff are busy and have many matters to handle. This can make clients anxious. If clients are ambulatory, they will often walk down the halls and see many different treatments being used on other clients such as intravenous tubes in the nose, stomach, arms, or head or oxygen machines. In the nurseries, one may find very small infants of less than five pounds being cared for by nurses as they work with a variety of complex machines, monitors, and tubes in the infants' small bodies. For many clients and their families the hospital culture is an unfamiliar, busy and strange way of living.

As American nursing students reflect upon nurses who functioned in general hospitals in the Early Era (1950s and 1960s), they will learn that patients (as they were called then) were often met at the entrance of the hospital. Nurses visited with them and their family or friends, and then oriented them to the unit and spent time listening to them. The physician also visited with the patient in a fairly friendly and informative manner. Nurses gave complete care related to feeding, bathing patients, and often walking with patients and knew the patient personally and professionally. The nurse of the Early Era could use her caring skills of presence and concern in which clients relied on the nurse as "their nurse." There was also less movement of patients to diagnostic and special treatment places than today. If patients went off the unit for special therapies, the nurse often accompanied the patient and stayed with them, bringing them back to the unit.

Today clients may be gone for several hours for extensive diagnostic and laboratory work and different kinds of treatment for cancer and other illness. The client has contact with many different kinds of therapists and specialists including nurses, physicians, pharmacists, radiologists, occupational and physical therapists, and others with nonprofessionals skills. The client's care and treatment may be the responsibility of many team members and/or managed care personnel. Most importantly, clients have very short stays today of approximately two to three days in the hospital and must be ready to recover outside the hospital. The goal is to get clients out of the hospital as soon as possible to reduce costs. The consequences of early hospital dismissals have not always had positive outcomes. There is also the reality that many clients, especially cultural immigrants, refugees, and the poor may not have home health care nor insurance to cover their hospitalization.

Currently there are claims that America has the best health care system in the world, but these views may not be supported by some consumers and clients because of the above factors. Granted, America has some excellent health services, especially for those who have money and can afford longer stays in the hospital, expensive treatments, medications, and other necessities. The gap between the "haves" and "have nots" is apparent. America has no national health program, so many clients are not covered for health care when they need professional care and treatments. Thus the crisis in the American health system prevails with President Clinton seeking national health coverage for all Americans. Major changes are being considered, but the outcome remains uncertain due to strong bipartisan political party interest, goals and games.

Nurses are acutely aware of the health crisis situation as they work directly with clients and families. They are concerned about early dismissals and trying to arrange referral services. Moreover, home care by family members may not be possible, and so many concerns and unresolved human caring problems prevail. Most nurses in large hospitals carry very heavy client care loads due to a cutback in nurse employees. Nurses monitor vital signs, machines, and respond to physicians', specialists', technicians', and clients' requests today. Nurses often have limited time to spend with clients or to provide desired caring modes such as presence, sustained surveillance, comfort measures, and other caring measures essential for health and well-being.[49] With the trend to cut back on health care services there is a heavy emphasis on primary care, case management, managed care, and introducing services. These services have their value, but they often limit the opportunity for clients to receive what they came to the hospital for namely, exquisite nursing care practices that are culturally congruent, meaningful, and beneficial to them.

Currently, metaphors predominate in hospitals as symbolic and meaningful expressions such as "Time is money;" "The bottom line is cost savings;" "Staff management is our goal;" and "That's all I can do now for anyone." Physicians often use these metaphor statements such as, "Let's give them (the clients) shot gun therapy;" "The client needs a blast of antibiotics;" "Let us use these magic bullets (pills);" "The game plan is you carry the ball;" "You can't win them all (referring to client recovery);" "Let's try this aggressive therapy;" "We need to fight the disease;" and many other metaphors and cultural sayings prevail in hospitals.[50,51] Such metaphors reflect that the culture of the hospital is like a war game or a sports game with detached and impersonal caring expressions for clients. Metaphors have become common linguistic expressions that convey a visual image of the practice modes in hospitals. Nurses and hospital staff need to reflect on these metaphors as part of the hospital culture and to be alert that such metaphors get communicated to clients with different meanings and concerns, especially clients from other cultures in the world.

As discussed in early chapters, there are clients from many different cultures in hospitals. Nurses are expected to care for these clients and to communicate effectively with cultural strangers. Since nurses often have contact with clients from as many as thirty different cultures in large urban hospitals in a typical day or night, many problems in understanding and working with clients occur. Cultural differences as a cause of major communication problems are usually identified and can lead to client dissatisfactions and slow recovery. Nurses' "common sense" or "being kind" are not adequate to care for the culturally different; some clients need culture-specific care practices. But still today in the United States, over ninety percent of hospital staff have had limited or no preparation in transcultural health care. Moreover, most hospital staff in the United States can speak and understand only one language. As a consequence, many serious communication, treatment, and caring problems can be observed in rural and urban hospitals and especially in community health agencies. Until staff are prepared in transculturalism these problems will not be alleviated or rectified, and quality care is threatened or not available.

The hierarchical male corporate organizational structure and decision-making process in the American hospital influences health care, nursing, and the image of hospitals. While egalitarian and coparticipation in client services is sought as an ideal in transcultural nursing, there are often only few good examples of collaborative direct client care practices. One also finds only a few female nurses as vice presidents of administration, nursing services, or corporate hospital boards, males hold most of the top positions. With the recent restructuring of hospitals, some of these nurses have been removed from their positions as "cost saving" strategies and their positions have been returned to males.

The concept of "managed care" and "case management" are the latest popular cultural goals in hospitals and clinic settings. These terms imply managed control largely of money resources to corporate managers, and so client services are tightly managed. Managed care is questionable to this author as it is incongruent with humanistic and transcultural nursing care practices. Hospital staff are caring for acutely ill clients, but there are limited professional nurses to provide transcultural caring modalities. The author's recommendations for partnership care, coparticipation experiences, and a focus on wellness and prevention must be considered for the welfare of clients.[52] Transcultural nurses have been active to support this trend, but it is difficult when other staff do not understand these important goals from a transcultural perspective.

With corporate organizations managing and influencing hospital administration and health care reform in the United States, there are several dominant hospital cultural values and practices that need to be identified within medically dominated and controlled university urban teaching, service, and research hospitals. These cultural values and practices can be summarized as follows: 1) cost control with cost effective practices; 2) managed care practices with well-documented measurable outcomes; 3) use of a great variety of high-technologies with staff monitoring complex sensitive computer equipment in client services; 4) early release and ambulation of clients to reduce costs; 5) promotion of self-care so clients can care for themselves at home; 6) competitive efforts among interdisciplinary professionals for large research grant funds to maintain hospital staff and programs; 7) maintaining multidisciplinary "team" work; 8) being effective and efficient with less monies; and 9) competing with other hospitals for available resources and services.

As one might surmise, many of these above hospital cultural health care values are not congruent with what many consumers hope for, especially clients of diverse cultures. As transcultural nurses continue to identify and respond to clients' emic cultural needs and values one can readily identify current gaps in health care services with the present cultural values and practices. Some of the missing dimensions are 1) the virtual absence of culturally based care focused on client-centered participation; 2) the lack of focus on care as the essence of nursing; 3) the limited focus on culturally diverse clients' needs; 4) limited attention to the holistic care needs of clients which go beyond the biomedical, technological, and physical needs of clients to sociocultural and other considerations; 5) the virtual absence of the generic group care of clients and families with professional care participation; 6) the absence of quality care with care practices that do not necessarily have to be measured, controlled, and manipulated, with presence, comfort modes, listening, and providing surveillance as only a few examples of caring modes to be used in transcultural nursing.

Today and in the future, a powerful and highly effective way to help clients recover by providing culturally congruent, sensitive, and meaningful care must become an integral norm, standard, and value of the new rural and urban hospital cultures for quality care. This need will be in greater demand in the twenty-first century as immigrants, refugees, and people from many diverse countries come to live in the United States. Health care can no longer be focused on traditional Anglo-American service, but will need to accommodate multicultural groups and individuals. This will pose enormous problems for health personnel who have never dreamed this might occur and who are unprepared for such changes. Culture shock, cultural problems, and legal suits can be anticipated unless hospitals and community health services are soon transformed to a multicultural focus with cooperative disciplinary practices. Hospital staff would soon begin to draw upon available transcultural nursing research and knowledge to improve client care and to build a new ethos of hospital culture. From our present transcultural research clients of many cultures unfamiliar to hospital culture are reluctant to go to a hospital as they believe it is still a place to get sicker or to die and that their culture needs will not be met unless they are Anglo-Americans and have money.[53] For example, Greek Americans were afraid to come to the hospital unless absolutely necessary and believed that it is difficult to get well and stay well in the hospital. African Americans and Mexican Americans have expressed similar concerns with the former often fearing surgery or taking powerful medications they believe could kill them, make them weak, or unable to function. High-tech equipment is often greatly feared by cultures such as the Old Order Amish, and Japanese women fear the use of ultrasound and CAT scans. Arab Muslim women fear being in hospitals if they are cared for by male nurses and physicians and they fear being left along in the room with males. Other clients fear they will not get the right foods to eat and so their cultural food taboos will be neglected, which could lead to sickness and death while in the hospital. Korean clients often fear that their "good family blood" will be taken from them and given to non-kin people. These glimpses of transcultural research knowledge need to be studied to facilitate the use of hospitals and other professional services by people of different cultures.[54] Many of these research findings and others have barely been used to provide culturally congruent nursing care.

In this chapter, the hospital culture and the culture of nursing were presented and discussed with a focus on the Early and Recent Eras in the United States. Today, it is imperative that nurses study and understand that hospital and nursing cultures can influence the effectiveness of the nurse practitioner, educator, and researcher. Nurses must remain alert to cultural variabilities within and between nursing and hospital cultures. The Four Tribes of Nursing demonstrated the regional variability of different cultural orientations across the United States. Most importantly, hospital cultures need to be studies and understood for meaningful and effective health care services in the future. Nurses prepared in transcultural nursing are in a unique and powerful position to transform hospitals and health care practices into client-centered transcultural health care services. Still today far too many American hospitals and health care practices are centered on Anglo-American professional, federal, and etic outside interest groups. All health personnel need to be alert to cultural differences and commonalties in order to provide meaningful, beneficial, and appropriate care to consumers. As consumers of different cultures begin to control health care services by their use or lack of usage, health personnel will realize the power of cultures. It is therefore imperative that health care reform begin and end with a focus on transcultural care practices. Nurses prepared in transcultural nursing are in a unique position to help bring about major and important reforms in American health care services.

*Note: In this chapter, unless otherwise specified, "American" will be used to refer to the people and culture of the United States of America.

References

1. Leininger, M., "The Traditional Culture of Nursing and the Emerging New One," *Nursing and Anthropology: Two Worlds to Blend*, M. Leininger, ed., New York: John Wiley and Sons, 1970, pp. 63–82.
2. Ibid.
3. Leininger, M., "Culture of Nursing and the Four Tribes," *Health Care News*, 1985, Detroit: Detroit Receiving Hospital, 1985.
4. Leininger, M., "Two Strange Health Tribes: Gnisrum and Enicidem in the United States," *Human Organization*, v. 35, no. 3, Fall, 1976, pp. 253–261.
5. Leininger, M., "USA Tribes of Nursing," *Journal of Transcultural Nursing*, v. 6, no. 1, 1994, pp. 2–5.
6. Leininger, M., *Transcultural Nursing: Concepts, Theories, and Practices*, New York: John Wiley and Sons, 1978a.

7. Leininger, op. cit., 1985.

8. Leininger, op. cit., 1978a.

9. Kalisch, B. and P. Kalisch, "Anatomy of the Image of the Nurse: Dissonant and Ideal Models," *Image-Making in Nursing*, C. Williams, ed., Kansas City: American Academy of Nursing, 1982, pp. 3–23.

10. Ibid., p. 5.

11. Kalisch, B. and P. Kalisch, "Improving the Image of Nursing," *American Journal of Nursing*, v. 83, no. 1, 1983, pp. 48–52.

12. Kalisch, B. and P. Kalisch, *The Changing Image of the Nurse*, Don Mills, Ontario: Addison Wesley Publishing Company, 1987.

13. Ibid., p. 7.

14. Ibid., p. 11.

15. Ibid.

16. Ibid., p. 17.

17. Ibid., p. 21.

18. Leininger, op. cit., 1970.

19. Leininger, M., "The Culture of American (USA) Nurses," unpublished paper, Seattle: 1992.

20. Leininger, M., "Cultural Differences Among Staff Members and the Impact on Patient Care," *Minnesota League of Nursing Bulletin*, v. 16, no. 5, November, 1968, pp. 5–9.

21. *The American Nurse*, Kansas City, Missouri: American Nurses Association, 1994.

22. Leininger, M., *Care: An Essential Human Need*, Thorofare, New Jersey: C. Slack, Inc., 1981, (republished, Detroit: Wayne State University Press, 1988).

23. Leininger, M., *Care: The Essence of Nursing and Health*, Thorofare, New Jersey: C. Slack, Inc., 1984a (republished, Detroit: Wayne State University Press, 1988).

24. Ibid.

25. Gaut, D., Conceptual Analysis of Caring," *Care: An Essential Human Need*, M. Leininger, ed., Thorofare, New Jersey: C. Slack, Inc., 1981, pp. 17–24.

26. Watson, J., *Nursing: Human Science and Human Care: A Theory of Nursing*, New York: National League for Nursing, 1988.

27. Orem, D. E., *Nursing: Concepts of Practices*, 2nd ed., New York: McGraw Hill Book Co., 1980, p. 35.

28. Leininger, M., "Editorial: Self-Care Ideology and Cultural Incongruities: Some Critical Issues," *Journal of Transcultural Nursing*, v. 4, no. 1, Summer, 1992, pp. 2–4.

29. Leininger, M., "Selected Culture Care Findings of Diverse Cultures Using Culture Care Theory and Ethnomethods," *Culture Care Diversity and Universality: A Theory of Nursing*, M. Leininger, ed., New York: National League for Nursing Press, 1991, pp. 345–368.

30. Leininger, op. cit., 1970, pp. 70–82.
31. Ashley, J., *The Hospitals Paternalism and the Role of the Nurse*, New York: Teachers College Press, 1976.
32. Leininger, M., "Leadership in Nursing: Challenges, Concerns, and Effects," *The Challenge: National Administration in Nursing and Health Care Services*, Tempe, Arizona: University of Arizona, 1974, pp. 35–53.
33. Ashley, op. cit.
34. Leininger, M., "Political Nursing: Essential for Health and Educational Systems of Tomorrow," *Nursing Administration Quarterly*, v. 2, no. 3, Summer, 1978, pp. 1–15.
35. American Nurses Association, "Salary Report," Kansas City, Missouri, ANA, 1994, pp. 3–4.
36. Leininger, op. cit., 1991.
37. Omeri, Akram, *Personal Communication*, Detroit: 1994.
38. Kerr, J. and J. MacPhail, *Canadian Nursing: Issues and Perspectives*, Toronto: McGraw Hill Ltd., 1988, pp. 1–65.
39. Ibid.
40. Baumgart, A., and J. Larsen, *Canadian Nursing Faces the Future: Development and Change*, St. Louis: The C. V. Mosby Co., 1988, pp. 1–18.
41. Kerr and MacPhail, op. cit., 1988.
42. Leininger, M., op. cit., 1985.
43. Ibid.
44. Leininger, op. cit., 1970.
45. Leininger, M., "Two Strange Health Tribes: The Gnisrum and Enicidem in the United States," *Transcultural Nursing: Concepts, Theories, and Practices*, M. Leininger, ed., New York: John Wiley and Sons, 1978b, pp. 267–283.
46. Leininger, op. cit., 1978a, pp. 1–35.
47. Kettter, Joni, "Restructuring Spurs Debate on Staffing Rations, Skill Mix," *American Nurse*, July/August, 1994, pp. 26.
48. Ibid.
49. Leininger, op. cit., 1984.
50. Stein, H. F., *Medical Metaphors and Their Roles in Clinical Decision Making and Practice*, Boulder: Westview Press, 1990, pp. 61–93.
51. Leininger, op. cit., 1991.
52. Leininger, M., *Care: Diversity and Uses in Clinical Community Nursing*, Thorofare, New Jersey: C. Slack, Inc., 1984b, (republished, Detroit: Wayne State University Press, 1988).
53. Leininger, op. cit., 1991, pp. 345–368.
54. Ibid.

Chapter 9

Gnisrun and Enicidem:
Two Strange Health Tribes in Acirema*

Madeleine Leininger, PhD, LHD, DS, FAAN, CTN, RN.

For many years anthropologists have been busy describing and analyzing strange and familiar cultures in the world. These accounts have been useful in understanding people having different rituals, beliefs, and values. But studying these cultures often leaves the anthropologist with a host of questions and with the desire to study further the culture's special or unexplained behaviors.

As a nurse and anthropologist, the author has had the opportunity to study two strange health professional tribes or cultures in the United States, namely, the Gnisrun and the Enicidem. These tribes have different declared interests but they have been greatly preoccupied and involved with illnesses, health, care (caring), formulating diagnoses, curing and with treatment regimes of the Naciremas. Although these two tribes are very large, they are somewhat loosely organized with many subculture groups as part of the Nacirema nation. Often their strange behaviors, rituals, and beliefs are not fully understood by the public citizen. Moreover, these two tribes do not seem to understand fully their own tribal behavior even though they have known and interacted with each other for more than a hundred years.

The Naciremas in the United States have been widely studied through time with respect to their general lifeways, values, and historical developments by several anthropologists and other social scientists. For example, Linton[1] originally studied the Nacirema culture in the 1930s, then Horace Miner[2] in 1956, and Spradley[3] in 1975. These accounts provide fascinating glimpses of the Naciremas, but none of these authors were members of the Gnisrun or Enicidem health tribes and have not studied their particular cultural ways. Accordingly, as a nurse and anthropologist and a longtime member of the Gnisrun tribe, the author has been discovering and documenting the strange tribal behaviors, practices, and beliefs of both the Gnisrun and Enicidem for slightly more than forty years as a participant-observer.

This chapter focuses on the above two tribes using comparative (modified) ethnonursing, ethnography, and ethnohistorical methods and available literature sources. In order to grasp the purposes of the two strange health tribes, readers are asked figuratively to step out of their own culture and to place themselves in another culture assuming the role of a stranger to the tribes. Readers are asked to view the two tribes like unknowns living on a distant planet and try to make sense of their strange actions, values, and lifeways. They need to use a new pair of glasses and different ways of knowing the two strange tribes with their unusual names and behaviors. This transcultural nursing study will provide some new insights about the two tribes. One must keep in mind there is not right or wrong, good or bad, ethical or unethical behavior, but rather *interesting* behavior expressions and ways of living. Already the reader has noted the strange terms, Gnisrun and Enicidem, to identify the two tribes. These names are used to distance oneself from the tribes and to get a fresh perspective of them like anthropologists or transcultural nurse researchers in doing field studies of cultures. Throughout the chapter the reader may find the behavior and lifeways of the tribes to be amusing, sometimes alarming, and at still other times totally baffling. Dueto space limitations only the dominant features of these two tribes are presented.

The Gnisrun Tribe

The Gnisrun tribe is the largest health professional group in the United States with about one million in Nacirema and nearly 4.5 million in the world. They are a rather unusual tribe in that they are gender-biased, nearly ninety-two percent female, and predominantly of white Anglo-European heritage.[4] Only recently have they taken steps to recruit actively males and "minorities" to enter their sacred tribe. The small numbers of males who have gained membership into the Gnisrun tribe have largely occupied administrative, anesthetist, manager, or top clinical specialist positions. In contrast, only selected females in the Gnisrun tribe are in top administrative positions unless they have proven themselves over the years or competed successfully for male roles or positions. The Gnisrun tribe has also recruited sesruns to Nacirema land from the Philippines, Europe, Southeast Asia, and other places in the world to meet shortage demands largely in hospitals and clinics. Interestingly, the sesruns from foreign lands seldom hold top administration or high salaried positions unless they work for many years and imitate Anglo-sesruns normative behaviors, values, and lifeways.

Anthropologically speaking, the Gnisrun social organization reflects many loose nomadic bands in that they are made of groups who usually have no lasting ties to a geographic area but are usually free to travel within and outside of Nacirema land and overseas. Some members of the Gnisrun tribe tend to roam extensively according to their specialty skills, personal interests, for economic gains, and for other family, personal, or professional interests. Although the tribe is loosely united by professional organizational ties, sesruns are expected to show professional loyalty to their local and national groups and especially to their specialty or functional groups. Most sesruns are dedicated to their work as they function in health departments, clinics, or in schools of nursing, but some members claim that professional dedication is not a norm when sesruns work only for new home appliances, care, and monetary gains. Some in Nacirema land view sesruns as an oppressed group subjugated by male dominance and power, and especially by oppressive Enicidem tribal members. As a consequence, female sesruns have had to resist such oppressive male forces by defending themselves. Feminists sesruns have become strong and vocal groups in recent years to defend their rights and values. Likewise male sesruns have become organized to protect their interests.

The Gnisrun tribe is primarily matrilineally organized with matriarchal leaders and followers and some male leaders. Many tribal members live in apartments or in homes largely in urban settings. The Gnisrun tribe trace their descent from the great nineteenth century British founding leader known as Elagnithgin. They tend to revere this woman as their tribal leader, cultural heroine, and leader who inspired sesruns worldwide. In fact, each year the tribe members reaffirm their firm allegiance to this leader in May, and they have ceremonial activities, conferences, and make special public acclamations in their sacred temples, in schools of nursing, hospitals, or where sesruns work. The members treasure Elagnithgin's small sacred book, *Notes on Nursing*, which contains the early sacred credos, laws, principles, and cultural values of the Gnisrun tribe.[5] Some even claim the book has a theory, but this idea has been challenged by theory experts. Elagnithgin's status, words, and sacred paraphernalia can be found in several Gnisrun repositories and temples within North and South Nacirema, Europe, and other places in the world.

Over the past few decades, there have been a few bold scholars within and outside the profession who question the significance of Elagnithgin's contributions to the discipline and profession. Some believe it has been overestimated and still others uphold her ideas as "profound".[6,7] Nonetheless, her influence can be seen in many Gnisrun schools. For example, some young initiates are expected to wear Elagnithgin's white uniforms and caps for graduation ceremonies, and to hold the Elagnithgin lamp while reciting the Elagnithgin Egdelp. This ceremony is often viewed as a powerful identification rite for sesruns to proclaim their identity and follow the sacred beliefs of the tribe.[8] In recent years, there has been considerably slippage or abandonment of this Elagnithgin ritual as most sesruns are enrolled in university programs, wear university academic gowns and caps, and follow the university norms and practices of commencement. Interestingly, some sesrun leaders are not sure if this university rite is effective to make them a "true professional," and so they may hold a separate Elagnithgin ceremony with recitation of the Elagnithgin Egdelp. The ambivalence about the significance of the two traditional and universal ceremonies still prevails among some sesruns and faculty. Why such confusion should reign is baffling to progressive and modern sesrun leaders and often to the public.

Upon completion of the basic Gnisrun programs of study, recent sesrun initiates are expected to serve in staff positions in a variety of ecological niches such as hospitals, clinics, community health settings, military services, and in other new kinds of health services. But when sesruns complete master, doctoral, and post-doctoral programs, they seek top positions such as in advanced clinical specialties, administration, research, and academe. Those with doctoral degrees seek positions in universities or in top federal or national agencies. Currently, sesruns with advanced degrees are in great demand as primary care practitioners, managed care experts and in several nontraditional Gnisrun roles. With the Gnisrun tribe, there are many splinter groups or subclans who tend to view differently the abilities and competencies of practical, associate, baccalaureate, and graduate sesruns. For example, some subclans believe graduates with associate degrees are more competent than baccalaureate graduates. There are also clinical subclans with master and doctoral preparation who are so competent and confident that they have established their own independent professional services. Such action may be quite frightening to other Gnisrun subclans, but especially to naicisyhps who want to regulate and control sesrun spheres of functioning. Some naicisyhps believe that these sesrun are competing for their money and capturing their patients "cold-handed." As a consequence interprofessional competitive behaviors between the two major health tribes can be found. These sesruns see themselves as entrepreneurs and as independent practitioners who can offer directly to the public caring and health services which are different from the services of naicisyhps.

Historically, there is evidence that the gnisrun tribal members have been gradually taking over (or, as some may contend, stealing) some traditional rituals, practices, treatment modes, and paraphernalia from the Enicidem tribe. There is evidence for this in several areas, but especially with sesrun conducting physical client assessments, administering complex treatments, taking and transfusing blood, providing firsthand emergency or acute care services, providing health counseling, wearing stethoscopes around their necks, and giving direct instruction to clients and others about medical diseases, symptoms, and treatments—all similar to what naicisyhps have done in the past. Gnisrun tribal members often demonstrate their sesrun competencies and skills in the use of technological equipment and in psychophysical activities and therapies as an integral part of their professional services. Gnisrun tribal members contend these are naturalistic, congruent, and expected role practices of modern Gnisrun services. In recent years, transcultural sesruns, led by their leader Regniniel, are providing an entirely new kind of service to clients of diverse cultures. This service transcends traditional sesrun practices to provide culture care to people who speak different languages and have different culture care needs. Some sesruns have been slow to recognize this service, however, young sesruns are excited about this new area of practice and are beginning to use many transcultural ideas in their practices. In addition, some faculty are incorporating these ideas into Gnisrun curricula. In contrast, the Enicidem tribe has been extremely slow to use ideas related to transculturalism in their practices. Many anthropologists are amazed at the tremendous progress of Regniniel and her followers in making Gnisrun care sensitive and congruent to clients of diverse cultures.

Ideally, the Gnisrun and Enicidem are expected to work together and respect and value one another's contributions in human services. Their manifest behavior, however, often reveals that they tend to compete with subtly exchange verbal feuds regarding role activities and autonomous functioning with naicisyhps. Lately, some Gnisrun tribal members have been claiming that the naicisyhps are stealing their "caring rituals" and their practices related to health promotion and maintenance. Interesting, in public contexts, the two tribes will give verbal recognition to each other and proclaim they work closely together, however, in day-to-day hospital practices, one can identify some conflicts and tensions largely due to the perceived encroachment on one another's practice turfs. In recent years, the two tribes seem to be going their own ways with autonomous practices, but today they are expected to collaborate and function together as multidisciplinary practitioners.

A Glimpse: The "Old" Gnisrun and Enicidem Tribes

In reflecting on the "old" (pre-1970) Enicidem and Gnisrun tribal cultural behavior, values, and norms, some interesting features and attributes still can be identified between the two tribes. In the old Gnisrun culture, tribal members were largely enculturated and socialized to be passive, deferent, compliant, and dependent upon authority figures.[9] They were mainly other-directed and looked for acceptance, rewards, and sanctions largely from non-nurses and other outside their group, and especially sanctions from Enicidem tribal members. Accordingly, most female sesrun who worked in hospitals were controlled by and deferent to the naicisyhps in most of their decisions and actions, and were often referred to as "handmaidens of the naicisyhp" or as their "arm-and-leg extensions."[10] Gaining power from a naicisyhp was often the unspoken and desired wish of sesrun, and especially for strong sesrun leaders seeking autonomy and independence. Sesrun took written and verbal orders from naicisyhps despite the fact the sesrun often knew what was best for patients. In the "olden days" a sense of duty and obligation was evident along with deference to authorities. Most sesrun felt they were powerless to change major decisions or to questions the naicisyhp's orders unless they had a trusting relationship with him, and even then it was risky.[11] The

Enicidem tribal members were strongly in control of the hospitals with their patriarchal domination and power unless in a religious-run female hospital. Many female sesrun felt helpless to change the power and accepted medical power as a "given." Today most sesruns would call such behavior discrimination, oppressive male dominance, sexism, chauvinism, and bureaucratically unjust controls that limit sesrun's freedom to act and make good decisions for the benefit of clients and the profession.

In the 1940s the author frequently recalls how sesrun would always let a naicisyhp enter an elevator or room first, defer to his ideas, and get everything ready for the naicisyhp before he came for "ward rounds". In fact, the sesrun would line up the naicisyhp's charts so that he could quickly scan them and scratch some illegible orders on the charts which the sesrun called "chicken scratches," which they would spend considerable time trying to decipher. Sesrun were also expected to "trail after" the naicisyhp as he visited "his patients" on the ward. She would help him identify and remember the patient's name, condition, behavior, treatment status, and subtly advise him of what the patient needed. Most sesrun would remain with the naicisyhp until he left the unit, and some would even provide coffee or food snacks and actually "care for him" until he left the unit. Occasionally a sesrun would receive a "thank you" from the patriarch. To this investigator, sesrun in the "olden days" spent considerable time caring for and about naicisyhps to please them as they assumed total nursing care for patients. The sesruns of the "olden days" knew well how to provide complete or total quality care to patients, but they also had to care for naicisyhps to make things run smoothly, and this was an added responsibility. Rewards for the sesruns were minimal except for an occasional box of candy, smile, or positive nod or remark from a naicisyhp which the sesrun appreciated. Amid the many deferent sesruns caring for naicisyhps, there were some very strong leaders who were autonomous, leaders, brave, and authoritarian. These sesrun leaders would assert themselves with a naicisyhp and tell him what was needed for patients and the unit, and the naicisyhp would rely on them. They usually had been functioning in the system a long time, and everyone knew and respected these sesruns as they knew what was best for patients, sesruns, and other staff in the system, and how to handle naicisyhps. They were the inspiration for future sesrun models to empower them.

In the pre-1970s days, it was fascinating to observe that when a well-known naicisyhp or "chief" entered the sacred temple of the hospital to examine "his" patients, he would make explicit decisions and definitive pronouncements about the patient before other novice naicisyhps or "lesser chiefs". This "great chief" in command would order new or unusual medications and treatments, and would make the lesser chiefs want to follow and extol his powerful abilities and attributes. Theoretically, the greater the "chief's" perceived status and actions, the larger the number of lesser chiefs who would follow and listen to his sacred utterances. Accordingly, many sesruns would follow the "great chief" on his ward rounds to grasp some of his utterances about the patient and to hear the unusual "orders" for his patients as he recited them at the bedside. There was an implicit expectation that all sesruns and novices should honor and give respect to the "great chief". Indeed, if the lesser chiefs did not reflect obedience and respect, one could expect verbal reprimands in front of other peers or the patients. Remaining compliant, deferent, passive, and dutiful to the "chief naicisyhp" or specialist was clearly expected by sesruns and others, and only a few brave sesruns would ever challenge his authority, decisions, or actions. In those days, it was rare to see a female naicisyhp or female chief on the wards. But where these female naicisyhps existed, they tended to act like the male chief leaders and struggled to be recognized by them.

Recent Nursing Culture

During the past two decades several noteworthy changes have occurred in the Gnisrun tribe largely due to sesruns pursuing advanced degrees in institutions of higher education, the rise of feminism empowerment strategies, and the creative work of sesrun leaders to gain more freedom, rights, power, and equal opportunities. Nacirema sesrun have become politically active and many have become assertive in attaining and maintaining their rights and to being autonomous and independent in their actions and decisions.[12,13] Today, many of these sesrun are making their own professional and personal decisions, determining their future plans, and working to realize their goals. This shift in sesrun behavior has been alarming to those naicisyhps who still expect sesrun to be dependent, subservient, and "handmaiden" females to them as in "the good old days". As a consequence, female sesruns who are functioning in a more independent way, have observed that some naicisyhps experience culture shock and want to control sesruns and their practices. These Enicidem tribal members are not fully cognizant of how or why these changes have occurred so quickly with sesruns, but they believe it is because they attended universities instead of continuing to be in an apprenticeship hospital role with them learning about medicine and treatments under naicisyhp guidance. Accordingly, some naicisyhps have tried to entice and capture these sesrun to work for them by calling them "Medical Assistants," "Medexes," "Registered Medical Technicians," and other similar names.[14,15] They have offered sesruns high salaries and encouraged them to practice their sacred medical rites. And, indeed, some sesruns have become enamored with these offerings and learning sacred medical techniques from the great naicisyhps with special rewards. These sesruns have become "mini" or "junior doctors," and are earning higher salaries than university-prepared graduate sesrun as they virtually run the naicisyhps' clinics when they are gone. Some of these medical enticements have "worn off" for some sesruns, and they are returning to the Gnisrun tribe for fear of losing their Gnisrun tribal identity, and security. While this movement was occurring, many Gnisrun tribal leaders saw the behavior of the Enicidem tribe as "co-optation," "professional cannibalism," "power misuse," and as unethical or unacceptable practices of the 1970s and early 1980s. Some sesrun leaders exchanged fierce tribal words, made legal threats, and spoke publicly to deter Enicidem tribal members from taking and misusing sesruns. Gradually the niacisyhps backed off so that today the "stealing or capturing" of sesruns has become less evident. But the Gnisrun members always anticipate that another similar coup might occur by naicisyhps when they get desperate for help and want to control or regulate sesruns to meet their needs. Thus, interprofessional tensions or concerns always seem to be below the surface in Enicidem and Gnisrun tribal relationships as the latter continue to assert their professional freedoms and practices.

The image of the Nacirema sesrun is changing to that of being an autonomous, intelligent, and capable professional who is not the same as a naicisyhp. As sesrun became more assertive and self-directed, they established their own practices and lifestyle. Many sesrun in academe are models by establishing their own research and teaching pursuits and helping future sesruns to carve similar independent activities and to use nursing knowledge. There are, however, some differences between the clinical subclans and academic ones with their "town" (clinical) and "gown" (academic) beliefs, norms, and practices revealing some major gaps and questionable goals. This has lead to intertribal and interclan tensions between academic and clinical sesruns. In addition, some sesrun subclans or lineages such as midwives and oncology and cardiac specialists are aligning themselves because of their clinical interests and strong political and clinical specialty alignments. Accordingly, social and political tensions and actions can be observed between these sesrun groups with "up-one" female goals, competition, and jealousy. Diverse views about these political groups and their goals have been of concern to the ANA and NLN parent organizations, especially as they seek unity and want a strong, united professional voice. Concomitantly, there are a number of strong political and social friend alignments among political sesrun groups which tend to reinforce individual and small group political goals by their social relationships, lesbianism, and by "scratching one another's back," to promote each other, and often to gain important national, local or international positions.[16] Such interclan political sesrun activities and competition struggles have been especially observed as tribal members enter the sacred Academy of Gnisrun of the ANA or become deans or leaders of major public organizations, institutions, or agencies in Nacirema land. Some of the political work is done under the guise of advancing feminism. Male sesruns are often frightened by such strong feminist's pursuits and their aggressive way, and they tend to withdraw or not "tangle" with these sesruns. Hopefully, some of these interclan and subclan social, political, and gender pursuits will decrease in the 1990s so that equal rights will prevail among male and female sesruns in order to advance the discipline and professional goals. A critical problem still remains, however, and that is related to reducing female jealousy, harassment, and petty criticisms among female sesruns in the Gnisrun tribe. This problem has been limitedly addressed.

In the early 1980s a small lineage group in the Eastern area of Nacirema land declared that it was time for all sesrun to identify the major concepts of the Gnisrun knowledge and declared that "nursing, health, environment, and person" were the major paradigm concepts.[17] However, some sesrun vehemently opposed this presumptive stance and held that human care was the central focus to explain and predict nursing.[18,19,20] Today, human care (caring) and caring science is being recognized and valued, and care is being reaffirmed and valued as a central feature of nursing. The author, as an early leader in promoting caring as the dominant and central domain of Gnisrun, found that female sesruns were exceedingly slow to recognize, value, and study human care because they perceived care as too feminine, soft, and not medical.[21] Despite these care resistors, humanistic, and scientific care continues to be studied today as the major substantive and epistemic base of Gnisrun knowledge and the metaparadigm of nursing. Sesruns of the 1940s and 1950s are pleased to see this vitalization of care as central to nursing and to discover the many embedded ideas and meanings of human care. With the advent of developing and using nursing theories by academically prepared sesrun, the nature and direction of the field is changing. Some sesrun groups traditionally aligned themselves politically and intellectually by showing great allegiance to four theorists, i.e., Orem, King, Roy, and Rogers. Today more sesruns are valuing Watson, Leininger, Newman(s), and Parse theories. Sesrun students are especially demanding Regniniel's theory of Culture Care to help them care for many new immigrants and strangers in their community. The use of nursing theories has had a positive and significant impact in guiding Gnisrun practices and advancing discipline knowledge.

Another cultural movement occurring with sesrun is the focus on Gnisrun diagnoses and assessment rituals. The diagnosis cultural movement of NANDA appears to be mainly a linguistic twist to the medical disease nomenclature with use of similar medical terms and classificatory modes.[22] The author contends that this latest diagnosis movement will soon become extinct. Already the ritual has required much time, money, and intellectual effort with limited benefits. With the diagnosis ritual, some sesruns assume that all humans are alike and fail to identify cultural differences in assessing, diagnosing, and understanding people of diverse cultures. Unfortunately, these sesrun have been uninformed of cultural differences to realize that without substantive transcultural nursing knowledge, Western-based diagnoses lead to serious problems for clients in making accurate nursing assessments.

Today, as one walks through a modern Nacirema hospital, one finds many sesrun extremely busy in critical or intensive care units as they monitor complex machines and watch clients' vital signs. Some of these sesrun are almost in a cultural trance or possessed by high-tech rituals and monitoring task activities. Some sesruns are diligently mastering medical diagnoses and many treatments with high-tech instruments. As a consequence, there are many cases of sesrun "ritual burn out" and soon sesruns suddenly leave the high-tech world for new and different experiences. A sesrun stated: "I feel at times as if the machine cast a spell on me and completely determined what I did for patients." Other sesrun are concerned that they were spending more time monitoring machines, giving pills and treatments, or doing medical procedures than providing direct and intimate care to clients. Some of these sesruns are realizing that giving "hands on care" and understanding care phenomena is what nursing is or should be about as human caring is what clients want most of sesruns. Moreover it is the most satisfying and creative aspect of nursing.

In some modern hospitals sesrun express concern that pharmacists are taking over Gnisrun functions by dispensing, monitoring, recording, and evaluating pills given to clients. There are mixed feelings with both happy and unhappy views of this trend. Some sesruns notice that social workers are encroaching upon sesrun domains and activities by being health counselors and even home care instructors. While such practices exist, they seldom are openly discussed with pharmacists or social workers. Direct confrontation does not usually take place until an incident, crisis, or legal problem occurs in a hospital or home situation and is often addressed under the rubric of "quality care assurance" practices.

Still another recent trend is that all health professionals are to function as a multidisciplinary team for the client's benefit. This is an ideal, and what becomes manifest is usually that each discipline does its own thing and holds its own perceived turf and assumed knowledge boundaries. Some female health professions including Gnisrun, see the multidiscipline movement as another oppressive Enicidem movement in the health sciences. Since some Gnisrun tribal members have been launching their own independent practices for more than a decade, this latest multidisciplinary trend is of concern to sidetrack sesruns professional work. Advanced primary care sesruns are, therefore, questioning the goals of multidisciplinism as they establish their roles and their economic, political, and professional careers.

Unionization practices with strikes, marches, and walkouts have generally improved the economic and working conditions for sesrun in hospitals and universities. The initial idea of sesruns striking was shocking to the public as it did not fit the traditional image of sesruns as "angels of mercy" or compliant women. Sesrun are also taking a leadership role for Nacirema health practices and for promoting national health care policies and services in Nacirema land. The sesrun's desires to serve all clients and to use their specialty skills and independent decisions backed with nursing care science knowledge are clearly evident in the 1990s era. It is also evident that more Nacirema consumers are seeking and valuing sesrun services with children, aged, chronically ill, handicapped, and those who are from different cultures. These trends are encouraging and signify a major public turning point to recognize the important contributions and expertise of sesruns.

The Enicidem Tribe

The Enicidem tribe has been historically well established over hundreds of years and is known as one of the most powerful tribes in Nacirema land and in most places in the world. Traditionally, the tribe has had great power, authority, and control over the diagnosis, pathological states, and treatment regimes of humans. Tribal members known as naicisyhps function in hospitals, health agencies, clinics, and in many more places related to medicine or medical health matters. Their great historical leader known as Setarcoppih and his many followers set the standards, norms, and practices which have been maintained through the years. Historically, the Enicidem tribe received its special credo, values, and norms of practice from Setarcoppih.[23] This leader had sacred and profane messages for the tribal members through the Citarcoppih Oath, which all members were expected to follow in their profession. Indeed, if any member happened to fail to abide by this Oath, he would lose favor with the Enicidem tribe and could be dropped as a member. Through time, Setarcoppih and the Oath have served as powerful moral, ethical, and legal guides for tribal members' decisions and actions.

It is important for the reader to realize that the Enicidem tribe is a very old tribe with a great historical legacy having its origin and forms of primitive practice dated back to the year 450 B.C.[24] Egyptian artifacts, other archeological evidence, and cultural norms reflect a very long history of this profession serving and maintaining the human species. Through the ages, there have been many outstanding Enicidem tribal scientists and leaders as diagnosticians and therapeutic curers. These medical specialists or generalists have received public recognition, social status, and access to considerable money to uphold their practices, accumulate wealth, and maintain social prestige. Indeed, some Enicidem tribe members have moved into key political positions using their power, money, and status to gain top public and political leadership positions. One will find that a male naicisyhp may be a mayor, governor, senator, congressman, or president of a university, and hold many key positions in society. Unquestionably, their status, money, and political interests have helped the Enicidem tribe gain such prestigious positions, often with wide public acclaim. The Enicidem tribe contrasts with Gnisrun tribal members in Nacirema land who are mainly females and who still today hold very few top executive, political or public positions. It is always amazing and almost magical how male Enicidem tribal members move up the professional, sociopolitical ladder almost over night and can use their power and wealth in diverse ways.

It is also of interest to note that the Enicidem tribe has had mainly Anglo-European white male members for many years; however, in recent decades with affirmative action, the tribe has markedly increased the number of women and cultural minorities into their sacred tribe. The Enicidem tribe have also been highly successful at gaining high salary incomes (often more than $200,000 annually), and so they have successfully attracted into and retained some women and minorities in the tribe. Unfortunately, most sesrun with comparable preparation and experience today earn considerable less than the Enicidem tribal members (usually $45,000 to $85,000 annually for top sesrun positions) despite their heavy professional responsibilities and workloads. Such inequities have remained a major bone of contention with the sesruns, especially since both tribes are ideally expected to function effectively together in a collaborative and cooperative relationship.[25] Such salary differentials and inequities in public recognition and awards for sesrun human caring and medical curing services have led to non-egalitarian relationships and problems in cooperative teamwork.

The Enicidem tribe with its many clan and subclan "specialties" have been extremely powerful in Nacirema land and in most worldwide health systems. Their leaders enjoy strong visibility and public images almost like a powerful Czar or prestigious religious leader. They support their professional members, but dislike competitors such as shamans and folk healers who actually preceded them in their field. Today, many folk healers who have remained active in local folk healing practices are entering the sacred Enicidem world through the influence of transcultural nurses and medical anthropologists. Only a few Enicidem tribal members are valuing transcultural generic or folk healing practices and the role of indigenous healers.

It has been interesting to observe in recent years that Enicidem tribal power has begun to wane in Nacirema land due to several factors such as: 1) the public's deep concern about exorbitant medical, health care, and naicisyhp costs; 2) the difficulty of accessing Enicidem services; 3) the past preoccupation of the tribe of focusing mainly on diseases, symptoms, pathological conditions, and expensive diagnostic procedures and treatments; 4) consumers' desires to change medical practices to be more caring, humanistic, folk-like, and personalized; 5) the desire of consumers to learn about preventing illnesses and ways to preserve health; and 6) the increase of legal suits due to questionable medical treatments, costs, and malpractice claims.[26,27] For these reasons and others many Nacirema consumers are calling for health care reform. Many consumers are demanding more voice, control, and a major reform of the costly and questionable medical or health care system. Consumers want greater access to and greater availability of health services, especially medical services for the poor, homeless, elderly, infants, underrepresented cultures, or for others who need long term care services.[28]

But partisan controversial views exist on health care reform goals and methods. Legal suits against Enicidem members have markedly increased in the last two decades, which is forcing some members to retire or leave the profession. It is unfortunate that some excellent and competent naicisyhps have left the profession due to actual or potential legal threats, rising insurance rates, high liabilities, and loss of control over their practices. This state of affairs is of deep concern not only to naicisyhps, but to Nacirema consumers who want good medical and health practitioners. Despite this serious matter, there are Enicidem tribal members who are continuing to function and to make noteworthy medical contributions and discoveries to advance medical practices. Their scientific discoveries are often quickly pronounced in television media and in their sacred journal, *The New England Journal of Medicine*. As one looks further at Enicidem tribal members functioning in hospital and university health science settings, one can identify a stratified system of leadership, political norms, and controls.[29] The Enicidem leaders who specialist in clinical areas such as surgery, internal medicine, and new or rare specialties have considerable dominance and control over many professionals and staff members in hospitals or clinics. But today, large corporations and insurance companies are taking over some hospitals and community agencies. Large urban university hospitals are stratified organizations with most control exerted by specialty naicisyhps. Anthropologically speaking, one still finds "Big Chiefs" and "Little Chiefs" who are the big and little tribal members or clans and subclans, with the Little Chiefs becoming more independent than in earlier days. Nonetheless, the Little Chiefs, medical students, and residents are expected to show deference and respect to nationally recognized leaders for their practices, research, and clinical skills. The Little Chiefs still need to undergo rigorous enculturation practices to become recognized as a Big Chief by listening to and observing their behavior in the hospital and new kinds of medical services. Upon completion of the Enicidem tribal learnings, lesser chiefs must undergo special ceremonial rites of passage with rigorous national examinations. Enicidem tribal members have their own ceremonies in Nacirema universities. They establish their own time for graduation ceremonies and rules. They seldom follow the prescribed university schedule required of all other disciplines except for law graduates. This exception is often questioned by many other disciplines in the university, but still has not been changed. Enicidem graduates are usually very proud to have studied under great naicisyhps or recognized Big Medical Chiefs, and this fact is often recognized at commencement exercises. It contrasts sharply with the Gnisrun tribal graduates who seldom extol or mention their major mentors or leaders with whom they studied in university settings in any private or public ceremony.

Interestingly, the social organization of most Enicidem schools follows a similar stratified ranking system except that the dean of the Enicidem school (a very high-ranking chief) exerts tremendous authority, influence, and power over all other health professionals and even over other academic disciplines in most universities.[30] The Enicidem dean's power can be noted in getting academic positions, research monies, and material and other human resources. This power is in marked contrast with most female Gnisrun deans who struggle to get power in university systems and are often threatened with being placed under the control of an Enicidem tribal member, especially when university leaders do not know or understand Gnisrun professional goals and practices. Gnisrun deans and senior faculty have often fought for autonomy and, metaphorically, a place in the sun amid male Enicidem tribal leaders.[31,32] The problem has become even more difficult when these Enicidem tribal members become presidents of the universities. Some courageous Gnisrun deans have made their mark in this incredible power struggle so that today many Enicidem leaders are respecting Gnisrun goals and that the discipline is different from theirs. As one of the early sesrun leaders and an early feminist leader who worked to make this shift occur, the author can attest it was a very difficult political struggle.[33]

It has always been fascinating to hear the public refer to "their doctors," and to follow their orders in whatever they say as if their lives fully depended upon them. Such expressions of possessing and abiding by "their doctor" can be heard in beauty salons, social gatherings, public meetings, and in many other contexts. It is always amazing to sesruns why the public fails to recognize sesruns, as they have worked most directly, intimately, and often more continuously with consumers in hospitals, clinics, and homes for more than one hundred years. They are usually the healers in the care and cure process. This public recognition of sesruns is gradually being recognized with focused public media programs on sesruns.

One would be remiss not to mention a few Enicidem tribal rituals that some Gnisrun tribal members tend to follow yet today. For example, a number of naicisyhps expect clients to disrobe and don a white or colored hospital gown that is open in the front or back preceding a physical examination to determine the client's disease condition, or state of pathology. This ritual is often annoying to Anglo-Naciremas, but even more shocking or disturbing to cultural minorities. For example, it is a cultural taboo for Arab female clients to expose their bodies to male naicisyhps or sesruns.[34] For other cultures such as Hispanics and Philippine clients who believe in the "hot-cold" theory of Twellness or illness, one loses body temperature by such practices, plus it is most embarrassing to expose one's "privates" to a stranger. These rituals are being changed by transcultural sesruns who are creatively making care and assessments culturally acceptable to clients of diverse cultures.[35] But since transcultural sesrun specialists are still few in number and a "new species" in most hospitals, their impact is slowly being recognized and valued. The tide is turning, however, with transcultural sesrun specialists and generalist sesruns making a noteworthy difference where they are employed.

In addition, clients are often exposed on admission to a series of laboratory tests by naicisyhps to determine pathologies and for their legal protection. Most recently these tests have increased due to an increase in legal suits by consumers. The client is also expected to answer a series of questions which may reveal information viewed as sacred or private. Some clients have difficulty telling the naicisyhp or sesrun about emotional problems, because they are cultural secrets, taboos, or private information, or because clients fear being demeaned by a professional who does not understand their culture and special linguistic terms.

Still today, most naicisyhps and some medically oriented sesruns tend to focus upon diagnosing diseases, explaining symptoms, and discerning pathological states. This focus is often in conflict with some clients who value and want to find ways to maintain their health, prevent illnesses, and adapt to new or changing cultural and social circumstances. Indeed, some clients feel they have to declare themselves quite ill to get an appointment to be heard or to talk about their concerns. As a consequence, clients are beginning to seek sesruns who focus on human caring, health, and well-being. The differences between the Enicidem and Gnisrun tribal philosophies of health care services and domain of practice is becoming clearer, especially if sesruns would shift more noticeably and firmly to human care science, preventive and health care practice modes. At the same time, clients respect and value naicisyhps who can remove and replace practically all organs with considerable skill, perform almost unbelievable surgical interventions, or use complex treatments for the consumer's benefit. Indeed, some wealthy clients fly thousands of miles from overseas to have an Nacirema naicisyhp remove an object, treat a disease, or perform an unusual procedure or other highly specialized medical service. Likewise, some clients seek outstanding sesrun specialists who are skilled in midwifery, parent care, medical-surgical caring services, transcultural and other areas of Gnisrun practices. There is an emerging complimentarity in caring (largely nursing), and curing health services (largely medical) beginning to emerge to support and justify the Gnisrun and Enicidem tribes in the health sciences and in academic disciplines.

While many more fascinating revelations could be revealed about the two largest health care tribes in Nacirema land and in the world, the author has provided a glimpse of their strange lifeways, beliefs, norms, and practices. By now the reader recognizes that the Gnisrun tribe is "nursing," Enicidem tribe "medicine," and Nacirema "American," spelled backward, as one looked at these dimensions with new glasses. This different approach to study professional cultures from an anthropological and transcultural nursing perspective provides new insight now often recognized when one lives and is an integral part of one of the tribes. Intergroup tribal conflicts, confrontations, and concerns will undoubtedly continue in the future between the two tribes, and such tensions could be viewed as a positive means to strengthen the goals and image of each discipline. In general, there is a growing genuine respect for and appreciation of the great need and contributions of each professional tribe. Most assuredly, the Gnisrun and Enicidem tribes will not become extinct, as they are essential to human care, cure, healing, and the survival of Homo sapiens. It is, however, reasonable to predict that both tribes will need to make significant changes to respond to a growing and intensely multicultural world and with consumer demands for health care reform that is more accessible, congruent, and less costly. The two American tribes are ethnocentric, believing their ways are the best and superior to other kinds of health services within and outside North America. Thus worldview is far too narrow, reflecting a need for nurses and physicians to broaden their view to a transcultural one and discover what other world health systems are doing. Transcultural nursing leaders who have developed the field as a formal area of practice, see the need for this expanded worldview and for the critical need for transcultural education and practice for *all* health professions, and hopefully by the year 2010. Nursing has had nearly three decades to establish transculturalism; whereas medicine has just begun to consider formal education preparation for medical students. Transcultural practices into medical education and clinical practices has yet to become a reality. The need for transcultural education will be even more crucial as clients, nurses, and physicians continue to come from virtually every place in the world to America. The demand for nurses and physicians to have transcultural knowledge and skills will markedly increase with global movements of people. In general, the future for both tribes seems promising, but each discipline needs to reexamine its professional goals and practices and shift to the globalization of transcultural health education and practices.

Note: This is a revised version of the original article published in the first edition of *Transcultural Nursing: Concepts, Theories, and Practices*, New York: J. Wiley and Sons, Inc., 1978, and recently published in the *Journal of Transcultural Nursing*, Memphis: University of Tennessee Press, v. 2, no. 2, Winter, 1991, pp. 32–39.

References

1. Linton, R., *The Study of Man: An Introduction*, New York: Appleton-Century-Crofts, 1936.

2. Miner, H., "Body Ritual Among the Nacirema," *American Anthropologist*, v. 58, 1956, p. 503.

3. Spradley, J. *Naciremas*, Boston: Little, Brown, 1975.

4. Leininger, M., "The Culture Concept and American Culture Values in Nursing," *Nursing and Anthropology: Two Worlds to Blend*, M. Leininger, ed., New York: John Wiley and Sons, 1970, pp. 51–63.

5. Nightingale, F., *Notes on Nursing: What It Is and What It Is Not*, London: Harrison and Sons, 1859.

6. Smith, F. B., *Florence Nightingale: Reputation and Power*, London: Croom Helm, 1982.

7. Leininger, M., *Reflections on Florence Nightingale with a Focus on Human Care Knowledge and Leadership*, Philadelphia: J. B. Lippincott Co., 1992.

8. Leininger, M., "Two Strange Health Tribes: Gnisrun and Enicidem in the United States," *Human Organization*, v. 35, no. 3, Fall, 1976, pp. 253–261.

9. Leininger, M., *Transcultural Nursing: Concepts, Theories, and Practices*, New York: John Wiley and Sons, 1978.

10. Nightingale, op. cit.

11. Ashley, J., *Hospitals, Paternalism and the Role of the Nurse*, New York: Columbia University, Teacher College Press, 1976.

12. Ibid.

13. Kalish, P. and B. Kalish, *Changing Image of Nursing*, California: Appleton-Lange, 1984.

14. Leininger, M., "The Tribes of Nursing," *Health Care Weekly Review*, Southfield, Michigan, v. 2, 1983, p. 3.

15. Leininger, M., "Primex: Its Origin and Significance," *American Journal of Nursing*, Kansas City, 1973a, pp. 1274–1277.

16. Leininger, op. cit., 1983.

17. Fawcett, J., "The Metaparadigm of Nursing: Present Status and Future Refinements," *Image: The Journal of Nursing Scholarship*, v. 16, no. 3, 1984, pp. 84–87.

18. Leininger, M., *Care: An Essential Human Need*, Detroit: Wayne State University Press, 1984a. (First published by Charles Slack, Inc., 1981).

19. Leininger, M., *Care: The Essence of Nursing and Health*, Detroit: Wayne State University Press, 1984b. (Reprinted 1988).

20. Watson, J., *Nursing: Human Science and Human Care: A Theory of Nursing*, Norwalk, Connecticut: Appleton-Century-Crofts, 1985.

21. Leininger, M., *Culture Care Universality and Diversity: A Theory of Nursing*, New York: National League for Nursing Press, 1991.

22. Leininger, M., "Issues, Questions, and Concerns Related to the Nursing Diagnosis Cultural Movement from a Transcultural Nursing Perspective," *Journal of Transcultural Nursing*, v. 2, no. 1, Summer, 1990, pp. 23–32.

23. Richards, D. W., "Hippocrates and History: The Arrogance of Humanism," *Hippocrates Revisited*, R. J. Bulger, ed., New York: Mecom Press 14, 1973.

24. Ibid.

25. Leininger, M., "This I Believe: About Interdisciplinary Health Education for the Future," *Nursing Outlook*, v. 19, 1971, pp. 787–791.

26. Leininger, M., "Health Care Systems for Tomorrow—Possibilities and Guidelines," *Washington State Journal of Nursing*, v. 45, no. 1, 1973b, pp. 10–16.

27. *Healthy People 2000*, Superintendent of Documents, Washington, D.C.: Government Printing Office, 1991.

28. Ibid.

29. Pellegrino, E. D., "The Academic Role of the Vice President for Health Sciences: Can a Walrus Become a Unicorn?" *Journal of Medical Education*, v. 50, 1975, pp. 221–228.

30. Ibid.

31. Leininger, M., "Psychopolitical and Ethnocentric Behaviors in Emerging Health Science Centers," American Anthropological Association Annual Meeting, Mexico City, November 1969.

32. Leininger, M., "The Leadership Crisis in Nursing: A Critical Problem and Challenge," *The Journal of Nursing Administration*, v. 4, no. 2, March-April, 1974, pp. 28–34.

33. Ibid.

34. Luna, L., "Transcultural Nursing Care of Arab Muslims," *Journal of Transcultural Nursing*, v. 1, no. 1, Summer, 1989a, pp. 22–26.

35. Leininger, M., "Transcultural Nursing: A Worldwide Necessity to Advance Nursing Knowledge, and Practice," *Nursing Issues*, J. McCloskey and H. Grace, eds., 3rd ed., Boston: Little Brown and Co., 1989.

Chapter 10
Cultural Perspectives of Pain

Antonia Villarruel, PhD, RN

The purpose of this chapter is to explore the interactive components of the human phenomenon of pain. Aspects of pain beliefs, mode of pain expression, assessment of pain, and care associated with pain will be explored from a cultural perspective. An understanding and respect for the diversity of expressions and meanings that exists between nurses and clients is a critical dimension of nursing practice.

Pain has been defined as an unpleasant sensory and emotional experience arising from actual or potential damage or described in terms of such damage.[1] Pain has also been described as an emotional experience, a result of imbalances within the body or the universe, a punishment from God, and inevitable fate, whatever the experiencing person says it is.[2] Regardless of the definition used, *pain is a universal human experience.* All humans during the course of their life span will encounter situations in which pain is inevitable. Neonates, infants, children, the elderly, men and women differ in what experiences they regard as painful, how pain is expressed, the type of action or reaction, and the expressions of care that may be taken in response to pain. With the universality of the experience of pain there is also diversity that exists among people in the perception, meaning, attitude, expression, and care associated with pain. The challenge to nurses is to consider both the universal and diverse pain modes while working with clients.

Pain is also a phenomenon that is universal to nursing practice. Nurses in the context of their practice frequently encounter people who are or will be experiencing pain. Examples of such encounters include situations in which pain occurs as a result of a specific illness, e.g. rheumatoid arthritis, the treatment related to the illness, e.g. joint and muscle pain associated with physical therapy, abdominal discomfort associated with certain medication regimes, or experiences associated with the illness itself, e.g. progressive decrease in function and resulting inability to engage in previously enjoyed activities. In whatever context, nurses are faced with the challenge of interpreting a diversity of responses to pain in order to assess the meaning of the pain from a clinical perspective. Of equal importance, nurses must strive to interpret pain behavior and meaning from the perspective of the client.

While many nurses may try to elicit the individual's perspective in relation to experience of pain, the nurse also interprets and seeks to validate or legitimize the presence of pain. This interpretation by the nurse is based in part on clinical knowledge, such as whether a particular disease or injury is likely to cause pain; the accompanying presence of clinical symptoms which may indicate pain, for example, an increase in blood pressure, heart rate, and respirations, tenderness, or inflammation; behavior perceived as congruent with a report of pain, such as screaming, lethargy, or a decrease or disinterest in normal activities. The nurse's decision as to whether pain exists and the nature and intensity of pain may or may not be congruent with the perspective of the person who is experiencing the pain. Conflict, manipulation, and frustration on both the part of the nurse and the individual experiencing pain are likely outcomes that result from an incongruence in perspectives. Situations like this will continue to be inherent in encounters with pain until nurses consistently consider and value the individual's perception and expression of pain. Further, nurses must seek to understand and respect the perspective of the individual experiencing the pain and the context in which pain is being presented. It is only when the potentially divergent and conflicting perspectives of the nurse and client are equally considered and valued, that effective and appropriate nursing care can be designed.

The assessment of pain and the effectiveness of nursing care are dependent on the nurse's understanding and acceptance of an individual's perception, expression, and care associated with pain. While this can be said to be true of any nurse-client interaction, this becomes a critical factor in relation to pain experiences. The individual's subjective experience of pain, expressed overtly and convertly, is assessed by nurses. It is only when nurses sanction the expressions as indicative of pain that subsequent care and comfort of the individual will ensue. Nurses have it within their means and within the scope of nursing practice to acknowledge pain and promote comfort, care, and healing, or to ignore an individual's pain and thus cause or prolong suffering. Clearly, the issues surrounding the care of people in pain are complex. The individual and interactive physiologic, psychological, social, spiritual, cultural, and ethical dimensions that come into play during such encounters between clients and nurses during a pain experience are generally not well understood and often appear to be in conflict. A useful context to begin to unravel the complexities involved in the pain experience is within the context of culture. According to Leininger, "culture refers to the learned, shared, and transmitted values, beliefs, norms, and life practices of a particular group that guides thinking, decision, and actions in patterned ways.[3]

Expressions, meanings and care associated with pain are learned in early childhood within the cultural context of the family.[4] What constitutes pain, how one is supposed to respond or react to pain, and the actions to be taken during pain occurrences (if any), under specified circumstances, for particular results are learned in early childhood in the family context. How and if individuals and families perceive and react to physical distress, such as an experience of pain, and how this is understood as a problem of health and illness, are influenced by cultural group membership.[5,6] Pain, therefore, can be said to have meanings that are culturally derived. Culture also influences a nurse's perception, meaning, and decision-making regarding the care of persons who are experiencing pain. Nurses, within the course of their nursing education and subsequent practice, also learn what situations are likely to cause pain, the relation of pain to particular disease states, and the type of action and care to take under specified and prescribed circumstances. Nurses, however, must also be cognizant of similarities and differences in beliefs and practices associated with pain between themselves, and the clients and families for whom they care during pain situations. If the cultural meaning of pain is very different for the nurse, client, and family, then the assessment, care, and evaluation of specific actions to alleviate pain are difficult.[7] An awareness and understanding of the interrelation between the culture of the client and family, and the culture of the nurse is critical in order to determine the need for and goal of care, and also for the design of specific care strategies.

In this chapter further discussion of the interactive elements of culture and pain from a transcultural nursing perspective will be taken. Leininger's theory of cultural care diversity and universality will be used as the organizing framework from which the diversity of the meanings, expressions, and care associated with pain can be viewed. Existing research and practice examples will be utilized as a basis to identify areas for further knowledge development as well as strategies for designing culturally congruent nursing care In relation to pain.

Theory of Cultural Care Diversity and Universality

A major premise of the theory of cultural care diversity and universality, is that care is a powerful means to help clients recover from illnesses or unfavorable human life conditions, such as pain.[8] Further, care and culture are viewed as inextricably linked together and thus, cannot be separated in nursing care actions and decisions.[9] The importance of considering cultural factors in nursing assessment and subsequent care can also be viewed from the reference of cultural pain. *Cultural pain refers to the insensitivity of an individual or group towards an individual who has different beliefs or lifeways, and which leads to discomfort or an unfavorable response.*[10]

Leininger[11] stipulates that knowledge of meanings and practices derived from world views, social structure factors, cultural values, environmental context, and language and ethnohistorical factors are essential to guide nursing decisions and actions. Based on this cultural knowledge, the nurse directs nursing care decisions and actions directed toward 1) preservation and maintenance, 2) accommodation and negotiation, and 3) repatterning and resctructuring.[12] 'The purpose of action is directed toward the delivery of culturally congruent care and subsequently beneficial client outcomes. The relevance of this theory and underlying premises can be seen clearly in dealing with the complexities of caring for clients experiencing pain. Further, the inadvertent infliction of cultural pain by the nurse can perhaps be avoided when the cultural dimensions of pain are considered when caring for people experiencing pain.

The Sunrise Model, a conceptual picture which depicts the components of the theory of cultural care universality and diversity, serves as a useful guide for practice and research to understand the multiple influences on the care and health of individuals, families, and groups who are experiencing pain. The sunrise model can also be used as a guide for conducting cultural assessment in relation to different aspects of pain. It will be used as a framework from which to understand and examine existing research related to care patterns and expressions of individuals, families, and groups related to pain. In addition, the model will be used as a guide to direct nurses's thinking in recognizing and understanding the multiple influences on the care patterns of nurses and on nursing systems in relation to pain, and to stimulate new kinds of practice and research. Cultural influences on meanings, expression, and responses associated with pain.

Both in practice and research an individual's cultural background has long been recognized as a major determinant of how the individual perceives and reacts to painful situations.[13] From the perspective of Leiningers theory, the worldview of people, that is, the way people tend to look upon the world, influences the value stance about their life and the world about them,[14] relation to pain, cultural and social structure dimensions such as cultural values and lifeways, religious and philosophical factors, economic factors, and environmental context are but a few of the influences that affect the expression and care associated with pain. Thus, from a theoretical standpoint, an understanding of these various factors is a critical dimension that will facilitate the understanding of an individual's expression of pain, and the type of care that is congruent with individual's particular worldview. Additional theoretical support for the link between pain and culture has been provided for in the development of the gate control theory.[15] This widely accepted and revolutionary theory of pain transmission and modulation postulates that factors such as prior pain experiences, environmental cues, and psychological character can trigger mechanisms within the central nervous system These mechanisms affect the transmission of individual's nerve impulses which influence an Individuals perception and tolerance of pain, in other words, this theory provides a basis for understanding why two individuals who experience the same pain stimulus, such as an injection, might indicate that they are experiencing different levels of pain intensity. In addition, differences in the amount of pain individuals are able to tolerate can be accounted for in this theory. The significance of this theory is that a direct neurophysiological link between culture and pain, physiological impulses and sociocultural factors, been proposed.[16] Addition, in theory and practice there exists support for the link between culture and pain, there are relatively few studies In which the effects of culture on the pain experience have been explored. Probably the most cited study in the area of culture and pain is the work of Zborowski.[17] In this landmark study qualitative interviews were conducted with men hospitalized with a chronic pain condition. These men were members of four distinct ethnocultural Jewish, Italian Irish, and Old American. In addition, interviews with healthy respondents from the respective ethnocultural groups, nurses and family members who were involved in the pain experience, and participant observation were utilized.

A major premise of Zborowski's[18] study maintained that attitudes toward pain are related to cultural patterns; as cultural patterns differ, so then will attitudes toward pain. Findings from this study support the premise that differences exist between cultural group members in relation to reactions and meanings associated with pain. As an example of differences in reactions toward pain, emotional descriptors of pain occurred more frequently in interviews with Jews, while Italians admitted to freely showings pain by crying, complaining, or being demanding. Old American, in contrast, tended to be more stoic and hide their pain. Differences in behavioral responses by members of the same cultural group were recognized and seen as influenced by factors such as environmental contexts, e.g. hospital vs. home, and interethnic variables such as the degree of Americanization, differences in socioeconomic background, education and religiosity.

Attitudes toward pain in the four cultural groups were also identified. Similar future-oriented anxiety toward pain was found in both Jewish and Old American clients. Both groups indicated concern, not necessarily for the pain, but for the implication of the pain in relation to their general health. In contrast, Italians, concerned with the sensation of pain and sought immediate and complete relief. A major contention of this study is that pain behaviors vary among cultural group members, but have similarities across cultural groups. In contrast, attitudes toward pain are similar among cultural group members, and vary among cultural groups. Zborowski[19] maintained that similar reactions to pain do not necessarily reflect similar altitudes toward pain, thus accounting for the universality of responses and diversify in attitudes toward pain. Secondly, while similar reactions to pain may be employed across cultural groups, they serve different functions and purposes, which are influenced by cultural beliefs and patterns.

Much of the research since this study, which was conducted in the early 1950s has been focused on identifying differences in pain responses among cultural groups. Both differences and similarities among cultural groups have been found in relation to pain anxiety and pain attitudes,[20] tolerance,[21] responses,[22, 23] perception,[24] pains coping behaviors.[25] Despite this growing body or research, further work is needed to determine the similarities and differences among cultural groups. Most importantly, there is a need to study how culture influences attitudes, beliefs, expressions, and care associated with pain. While studies which compare meaning and behavior of pain between cultural groups is necessary, a critical area of study is to understand the cultural context from which meanings, behaviors, and expressions of pain can be understood.

A relevant direction for studying the relation between pain and culture would thus be a transcultural approach. In utilizing this approach, the experience of pain could be Interpreted and more fully understood within cultures. Subsequently, those elements that are universal and diverse in relation to pain experience across cultures could be delineated and serve as a guide for designing nursing care decisions and actions aimed toward preservation/maintenance, accommodation/negotiation, or a repatterning/restructuring. The resulting actions would be directed toward the delivery of culturally competent and congruent care that would also result in the effective management of pain.

Several studies with a transcultural focus that are relevant to pain have been conducted. One such study examined perceptions and responses of Arab Americans to pain.[26] While the method used in the study was not presented, perceptions and reactions to pain were discussed in relation to family and kinship ties, in addition to language and environmental context. Findings from this study indicated that Arab Americans view pain as unwelcome and unpleasant. Responses toward pain were thus directed at avoiding pain situations, controlling existing ones, and attending to pain immediately.[27] Expressions of pain were influenced by the environmental context and the presence of family members. For example, responses in the presence of family members were characterized by loud moans, screams, and gasps for air, but were considerably more subdued in the presence of members outside the family. In contrast, certain pain episodes, such as in the case of labor and delivery, required a public expression of pain. Descriptions of pain by Arab Americans tended to be more encompassing than just the primary site of injury or pain, involving references to the entire body, life, and overall functioning. In addition, metaphors of pain and fire or flame were made in relation to describing a burning sensation of pain.[28]

In another study ethnohistorical methods were used as a means to discover beliefs related to pain in ancient Mesoamerica.[29] Major themes which emerged from this study included: pain was an accepted, anticipated, and necessary part of life; humans had an obligation to endure pain; the ability to endure pain and suffering stoically was valued;

the pain was experienced by a person was in part predetermined by the gods; pain and suffering were viewed as a consequence of immoral behavior, methods of pain alleviation were directed toward maintaining balance within the person and the surrounding environment.[30] Links between themes from this ethnohistorical study and existing research findings related to pain in Mexican Americans were congruent. In addition, these findings provide support for the proposed relation within Leiningers model of the relation between the ethnohistorical context and care patterns and expressions of culture patterns.

While transcultural studies related to pain are sparse, pain was found as a theme that emerged in several studies. For example, pain as it relates to health was a major theme in a transcultural nursing study conducted to discover the health meanings and practices or older Greek Canadian widows.[31] In this study widows defined health as a state of well-being, ability to perform daily role activities, and avoidance of pain and illness. In addition, practices to prevent and treat illness included remedies to alleviate and treat pain. Quinine and chamomile tea were two remedies identified by this group to alleviate pain and cramps.[32]

Expressions and behaviors related to pain of Japanese Americans (Nissei) were presented in the context of beliefs related to cancer.[33] A frequent observation of nurses in relation to Nissei clients is that they often appear stoic In situations that are likely to cause pain. This stoic behavior, however, does not necessarily mean that within the culture there is a high tolerance to pain, but, rather, there are cultural norms which determine how pain should be expressed. For example, within the culture, the belief does exist that one should be able to withstand discomfort, thus, expression of pain indicates that one is weak of character.[34] Important to consider when interpreting behavior associated with pain are cultural norms and expectations as to how one should express oneself in health-illness situations such as pain.

Much can be understood about the cultural meaning of pain by the language used to communicate experiences with pain. For example, within Chinese culture a term sometimes used to describe pain associated with the death of a close relative is *suan* translated literally as sourness.[35] Within the Chinese belief system 'the heart is seen as the center of emotions, thus, all emotions, good and bad, seen as originating there. An additional element of Chinese culture is that the symptom is viewed as the primary illness problem.[36] Therefore, care associated with a Chinese client must focus on the symptom (the taste of sourness in the heart), rather than the cause of the symptom (loss or sadness). As the symptom and cause are culturally defined, so, too, must there be accompanying cultural prescriptions for the treatment of such a condition. Knowledge of cultural care practices associated with pain are critical for the design of culturally relevant care.

Research and practice implications

From a research perspective, the importance of delineating the cultural context in relation to pain can be seen in the diversity of meaning, expressions, and care as presented in these select studies. Further research in this area, utilizing a transcultural approach would be useful in delineating the role of culture in relation to the experience of pain.

From a practice perspective, the diversity of meanings, expressions, and care associated with pain, provide support for obtaining a comprehensive assessment of the individual's perception of pain. The following questions can be used as a guide by the nurse to discover both individual and group perspectives of the pain experience:

What do you think caused the pain?

What have those close to you told you about your pain (what caused it, how should it be cared for, who might you go to for care)?

What ways do you let others know you are in pain?

How do others know you are in pain?

What words do you use to describe pain?

What are the methods that you usually rely on when you are in pain at home, in the hospital, or other settings?

Who are the persons you turn to when you are in pain? (Describe a situation in which you went to them for help or care.)

What do you (others) think should be done (for you, by you, by others) when you are in pain?

What do you (others) think might be useful in caring for you while you are in pain?

What does pain mean in your culture? (Why do you think people have pain? What are some causes of pain?)

What are some ways in which people in your culture care for people who are in pain? (What things are done for people when they are in pain? Who should do these things?)

If you (others) were experiencing pain, under what conditions would you (others) ask for help or care?

From whom would you seek help or care?

What result would you hope from the care?

How are people supposed to act when they are in pain? (Is this the same for men, women, and children?)

These questions will hopefully stimulate thinking by nurses as to how to uncover the cultural influences of pain for the individual client. Information gained from the use of these questions and similar lines of inquiry in nurse-client interactions will serve as a useful basis for the delivery of culturally congruent care.

Cultural influences on nurses' perceptions and care associated with pain

Within the theory of Culture Care Diversity and Universality, there is a proposed relation between cultural and social structure dimensions, care patterns, and health systems. In relation to nurses these dimensions ultimately influence nursing professional systems, the individual practitioner of nursing, and ultimately the health and well-being of the client.[37] Components of generic care and care systems, nursing care and care systems, and professional systems interweave and influence nursing care decisions and actions. This dynamic interaction is clearly demonstrated in nursing care decisions related to pain.

Influences on individual nurse's interpretation of pain and suffering have been identified. Characteristics of the nurse, characteristics of the client, and environmental context are important factors that affect not only a nurse's interpretation of the patient's pain and suffering, but also affects what care decisions and actions are made.

The work of Davitz and Davitz[38] has been foundational in recognizing the multiple factors influencing nursing care decisions related to pain. A major assumption of this research proposed that inferences of suffering are made on the basis of observations and mediated by a system of explicit and implicit beliefs. Explicit beliefs include elements related to the nature of pain, such as cause, intensity and duration. Implicit beliefs are associated with elements of the nurse and client, such as ethnic/cultural background, gender stereotypes, and religious beliefs.

In a study conducted with American nurses, vignettes were presented in which the physical condition, age, and gender of the client were similar, but patients differed in relation to ethnic and religious group membership (i.e. Oriental, Mediterranean, Black, Spanish, Anglo Saxon/Germanic, Jewish).[39] Results of this study indicated that nurses' inferences in relation to both the amount of pain and psychological distress differed according to ethnic group and religious membership. Nurses reported higher levels of pain and psychological distress in Jewish and Spanish clients, while the lowest levels of both dimensions were reported for Oriental and Anglo-Saxon/Germanic clients.

Other studies conducted in this area have identified client variables of age,[40] gender,[41] cultural group membership,[42] type of illness or injury[43] evidence of pathology,[44] and verbal and nonverbal communication patterns of clients,[45] as influencing nurses' inferences of suffering. In addition, client characteristics (e.g. size. age, gender, individual pain tolerance) clinical observations (e.g. surgery type, vital signs, overall condition and complications) and medication considerations (response to and time of last medication) were seen as factors influencing the amount and type of medication administered by nurses to clients presented in vignettes.[46]

Similarly, individual characteristics of nurse have been found to influence nurses inferences of pain experienced by clients. The influences of nurses cultural background on inferences related to pain and suffering were examined cross-culturally.[47] Nurses from Korea, Puerto Rico, Japan, Uganda, India, Nigeria, Thailand, England, Israel, Belgium, Taiwan, Nepal, and the United States were similarly asked to rate the amount of pain and psychological distress of clients as presented in vignettes. Efforts were made to ensure that instruments were relevant to all cultural groups of nurses. Differences among groups were found both in their rating of pain and psychological distress. Ratings of physical pain were lowest among nurses from Belgium, the United States, and England while nurses from Nepal and China were lowest in their rating of psychological distress. Differences among ratings of pain differed by national group membership of the nurses and the gender of the patients presented in the vignettes.[48]

Other nurse characteristics have been studied to examine their influence on nurses interpretations of pain. Such factors have included age, personal experiences with pain, cultural and religious background, level of education, years of nursing experience, and relative job satisfaction.[49, 50, 51, 52] While inferences of pain and psychological distress differ among nurses, findings are neither conclusive nor consistent as to what characteristics of the nurse or client influence nurses' perceptions.

The importance of this body of work has been to recognize that individual and group characteristics of nurses and clients affect how pain is interpreted. While further study in this area is needed, the influence of cultural group membership on the norms of pain expression and on behavior from the perspective of the client and nurse is evident. Nurses must begin to recognize that the interpretation of pain is influenced by characteristics of both the client and the nurse. Differences in pain perception can not always be accounted for by looking solely at physiological indicators.

The environmental context in which the nurse practices is also a factor within the theory of Culture Care Diversity and Universality which is proposed to affect nurses, nursing care systems, and ultimately nursing care decisions and actions. In relation to pain, the context in which the nurse practices, whether in the hospital or community, working with infants or the elderly, also influences what reactions to pain that are viewed as acceptable by nurses and what care measures are deemed as appropriate. For example, while crying and screaming may tend to be viewed as an expected and acceptable response from a young child who is receiving an injection, a similar reaction from an adult receiving an injection may be viewed as an inappropriate response. An example related to differences in care of clients in pain potentially exists between hospice and hospital settings. The frequency and quantity of narcotic administration may tend to be greater in a hospice setting, where the primary goal of care is for comfort. In a hospital setting, while comfort is a goal, concerns about narcotic administration and addiction, respiratory depression, or overdosing, are influencing factors which may tend to decrease both the amount of medication ordered and the frequency with which it is administered.

Unit culture has been identified as a factor that influences nursing care related to pain. Unwritten standards of care, cooperation among the multidisciplinary team, and administrative support are all components of unit culture that affects care related to pain.[53] For example, nurses may place a high priority on efforts to relieve pain in environments where they are held accountable by their coworkers, peers, and families for adequate pain relief. In contrast, nurses may not be as attentive to providing pain relief for clients in environments where adequate pain control is not viewed as important, or under the control of nurses, and where such efforts to alleviate pain are not recognized.

In addition to the influences on the nurse and client, and the influences of the cultural context on both the nurse and client, the interactive cultural elements between the nurse, client, and environment must be considered. Involved in the assessment of pain is an interpretive process from which the professional, such as the nurse, sanctions the validity of the pain that the person experiences. Yet, inferences made by nurses in relation to if pain exists, the severity of the pain, and the action that should be taken, are not always congruent with the perspective of the client. In addition, the type of care designed for the client by the nurse may not be congruent with the client or within the environmental context.

A few examples will be given to illustrate these multiple components and interactions. A nurse might come to the conclusion, for example, that a person who does not ask for p.r.n. pain medication is not in pain. Other factors, however, such as fear of becoming addicted to narcotics, or the need to be perceived as good and strong, may more accurately reflect the perspective of the client.

In a related situation a client may indicate to the nurse that he/she is in pain. Yet, if after a thorough assessment, the nurse is unable to relate the pain to a particular condition or disease state, or detect the presence of other clinical indicators of pain, such as a change in vital signs, diaphoresis, or decreased activity, the nurse might conclude that the complaint of pain is an expression of loneliness, depression, or reflects an attempt to manipulate or perhaps gain attention from others. The nurse, based on this decision, may choose not to take any action directed toward alleviating the client's pain. From the perspective of the client, the following example could also illustrate the concept of cultural pain. The client may perceive the nurse as insensitive to his or her condition. In addition, if the client is from a cultural group that is different from the nurse the client could interpret the nurses' lack of response or consideration of his/her pain, as a rejection of the client because of the differences in cultural background.

An individual may be used to dealing with pain in a certain manner, but may alter his or her behavior in order to influence nurses to act in a certain manner. For example, a person experiencing pain, who is and quiet and utilizes forms of distraction, such as reading, watching television, or talking with friends or family to deal with pain, may find it difficult to have health care professionals believe he or she is experiencing pain. Comments from nurses or other health care providers such as, "You don't look like you're in pain." "The pain must not be that bad if you were sleeping," "Maybe you're just anxious, because you were fine when your friends were here.". are indicators to individuals as to what expressions and behaviors will elicit care from nurses, such as medication administration. Thus, in order to be consistent with a nurse's view of how pain should be conveyed, the client may begin to moan, cry, rock, and guard the affected site. Although this behavior may not be consistent with the patient's pattern of expression, it is only when this behavior is consistent with that of the nurse, or understood by the nurse, that care decisions and actions will be initiated by the nurse.

These are but a few examples, from research and practice, which illustrate the multiple dimensions nurses need to consider in caring for clients experiencing pain. These examples are characteristic of the complexities involved in the nursing care of people who are experiencing pain. The research presented in this chapter also reflects the challenges researchers and practitioners face in relation to the care of people experiencing pain. At a minimum, it is critical for nurses to recognize that there are multiple factors that influence a person's expression, meaning, and care as it relates to pain. In addition, nurses must recognize that these same factors influence the nurse's perception of the patient's pain, and that these perspectives may not always be congruent and will often be in conflict.

The theory of Culture Care Diversity and Universality provides a useful framework to guide both practice and research in relation to caring for people in pain. Clearly there is a need for transcultural nursing studies related to pain, specifically in relation to: I) the discovery of meanings, expression, and care patterns as they relate to pain across cultural groups; 2) the discovery of which and in what manner meanings, expressions, and care are influenced by cultural and social structure dimensions, both in relation to the nurse and the client; and 3) understanding the influence of the cultural context in relation to pain from the perspective of the nurse and client. At the same time, nurses in practice settings must develop nursing care decisions and actions that will result in the delivery of culturally congruent care. In other words, care should be designed that will be congruent with the beliefs, values, and lifeways of the client in order to assist them in achieving beneficial outcomes, such as wellness, or to assist them in their acceptance of pain outcomes. A nurse's knowledge of culture care can assist in the creative discovery and use of means to care for clients experiencing pain. The comfort of clients is dependent on the nurse's ability to understand and respect the diversity of meanings and expressions of pain.

References

1. Mersky, H. Classification of Chronic Pain: Description of Chronic Pain Syndromes and Definitions of Pain Terms. *Pain Supplement,* Vol. 3., 1986.

2. Meinhart, N.T. and McCaffery, M. *Pain: A Nursing Approach to Assessment and Analysis.* Norwalk, CT: Appleton-Century-Crofts, 1983.

3. Leininger, M. Leininger's Theory of Nursing: Cultural Care Diversity and Universality. *Nursing Science Quarterly,* Vol. 1, No. 4, 1988, pp. 52-160.

4. Abu-Saad, H. Cultural Group Indicators of Pain in Children. *Maternal Child Nursing Journal,* Vol. 13, 1984, pp. 187-196.

5. Klienman, A. *Patients and Healers in the Context of Culture.* Berkeley, CA: University of California Press, 1980.

6. Klienman, A. *Nursing and Anthropology: Two Worlds to Blend.* New York, NY: John Wiley & Sons, 1970. (Reprinted by Greyden Press, Columbus, OH, 1994.)

7. Larkins, F. The Influence of One Patient's Culture on Pain Response. *Nursing Clinics of North America,* Vol. 12, 1977, pp. 663-668.

8. Leininger, M. *Transcultural Nursing: Concepts, Theories, and Practices.* New York, NY: John wiley & Sons, 1978.

9. Op cit. Leininger, 1988.

10. Leininger, M. Presentation at Transcultural Nursing Society Annual Meeting, University of Utah, Salt Lake City, 1984.

11. Leininger, M. *Cultural Care Diversity and Universality: A Theory of Nursing.* New York: National League for Nursing, 1991.

12. Ibid.

13. Lipton, J. and Marbach, J. Ethnicity and pain experience. *Social Science Medicine,* Vol. 19, 1984, pp. 1279-1298.

14. Op cit, Leininger, 1988.

15. Melczak, R. and Wall, P.G. Pain Mechanisms: A New Theory. *Science*, Vol. 150, 1965, pp. 971-979.

16. Bates, M. Ethnicity and pain: A biocultural model. *Social Science Medicine*, Vol. 24, 1987, pp, 37-50.

17. Zborowski, M. Cultural components in response to pain. *Journal of Social Issues*, Vol. 8, pp. 16-30, 1952.

18. Ibid.

19. Ibid.

20. Weisenberg, M. Kriendler, M. Schachat, B. and Werboff, J. Pain: Anxiety and Attitudes in Black, White, and Puerto Rican Patients. *Psychosomatic Medicine*, Vol. 37, 1975, pp. 123-135

21. Woodrow, K.M., Friedman, G.D., Sieglaub, A.B. and Collen, M.F. Pain Differences According to Age, Sex, and Race. *Psychosomatic Medicine*, Vol. 34, 1972, pp. 548-556.

22. Flannery, R.B., Sos, J., and McGovern, P. Ethnicity as a Factor in the Expression of Pain. *Psychosomatics*, Vol. 22, 1981, pp. 39-45.

23. Lawlis, G.F., Achterberg, J., Kenner, L., and Koepte, K. Ethnic and Sex Differences in Response to Clinical and Induced Pain in Chronic Spinal Pain Patients. *Spine*, Vol. 9, 1984, pp. 751-754

24. Greenwald, H.P. Interethnic Differences in Pain Perception. *Pain*, Vol. 44, No. 2, 1991, pp. 157-164.

25. Moore, R. Ethnographic Assessment of Pain Coping Perceptions. *Psychosomatic Medicine*, Vol. 52, 1990, pp. 171-181.

26. Reizan, A. and Meleis, A.I. Arab-American Perceptions of and Responses to Pain. *Critical Care Nurse*, Vol. 6, 1986, pp. 30-36.

27. Ibid.

28. Ibid.

29. Villarruel, A.M. and Ortiz de Montellano, B. Culture and Pain: A Mesoamerican Perspective. *Advances in Nursing Science*, Vol. 15, No. 1, 1993, pp. 21-32.

30. Ibid.

31. Rosenbaum, J.N. The Health Meanings and Practices of Older Greek-Canadian Widows. *Journal of Advanced Nursing*, Vol. 16, No. 1, 1991, pp. 320-1327.

32. Ibid.

33. Kagawa-Sincer, M. Ethnic Perspectives of Cancer Nursing: Hispanics and Japanese-Americans. *Oncology Nursing Forum*, Vol. 14, No. 3, 1987, pp. 59-65

34. Ibid.

35. Op cit, Klienman, 1980.

36. Ibid.

37. Op cit, Leininger, 1991.

38. Davitz L. and Davitz, J. Culture and Nurses' Inferences of Suffering. L.A. Copp (Ed.) *Recent Advances in Nursing Perspectives on Pain*. NY: Churchill Livingstone, 1985.

39. Davitz, I.J. and Pendelton, S.H. Nurses Inferences of Suffering. *Nursing Research*, Vol. 18, 1969, pp. 100-110.

40. Mason, D.J. An Investigation of the Influences of Selected Factors on Nurses: Inferences of Patient Suffering. *International Journal of Nursing Studies*, Vol. 18, 1981, pp. 251-259.

41. Cohen, F.L. Postsurgical pain relief: Patients Status and Nurses' Medication Choices. *Pain*, Vol. 9, 1980, pp. 256-274.

42. Acheson, E.L. Nurses's Inference of Pain and Distress for Culturally Different Patients. *Oklahoma Nurse*, Vol. 34, 1989, pg. 7.

43. Dudley, S. and Holm, K. Assessment of the Pain Experience in Relation to Selected Nurse Characteristics. *Pain*, Vol. 18, 1984, pp. 179-186.

44. Halfens, R., Evers, G. and Abu-Saad, H. Determinants of Pain Assessment by Nurses. *International Journal of Nursing Studies*, Vol. 27, No. 1, 1990, pp. 43-49.

45. Baer, E. Davitz, L.J., and Lieb, R. Inferences of Physical Pain and Psychological Distress in Relation to Verbal and Nonverbal Patient Communication. *Nursing Research*, Vol. 19, 1970, pp. 388-392.

46. Op cit, Cohen, 1980.

47. Davitz, L.N., Sameshima, Y., and Davitz, J.R. Suffering as Viewed in Six Different Cultures. *American Journal of Nursing*, Vol. 76, 1976, pp. 1296-1297.

48. Ibid.

49. Op cit, Dudley and Holm, 1984.

50. Op cit, Halfens, Evers, and Abu-Saad, 1990.

51. Op cit, Mason, 1981.

52. Holm, K. Cohen, F., dudas, S., Medema, P.G. and Allen, B. L. Effect of Personal Pain Experience on Pain Assessment. Image: *Journal of Nursing Scholarship*, Vol. 21, 1989, pp. 72-76.

53. Foster, R.L. The Effect of Unit Culture on Nurses' Managment of Children's Pain. *Journal of Pain and Symptom Management*, Vol. 6, No. 3, 1990, pg. 202.

Chapter 11
Transcultural Mental Health Nursing

Madeleine Leininger, PhD, LHD, DS, FAAN, CTN, RN.

As one of the early pioneers in psychiatric nursing and the author of one of the first comprehensive psychiatric nursing textbooks, *Basic Psychiatric Concepts in Nursing*, in 1960, it has been encouraging to see several changes in psychiatric mental health nursing.[1] The area, however, that has needed a major change is to incorporate cultural care dimensions of mental health to meet diverse client needs and expectations. This need became clearly apparent to me while trying to use Western Euro-American psychoanalytical and other general psychiatric concepts to care for disturbed children and adults of different cultures in the mid 1960s. It was these children with their uninhibited comments and actions who told me that there were differences among African, Jewish, German, Appalachian, and Anglo-American children which needed to be studied and recognized. Transcultural differences among the children in daily caring experiences were extremely difficult to overlook or deny. As an experienced psychiatric nurse interested in helping people, this reality left me in culture shock and feeling helpless and concerned. My basic and advanced psychiatric nursing preparation had been inadequate and incomplete with the absence of cultural factors and transcultural nursing theory, knowledge, and practices.

Discovery of the Need for Changes

The above culture shock experience led me to realize more fully in my conversations with the well-known cultural anthropologist, Margaret Mead, that anthropological theories and research of diverse cultures could help nurses to understand and greatly expand psychiatric nursing knowledge, research, and practices. Following five years of doctoral study in anthropology, as the first nurse with graduate preparation in nursing to complete a Ph.D. program in cultural anthropology, I began to learn about different cultures with diverse beliefs about mental health and illness. I soon became deeply concerned that many people seeking help in psychiatric hospitals or in private psychotherapy could well be misdiagnosed, misunderstood, or not cared for adequately due to Western ethnocentric psychiatric viewpoints and practices and the absence of cultural knowledge. Major differences in the culture care patterns, expressions, and beliefs related to mental health and illness also were of concern to me for in the 1940s and 1950s psychiatric nurses were largely focused on diagnosing psychiatric diseases and in learning about ways to be a competent clinical specialist and therapist in psychiatric nursing. It also became apparent that the psychiatric nurses could no longer mainly rely on the mind-body or psychophysical aspects of psychiatric nursing. Thus the field of transcultural nursing was established as a formal area of study and practice to learn comparative culture care, and especially to expand and initiate new knowledge into psychiatric nursing.[2,3]

The cultural dimensions of human care from a holistic care viewpoint needed to be incorporated into all aspects of psychiatric research and practice. To continue with the partial and narrow Western psychiatric perspectives and with the APA nomenclature of prescribed treatment regimens was inadequate for multicultural clients. Indeed, I predicted that mental health programs would fail because clients were coming from many different cultures by the early 1960s and few knew how to care for them. Global migrations and immigrations of clients were already leading to major cultural value conflicts and stresses in psychiatric settings. One could predict more serious problems related to misdiagnoses and mistreatment of cultural strangers in the future in most places. This reality along with the need to educate nursing students and faculty to transcultural mental health dimensions in all areas of learning were greatly needed and clearly evident.

The need for transcultural mental health nursing was even more essential in health care institutions and in communities with multiple cultures and subcultures. Transcultural mental health preparation of staff was essential because of many people coming from virtually every place in the world and even more predicted in the next century. Accordingly, the critical problem was to prepare nurses with a transculturally based framework so they could function with clients of culturally different backgrounds. Psychiatric nurses needed to change from treating clients from a unicultural viewpoint or as if they were all alike and came from one dominant culture. This "all alike view and approach" was woefully inadequate to meet the needs of consumers from diverse cultures who expected and wanted their cultural values, beliefs, and practices respected and acted upon in culture specific ways.

Unquestionably, nurses with preparation in transcultural nursing would be using different knowledge and skills related to cultural specific beliefs, values, and lifeways of people. Mental health nurses need to change their practices to fit with and be relevant to clients' cultural background. Many psychiatric nurses also need to study anew their traditional practices from and refocus on transcultural mental health nursing. Available transcultural knowledge could be used by psychiatric nurses to assess clients within a much broader and yet culture-specific way as they learned about specific cultural values and beliefs and mental illnesses, recovery, and prevention processes. Psychiatric nurses needed to become skilled in doing culturalogical holistic mental health assessment and to draw upon the clients' culture care knowledge and experiences. Learning about the assets and strengths of a culture and their beliefs and lifeways would provide comparative Western and non-Western psychiatric knowledge. These factors and others have slowly led to nurses pursuing the study of transcultural comparative mental health knowledge and skills.

Questions for Reflection

In shifting to a transcultural psychiatric nursing perspective, several questions immediately come to mind such as: 1) What universal (or common) and diverse mental stresses, conflicts, and behaviors tend to recur in different nursing contexts and cultures? 2) What are the meanings and clients' interpretations of these stresses or conflicts and how do clients believe their concerns could be reduced or altered? 3) What are the emic (insider's knowledge) and etic (outsider's) interpretations of cultural conditions, clashes, or conflicts from a holistic viewpoint of an individual or group? 4) What constitutes mental illness or pathologies of specific cultures such as the Turks, Arabs, Mexicans, Italians, Russians, Czechs, and many other cultures? 5) What explanations and interpretations are known in these cultures about mental health, illness, treatment, and culture care? 6) What similarities and differences exist between Western and non-Western cultures related to mental health that could provide guidelines and principles for transcultural mental health nursing? 7) What generic folk care practices need to be incorporated into transcultural mental health nursing practices and how do these practices differ from current professional psychiatric practices or therapies? 8) How can generic and professional mental health nursing practices be synthesized to be beneficial to clients? 9) What problems exist with the present day use of nursing diagnoses (NANDA or others) to identify, understand, and accurately care for clients from diverse cultures? 10) Why do some cultures or subcultures never use or accept psychiatric care? 11) What culture-specific mental illnesses exist in cultures? 12) What are the benefits of culture-specific mental health nursing?

These questions can lead the nurse to new discoveries related to nursing practices. The Theory of Culture Care Diversity and Universality is a valuable guide to discover comparative transcultural mental health knowledge and ways to provide mental health nursing practices that are culturally congruent to specific cultures. Research studies focused on the meaning of mental health and illness in different cultures are extremely important in developing mental health caring and therapy goals. Psychiatric nurses with traditional professional education will need to reexamine their own cultural myths, biases, and practices in light of extant transcultural nursing concepts, principles, and research findings about diverse cultures. The use of emic and etic interpretations and experiences offers many stimulating challenges for nurses, especially those who are familiar with the Theory of Culture Care Diversity and Universality open to designing new ways to care for the mentally ill or troubled.

Fundamental Principles for Transcultural Mental Health Nursing

Currently, transcultural mental health nurses can draw upon the body of transcultural nursing knowledge to guide them in their teaching, research, and practice. A comparative focus on mental health differences and similarities among cultures help the nurse to think anew about her (his) ideas and practices of transcultural nursing concepts of cultural imposition, cultural blindness, cultural conflicts, cultural values, cultural beliefs, and cultural lifeways and can provide information to understand clients and to develop transcultural mental health nursing practices. There is also a growing body of transcultural research knowledge of diverse cultures that can be used or considered in developing mental health practices. This information is found in many chapters in this book and in other reference sources. Let us next turn to some fundamental principles and ideas to support and develop transcultural mental health nursing.

The first principle is to understand and respect cultural differences and care for clients from any culture as human beings. To understand the "why" of beliefs and actions helps the nurse to know why many differences exist in people care is important. The nurse needs to recognize that differences have meanings which can generally be understood with transcultural nursing and anthropological knowledge. Understanding cultural differences means the nurse is capable of using ideas appropriate to a specific culture. Recognizing cultural variabilities and similarities with mental expressions is difficult without some holding cultural knowledge to reflect upon in an assessment or therapy session. Interactional data may be helpful, but it is often of limited assistance in understanding specific cultural values, beliefs, and practices.

The second important principle is that the nurse should endeavor to understand her (his) own culture values, beliefs, and lifeways in order to make accurate client assessments and interpretations. Without awareness of the nurse's own culture, misinterpretations and inaccurate decisions and actions can readily occur, which often leads to unfavorable consequences. Cultural informants are generally sensitive to how their beliefs and actions are interpreted and to professional biases, prejudices, and disbeliefs of the clients' views. It is often difficult for clients to convince health personnel regarding which beliefs are "normal" and accurate from the clients' perspective, and which are "abnormal" or distorted. Nonetheless, the mental health nurse needs to make sense out of diverse information as she (he) reflects on cultural norms and rules of the client's culture as well as the therapist's culture. Misinterpretation of cultural background factors often leads to cultural insensitivity and to many unfavorable outcomes. The nurse needs to understand her (his) cultural values and behaviors in order to be make accurate assessment and to work effectively with clients.

The third principle is to identify and work with a transcultural nurse mentor to help the nurse practitioner or specialist to be fully effective in his (her) work. Transcultural nurse mentors can be of great assistance to help novice nurses reflect upon their own cultural attitudes and practices in order to consider the context of behavior and what may be relevant to help the client. Learning about non-verbal and verbal cues from clients is important to understand and interpret fully what clients say or do within their cultural frame of reference and context. Making mental health nursing practices meaningful within the client's cultural context from the initial contact until the end of the relationship is extremely important and dependent upon the nurse's knowledge of the culture and the use of mentor perspectives. Rigid professional attitudes, policies, or the lack of accommodation to meet the client's cultural needs can lead to disturbing, violent, or uncooperative behavior. The three modes of the Culture Care Theory using 1) culture care preservation or maintenance strategies, 2) culture care accommodation or negotiation, and 3) culture care repatterning or restructuring are most useful guides for nursing action and interaction in the care of the mentally ill client and his (her) family.

The fourth transcultural nursing principle is to learn about the client's cultural context, multiple social structure factors, and the worldview, which can greatly influence mental health behaviors. Understanding the cultural context of the mentally ill means grasping the totality of the client's environment and situation which is meaningful to him (her) now and in the past. What makes the client upset or ill is usually context specific. The nurse needs to consider *low cultural context* in which the client will give a lot of verbal explanations and use many words and symbols to convey their ideas. In contrast, a client from a *high cultural context* will have very limited verbal comments but will expect the nurse to understand without using verbal explanations. Usually the low cultural context reflects more traditional values, beliefs, and explanations known to many in the community. Knowledge and assessment of the cultural context has a great influence on the perceptions and behavior of the client.

The fifth principle is to allow time and maintain patience as one works with clients of different psychocultural expectations, values, and lifeways. Adjusting to client's from several cultures may be stressful to some nurses as it requires alertness, sensitivity, and a conscious centering on the client, his (her) culture, and responding appropriately to the client's needs. Periodic assessment of the client alerts the nurse to be aware of changes in client's behavior over time and of changing client needs. Using client cultural data in thoughtful and appropriate ways necessitates patience, reflective thinking, being mindful of the situation and to become culturally sensitive and knowledgeable about the client.

Sixth, the nurse must learn about the different cultural illnesses and wellness states of different cultures and subcultures and respond knowingly to these conditions in a sensitive and appropriate way. Since our *Western APA Diagnostic and Statistical Manual* seldom includes culture-bound illnesses, syndromes, or conditions, such as running amok, susto, evil eye, intentional death, spiritualism, stoicism, and other cultural behaviors, the nurse must learn about these non-Western or culture-bound conditions. Cultures also tend to have different thresholds for expressing particular deviant behaviors which they may not consider to be pathological, psychotic, or even neurotic. Hallucinations and delusions are often not expressed in the same transcultural manner with other cultures. Most importantly, it is often the cultural context, situation, or event that influences whether cultural behaviors are viewed as "normal" or "deviant." Some cultures tend to accept specific and deviant behaviors more readily than others and without fear or concern. Transcultural mental health nurses would need to be open to recognize diverse cultural expressions of what may be known as normal or abnormal in a culture.

Cultural variability also exists which may make the nurse uncomfortable when clients change their behaviors in varying ways in different contexts and with different people due to status and role expectations. Psychopathological conditions may not exist in some cultures or may be expressed differently in cultures. Assertive, aggressive, and some forms of violent behavior are often viewed differently in cultures as "normal" adaptive or normative behavior, often as necessary to survival or to fulfill social and cultural obligations. Counter-revenge feuds and "game like" aggressive actions may be an integral part of a client's cultural behavior and not an indication of illness. Major discrepancies and variations with diagnosis and symptoms of clients in different cultures may be baffling to a mental health nurse until they study and use transcultural knowledge. Discrepancies in the treatment, prognosis, and care of clients can greatly vary in cultures. Fitting symptoms and signs of Western categories to a non-Western culture or nomenclature may not give an accurate and reliable transcultural taxonomy or means to help clients in effective ways.

It is also important for the mental health nurse to know that psychological and medical anthropology are branches of anthropology. Researchers in these fields have been studying mental illnesses and diseases in different cultures for many decades. These psychologists and medical anthropologists tend to focus mainly on what constitutes "normality" and "abnormality" in different cultures.[4] Anthropologists focus in depth on social structure factors such as politics, religion, and cultural beliefs to assess the impact of these factors upon the client. Anthropologists are also interested in describing and studying the functions of the healers and curers in different cultures in treating cultural conditions. Psychological anthropologists are interested in the effect of forced migrations, refugees, urbanization, and cultural context changes on clients and the impact of medicalization and high technologies on people of different cultures. Psychiatrists prepared in anthropology tend to look at these dimensions along with anthropological ideas related to biochemical and physiological stresses and different cultural treatment modes of cultural illnesses. Illnesses and cultural coping abilities and cultural adaptations to life experiences are also of interest to anthropologists.

Currently, psychiatrists seem to be holding to the stance that mental diseases are genetic or due to biochemical factors. This theme has been dominating the medical professional and public media. Transcultural nurses are most interested in culture-specific factors or factors external to the mind and body which affect the client's behavior and attitudes toward others in community and hospital cultures.[5] Helman, a British anthropologist, holds that the relationship of culture to mental illness tends to define what is "normal" and "abnormal" in a particular culture, and there is a close relationship between culture and the way mental illnesses are recognized, explained, and treated by members of the culture.[6] Transcultural nurses draw largely upon external and interpersonal forces based especially on their research care findings. They remain attentive to human caring, environmental living factors, social context, and health or well-being factors from a nursing perspective.

Psychocultural Specific Mental Health Conditions

During the past several decades much has been written by transcultural nurses, anthropologists, psychologists, and a few psychiatrists about culture-specific expressions of mental illness and the relationship of culture to personality. The works of Helman;[7] Marsella, Tharp and Ciborowski;[8] Peterson;[9] Peterson et al.;[10] Leininger;[11,12,13] Mead;[14] Glittenberg;[15] Barnauw;[16] and Moore, VanArsdale, Glittenberg, and Aldrich.[17] The relationship between the individual and the culture has led to many speculative ideas and informative ethnographic data to establish therapeutic care practices.

Psychiatric nurses have been slow to recognize and systematically study mental health and illness from a culturalogical perspective. The author contends this is largely due to the lack of preparation in anthropology and transcultural nursing and the close identification of psychiatric nurses with psychiatrist's work and therapies. Many psychiatric nurses remain absorbed in studying psychiatric medical diseases and psychoanalytical modes of therapy in order to institute independent and collaborative treatment practices. In addition, some psychiatric nurse therapists have relied heavily upon the importance of psychoanalysis and the psychotherapy practices.

Psychoanalytical, neo-Freudian, and other psychiatric schools of thought have greatly influenced psychiatric nursing education and services. The cultural dimensions, however, have been neglected except for work of the author and a few recent psychiatric nurses who have had anthropological preparation and have studied and developed transcultural mental health nursing. Leininger;[18,19,20,21] Glittenberg;[22] and Campinha-Bacote;[23,24] have been some of the major leaders to establish transcultural mental health nursing education and practice. In fact, the psychocultural nursing research conducted by Leininger in the mid 1960s was the first study to show the benefits of focusing on cultural factors and mental health.[25]

In Leininger's initial ethnonursing study of the Gadsup of the Eastern Highlands of New Guinea in the 1960s, she observed the absence of schizophrenic behavior in the people of the two villages where she lived and studied for more than one year. The Gadsup had short-term transient depression behavior which was usually related to the loss of a loved kinsman, child, spouse, or significant village leader. The absence of many Western illnesses was apparent and could be explained from ethnographic and ethnonursing research findings related to the cultural context and to culturally constituted values and beliefs of the people. A caring ethos and nurturant childcare by women with strong protective care by men among their kinsmen and lineages were other important factors.[26] In addition, the rhythm of Gadsup daily life was quite regularized and predictable, which gave them security and reassurance in knowing what rules of living to follow and clear expectation for action modes. Intertribal feuds and sorcery acquisitions existed which were related to normative beliefs and explicit village rules of behavior for all Gadsups.

In recent years, the Gadsup have had increased contact with outsiders or strangers from other countries. The author found in her last visit in 1992 signs of unrest, violence, paranoid-like behaviors, extended family anxieties with signs of confused and anxious behaviors that were largely related to foreigners in their villages or nearby. One could also identify some paranoid or suspicious behavior was almost justifiable due to outsiders encroaching upon the Gadsup lands, lifeways, and use of their natural resources and humans without giving anything in return to the Gadsup villagers. In fact, a young male group known as the "rascals" have launched an aggressive movement with violent acts to regain the indigenous rights, land, and money.[27] Sick behavior cannot be viewed as psychiatric or irrational by the people, but *must be understood within their cultural context and experiences with Western exploiters.*

In the next section some culture-specific psychocultural expressions related to mental health will be highlighted to help the reader understand the influence of culture on mental health or illness in different cultures. Many of these culture-specific findings come from the author's research and those of doctoral transcultural nursing students.[28]

1. Mexican Americans

Mexican Americans tend to have less incidence of mental illnesses, which appears to be largely due to their close extended family ties, support for their cultural values and beliefs, and role of religion and kinship to allay anxieties, stresses, and unnecessary conflicts. Many Mexican American stresses were related to poverty, unemployment, and urban problems which can bring about periods of depression, overweight conditions, and potential suicide. Research among Mexican Americans reveals that alcohol is frequently used with negative outcomes. The male *machismo* often reveals men taking too much alcohol in order to express their masculinity, bravery, or power. Mexican American women tend to relieve their mental stresses or conflicts with family, support, use of folk healing modes, and especially herbal drinks. Some Mexican American women have panic expressions which they blame upon external forces that led to problems and failures. Mexican Americans petition God and many saints to help them cope with daily mental and cultural problems related to death or losses and to family stresses. The cultural phenomenon of susto, magical fright, can be precipitated by sudden or unexpected accidents or critical social life situations. Casting the evil eye (*mal ojo*) is another potential conflict that can lead to mental illness. The evil eye is caused when strangers overpraise or envy a newborn. The cultural condition often is caused unintentionally by nurses, physicians, and others who do not understand the Mexican cultural beliefs and lifeways.

2. Appalachians

Appalachians come from the rural mountains and hills of the eastern United States. They often move into urban areas seeking employment. The intense and fast moving large city culture often lead Appalachians to feel alone and depressed. They experience what they call the "blues" but usually do not become psychotic. They have a deep sense of being separated from their kinsmen and friends in the rural "hollows" of their homeland. Appalachians often talk about the fear of urban crime and not leaving their homes at night unless absolutely necessary. Elderly Appalachians were especially afraid to go out at night in the urban environment. The Appalachians often talk about a "case of nerves" or of trying to understand how to cope in violent urban and stressful environments. The author found in her research that many of the urban Appalachians were very neglected and unknown white people by health personnel. However, the Appalachians were experiencing great poverty and isolation, especially in urban locations. They had limited resources and many lived below the poverty level of $5,000 per year. Appalachians were generally uncomfortable with Anglo-American and multicultural urban values, beliefs, and lifeways because they were so strange to them. The need for transcultural caring values of 1) keeping close ties with kin from the hollow; 2) relying on their personalized region; 3) using folk remedies; and 4) protecting themselves from harmful strangers, were desired and important for Appalachians to maintain their mental health and survival in an urban context. Appalachians wanted transcultural nurses to be with them as they understood their cultural values and lifeways and they listen to them.

3. African Americans

The psychological, psychiatric, and some anthropological literature on African Americans and "Blacks" show considerable variability in research findings and interpretations. Hence, nursing students are encouraged to read extensively on this subject because this short account is in no way complete enough to show variabilities among a large and growing African American culture. Moreover, controversial issues exist related to mental health and illness with African Americans. Hence, only a brief summary of a few dominant themes is given here.

In general, there is a great lack of in-depth understanding about African Americans and those who are called "Black" due to cultural, biological, racial (phenotypes and genotypes) and diverse life experiences. The transcultural mental health nurse must study acculturation and ethnohistorical factors in-depth to grasp the general picture and change in African American culture over time. They must go beyond hair, body size, and skin color differences and dwell on the past and present cultural life experiences influencing African Americans' lives, especially in large urban cities. Understanding the Sunrise Model components of the worldview and diverse social structure factors are relevant influencers of mental health of African Americans. There are also major differences between rural and urban African Americans, who experience different kinds of mental stresses as they move from rural to urban environments.

Studies show that the major mental health problems for urban African Americans are related to alcohol and drug abuse which have led to street deaths, homicide, and physiological diseases such as hepatitis, and liver cirrhosis, heart disease, cancer, and a host of other pathological conditions.[29,30] Some studies hold that the urban African American extended family no longer exists and where this occurs, family instability is evident leading to the lack of strong male and female sex role identification and survival skills in a crime oriented urban society. Today, many African American fathers and mothers are often absent from their homes due to outside work for economic survival. This has undoubtedly had a major influence on maintaining cultural values and helping children survive and cope with life in a persistent changing world. In the past, African American families provided food, shelter, clothing, counseling, and environmental support through extended family ties. The absence of family ties in urban homes has influenced the mental health and well-being of African Americans.

There are also reports of an increase of human immunodeficiency virus (HIV) infection in some large African American urban communities. Hypertension, stroke, and other pathological conditions have frequently been traced to cultural, social, economic, and political factors which have had a deleterious impact upon the general health and survival of African Americans in large urban contexts.[31]

A transcultural mental health nurse needs to become knowledgeable about sociocultural, political, economic, and other factors which influence African American lifeways. The nurse should study specific cultural values, beliefs, and lifestyle practices as well as folk beliefs, related to witchcraft, voodoo, and other African heritage expressions. It would be important to understand hexes and voodoo practices in relation to mental illness and health. Voodoo teaches that illness or death can come to an individual or group through supernatural forces.[32] It may be referred to as root work, black magic, being hexed, fix, a spell, or witchcraft. The affected person may talk about being nauseated, vomiting, diarrhea, or having muscle weakness or convulsions. "Falling out" may also be identified by African Americans as a sudden collapse, inability to talk, and sometimes paralysis. These culture-related expressions often lead to misdiagnosis and inappropriate treatment and nursing care actions. Nurses with transcultural perspectives and knowledge can identify these kinds of cultural conditions that can influence African American holistic health and well-being. Drawing upon African folk (emic) knowledge is extremely important to understand the client and family, and to alleviate cultural and mental stresses which sometimes mimic aspects of mental disorders.

4. Vietnamese

Vietnamese generally find that Western psychiatric treatment and mental health care is strange and questionable. If Vietnamese are seen in a psychiatric setting, their concerns are often misinterpreted or misdiagnosed by nurses and physicians who fail to understand Vietnamese culture values, beliefs, and lifeways. Vietnamese hold that the mind, body, and soul are integrated and cannot be viewed as separate entities. The idea of psychiatric nurses or physicians separating the mind, body, and soul is disturbing to Vietnamese immigrants and refugees should seek Western psychiatric help. The idea closes to Western mental illness might be a "case of nerves" or having "something wrong with the nervous system." Some Vietnamese view such conditions as mainly a weakness of the nerves. Moreover, the head with many different spirits is sacred, and needs to be considered in surgical and medical conditions and treatment modes a spiritual focus.

Many Vietnamese clients which the author and other transcultural nurses have studied have encountered great difficulty with hospital personnel due to language and cultural value barriers. Vietnamese Americans tend to suppress or deny their feelings about problems because nurses are viewed as strangers. They will often talk about somatic concerns rather than their private cultural life situations or personal and family losses. Experiencing "cultural pain" as defined in this book has been typically found with Vietnamese refugees who have endured severe cultural tensions and hardships. Spending time with the Vietnamese client and family to help them get comfortable with the nurse is important. Then they will talk about their losses and concerns and how to use their folk remedies, foods, herbs, and teas. Posttraumatic stress disorder (PTSD) is commonly used by psychiatric staff to fit Vietnamese refugees with a Western label.[33] Nurses using the Culture Care Theory will want to focus on the assets or strengths of Vietnamese clients and especially their families when dealing with mental stresses or conflicts. Cultural pain is often due to loss of kinship or family members, inability to get work, and lack of respect. The nurses will also need to deal with feelings of loneliness and separation which refugees experience as well as leaving their homeland and adjusting to a very different culture.

Feelings of hopelessness, distress, grief, fatigue, mood swings, and somatic complaints can be found as dominant mental concerns with many Vietnamese refugees and immigrants. Vietnamese culture care values related to kinship factors, religious beliefs, and their present or past ethnohistory and environmental contexts are all important areas for the nurse to focus upon with Vietnamese. This broad holistic approach reflected in the components of the Sunrise Model can be extremely helpful to guide the nurse in discovering and understanding concerns, stresses, and present life situations. The Vietnamese traditional beliefs, values, and lifeways and ways they prevent illness through cultural taboos are important. Helping Vietnamese and other Asian clients to regain their mind-body-soul equilibrium (or balance) should also be a major goal in nursing care. Western forced psychiatric disease labels and nursing diagnostic categories (NANDA) are usually inappropriate for nurses working with clients from Southeast Asia. Providing a quiet area for reflection and talking, avoiding negative criticism (saving face), and encouraging the client to share ideas about their family or work situations are often ways to achieve culturally competent and sensitive nursing care.

Above are only selected examples of some of the factors which the nurse needs to consider to provide culture-specific and culturally congruent mental health care. Many more cultural examples could be presented, but the reader will find that other chapters in the book will be of great help in understanding other cultures and potential mental health concerns and needs. Using transcultural concepts, principles, and the Culture Care Theory, the nurse can move from cultural awareness through systematic cultural assessments to applying transculturally based knowledge to provide culturally competent and congruent care for clients of diverse or similar cultures. Unquestionably, knowledge of the different cultures is essential for sound nursing decisions and actions. Mental health cultural skills from a comparative view will increase in-depth cultural knowledge. The nurse should remain alert at all times to similar and different Western and non-Western psychiatric diseases and psychiatric nursing practices and use emic data to guide nursing actions.

For most psychiatric nurses, today, transcultural nursing is essentially a new and exciting area of study and practice. It is most rewarding to enter the world of cultural strangers and understand their expressions of mental illness and wellness in different cultures. It is indeed rewarding and stimulating to assess and deal with intercultural variabilities, beliefs, and practices in relation to the effectiveness of one's care practices, especially bearing upon transcultural acculturation, enculturation, and assimilation aspects. Today and in the immediate future, considerably more formal education and direct mentorship will be required of psychiatric nurses to advance their practices and become competent and effective in transcultural mental health. Until this occurs, clients of diverse cultures may be jeopardized in receiving appropriate and beneficial mental health care.

References

1. Hofling, C. and M. Leininger, Basic Psychiatric Concepts in Nursing, New York: John Wiley and Sons, Inc., 1960.

2. Leininger, M., Transcultural Nursing: Concepts, Theories, and Practices, New York: John Wiley and Sons, Inc., 1978a.

3. Leininger, M., Culture Care Diversity and Universality: A Theory of Nursing, New York: National League for Nursing Press, 1991.

4. Kottak, C., Anthropology: The Exploration of Human Diversity, 5th ed., New York: McGraw Hill, Inc., 1991, pp. 354–367.

5. Leininger, M., *Discovery and Uses in Clinical and Community Nurses*, Detroit: Wayne State University Press, 1984, (reprinted by Charles Slack, 1988).

6. Helman, C. G., *Culture, Health, and Illness*, London: Wright, 1990.

7. Ibid., pp. 214–215.

8. Marsella, A., R. Tharp, and T. Ciborowski, eds., *Perspectives on Cross-Cultural Psychology*, New York: Academic Press, 1979.

9. Peterson, P., *Handbook of Cross-Cultural Counseling and Therapy*, Westport, Connecticut: Greenwood Press, 1985.

10. Peterson, P., N. Sartorius, and A. Marsella, *Mental Health Services: The Cross-Cultural Context*, Beverly Hills: Sage Publications, 1984.

11. Leininger, M., "Witchcraft Practices and Psychocultural Therapy with Urban United States Families," *Human Organization*, v. 32, no. 1, 1978b, pp. 73–80.

12. Leininger, M., "Transcultural Interviewing and Health Assessment," *Mental Health Services: The Cross Cultural Context*, P. Peterson, N. Sartorius, and A. Marsella, eds., Beverly Hills: Sage Publications, 1984, pp. 109–135.

13. Leininger, M., "Transcultural United Health Nursing Assessment of Children and Adolescents," *Psychiatric and Mental Health Nursing With Children and Adolescents*, C. Evans, ed., Gaithersburg, Maryland: Aspen Publishers, Inc., 1990.

14. Mead, M., *Coming of Age in Samoa*, New York: New American Library, 1961, (originally published 1928).

15. Glittenberg, J., "Cultural Heroes Aid in Coping," Unpublished paper, *Psychiatric Nurse Clinical Symposium*, Denver: April 18, 1979.

16. Barnauw, W. V., *Culture and Personality* (4th ed.), Homewood, Illinois: Dorsey Press, 1985.

17. Moore, L., P. VanArsdale, J. Glittenberg, and R. Aldrich, *The Biocultural Basis of Health: Expanding Views of Medical Anthropology*, Prospect Heights: Waveland Press, 1989.

18. Leininger, M., *Nursing and Anthropology: Two Worlds to Blend*, New York: John Wiley and Sons, Inc., 1970.

19. Leininger, op. cit., 1978a.
20. Leininger, M., "Gadsup of Papua New Guinea Revisited: A Three Decade View," *Journal of Transcultural Nursing*, v. 5, no. 1, Summer, 1993, pp. 21–30.
21. Leininger, op. cit., 1991.
22. Glittenberg, I., *Shamans, Exorcists, and Psychotherapists: Common Healers*, unpublished paper, Denver: University of Colorado School of Nursing, 1977.
23. Campinha-Bacote, J., "Cultural Competence in Psychiatric Mental Health Nursing: A Conceptual Model," *Nursing Clinics of North America*, v. 29, no. 1, March, 1994, pp. 1–8.
24. Campinha-Bacote, J., "Voodoo Illness: A Review," *Perspectives in Psychiatric Nursing*, v. 28, no. 1, 1992, pp. 11–17.
25. Leininger, op. cit., 1970.
26. Ibid.
27. Leininger, op. cti. 1993 pp. 21-30.
28. Leininger, op. cit. 1991 p. 362.
29. Ronan, L., "Alcohol-Related Health Risks among Black Americans," *Alcohol Health and Research World*, 1987, pp. 36–89.
30. Bailey, E., *African Americans Health in Urban Community*, 1991.
31. Leininger, op. cit., 1991.
32. Bailey, op. cit.
33. Tran, T. M., *Indochinese Patients*, Falls Church, Virginia: Action for Southeast Asians, 1980.

Chapter 12
Ethical, Moral, and Legal Aspects of Transcultural Nursing

Madeleine Leininger, PhD, LHD, FAAN, CTN, RN

> *When nurses understand and incorporate ethics of care from a transcultural nursing perspective into all aspects of nursing, we will have achieved one of the greatest and most meaningful services to humankind. We shall await that day with great joy.*
>
> Leininger, 1988

This chapter focuses upon selected aspects of transcultural differences and similarities with respect to values, beliefs, and practices of Western and non-Western cultures with nursing implications. Understanding ethical, moral, and legal values, norms, and practices among human cultures is a major challenge for nurses as is making appropriate nursing care decisions or actions. Some examples of cultural differences are presented to help nurses understand *why* clients may hold firmly to their ethical and moral values in life-and-death situations.

In this paper, "ethics" refers to how *individuals or groups* should or ought to behave, *whereas* morals *refers to individuals or groups need to conduct themselves with respect to what is held to be good, bad, right, or wrong.*[1] *"Legal" describes those claimed rights and acts of individuals or groups that are enforced, maintained, or regulated by law.*[2] Ethical and moral expressions, values, and beliefs tend to be buttressed by multiple factors, especially by religious beliefs, philosophical views, and specific cultural values, but usually vary transculturally.

Worldwide General and Professional Concerns

The topics of ethics, morals, and legal actions are of interest to all health professionals because they influence the welfare and survival of those served in professional relationships. But health professionals are not alone, as government officials, politicians, and most scientists and humanists are expected to be alert to the ethical and moral dimensions of their work and interests. Moreover, in recent years, world leaders and citizens have become increasingly vocal about violations of human rights and injustices reflecting unethical behaviors. Many have demanded that unethical or immoral behavior be seriously addressed at local, national, and worldwide levels. Ethical and moral behaviors have been a growing concern in all areas of human relationships and in worldwide affairs.

With rapid modes of communication and transportation, people from many different cultures are coming in close contact with one another and trying to relate in understandable ways. However, among world strangers major differences in beliefs, values, and actions often lead to tensions, conflicts, and misunderstandings. As a consequence, ethical, moral, and legal behaviors can often be identified among cultural strangers in business and a variety of work and recreation places. While one might assume or hope that all humans have similar ethical and moral behaviors to guide their actions, this is not the case. In fact, there are more diversities than one can imagine among cultures worldwide due to different values, lifeways, and enculturation processes. However, it is always important to search for common values amid cultural diversities. Hence, it is imperative to learn about transcultural differences and similarities with respect to ethical and moral behaviors among human beings worldwide.

Currently in nursing there has been an increased focus on moral, ethical, and legal issues related to nursing care services during the past decade. Many of these issues have come to the foreground due to the marked increase in working with clients using a vast array of new technologies, medicines, treatments, and care practices. The ethical problems arise as the nurse attempts to help cultural strangers with their particular behavior and needs from different cultures or subcultures. Today, many clients are quick to identify if their ethical rights have been threatened or violated in health care services. They may seek clarification, pose ethical questions, or seek restitution for any ethical offenses. Since nurses work so closely with clients in life, death, and in a variety of daily and nightly contexts, they are exposed to ethical and legal affairs. Some nurses are very sensitive to violating the client's ethical rights, while other nurses may try to avoid the issue or not be concerned. Ethics courses are increasing in schools of nursing to alert nurses to ethical and moral issues in education and service settings. It is of interest that in the 1940s to 1960s many nurses had ethics courses in their programs, but in the high technology era of the late 1960s, there was limited time for such instruction. Today, there is a renewed emphasis on nursing ethics due to many consumer professional issues. A number of nurse ethicists such as Aroskar,[3] Carper,[4] Curtin and Flaherty,[5] Davis,[6] Fowler,[7] Fry,[8,9] Gadow,[10] Leininger,[11,12,13] Ray, [14,15] Veach and Fry,[16] Watson[17] and Watson and Ray[18] are teaching their philosophical views, theories, principles and practical ways to help nurses deal with ethical issues in their clinical, research, education, and consultation practices. There are other nurse ethicists who address a variety of nurse/client and other issues. In addition, the scholarly thinking of other ethical and moral theorists or philosophers continues to influence the thinking and writings of nurses such as Beauchamp and Childress,[19] Callahan,[20] Gilligan,[21] MacIntyre,[22] Noddings,[23] Pellegrino et al.,[24] and Toulmin.[25] As a consequence, ethical knowledge is being discussed and studied in most schools of nursing, especially in the United States.

One of the most critical and neglected areas in teaching and research is in transcultural nursing's ethics and moral dimensions. Since the advent of transcultural nursing, only a few research studies have been done, and many schools of nursing have not examined the important feature of ethics. How different cultures define, interpret, and practice ethical and moral behavior is only slowly entering nurses' thinking and practices. The author, however, initiated this focus as an important and essential dimension of nurses' consideration when the field was launched and with writings since the 1960s.[26,27] Transcultural knowledge is providing nurses with many contrasting ethical insights about illnesses, treatments, and death issues, in different cultures.[28] Transcultural nurses are encouraging other nurses to study ethical and moral nursing care issues and how to resolve or prevent serious ethical dilemmas in clinical practices.[29]

Importance of Transcultural Ethical, Moral, and Legal Care Knowledge

The author takes the position that the transcultural ethical, moral, and legal aspects of nursing care are largely unknown yet are the most important issues for professional nurses today. Nurses are challenged to learn about diverse cultures and how different people know and practice ethical, moral, and legal in situations. Moreover, nurses are challenged to learn that ethical behaviors and values are difficult to learn because they are largely embedded in clients' cultural beliefs and practices. Hence, some specific examples are necessary to understand ethical values and beliefs along with any commonalities among clients.

One of the prevailing myths or beliefs among nurses is that Western ethical and moral philosophies exist worldwide, or "should" despite the fact that great differences among cultures are universal, and that these values can be used in caring for clients from any culture whether from Africa, the Middle East, Southeast Asia, or South America. This myth or belief can lead to serious ethical and legal problems, as there is far more diversity than similarity in ethical and other aspects of cultural behaviors. Nurses need to learn about ethical diversity among cultures with respect to their values, morals, and legal rights. Otherwise, problems related to cultural imposition practices with unfavorable consequences can result in clients receiving unsatisfactory care. Ethical rights can be readily violated or not taken into consideration. *The reality is that cultures have their own ethical beliefs and moral rules or standards to guide, interpret, and support their actions and decisions, and these cultures make judgments and decisions according to these ethical norms.*

Ethical knowledge of different cultures remains largely the missing dimension in most schools of nursing along with theory and research in transcultural ethical expressions and patterns. Nurses need to discover what constitutes ethical or moral decisions or behaviors for Africans, Asians, Greeks, Jews, and other cultures in the world. However, where transcultural nursing is taught, considerable emphasis is given to nurses discovering ethical expressions and meanings. The theory of Culture Care with the Sunrise Model has been extremely helpful in their discovery because multiple influencers are studied.[30]

With the trend of increased multiculturalism worldwide, transcultural ethical knowledge has become extremely important to nurses in order to provide culturally meaningful and ethically responsible care. Transcultural ethical and legal ideas should be taught early in nursing so that students will be alert to differences in ethical values and practices among clients. Today clients and their families become upset when nurses are insensitive to or unaware of their ethical beliefs and perform actions that are offensive or inappropriate. Some clients view making a wrong assessment or diagnosis as unethical which may occur when nurses are not knowledgeable about cultures.[31] Moreover, nurses need to understand the client's ethical beliefs in life and death situations especially when planning and providing direct care to clients. Inappropriate ethical decisions and care practices can lead to major legal suits. Family members often identify when ethical or moral values were violated or not respected especially in critical care situations when life and death are major concerns. But there are many more situations in which the professional nurse needs to be knowledgeable about the transcultural ethical and moral values of clients in order to provide culturally congruent care.

As nurses learn about cultures and their humanistic care needs, they will realize that cultures live by different codes, beliefs, principles, standards, rules, and values according to their worldview and social structure factors. These values are learned and passed on *intergenerationally* often giving people a stable *anchor or blueprint for living and dying.* Such cultural values support ethical and moral decisions by which humans have almost automatic guides when the threat of illness, disability, treatment, or death occurs. *Cultures,* therefore, have *ethical guides that enable them to respond to many situations in a "given" or natural way to strangers and non-strangers.* Ethical cultural values are very important and are generally derived from one's religious beliefs, kinship norms, and reinforced during living patterns. At no time should the nurse assume that all cultures or people are essentially alike and should be dealt with alike in nursing care. *Cultural variability* is important to remember. Most importantly, the nurse can learn about clients' ethical and moral values and legal constraints. This knowledge can be used in specific and creative ways to be an effective practitioner.

As the nurse learns and discovers different transcultural ethical, moral, and legal care knowledge, several questions should be considered: 1) What are some of the diverse beliefs, meanings, forms, expressions, symbols, metaphors, and values of ethical and moral care? 2) What are ethical and moral values universal or common among several cultures a nurse may work with? 3) What is the meaning of the dominant ethical values to the client, family, and community? 4) What highly sensitive ethical behaviors or rules does the nurse need to consciously respect? 5) Are there gender differences regarding who carries out ethical or moral duties or procedures? 6) How can the nurse's moral or ethical behavior get in the way of clients receiving appropriate care in accord with the client's ethical values? These questions and others help one to learn about and preserve important ethical behaviors important to the culture. In addition, nurses must actively listen and observe what clients do, say, and philosophize about life and their world of living to learn about ethics.

Although ethical, moral, and legal knowledge can be generated from several different sources and disciplines, rich sources are ethics, transcultural nursing, anthropology, philosophy, humanities, and comparative international law. Anthropologists have been studying cultures and ethical moral behavior for nearly a century, and their work is important to gain a comparative perspective. The early work of Boas,[32] Herskovits,[33] and Kluckhohn,[34] and the more recent work of Downing and Kushner,[35] Haviland,[36] Lanham,[37] and Leininger,[38] are a few examples of work by scholars about ethics in different cultures. These researchers of ethical behaviors have identified how some cultures have established and maintained certain ethical and moral rules, rights, and legal sanctions related to the prevention of illnesses, death, and avoiding major cultural conflicts with health care personnel. For example, most cultures such as Native Americans and Canadians, have explicit legal and ethical rights and ways to protect their health, lives, land, food, property, and children. This body of knowledge awaits transcultural nursing's discovery. They also know how to handle others when their rights are violated. People will often fight to defend their ethical rights, even at the cost of human lives and property damage. In general, *ethical, moral, and legal rights are stronger and more resilient in most cultures than many persons might suspect.*

Some transcultural nurse researchers have been studying the way cultural values and beliefs influence ethical health care practices since the early 1960s.[39,40,41,42,43,44,45] For example, Luna found that Arab Lebanese Muslim women held that it was unethical for Anglo-American nurses to press for bonding between a newborn infant and the father in a hospital nursing context, as it was counter to their cultural values.[46] Among the Old Order Amish, Wenger found it was unethical to take pictures and use them for public purposes or to use high technologies in hospital nursing care without the appropriate person's consent.[47] The author discovered that the Gadsup people of New Guinea would consider a female nurse unethical if she revealed sex secrets to males in the village.[48] She also found that Arab Muslim clients make their own decisions when a loved one is dead and that these beliefs must be respected by health personnel and to avoid cultural imposition practices. Such examples and many others are found in transcultural nursing research studies.

Transcultural nurses and anthropologists who are aware of the moral, ethical, and legal values of specific cultures will usually take a position to make this knowledge known to outsiders who attempt to violate the ethical rights of people. This protective stance is important when health professionals are unaware of culture-specific rights related to death, birth, marriage, abortions, circumcisions, gender, and even the community rights of cultures living in specific geographic areas. Ethical values about abortion, assisted death and euthanasia practices with the aged are sensitive issues in most cultures, and there are norms to reinforce their values. The author recalls that the Gadsup villagers of New Guinea were stunned to learn that Western women requested and had abortions. This was a cultural shock because the Gadsup women greatly value life, children, and actively protect their newborns. Gadsup mothers and their kinswomen do everything possible to have healthy infants and consider it wrong to kill any fetus in the womb. Or consider Eskimos who do not view a fetus as human, until it is named, and so their ethical position is different. A number of cultures believe that a fetus is human from the time of conception. Such ethical positions may contrast with those of "pro choice" and "pro life" supporters in the United States.

There are also major ethical problems which nurses may experience in functioning in the Middle East or in Indonesian Arab Muslim cultures, for example the removal of body organs to do an organ transplant violates body integrity and their religious beliefs. For Arab Muslims, the ethical principle is to keep the entire body (including all organs) intact and in a natural position, as the whole body needs to be together at death for their beliefs in reincarnation. They also believe that it is unethical for physicians and nurses to tell the Arab client with cancer about the malignancy conditions, for it is Allah who knows and is guiding the Arab client's destiny, not professionals.

As nurses study different cultures, they are challenged to search for both universal or common features as well as diversities among and between cultures. This provides a comparative view and alerts the nurses to shared ethical values as well as differences. It is the shared ethical and moral values that can be the common links to peace, harmony, or general understanding. The nurse will find the theory of Culture Care Diversity and Universality provides an important framework to discover transcultural ethical care differences and similarities.[49] With the use of the theory, the nurse will be able to search for different areas such as the worldview, religious, kinship, education, cultural values, professional experiences, and other areas that influence ethical and moral factors. The theory also helps nurses to contrast emic and etic client and nurse views about the sources of ethical, moral, and legal conflicts.

Another challenge for nurses is to study Western and non-Western philosophies and worldviews of the ways cultures know, give meanings, and use ethical and moral guides in their life. Nurses will find that in the Western cultures, there are generally *normative, descriptive, utilitarian, deontological ways* to interpret or explain ethical behavior, but the nurse should *not* assume these are universal ethical principles and typologies. In many non-Western cultures ethical and moral behaviors are embedded in principles about the philosophy of life, spirituality, religion, kinship, politics, and in relation to culturally specific contextual situations. For example, the Gadsup of New Guinea rely on distributive values that are context-based and those based on ancestral directive, which were passed on to them as ethical guides of what to do or avoid.[50] In other non-Western cultures such as in South East Asia, there are multiple spirits that guide the Vietnamese behavior. Ethical and moral guides to behavior tend to vary in Western and non-Western cultures.

Another related and major concern in nursing is the problem of cultural imposition nursing practices which influence the nurse's decisions with clients and the outcome of nursing care. As defined earlier, cultural imposition refers to the tendency to impose one's own values, beliefs, and practices on another culture due to the belief that they are superior to or better than those of another person or group.[51] If nurses are not knowledgeable about the different ethical values of a culture, one can anticipate that cultural imposition practices will occur. Such imposition practices tend to lead to client dissatisfaction, non-compliance, stresses, and a host of other problems, some of which can lead to legal problems.

Currently, one can identify several examples of cultural imposition practices in different nursing care contexts. In order to reduce or prevent such problems and negative consequences, the nurse needs to consider these self-examination questions: 1) What are my ethical beliefs and practices and how can they influence the client's health and well-being? 2) How can nurses with strong ethnocentric values, biases, and actions prevent ethical dilemmas that lead to cultural imposition practices and conflicts? 3) In what kinds of clinical contexts do nurses tend to impose their professional and personal ethical beliefs or values on clients, families, or groups? 4) In what ways can nurses prevent cultural imposition or best handle ethical or moral dilemmas? and 5) What are the potential legal consequences associated with the nurse who violates a client's ethical values? If the nurse begins with these questions and then tries to remain nonjudgmental using an open learning attitude toward the client, many weighty ethical problems can be avoided or resolved.

Today, many nurses are traveling to and often working in unfamiliar cultures or with "cultural strangers." Understanding the world of strangers who have different ethical values and beliefs can be unsettling to nurses who like to be confident of their knowledge and skills. Nurses need to do their homework, especially before traveling to foreign countries. They need preparation in transcultural nursing and to take selected anthropology courses to learn about the ethical values and lifeways of the people where one plans to work. This approach can reduce ethical stresses, conflicts, and imposition practices by preventing problems and offensive acts. Since ethical values are seldom written down as medical entities, the nurse needs to reflect upon the culture's religious beliefs, values, and lifeways as well as to learn from the people about ethical values. If cultural strangers show signs of being annoyed, refuse to accept help or avoid professional care, the nurse takes these signs as areas of potential ethical conflicts and tries to understand them with a transcultural nurse mentor. By listening attentively to the clients' explanations and interpretations of why they do what they do and why they believe in their practices, the nurse can usually facilitate positive relationships. Most importantly, the nurse searches to understand specific ethical values, cultural sanctions, cultural taboos, and specific religious conflicts. Some clients may also be candid and explain their reasons for refusing certain nursing practices. The nurse's attitude of genuine respect, a caring interest, and sincerity with clients are usually most valuable in ethical care practices.

Discovering the specific emic reasons underlying the client's unusual behavior often opens a whole new world of new insights. The nurse will also need to learn how to be non-judgmental and to suspend personal ethical beliefs and practices in order to prevent premature judgments about the client's behavior. Imposing professional ethical values onto the client or the family often occurs unintentionally or because the nurse does not know the client's cultural and ethical values. It is essential that nurses be aware that some clients will be most hesitant to share any ethical and other cultural values because they fear that health professionals may misinterpret, demean, or devalue them, or even deprive them of nursing care. For example, the nurse's ethical beliefs about abortion, AIDS, blood transfusions, folk remedies, gay or lesbian behavior, and other areas may lead to conflicts with the client if the nurse expresses her (his) views about these matters and expects the client to believe they are the right ones. In talking about or trying to provide health teaching to a client, the nurse can discover the client's ethical, moral, or general human rights, and secrets. These cultural secrets will only be shared if the client trusts the nurse or has moved from a stranger to friend role.[52] Moreover, since some ethical values and beliefs are complex and seemingly ambiguous, they may have to be understood by examples provided by letting the client describe situations or give examples. Some clients like to tell stories that give examples of their ethical beliefs. This often takes patience, time, and focused observation along with a genuine interest to learn about ethically based situations. The nurse should always recheck with the client to be sure in understanding ethical behaviors in context.

Selected Culture-Specific Ethical and Moral Care Values

As stated above, transcultural knowledge is essential to discover ethical and moral values and their transmission to offspring over time. Ethical values are usually passed on intergenerationally through enculturation and socialization practices. Rewards are often given to children and adults when they learn acceptable moral and ethical culture behaviors. Some cultures are quite conscientious in teaching and monitoring ethical behavior to their people throughout the life cycle such as the Old Order Amish, Orthodox Jewish Americans, and Hutterites. Other cultures, such as Anglo-Americans tend to be less conscientious in teaching ethical and moral values, especially in recent years. Japanese in their homeland teach ethics and morals in explicit ways and for longer periods of time than most parents in the United States. In a course called *Dotoku* (referring to ethics), Japanese students receive ethical and moral instruction related to group perseverance, diligence, quietness, patience, respect for elders, and teamwork.[53] These ethical values are mainly derived from their social structure and worldview, but especially from their religious beliefs and kinship relationships. Such ethical values have guided the Japanese for many years and many generations in decision making and actions. The Japanese culture shows tenacity in teaching ethical values and principles, which has promoted cultural identity and other benefits to the people in the work and home contexts.

In the United States and in Japan, the author has studied care expressions of Japanese American individuals and families in different nursing contexts and found behaviors similar to those cited above. Ethical care values of deference to and respect for the elderly, reciprocal kindness to one another, benevolence, and a tendency to forgive easily were documented with the Japanese American clients.[54] A dominant ethical care value of Japanese families is to show respect for the elderly, which was clearly apparent in Japanese hospitals. In fact, the care values of deference to and respect for the elderly were held as moral imperatives and responsibilities for family caregivers to be maintained with first, second, and third generations. While there were some slight variations with the present generation, still these values remained dominant ones and served as ethical expectations of professional nursing staff in order to provide culturally congruent and acceptable care.

In an industrial context, the ethical values of respect and deference were also identified by the author as important to the Japanese employees in a large car manufacturing plant in the Midwestern area of the United States. These employees had recently come directly from Hiroshima and Tokyo, Japan. They showed markedly deferent behaviors toward and for one another, but especially toward older employees in authority or in responsible positions. There was also strong reciprocal loyalty toward each other and an attitude of being one big corporate family. These values were predominant ethical care values for the Japanese employees, but especially for the Japanese managers. The Japanese president of the company was greatly respected for his benevolent and responsible role with his employees, and the latter showed reciprocal deference to him. In this action based research study of the Japanese, it was clear that explicit institutional goals of the plant were made known and were expected to be followed. There were a few Anglo-American employees in the plant who had great difficulty adjusting to these Japanese ethical care values because they valued individualism, competition, self-reliance and less respect for those in authority.[55] These Anglo-American cultural values were in direct conflict with the Japanese care values and their ethical mode of functioning. As a consequence, the Anglo-American employees were concerned about their rights and beliefs and ways to change the Japanese to their ethical norms and values. Through transcultural nursing consultation, the Anglo-American employees began to recognize the cultural differences and to work with the author's theoretical idea of culture care accommodation in order for both cultures to have work satisfaction.

Another illustration of the meanings and expressions of ethical care was discovered in Luna's recent study of Arab Lebanese Muslims in three urban culture contexts.[56] Luna's study covered a three-year period and was focused on identifying the meanings and expressions of culture care with Arab Lebanese Muslims, including their moral and ethical care behaviors. The researcher identified that their ethical and moral decisions were clearly derived from the Qur'an, which is the holy scripture containing the tenets of Islamic religious beliefs and practices. The Qur'an guides Arab Muslims in their ethical care practices. Luna found that care was viewed as an ethical responsibility and a moral obligation. For example, male Arab Lebanese Muslims were expected to honor, protect, and to be an economic provider and protector of the Lebanese family. Female Lebanese Arab Muslims emphasized and practiced ethical care as *family honor, unity, and social and domestic family responsibility.* These ethical care responsibilities with gender differences were clearly embedded in their religious, kinship, and social responsibilities. Accordingly, Arab Lebanese children were taught at an early age to learn these ethical and moral care values in order to protect themselves, to guide them in their daily relationships and acceptable Arab behaviors. These ethical care values would need to be respected as nurses cared for the Arab Lebanese Muslims.

Prior to Luna's research, hospital and clinic nurses as well as physicians and social workers were unaware of how much Arab Lebanese used these culture-based ethical care values while in the hospital. Some nursing staff had been frustrated trying to get Arab Lebanese clients to cooperate, comply, or to understand what the staff wanted them to do, and so cultural imposition practices were apparent in client/nurse relationships. It was clear that the Arab Lebanese could not change their dominant ethically based behavior over night, nor were they willing to do so. As a consequence, mutual avoidance was evident between nurses and clients. Other ethical care expectations of many Arab clients made them uncomfortable with nurses, such as when the nurse gave medications to them with the left hand rather than the right hand, the left hand is held to be associated with dirtiness and the right with cleanliness. Respecting ethical care proscriptions derived from religious beliefs, helped nurses to give appropriate caring practices to the Arab Lebanese which they, in turn, valued and appreciated. It was clear that when nurses understood the Arab Muslim ethical values and rights, the clients responded in cooperation and a satisfactory manner. It is this body of transcultural nursing ethical knowledge that can help nurses to provide culture-specific and congruent ethical care decisions and actions. It also helps the nurse realize that not all cultures have the same ethical, moral, and legal expectations.

In the author's search for universals or commonalities of shared ethical care knowledge, there was evidence from 1983–89 with Mexican Americans, a few Native American groups, Chinese Americans, Arab Lebanese, and Vietnamese Americans that they shared some similar ethical care values. The commonly held values were filial respect, obedience, and deference to their elderly, but with slight differences in cultural care expressions and meanings. It was of interest that Chinese Americans who had been in America for five years retained strong ethical care practices with moral obligations to be obedient, compliant, and deferent to their elderly and to any older Chinese government official in the United States. From the five cultures cited above, there were explicit prescriptions for what ought to be or should be ethical caring behaviors and with moral commitments of what made their actions right or wrong. These cultural informants were pleased to identify and explain to the nurse the meanings of such care expectations from their religious beliefs, kinship practices, and explicit cultural values, which supported filial respect for and obedience to elders. These ethical and moral care values identified are used today to guide nurses in giving culture-specific and ethically congruent nursing care to clients of these five cultures in several nursing settings. In the hospital context, the author's research findings revealed that Anglo-American nurses showed less evidence of overt respect for clients of the five cultures, but especially for Anglo-American elderly.[57] For Anglo-American hospital nurses, care of the elderly was often viewed as a duty or task, with many nurses expressing a preference to care for young or middle-aged clients. Anglo-American nurses encouraged the elderly to be self-reliant and to be self-care givers which followed Orem's Self-care deficit theory that nurses had been encouraged to use in their professional nursing education. For the Mexican and Vietnamese elderly clients the concept and practices of self-care were very difficult to accept as self-care was not congruent with their traditional cultural values and ethical expectations. It was also discovered that Anglo-American nurses tended to avoid Vietnamese and Chinese clients who could not speak English. These clients, therefore, felt neglected. They wanted members of their extended family to come and care for them in the hospital. In general, most professional nurses were handicapped in giving appropriate culture care to elderly clients of the five cultures because of their lack of ethical cultural knowledge, language, and transcultural nursing skills.

In the American nursing literature and in the Code of Ethics of Nursing there are ethical guides for patient care.[58] Some of these ethical statements pose problems as some do *not* fit other cultures or are inappropriate to the culture. These values, however, are viewed as essential professional ethical values as a code to guide all nurses and cultures. There is a great need to incorporate transcultural nursing ethical research findings into all areas of nursing to prevent cultural imposition and other problems. Thus, an urgent need remains for discovering transcultural ethical and moral values of Western and non-Western cultures along with culture care concepts, principles, and practices. Such culturally based knowledge is essential for direct client nursing care throughout the life cycle. There is also a need to *shift* nurses from relying mainly on their *own cultural values* to consider and use *multicultural ethical values* and practices for newcomers and others who do not plan to change their value system. The use of *culture-specific ethical values* can reduce ethical conflicts, prevent legal suits, and insure beneficial, satisfying, and culturally congruent nursing practice. Transcultural nursing education on ethical values has become imperative for all nurses in order to prepare a new generation of nurses to be culturally knowledgeable, competent, flexible, and reliable especially to cultural strangers. Remaining open-minded and flexible to cultures within and outside one's country is essential. When this occurs, one can find considerable growth and stimulation among nurses and great satisfaction in people care.

Contextual Spheres of Ethical Culture Care

In this last section five contextual spheres of ethical and moral culture care will be briefly discussed from different perspectives: a) personal or individual, b) professional or group, c) institutional or community, d) national, cultural, or societal, and e) worldwide human culture.[59] These five spheres can be viewed as different contexts which give meaning to and influence ethical, moral, and legal decisions or actions. They are the reality contexts or perspectives in which nurses and clients function, and which provide a basis to understand and accurately assess ethical behavior. These five contextual spheres of knowing and understanding can be used to guide nursing decisions and actions related to ethical and moral decisions.

As nurses consider these contextual spheres of ethical, moral, and legal behavior, they will recognize the author's principle that understanding and responding to different contexts is essential for effective and therapeutic nursing care practices. Each of the above spheres reflects different cultural frames of reference for meaningful ethical nursing care decisions and actions. For example, in the United States, Americans maintain a dominant focus on the individual's personal views, rights, beliefs, and actions. Ethical decisions tend to be referenced to individuals as the sphere of knowing or understanding. In contrast, in the People's Republic of China, the Chinese maintain a dominant reference to collective societal good. Any decisions regarding individual rights become part of a communal obligation and communal rights of the central government which are made known and explicitly used as normative cultural rules and regulations. While ethical rights and freedoms in China are being sought by some individuals in their homeland, still the dominant norm is to subordinate individual action to collective or large group needs in Chinese society. Other non-Western cultures may also value collective cultural rights over individualism, as is the case with cultural groups in the Middle East, Southeast Asia, and areas in Latin America. The dominant Chinese culture care values of obedience and compliance were observed and documented in the People's Republic of China and with recent Chinese American immigrants living in the United States.[60] Interestingly, these same cultural values were evident during the June 1989 pro-democratic student's movement in China, in which the central political committee of the communist government (Politburo) denied the individual or personal wishes of students as they rallied for a democratic government. Such strong collective central government rules were of deep concern to many Americans who greatly value individual freedom and the right to be heard, make choices, and receive due free speech considerations. For American students, the Chinese cultural norms and ethical values of obedience, compliance, and deference to authority have been extremely difficult to accept. The author also discovered in her research that Chinese American students who had come from China since 1980 and were studying at a Midwestern university had retained values of obedience and deference to their government in many overt and covert ways.

In the Western world of nursing, especially in the United States, a nurse's individual and professional values and perceived personal rights are dominant ethical values which tend to govern what a nurse should or ought to do or be. American and most Canadian nurses often become upset, protest, or march if their perceived individual or professional rights are violated. Institution or group ethical norms or values are often questioned and viewed with suspicion if too authoritative leaders prevail, as it is a potential threat to the individual's rights and autonomy.

Most nurses deal with at least three major sets of ethical spheres of rights. First, there are the *personal culture values* that the nurse has learned in the family culture context in the early and ongoing life with the family. Second, there are *professional cultural values* that the nurse learns while in schools of nursing. Third, the nurse is expected to live by and value the *societal or dominant cultural values*, such as the American cultural lifeways and ethical expectations.[61] This latter set of values cannot be ignored as nurses and the nursing profession are expected to serve society as a public citizen in hospitals, agencies, or wherever they are employed. In addition, I hold that nurses belong to a *worldwide human culture* in which there are certain obligations and expectations to be sensitive to and respond to worldwide caring needs of people. This global or worldwide sphere of ethical values has yet to be fully studied, but is being pursued with the theory of culture care and universal professional care values, if any exist. As the professional nurse travels, reads, and functions in a global nursing context, her (his) ethical and moral awareness should become evident. Transcultural nurses are playing a major role to help nurses extend their thinking and knowledge beyond their local or national culture and consider global sets of ethical, moral, and legal viewpoints. When this goal is fully accomplished, one will find nurses ready and able not only to respect diverse cultural values and beliefs but function more effectively in different cultures. Nurses will learn how to become more flexible and to accommodate or restructure values to meet cultural past and new expectations. Thus, different contextual ethical spheres of knowing and experiencing are important to understand and act upon to function in a multicultural world. Transcultural perspectives of ethical knowledge and the use of appropriate culture care ethical practices are becoming more and more essential to nurses competencies and expectations. When this expectation is reached, one can predict less cultural burnout, fewer cultural imposition practices, ethical offenses, and serious legal problems. Instead, clients and nurses will have become co-participants to provide culturally congruent nursing care.

In the above different contextual spheres of ethical thinking and decision making, the nurse may need to compromise or accommodate different ethical values for another person's perceived good or benefit. Sometimes, the nurse works out what Ray called a "bonding" relationship with the client in which the nurse and client come to a consensus that is mutually agreeable.[62] Sometimes, nurses avoid ethical dilemmas by not dealing with them directly or by figuratively running away because of ethical conflicts or dilemmas. Some nurses live in an uncomfortable confusion due to a lack of awareness of such ethical and moral problems, and this greatly reduces the nurses' effectiveness, development of professional skills, and work satisfactions.

Turning to the author's extensive research of nearly twenty cultures over the past three decades (1960–1995), she found that the client's ethical and cultural values were often limitedly assessed by nurses.[63] Clients however, were fairly perceptive to identify the nurse's values and often the institution's cultural norms, values, and what was ethical or not appropriate to use in hospital or community agencies. The client's ethical personal and local cultural care beliefs and values tended to get limited attention by the hospital staff. If clients acquiesced to nurses', physicians', or institutional covert ethical norms, there were often signs of clients being restless and dissatisfied when their own cultural norms failed to fit or comply with the values of the professional staff. It was also difficult for some nurses and physicians to accept and respect the clients' rights or to make appropriate cultural decisions. In the hospital context, clients tended to yield to the professional staff's ethical values and choices, or to the hospital norms because they feared they would not receive care or treatment if they asserted their own rights or choices. So clients usually complied with health personnel's desires in order to assure themselves that they would get some care and/or treatment regimes. They felt vulnerable, however, and would often not request some essential physical care and treatments. Such practices reveal ethical issues that need to be recognized and dealt with by nurses and other personnel. Today, with acute illnesses of clients and the high cost of hospital services, American clients often feel they need to leave the hospital as soon as possible. However, nurses often recognize that clients are not always ready and able to leave a few days after major surgery. Clients from other cultures often believe in staying longer. Some clients feel they are at the mercy of the nurses and physicians because they are not on their home turf while in the hospital, and so they must make safe decisions and not strongly assert themselves to staff or they may not remain in the hospital. Several clients in the hospital study told the researcher that it was almost impossible to refuse whatever was offered to them by the nurse or physician because if they refused something or did not comply, they would probably not remain in the hospital for what they felt was important to their health. Some clients felt that if they did not comply, they would be treated in a non-caring way, and so it was usually best to comply, keep silent or not cause problems, even though some ethical beliefs and values were impinged upon.

The author also discovered that in some cultures such as the Philippine, Korean, and mainland Chinese, clients want and expect the physician and nurse to *make decisions for them.* This is especially evident when they are in the hospital and because of their cultural value beliefs to be deferent and obedient to those in authority. This contrasts with Anglo-American clients who value *making their own independent decisions* as their American cultural and ethical right of freedom. Middle and upper class Americans are becoming more active not only in choosing their hospitals, physicians, nurses, and other therapists, but also in trying to reform the health care system. The "Patient's Bill of Rights" is a document which reflects the client's growing rights to protect their rights and freedoms while in some hospitals. In the future, such major ethical and cultural value differences need to be recognized and responded to for culturally congruent nursing care.

Given these above differential contextual spheres that influence the nurse's ethical decisions, the nurse should consider what ethical decisions are appropriate or inappropriate in these different contextual spheres of functioning. Is there a hierarchical ordering in which one sphere supersedes the other in different cultures? What happens if the "traveling nurse" follows Western personal or national types of universal-like ethics in an unknown non-Western culture, such as the Republic of South Africa? How will the nurse know what is ethically or morally desired for the client, or for the majority of clients in the strange cultures in which the nurse is employed? Or, if the nurse makes an ethical care decision from a deontological stance, how congruent will this decision be with what is *best for the individual* unless the nurse knows the individual's personal values, beliefs, and practices, let alone his national cultural values? What is the ethical or philosophical source of Western public health policies, and do they violate ethical values of non-Western cultures? These are some untapped ethical and moral nursing research questions that merit systematic study in the future.

As more nurses become prepared in transcultural nursing and ethics courses, ethical knowledge theories, principles, codes, and covenants will enable nurses to use comparative ethical knowledge. *Nurse ethicists who have not been prepared in transcultural nursing will need to reexamine their knowledge and theoretical stance transculturally.* An encouraging development is that qualitative paradigmatic research methods such as phenomenology, ethnonursing, and use of metaphors, narratives, and life histories will continue to be extremely valuable to discover the embedded or hidden ethical, moral, and legal values that exist in human cultures.[64] Subjective, intuitive, and non-verbal ethical and moral meanings and expressions will be important to understand ethical, moral, and related cultural behaviors. Ethical behavior remains extremely difficult to measure. Most assuredly, transcultural ethical, moral, and legal research studies will need to increase markedly in nursing research in order to serve people in meaningful ways in the future.

In this chapter, the author discussed that transcultural ethical, moral, and legal knowledge and nursing competencies are largely missing or neglected areas in nursing education and practices. Still today, Western nurses tend to rely on their own cultural values as ethical guides as means to care for non-Western cultures, despite major differences in ethical beliefs and practices. Many examples were presented to show differences and some similarities among cultures. The theory of Culture Care and qualitative research methods were identified as valuable means to discover and understand ethical, moral, and legal aspects of human care. Understanding and appropriately responding to people of diverse ethical and moral expectations require nurses to be alert to such valued differences in order to insure congruent, beneficial, and effective nursing care and to avoid cultural offenses and legal suits. To discover the utmost aspects of what helps clients from diverse cultures face life-and-death issues bears directly on the necessity of understanding ethical, moral, and legal beliefs and practices. This is an essential goal for nursing in our intense multicultural world.

Note: This paper was derived from the author's article entitled "Culture: The Conspicuous Missing Link to Understand Ethical and Moral Dimensions of Human Care" published in the book: *Ethical and Moral Dimensions of Care*, M. Leininger, ed., Detroit, Wayne State University Press, 1988, pp. 49-66.

References

1. Leininger, M., "Culture: The Conspicuous Missing Link to Understand Ethical and Moral Dimensions of Human Care," *Ethical and Moral Dimensions of Care*, M. Leininger ed., Detroit: Wayne State University Press, 1988a, pp. 50–51.

2. *Webster's New World Dictionary of the American Language*, College ed., New York: The World Publishing Company, 1981.

3. Aroskar, M., "The Interface of Ethics and Politics in Nursing," *Nursing Outlook*, v. 35, no. 6, 1987, pp. 268–72.

4. Carper, Barbara, "The Ethics of Caring," *Advances in Nursing Science*, v. 1, no. 3, 1979, pp. 1–19.

5. Curtin, L. and J. Flaherty, *Nursing Ethics: Theories and Pragmatics*, Bowie, Maryland: Robert J. Brady Co., 1982.

6. Davis, A.J., "Compassion, Suffering, Morality: Ethical Dilemmas in Caring," *Nursing Law and Ethics*, v. 2, no. 6, 1981, p. 8.

7. Fowler, M., "Ethics Without Virtue," *Heart and Lung*, v. 15, no. 5, 1986, pp. 528–30.

8. Fry, S., "Moral Decisions and Ethical Decisions in a Constrained Economic Environment," *Nursing Economics*, v. 4, no. 4, 1986, pp. 160–63.

9. Fry, S., "The Ethics of Caring: Can it Survive in Nursing?," *Nursing Outlook*, v. 36, no. 1, 1988, p. 48.

10. Gadow, S., *Existential Advocacy—Philosophical Foundation for Nursing*, San Francisco: Image Ideas Publication, 1980.

11. Leininger, op cit., 1988a, pp. 37–61.

12. Leininger, M., *Ethical and Moral Dimensions of Care*, Detroit: Wayne State University Press, 1988a, pp. 49-66.

13. Leininger, M., *Care: The Essence of Nursing and Health*, Thorofare, New Jersey: Charles B. Slack, 1984, reprint, Detroit: Wayne State University Press, 1988.

14. Ray, M. A., "Health Care Economics and Human Caring in Nursing: Why the Moral Conflict Must be Resolved," *Family Community Health*, v. 10, no. 1, 1987, pp. 35–43.

15. Ray, M. A., "Discussion Group Summary: Ethical Dilemmas in the Clinical Setting—Time Constraints, Conflicts in Interprofessional Decision Making," *The Ethics of Care and the Ethics of Cure: Synthesis in Chronicity*, J. Watson and M.A. Ray eds., New York: National League for Nursing, (Pub. #15-2237), 1988, pp. 37–39.

16. Veach, R. and S. Fry, *Case Studies in Nursing Ethics*, Philadelphia: J.B. Lippincott, 1987.

17. Watson, J., *Nursing: Human Science and Human Care. A Theory of Nursing*, Norwalk, Connecticut: Appleton-Century-Crofts, 1985.

18. Watson, J. and M. A. Ray, *The Ethics of Care and the Ethics of Cure: Synthesis in Chronicity*, New York: National League for Nursing, (Pub. #15-2237), 1988.

19. Beauchamp, T. and J. Childress, *Principles of Biomedical Ethics*, 2d ed. New York: Oxford University Press, 1983.

20. Callahan, D., "Autonomy: A Moral Good, Not a Moral Obsession," *Hastings Center Report*, v. 14, no. 5, 1980, pp. 40–42.

21. Gilligan, C., *In a Different Voice: Psychological Theory and Women's Development*, Cambridge: Harvard University Press, 1982.

22. MacIntyre, A., *After Virtue*, Notre Dame, Indiana: University of Notre Dame Press, 1981.

23. Noddings, N., *Caring: A Feminine Approach to Ethics and Moral Education*, Berkeley: University of California Press, 1984.

24. Pelligrino, E., P. Mazzarella, and P. Corsi, *Transcultural Dimensions in Medical Ethics*, Frederick, Maryland: University Publishing Group, Inc., 1992.

25. Toulmin, S., "The Tyranny of Principles," *Hastings Center Report*, v. 11, no. 6, 1987, pp. 31–39.

26. Leininger, M., *Culture Care Diversity and Universality: A Theory of Nursing*, New York: National League for Nursing Press, 1991a.

27. Leininger, op. cit., 1988a, pp. 49-66.

28. Leininger, M., "Cultural Care: An Essential Goal for Nursing and Health Care," *American Association of Nephrology Nurses and Technicians*, v. 10, no. 5, 1983, pp. 11–17.

29. Leininger, M., *Care: Discovery and Uses in Clinical and Community Nursing*, Detroit: Wayne State University Press, 1988b.

30. Leininger, op. cit., 1991a, pp. 1–45.

31. Leininger, M., "Issues, Questions, and Concerns Related to the Nursing Diagnosis Cultural Movement from a Transcultural Nursing Perspective," *Journal of Transcultural Nursing*, v. 2, no. 1, Summer, 1990, pp. 23–32.

32. Boas, F., *Race, Language and Culture*, New York: Free Press, 1966.

33. Herskovits, M., *Cultural Dynamics*, New York: Knopf, 1964.

34. Kluckhohn, C., *Mirror for Man*, Greenwich, Connecticut: Fawcett Press, 1970.

35. Downing, T. and G. Kushner, *Human Rights and Anthropology*, Cambridge, Massachusetts: Cultural Survival, 1988.

36. Haviland, W.A., *Cultural Anthropology*, 5th ed. New York: Holt, Rinehart, and Winston, 1987.

37. Lanham, Betty B., "Ethics and Moral Precepts Taught in Schools of Japan and the United States," *Japanese Culture Behavior: Selected Readings*, J. Libra and W. Libra eds., Honolulu: University of Hawaii Press, 1986, pp. 280–96.

38. Leininger, op. cit., 1988a, pp. 49–66.

39. Ibid.

40. Leininger, M., *Transcultural Nursing: Concepts, Theories, and Practices*, New York: John Wiley and Sons, 1978.

41. Leininger, op. cit., 1974.

42. Leininger, op. cit., 1991a.

43. Horn, B., "Transcultural Nursing and Childrearing of the Muckleshoot People," *Transcultural Nursing: Concepts, Theories, and Practices*, M. Leininger, ed., New York: John Wiley and Sons, 1978, pp. 223–39.

44. Luna, L., *Care and Cultural Context of Lebanese Muslims in an Urban US Community: An Ethnographic and Ethnonursing Study Conceptualized within Leininger's Theory*, Ph.D. Dissertation, Wayne State University, 1989.

45. Wenger, A., *The Phenomenon of Care in a High Context Culture: The Old Order Amish*, PhD Dissertation, Wayne State University, 1988.

46. Luna, op. cit., 1989.

47. Wenger, op. cit., 1988.

48. Leininger, M., "Transcultural Care Principles, Human Rights, and Ethical Considerations," *Journal of Transcultural Nursing*, v. 3, no. 1, 1991b, pp. 21–24.

49. Leininger, op. cit., 1991a, pp. 345–372.

50. Leininger, M., "Culture Care of the Gadsup Akuna of the Eastern Highlands of New Guinea," *Culture Care Diversity and Universality: A Theory of Nursing*, New York: National League for Nursing Press, 1991, pp. 231–238.

51. Leininger, M., "Becoming Aware of Types of Health Practitioners and Cultural Imposition," *Journal of Transcultural Nursing*, v. 2, no. 2, 1991 c, pp. 32–39.

52. Leininger, op. cit., 1991a, pp. 91–93.

53. Lanham, op. cit., 1986, pp. 284–296.

54. Leininger, op. cit., 1991a, p. 359.

55. Ibid.

56. Luna, op. cit., 1989.

57. Leininger, op. cit., 1991a, p. 355.

58. Viens, D., "A History of Nursing's Code of Ethics," *Nursing Outlook*, v. 37, no. 1, 1989, pp. 45–49.

59. Leininger, op. cit., 1988a, pp. 61–64.

60. Leininger, op. cit., 1991a, p. 361.

61. Leininger, M., *Transcultural Ethnonursing and Ethnographic Studies in Urban Community Contexts*, (unpublished) Detroit: Wayne State University , 1960–1993.

62. Ray, op. cit., 1988.

63. Leininger, op. cit., 1960–1995.

64. Leininger, M., *Qualitative Methods in Nursing*, Orlando: Grune and Stratton, Inc., 1985.

Section III:

Culture Specific Care of Different Cultures

Chapter 13
Arab Muslims and Culture Care*
*Linda J. Luna, PhD, CTN, RN.***

Caring for Arab Muslims poses a real challenge to most nurses today since Western awareness about their complex cultural beliefs, values, and lifeways is just beginning to develop. Muslim religious values and the worldview of Islam are markedly different from the values which underpin life in the Western world. Understanding Arab Muslims, therefore, requires that nurses learn about the religious and cultural values, social structure features, as well as the health care beliefs and practices of Arab Muslims. The central and important goal of transcultural nursing necessitates learning about the culture and then developing care practices that are culturally congruent with the values of the people.

Today, more nurses are beginning to recognize the importance of transcultural nursing and the evolving body of knowledge about the influence of cultural factors on health and care behaviors and lifeways. Such knowledge is extremely imperative in professional practice in order to bridge the gap between the experiences and worldview of the nurse and that of the client or the family whose cultural values, lifeways, and worldview may be quite different from those of the nurse.

In this chapter some fundamental transcultural concepts and ethnonursing insights will be presented to help nurses understand and care for Arab Muslim clients. Leininger's Culture Care theory with a focus on worldview, ethnohistory, social structure (especially religion and kinship), language, cultural values and beliefs and environment will be presented.[1] Transcultural nursing care guidelines and practical applications to support ways to provide culturally congruent care will be offered as derived from the literature and from the author's research of Middle Eastern peoples and from direct field experience with several Arab cultural groups in a large community in the United States. These experiences and the author's current residence in the Middle East have been most valuable to understanding the importance of transcultural nursing knowledge and to developing clinical skills to care for Arab Muslim clients.

Leininger's theory of Culture Care Diversity and Universality provided the theoretical frame of reference for this chapter and the author's research. The theory was used to discover and understand cultural values and lifeways of the Arab Muslims through an analysis of social structure, worldview, language and environmental features.

Leininger holds that care is essential to human health and well-being and is the major feature which distinguishes nursing from other disciplines.[2] The goal of the theory is to provide culturally congruent care to individuals, families, and cultural groups. While the concept of care is central to Leininger's theory, the concept of health is also studied in relation to care to discover the relationship of health (well-being) to care. Health and care behaviors are held by Leininger to vary transculturally and take on different meanings in different cultures.[3] Leininger postulates that if one understands the meanings and forms of care, one can predict the health or well-being of human beings.

Culturally congruent nursing care requires in-depth knowledge and direct experiences with cultural groups. Congruent and effective nursing care needs to be grounded in transcultural knowledge to achieve care congruence and health. The three nursing care decisions or actions which Leininger holds to provide culturally congruent care for clients and which were studied by the author were: 1) Culture care preservation and/or maintenance; 2) Culture care accommodation and/or negotiation; 3) Culture care repatterning and/or restructuring. These three modes or patterns of care are helpful to consider as the nurse uses knowledge from Arab Muslim clients to plan and give nursing care. If these modes of action are used, Leininger predicts there will be fewer signs of cultural conflict and stress between the nurse and client, and fewer negative responses from clients in nursing care practices. Culturally congruent care will reflect the nurse's knowledge of and sensitivity to clients' cultural lifeways. Clients will find nursing care more acceptable and satisfying. Accordingly, the nurse will fee more satisfied and rewarded in her(his) care practices.

Learning about Arab Muslims

At the outset it is important to state that a review of nursing care literature revealed no research related specifically to the Arab Muslim culture and to nursing care phenomena. This is of interest as Islam is the second largest of the world's religious cultures with an interesting and important ethnohistory. Moreover, there are many misunderstandings and myths about Islam and Arab culture. Thus, some general facts and ideas about Islam and Arab Muslims are in order.

It is important to realize that considerable variability exists within the Arab Muslim culture as Arabs come from a number of countries throughout the Middle East, parts of India and North Africa and they have different lifeways and cultural patterns. Because of such variabilities, some ideas may not be directly applicable or relate specifically to all Arab Muslim groups in the world. In this chapter only some knowledge about Arab Muslims in the United States will be discussed, rather than focusing on all Arab Muslim cultures and their variabilities worldwide.

To begin, the nurse needs to know which groups are represented by the term "Arab Muslim." Frequently, the terms "Arab" and "Muslim" are used as being synonymous, which is not acceptable. Not all Arabs are Muslim, and not all Muslims are Arab. To understand this statement, let us explore further the differences and some ethnohistorical facts.

Most Arab scholars view the Arab world as stretching from Morocco to the Arabian Gulf. Although reference is made to the "Arab World," there exists no one single Arab nation, but rather a number of separate Arab states. Countries which make up the Arab world are the countries of North Africa including Morocco, Algeria, Tunisia, Libya, Egypt, Somalia, Sudan, Djibouti and Mauritania; the Middle Eastern countries of Lebanon, Syria, Iraq, Jordan and Saudi Arabia; and the states and territories bordering the southern and eastern edge of the Arabian peninsula such as the Yemens, Bahrain and Kuwait.[4] Although most inhabitants of these Arab countries are Muslim, there are several million Christian Arabs who reside within these boundaries, including the Maronites of Lebanon and the Chaldeans of Iraq. A commonly accepted meaning for the term "Arab" is "any person who resides in the area stretching from Morocco to the Arabian Gulf, who speaks Arabic, and who takes pride in the Arabic culture and the Arabs' historical accomplishments."[5]

In contrast, a Muslim is a practitioner of the faith of Islam. Most Muslims, however, are not Arab.[6] With the expansion of Islam in the seventh century, the religious culture moved out of the Arabian peninsula in all directions to embrace many cultural groups. Today the largest Muslim states are situated outside the Middle East in Indonesia and the Indian subcontinent.[7] Pakistani and Indonesian Muslims, however, are not Arab Muslims. Arab Muslims are Muslims who originate from any of the previously mentioned countries which comprise the Arab world—i.e., Lebanese Muslims, Saudi Muslims, Egyptian Muslims, etc. In fact, Arabs constitute only twenty-five percent of the world's Muslim population, a fact which surprises most people.[8]

Muslims are divided into two major and legitimate religious orthodoxies, the Sunni and the Shi'a, plus a number of smaller orders. The Sunni constitute the largest group of Muslims, whereas the Shi'a are a minority. With regard to the major beliefs and practices of Islam, however, there is little difference between the two groups. The few points of divergence revolve around the issue of early leadership following the death of the prophet Muhammad. The nursing concepts and research findings addressed in this chapter apply to both groups of Arab Muslims, the Sunni and the Shi'a, as well as to the smaller group.

Ethnohistorical Aspects of Arab Muslim Immigration

There are currently no reliable statistics as to the number of Arab Muslims in the United States. Various sources give estimates on the number of Arabs as a whole, while others approximate the total number of Muslims. Naff attempts to separate the two by citing the approximate number of Arabs in the United States to be roughly two million, ten percent (or 20,000) of whom are Muslim.[9] There appears to be a consensus among Arab writers that such figures are a conservative estimate, since several ongoing regional wars in the Arab world during the past decade have served as motivating factors for migration for many Arab Muslims.

Early Arab immigrants to the United States were primarily Christian. Haddad contends that the first major influx of Arab Muslims to the United States occurred between 1875 and 1912.[10] The incentive for migration at this time was to achieve financial success similar to that reported by the earlier arriving Christians. Most of the early Muslim immigrants were single males who planned to return to their homeland after accumulating a certain amount of wealth. Many of these early arriving Muslim males did return home, however, a significant number stayed on in American and were instrumental in establishing institutions and organizations to preserve the Islamic faith. A second wave of Muslims came to the United States before World War II, followed by a third wave (1947 to 1960), and a fourth from 1967 to the present.[11] During these periods various political and economic factors in the Arab world, such as wars and coups d'etat, as well as an expanding American economy and changes in the United States immigration laws, provided incentives for Arab Muslims to migrate.[12]

Many Arab Muslim scholars tend to emphasize a distinction between early arriving immigrants and those who came in later years, with the latter identified as better educated and with greater numbers from the professional class. Haddad notes that such a distinction may be exaggerated, since many later immigrants were not professionals, but rather were part of the flow of "chain immigration" of relatives joining other family members in the United States.[13] Chain migration continues to characterize the migration patterns of most Arab Muslims with the exception of Yemenis, who are primarily men who come to work, save money and return to Yemen.[14]

Like most cultures with strong religious beliefs which attempt to survive in new lands, the early growth of Islam in America showed an adaptation of traditional practices to a new environment. In keeping with American practices, various social events and fund-raising activities began to be conducted at the mosque and women took on more active roles in various aspects of mosque life which generally were not open to them in their native countries.[15] Since the early 1970s, events in the Middle East, particularly in Iran, have precipitated a strong tendency among many Muslims to return to the essential teachings of Islam. There has been a movement in many Muslim communities in the United States toward reform or reviving traditional Islamic practices. Many new immigrants, as well as an increasing number of earlier arrivals, are reaffirming their total commitment to Islam as a way of life. In order to provide effective nursing care, nurses need to be aware of these changes and the increased religious awareness on the part of many Arab Muslims.

The Worldview of Islamic Culture and Nursing Considerations

To care for Arab Muslim clients effectively, nurses need to be aware of the worldview of Islam as a cultural influence upon the daily life of the people. The worldview of a cultural groups is their way of looking at reality and the world around them. One aspect of worldview is the role of religion, as it gives meaning to living, dying, and the maintenance of health and care practices.

The religion of Islam began in the center of Arabia during the seventh century and is a monotheistic religion—to associate other gods with Allah (God) is a capital crime. This term "Islam" is an Arabic word meaning "the act of submission is resignation or resignation to God."[16] For the Muslim believer, the Qur'an (or holy book of Islam) is the absolute authority of the word of God, and understanding this tenet is essential to understanding Arab Muslim clients. To Muslims, "the Qur'an is the actual word of God transmitted by the angel of prophecy, Gabriel, to the prophet Muhammad, who transmitted it to the people."[17] As such, it lacks any tampering or changing by human leaders. Muslims resent reference to Islam as Muhammadanism, since the term implies divinity to Muhammad. According to Muslim belief, Muhammad was merely a man and the messenger of God, but he was in no sense divine.

The single most important feature of the worldview of Islam is the concept of *Tawhid*. *Tawhid*, a verbal noun which derives from the root *wahada*, carries the meaning of "unity" or "intensive unification."[18] The idea of unity refers to the unity of the Supreme Being (Allah) and the subsequent unity of nature. *Tawhid*, or the doctrine of absolute unity, implies that only God is ultimate and worthy of worship.[19] The existence of God is not in isolation; rather all the world is united in God. *Tawhid* is the fundamental principle of Islam from which all other principles are derived. The obedient Muslim lives his life in a way that reflects *Tawhid* in the unity of mind and body, a tenet which is essential to grasp in planning nursing care interventions.

Tawhid implies that all Muslim believers are a single brotherhood, the *ummah*, which knows no superiority in terms of color or ethnicity. Prayer and recitation of the Qur'an are said daily by Muslims all over the world in the Arabic language, even though Arabic is not the mother-tongue of most Muslims. An Arab Muslim, however, has no superiority over a non-Arab Muslim, rather all are members of a universal community of Islam, the *ummah*. This "unity in diversity" is a distinctive feature of the permeating worldview of *Tawhid*, and is the major reason why many people from minority cultures are attracted to the religion of Islam.

The moral and ritual obligations which help Muslims lead a disciplined life are summed up in five main duties known as the pillars or foundations of Islam:[20]

1. The first is a confession of faith: "There is no God but God, and Muhammad is the prophet of God." The confession of faith is uttered on a number of occasions, such as birth and death.
2. Prayer is the second duty of Muslims, said at five specified times each day.
3. The third pillar is the obligation of alms giving. The Qur'an stipulates that one should share with the less fortunate the blessings of wealth which God has given one.
4. The fourth duty required of Muslims is fasting during the holy month of Ramadan, during which no food or drink is taken during daylight hours. Many Muslims extend this to oral medications, although according to Islamic law, the ill are exempt from the obligation of fasting.
5. The pilgrimage to Mecca, the holy city of Islam, is the fifth duty which every pious Muslim strives for at least once in a lifetime.

The above duties for Muslims are a large measure of fulfillment, well-being and health, and are a source of guidance in today's perplexing world.

Within Islam, the concepts of *halal* and *haram* are important to understanding Muslim culture. *Halal* describes those things that are permissible or lawful according to the tenets of Islam, and *haram* describes those things that are forbidden.[21] For example, the code of *halal* applies to the manner in which meat is slaughtered. To be considered *halal* and lawful for consumption, an animal must be slaughtered in accordance with certain Muslim prescriptions—i.e., the use of a sharp knife to spare the animal unnecessary pain, recitation of verses from the Qur'an, and facing toward Mecca. However, the code of *halal* is demanded in other activities also, such as in manner of dress. According to Islamic doctrine, clothing and adornment must take into consideration the principles of decency, modesty and chastity for both men and women.

There are many nursing implications related to the worldview of Arab Muslims which should be kept in mind as nurses care for Arab Muslims. Like members of any religious groups, the intensity of an individual's belief and faith may vary. For example, the devout Arab Muslim who has a diabetic condition may find the sense of spiritual health and well-being brought about during the fast of Ramadan equally as important as maintaining a diet which balances insulin requirements. Maintaining spiritual health and well-being is important since the concept of *tawhid* implies that physical health is not separate from the spiritual dimension—i.e., there is mind-body unity. The Arab Muslim view of health, therefore, correlates with the worldview concept of unity reflected in *tawhid*. In working with an Arab Muslim client who has a diabetic condition and who wishes to fast during Ramadan, the nurse could use Leininger's decision-action mode of culture care restructuring in an effort to allow the client to retain his beliefs and practices, but reconstructing ways in which dietary and metabolic needs can be met in order to prevent insulin imbalances and to maintain holistic health.

Still another nursing consideration centers around the performance of prayer. Before entering into obligatory prayer, the Muslim believer carries out ritual cleansing according to Islamic tradition. This ritual cleansing includes washing the feet up to the ankles, washing the arms to the elbows, and washing the face and the inside of the ears.[22] A part of the worship ritual includes removing the shoes and facing toward Mecca. For women, covering the hair is also required. Some Muslims may not feel the need for daily prayer, while others may see this practice as essential to recovery or maintenance of health and well-being. During the culturalogical assessment, the nurse should assess the client's wishes regarding prayer and the desired frequency. If prayer is desired, the nurse may provide assistance with the ritual cleansing or allow a family member to assist, especially if the client is of the opposite sex. Providing a basin of water and finding a quiet place for the client to perform the religious duty supports culture care accommodation as an important nursing intervention. Religious articles such as prayer rug or a copy of the Qur'an are often brought from home for the Arab Muslim client. These articles should be treated with respect, and nothing should ever be placed on top of the Qur'an, as it is a sacred object.

For many Arab Muslims, observing the fast of Ramadan and performing the religious obligations of prayer are important cultural expressions for maintaining health and preventing illness. The nurse should attempt to assess the meaning and importance to the client of these rituals, since for many Arab Muslims, they function as more than simple acts of worship. Fasting and prayer help to maintain a pure heart, a sound mind, and a clean, healthy body.

The culturally knowledgeable and sensitive nurse will realize the concern of many Arab Muslim females for modesty. Taking measures to provide culture care accommodation and culture care preservation by respecting the female's modesty should be an integral part of nursing care. The traditionally orientated female usually expects to have female care givers. The nurse should remain with the female client during any type of examination or procedure and give special attention to draping and preventing unnecessary exposure of the body. The Muslim female may desire to have another female relative present, and occasionally she may wish to have her husband present during a health examination, especially if the health provider is a male.

Language Significance, Symbolism, and Nursing Care

In caring for Arab Muslim clients, language expression and use can serve to facilitate care. Language is more than simply a medium of communication. It is a means to understand the cultural values and beliefs, worldview, and perceptions of health and care.

To Arab Muslims, Arabic is regarded as the most perfect of all languages, since it was the vehicle through which the message of Islam was revealed. Inherent in the religious significance of Arabic is the conviction that the Holy Qur'an cannot be translated into other languages without losing a great deal of meaning. For this reason, Muslims, regardless of their native tongue, pray and recite the Qur'an in Arabic. Knowledge of the Arabic language brings a great deal of prestige to the Muslim who can speak and read it.

The Arabic language has developed in three forms. There is a distinction between various regional dialects of Arabic, a modern standard Arabic utilized by radio, television, and press media, and the classical written Arabic of the Qur'an. All spoken dialects are considered inferior to the classical form, which is regarded as ideal and complete, being the revealed word of God.

Although Arabic is a relatively difficult language to learn, the Arab Muslim client who speaks no English appreciates, respects, and is influenced by the nurse who makes an effort to communicate in Arabic. Facility in Arabic does more than use the language for exchanging ideas; it creates a positive atmosphere of acceptance that is conducive to constructive communication and caring modes. For many clients, language poses a tremendous barrier when attempting to enter the Western health care system. For this reason, many available community services are frequently unused by Arab Muslim clients. Bilingual staff and translators are helpful in dealing with the non-English speaking client, however, learning a few simple phrases and greetings in Arabic will facilitate establishing and maintaining a caring relationship with the client and the family.

Every culture and religion has its own set of symbols which give insight into underlying cultural norms and values. By assessing the client's symbolic construction of reality, the nurse can get close to thoughts, actions, and feelings of the client and can deal with barriers that might otherwise interfere with effective nursing care. A variety of symbolic icons, objects, and forms of human expression provide support in the life of Arab Muslims. As mentioned earlier, religion is all-pervasive. Seldom does an Arab Muslim make a promise or plan of action without uttering the term *Inshallah* (if God wills).[23] The utterance reflects the Muslim belief in divine authority for all intended actions.

Prayer beads are a common symbol of Islam used by both males and females. Similar to a rosary, the string usually consists of thirty-three beads and is used in private worship to recall the ninety-nine attributes of God listed in the Qur'an. The use of prayer beads is a reminder to Muslim clients of the nearness of God and thereby serves to reduce anxiety and provides a sense of peace and well-being.

From the very beginning of Islam, there has been a reluctance among Muslim artists to render reality in human or anthropomorphic form. Any symbolic representation of the prophet Muhammad or his family is avoided; instead, reality is depicted through abstract art and calligraphy. Again, the concept of *Tawhid* is inherent in the geometric patterns known as arabesque, which have no beginning and no end, thus, giving the impression of infinity. The purpose of such art for Muslims is to direct one toward the remembrance of God.[24]

A variety of cultural values are inherent in the above concepts of language use and symbolism. The nurse should be particularly attentive when giving care to Arab Muslim clients, to any treatments or interventions which conflict with the clients' cultural values.

Social Structure Factors and Nursing Care

To fully comprehend any culture, and especially Arab Muslim culture, social structure is an important element. Religion is one major factor of social structure for the Arab Muslim client. Another important aspect is family and kinship. The nurse needs to recognize the centrality and importance of the family as the major unit of social organization for Arab Muslim culture. The Arab Muslim is born into an extended family which fashions and uses kinship ties to achieve various daily activities and goals throughout life. It is largely within the family that a person derives his/her sense of identity. In all matters the individual is expected to place family or group concerns before any individual concerns.[25] This often means making great personal sacrifices in order to put the good of the family foremost. However, certain advantages are inherent in such a system. Fashshur points out that an extended family provides multiple role models for children varying in age, sex, and other personal and social attributes.[26] Furthermore, the extended family serves many of the naturalistic caring functions which are delegated to institutions in the West—i.e., money lender, job placement center, and nursing home.

Age commands a great deal of authority in an extended Arab Muslim household. Elderly parents usually live with the oldest son, since it is considered disrespectful for old parents to live alone. According to the Qur'an, taking care of one's family is as important as other religious duties.

Until recently, nursing homes or homes for the aged were unknown in the Arab world. Even though a few such institutions now exist, for example in Egypt, the idea of sending one's parents to a nursing home is still unpopular. Elkholy notes that senility among the aged appears to be a rare occurrence in the Middle East, since the elderly gain status with age rather than experiencing loss of self-esteem and self-worth, as is often the case with the elderly in the West.[27]

Islam and the teachings of the Qur'an provide cultural rules which guide family living and influence care practices. The nurse should be aware of these cultural norms and function within their orientation. Arab Muslim culture strongly upholds the married state this is reinforced by the Qur'an teaching that "men and women are created mates, a pair, to treat each other with affection and compassion within the bonds of matrimony."[28] Celibacy, for the purpose of dedicating one's life totally to God's service, is not highly regarded in Islam. Instead, Muslims are encouraged to marry, since the single state is considered unnatural and potentially leads to sin.[29]

Arab Muslims value and have a strong procreation orientation which is supported by Islamic beliefs. Children are regarded as God's greatest gift since they bring continuation of life. Although the Qur'an makes no reference to contraception, birth control and family planning are traditionally sensitive topics since there tends to be a strong belief that the number of children to be born is determined by Allah. It is usually not within the traditional role of the Muslim woman to decide alone on a family planning method. The husband is generally consulted, but the attitude toward birth control and family planning will vary with acculturation, education, and according to the country of origin. Abortion is not allowed under Islamic law. Traditional Arab values tend to emphasize the birth of a male child over a female child. The birth of a son is usually an occasion for rejoicing and celebration, while the birth of a girl may be greeted with silence. This distinction between sons and daughters may be explained by recognizing that in the Arab world, girls tend to grow up, marry, and move to another's house. Daughters, when married, spend their lives building up another's house, while sons build up the house of the parents. While some nurses with feminist values may abhor the overindulgence of the male child, the culturally knowledgeable and sensitive nurse will be cautious and refrain from inflicting any ethnocentric biases or judgmental attitudes toward the Arab Muslim mother who responds to the birth of a daughter with indifference. To avoid cultural imposition, the nurse should recognize that such behavior is reflective of social structure features which for centuries have given importance to males for their roles in family continuity.

Cultural Food Values and Care Considerations

Cultural values and beliefs regarding food and nutrition are important factors to consider in nursing care. Functions, beliefs, and practices of food-use vary cross-culturally.[30] The nurse needs to assess the use and function of food as one important element in understanding behavior.

As with other religious groups, Arab Muslims subscribe to a number of dietary rules and taboos derived from religious law. Under Islamic law the consumption of pork, alcohol, and improperly slaughtered meat (meat that is not *halal*) is forbidden. Since few hospitals provide *halal* meat on the menu, the Muslim who observes strict dietary regulations may select a vegetarian diet when hospitalized. Furthermore, many American processed foods use pork products such as lard, which poses a problem for the Muslim client. Using Leininger's culture care accommodation mode of decision-action, the nurse should assess with the client the extent to which dietary restrictions are observed, and then take steps to accommodate the client in the choice of food. Most Muslims when hospitalized expect and appreciate accommodation to their dietary laws, even though they may be less diligent in other religious practices.

Food and diet vary considerably throughout the Arab world, however, in all Arab Muslim cultures, food is closely associated with hospitality and care. The traditional sign of Middle Eastern hospitality is the serving of a small cup of Arabic (Turkish) coffee to every visitor, regardless of the time of day. Certain rules of etiquette govern the serving of coffee. The elderly are served first and generally men before women, although this may vary throughout the Arab world. To refuse a cup of coffee from one's host is considered extremely disrespectful and uncaring.

Bread is a major staple of diet of most Arab Muslims. While many families purchase bread daily from an Arab bakery, many Muslim women in the United States continue to make bread at home in the traditional fashion. Bread is generally eaten at every meal and symbolizes the abundance of God's blessings. Should a piece of bread accidentally fall to the floor, the Arab Muslims must pick it up and touch it to the lips and forehead while uttering praise to God for giving bread to eat.

A field study conducted by the writer with Lebanese Muslims in a large, urban United States city revealed diet to be the area of least acculturation, in that the people have maintained the food habits of their native country.[31] Neither frozen nor canned foods were eaten with any regularity. Instead, foods were cooked fresh daily and a variety of spices and herbs (i.e., za'atar, yansoun, na'ana) are used for both cooking and medicinal purposes.

Meleis notes that "American food is thought to be too bland for Arab patients", and therefore, food is often brought into the hospital from home.[32] Hospitals which provide services to a large Arab population need to consider employing a transcultural nutritionist or transcultural nurse to facilitate effective caring practices, since food is closely linked to health and well-being.

Health, Illness, and Care Beliefs and Practices

According to Leininger, health, illness, and care are largely cultural phenomena with meanings which vary significantly according to cultural background. Care is seen as influencing the health state of individuals, families, and groups, whereas health tends to be congruent with and reflect many care practices and philosophical orientations.[33] Health includes more than just physical and psychological dimensions, and encompasses important social and cultural aspects of well-being also. Understanding health, illness, and care from a cultural frame of reference is important according to Leininger, since culture provides the framework for human behaviors including health and care practices. Prior to initiating a plan of care, it is imperative that nurses assess the clients' perceptions of their health-illness state in light of their cultural values, beliefs, and patterned lifeways. These *emic* interpretations are important for guiding the modes of nursing interventions.

Several traditional beliefs regarding health and illness still prevail among many Arab Muslims. One example is the phenomenon of the "evil eye" (*ain il-hasud*), as one of several supernatural origins of disease or misfortune. Referred to in the Qur'an, central to the phenomenon is the belief that one can project harm or misfortune on another by admiring that person's possessions with jealousy or envy. Any form of admiration thus becomes suspect as a potential vehicle for casting the evil-eye, and blue-eyed persons and women are particularly thought to have the power.[34] Aswad, based on anthropological fieldwork in a Muslim village in Turkey, identified that the evil-eye is often attributed to the in-marrying female who has access to family secrets upon marriage but who retains a strong bond to her natal family.[35] In order to avert the evil eye such things as blue beads or charms with verses from the Qur'an are worn. These should not be removed unless it is unavoidable, since the client may then consider himself/herself particularly vulnerable to evil forces within the environment. The nurse can avoid contributing to any suspicions of casting the evil eye by refraining from overt expressions of admiration for an infant and by uttering the term "*Bis-mallah*" (God's blessing) and touching the infant.

Visiting patterns on Arab culture have been recognized by a number of anthropologists as constituting important social and political functions.[36,37,38] Through ethnonursing research with Arab Muslims in the United States, the writer discovered that visiting as an important sign and reflection of caring behaviors was expressed in a variety of beliefs and actions. For example, traditional practices in the Middle East necessitate the visiting of the sick by relatives, neighbors, and friends. These visits constitute a social obligation to the point that illness often becomes a social gathering—a time when family and friends come together and social ties are renewed. When an individual is hospitalized, there is a more deeply felt obligation of family and friends to visit. Islam teaches that visiting a sick person, along with other good deeds, is an act through which a believer obtains nearness to Allah.[39] To fail to visit at the time of illness is considered damaging to the social relationship and may result in a complete severing of social ties. Although visiting is expected on other occasions such as marriage or birth, failure to do so at these times may affect the relationship, but it usually does not result in complete severing of relations.[40]

Rather than label the Arab Muslim family problematic because large numbers of visitors show up at visiting hours, an awareness of the cultural and religious obligation to visit the sick should be kept in mind by the nurse along with the inherent therapeutic benefits to the client. The nurse should anticipate this critical cultural need and provide a comfortable location in the hospital setting that would accommodate several visitors. Attention to these essential, indigenous acts of care/caring by family and friends should be anticipated, recognized, and accommodated rather than criticized if the goal of culture care congruence is to be attained.

Attitudes toward death and dying and the cultural expression of grief are other important areas that the nurse needs to consider in providing culturally sensitive care to Arab Muslim clients. Traditional Muslim beliefs support the deterministic position that whatever happens in life is a result of destiny, or God's will. Therefore, a traditionally-oriented Muslim may believe that the time of death is predetermined; when death is to occur, there is nothing that can change it.[41] However, a sense of hope always remains, since it is believed that only God knows when death will occur. The nurse can assist Arab Muslim clients in maintaining a sense of hope by avoiding the utterance of a potentially fatal outcome or avoiding the communication of a terminal diagnosis to a client or the family.[42] The subject of death is usually avoided, since there is a belief among some that to "speak of death is to bring it about."[43] For this reason, the nurse should be extremely cautious in counseling Arab Muslim clients with terminal cancer or other fatal illnesses. Western models which encourage terminal clients to talk about approaching death may be inappropriate in the context of Arab Muslim culture.

Death in the Arab Muslim culture is another occasion that enhances the solidarity of family and social relationships and allows for the expression of grief.[44] Traditional rituals of grief differ among urban and village residents throughout the Arab world. In the past, death of a villager was traditionally accompanied by loud wailing, crying and moaning of female members, and often tearing of the hair and clothing. Although this tradition is undergoing change, visiting by family and friends for several days after death remains an expectation, and as with illness, is a social obligation. Another custom which continues is the wearing of dark colors by female relatives during mourning. Ceremonies and mourning for the deceased may extend for a period of forty days up to one year following death.

According to Islamic law, a Muslim who dies does not own his body, therefore, organ donation or transplantation is usually not considered, nor are postmortem examinations.[45] Burial, rather than cremation, is considered the only lawful means of disposing of the body. The nurse may discover that a Muslim family may prefer a family member or friend to carry out the task of preparing the body after death, since special rituals of washing the body and wrapping it in a special cloth shroud are part of Islamic belief.

Summary

Nursing care of the Arab Muslim client can be extremely rewarding, providing the nurse is knowledgeable about important features of the culture. Knowledge of the complex social structure features, worldview, language, and cultural values are critical in promoting a sense of care for Arab Muslim clients. The centrality of religion and the family are closely interrelated and reflect many aspects of health and care. This chapter has presented an overview of some of these features. The importance of culturalogical assessment for each client and family cannot be overemphasized, since cultural background, education, and degree of acculturation lead to variation in cultural patterns. Although this chapter has focused on the Arab Muslim client, it should be kept in mind that due to cultural similarities among Arabs, some of the patterns apply to Arab Christians as well. The use of Leininger's theory and the Sunrise Model for modes of nursing action are most valuable to assess and make decisions regarding care that is culturally-specific and congruent to the Arab Muslim client. Only through the use of transcultural nursing care knowledge and sensitivity to clients can nurses be more effective in meeting the care and health needs of this distinct cultural group. Leininger's theory of Culture Care and the Sunrise Model have been most useful to discover transcultural knowledge and understand the Arab Muslims' worldview and social structure factors along with their language, history, and the environmental context in which their health and well-being are expressed and become known.

Footnotes

*This chapter was written prior to the Persian Gulf War (1991–1992).

**Dr. Linda Luna is Director of Nursing Education and Research at King Faisal's Specialist Hospital and Research Center in Riyadh, Kingdom of Saudi Arabia. She has been employed in this center since 1991 as a transcultural nurse specialist, educator, and researcher. She obtained her Ph.D. focusing on transcultural nursing at Wayne State University, College of Nursing, studying under Professor Leininger.

References

1. Leininger, M., "Leininger's Theory of Culture Care Diversity and Universality: A Theory of Nursing," *Nursing Science Quarterly*, v. 1, no. 4, 1988, pp. 152–160.
2. Leininger, M., "The Phenomenon of Caring: Importance, Research Questions and Theoretical Considerations," *Caring: An Essential Human Need*, M. Leininger, ed., New Jersey: Charles B. Slack, 1981, pp. 3–15.
3. Ibid., 1988.
4. *Who Are The Arabs?*, New York: The League of Arab States: Arab Information Center, 1986.
5. Almaney, A. and A. Alwan, *Communicating with Arabs*, Prospect Heights, Illinois: Waveland Press, 1982.
6. Adams, C., "Islamic Faith," *Introduction to Islamic Civilization*, R. Savory, ed., New York: Cambridge University Press, 1979, pp. 33–44.
7. Fry, G. and J. King, *Islam: A Survey of the Muslim Faith*, Grand Rapids, Michigan: Baker Book House, 1980.
8. Martin, R., *Islam: A Cultural Perspective*, New Jersey: Prentice-Hall, 1982.
9. Naff, A., "Arabs in America: A Historical Overview," *Arabs in the New World*, S. Abraham and N. Abraham, eds., Detroit: Wayne State University Center for Urban Studies, 1983, pp. 8–29.
10. Haddad, Y., "Muslims in the United States," *Islam: The Religious and Political Life of a World Community*, M. Kelly, ed., New York: Praeger, 1984, pp. 258–274.
11. Ibid., p. 260.
12. Abraham, S., "Detroit's Arab-American Community: A Survey of Diversity and Commonality," *Arabs in the New World*, S. Abraham and N. Abraham, eds., Detroit; Wayne State University Center for Urban Studies, 1983, pp. 84–108.
13. Haddad, Y., "Arab Muslims and Islamic Institutions in America: Adaption and Reform," *Arabs in the New World*, S. Abraham and N. Abraham, eds., Detroit: Wayne State University Center for Urban Studies, 1983, pp. 64–81.
14. Aswad, B., *Arabic Speaking Communities in American Cities*, New York: Center for Migration Studies, 1974.
15. Haddad, op. cit., 1983,
16. Ahamad, K., *Islam: Its Meaning and Message*, London: Redwood Burn Limited, 1975.
17. Hassan, R., "Peace and Islamic World View," *Occasional Papers*: Proceedings of International Conference—The Quest for Peace Beyond *Ideology*, M. Max, ed., Detroit: Wayne State University, 1981, pp. 11–14.

18. Al Faruqi, L., "Unity and Variety in the Music of Islamic Culture," *The Islamic Impact*, Y. Haddad, B. Haines, and E. Findly, eds., New York: Syracuse University Press, 1981, pp. 175–194.

19. Al Farqum, I. and L. Al Faruqi, *The Cultural Atlas of Islam*, New York: MacMillan Publishing Company, 1986.

20. Bates, D. and A. Rassam, *Peoples and Cultures of the Middle East*, New Jersey: Prentice-Hall, 1983.

21. Ibid.

22. Fry and King, op. cit.

23. Weekes, R., *Muslim Peoples: A World Ethnographic Survey*, London: Greenwood Press, 1978.

24. Al Faruqum and Al Faruqi, op. cit.

25. Barakat, H., "The Arab Family and the Challenge of Social Transformation," *Women and the Family in the Middle East: New Voices of Change*, E. Fernea, ed., Austin, Texas: University of Texas Press, 1985, pp. 27–48.

26. Bashshur, R., "Aspects of Family Organization and Personal Adjustment in Arab Society: Contrasts Between Traditional and Western Models," unpublished paper, 1986.

27. Elkholy, A., "The Arab American Family," *Ethnic Families in America: Patterns and Variations*, C. Mindel and R. Habenstein, eds., New York: Elsevier, 1981, pp. 145–162.

28. Marsot, A., "The Changing Arab Muslim Family," *Islam: The Religion and Political Life of a World Community*, M. Kelly, ed., New York: Praeger, 1984, pp. 243–257.

29. Ibid.

30. Leininger, M., *Transcultural Nursing: Concepts, Theories, and Practices*, New York: John Wiley and Sons, 1978.

31. Luna, L., "Health and Care Phenomena Among Lebanese-American Muslims," unpublished field study, Detroit: Wayne State University, 1986.

32. Meleis, A., "The Arab-American in the Health Care System," *American Journal of Nursing*, v. 81, 1981, pp. 1180–1183.

33. Leininger, M., personal communication, March, 1986.

34. Spooner, B., "The Evil Eye in the Middle East," *The Evil Eye*, C. Maloney, ed., New York: Columbia University Press, 1976, pp. 76–84.

35. Aswad, B., "Key and Peripheral Roles of Noble Women in a Middle Eastern Plains Village," *Anthropological Quarterly*, v. 47, 1974, pp. 9–27.

36. Altorki, S., *Women in Saudi Arabia: Ideology and Behavior among the Elite*, New York: Columbia Press, 1986.

37. Aswad, B., "Visiting Patterns among Women of the Elite in a Small Turkish City," *Anthropological Quarterly*, v. 47, 1974, pp. 9–27.

38. Joseph, S., "Women and the Neighborhood Street in Borj Hammoud, Lebanon," *Women in the Muslim World*, l. Beck and N. Keddie, eds., Cambridge: Harvard University Press, 1978, pp. 541–557.

39. Al Muzaffar, M., *The Faith of Shi'a Islam*, Great Britian: The Muhammadi Trust, 1982.

40. Altorki, op. cit.

41. Baqui, M., "Muslim Teachings Concerning Death," *Nursing Times*, v. 75, no. 14, 1979, pp. 44–45.

42. Meleis, A. and A. Jonsen, "Ethical Crises and Cultural Differences," *The Western Journal of Medicine*, v. 138, no. 6, 1983, pp. 889–893.

43. Racy, J., "Death in an Arab Culture," *Annals of the New York Academy of Science*, v. 164, 1969, pp. 871–880.

44. Fakhouri, H., *Kafr El-Elow: An Egyptian Village in Transition*, Prospect Heights, Illinois: Waveland Press, 1972.

45. Henley, A. and J. Clayton, "Religion of the Muslims," *Health and Social Service Journal*, v. 97, 1982, pp. 918–919.

Chapter 14

Anglo-American (USA) Culture Care Values and Perspectives*

Madeleine Leininger, PhD, LHD, DS, FAAN, CTN, RN.

If we are to work effectively with people of diverse cultures, we must first understand our own cultural heritage with its values and lifeways as a means to understand other cultures. This understanding should reflect differences and similarities in order to know and appropriately respond to the wonderful gift of diversity among human beings.

Leininger 1969

The Anglo-American way of life tends to become obscure because many contend that if one lives in the United States, "all Americans are alike and there are no differences among them." This is a myth as there are cultural differences and variations among Americans by virtue of their diverse cultural heritage, specific values, and cultural patterns. Within the American culture are the Anglo-Americans who are largely Caucasian immigrants from many places in the world whose lifeways reveal special beliefs, values, and practices that have prevailed for many generations. It is fascinating to discover how this large and dominant culture has influenced health care practices in the United States and in other cultures. Indeed, Anglo-American cultural values and patterns have been so pervasive that one assumes they represent "the American way of life." However, many Americans are unaware of the specific characteristics of traditional Anglo-American culture and how these values are different from those of other cultures in the United States. One of the greatest nursing challenges and purposes of this chapter is to understand the Anglo-American culture with its complex and diverse features and largely of caucasian heritage.

The Challenge and Importance of Understanding Anglo-Americans

The original term Anglo is derived from the Latin and refers to one of the four Germanic peoples together with the Saxons, Frisians, and Jutes who invaded England

335

from the third to the sixth century as the Romans retreated. These Germanic tribes displaced the native Celts who eventually referred to all their Germanic conquerors as Anglo-Saxons.[1,2] When the colonists immigrated to America from England beginning in the 1600s, they brought English cultural values, language, and many beliefs to the United States. Gradually, these Anglo-Saxons or English people became known as Caucasians; Anglo-Americans are often referred to as "WASPs", i.e., White, Anglo-Saxon, Protestants.[3,4,5] This large cultural group, along with others who are not Protestant, has for nearly four centuries profoundly influenced and shaped the legal, economic, educational, religious, political, and cultural values in the United States of America.

The genetic and physical features of Anglo-Saxons are quite heterogeneous with Mediterranean, Alpine, and Nordic racial features with influences of the Celtic, Teutonic, and Scandinavian peoples. The Anglo-Saxon culture prevailed over successive waves of immigration to America, much as the Anglo-Saxon world of early England absorbed Celts, Norse, Danes, and Frenchmen.[6] Arsenberg and Niehoff maintain that the United States has several streams of culture flowing side by side but assert there is still a national, white middle-class with its origins in Western European cultures. They state:

> *The language is English, the legal system derived from English common law, the political system of democratic elections comes from France and England, the technology is solidly from Europe, and even more subtle social values, such as egalitarianism (though modified) seem to be European derived. Anglo-Saxon civil rights, the rule of law, and representative institutions were inherited from the English background.[7]*

Essentially the English were the first Europeans to colonize the Americans in large numbers even though they were preceded in the Southwest by smaller numbers of Spaniards. Since the English gave the Anglo-Saxon label to Anglo-Americans, their origins were derived from the original inhabitants of the British Islands who were subdued by the Celts.[8] The latter ancestors first appeared in central Europe and later moved to northern France, southern Britain, and finally Ireland. But as these people immigrated to the United States, they became known as "Anglo-Americans." According to Arsenberg and Niehoff, and McGill and Pearce, Anglo-Americans had British roots that led to cultural values such as the nuclear family that were largely derived from pre-industrial Britain. These cultural values and others became part of the Anglo-American values in the United States.[9,10]

For several decades, anthropologists and sociologists have been studying Anglo-American core values.[11,12,13,14,15,16,17,18,19,20,21] These scholars with their rich descriptions, theories, and narrative accounts have been extremely helpful to grasp the general features of Anglo-American culture and to identify differences among other cultures in the United States and elsewhere such as the Japanese, Chinese, Russians, and others.

Understanding the overt or subtle differences about Anglo-Americans can help nurses to prevent cultural clashes, imposition practices, cultural stresses, and other problems that may arise between nursing staff and clients. In addition, knowledge of Anglo-Americans has been extremely valuable to facilitate communication, guide decision making, and to prevent gross misunderstandings between cultures within and outside the United States.

It is strange but true that most Anglo-American cultural values and patterns of thinking and acting are usually not studied until outsiders comment or raise questions about "Anglo ways." Most Anglo-Americans take for granted their culture as a part of their lifeways and they fail to recognize its unique features. Sometimes people from very different backgrounds speak of Anglo-American behavior as strange, peculiar, or even bizarre. Becoming aware of such differences of Anglo-Americans in relation to other cultures is important so that not all people in America are viewed alike. For example, the author has often heard outsiders say that Anglo-Americans tend to be so individualistic and autonomous that they have difficulty valuing or conforming to group norms and other ways of living outside the United States. Some non-Anglo-Americans view Anglo-Americans as highly materialistic and too competitive. Other outsiders or visitors find that "Anglos" tend to take many kinds of pills too avoid any physical pain or suffering. Anglo-Americans who travel to very different cultures in the world also discover that other cultural groups dress and act differently than themselves. Such differences noted by outsiders about Anglo-American culture makes one pause to understand the why of the intercultural differences. Gaining knowledge and understanding one's own culture and that of others remain the hallmark of professional nurses and scholars, but especially of transcultural nurses as they work with people of many different cultures.

Since the mid 1950s, the author has been studying and observing Anglo-Americans and any changes in their values, beliefs, and communication modes in order to advance transcultural nursing knowledge and improve nursing care practices.[22,23] Identifying differences and similarities of Anglo-American and other cultures is helping to dispel the "all alike American syndrome" in nursing and helping nurses be attentive to differential client care practices. Some of the greatest problems of Anglo-American nurses have been ethnocentrism and cultural blindness in which nurses fail to recognize cultural variations among Americans. Anglo-Americans tend to be lumped and dumped together as all alike without awareness of subtle and major differences. Such tendencies have led to intercultural problems, ineffective nursing care practices, and on-going cultural clashes and sometimes legal suits. Cultural awareness of Anglo-Americans is essential to develop nursing competencies, for it is difficult to be knowledgeable or an advocate of clients without understanding their cultural values.

At last Anglo-American nurses are realizing that today most United States hospitals, clinics, community agencies, and corporate institutions have historically been largely established and maintained with the dominant unicultural Anglo-American values and practices. This is evident in nursing education and practice and in hospitals, health care agencies, and most organizational structures dealing with health care. But among these Anglo-American values, there are specific cultures that need to be recognized such as Swedish, Danish, Finnish, German, Italian, Greek, and many other Anglo based cultures. These cultures are part of the general Anglo-American cultures that need to be considered in client care and staff relationships. But transcending these cultures are some common Anglo-American values, beliefs, and practices that are shared and have been passed on to succeeding generations as dominant Anglo-American values as cited above in many references by Anglo-American specialists on this culture. Knowledge of the dominant or overriding Anglo-American culture is essential to grasp this pervading way of American life. However, the nurse needs to be attentive to the subtle and gross differences that may be evident as one works closely with specific representatives of the culture. Nurses cannot neglect the dominant Anglo-American culture if they are to be effective, competent, and sensitive transcultural nurses. Let us turn to some of these dominant Anglo-American cultural values in the United States.

Anglo-American Cultural Values

Since cultural values are the powerful directive forces that give meaning and direction to human action and decisions, Anglo-American cultural values identified below are held to be essential to understanding and practicing nursing. The values identified below came from the author's three decades of research on Anglo-Americans with a focus on culture care meanings and actions. These values are reaffirmed from anthropological research and writings such as those by DuBois, Fried, Gorer, Hall, Kluckholn and Kluckholn, Mead, Nash, and Stewart and Bennett.[24,25,26,27,28,29,30,31,32] Anglo-American cultural values will be identified and then discussed with a focus on transcultural nursing care meanings and practices, largely from the author's research and experiences.[33,34]

Dominant Anglo-American Middle and Upper Class Cultural Values [35]

1. Individualism and self-reliance
2. Independence and freedom
3. Competition, assertiveness, and achievements
4. Materialism
5. Dependence on technology

6. Equal gender roles and rights
7. Instant time and action (doing)
8. Youth and beauty
9. Reliance on "scientific facts" and numbers
10. Generosity and helpfulness in crises

Unquestionably, Anglo-Americans value individualism, freedom and being fairly autonomous in thinking and actions. They like their individualistic freedom to speak, act, and be on their own, and generally dislike being treated as a collectivity or group. Personal identity and uniqueness as individuals is important to most Anglo-Americans. Nash contends that they are the most individualistic people in the world, which he holds comes from their traditional English pre-industrial norms and American industrialism.[36] Anglo-Americans not only want to be recognized as individuals, but as being self-reliant, independent, and self-determining persons. They value privacy and having their own material goods with them. Most adult middle and upper class Anglo-Americans socialize, reward, and promote with children the idea of being unique with their own things and name and being self-reliant and autonomous. Such values are taught at home at an early age and are reinforced in schools and work. For example, many Anglo-American children are taught at a very early age to feed themselves, brush their teeth, dress, make decisions, and talk independently in their unique ways. Children learn early what belongs to them as their possessions and their rights. Such child-rearing practices and others related to individualism, self-reliance, freedom of speech, and autonomy tends to contrast sharply with Chinese, Vietnamese, and many other non-Western cultures in which children are taught to value being part of a group (often large families), living communally and sharing material goods.

Anglo-Americans dislike being constrained or having their freedom infringed upon by others, especially by government and institutional policies or practices. Speaking openly about almost any matter is valued, defended, and protected by Anglo-Americans. Hence policies or decrees that limit such expressions are often resisted, avoided, or responded to negatively. Political ideologies and practices such as Marxism or working for the collective good tend to be questioned by most older Anglo-Americans. Accordingly, Anglo-American nurses usually resent autocratic or oppressive leaders that suppress their individual rights, autonomy, freedom, or special ways of doing things.

The Anglo-American cultural values of competition, achievement, and assertiveness are part of their way of life. Competition and achieving measurable outcomes are supported. Likewise, Anglo-American nurses have become more competitive in recent years and like to show their achievements, worth, and measurable gains in products or symbols. Most support women's rights and professionally upward-bound goals at work, college, or in public arenas. Anglo-American nurses pursue their competitive and assertive efforts to achieve by tapping available rewards and by competing with other individuals and groups in the work or home place. "Playing the game" and gaining access to key people, positions, and awards have become important to Anglo-American nurses of the new era.

The Anglo-American values of achieving, being competitive, and getting key positions, honors, or rewards may be directly at odds with nurses and clients of other cultures who do not value these attributes. For example, traditional Native Americans in the United States and Canada generally do not promote competition and achievement because they believe these values lead to disharmony with others and their environment. Being aware of such differences among cultures can prevent major cultural clashes, offensive acts, non-compliance, and negative nursing experiences. These values are also important in nursing education and administration, especially when nurse leaders are promoting competition and achievement activities between students, staff, and others. Nurses from non-Western cultures that value cooperation, interdependence, and avoiding open competition, often experience cultural strain, conflicts, and dislike for their work. Transcultural nurses can be helpful to bring about awareness and understanding of cultural value differences to nursing staff and to educators who are not knowledgeable of such cultural factors. Indeed, there are many incidences and unfavorable outcomes that can be identified in schools of nursing and in health services where competitive actions and fierce competition behaviors fail to be recognized, let alone dealt with in nursing situations.

Other dominant Anglo-American middle and upper class values are materialism and reliance upon technological goods and equipment. Anglo-Americans value having material goods and a great variety of high-technology products as conspicuous items in their homes and work environments. Many Anglo-Americans feverishly work to get money for many different material items and technological electrical products that are held to make work easier and more efficient. There are often several cars, television sets, freezers, and a great variety of electrical kitchen appliances in middle and upper class Anglo-American homes. Electronic gadgets are viewed today as essential and justified. Moreover, Anglo-Americans may buy several varieties of small technologies to be sure there is always one to replace the other. Moreover, as new technologies come on the market, the old one, which is often still functional, tends to be discarded. Cultural anthropologists have been studying this behavior and found that most Anglo-Americans dispose of more material and technological goods than any other culture or country in the world.[37] Future archaeological digs will undoubtedly reveal lots of technologies, aluminum cans, and many plastic products as belonging to the twentieth century Anglo-Americans. Being modern, progressive, and successful often is associated with automation and with new products on the market, but it also reflects the conspicuous consumption of middle and upper class Anglo-Americans as wasteful and reflecting a "throw away" culture. Having the newest, latest, and most efficient technologies in Anglo-American middle and upper class homes, offices, and places of leisure is highly desired. Such vast amounts of materials goods and electronic equipment contrast sharply with the poor and often with other cultures within and outside the United States that have virtually no material goods and technologies. In fact, these cultures could live for months or years from what is thrown away by Anglo-Americans in material goods and foods. Moreover, the poor or homeless in American hunt for and scrounge around in garbage cans and other places to survive. Living on "toss aways" is a way of daily and nightly life for some people in America and in other countries where conspicuous material goods are discarded. The electronic and technological culture has become a dominant hallmark of Western cultures.

Speaking more specifically to technologies in hospitals, clinics, and more recently in homes, there are many kinds of high-technological electric equipment such as computers, x-ray machines, special instruments, and a great variety of powerful technologies to assess and promote medical treatments. Health care systems have become technology centers with health personnel being dependent upon such equipment for professional services. Technologically dependent home care is beginning to flourish and will require a variety of small but effective and safe technologies. Hospitals continue to buy the latest and most effective technologies as their budgets permit. We shall see similar purchases in wealthy homes for their own private and instant diagnostic and treatment uses. But not all cultures believe in and use such technologies. For example, the Old Order Amish do not value the use of high technologies unless for very specific reasons. If the Amish are greatly threatened by the loss of a family member's life, they may decide to use selected hospital services and high technologies. Generally, such considerations are weighed carefully so that the use of technologies does not violate their religious beliefs and caring values.[38] Nurses prepared in transcultural nursing often alert other nurses to these areas of cultural conflict so that the client and the family are not offended or demeaned for not using high technologies and other hospital or health products. Moreover, if such technologies are used with ignorance or error, one must carefully assess the influence on their total well-being or threats to survival.

Another dominant Anglo-American value is that males and females should be treated with equal respect, rights, and role opportunities in the home or work place. Equal gender rights and opportunities are promoted and defended for Anglo-American women whose rights can be violated, neglected, or oppressed. During the past two decades the feminist movement in the United States has been an active pursuit in many different education and service centers. Anglo-American women have been active to obtain salaries comparable to their male counterparts and to seek some of the top positions traditionally held by men in diverse organizational settings. Anglo-American nurse leaders have been especially active in making men and women aware of their behaviors and especially to reduce expressions and behaviors offensive to women. Many nurses have worked hard to free themselves from being dominated by male physicians and other patriarchal health personnel. Progress is being made as there are more signs of nurses moving into top leadership positions, gaining access to better employment environments, and getting salaries equal to those of men. There are, however, gender gaps in salaries with women doing the same kind of work but receiving less pay.

But the struggle of Anglo-American women and nurses is an enigma for women and men in other cultures. For some non-Anglo-Americans the push by women for equal rights with men is frightening as gender differences are important in other cultures. Some non-Anglo-American nurses are shocked to find Western nurses imposing and pushing for equal rights, for they also know of the serious consequences if women dominate men or drastically change their cultural roles and behaviors. Abuse and battering of women often occurs when male spouses in some cultures learn about drastic changes in their women's roles. There are, however, some women in other cultures interested to change their traditional gender practices and they often seek out Anglo-American nurses to help them. Transcultural nurses are extremely important to help these nurses from diverse cultures because they have knowledge of the culture and remain aware of cultural differences and consequences of changes. Transcultural nurses have ethical and moral responsibilities to protect those who may not understand transcultural values, beliefs, and practices. Assisting clients who have different gender values than Anglo-Americans is, therefore, an ethical responsibility so that culturally congruent practices can be appropriately established. Some Anglo-American feminist leaders who have not been prepared in transcultural nursing may have difficulty with the role expectations of transcultural nurses, especially as an ethical responsibility. At the same time, males are changing some of their traditional values and practices in different cultures and they too need nurses with knowledge of past and current transcultural changes.

As one turns to another Anglo-American value, the metaphors "time is money" and "time must not be wasted" reveal that time is a dominant value in our culture. If time is not appropriately used and respected, Anglo-Americans often become angry, frustrated, restless, and upset. Moreover, maintaining time schedules and expectations can lead to being seen as competent, successful, and efficient. Anglo-Americans want time savers or extenders to help them achieve and be successful. Figuratively, time dictates where one should be day and night. Many Americans today are *born into the world by the clock, work by the clock, get married by the clock, and can die by the clock.* Time truly pervades Anglo-American lifeways. Transculturally, the power of time and its uses are more evident in this culture than in many cultures of the world.

Reflecting on time, the contrast with the Papua New Guinea people with whom the author lived and studied for nearly two years, was clearly apparent. The Gadsup had no mechanical or electronic time pieces. They had no sense of Western clock time in their daily and nightly activities in the early 1960s. Only very recently do they know and use clock time in our Western views and practices. In fact, the Gadsup had never seen a watch until the author showed them hers in the early 1960s. The Gadsup, however, did have a general concept of time by their daily activities of living by the rising and setting of the sun, changes in plant growth, and other changes in their activities, physical environment, and historical events. Likewise, there are other cultures in the world in which time is not central to lives and well-being. Such time differences and awareness are extremely important to provide culturally congruent and satisfying care and to establish a well-being rhythm of people's lifeways based on the time concept of their culture.

Transcultural nurses are usually aware of differential time concepts and alert nurses to time differences. In some hospital contexts, Anglo-Americans may consider that they receive good care when nurses respond instantly to their calls; whereas clients from different cultures have a concept of time that means "the nurse will come in time," but more importantly they "will have a compassionate and caring attitude toward me when they come." If Anglo-American clients are delayed for more than ten minutes they become impatient and angry and may want to leave the hospital or threaten a lawsuit.

The concept of time is closely related to another Anglo-American value, namely that of doing. Being active and doing something have been strong normative expectations for Anglo-Americans and especially nurses.[39] Nurses are often evaluated on how much they do, what activities they have completed, or how many things they have done. Doing is related to success, acceptance, and satisfying persons in authority. With the present emphasis on quantifiable, measurable outcomes and costs, nurses feel compelled to produce what they have done or how much they have done in clinical areas or in educational settings. This Anglo-American value of doing and measuring often comes into great conflict with the professional nurse who practices non-doing activities and of being naturalistic and humanistic. Caring nurses value listening to, giving time, and offering presence to clients of different cultures plus other caring modes and practices, but this is difficult when they are pressured for time and to produce something. These nurses often receive unfavorable response when they are caring for client's in non-doing activities. The pervasive Anglo-American nursing value of doing something may be very difficult in caring for Mexican, Vietnamese, Philippine, Korean, Taiwanese, Chinese, and Native Americans. The meaning and uses of time with clients, staff, nurses, students, administrators, and others need to be studied and understood with respect to specific cultural values, uses, and the importance of doing or non-doing in different nursing contexts and with clients of diverse cultures.[40] Nurses prepared in transcultural nursing can be extremely helpful for competent nursing practices and to deal with the meaning of time in different cultures.

Youth and beauty are major cultural values of Anglo-Americans. These values can be noted with attention given to infants, small children, and young adults receiving health care in hospitals and other health agencies. Health personnel often show that they like to care for youths but may dislike caring for the elderly. In fact, elder abuse and neglect may be evident in the ways elderly Anglo-Americans receiving care are served food and in the ways of communicating with them in homes or places for the elderly. These practices may be quite different from those experienced by non-Western elderly who are deeply respected, valued, and cared for with kindness and affection in cultures such as the Philippine, Japanese, Korean, and Thai. In these cultures, the elderly are given much respect for their wisdom and age by their people. The emphasis on the attractive or beautiful one leads care givers to make Anglo-American elders appear youthful or younger looking than their normal age by hairstyles and excessive makeup. These tendencies of Anglo-Americans to keep people young, beautiful, active, and vibrant often are a dominant part of health care norms and practices. There are however, counter-cultural groups in America and elsewhere who value almost the opposite of the values of beauty and youth. These groups need to be understood for what they value.

Transcultural nurses who are knowledgeable about cultural variations among people, but especially regarding the meaning of beauty and youth can help health personnel be sensitive to the fact that there are often considerable nursing care services with the idea of aesthetics and youth. What constitutes youthfulness and beauty is generally *culturally constituted and varies transculturally.* To devalue the expressions of elder age and to give favoritism to the young may lead to cultural clashes, conflicts, uncooperativeness, and demeaning behaviors toward those affected. To value beauty and youthfulness in accord with cultural beliefs and practices could well lead to improved human relationships and culturally congruent care practices.

Still another dominant Anglo-American value is to rely on scientific facts and numbers gleaned from research studies, newspaper articles, reports, and television media as the truth. Getting facts in quantifiable numbers and by logical or objective means is greatly valued by Anglo-Americans, and only recently are they beginning to value non-quantifiable behaviors. Subjective, symbolic, non-numerical, or spiritual qualities of life and living may not be viewed as reliable, accurate, or the real truth. The public media also extols scientific facts, statistics, and measurable indicators as the only truths in the world. The realization that scientific facts can be manipulated and altered to fit certain motives or goals may be hard to accept. To think that different cultures have different ways of knowing what is true may also be hard to accept. Today, nurses are learning to use qualitative methods and discovering that culture and ways of knowing may be quite different from measuring everything. Qualitative researchers know that human knowledge cannot always be reduced to finite or measurable numbers and outcomes. Learning that non-Western cultures know and understand reality and non-realities in different ways is important in transcultural nursing. Understanding the meaning of culture care usually necessitates the use of naturalistic qualitative research methods and approaches to enter into and remain effective in the lifeways of most cultures.

Finally, Anglo-Americans value and are known for being generous to others especially in times of crisis, suffering, gross neglect, disability, or in tragic situations. Anglo-Americans are often known for generosity and willingness to share in times of major natural or artificial catastrophes related to floods, storms, explosions, and accidents. Anglo-Americans continue to help other countries who have experienced famine such as Rwanda in 1994, but also where floods, hurricanes, tornadoes, fires, and other kinds of major loss or suffering have occurred. They will also "pitch in" to give direct help to people in times of loss, famine, war, earthquakes, and other catastrophes. Anglo-American church groups, nurses, physicians, and others often come forth to show compassion and direct assistance. The values of giving and sharing money and other resources are often well known by others in the world. These are very positive values which give Anglo-Americans an altruistic and caring image. As a consequence, many cultures in the world expect Anglo-Americans and other Americans to be altruistic and generous in money, material goods, and direct assistance. Most Americans respond to such cultural expectations and take pride in being generous when they can or in sacrificing to others in desperate need.

In this chapter, a number of Anglo-American cultural values have been discussed with the intent of helping nurses understand the importance of dominant Anglo-American cultural values. Granted, there are cultural variabilities among Anglo-Americans but patterns and dominant values can be identified. It is also important to realize there are variations with rural and urban Anglo-Americans, but these dominant values tend to prevail with subtle differences. To know one's own culture with the attributed tendencies and action modes is essential in preventing cultural clashes and unfavorable nurse-client and family care practices. It is always an important transcultural principle to know one's own cultural values as a first and wise step before caring for other cultures. Moreover, if one know his/her own values this can facilitate entering the world of the stranger and being alert to cultural variabilities and explications of the other. Such transcultural culture care knowledge and appropriate skills are the hallmarks for providing culturally sensitive, responsible, and competent care.

---

* In this chapter the term Anglo-American refers to those Caucasians in the United States who trace their heritage largely from Europe. It does not include many other immigrants and Caucasians who have recently become citizens of the United States.

References

1. Blair, P. H., An Introduction to Anglo-Saxon England, 2nd ed., New York, Cambridge University Press, 1977.

2. Baugh, A. C. and T. Cable, A History of the English Language, 3rd ed., New Jersey: Prentice Hall, Inc., 1978.

3. Anderson, C. H., White Protestant Americans: From National Origins to Religious Groups, New Jersey: Prentice Hall, Inc., 1970.

4. Baugh and Cable, op. cit.

5. Winawer-Steiner, H. and N. A. Wetzel, "German Families," Ethnicity and Family Therapy, M. McGoldrick, J. K. Pearce, and J. Giordano, eds., New York: The Guildford Press, 1982, pp. 247–268.

6. Anderson, op. cit.

7. Arsenberg, C. M. and A. H. Niehoff, "American Cultural Values," The Nacirema: Readings on American Culture, J. P. Spradley and M. A. Rynkiewich, eds., Boston: Little, Brown, and Co., 1975, pp. 363–378.

8. Anderson, op. cit.

9. Arsenberg and Niehoff, op. cit.

10. McGill, D. and J. K. Pearce, "British Families," Ethnicity and Family Therapy, M. McGoldrick, J. K. Pearce, and J. Giordano, eds., New York: The Guildford Press, 1982, pp. 457–482.

11. Boorstin, D., The Americans: The Colonial Experience, Vol. 1, New York: Random House, 1958.

12. Boorstin, D., *The Americans: The National Experience*, Vol. 2, New York: Random House, 1965.

13. Cohen, M., *American Thought: A Critical Sketch*, New York: Collier Books, 1954.

14. DeBois, C., "The Dominant Value Profile of the American Culture," *American Anthropologists*, v. 57, Part 1, December 1955, pp. 1232–1239.

15. Gorer, G., *The American People: A Study in National Character*, New York: W. W. Norton, 1948.

16. Goodenough, W. H., *Cooperation in Change*, New York: Russell Sage Foundation, 1963.

17. Hall, E., *Beyond Culture*, New York: Anchor/Doubleday, 1976.

18. Hsu, F., *Americans and Chinese: The Two Ways of Life*, New York: Schuman, 1953.

19. Kluckholn, C., "American Culture: A General Description," *Human Factors in Military Operations*, Chevy Chase, Maryland: John Hopkins University, 1954.

20. Kluckholn, C., "The Evolution of Contemporary American Values," *Daedalus*, no. 2, 1958, pp. 78–109.

21. Leininger, M., "The Traditional Culture of Nursing and the Emerging New One," *Nursing and Anthropology: Two Worlds to Blend*, M. Leininger, ed., New York: John Wiley and Sons, 1970, pp. 63–82.

22. Ibid.

23. Leininger, M., *Transcultural Nursing, Theories, Concepts, and Practices*, New York: John Wiley and Sons, 1978.

24. Dubois, op. cit.

25. Fried, M., *Readings in Anthropology, Vol. II: Readings in Cultural Anthropology*, New York: Thomas Y. Cromwell, 1959.

26. Gorer, op. cit.

27. Hall, op. cit.

28. Kluckholn, C. and F. Kluckholn, "American Culture: Generalized Orientations and Class Patterns," *Conflicts of Power in Modern Culture: Seventh Symposium*, New York: Harper and Bros., 1947.

29. Mead, M., *Sex and Temperament in Three Primitive Societies*, New York: William Morrow and Co., 1963.

30. Mead, M., *And Keep Your Powder Dry*, New York: William Morrow and Co., 1965.

31. Nash, D., *A Little Anthropology*, Englewood Cliffs, New Jersey: Prentice Hall Press, 1989.

32. Stewart, E. and M. Bennett, *American Cultural Patterns: A Cross Cultural Perspective*, Yarmouth, Minnesota: Intercultural Press, Inc., 1991.

33. Leininger, M., *Care: An Essential Human Need*, Detroit: Wayne State University Press, 1988a. (Originally published, Thorofare, New Jersey: C. Slack, Inc., 1981).

34. Leininger, M., *Care: The Essence of Nursing and Health*, Detroit: Wayne State University Press, 1988b. (Originally published, Thorofare, New Jersey: C. Slack, Inc., 1984).

35. Leininger, M., *Culture Care Diversity and Universality: A Theory of Nursing*, New York: National League for Nursing Press, 1991, p. 355.

36. Nash, op. cit.

37. Rathje, W. and C. Murphy, *Rubbish: The Archaeology of Garbage*, New York: Harper Collins Publications, 1992.

38. Wenger, A. F., "The Culture Care Theory and the Old Order Amish," *Culture Care Diversity and Universality: A Theory of Nursing*, M. Leininger, ed., New York: National League for Nursing Press, 1991, pp. 147–178.

39. Leininger, op. cit., 1970, pp. 56–57.

40. Leininger, M., "Cultural Differences among Staff Members and the Impact on Patient Care," *Minnesota League for Nursing Bulletin*, v. XVI, no. 2, November, 1968, pp. 3–4.

Chapter 15
Philippine Americans and Culture Care
Madeleine Leininger, PhD, LHD, DS, FAAN, CTN, RN.

The number of Philippine immigrants to the United States has steadily increased since World War II, and among them are Philippine nurses who are one of the largest groups of foreign-born nurses practicing in the United States.[1,2] Philippine nurses have come to this country largely for economic and political reasons, but also to advance themselves through American nursing education and practice experiences.[3,4] With the increase of Philippine nurses in nursing service and educational contexts, there have been signs of intercultural tensions and conflicts largely related to misunderstandings.[5,6] Differences in cultural beliefs, values, and lifeways between Anglo-American and recent Philippine nurse immigrants have been frequently identified in hospitals, clinics, and schools of nursing. For example, Anglo-American nurses who are assertive in the work situation, and who also value individualism, autonomy, and competitiveness often come in conflict with Philippine nurses who do not value these attributes. Instead traditionally oriented Philippine nurses tend to value ways to maintain smooth working relationships and be deferent to those in authority. Such cultural differences may prevail in the work situation, but may not always be recognized with the busy daily activities of the nurses. These differences are, however, the source of tension, nurse burnout, distrust, and other problems that limit nurses' effectiveness. Moreover, intercultural staff problems can lead to work dissatisfaction and resignations and reduce the quality of nursing care to clients.

In this chapter the author shares her nursing research findings of the Philippine people living in a large urban Midwestern community and also draws upon related nursing and anthropological studies focused on Philippine health and nursing care aspects. To date, there have been very few nursing studies of Philippine nurses and client care until the author's study in the mid 1980s and those of her students in recent years. The need, however, for discovering cultural factors in nursing care and the education of Philippine and other nurses has been clearly evident for several decades. This need has been evident with the active recruitment of Philippine nurses to meet nurse shortages in the United States and other countries since Philippine nurses are the largest immigrant group.[7,8] The lack of research in this area has been due, in part, to the tendency to overlook the importance or role of Philippine nurses as immigrants from their homeland to a strange country such as the United States. Moreover, nurse researchers with no preparation in transcultural nursing have been handicapped in studying Philippine nurses and understanding the meaning of their behavior and needs. With the advent of transcultural nursing, interest in this neglected culture has grown. Spangler's recent study and that of the author are two major studies of importance.[9,10] In this chapter the author will draw upon these findings and other available sources to help nurses understand the Philippine culture in order to improve client care and intercultural nurse relationships. The author's consultant visits in the Philippines (beginning in the 1970s), her work as advisor to the Philippine Nurses Association in the United States plus her educational and service experiences will also be drawn upon.

Ethnohistorical Dimensions

Philippine nurses who immigrated to the United States came from the Philippine Islands, which are located in the Pacific Ocean near the eastern edge of Southeast Asia. There are 7,100 islands in the Philippines, only some of which are inhabitable. Nearly fifty million people live in three main regions of the Philippines, namely, Luzon, Mindanao, and the Visayas.[11] There are eight major language groups and 87 dialects. Manila is the capital of the Philippines, and is the industrial and education center of the country.

The Philippine people were influenced by several groups who immigrated to the islands beginning in the seventh century such as the Indonesians, Malayans, Chinese, Japanese, Spanish, Europeans, and North Americans.[12] These peoples came to the Philippines for trade, war, exploration, conquest, and many other purposes. Prior to the 1500s little was known about the Philippines until the Spanish and Portuguese reported on them. Magellan claimed the islands for Spain in 1521, and with the Spanish conquest came Christianity and Roman Catholicism. The Philippine Islands were named after Philippe II of Spain, and the islands were initially placed under the administration of the viceroy of Mexico as part of Spain's New World empire.[13] With Spanish control for three decades, trade with China, Japan, and other Southeast countries began to increase. Roman Catholicism became the major religion in the Philippines under Spanish rule. The Portuguese, Dutch, and British made attacks on the Philippine Islands and occupied them finally in 1762.

After several revolts by the South American colonies against Spain, the people of the Philippines became critical of Spanish rule, the clergy, and forced labor. This led to the emergence of a nationalist movement under Jose Rizal (1861–1896), and after his execution General Emilio Aguinaldo resigned. Then came the Spanish-American War of 1898, and later the United States gradually passed acts to give the Philippine people more autonomy and freedom. Manuel Quezon was elected the first president of the Commonwealth.[14] Independence, however, was not given to the Philippines until after the end of the wartime occupation of the country by the Japanese (1942–1945). During World War II, nearly 40,000 Philippinos were killed. On July 4, 1946 the Republic of the Philippines was proclaimed and Manuel Roxas became the Republic's first president.[15] Since then, the Philippine people have been threatened by communist guerrillas and with autocratic leaders such as Carlos Garcia and Ferdinand Marcos. In 1985 Corazon Aquino became the first woman president of the Philippines and took office with the goal of providing a democratic government.

Theory and Research Method

The author used the Culture Care Theory and the ethnonursing research method to study twenty key and thirty general Philippine informants living in an urban Midwestern city from 1984 to 1986. Since the theory and method have been presented in earlier chapters, they will not be discussed here.

Worldview, Social Structure, and Related Factors Influencing Philippine Culture Care

Worldview, Religious, and Kinship Factors

The majority of Philippinos have a deep sense of loyalty and pride in their country, language, kinship ties, philosophy of life and religion. Accordingly, informants in the author's study viewed the world as a gift from God which they were to care for an respect and in which to live in harmonious relationships with one another. The majority of Philippinos are Roman Catholic, with nearly eighty percent belonging to this faith. Approximately nine percent are Protestant, six percent Muslim, three percent animist, and two percent of other religious views.[16] It is of interest that when the Spaniards found the Muslims in the southern Philippines, they called them Maros after the Muslim Moors of Spain and Morocco. The Maros fought the Spanish, disliked Americans, and continued to defend the Manila government. Roman Catholicism has greatly influenced the daily lives of Philippinos, and they have many religious ceremonies and feasts. The informants reaffirmed the importance of Catholicism and frequently told the researcher how it helped them deal with political oppression, economic pressures, illnesses, uncertainties, and recurrent stressful life problems. A typical comment was, "I always leave my life in the hands of God, and God will take care of me." The majority of key and general informants (ninety-two percent) regularly attended church and religious ceremonies. Caring ideas were closely linked to the informant's religious beliefs, especially to be deferent and respectful to authority and to maintain charitable and smooth relationships with others.

Strong kinship ties have always been evident with the Philippinos and this was true with the key and general informants as they talked about the great importance of extended family members and depending on each other. The care constructs of mutual help, kin obligations, compassion, and direct care were expected norms in daily kinship relationships. This finding confirmed DeGracia's comment of Philippino families showing: a) unquestioned respect for and deference to authority; b) strong family unity with social control over its members, and c) an emphasis on extended family obedience to preserve and give the family a good name.[17] Acts of disloyalty, misconduct, or delinquency were held to bring shame to the extended family members in the author's study. Informants told how family members are obligated to provide assistance to their kin and to show respect for one another, mutual aid, and support in times of crisis and threats of illness. One Philippine American informant, who has lived in the United States for more than ten years, said, "Our family in the Philippines remains important and we have many extended family members back home that we help." The informants told how they spent much time together and shared food, advice, and money in their urban homes in the United States as they had when they lived in the Philippines. The researcher's study revealed that many elderly family members were being cared for in their homes, and none were reported to be in commercial nursing homes, as this is counter to their beliefs. The informants did not endorse the idea of nursing homes for their elderly because it is the responsibility of the extended family members to care for them in their homes. Most evident was the fact that children were socialized to care for and respect their kin especially their elders. The informants were proud of and talked enthusiastically about their elders and all family members, as well as about good times together. The Philippino informants were expected to keep close family ties and maintain a deep sense of loyalty, mutual respect, and obligation to each other. Accordingly, they would share anything they had with one another.

There were several important culture care values which were derived from the Philippine religious kinship and worldview to support extended family relationships. These caring values were held to be very important to support family well-being, healthy lifeways, and smooth relationships. The major cultural value of *pakikisama* was identified which refers to maintaining smooth harmonious interpersonal relationships, and to get along with others. The term *pakikisama* is a caring value and means "to go along with." Philippinos are taught how to get along with each other and practice *pakikisama* in all their relationships. Conceding gracefully and without conflicts or disharmonious relationships was important to all key and general informants in the study.

Amor propio was another cultural concept identified; it refers to personal esteem, honor and "saving face." Traditionally, it has been important to preserve social relationships, maintain a sense of self-esteem and save face. Maintaining Philippine self-esteem and avoiding social shame, or hiya, was discussed with the researcher by all informants. Several said, "One must not shame (hiya) oneself for others. Shaming or depreciating another Philippino could cause the person to lose face and experience a loss of *amor propio*.

Still another closely related idea was *utang na loob*. The term refers to an obligation in which one person is expected to help another by mutual reciprocity.[18] The recipient of help is morally bound to repay the helper at some time, and this was known and valued by all families studied. A "give and take" among relatives and other friends was expected as they cared for one another, with expectations of money or instant repayments of any kind. If a monetary debt was incurred, the recipient was not expected to repay the money or kindness until a later time, and then it was like receiving a give during a time of need. Finally, there was the cultural care value and belief of *bahala na*, or to "leave oneself to the will of God." This value permeated the thinking and explanations given to the researcher by many informants. It referred to accepting the will of God and resigning oneself to His will.[19]

From a political viewpoint, Philippinos have traditionally experienced many different kinds of political leaders and government ideologies with practices of threats, violence, and unexpected actions. Their ethnohistory has reflected past patterns of political conflicts and clashes related to government affairs, and the people have coped with diverse changes.[20] Maintaining respect for those in political roles of authority was difficult, when one did not especially like their way of functioning. Several informants expressed their concerns about this matter. Data for this study were collected during the Marcos regime, and most informants were very guarded about sharing any political ideas for fear of retribution to themselves or harm to their families in the Philippines. Indeed, the informants were quite afraid, tense, and very restless about the political condition of their homeland and the political power of the Marcos regime during the 1980s. In fact, ninety percent of the key and general informants said they came to the United States to avoid political oppression, violence, and killings. In addition, they spoke about their desire for better jobs to improve their economic situation, buy a home in America, and send money back to their Philippine kinsfolk.

Traditionally, the Philippine people lived in rural communities and were dependent upon a subsistence farming income from small plots of land. The economic pattern of living was valued. Many informants in the study missed this lifeway while living in a large urban community where only a few had gardens, called their "small farms." Agriculture had also been their traditional means of livelihood by raising crops such as copra, rice, corn, abaca, sugar, fruits, vegetables, and tobacco in the Philippines. Land use was valued, but it was always a major and long-standing problem in their homeland. Key and general urban informants living in the United States said it was difficult to adapt to a complex urban life with high-technologies and complex jobs and to work with Americans and their competitive work ethic. Approximately eighty percent of the informants were middle class professionals, i.e., nurses, engineers, common laborers, and tradesmen who were pursuing additional education in order for them to be retained in their professional positions. All the informants said they saved money to buy (or build) a home with modern plumbing, appliances and other conveniences. They were very pleased with how their frugal lifeway had enabled them to purchase a home and be financially successful in the United States. However, all the informants missed their farms with homegrown vegetables and fruits, which they talked about often, and the elderly especially remembered their vegetable farms "back in the homelands" in the Philippines.

Education has been traditionally valued by most Philippinos in the past and still is valued today in the United States. All the informants talked about their eagerness to go to school or college and become a "good professional." All the informants except those over sixty-five were or had been recently involved in educational programs or courses. Educational preparation was held to be extremely important for Philippinos to get ahead and to retain good positions in urban society. None of the informants had top administrative positions in the city. Parents were most supportive of their children getting an education and felt it was their responsibility and obligation to educate them. The informants spoke of initial problems with learning English, but they had mastered the language over time. Older Philippinos learning English relied on younger adults or children to learn the new language. Families were very proud and supportive of their children who had earned a degree or received a diploma, and these awards were framed and placed in a prominent place in their living rooms.

Dominant Ethnocare Values, Beliefs, and Practices

From many interviews and observations of the Philippine informants in their natural and familiar home settings and in other life situations, several dominant culture care constructs were discovered and confirmed.[21,22] These care constructs were ideas embedded in the worldview, social structure, environmental context, and language. The informants often shared their ideas about care, health, and illness in their home settings, often while having tea with the researcher. Their warm and gracious hospitality was always evident, and they were pleased to talk about differences and similarities of living in the Philippines and the United States. Care meanings were important to talk about especially their kinship and religious practices. They also talked about the non-caring political behavior of authoritative and aggressive leaders in the two cultures.

The *first important* care construct of Philippine informants in this study was that caring means to *maintain smooth and harmonious relationships with others, but especially with family members.* One was a caring individual or family member if one could maintain favorable relationships with others at home, in the hospital, at work, or wherever one functioned or lived. To be caring was to avoid unnecessary conflicts, confrontations, and disruptions. The cultural concept of *pakikisami*, or "getting along," was a dominant guide of ways to relate to others. The informants held that a caring person would get along with others be gentle, and able to control stresses and conflicts in order to remain well or healthy and prevent illnesses, tensions, and shame. Philippino caring ways would also support self-esteem and ways to be healthy or remain well. (They used the latter terms interchangeably.)

The *second meaning and action mode* about care or caring was to show *respect for others.* All Philippine informants held a strong belief that care meant showing respect for those you lived and worked with but especially for one's families, the elderly, and those in authority. The older informants aged 55 to 65 years gave several examples of respect for the elderly such as being attentive to, giving assistance and helping older family members. To be a caring person or group member one should be able to anticipate and offer assistance to others. Respect was a positive signal that one could give to others in time of need in a manner that was supportive. Preserving one's self-esteem and that of the family was a desired goal, especially because one respected the person as God's representative.

The *third dominant* care construct by the Philippine informants was that care meant *reciprocity. Care as reciprocity meant giving to others in time of need or when assistance was evident.* Reciprocity as care was giving help freely without hesitation or reservation and not expecting immediate return. Reciprocity was giving and receiving between individuals or the family group in a sincere and spontaneous way. Reciprocity as care was like a gift to another that was not expected or requested from the giver. Informants disliked it if they gave Anglo-Americans something and the latter felt they had to pay them back immediately. Reciprocity with a Philippino caring ethos meant giving in anticipation and without an immediate "give-back". Reciprocal caregiving should always fit the time, occasion, and event. Philippine nurses who perform acts of reciprocity as caring would never expect to return immediately acts of kindness, but rather would wait until a need arose. Moreover, caring acts needed to be given graciously and sincerely by the caregiver. In traditional Philippine lifeways, the care giver is often obligated to receive help at a later time. The concept of *utang na loob*, or the "give and take" of a relationship, was upheld by all informants. The informants spoke about the qualities they liked about a nurse who showed proper mutual reciprocity and could combine this attribute with respect for others. Several examples were given of the nurse caring for the elderly and providing respect, but also reflecting the "give and take" between the nurse and the older client, whether ill or well. Care as reciprocity was an important means to attain well-being. Unfortunately, in this country, Philippine reciprocity tends to be viewed by Anglo-Americans as a debt to be paid back, which was disliked by Philippine nurses who knew reciprocity from their cultural orientation.

The *fourth dominant meaning of care was preserve one's self-esteem or face (amor propio) and also avoid shame (hiya).* A caring person or family would not demean or threaten the self-esteem of another because one needed to "save face." A caring person was careful not to reprimand another person or group in public situations as this would lead to being a non-caring person and shaming consequences. For example, if a nurse were to reprimand a Philippine nurse in front of other nurses, this would be most hurtful and shameful to the Philippine nurse and a source of conflict and tension. This was often observed between Philippine nurses and Anglo-Americans in the hospital and was identified as non-caring behavior. A caring nurse would be aware of *hiya* and avoid inducing shameful feelings in another. Shaming Philippine individuals and older men and women was always viewed as non-caring behavior which should be avoided at all times, because it decreased one's self-esteem and honor and led to intercultural negative feelings about the persons involved.

Another caring construct discussed by the informants was the obligation to care by providing physical comfort to those who showed signs of restlessness and discomfort. Spangler's recent study clearly showed that Philippine nurses knew how to anticipate and provide physical comfort measures to the sick, helpless, and those experiencing pain as an obligation to care.[23] A variety of thoughtful strategies were evident to provide physical comfort measures to clients in the hospital that led to the clients' well-being, recovery, and relief of pain and other discomforts. Care as providing physical comfort measures was often demonstrated by acts of tenderness as caring. Physical comfort and tenderness as care in the author's study reflected a combined skill of using gentle touches to help others with a compassionate and kind attitude. Gentle touches were soft and given in a sustained manner, said several key women informants. Such touches were contrasted with those given by Anglo-American nurses, who were inclined to touch in a hard or firm manner. Gentle nursing care meant moving in a slow and deliberate touching way with thoughtful consideration of the person. Being quiet, providing privacy, and being pleasant were also viewed as caring and were linked with gentleness and physical comfort measures. Philippine nurses were skilled in providing generic caring modes which Anglo-American and other nurses could learn from Philippine caring practices.[24]

Culture-Specific Nursing Care

Using the above specific care findings generated from transcultural nursing research, the theorist predicted that such generic care constructs could lead to professional, culturally congruent care if used in a specific and conscientious way by nurses. The nurse would need to consider ways to use these specific care constructs in relation to the three predicted or advised modes, namely, culture care preservation or maintenance, culture care accommodation or negotiation, and culture care repatterning or restructuring when caring for Philippine American clients.[25] *Culture care preservation* would be important in order to use care related to saving face and self-esteem and thus avoiding shame. The nurse would preserve respect for and deference to Philippine clients in giving culture-specific care. In addition, the care construct of mutual reciprocity or the give and take in nurse-client relationships would be very important. Providing mutual reciprocity and maintaining self-esteem would need to be given full consideration in the care of Philippine clients in this country or in their homeland. The nurse would need to maintain ways to provide physical comfort measures and tender, gentle touches to Philippine clients in the hospital, home, or wherever cared for. Comfort care should be provided in a quiet, gentle, and respectful way without reducing self-esteem or making clients feel shamed. All of these culture care values would need to be considered culture care preservation and maintenance measures by the nurse to provide culturally congruent nursing care practices.

With the above dominant care constructs in mind, the nurse would consider *culture care accommodation or negotiation in caring* for Philippine clients. The nurse could provide culture-specific care with this modality by accommodating the client's expressed desire for fish, rice, vegetables, and other "hot-cold" foods to restore or maintain their health. Sometimes there may be medical reasons why these foods may not be given, but frequently they can be given as therapeutic healing modes to Philippine clients. Several informants talked about Anglo-American nurses and physicians who were not aware of their folk food preferences and how staff needed to accommodate their food preferences. Some were afraid to mention that they wanted such foods for fear of being shamed or losing self-esteem if their ideas were rejected. Nurses should understand and provide these important culturally-based foods. Over ninety-five percent of the informants who had lived in the United States for more than ten years and were clients in the hospital, said they longed for their native foods, but had difficulty getting the foods, especially rice and fish. They believe their native foods help them to recover and were much more nutritious than many of the American hospital junk foods such as potato chips and fried hamburgers. They felt Americans should eat more native Philippine foods to maintain their health. Culture care accommodation was a recurrent suggestion by informants with foods, folk healing medications, and respect for using all the caring modes described above, such as nurses accommodating respect for privacy and comfort measures as needed.

Culture care repatterning or restructuring would be used when new professional treatments and caring patterns needed to be modified or changed in relation to caring for Philippine clients. These would greatly vary with each Philippine client who became ill or who was ill but living at home. If self-esteem had been lost or threatened, the nurse would consider with the client how to reestablish and repattern self-esteem in order to prevent exposure to shaming incidents in the hospital or home. The nurse would need to be cognitively aware of ways to repattern or restructure any of the dominant care constructs already identified and described above. This would require creative thinking and planning by the nurse with the client's family in order to provide culturally congruent care. The nurse could develop a plan with a Philippine client to repattern his life due to a strong fear of loss of self-esteem to regain self-esteem or self-respect. These factors would be especially important in dealing with pain as Philippine clients do not like to complain, especially about pain. The Philippine elders contended that pain was a gift from God and should be accepted as suffering for God, but if pain was strong, the nurse should offer the client a little pain relief. Philippine clients become discouraged and some depressed if they cannot maintain their self-respect and deal with insults and offensive interpersonal situations.

Some general culture care principles to provide culturally congruent care to Philippine clients with traditional cultural values would be the following:

1. Show deference, respect, and kindness to clients, especially the elderly. Consider that the elderly prefer to be cared for in their home by extended family members rather than in a nursing home;
2. Involve and facilitate extended family members in nursing care activities whether at home or in the hospital as essential for the client's wellness or ability to face death;
3. Consider ways to maintain non-aggressive relationships with Philippine clients and avoid open confrontations and the loss of self-esteem;
4. Respect clients who value privacy and quiet periods of time as essential to their recovery or well-being;
5. Accept gifts that reflect mutual reciprocity without feeling compelled to immediately return a gift;
6. Ask clients how they would like to be cared for, what comfort measures they would like to receive;
7. Consider that pain may be viewed as a gift from God, and often the client can endure more pain than most Anglo- or Jewish Americans. However, small doses of medications to relieve postoperative or chronic suffering may be essential to clients.

The above nursing care considerations are important to provide culturally congruent care to many Philippine clients, especially those who value their past lifeways and practices. If the Philippine client is fully acculturated to another group's lifeways, some altering in the caring approaches would be needed.

Folk Health Beliefs, Values, and Nursing Care

Folk health beliefs and values continue to play an important part in Philippine caring and health ways. Many of these folk values are based on the "hot-cold" theory related to illness and wellness states. Excessive exposure to heat or cold, such as being out in the sun, taking a hot shower, exposure to intense anger, fright, or excitement, is believed to be harmful because it leads to imbalances and illnesses. If a client experiences these extremes or imbalances, the nurse needs to consider ways to counteract excessively hot or cold states with the goal of helping the client regain a balance or normal state. Hospitals are often viewed as places where clients are exposed to excessive amounts of heat or cold with food, air, or treatments which can lead to imbalances and illnesses. Nurses should be aware that air conditioning and excessive temperatures in the clients' room are of concern to Philippine clients and their relatives.

In Jacano's ethnography of a barrio in the Philippines he found that the people believed that hot air is absorbed through the pores and goes to the brain to produce mental illness.[26] Likewise, key informants in the author's study spoke about excessive heat that makes them ill in the work place, at home, or in the hospital. They also told how the wind was associated with spirits (*ingkanto*) and leads to pains and aches by penetrating the body. These folk beliefs are considered in the nursing care with other care constructs discussed above and with thought that some clients have beliefs in folk practices stronger than others. The author's culturalogical assessment guide helps to determine the extent and focus of folk beliefs.

Stern et al. in their study identified several folk beliefs and practices related to pregnancy and childbearing such as the belief in keeping the baby small for an easier delivery, avoidance of dark-skinned fruits and vegetables during pregnancy to prevent darkening the skin, and using chicken soup to stimulate breast milk.[27] Their study provides additional guidelines to consider with mothers during childbirth. Similar folk practices and beliefs were identified by the author along with a variety of folk herbs, medicines, and mother care practices based on traditional or generic folk care. For example, the mothers spoke about "winds hangin" to cause potential mother-infant problems. The importance of family privacy and keeping the mother and child warm and out of drafts after childbirth were also discussed. These informants confirmed that the nurse would be giving good care if these factors were known and acted upon.

Several key informants told how they used home remedies to allay stress and pressure problems not that they are living in an urban environment. They compare it with their past living in rural Philippine communities, which were peaceful and quite. They identified different folk illnesses that are still due to hot and cold imbalances and threats, and they often use folk home treatments and medicines to counteract these illnesses and restore their health. Many informants talked about cold winds in the winter that caused abdominal cramps, colds, pneumonia, and high fevers. They were combining their generic folk and a few professional healing modes, but still relying on the former due to costs, efficiency, and easy access.

Several Philippine informants in the study were deeply concerned about the tendency of some psychiatrists, nurses, and other mental health personnel to view their behavior as "psychotic," "paranoid," or "severely depressed" when they were quiet and uncomplaining. These key informants talked about their quiet manner and reluctance to share ideas with professional strangers, especially psychiatric staff, "because they do not understand our lifeways and often misdiagnose us." Remaining quiet and answering questions from physicians made them uncomfortable as the questions often did not fit their cultural frame of reference. Many disliked referrals to psychiatrists because their statements and the cultural lifeways of their families were misunderstood. This was evident with Philippine informants who had lived in the United States for more than twenty years. Nurses and others in the mental health field need to be aware of these potential cultural problems and misunderstanding clients' behaviors that seem strange or different. Being passive and quiet may not be psychotic. Philippine informants said they had to learn how to protect themselves against strangers in order to remain well and to help outsiders understand their cultural patterns and learned lifeways. The professional nurse also needs to realize that most non-Western cultures do not believe in treating the mind separately from the body. They have long viewed the person as a cultural and holistic being rather than treating clients as having separate mind and body parts. Such a mind-body dichotomy is often very strange to cultural groups such as Philippinos who expect to be viewed as a *total* functioning and whole person.

Transcultural Clinical Nursing Considerations

In this last section, a few common and recurrent problems occurring between Philippine and Anglo-American nurses will be identified from the author's research, other studies, and from direct clinical experiences with clients and nurses.

It is well known that Anglo-American nurses value assertiveness, independence, direct confrontations, competition, autonomy, technological efficiency, and individualism. These cultural values also reflect many of the dominant cultural values of middle class Anglo-Americans. These values, however, may often be in conflict with the values of Philippinos and lead to serious problems between Anglo- and Philippine American nurses. In Spangler's recent comprehensive study of cultural values and practices of Anglo-Americans and Philippine Americans in a hospital context, she identified such concerns and problems.[28] Her study clearly revealed the differences between Anglo- and Philippine Americans as well as some areas of similarity, with the use of Leininger's Culture Care Theory to focus on cultural values and nursing care practices in the two cultures. (The reader is encouraged to read Spangler's chapter in Leininger's book *Culture Care Diversity and Universality: A Theory of Nursing*). Philippine nurses do not espouse all Anglo-American values, but rather rely on maintaining their cultural values discussed above, such as maintaining smooth relationships, indirect communication, respecting authority, remaining quiet at times, avoiding shame, and maintaining self-esteem. In clinical settings, Anglo-American nurses often expect Philippine nurses to be like them and to know how to be confrontational, efficient, quick, and politically assertive. Anglo-American nurses may not realize how offensive these behaviors may be to Philippine nurses who are new to this country or dislike some American values. Moreover, Anglo-American nurses in clinical settings often do not like Philippine nurse to be passive and talk and stay together. Such Philippine behaviors and practices are often viewed by Anglo-American nurses as being clannish, resistant to American ways, and showing a dislike for Anglo-American nurses. When Philippine nurses on a clinical unit speak in their native language and exclude Anglo-American nurses, this often leads to feelings of distrust and interpersonal tensions that may continue and influence staff relationships and client care management practices.

In several nursing service consultations in the United States during the past two decades, the author has identified several recurrent themes of difficulty between Anglo-American and Philippine nurses. Anglo-American nurses often complain about Philippine nurses being too passive, quiet, groupish, and dependent on physicians. Philippine nurses complain that Anglo-American nurses are far too aggressive, confrontational, direct, and non-caring in their ways. They also feel that sometimes that are given the less than desirable nursing tasks which Anglo-American nurses dislike doing. Many Philippine nurses were aware of intercultural tensions and their struggles to preserve their self-esteem and confidence and to avoid being confronted in public settings or before other nurses in conferences. Philippine nurses often feel powerless to deal with these situations, and some viewed them as signs of discrimination or prejudice. Some Philippine nurses told how depressed they were with such encounters and the loss of self-esteem and respect. Some Philippine nurses had resigned and others had been dismissed from the nursing unit when tensions or conflicts were excessive. Covert anger and resentment could be identified between Anglo- and

Philippine American nurses, but these transcultural problems were never openly discussed on the nursing units. The Philippine nurses disliked the fact that they held no top administrative positions such as head nurse or supervisor. This was of concern to some Philippine nurses who had been employed for many years on a unit. In talking with Anglo-American nurses, it was evident that they thought the Philippine nurses' deference to authority, quiet manner, and passivity was largely related to limited nursing education and preparation in American lifeways. It is also important to remember that if Philippine nurses are excessively shamed or pushed too far when trying to get them to something they dislike, they can become angry and make their position known in a firm and direct manner.

In sum, understanding transcultural nursing problems, behaviors, and patterns of interaction between Anglo- and Philippine American nurses is extremely important to facilitate quality nursing care. The transcultural nursing knowledge generated from research with the use of the Culture Care Theory disclosed many valuable and important insights to guide nursing practices. Culture care values, meanings, and actions need to be used to provide congruent care and improve nurse and client relationships. Nurses need to be knowledgeable about traditional and changing Philippine cultural values and caring lifeways through culturalogical assessments to improve nursing practices. Both Philippine and Anglo-American nurses have unique contributions to share to advance and improve human caring modalities, but the challenge is to recognize these contributions and use them appropriately in nursing care contexts.

References

1. Anderson, J. N., "Health and Illness in Philippino Immigrants," *The Western Journal of Medicine*, v. 6, no. 139, 1983, pp. 811–819.

2. Spangler, Z., "Culture Care of Philippine and Anglo-American Nurses in a Hospital Context," *Culture Care Diversity and Universality: A Theory of Nursing*, M. Leininger, ed., New York: National League for Nursing Press, 1991a, pp. 119–146.

3. Leininger, M., "Ethnocare, Ethnohealth, and Ethnonursing of Arab, Polish, Italian, Greek, Appalachian, Mexican, Philippine, and African Americans in a Detroit Metropolitan Community," unpublished manuscript, Detroit: Wayne State University, 1984.

4. Cameron, C., "*Relationship Between Select Health Beliefs, Values, and Health Practices of Philippine Elderly*," post-masters field study, Detroit: Wayne State University, 1986.

5. Spangler, op. cit., 1991a.

6. Leininger, M., "Cultural Care: An Essential Goal for Nursing and Health Care," *Journal of Nephrology Nursing*, v. 10, no. 5, 1983, pp. 11–17.

7. Spangler, op. cit., 1991a.

8. Anderson, op. cit., 1983.

9. Spangler, Z., "*Nursing Care Values and Practices of Philippine-American and Anglo-American Nurses Using Leininger's Theory*," post-masters field study, Detroit: Wayne State University, 1991b.

10. Leininger, op. cit., 1984.

11. Thernstrom, S., *Harvard Encyclopedia of American Ethnic Groups*, Cambridge: Belknep Press, 1980.

12. Weddel, C. E., and L. A. Kimball, *Introduction to the Peoples and Cultures of Asia*, Englewood Cliffs, New Jersey: Prentice-Hall, Inc., 1985, pp. 304–307.

13. Ibid.

14. Ibid., pp. 305–306.

15. Ibid., p. 306.

16. Ibid., p. 305.

17. DeGracia, R., "Health Care of the American-Asian Patient," *Critical Care Update*, 1982, p. 20.

18. Melendy, H. B., *Asians in America*, Honolulu: University of Hawaii Press, Wayne Publishers, 1977.

19. Ibid.

20. Kroeber, A. L., *Peoples of the Philippines*, Westport: Greenwood Press, 1973.

21. Leininger, op. cit., 1984.

22. Leininger, M., *Culture Care Diversity and Universality: A Theory of Nursing*, M. Leininger, ed., New York: National League for Nursing Press, 1991, p. 358.

23. Spangler, op. cit., 1991b.

24. Ibid.

25. Leininger, op. cit., 1991.

26. Jacano, F. L., *Growing Up in the Philippine Barrio*, New York: Holt, Rinehart and Winston, 1969.

27. Stern, P. N., V. P. Tilden, and E. K. Maxwell, "Culturally Induced Stress During Child-Bearing: The Philippino-American Experience," *Issues in Health Care of Women*, v. 2, 1980, pp. 67–81.

28. Spangler, op. cit., 1991b.

Chapter 16
Culture Care of Mexican Americans

Antonia Villarruel, PhD, RN. and Madeleine Leininger, PhD, FAAN, CTN, RN

In this chapter an overview of selected aspects of the Mexican American social structure and worldview is presented to show their influence on Mexican American health care patterns and nursing needs. Components of the Mexican American folk health system and associated care patterns are an area of focus in relation to transcultural health and nursing care of Mexican Americans. Culture care values, beliefs, and research findings are essential to assist the nurse in providing culturally congruent, effective, and competent nursing care to a growing and diverse population in the United States. In this chapter some values, beliefs, and lifeways are related to or show to have features similar to other Hispanic subcultures. However, this chapter also demonstrates in-depth considerations which are culture-specific to Mexican American.

Mexican Americans: An Ethnohistorical Context

Mexican American culture consists of a complex melding of the history, traditions, and beliefs of three distinct peoples from Mesoamerica, Spain, and the United States. First, there existed an Indian or native heritage of Mesoamerica that spanned thousands of years before Christ until the arrival and eventual conquest of this region by the Spanish in the sixteenth century. The blending of Spanish and native Mesoamerican heritage created the major strands of the culture of contemporary Mexico. The Mexican presence in the United States, as a result of conquest by the United States and continued migration of Mexicans to the north, introduced another cultural strand to the fabric of Mexican American culture. The current social structure, beliefs, health and care expressions of Mexican Americans were influenced by each of these distinct cultural strands. It therefore becomes necessary to understand the influences of these cultural forces in relation to existing Mexican American culture.

In order to understand the ethnohistory of Mexican Americans, it is important to consider Mesoamerica and Spain. Geographically, Mesoamerica is comprised of the territory known today as central Mexico, Guatemala, Honduras, and El Salvador. While a host of distinct cultural groups have inhabited this land over time, such as the Olmecs, Mayans, and Aztecs, a number of features were unique to this area. These features included a complex yet precise calendar system, a religion based on the worship of an extensive pantheon and which practiced human sacrifice as a form of worship, a ball-game played on special courts, extensive knowledge of astronomy, the cultivation of maize, the use of cocoa beans for trade, hieroglyphic writing, and the extensive use of plants and minerals for the treatment of illness.[1,2]

In addition, people from this area, past and present, share a rich cultural and historical tradition which includes shared beliefs in such concepts as duty; destiny or fate; duality and equilibrium; and the reciprocal and circular relationship among humans, nature, and the supernatural. These beliefs and principles are illustrated in the following example. A recurring theme in views of the order, organization, and structure of the universe was the dual opposition of contrary elements. The universe was thought to be divided by a horizontal plane which separated the "Great Mother" and its related elements (e.g., cold, below, underworld, darkness, weakness, night, death, wind, sharp pain) from the "Great Father" and its related elements (e.g., hot, above, heaven, drought, light, strength, large fire, life, flower, irritation, stream of blood-life, perfume).[3] The structure of the human body was seen as parallel to the structure and organization of the universe, with certain parts of the body and conditions associated with parts of the universe. In addition, it was believed that there was a link between the universe and humans, in that behavior of persons affected the equilibrium and stability of the cosmos, and, conversely, forces in the cosmos could affect human behavior and functions.[4] The maintenance of equilibrium directed human behavior in relation to one's health and well-being. In addition, humans had an obligation to maintain balance and equilibrium within their lives, as this affected the stability of the universe. The value of worth of an individual was viewed in the context of their relation and contribution to others.

Spain's discovery and eventual conquest of Mexico marked the start of the destruction of many elements of this long-standing civilization. The conversion of Indian civilization to Christianity became the theoretical justification for the Spanish presence in Mexico and for the subjugation of its people.[5] The securing of riches as a means of service to Spain was also an explicit purpose which supported the exploitation of the indigenous people and land of New Spain.[6] Efforts to convert the Indians to Christianity and to subjugate them to a new rule resulted in the massive destruction of native art, architecture, books, monuments, and temples because they were viewed by the Spanish as pagan and even satanic. One exception to this destruction of Indian culture was the native knowledge of and beliefs about medicinal plants which were incorporated into the Spanish medicinal system. The adoption of this aspect of the culture by the Spaniards may partially explain the contemporary cultural commitment to and use of herbal remedies by Mexicans.[7]

The adoption by native Mesoamerica of elements of Spanish culture, including Christianity and beliefs about illness, was facilitated by a congruence in the beliefs of the two cultures.[8] For example, similarities in religious beliefs existed between a) the multiplicity of Catholic saints and the extensive pantheon of the Aztecs, and b) the Christian belief in personal sacrifice as a means for individual redemption and the Aztec belief in sacrifice aimed at the collective good of the universe.[9,10] In relation to health and illness, similarities between Aztec and Spanish beliefs included a) causes of illness based on a hot-cold classification and b) the existence of diseases affecting children believed in Aztec culture to be caused by the invisible emanation from the liver, and in Spanish culture to be caused by evil eye (*mal de ojo*).[11,12] These are a few examples of two distinct cultures of ancient Mesoamerica and Spain and the way they blended to form the culture of the Mexican people. It is important to recognize that, in addition to the blending of cultures, some beliefs, values, and customs unique to ancient Mesoamerica and also those unique to Spain remained relatively intact.[13] These culturally distinct strands of the two civilizations were also integrated into the culture of the Mexican people.

In describing the perception of the United States by Mexico and other Latin American countries, the renowned Mexican novelist Carlos Fuentes writes, "…we have admired democracy, we have deplored empire. And we have suffered the actions of this country (U.S.) which has constantly intervened in our lives in the name of manifest destiny, the big stick, dollar diplomacy, and cultural arrogance."[14] This statement of Mexico/United States relations is given to help the reader understand the ambivalent and often uncomfortable relations between members of these two cultural groups.

The southwest region of the United States was first settled by the Spaniards who established settlements in 1598 in the area known today as Santa Fe, New Mexico. It was several hundred years later, in the 1820s, that citizens of the United States began settling in what was then Mexican territory. Shortly thereafter, the United States defended the recently established Republic of Texas against the Mexican army in the Mexican-American War (1846–48). Mexico, defeated in this war, ceded to the United States, territory which comprises present-day Arizona, California, Texas, New Mexico, Utah, parts of Colorado, Nevada, and Wyoming, in the Treaty of Guadalupe Hidalgo (1848). While a provision of the treaty provided protection for those of Mexican descent, including land, property, legal, civil, linguistic, religious, and cultural rights, these provisions were never honored, and these basic rights were denied Mexicans. In part because of the lost property interests in Texas and the southwest region of the United States, Mexicans became an economically segregated working-class group.[15]

Since that time, a number of socioeconomic and political conditions in Mexico and the United States such as the Mexican Revolution of 1910, the Great Depression,

World War II, the demand for cheap agricultural and industrial labor in the United States, and most recently, the North American Free Trade Agreement, have dictated the allied or adversarial nature of the relationship between these two countries. In addition, these events have also influenced the extent to which Mexicans migrate to the United States in search of economic opportunities, the permeability of the United States/Mexico border, and the extent to which Mexican migrants and United States citizens of Mexican descent are welcomed by their northern neighbor. It is because of this long history of unwelcome intervention, domination, oppression, and broken promises that Mexicans look to Americans with strong suspicion and distrust. At the same time, Mexican Americans have continued to maintain a high degree of cultural survival and pride.

It is critical to recognize that the Mexican American population is not a homogeneous group. Length of time in this country, reason for migration, geographic residence, and level of acculturation are all factors which account for considerable diversity. Distinct sociopolitical profiles have been suggested to describe the diversity among Mexican Americans and include: a) Mexican Americans born in the United States, who are either fully bilingual and bicultural, or, who have little knowledge of the Spanish language and may not identify strongly with Mexican American values or traditions; b) United States born Hispanics who live in the border states; c) immigrants who have moved to the United States from urban cities in Mexico to seek better economic and educational opportunities; and d) Mexican undocumented workers, recently emigrated from rural Mexico.[16] These factors influence the degree to which Mexican Americans will retain features of their Mexican American culture and/or adopt elements of American culture.

Mexican Americans Today

Mexican Americans are one group included in the commonly used umbrella term, "Hispanic". Other groups which are included in this categorization utilized by the Bureau of the Census in 1980 include persons of Puerto Rican, Cuban, Haitian, Central (Caribbean), South Americans, and others of Spanish cultural heritage, regardless of race. This broad categorization reflects long-standing efforts to accurately reflect the general sociocultural and ethnographic characteristics of Hispanics in the United States. While Hispanic subgroups share similar characteristics, for example, Spanish ancestry and language, there is much diversity that exists among them. Unfortunately, national surveys and statistics, and research studies are only beginning to differentiate among subgroups. Because there is a critical lack of data on Hispanic subgroups, it is necessary to study and examine individual Hispanic subgroups, and to be cautious in relation to generalizations that are made from studies that do not differentiate among Hispanic subgroups.

Cultural Characteristics and Demographics

Currently, Hispanics comprise 9% (22.3 million) of the United States population and are one of the most rapidly growing minority groups; estimates project that by the year 2050, Hispanics will comprise 19 to 24% of the United States population.[17] The majority of Hispanics are Mexican Americans (63%) and they are the largest group of mainland Hispanics in the United States.[18] While Mexican-Americans live in all fifty states, the majority of Mexican Americans live in California (43.3%), Texas (28.8%), Arizona and New Mexico (9.2%); nearly 90% of Mexican Americans in the United States reside in urban areas.[19] Other Hispanics such as Cubans, Puerto Ricans, and Haitians live in the southeastern United States in a warm climate similar to their native homeland, and many live in New York and nearby areas for employment and immigration reasons. These Hispanic cultures are important and need to be studied for differences and similarities in relation to Mexican Americans.

Mexican Americans are a relatively young population, having the youngest median age (24.3 years) among non-Hispanic and Hispanic subgroups.[20] In relation to family composition, the average family size of Mexican Americans (4.06 persons) is the largest of any Hispanic subgroup, while the percentage of female led households (19.1%) is the lowest.[21]

Hispanics remain the most undereducated segment of the United States population, and current trends indicate that the gap between Hispanics and non-Hispanics is widening. While educational attainment levels have been improving for African Americans and the Anglo-American segment of the population, Hispanics continue to enter school later, dropout at an earlier age, receive proportionally fewer high school diplomas and college degrees, and as a result, are more likely to be illiterate.[22]

The education of Hispanics, in particular Mexican Americans, has influenced the types of employment available to this population. While Mexican American workers do primarily unskilled labor, the percentage of Mexican American men who work or seek work was higher than the percentage of non-Hispanics (79.6% for Mexican Americans in contrast with 73.9% for non-Hispanics).[23] Despite a strong labor participation by all Hispanic subgroups, the rates of poverty are higher for Hispanic children (36%) and families (25%), than non-Hispanic children (18%) and families (9%).[24]

The over-representation of Hispanics in low-paid and low benefit occupations impacts on the degree to which Hispanics are health insured. Because health insurance benefits are not provided for many employed Hispanics, and because employment will render many Hispanics ineligible for Medicaid benefits, there is a higher proportion of uninsured among Hispanics. While only 14% of the United States population does not receive either a private or public form of insurance, 34% of Mexican Americans are uninsured.[25] Factors such as poverty and low health insurance coverage clearly affect access of Mexican Americans to adequate health care. Limited access to care is reflected in low physician utilization rates, and low utilization of health promotion and disease prevention services such as prenatal care.[26] It is of interest that despite the presence of multiple risk factors including limited utilization of prenatal services by Mexican Americans, there exist surprisingly low rates of infant mortality and incidence of low birth weight babies for this population.[27] This is an area that requires further study as it may well indicate cultural practices and characteristics that facilitate a health outcome for both mother and infant. The above factors provide a picture of Mexican Americans as a primarily young, growing population, who hold unskilled jobs and are often poor. Nonetheless, they maintain a strong work ethic and deal with many serious socioeconomic and cultural barriers related to health and education.[28]

Social Structure and Worldview

Reflecting upon Leininger's Culture Care theory with the Sunrise Model, the nurse considers worldview and social structure factors. The Mexican worldview is focused on their extended family, belief in God's help, and that one must deal with present time reality.[29] With respect to kinship and social factors, the family unit is central to the culture of Mexican Americans. It is characterized by the cultural value of familism, which refers to the extension of kinship relationships beyond the nuclear family and characterized by affiliation, interdependence among members, the values of cooperation, respect for others, and equality.[30,31,32,33] The concept of familism is reflected in cultural patterns that cross rural-urban settings, class lines, and different levels of acculturation.[34,35,36,37] The concept of familism extends beyond the nuclear to extended family. The composition of the extended family often consists of relatives such as cousins (*primos*), and aunts and uncles (*tios*) or non-relatives who are brought into the family network, often related to religious rites of passage such as baptism, confirmation in which the title *comadre* (godmother), and *compadre* (godfather) are used. Extended family members function to provide emotional and financial support for Mexican Americans by sharing housing or taking responsibility for raising a child from the nuclear family for a short or extended period of time.

The family unit within Mexican culture is further characterized by a hierarchical structure and child-rearing patterns that assign roles, responsibilities, and expectations on the basis of age and gender.[38,39] For example, both men and women have prescribed roles within the family. Women traditionally maintain the household, while men are directly responsible for supporting the family financially and serve as the primary spokesperson and protector of the family. As children are enculturated, they learn these roles and responsibilities. For example, a young girl is expected to assist her mother with household tasks such as cooking, cleaning, and caring for younger siblings. As young boys grow older, they are expected to watch their siblings, especially younger or older sisters, when they are away from home. Responsibilities and respect are accorded based on age and especially with the elderly who receive much respect (*respeto*).

With respect to religion and spiritual beliefs, Mexican Americans believe that God, fate, or luck is responsible for certain life events, including illness, recovery, and death. These beliefs are traced to tenets of Catholicism and ancient Mesoamerican lifeways. Mexican Americans believe that certain life events are beyond the control of the individual and that prayers, bargaining, or promises to God, The Virgin (*la Virgin*) of Guadalupe, or the Virgin of San Juan de los Lagos and other patron saints are necessary to change, guarantee, or prevent the course of certain life events for themselves of extended family members.

There are certain cultural values, personhood (*personalismo*), and respect (*respeto*), that are very important to consider in communication with and care for Mexican Americans. Respect (*respeto*) is a concept which dictates the appropriate deferential behavior toward others, according to factors such as age, gender, social position, and is an element of positive interpersonal and reciprocal relationships.[40] For example, elders and health care providers are addressed by their titles, i.e., Mr. (*Señor*), Mrs. (*Señora*), or doctor. The content of communication is acknowledged and considered, open disagreement or minimizing a person's concern is seen as a sign of disrespect. Because of the social status of health care providers, they are often given respect immediately. There is, however, an obligation to respect Mexican-Americans to maintain an effective and congruent relationship.

A related concept to consider in establishing and maintaining effective communication, is the concept of personhood (*personalismo*). This refers to the preference of personal contacts over interpersonal and institutional contacts.[41] The concept is demonstrated in provider-client relationships when providers: a) appear to be unhurried; b) take the time to ask about some aspect of the personal life of the client, such as the health of a family member; c) share small aspects of their personal life with the client; or d) acknowledge the skill or some strength of the client (e.g., "I can tell you take good care of your daughter"). While the concepts of *personalismo* and *respeto* may appear trivial, or else characteristic of any nurse-client interaction, they are very critical care values in order for the nurse to provide culturally sensitive, congruent, and responsible care to Mexican Americans and Mexicans.

Culture Care and Health Research Guidelines

During the past decade a number of transcultural nurses have been studying Mexican Americans mainly in urban and suburban communities. Studies by Dugan,

Leininger, Stasiak, and Wenger focused on caring and health beliefs and practices of urban Mexican Americans.[42,43,44,45] Most of these researchers used Leininger's Culture Care theory and the ethnonursing and ethnography research methods. In this section some of Leininger's and Stasiak's major findings will be presented, and the reader is encouraged to read further on these studies.[46] From Leininger's and Stasiak's ethnonursing investigation about human caring and health, several dominant care themes were found to guide nursing care decisions and actions. Research theories will be highlighted below based on these studies.

Theme One: Caring was expressed as filial love or love of family and being involved with extended family. Filial love as a caring attitude and action mode was observed and documented with the entire extended family members including fictive kin. The godparents (padrinos) *had special caring relationships with the parent which were built upon spiritual ties known as* compadrazgo. *The religious and kinship aspects of the social structure as well as worldview and language had a powerful influence on care and caring modalities, which in turn were confirmed by many key and general informants to promote healing, health, and well-being. These findings were also supported by other nurse investigators, i.e., Dugan and Wenger.[47,48] Caring for others was the predominant mode of caring in the studies and was expressed by individuals and family members being attentive to family and kin, being assistive to others, and being supportive of family needs and concerns.[49]*

Theme Two: Care meant succorance or the means to provide direct aid to the family in different ways. Care as succorance meant not only being with extended family members, but also providing food and other needs in order to keep well or to provide for the well-being (bienestar) *to others in a direct way. Succorance was a caring mode with health and healing outcomes or benefits to others served.*

Theme Three: Caring meant respect for gender differences, in that the mother was a domestic, inside the home, carer in decisions and actions; whereas the father was the protective carer dealing with matters often outside the home or largely in the public (political-economic) arena. The Mexican American mother performed many caring acts in the home to care for children, adults, and especially the elderly by filial direct care activities. She used folk care practices including medicines, and home treatments with Mexican hot/cold foods, and general succorance activities. In contrast, the Mexican American father maintained a protective carer role. He remained mindful of outside political influences and economic conditions that could influence the extended family's welfare and with respect to the larger cultural neighborhood values and norms. The father and other Mexican American males expressed their masculine behaviors to maintain protective care from outside unfavorable conditions. The mother and extended family females maintained caring modes in the day-to-day home situation. The nurse with a transcultural focus would need to be aware of these research findings with all informants.

Theme Four: Caring meant the use of folk (generic) rituals and practices to promote healing, health, and well-being for others and to consider professional caring practices. Generic or folk care was used more often than professional caring services in the urban-suburban Mexican American community due to preference, availability, accessibility, and low cost. Most importantly, Mexican Americans trusted the folk care with "home remedies that have always worked for us," such as herbs, hot/cold foods, massage, and "medicines." Signs of distrust of professional caregivers were often related in narratives about not being understood in the hospital with their beliefs, values, and lifeways. Language barriers and fear of not being respected in the hospital were major concerns related to trust and anticipate quality nursing care. Most informants demonstrated belief in the hot and cold theory and wanted foods and treatments directed toward preserving or making accommodations for hot/cold foods, especially while in the hospital, to promote health and healing. The informants recognized that many of their indigenous folk healers came from Mexico some decades earlier, but they still sought the Mexican herbs and medicines from anyone going to or coming from Mexico. However, if no folk or generic care and cure modes were available, then they would rely on or "test" professional offerings.

These above caring themes provide guidelines for culturally congruent care related to Leininger's three modes of nursing care decisions and actions. Use of the three modes can lead to providing culturally congruent care—the goal of the theory. In all of the above studies, the researchers found the informants were eager for the nurse and others to preserve and maintain their care practices as they were supported mainly by their religious and family practices. Several families wanted cultural accommodations made by nurses in hospital or clinic services. Respect for and attention to spiritual and kinship needs were critical. But in addition, folk healing and linking generic and professional care practices in the home were desired. Stasiak's chapter provides an excellent summary of examples of implementing the three modes of nursing care for culturally congruent nursing care.[50]

Generic (Folk) System: Curanderismo and Curanderas

Since the generic (folk) system remains important to Mexican Americans and especially to link professional care with it, more information about generic care is needed. The concept of *curanderismo* is described in the anthropological, health science, and transcultural nursing literature. It is a syncretic, eclectic, and holistic mixture of beliefs derived from Mesoamerican, Spanish, spiritualistic, homeopathic, and modern "scientific medicine" or empirical observation.[51] The curanderismo is a system based on the knowledge of herbal remedies, Spanish prayers, altered states of consciousness, and healing rituals that include the use of Indian costumes and Catholic rituals.[52] The folk practitioner (*curandera*) combines his skills and familiarity with empirical and ritualistic remedies and derive their ultimate healing power and abilities from God.[53] Nurses need to understand these ideas because they are important components of caring and healing practices. Some of the major tenets basic to the healing practices of curanderismo include:

1. The body and mind are inseparable.
2. Religious, interpersonal or sociological, supernaturalistic, and naturalistic balance and harmony are important.
3. The body and soul are separable.
4. There exist interaction and communication modes between the natural and supernatural worlds.
5. The patient is an innocent victim.
6. The healer (curandera) is expected to interact openly with the patient.
7. The curandera is expected to use healing powers for good only, as they can be taken away from God if they are abused.
8. The devotion of the curandera to God, their piousness and devotion are crucial facets in their abilities to heal.[54,55,56,57,58,59]

The first five statements are concerned with basic beliefs about health and illness, while the last three address the role of the curandera. It is of interest that these tenets are congruent, if not identical with, tenets of Mesoamerican religion and medicine and Catholic (with the exception of the separation of body and soul) traditions.

Central to the healing practices of the curandera, is the idea that illness is a manner in which to emulate the life of Christ.[60] Invoking the name of Christ, the ritualistic signs of the cross, the use of candles, altars, charms, confessions, and statues of the saints, Christ, and Mary, are used to strengthen the patient, to foster acceptance of suffering, and to promote faith in God.[61] It is the belief in the curandera's connection to the sacred that supports the client and enables him to benefit from the healing powers of God and the saints.[62] Failure to facilitate a cure is not viewed as a weakness of the curandera, but rather as an expression of the will of God.

Religious symbols are but one of the healing practices that are used by the curandera. Herbs, the regulation of diet, the manipulation of joints and bones, as well as massage are common skills known and utilized by many curanderas. Often, the basis for their use is directed towards maintaining or restoring balance and harmony within one's body and life. Because illness is considered a family matter in Mexican American culture, the involvement of family members is promoted, supported, and often times requested by the curandera during a healing session.

The effectiveness of the curandera is often attributed to the feeling of security and trust that is conveyed in addition to the impression they give indicating they are in total control of the situation.[63] The cultural expectation or belief that the client is a passive entity or victim of illness, places the curandera in a position to assume the control. Again it is the belief in the curandera's close relationship with God that empowers the curandera in healing situations. Curanderas have been associated with and effective in treating: a) culture bound syndromes such as evil eye (*mal ojo*), ball in stomach (*empacho*), fallen fontanel (*caida de mollera*), and social fright (*susto*); b) certain "medical" illnesses, such as febrile illnesses, convulsions, ulcers, and musculoskeletal disorders; c) psychophysiological disorders; d) socially disruptive behaviors; and e) infant deliveries.[64,65] While the majority of literature addresses the role of curanderismo in treating culture-bound syndromes and certain psychiatric disorders, Tamez contends that there are other illnesses that curanderas are utilized for and effective in treating.[66] Because of the nature of the illnesses, being perhaps more sensitive in nature, they are not as visible to the researchers, and are thus easily missed or overlooked.

The existence or persistent use of curanderas and curanderismo in Mexican American culture has been attributed to several factors. The unavailability or inaccessibility of the professional health systems; the ineffectiveness of or dissatisfaction with professional health systems; the authoritarian structure of the Mexican family, social, and religious life; the low rate of assimilation of Mexican Americans with dominant American societal values; the congruence of curanderismo with Mexican American beliefs about health, illness, and healing practices; and the perceived effectiveness of curanderas in dealing with specific illness, are all factors that have been identified in the literature.[67,68,69,70,71] In much of the research literature, however, there is contradictory evidence as to the prevalence of this folk health care system in the United States. Findings from several studies indicate that there is a persistence of traditional Mexican American beliefs about health and illness, folk remedies, and use of folk healers such as curanderas.[72,73,74] Other studies have suggested that belief in traditional Mexican American folk illnesses is declining, but more apparent is the less frequent use of traditional folk healers, such as curanderas.[75,76,77,78]

A synthesis from both research groups reveals several patterns. The research indicates a persistence in the folk etiology of illnesses and certain types of folk practices (e.g., use of herbs), but some modifications in beliefs have occurred due to the influence of professional health care practices. The use of folk healers, such as curanderas appears to be less persistent, which may, in part, be related to acculturation, the decreased availability of curanderas, and an increased reliance on the popular and professional health care services according to Keefe and Perrone, et al.[79,80] An alternative explanation supported by recent field study by Villarruel suggests that treatment for certain illnesses and use of certain treatments such as herbs and teas which were traditionally dealt with by a curandera, may have been taken over by family or extended family members. In general, the above research supports the conclusion that integration of the generic (folk) health care system of Mexican Americans and professional health care systems is slowly occurring.

Generic Nursing Care Considerations for Mexican Americans

In light of the above ethnohistory, worldview, social structure, cultural values, and folk beliefs and practices of Mexican Americans, these summary points are offered to provide culture-specific and congruent care:

1. The nurse should give major consideration to the extended family as partners or participants in nursing care plans, decisions, and actions. Discussion and involvement of the family members in client care in the hospital or home are important. Involving family members in feeding, bathing, walking with, and other caring activities with the client are important. In addition, the mother's role as the inside family caregiver and the father's role as the protective carer largely outside the home needs to be assessed and considered.

2. The nurse should support, where possible, the cultural beliefs, values, and practices in nursing unless they are in serious conflict with well-known professional knowledge and are known to be not beneficial to the client and family. Since a prevalent belief among Mexican Americans is that health and well-being are a reflection of God's will or an indication of good favor with Him, prayer and spiritual care with the family are important. Belief in the balance of "hot and cold" elements is an important consideration in nursing care activities, eating, sleeping, and medical or nursing treatments. The client or family often can teach nurses about hot and cold foods and treatment measures. Active listening and respect for the client's cultural beliefs are most important. Since illness is often thought to be due to prolonged exposure to hot or cold substances or hot and cold air, the room temperature, drafts, and use of proper foods to redress imbalances are important. Cold is generally thought to harm the body from without; whereas excessive heat can lead to diseases such as cancer and paralysis.[81,82]

3. The nurse should keep in mind the present time orientation of Mexican Americans and place less emphasis on the future plans and goals for the client and his family.

4. Transcultural nursing research has shown that Mexican Americans value other care with presence, touching, being together with the family as a unit, and face-to-face relationships as caring modalities. The nurse needs to be cognizant of these culture-specific care values and use them in nursing practices.

Permitting more than one person to visit the client and remain with the sick person are a few culture-specific care needs.

5. Mexican Americans value modesty and may feel threatened by a lack of respect during physical examinations, or may feel overexposed during nursing care or medical procedures. Some women may feel embarrassment when a physical examination is conducted, especially by a male nurse or physician. Exposure of the body, touching the genitalia, especially by those of the opposite sex, is often disturbing to Mexican Americans. Men may be reluctant to use condoms, and women with Catholic beliefs may strongly resent birth control measures, especially artificial devices.

6. Speaking and understanding Spanish to Mexican Americans is important to facilitate communication and action modes. Nursing students and staff are strongly recommended today to learn Spanish and especially if they will serve Mexican Americans, Cubans, Puerto Ricans, Haitians, or other Hispanic groups.

Concluding Comments

In this chapter a number of important ideas were presented about Mexican American beliefs, values, and lifeways. An overview of one Hispanic subgroup, Mexican Americans, was provided from an ethnohistorical perspective living in different environmental contexts over time. Several research studies by transcultural nurses and other social scientists were presented to be considered by the nurse in providing client care. Today Mexican Americans are the second largest minority group in the United States and are anticipated to be the largest by the year 2020. Many Mexican Americans have retained their cultural values and beliefs through the years with pride. The cultural concepts and values of respect (*respecto*), confidence (*confianza*), pride (*orgullo*), extended family involvement, belief in God, and other dominant values make Mexican Americans and other Hispanic cultures unique in their cultural lifeways. Most importantly, several dominant culture care values and practices were presented to guide nurses in their decisions and actions with Mexican American clients. Folk healers were discussed with their religious beliefs and practices. These research findings offer important guidelines for nurses to provide culture-specific and congruent care to Mexican Americans. Although other related Hispanic cultures such as Puerto Rican, Haitian, and Cuban were not specifically discussed in this chapter, many ideas represented here may serve as general guides for the nurse in caring for clients, as they are all part of the Hispanic group. However, nurses must realize these other cultures are not identical to Mexican American and must be understood within their own cultural ethnohistory values and beliefs.

The plight and experiences of Mexican Americans and other Hispanics in the United States are of concern and need to be understood by nurses and other health care providers. In addition, language barriers, poor housing, low salaries, lack of jobs, limited educational opportunities, and discrimination are all contemporary problems that influence health and well-being of Mexican Americans. Amid these problems or barriers, the Mexican American values of the extended family: providing other-care, family togetherness, celebration of family and religious holidays, love of children, respect for others in authority and the elderly, deep spiritual beliefs, and tenacity for life, love, and living must be viewed by non-Hispanics as great assets for a thriving and growing culture. We have much to learn from Mexican Americans. The nurse with transcultural knowledge and skills will recognize these realities as Mexican Americans continue to live, grow, and contribute to the multicultural world of the United States and elsewhere.

References

1. Coe, M., *Mexico, 3rd ed.*, New York: Thames and Hudson, Inc., 1984.

2. Schele, L., and M. E. Miller, *The Blood of Kings: Dynasty and Ritual in Maya Art*, Fort Worth: Kimball Art Museum, 1987.

3. Lopez-Austin, A., *The Human Body and Ideology of the Ancient Nahuas: Volume I and II*, B. Ortiz de Montellano and T. Ortiz de Montellano, trans., Salt Lake City: University of Utah Press, 1988. (Original work published 1980).

4. Ortiz de Montellano, B., "Aztec Religion and Medicine," *Healing and Restoring: Health and Medicine in the World's Religious Tradition*, L. E. Sullivan, ed., New York: Macmillan and Co., 1989a, pp. 359–394.

5. Manrique, J. A., "The Progress of Art in New Spain," *Mexico: Splendors of Thirty Centuries*, New York: Metropolitan Museum of Art and Bullfinch Press, 1990.

6. Diaz del Castillo, B., *The Conquest of New Spain*, J. N. Cohen, trans., Baltimore: Penguin, 1963.

7. Finkler, K., *Physicians at Work, Patients in Pain: Biomedical Practice and Patient Response in Mexico*, Boulder: Westview Press, 1991.

8. Ortiz de Montellano, B., *Syncretism in Mexican and Mexican American Folk Medicine*, Department of Spanish and Portuguese, 1992 Lecture Series, Working papers, 5, University of Maryland, 1989b.

9. Ortiz de Montellano, B., *Aztec Medicine, Nutrition, and Health*, New Brunswick: Rutgers University Press, 1990.

10. Mirande, A., and E. Enriquez, *La Chicana: The Mexican American Woman*, Chicago: The University of Chicago Press, 1979.

11. Ortiz de Montellano, op. cit., 1989a.

12. Ortiz de Montellano, op. cit., 1989b.

13. Ibid.

14. Fuentes, C., *The Buried Mirror: Reflections on Spain and the New World*, New York: Houghton Mifflin, 1992.

15. Moore, J., and H. Pachon, *Hispanics in the United States*, Englewood Cliffs, New Jersey: Prentice-Hall, 1985.

16. Martinez, C., "Mexican-Americans," *Clinical Guidelines in Cross-Cultural Mental Health*, L. Comas-Dias and E. H. Griffith, eds., New York: Wiley & Sons, 1989, p. 38.

17. United States Bureau of the Census, Department of Commerce. *The Hispanic Population in the United States: March 1991*, Current Population reports, Series P–20, N. 455, 1991.

18. Ibid.

19. Ibid.

20. Ibid.

21. Ibid.

22. National Council of La Raza and Labor Council for Latin American Advancement. *Hispanics and Health Insurance, Volume 1: Status*, Washington, D.C., 1992.

23. United States Bureau of Census, op. cit.

24. Ibid.

25. Ibid.

26. United States Department of Health and Human Services. *Health United States 1990*, Hyattsville, Maryland: DHHS Pub. No. (PHS), 1991, pp. 91–1232.

27. Ibid.

28. National Council of La Raza and Labor Council for Latin American Advancement, op. cit.

29. Leininger, M., *Culture Care Diversity and Universality: A Theory of Nursing*, New York: National League for Nursing Press, 1991.

30. National Coalition of Hispanic Health and Human Service Organizations (COSSMHO). *Delivering Preventive Health Care to Hispanics*, Washington, D.C., 1988.

31. Falcov, C. J., "Mexican Families," *Ethnicity and Family Therapy*, M. McGoldrick, J. K. Pearce, and J. Giordana, eds., New York: Guilford Press, 1982, pp. 134–163.

32. Sabogal, F., G. Marin, R. Otero-Sabogal, B. V. Marin, and E. J. Perez-Stable, "Hispanic Familism and Acculturation: What Changes, What Doesn't?" *Hispanic Journal of Behavioral Sciences*, v. 9, 1987, pp. 397–412.

33. Kegan, S., and G. L. Zahn, "Cultural Differences in Individualism," *Hispanic Journal of Behavioral Sciences*, v. 5, 1983, pp. 219–232.

34. Scheper-Hughes, N., and D. Steward, "Curanderismo in Taos County, New Mexico: A Possible Case of Anthropological Romanticism?" *The Western Journal of Medicine*, v. 139, 1983, pp. 875–884.

35. Domino, G., and A. Acosta, "The Relation of Acculturation and Values in Mexican Americans," *Hispanic Journal of Behavioral Sciences*, v. 9, 1987, pp. 131–150.

36. Mindel, C., "Extended Familism Among Urban Mexican Americans, Anglos, and Blacks," *Hispanic Journal of Behavioral Sciences*, v. 2, 1980, pp. 21–34.

37. Kranau, E., V. Green, and G. Valencia-Weber, "Acculturation and the Hispanic woman: Attitudes Toward Women Sex-Role Attribution, Sex-Role Behavior, and Demographics," *Hispanic Journal of Behavioral Sciences*, v. 4, 1982, pp. 21–40.

38. Zapata, J., and P. Jaramillo, "The Mexican-American Family: An Alderman Perspective," *Hispanic Journal of Behavioral Sciences*, v. 3, 1981, pp. 275–290.

39. Jaramillo, P., and J. Zapata, "Roles and Alliances within Mexican-American and Anglo Families," *Journal of Marriage and the Family*, v. 49, 1987, pp. 727–735.

40. COSSMHO, op. cit., 1988.

41. Ibid.

42. Dugan, A. B., "Compadrazgo: A Caring Phenomenon Among Urban Latinos and its Relationship to Health," *Care: The Essence of Nursing and Health*, M. Leininger, ed., Detroit: Wayne State University Press, 1988, pp. 183-194.

43. Leininger, M., *Nursing and Anthropology: Two Worlds to Blend*, New York: John Wiley & Sons, 1970.

44. Stasiak, D. B., "Culture Care Theory with Mexican-Americans in an Urban Context," *Culture Care Theory Diversity and Universality: A Theory of Nursing*, M. Leininger, ed., New York: National League for Nursing Press, 1991, pp. 179–201.

45. Wenger, A. F., *Ethnocare of Mexican-Americans*, Field study report, Detroit: Wayne State University, 1986.

46. Leininger, M., "Selected Culture Care Findings of Diverse Cultures Using Culture Care Theory and Ethnomethods, *Culture Care Diversity and Universality: A Theory of Nursing*, M. Leininger, ed., New York: National League for Nursing Press, 1991, p. 356.

47. Dugan, op. cit.

48. Wenger, op. cit.

49. Stasiak, op. cit.

50. Ibid.

51. Maduro, R., "Curanderismo and Latino Views of Disease and Curing," *Western Journal of Medicine*, v. 139, no. 9, December 1983, pp. 868–874.

52. Gomez, G., and E. Gomez, "Folk Healing Among Hispanic Americans," *Public Health Nursing*, v. 2, 1985, pp. 245–249.

53. Tamez, E., "Curanderismo: Folk Mexican-American Health Care System," *Journal of Psychosocial Nursing and Mental Health Services*, v. 19, 1978, pp. 21–25.

54. Gomez and Gomez, op. cit.

55. Gonzalez-Swafford, M., and M. Gutierrez, "Ethno-Medical Beliefs and Practices of Mexican-Americans," *Nurse Practitioner*, v. 8, 1983, pp. 29–30.

56. Kiev, A., *Curanderismo: Mexican-American Folk Psychiatry*, Toronto: The Free Press, 1968.

57. Maduro, op. cit.

58. Perrone, B., H. H. Stockel, and V. Krueger, *Medicine Women, Curanderas, and Women Doctors*, Norman: University of Oklahoma Press, 1989.

59. Gomez and Gomez, op. cit.

60. Ibid.

61. Kiev, op. cit.

62. Maduro, op. cit.

63. Perrone, Stockel, and Krueger, op. cit.

64. Gomez and Gomez, op. cit.

65. Tamez, op. cit.

66. Ibid.

67. Gomez and Gomez, op. cit.

68. Gonzalez-Swafford and Gutierrez, op. cit.

69. Kiev, op. cit.

70. Martinez, C., and H. W. Martin, "Folk Diseases Among Urban Mexican-Americans: Etiology, Symptoms, and Treatment," *Journal of the American Medical Association*, v. 196, no. 2, 1966, pp. 147–150.

71. Tamez, op. cit.

72. Kosko, D., and J. Flaskerud, "Mexican-American, Nurse Practitioner, and Lay Control Group Beliefs about Cause and Treatment of Chest Pain," *Nursing Research*, v. 36, 1987, pp. 226–230.

73. Slesinger, D., and M. Richards, "Folk and Clinical Medical Utilization Patterns Among Mejicano Migrant Farm Workers," *Hispanic Journal of Behavioral Sciences*, v. 3, 1981, pp. 59–73.

74. Martinez and Martin, op. cit.

75. Trotter, R., "Folk Remedies as Indicators of Common Illnesses: Examples from the United States/Mexico Border," *Journal of Ethno-Pharmacology*, v. 4, 1981, pp. 207–221.

76. Marin, B., G. Marin, A. Padilla, and C. de la Rocha, "Utilization of Traditional and Non-Traditional Sources of Health Care among Hispanics," *Hispanic Journal of Behavioral Sciences*, v. 5, 1983, pp. 65–80.

77. Keefe, S., "Folk Medicine Among Urban Mexican-Americans: Cultural Persistence, Change, and Displacement," *Hispanic Journal of Behavioral Sciences*, v. 3, 1981, pp. 41–58.

78. Higginbotham, J. C., F. M. Trevino, and L. N. Ray, "Utilization of Curanderos by Mexican-Americans: Findings from H. Hanes 1982–84," *American Journal of Public Health*, v. 80, Suppl., 1990, pp. 32–41.

79. Keefe, op. cit.

80. Perrone, Stockel, and Krueger, op. cit.

81. Harwood, A., "The Hot-Cold Theory of Disease," *JAMA*, v. 216, no. 7, 1971, pp. 1153–1158.

82. Wilson, H. and C. Kneisl, *Psychiatric Nursing*, Reading, Massachusetts: Addison-Wesley Publishing Co., 1988.

Chapter 17
African Americans and Cultural Care
Marjorie Morgan, PhD, CNM, CTN, RN

One of the largest minority groups living in the United States today is that of the African Americans. It is important that professional nurses understand this culture in order to provide culturally congruent nursing care. Because of the variability among African Americans living in different places in the United States, the nurse needs to take into account both the diverse and common beliefs, values, and lifeways of the people when assessing and planning nursing care for them.

The worldview of African Americans comes from their cultural heritage and cultural experiences in the United States. The worldview of most nurses comes mainly from living in this country, but also from nursing education and clinical practices. When an African American seeks professional services, the nurse and client may have difficulty understanding each other unless the nurse has knowledge of the African American culture. Differences in cultural caring values, beliefs, and practices between the nurse and client may lead to cultural conflicts and less beneficial care for the client. If the nurse does not understand and accept the cultural characteristics of the client, the client may decide to reject the nursing care that is offered.

In this chapter, Leininger's Theory of Culture Care Diversity and Universality will be used to identify patterns of care through beliefs, values, and practices of African Americans. This theory is useful to help nurses learn about care that can contribute to the health and well-being of African Americans. In the process of learning about this culture, the author realized that the lifeways and beliefs of the people tend to be embedded in the religious, political, economic, and other aspects of the social structures of the people. In addition to social structures, the language and environmental context of African Americans have to be considered to get an accurate picture.

In the use of the Leininger theory, the generic folk care and health beliefs are contrasted with beliefs of nurses and other professional health care providers. Understanding these contrasting folk care and health beliefs, values, and practices enables nurses to use the knowledge to make nursing care decisions. Through the use of culture care knowledge, the nurse can provide practices that facilitate three different modes of action or decisions. These are nursing care preservation/

maintenance, accommodation/negotiation, or repatterning/restructuring. Using these modes of care, the nurse can provide culturally congruent and culture-specific care to African American clients.[1]

Ethnohistory and the African American Caring and Health Ways

Nurses who practice transcultural nursing consider it important to know the history of a people in order to understand the way in which the people view their world and their health care. For example, many of the folk remedies of African Americans came from the time that their ancestors spent in slavery in the United States. Since there were often no physicians and nurses available to the slaves, they had to depend on remedies that they brought with them from Africa. This system of folk healing was then passed down from generation to generation until the present time, when many of the same remedies are still in use.

The history of African slavery began in 1444 when Henry the Navigator took 165 Africans to Portugal on a slave ship. The practice of moving people from West Africa in slave trade lasted for approximately four centuries. Many Africans were brought to the New World where they were held as slaves in North and South America and the Caribbean. At the same time many European countries were involved in the colonization of these areas. Osborne, as quoted by Sherlock, stated that the three institutions of African slavery, European colonization, and a plantation economy gave impetus to the Creole society which was common to the Caribbean, southern United States, and Central and South America.[2,3]

From this history and from Creole society grew the belief and value systems of many African Americans. Snow said that the elements of their health belief system come from a variety of sources including "European folklore, Greek classical medicine, the cultures of West Africa, and modern scientific medicine."[4]

Plantation owners and overseers came from Europe, so the slaves combined the European folklore that they learned from their masters with their African remedies to deal with injury and illness. Often the European methods included the Greek classical remedies since most Europeans had been educated in the Greek and Roman tradition. Years later as African Americans left the rural areas of the South to find work in the urban North and the West, more reliance on the biomedical system began to be seen as the people became more acculturated to the dominant American way of health. However, many of the folk practices from the rural South are still found wherever African Americans live.

In 1870, after the Civil War the Fifteenth Amendment to the United States Constitution gave former slaves the right to vote. Civil rights legislation of 1875 opened public accommodations and jury duty to the same people. However, ways were found by the white majority of Americans to deny these rights. Dr. Martin Luther King, Jr., and the Civil Rights movement were instrumental in getting the 1964 civil rights bill passed by Congress. This legislation banned discrimination in jobs, schools, public accommodations, and voting. While racism is still found in the United States, African Americans have carved out a niche in the society through the exercise of their rights. Many elected officials are African American. Better educational opportunities have enable more African Americans to reach their dreams of professional life. However, as an African American colleague stated, "many" still does not translate into "the majority."

More recent history of African Americans has included a rise in Afrocentric awareness as the concepts of plurality and cultural heritage consistency have begun to gain prominence in the United States. The old American belief in the "melting pot" as being the proper means to enfold new and different cultures into the fabric of the land has been questioned. Nathan Glazer and Daniel Patrick Moynihan in 1963 asserted that Negroes were Americans with no African beliefs and practices left to value.[5] Mazrui, writing in 1986, saw a new pride rising and re-Africanization occurring after years of attempts by the Western world to dis-Africanize Black Americans.[6] More African Americans are now learning about their cultural heritage in schools and colleges throughout America. But all too often the history of African Americans is usually limited to that provided during "Black History" month or that taught to African American students who have the time and money to fit such a course into a plan of study. Black history has been limitedly integrated into formal American history courses.

Nurses who understand the care, health and illness beliefs, values, and practices that arose from the ethnohistory of African Americans can plan and provide better nursing care. Knowledge of social structures, worldview, and environmental context also help the nurse to identify and understand beliefs, practices, and values. These factors will be considered next.

Social Structures, Worldview, Health, and Care

Studying human care with reference to the African American worldview and social structures can be a challenging yet most stimulating learning endeavor in light of the diversity that exists among African Americans in the United States. Bloch has stated that factors such as "social class, age, sex roles, region or location in the United States, socialization patterns, individual life experiences or circumstances, and ongoing changes in the cultural environment" all contribute to variation in the African American group of people.[7] But among these variations some common characteristics in beliefs, values, and practices prevail.

In the United States there are 29.9 million African Americans who make up 12.1% of the American population. The majority live in industrial Midwestern and

Northeastern cities of the United States and in the rural South. About 53% live in the Southern states where in-migration is equal to out-migration.[8]

No matter where in the United States African Americans live, one of the most important social structure features in this group is the extended family and its kinship ties. The extended family is one that includes not only people related "by blood," but also those who are brought into it as fictive kin, such as boyfriends, preachers, family friends, and many others. Close friends from organizations such as sororities, fraternities, and church are considered "brothers" and "sisters" or "aunts" and "uncles." The concept of "my brothers and sisters" and "my aunts and uncles" must therefore be considered to include many who may not be related by biological ties. A review of pertinent literature shows that this African American family closeness often goes beyond geographical, legal, political, and economic borders. Members of the extended family lend support to one another by gifts, childcare, financial help, home repairs, and advice for personal problems.[9,10,11,12,13] Stack discovered in her study that families in an indigent African American community practiced cooperative sharing and swapping of goods and services within the kinship system as strategies for survival.[14] Families that have been separated by members moving from one geographical area to another find that family reunions, marriages, and funerals are valuable times to maintain the family.[15] These celebrations and rituals also reinforce bonds of solidarity and closeness in caring for each other in the African American community.

Many researchers have explored the basis for the strength of the extended family in the African American community. Some argue that the African American family has its roots in Africa,[16,17] while others view the influence of the American political, economic, and social struggles as contributing to the values and characteristics of the family.[18,19,20]

Aschenbrenner found that the values related to the family were: "1) a high values placed on children; 2) the approval of strong, protective mothers; 3) the emphasis on strict discipline and respect for elders; 4) the strength of the family bonds; and 5) the ideal of an independent spirit."[21] There is evidence of a caring ethos among extended family members that strengthens many African Americans in times of crisis and that enables them to face daily living and survival.

Specific statements related to the family and health care were given in articles by African American nurses Bloch and Thomas.[22,23] When a member of a family is ill, the family is less likely than in some other cultural groups to see this as a burden, but will instead view the problem as a family illness. Both authors state that there is a strong tradition of having kinfolk "sit up" with a family member who is ill.[24,25] The family in the African American community usually has one person who is given the duty of making the major decisions, including those related to care and health concerns, for other family members. Sometimes health decisions are refused until this person is consulted.[26]

Religion is another important factor of the social structure that influences the care and health values, beliefs, and practices of African Americans. A belief in a higher power extends to every facet of life including health. Many African Americans believe that without the power of God no one can be healed or saved from death. Gospel and African American folk music reflect this belief in God's or Jesus' healing power.

The moral teachings from the church can lead to good caring and health practices. Health is attributed to "living right." For example, by not doing too much "partying" and by doing good deeds health will come as a "blessing from God."[27]

That God, health, and illness are closely connected can be found in the work of several researchers. Leininger reported statements from her informants such as "If you follow what is in the Bible, you will be well and stay well;" "The Bible teaches you how to keep well and avoid evil thoughts and actions that could make you ill;" and "One has to let Jesus be the healer...People who are not working with Jesus have to use other people to heal them."[28] Roberson stated that Bible passages were frequently cited as sources for particular health beliefs by her informants. One of the key beliefs that she found was that God does nothing bad to people but that he can turn a person over to the devil who can then cause malevolent illnesses.[29]

The ability of God to give relief from illness is found in William's ethnography of members of a Black Pentecostal Church. He quoted several of his informants on God and illness. One person testified, "When my bronchial tubes were stopped up and I could not breathe for myself, I needed an artificial respirator and God got in them tubes." Another person said, "I got a sore throat yesterday. God is a throat specialist."[30]

African American churches are not only places of worship, they often function as "an escape mechanism from the harsh realities of daily life."[31] Church activities furnish opportunities for many African Americans to have roles of respect such as preacher, deacon, usher, choir leader or member, or Sunday School leader.[32] The minister, along with the deacons, members of missionary circles, choir members, Sunday School teachers, and others will often expect and be expected to visit a member of their congregation who is ill. These people offer encouragement and meet the spiritual needs of the person and the family in stressful situations such as an illness.[33,34]

There is, however, some diversity in the religious beliefs of African Americans, and nurses should not assume that all clients are Christian. Some African Americans are followers of Islam, and some embrace the Jewish faith. Getting information from clients about their religious beliefs is part of the culturological assessment.

Education is another aspect of social structure that is extremely important to African Americans. Older members of the group have a great desire for their children to obtain good educations as a means for advancement in society.[35] In 1986 the median educational attainment for both males and females in the African American population was twelve years or more.[36] During the past three decades the illiteracy rate in the United States has dropped appreciably and college enrollment has increased noticeably. However, the number of males enrolled in institutions of higher learning has dropped markedly thereby negating some of the benefits of African American enrollment.[37] This increased opportunity for education has not translated into an equitable situation in the job market for African Americans. According to Sidell, only 47% of African American college graduates earn income equivalent to that earned by Anglo-Americans with high school educations.[38]

Many authors have advanced the idea that economic factors have a major effect on the lifeways of the African Americans and on their health.[39,40,41] During a twenty year period between 1962 and 1982, the percentage of African Americans living below the poverty level was twice that of Anglo-Americans.[42] Sidell stated, "If you're poor, you're more likely to be sick, less likely to receive adequate medical care, and more likely to die at an early age. The effects of poverty on health and general well-being are clear-cut and profound."[43]

Several recent studies have shown that the inability of many African Americans to get health care within the professional system is due to their impoverished economic state.[44,45] While many factors may be related to the high morbidity and mortality rates in the African American population, lack of professional care due to poverty contributes to the high rates of heart disease, cancer, hypertension, tuberculosis, and infant deaths in this group according to these researchers.[46,47,48] The author has found in her practice of nurse-midwifery that many pregnant African American mothers do not receive needed prenatal care due to lack of medical insurance, money, transportation, and other factors associated with poverty.

Poverty also contributes to concern with the present rather than with the future. Living with poverty forces many African Americans to think about the day-to-day necessities of life rather than what might happen in the future. The nurse will soon learn that for some African Americans taking time off from work for nursing care, or medical treatment, is not considered important when money has to be earned for food, shelter, and other basics for the extended family and especially for the needs of the children and the elderly. Sometimes health care has to receive less attention.

The cultural philosophy of being present- rather than future-oriented is sometimes combined with a fatalistic view about illness and pain. Considering these values and philosophical beliefs, the positive effects of preventive and continuing health care as taught by nurses and other health care providers are often difficult for the African American client to understand.[49,50]

African Americans and the Folk Health System

The inability of some African Americans to get professional health care does not mean that the people do not get any health care. Instead African Americans have long had a folk health care system. This folk system is the traditional way of caring and healing. Most people seek out extended family members, friends, and neighbors for advice on illness, caring, and curing. There is also use of folk health practices and healing ways brought originally from Africa. Herbs and nonprescription drugs are often used. Assistance may be sought from folk practitioners and faith healers, with reliance on the professional health system only during extreme injury or illness.[51] In a recent study in an urban community, Bailey discovered a cultural pattern of health care-seeking.[52] Six steps taken by African Americans faced with illness were: 1) the illness appears; 2) the individual waits for a certain period of days; 3) the body is allowed to heal itself while the individual uses prayer or traditional, general healing regimens; 4) the individual evaluates daily activities and may try to reduce work or stress; 5) the individual seeks advice from a family member or some friend (church leader and/or traditional, generic healer included); 6) the individual finally attends a health clinic or family physician.[53]

Caper's study also found that many African American people use their religious beliefs, friends and neighbors, root doctors, spiritual healers, and magic vendors before they seek professional health care. She reported that her informants felt that the treatments provided by generic or folk healers seemed to "lie closer to the everyday experiences and world views of the clients than the more esoteric explanations based on a biomedical model of health and illness."[54] Mothers and grandmothers are often consulted especially in health care related to babies. For example, advice is frequently sought for such things as colic. Leininger said that the informants whom she interviewed in the southern part of the United States gave several cognitive reasons for beliefs related to professional health care. She reported that the people did not trust such care, since they felt that it was dangerous, unfriendly, slow, costly, strange, and that they were not treated as "whole" people. They preferred to trust generic, traditional care and used many folk care practices to maintain well-being and health.[55]

African American Curing Ways and Health Belief System

In order to identify ways in which African Americans remain well or become ill, Leininger's theory for studying care values, practices, and beliefs is important. Some of the beliefs and practices within the African American folk system of health care and curing came to the United States from Africa and have been passed down from generation to generation as part of the transmission of culture.

For African Americans good care can lead to good health. Good care and good health depend on being in tune with nature and its forces.[56,57] Illnesses are classified as natural when they have natural causes. In these the person has faced the forces of nature, that is air, food, water, and weather, without adequate protection. Illnesses are caused by such things as exposure to cold air, rain, heat, impurities in the air, or bad food or water.[58,59]

An example of a natural illnesses is arthritic-type pain. The cause of the pain is seen as exposure to cold air or to rain. Prevention is to bundle up with heavy clothes, carry an umbrella, or to stay indoors during inclement weather. Even when exposed to the elements as a youth, such illness may be revealed much later in life. A close African American friend of the author was told by older women that she was running a risk of getting arthritis when she didn't remain in the house for six weeks after her child was born.[60]

In the face of illness brought on by natural forces, books, such as the *Farmer's Almanac*, which contains information on the position of the planets, the phases of the moon, and weather forecasts may also be consulted. These natural forces are seen as important factors that can affect the health and well-being of people.[61,62] The author also found in her own research that many books which related to holistic health care are being written by and for African Americans and sold in African American bookstores. These books contain instructions for herbal remedies and ways to use heat and cold, crystals, massage, and meditation in generic health care. These can be considered as generic care modalities to improve the health and well-being of African Americans.

The opposite of natural illness is unnatural illness. Unnatural illnesses are caused by evil influences on the person in the form of witchcraft, hoodoo, voodoo, or rootwork. While the professional health care personnel work to treat and possibly cure natural illnesses, they usually have limited effect on unnatural ones. For these illnesses, generic or traditional healers must be consulted.[63, 64]

Health is also seen as being synonymous with good luck. Traditional healers use roots, herbs, potions, oils, powders, tokens, rites, and ceremonies in their healing practices. These healers will often combine secular and religious rituals in their care and curing of African Americans. The patient is sometimes told to go to a candle store to get oils, incense, candles, soaps, and aerosol room sprays to repel evil forces. In the southern part of the United States where the author practiced nursing, the door and window frames and sills were painted light blue on many houses in the African American community. This was to keep out the "haunts," "haints," or evil spirits that can cause unnatural illnesses.

When African Americans enter the professional health care system, they often bring these beliefs with them. Bloch suggested that when an African American goes to a professional health care giver, the nurse or doctor should assume that the client has already tried some generic healing methods. The professional needs to ask about what treatment has been used to be sure that there will be no conflict or incompatibility with the professional modes of helping the person.[65]

Language and the Power of Words

Language is an important aspect to be considered in studying a culture. Specific words and non-verbal expressions related to African American health beliefs, practices, and values are often expressed in nurse-client situations and in the cultural context. Many can be observed by nurses in the home, hospital, and clinic.

There is a specific system of thinking and expressing ideas about care, health, and illness in the African American culture. There are sometimes differences between Anglo-American and African American language which the nurse needs to recognize. Smitherman wrote that language is particularly important in the African American culture. According to the same author, Anglo-Americans depend on the written word to shape their lives, while African Americans use a spoken mode that is based on the African "orally-oriented background."[66] Smitherman continued that the power of life itself in Africa came from the concept of Nommo, or the "magic power of the word." The power of Nommo can be seen in the traditional African culture where "a newborn child is a mere thing until his father gives and speaks his name."[67]

This same importance of naming a baby can be seen in American hospital newborn nurseries. Distinctive names that reflect the African cultural background of the parents are often given to new boys or girls by their mothers, fathers, or grandparents.

In American hospitals and clinics many nurses and doctors report that they are too busy to spend more time with their clients to get to know them, to understand them, and to explain their illnesses and care to them. To many African American clients, who come from an oral tradition, this time spent for conversation is seen as more important than nursing and medical treatments, or record-keeping. African American patients think that the nurse does not care if she has not talked and listened to them. As Smitherman stated, "No medicine, potion, or magic of any sort is considered effective without accompanying words."[68] The nurse needs to be aware of the value of oral stories, legends, and personal experiences in caring for African American clients. These oral accounts enable the nurse to understand ways to link folk and professional care together.

Some African American clients in health care settings may use a style of communication that is cultural in nature, but foreign to the health care providers. The use of Black English, a distinctive language that reflects African heritage combined with historical factors of American life, may lead to misunderstandings in a health care setting and a lack of sensitive modes of caring. Smitherman wrote that eighty to ninety percent of African Americans use Black English some or all of the time. This varies with the geographical area in which the client lives, the age, and the educational background of the person.[69] Black English is a "highly oral, stylized, rhythmic, spontaneous language," with the meaning of words dependent on the context in which they are said.[70] If the nurse does not understand what is being said, it is important to clarify ideas with the patient and the family.

A particular problem can arise in treating African American clients related to their health and illness expressions. For example, the nurse needs to understand the various ways in which the term "blood" is used by some African Americans. Blood can be called high or low, rich or poor, thick or thin, up or down, clean or defiled, sweet or sour, or new or used.[71] Since the terms are used in so many different ways, with as an example "low blood," "low blood pressure," and "low blood count" being considered equivalent, the nurse needs to clarify what is meant when blood is referred to by the client.

The nurse can confuse clients of any cultural group with the use of highly technical health terms. This may result in the client not understanding, but pretending that he or she knows that is going on. Another reaction may be anger and suspicion of the nurse who is trying to communicate.[72]

The client may get frustrated when the nurse does not understand what the client is saying. Unfortunate, embarrassing situations can arise from not understanding terms such as "I've got to make water," indicating the need for urination. Another complaint of a client went untreated because the nurse did not realize that the client had a swollen gland, when the patient complained of having a "kernel".

From the above study of the worldview, social structures, language, and environmental context of African Americans, one can find patterns and expressions of care that contribute to health and well-being or that lead to illness. For example, the extended family has many caring ways such as being concerned about or for one's brothers and sisters. These attitudes and actions can lead to health and well-being as predicted in Leininger's theory. In addition, transcultural nurses have studied specific care meanings which will be discussed next.

The Meaning of Care

Several researchers have done ethnographic studies of African Americans and have determined the meaning and actions that express care in that population.[73,74,75,76,77] In Leininger's theory culture and care are directly linked and must be considered in planning and delivering of transcultural nursing care.

Leininger studied care phenomena among African Americans living in a rural area of the southern United States. She found that one manifestation of care came from "concern for others." Within this construct were patterns of providing for the needs of "brothers" and "sisters," being aware of others' needs, and helping others obtain these needs. Other expressions of caring were seen in "being present" in the community and of being "involved with" family and neighbors. She discovered that "touching" others within the community, particularly in times of sorrow and loss, is important to demonstrate care and caring. Finally, "sharing" showed caring in the African American group that she studied. This had such diverse meanings as the sharing of food, sharing religious experiences, sharing as a survival strategy, and the responsibility of family members to share.[78]

An example of lack of care was told during an interview with an African American postpartum client in a hospital. The client said that while she was in labor, she was largely left alone. Nonetheless the client kept turning on her call light, but the nurses would come in quickly and "do something" and then quickly leave the room. The physicians and nurses were troubled because the client was not dilating. Soon another nurse who had been taught about the African American values of presence, involvement with, and touching came in. Soon the client dilated and delivered a healthy infant. The client said that this "caring nurse" had given her the best nursing care she had ever had in that hospital. This example showed concern for, involvement with, presence, and touch, all care and caring constructs that had been identified in Leininger's research as being important to African Americans.[79] These care modes were used by the nurse to give quality nursing care.

In an indigent urban area, Stack reported that care was demonstrated by her African American informants by sharing of good and services but with the added activities of "swapping." While sharing generally implies the giving of something to another person without obligation, swapping entails an exchange relationship with the obligation to eventually return an item or activity of equal value to the giver. This type of caring activity provides what the author calls a "steady source of cooperative support to survive."[80]

In her research with extended families in Chicago, Aschenbrenner reported that both men and women agree that it is of "supreme importance" to care for and bring children up properly. Care for the young ones involves strict discipline and teaching them to have love and respect for their elders.[81] Osborne found that this respect for the elderly extends well into adulthood.[82]

The extended family often is multigenerational. Flaherty in a recent study reported on caring functions of grandmothers who took care of the infants of their adolescent daughters.[83] Four of these caring functions were managing activities to meet family needs, caretaking of the infant activities, coaching or role modeling the maternal role, and nurturing and loving the mother and the grandchild. Care was also shown to the daughter by assessing the new mother's attitude about mothering, assigning with expressions the mother's ownership of the baby, and patrolling the new mother's life style and life goals.[84]

The nurse of African American clients needs to understand the different values and modes of expressing care and caring within the culture. These nursing care actions and judgments can be made about ways to enter into the care when the client needs professional help.

Culturally Congruent Nursing Care

To plan for and provide culturally congruent nursing care, the nurse bases decisions on a cultural assessment to see if the client's health beliefs and practices should be accepted or need to be changed in some manner. From this assessment of the cultural beliefs, value, and practices of the client, the nurse uses Leininger's three modes of decision and action. These three modes are culture care maintenance/preservation, accommodation/negotiation, and restructuring/repatterning.

If current health care beliefs and activities are acceptable, then the nurse will use culture care maintenance or preservation. If there is need for change in the care of a client, a decision must be made as to whether and how the care can be modified with culture care accommodation or negotiation, or whether it needs to be changed by culture care restructuring or repatterning. A few examples of these modes for planning and carrying out nursing care will be presented.

In caring for the African American client, nurses should consider the cultural values of extended family and religious beliefs. The nurse should preserve the right of the client to draw upon these resources for strength and support. Culture care maintenance and preservation would be used to assure that the family and church members could stay with the client to express their concern for and involvement with the client.

Sometimes nurses have to use several modes to provide culturally congruent care. In the case of family and others visiting in the hospital, more than preservation may be needed. Accommodation to these caring needs may entail the nurse's using his or her skills to negotiate with physicians or case managers in the health care institution. This is particularly true if the client is an inpatient where there are hospital rules against visitors at certain times of the day or night. The nurse's knowledge of the cultural importance of family and religion to the African American client's well-being should strengthen her ability to teach the hospital authorities and other practitioners about this and to then use culture care negotiation effectively.

The cultural value in the African American community in relation to time needs to be considered in planning or providing nursing care. Nurses have been taught that being on time and paying attention to the clock is a fine value and attribute in American culture and in the nursing subculture. The African American patient may be inclined to adhere to a less rigid or more flexible time orientation. Nurses may maintain the cultural value of flexible time for their client by accommodating or negotiating with him or her about when a bath is desired or what time a tray should be served. On the other hand, this flexibility might not be therapeutic in regard to when a medicine or treatment is given. Here the nurse would discuss the matter and then develop a specific negotiation or repatterning plan with the client.

The trend for short-term hospital care has meant that many nurses are moving into the community to care for patients. This has made transcultural nursing care even more important as clients are less likely to change their usual folk health practices in their homes than they are in a strange and frightening environment such as the hospital. Evidence of the folk health system of African Americans may thus be more readily apparent when nurses go to the homes of their clients. Such things as religious statues, candles, oils, incense, and ointments may be seen at the bedside of clients. Many orthodox or professional practitioners of health care find humor in this and may ridicule the client about objects of this sort, or about generic health practices and practitioners. The transcultural nurse, however, will recognize the importance of incorporating the folk health practices and traditional healers of the clients into the planning and delivery of health care.

When giving care in the home, the nurse will often find an extended family that is multigenerational living under one roof. Health care interventions may be ineffective and ignored if the key members of the family are not consulted and included in the planning and delivery of care. Attention to the family and their beliefs, particularly the elders in the group, can lead to culturally congruent care that is meaningful and accepted more readily.

Most nurses realize that using derogatory, offensive, and discriminatory words to describe members of cultural groups will hinder the provision of culturally based care. However, a second form of giving offense which is sometimes not as apparent is stereotyping. To stereotype is to assign a trait or belief to all members of a group, rather than realizing that people are individuals and that cultural variabilities exist. Some of the stereotypical beliefs about African Americans is that they all eat watermelon and soul food, that all of the men play or favor basketball as a sport, that all live in dysfunctional families with no concern for their own or others' property, and that they all love gospel music. A striking example of stereotyping was given by one of the members of the Harlem Boys' Choir. He said that when the group travels many Anglo-

Americans ask the African American boys if they are a basketball team. The young man told his questioner that instead they are members of a choir that sings the works of many composers, including Mozart and Hayden. A cultural assessment by the transculturally oriented nurse regarding the individual and family that is mindful of the cultural beliefs, practices, and values can help prevent rigid stereotyping and increase awareness of cultural variability that prevails among African Americans.

While many nurses in the United States place high value on independence, technology, and legal factors in the society, African Americans view the family, religion, and economic factors as being more important. Nurses must realize this difference in worldview and use their transcultural nursing skills to meet the needs of their African American clients.

Summary

The purpose of this chapter was to discuss some of the cultural care, health, and illness beliefs, practices, and values that are found among African Americans in the United States. Because of the wide diversity of beliefs and practices in this population, nurses need to learn about the value and importance of using a culturological assessment when planning care for clients.

The cultural beliefs, values, and practices of African Americans are many and varied. The dominant cultural values are the extended family, religious beliefs, and education. Care beliefs and practices include concern for, involvement with, presence with, nurturing of, touching of, and sharing with other people, particularly those in the extended family, in the African American community, and the church. Transcultural nurses are prepared to incorporate these caring values, beliefs, and practices into professional nursing care with the generic folk care practices and beliefs. Transcultural nurse specialists can be helpful in guiding other nurses into this important way of caring for African Americans.

This chapter demonstrated the discovery of care values and practices through the use of the theory of Culture Care Diversity and Universality. Discovery of the care, health, and illness beliefs embedded within the social structures, worldview, language, and cultural context of African Americans provides a sound and reliable base to know and understand this culture. Several modes of intervention can be used such as culture care maintenance/preservation, accommodation/negotiation, and repatterning/restructuring. These modes are used to plan and give culturally specific congruent care. This is the goal of Leininger's theory and the goal of transcultural nurses in order that African American clients can receive quality care that helps them recover from illness and maintain their caring lifeways in society.

References

1. Leininger, M. ed., *Culture Care Diversity and Universality: A Theory of Nursing.* New York: National League for Nursing, 1991.

2. Osborne, O. H., "Aging and the Black Diaspora: The African, Caribbean, and African American Experience," M. Leininger ed., *Transcultural Nursing: Concepts, Theories, and Practices,* New York: John Wiley & Sons, 1978, pp. 317–333.

3. Sherlock, P. W., *West Indies,* London: Thames and Hudson, 1966.

4. Snow, L. F., "Popular Medicine in a Black Neighborhood," E. Spicer ed., *Ethnic Medicine in the Southwest,* Tucson: University of Arizona Press, 1977, pp. 19–95.

5. Glazer, N. and D. P. Moynihan, *Beyond the Melting Pot,* 2nd ed. Cambridge: M.I.T. Press, 1970.

6. Mazrui, A. A., *The Africans: A Triple Heritage,* Boston: Little, Brown and Co., 1986.

7. Bloch, B., "Nursing Care of Black Patients," M. S. Orque, B. Bloch and L. S. A. Monroy eds., *Ethnic Nursing Care: A Multicultural Approach,* St. Louis: C.V. Mosby, 1983, pp. 82–109.

8. U.S. Department of Commerce, Bureau of the Census, Statistical Abstract of the United States, 1991, *The National Data Book,* 11th ed. Washington, D.C.

9. Stack, C., *All Our Kin: Strategies for Survival in a Black Community,* New York: Harper and Row, 1974.

10. Billingsley, A., *Black Families and the Struggle for Survival,* New York: Friendship Press, 1974.

11. Leininger, M., "Southern Rural Afro American and White American Folkways with Focus on Care and Health Phenomena," M. Leininger ed., *Care: The Essence of Nursing and Health,* Detroit: Wayne State University Press, 1989, pp. 133–159.

12. Milio, N., *2226 Kercheval: The Storefront That Did Not Burn,* Ann Arbor: University of Michigan Press, 1971.

13. Ashenbrenner, J., *Lifelines: Black Families in Chicago,* Prospect Heights, Il.: Waveland Press, 1975.

14. Stack, op. cit.

15. McAdoo, H. P., "Black Kinships," *Psychology Today,* v. 12, pp. 67–79.

16. Ashenbrenner, op. cit.

17. Herkovitz, M., *The Myth of the Negro Past,* Boston: Beacon Press, 1958.

18. Glazer and Moynihan, op. cit.

19. Nobles, W. W. and Nobles, G. M., "African Roots in Black Families: The Social Psychological Dynamics of Black Family Life and the Implications for Nursing Care," *Black Awareness: Implications for Black Patient Care,* D. Luckraft ed., New York: American Journal of Nursing Co., 1976, pp. 6–11.

20. Martin, E. P. and Martin, J. M., *The Black Extended Family*, Chicago: The University of Chicago Press, 1978.

21. Ashenbrenner, op. cit.

22. Bloch, op. cit.

23. Thomas, D. N., "Black American Patient Care," *Transcultural Health Care*, G. Henderson and M. Primeaux eds., Menlo Park, California: Addison-Wesley Publishing Co., 1981, pp. 209–223.

24. Bloch, op. cit.

25. Thomas, op. cit.

26. Ibid.

27. M. N. Wicks, personal communication, July, 1990.

28. Leininger, op. cit., 1989.

29. Roberson, M. H. B., "The Influence of Religious Beliefs on Health Choices of Afro-Americans," *Topics in Clinical Nursing*, 1975, v. 3, pp. 57–63.

30. Williams, M.D., *Community in a Black Pentecostal Church*, Prospect Heights, Il.: Waveland Press, 1974.

31. Sidell, R., *Women and Children Last: The Plight of Poor Women in Affluent America*, New York: Viking, 1986.

32. Williams, op. cit.

33. Bloch, op. cit.

34. Williams, op. cit.

35. Bloch, op. cit.

36. Sidell, op. cit.

37. Ibid.

38. Ibid.

39. Ibid.

40. Funkhouser, S. W. and D. K. Moser, "Is Health Care Racist?" *Advances in Nursing Science*, v. 12, 1990, pp. 47–55.

41. Martin, M. E. and M. Henry, "Cultural Relativity and Poverty," *Public Health Nursing*, v. 6, 1989, pp. 28–32.

42. Snow, L., "Folk Medical Beliefs and their Implications for the Care of Patients," *Transcultural Health* Care, G. Henderson and M. Primeaux eds., Menlo Park, California: Addison-Wesley Publishing Co., 1981.

43. Sidell, op. cit.

44. Bailey, E. J., "Sociocultural Factors and Health Care—Seeking Behavior among Black Americans," *Journal of the National Medical Association*, v. 79, 1987, pp. 389–392.

45. Flaskerud, J. M. and C. E. Rush, "AIDS and Traditional Health Beliefs and Practices of Black Women," *Nursing Research*, v. 38, 1989, pp. 210–214.
46. Sidell, op. cit.
47. Bailey, op. cit.
48. Flaskerud, op. cit.
49. Bloch, op. cit.
50. Glazer and Moynihan, op. cit.
51. Thomas, op. cit.
52. Bailey, op. cit.
53. Ibid.
54. Capers, C. F., "Nursing and the Afro-American Client," *Topics in Clinical Nursing*, 1985, v. 7, no. 3, pp. 11–17.
55. Leininger, op. cit., 1989.
56. Snow, op. cit., 1977.
57. Bloch, op. cit.
58. Snow, op. cit., 1977.
59. Bloch, op. cit.
60. Wicks, op. cit.
61. Snow, op. cit., 1977.
62. Bloch, op. cit.
63. Snow, op. cit., 1981.
64. Ibid.
65. Bloch, op. cit.
66. Smitherman, G., *Talking and Testifying: The Language of Black America*, Detroit: Wayne State University Press, 1977.
67. Ibid.
68. Ibid.
69. Ibid.
70. Bloch, op. cit.
71. Snow, op. cit., 1981.
72. Bloch, op. cit.
73. Stack, op. cit.
74. Billingsley, op. cit.
75. Leininger, op. cit., 1989.
76. Milio, op. cit.
77. Ashenbrenner, op. cit.
78. Leininger, op. cit., 1989.
79. Ibid.

80. Stack, op. cit.
81. Ashenbrenner, op. cit.
82. Osborne, op. cit.
83. Flaherty, M. J., "Seven Caring Functions of Black Grandmothers in Adolescent Mother," *Maternal-Child-Nursing Journal*, v. 17, 1988, pp. 191–207.
84. Ibid.

Chapter 18
Culture Care Theory and Elderly Polish Americans

Marilyn McFarland, PhD, CTN, RN

Transcultural nursing research remains essential for nurses to advance knowledge of the elderly from diverse cultural backgrounds. Since the elderly will continually be a major subculture in the world in need of nursing care today and in the future, transcultural nursing research of the elderly remains crucial for quality care services. Understanding elders from their cultural background remains essentially a new area of study and practice for professional nurses.

This study examined care and health perspectives of elderly Polish Americans and how this knowledge can improve health care practices. Nurses who are knowledgeable about culture care and its influence on improving health will be able to see the benefits of providing culturally congruent care to the elderly. This study was based on Leininger's theory of Culture Care Diversity and Universality with use of her Sunrise conceptual Model.[1, 2] Several research questions guided this transcultural care study:

1. In what ways do the factors related to the social structure and worldview in Leininger's theory influence the care and health patterns of elderly Polish Americans?
2. What specific cultural care values, beliefs, and practices influence Polish American elderly health?
3. What Polish American care practices and expressions appear to be most congruent with healthy and beneficial lifeways for the elderly of this cultural group?
4. What nursing care implications can be identified from the ethnonursing data to provide culturally congruent care for the Polish American elderly?

Research Method

Informants

Data were gathered from extensive observations and in-depth interviews with three key and five general Polish American informants by the investigator along with an extensive literature study about Polish Americans. This study was an ethnonursing qualitative investigation using Leininger's method and enabling guides. The qualitative naturalistic inquiry method was chosen because of the absence of in-depth emic data about Polish American elderly. It was an appropriate way to enter the unknown world of this culture. They key and general informants ranged in age from 58 to 84 years old, and seven of the eight lived in a Polish neighborhood in a northern city in mid-Michigan which has a population of approximately 43,000 persons.[3] The data were collected by the investigator over a two-year period with three to four interviews and observation-participation-reflection times with the key informants. As data were collected, the focus was on theoretical premises, especially studying the worldview, kinship, and social, cultural, political, technological, economic, religious, and educational factors that seemed to influence the care and health of elderly Polish Americans. In addition, the generic and professional systems were studied.

Data Analysis and Evaluation Criteria

The data were analyzed in this study by using Leininger's four phases of data analysis.[4] The analysis began with collecting and documenting the raw data (first phase), then identifying descriptors (second phase), and discovering patterns (third phase), and ended with abstracting major themes (fourth phase). The Leininger-Templin-Thompson (LTT) computer software was used for coding and classifying the data.[5] Data analysis was an on-going process throughout the study.

The following qualitative criteria were used for analysis of the data: credibility, confirmability, meaning-in-context, recurrent patterning, saturation and redundancy, and transferability.[6] Credibility referred to the believability of the study findings established by the researcher through repeated engagements over a three month period with the informants. Confirmability was achieved by repeated accounts from the informants and by mutual agreement of the findings by the researcher and the informants. Meaning-in-context referred to the lifeways of elderly Polish Americans that reflected a tendency to recur in patterned ways. Saturation referred to evidence of having taken in all that could be known about the phenomena under study. Redundancy was related to saturation and referred to the tendency to get similar and repeated data. Transferability referred to whether the findings might have similar meanings in a similar context, but generalizability was not the goal of this qualitative study.

Orientational Definitions

Since the orientational definitions help the researcher to discover meanings from the informants, the following definitions were used:

1. Culture Care: Those supportive or facilitative acts specific to the Polish American culture which assist elders to improve their health and lifeways.[7]
2. Cultural Health: A state of well-being which is culturally defined and includes the ability to perform daily role activities.[8]
3. Polish American: Refers to any individual whose parents or grandparents were born in Poland and immigrated to the United States and who identifies himself/herself as a Polish American.
4. Culturally Congruent (nursing) Care: Refers to those cognitively based assistive, supportive, facilitative, or enabling acts or decisions that are made to fit with the cultural values, beliefs, and lifeways of elderly Polish Americans in order to provide or support meaningful, beneficial, and satisfying health care or well-being services.[9]
5. Emic: Refers to people's views expressed in their own words and actions.[10]
6. Etic: Refers to the outsider's or researcher's views.[11]

Theoretical Framework

This study was conceptualized within Leininger's theory of Culture Care Diversity and Universality.[12, 13] Leininger views care as a universal phenomenon but with some predicted diverse expressions, meanings, and patterns of care in different cultures. She contends that these care expressions, patterns, and meanings may take on different meanings in different contexts. The theory of Culture Care Diversity and Universality has been important to establish nursing knowledge about what is similar (more universal) and different (more diverse) about care within and among cultures. Leininger also predicts in her theory that professional nursing care combined with generic (folk) care would provide care that would be congruent with a particular culture's beliefs, values, and practices. It would lead to maintaining healthy lifeways for people. The goal of her theory is to provide culturally congruent care to clients of diverse cultures that would contribute to their health and well-being.[14, 15] For the elderly, this goal would be especially important to maintain their health. The care which is culturally congruent would also be predicted to be satisfying, meaningful, and beneficial to them.

The Leininger Sunrise conceptual Model was developed to depict various aspects of the worldview and social structure dimensions of a culture which influence care and ultimately the health status of people through the contexts of language, ethnohistory, and environment. The Sunrise Model serves as a cognitive map to guide the researcher in studying the theory in relation to these factors: technological, religious, kinship, and social factors, cultural values and lifeways, and political and legal factors.[16, 17] According to the theory these factors, as well as ethnohistory and environment, influence care patterns and expressions and, in turn, the health and well-being of individuals and groups. The theory is holistic and helps the researcher examine multiple factors infringing on the health and well-being of elderly Polish Americans in relation to human care. This broad theoretical view of the Polish American elderly's lifeways provided a comprehensive and holistic means to understand their total nursing care needs. Most importantly, if care of Polish American elderly is known from their emic point of view, professional nursing care (largely etic) could be predicted to be more congruent with their health and well-being.

Since the theory contributes to the transcultural nursing field, which focuses on comparative studies of cultures and their care patterns, values, and practices, knowledge of the Polish American elderly should contribute to transcultural nursing knowledge. Although this study explored care of the elderly in depth in one cultural group, transferability of the findings from this study with full cognizance of similar context might provide new and different transcultural gerontological knowledge.

Leininger's Culture Care theory rests on several premises which were used in this study and which focus on describing, explaining, predicting, and interpreting nursing phenomena from the people's emic perspective and contrasting data from the etic view. The following premises were used to guide this study.[18]

1. Culturally specific care is essential for elderly Polish Americans for their health, healing, growth, and survival.
2. The Polish American culture has generic (folk) care knowledge and practices that influence professional culture-care practices.
3. Polish American care values, beliefs, and practices are influenced by and embedded in the worldview; language; religious, kinship, political, educational, economic, and technological factors; cultural values; ethnohistory; and environmental context of Polish Americans.
4. Culture care meanings and patterns that influence the health and well being of Polish American elders can be used by nurses with Leininger's three modes to provide culturally congruent professional nursing care.

Ethnohistory, Worldview, Language and Environmental Context of Elderly Polish Americans

To help understand the Polish American elderly of today, an overview of their history and culture is first presented. The history of the culture provides background information to understand people in their past and present environmental contexts. It also gives clues to human care and health.

Two and one half million immigrants came to the United States from Poland during the late nineteenth and early twentieth centuries; and by 1972, between 5.1 and 6 million Americans claimed a Polish heritage.[19] According to the 1980 United States Census, over 8 million people claimed Polish American ancestry and the Polish people made up the eighth largest cultural group in the United States.[20] Most Polish immigrants who came to the United States during the late nineteenth and early twentieth centuries were village peasants, and they came to America primarily for economic and political reasons.[21] In 1600 Poland was the largest country in Europe, but in 1795 Poland was partitioned by the neighboring countries of Russia, Prussia, and Austria and ceased to exist politically. Austria, Russia, and Germany had little regard for the economic welfare of the Polish people under their rule.[22] By the late 1800s there was political discontent and great economic hardship in the three sectors of Poland, and many Polish people decided to emigrate.[23, 24, 25] All informants in this study were second- or third-generation Polish Americans whose parents or grandparents had come to the United States during the late nineteenth and early twentieth centuries.

One key informant, a third-generation Polish American woman, explained the hardships in Poland in the late 1800s and early 1900s:

> *My grandmother told me how the Poles suffered under Germany; the people had to use German exclusively in the schools and in the churches. They could practice Catholicism but not in Polish. There were strikes because the Polish people were forced to use German in the schools. The Russian sector was even worse, Poles were not educated at all, not even to read and write. In Austrian Poland life was very poor, as it was in all the sectors, but the Austrians were not so oppressive.*

A general informant, a sixty-five-year-old woman, reflected on the reasons her family came to the United States:

> *In 1880, my grandmother and grandfather and their four children left Poland because things were bad — not enough food and they were poor. My grandmother told me how here mother held on to the wagon as they left and cried for them not to go. She knew she would never see them again. It had to be really bad there to leave your families and know you would never be back.*

Polish immigrants often migrated into Michigan after brief stopovers in other states. Many came to Detroit, Grand Rapids and then smaller cities farther north where they found work as laborers. Even though most Polish people were originally farmers, they eventually sought factory work because it offered year-round employment.[26] A local Polish American priest, Bishop Povish, wrote, "The first occupation of the Poles (in this city) was in the sugar beet fields, then they went into the sawmills, the manufacturing of lumber products, and finally into the factories of the modern industries."[27]

A second-generation, sixty-four-year-old Polish American male general informant who was a retired electrician told the story of how his family eventually settled in the city and made their living:

> *My mother and father were born in Poland and came to the United States in the 1880s. My dad was sixteen when he came here with his parents...first to Chicago, where there was work in the steel mills, and then to this city. He met my mother in Chicago, married her there, and then they came (here) to do farm work in the sugar beet fields. Eventually he went to a factory. Dad was a sheep herder in Poland, but here the factory work in the foundry paid better than farm work.*

Polish immigrants typically settled in Polish neighborhoods that insulated new arrivals against the cultural shock of immigration. When the Polish arrived in this mid-Michigan city, they chose to live close to a large Polish American church built in 1874 on the southern edge of the city. One sixty-four-year-old female general informant commented on the Polish neighborhood which is still located around the parish church:

> *Well, everyone says the Polish neighborhood starts south of Columbus Avenue, but I really think it is pure Polish south of Seventeenth Street. We were on the edge of the city, so everyone in the neighborhood could have a garden and a cow. Most Poles who came here were farmers, so even though they worked in the factories, we did some farming, right here in the city. In the neighborhood we stayed close and lived close. All my aunts and uncles lived either across the street or around the corner.*

The fifty-one-year-old daughter of an eighty-four-year-old female general informant commented on the current Polish neighborhood:

> *A lot of Polish people still live in the neighborhood...our church, St. Stan's, has a lot to do with it. The church here is part of the Polish families. We attend St. Stan's and most people in this neighborhood do. My husband and I stayed in this neighborhood so our kids could go to the parochial school. This is why a lot of young families have stayed.*

Many people who live in this neighborhood still identify themselves as Polish Americans. According to the 1980 United States Census, of approximately 43,000 people who live within the city limits, 10,000 claimed Polish ancestry; 6,300 of these Polish Americans live in the traditionally Polish neighborhood within the city limits.[28]

Worldview includes the way people look outward toward others and their world to form a picture about their perspective life.[29] Bukowczyk explained that even though Polish Americans had made economic and political progress by the end of World War II, they tended to think in the passive voice the world acted upon them.[30] Their worldview was fatalistic and focused inward on their family, home and Polish American neighborhood and parish. The elderly Polish Americans in this study have broadened their worldview in recent years and have looked outward from the Polish American nieghborhood to the rest of the Untied States, Poland, and the world. More recently they have viewed themselves as a vital part of the larger world, and they are proud of their Polish American heritage.

Through the 1950s, parish schools taught the Polish language and Polish history. The parish school preserved the Polish language, encouraged students to acquire the cultural traditions of their parents, and developed familiarity with Polish history.[31] Although Polish is no longer taught in parish schools, Polish Studies programs in colleges and universities provide courses in the Polish language and history.[32] All elderly informants in this study spoke at least some conversational Polish and remembered when it became un-American to speak Polish. However, informants have expressed a new pride in the Polish language and in their ability to speak and read the language.

Review of the Literature on Polish Americans

A review of the literature on Polish Americans revealed several historical and ethnographic studies of this culture. There have also been several nursing studies published about this cultural group. The studies confirm that Polish Americans value their culture, traditions, and the Polish language, and are devoted to their Polish families, neighborhoods, and parishes.

There have been several historical studies of Polish Americans. In 1927 Thomas and Znaniecki conducted a sociological and historical study of the migration of the Polish people to the United States and the Polish immigrant experiences in the Polish American parishes of the early 1880s.[33] These authors described the Polish parish as much more than a religious association for worship under the leadership of a priest. They stated:

> *If [the parish] become the social organ of the community...it...assumes the*
> *care...of the group by organizing balls, picnics, and arranges religious services...It*
> *is the center of information for newcomers and acts as a representative of the Polish*
> *American community with other American institutions which try to ready the Polish*
> *community for political or social purposes.*[34]

Wytrwal compiled a social history of the Polish people in America. He focused on the economic and political factors in Poland and in the United States that influenced the Polish people to migrate. In the 1880s and early 1900s young Polish men were subjected to conscription into the armies of the three partitioning powers, and peasants were being forced off their land. At the same time, there were jobs available in American industry and the Polish people believed they could earn more money and make a better living in America.

Bukowczyk, after a dozen years of historical research, wrote a book about the Polish experiences in America.[36] He described Polish immigrants as rural people with customs and values oriented toward stability, family, security, and home. He reported that they were Roman Catholics and were fatalistic, prayerful, hopeful for a better afterlife, and they venerated the Virgin Mary, Poland's patroness. They lived in child-centered families and prized steady factory work, saved their money, and gave generously to their nuns, priests, and parishes. They valued a home of their own, their church, and children who would take care of them in their old age. Bukowczyk claimed that second-generation Polish Americans (those Polish Americans who were the first in their families to be born in the United States) were hard to describe as their culture had Polish and American elements. The third and fourth generations, he asserted, were the most difficult to describe. He stated, "Culturally, little about these young men and women was identifiable as Polish or Polish American."[37]

Researchers have recently conducted ethnographies of Polish Americans in various regions of the United States. Obedinski conducted an ethnographic study of Polish Americans in Buffalo, New York, and reported that Polish Americans were increasingly adopting an American style of life while retaining traditional family and religious practices.[38] Wrobel conducted an ethnographic study of Polish Americans in Detroit which focused on day to day life in a Polish American community.[39] He discovered a Polish American culture as a way of life that was distinct from both Polish and American cultures. He found the parish, family and neighborhood still paid a significant role in the lives of urban Polish Americans, fulfilling a variety of religious and social needs.

There have been several nursing studies on the care of Polish Americans. Rempusheski, in her ethnographic study of elderly retired Polish Americans in Arizona, found several care expressions related to traditional Polish American cultural values.[40] Ways to express caring described in her study were: 1) stopping by/visiting, 2) inquiring, 3) giving/bringing, [40] worrying/concern, 5) consoling, 6) cheering up, 7) listening, 8) remembering someone, 9) missing someone, 10) sharing joy, 11) sharing sickness, 12) thinking about someone, 13) advising/teaching, 14) praying for someone.[41] She found that although these elders had left their homes and retired to Arizona, they recreated the atmosphere of their Polish American neighborhood by forming and joining an Arizona Polish club where they socialized, reminisced, danced the polka, and celebrated Polish holidays.

It is important for nursing to identify the values of a culture, especially those values related to care and health. Leininger summarized the Polish American cultural values and care meanings from several transcultural nursing studies with Midwestern Polish Americans over the past decade.[42] The dominant emic cultural values identified were: 1) upholding Christian beliefs and practices, 2) family and cultural solidarity (other care), 3) frugality, 4) political activity, 5) hard work, 6) persistence, maintaining religious/special days, and 7) valuing fold practices. The culture care meanings identified were: 1) giving to others, 2) self-sacrificing, 3) being concerned about others, 4) working hard, 5) love of others, 6) family concern, 7) community solidarity, 8) health values of eating Polish foods, and 9) folk care practices.[43] In a videotape presentation of a culturological assessment of a third-generation Polish American informant, Stasiak and Leininger demonstrated that many traditional Polish American care values, meanings, and practices have remained a part of Polish American lifeways.[44] The videotape based on Stasiak's Polish intergenerational life history and nursing care of Polish Americans revealed the dominant emic care constructs of three generations of: 1) concern for and giving to others, 2) solidarity of the family or staying close, 3) helping others in need, 4) hard work and sacrifice, 5) eating natural foods, 6) folk care practices, and 7) prayer derived from the Polish American kinship, religious, and cultural beliefs and values. Stasiak's research supported Leininger's research findings with transferability evidence.

The author noted that many findings from the previous studies just reviewed still held true and were confirmed by second and third-generation Polish American informants in her study. Elderly Polish American informants continued to be devoted to their families, neighborhoods, and parishes and to express care in culturally congruent ways. During the data collection period, Poland was freed from Soviet domination, and all eight elderly Polish American informants expressed a renewed pride in Poland and in their Polish culture and a deep concern for the welfare of the Polish people.

Findings as Themes

The data resulted in the formulation of patterns and themes about the care and health of elderly Polish Americans. These themes reflected the findings that addressed the research questions, as well as other findings about Polish American lifeways related to their care and health mainly derived from observation and participation and reflection experiences and interviews with key and general informants. These discovered research themes are important to guide nurses in providing culturally congruent nursing care practices. Qualitative verbatim statements are presented to help the reader grasp the full world view and emic perspective of the informants.

Theme 1

Care was expressed by elderly Polish Americans by *observing Polish customs, searching for their Polish roots, and in the efforts made to use and preserve the Polish language.* These care expressions were derived from the informants' cultural beliefs, religious values, and old view, and were viewed as vital to the survival and well-being of their culture and the Polish American identity. The Polish informants feared that the loss of their customs and language would be detrimental to the health and well-being of themselves and their families. The practice of Polish customs and the celebration of religious holidays were valued by elderly Polish Americans and were often celebrated and sustained within the family and the church. A third-generation sixty-year-old female key informant spoke of the importance of religious holidays:

> *The Friends of Polish Culture is our local group of Polish Americans. We just celebrated our harvest festival,* dozynski. *We have another big celebration at Easter,* swienconka *(blessing of the Easter food). At Christmas we have a Christmas Eve dinner,* wigilia *(Vigil).*

One informant described the Christmas Eve dinner:

> *All of my kids will be home for Christmas. I will buy a large wafer about six inches wide, the* oplatek *[representing the sacred host], from the nuns. On Christmas Eve I will break off a piece and pass it to my oldest child; then she will pass it to the next one...It is an old Polish custom and a lot of Polish people here still do this. When the wafer is passed, you wish them good health.*

Elderly Polish American informants in this study expressed care for their families by planning and participating in traditional religious celebrations that included the practice of Polish customs. Elders believed that the practice of these customs and the celebration of religious holidays contributed to the health and well-being of family members and was essential to the survival of their lifeways and culture.

The search for one's history or roots has become a preoccupation for many Polish Americans. Six of the eight informants in this study have traveled to their European Polish homeland within the last ten years to find their relatives. These Polish American informants were raised in a close, tightly knit Polish American neighborhood where they spent most of their earlier lives focused upon their families, churches, parish schools, and making a living in local factories. One second-generation sixty-year-old Polish American female key informant explained to me, "When we were growing up, a lot of us never traveled as far as the next town [eight miles away], and if we did, it was a big deal." World view includes the way people look outward toward others and their world to form a picture about their perspective of life.[45] The elderly Polish Americans in this study have broadened their world view in recent decades and looked outward from their Polish American neighborhood to the rest of the United States, Poland, and the world. Elderly Polish Americans viewed themselves as a vital part of the larger world, and they were proud of their Polish American heritage. One second-generation sixty four-year-old male general informant said with pride, "Most people on this street have Polish names. I wouldn't change my name. I'm proud of being Polish American and proud of Poland." Local second- and third-generation Polish Americans were interested in political events in Poland and were interested in the welfare of the Polish people. One informant read from the local newspaper, "The mayor declared November 12, 1989

Polzan University Day." She explained that Polzan is the city's sister city in Poland. She described her family's interest in political events in Europe and in Poland:

> *I want you to know how very proud we are in this house...we are so proud of what has taken place in Germany...it is a direct result of what took place in Poland with Solidarity...Walesa addressed the United States Congress today...and met the President.*

Polish Americans were interested in the politics of Poland because it influenced the health and well-being of the Polish people. My informant explained, "We have a deep underlying interest in the welfare of the people in Poland...as my husband says, "All Poles are cousins."

The metaphor of the American melting pot idea had been firmly rejected by all informants of this study. They knew who they were and they were proud of being Polish Americans. They believed they had a unique contribution to make to their country and were not melting into a non-identifiable culture. They were also interested in and appreciative of the uniqueness of the culture of others as well. This broad world view was a reflection of their view of themselves and the way they saw others. One sixty-four-year-old third-generation female key informant explained:

> *I attended a multi-ethnic religious service at the park last summer. One of the priests talked about the melting pot theory. I was mad. I told him to look at the contributions of various people...I said look at the stained glass window in a church, look at the beauty, the color, and the shape of each piece of glass. They all have something to add to the whole.*

This informant valued her own cultural identity but valued the diversity in other cultures as well. This broad world view was reflected in the data from all eight informants and influenced the concern they expressed for the survival of diverse cultures. They recognized that the survival of all cultures, as well as their own, was essential to the health and well-being of all people.

Bigelow, a geographer who has studied ethnic subcultures in the United States, reported that the third and fourth generations of Polish Americans have intermarried with other Catholic nationalities.[46] He maintained that this has been detrimental to the maintenance of Polish-Catholic ethnicity. All the informants in this study reported that some of their children had not married Polish people, and they expressed concern that this has caused them to worry about the survival of Polish customs and the Polish language in their families. One third-generation sixty-three-year-old key informant explained that she had married a Polish man and that helped her maintain Polish ways:

> *I'm Polish and married a Polish guy...that has helped us preserve our Polish customs. We belong to the local Polish cultural group. I have no children but my sister has three kids, but they have not married Polish...they haven't even married*

Catholics. We both wonder who we are going to pass all this on to...all the Polish recipes, the customs, and the things we share as a family at Christmas and Easter.

Elderly Polish Americans were very attached to their language. Most second- and third-generation Polish Americans in this study learned to speak and read some Polish in parochial schools. Polish was spoken fluently by two key and two general informants with the remaining four informants speaking some limited conversational Polish. Some informants remembered when the nuns stopped teaching Polish. A third-generation sixty-four-year-old female key informant explained her experience in learning Polish, and the relationship of her knowledge of Polish to the care practice of helping others:

I learned Polish in grades one through four; then it was considered un-American to speak Polish so the nuns stopped teaching it...we are rethinking that now...twenty five years after high school I went to the local college and took several semesters to relearn Polish. I translate letters now back and forth for people who have relatives in Poland, so they can keep in touch; it is my contribution and I take no money.

She viewed this care practice as being beneficial to the health and well-being of Polish families, as well as essential to the survival of the Polish American culture.

The Polish language and Polish history and culture were no longer the focus in local parochial schools in this study. However, local Polish Americans have worked hard since 1972 to establish a Polish studies program at the local college. The view of Polish life historically presented in parochial schools in Polish neighborhoods was presented in a broader way in the local university. It included not only the Polish language and the views of Poland's past but also included views of life and cultural events in present-day Poland.

This new educational focus was reflected in the views of care and health and well-being expressed by elderly Polish American informants. Polish American elders have been maintaining the traditions of caring for and being concerned about the health and well-being of immediate family members, but they have extended their care and concern for the health and well-being of family members to Polish relatives, to the people of Poland, and to people from other cultures as well. The elderly informants viewed efforts to preserve the Polish language and traditions as essential caring practices to insure the survival of their cultural lifeways.

Theme 2

Care expressed and made meaningful by *visiting relatives in Poland, arranging for Polish relatives to visit in the United States, and by sending money, food, and medicine to them.* This theme was mainly derived from kinship and social values and practices. One eighty-four-year-old general informant related that even as late as the 1940s, her family was attempting to arrange immigration of their Polish kin to the United States:

> *My husband tried to get his cousin's family to come here right before W.W.II.*
> *I remember being told that we would have to share our home because these realities*
> *were coming from Poland...it was bad there...no meat, coffee, or soap,...but then*
> *the war came and after it was over, no one could get out.*

Today elderly Polish Americans express care for Polish relatives by visiting them in Poland and arranging for their relatives to visit in the United States. The same informant explained, "I kept writing to my husband's cousin and his wife...eventually we sent them money to come for a visit." A sixty-four-year-old general informant reported, "My sister traced my dad's relatives...she found my dad's brother in Poland about eighteen to twenty years ago. I have been back three time and my wife once." The care practice of visiting relatives in Poland and arranging visits of Polish relatives to the United States enhances the health and well-being of the Polish people and Polish Americans. One second-generation sixty-four-year-old general informant explained, "I found my older brother who had stayed behind in Poland after my mother and father came to the United States. The whole family was so glad I found him. I was glad we met each other before he died."

Polish American elder also expressed care by sending money and material items to relatives in Poland, many of whom they have never met. One informant explained the transfer of goods and money to Poland:

> *I have taken thousands of dollars to Poland. When people give me money to take*
> *to Poland, it means people really trust you. We have things worked out when we take*
> *money over; I have a picture of the person I am to give it to and that person has a picture*
> *of me. A lot of relatives send medicines to Poland...I sent cortisone ointment to my*
> *cousin. At Christmas time, I ship lemons, oranges and bananas. Two days a week we*
> *can drop off packages at an office in town here and they are shipped to Poland.*

The care that was expressed by Polish Americans through the transfer of food, medicines and money to Poland was done to enhance the health and well-being of their Polish relatives. One third-generation sixty-four-old female informant explained:

> *My cousin in Poland had horrible sores around her mouth. Even though*
> *health care is free in Poland, there is no medicine. After my cousin got the cortisone,*
> *her sores cleared up. She told me she was able to resume a healthy life.*

In this study, "giving to others" was an important care meaning and was practiced by Polish American elders. They have extended this care beyond their immediate families to relatives in Poland and even to the Polish people. Many elders raised and donated money for Polish relief. Some members of the Polish American community have acted as couriers to take American dollars to Poland. Second- and third-generation Polish American elders have extended the traditional care practice of giving to immediate family members to giving in relatives and others in Poland in order to improve the health and lifeways of Polish people.

Theme 3

Care meant spending time with, being there, doing for and reciprocating care with children, grandchildren, and other family members. This theme was derived from their cultural and kinship values, beliefs, and practices. Elderly Polish Americans still prize the home, family, stability, and security over the desire to make money or acquire material things. This was expressed by one third-generations sixty-three-year-old female key informant who worked part-time cleaning offices:

> *I think people [young Polish Americans] are too eager for money now. Polish people were poor when they came here and they still aren't rich. There are more important things than money. We [she and her sister] married poor when they worked hard...women didn't work in the past; we were home to care for our kids...it was important to be home when your kids came home from school. Today, kids are too eager for money...they think it is necessary for both a husband and wife to work...but a lot of what they buy isn't necessary. The care practices of spending time with or being there for their children and other family members were more important then than expressing care for one's family by making a great deal of money to buy material things. The elderly informants believed that caring in this manner was beneficial to the health of children and adults.*

Elderly Polish Americans relied on their families for care in the past and continue to do so today. One elderly informant explained how Polish families cared for each other in the Polish neighborhood when she was growing up. She explained:

> *In the neighborhood, we stayed close and lived close. All my aunts lived either across the street or around the corner. If someone had a baby, then someone just had to come across the street to help...if someone was sick it worked the same way.*

Two third-generation key informants who are sisters (fifty-eight and sixty-three years old) explained how Polish American families have continued to care for family members:

> *I care for my sister and she cares for me. We do a lot of things for each other. We both have sick husbands so we depend on each other...We care for our husbands...Polish American wives care for their husbands...a nursing home would be only if things were really bad. Husbands also would care for their wives if necessary.*

The seven informants (two key and five general) who had children all believed that their children would care for them if they became ill. When nursing home care was discussed, it was acknowledged as a possibility but only as a last resort. Polish American families continued the practice of taking care of elderly family members when they became ill. Polish American elders were confident that family members would be available to give care if their health was threatened or if they became disabled.

Nursing home placement of Polish American elderly family members had not been a traditional care practice in the past, and elderly Polish Americans viewed it as a care practice that would only be used if a family member was very disabled and could not be cared for in their own home or the homes of their children. The confidence elderly Polish Americans felt in the readiness of their families to give care made them feel secure, and they viewed this feeling of security as an essential part of their health.

Theme 4

Polish American *involvement in politics has allowed Polish Americans to care for elderly family members and other Polish elders in the community.* Political factors in the local city government have influenced the lives of second- and third-generation Polish Americans. A daughter of a second generation eighty-one-year- old female general informant commented, "In my mother's day, most people [Polish] were Democrats...but now they vote for the best candidate...but if all other things were equal between candidates, I'd vote for the Polish American."

Many Polish Americans have moved into political careers. A local historian stated, "Qualified Americans of Polish ancestry have held major posts in local government, including those of mayor, city manager, county executive, school superintendent, county treasurer and several city and county commissionerships."[47] Polish Americans who have held political posts in city government have been able to care for elders by arranging funding for a senior meal site at the local Polish parish. This site served a noon meal five days a week for senior citizens in the local Polish neighborhood an provided a place for elders to gather for social activities. The daughter of one elderly informant explained that senior meals and activities at the local parish kept elders active and got them out of their houses which she believed enhanced their health and well being.

Theme 5

Health for elderly Polish Americans meant being comfortable and secure, working hard, keeping active, and eating the right foods. These beliefs and practices were related to their cultural values. All eight informants viewed themselves as being in good health even though most were taking medication for chronic diseases such as heart disease, diabetes and arthritis. Good health meant being active rather than being free of disease. One second-generation informant explained, "I'm very healthy, I'm sixty-four and all I have is a little high blood pressure." His wife commented, "Good health is being mobile and having a clear mind." A third-generation sixty-four-year-old female key informant commented, "My health is pretty good. I take insulin for diabetes. I had back surgery a few years ago. I'm really stiff today...but I was out dancing last night...I didn't sit out a single dance."

According to Leininger, theoretical definitions of orientation are used in qualitative research rather than operations definitions and"...orientational definitions seek emic knowledge derived from the people and environmental contexts as the epistemological and ontological sources of cultural care knowledge."[48] Orientational definitions may be altered to fit the informants' frames of reference as a study progresses. The informants in this study *defined health as feeling well, being secure and comfortable, having a clear mind and being gable to do their daily activities.* This definition is consistent with Leininger's theoretical definition of health. Leininger stated, "Health refers to a state of well being that is culturally defined, valued and practiced and which reflects the ability of individuals (or groups) to perform their daily role activities in a culturally satisfactory way."[49] However, no informant used the term well-being when discussing health. On direct questioning about the term well-being several informants reported that they had heard the term mentioned but really could not define it. Health is an emic term that emerges from the data with a meaning that is culturally relevant to the informants, and well being is an etic term that the informants have heard mentioned by health professionals.

Elderly Polish Americans in this study identified links between their Polish traditions and lifeways and their views of health. The Polish American traditions of hard work, keeping busy, and keeping active were viewed by elderly informants as care practices to insure or maximize their health. One third-generation sixty-three-year-old female key informant explained:

> *Keeping busy is important to your health. It isn't good to think too much about your health or being sick. My husband has leukemia but we still go out. My sister's husband stays home and worries his heart, that isn't good.*

Another third-generation female key informant explained a similar view about keeping healthy, "To keep healthy I do housework and I walk. If I can, I park as far away from a store that I can so I will walk." One second-generation sixty-four-year-old general informant who was retired from his job that required physical exertion explained, "I keep healthy now by exercising and working out at the health club."

All Polish American elders in this study discussed food preparation and production in relationship to their health. Attention to the healthy preparation of foods was viewed as an important care practice both for themselves and for their families. There was concern expressed by several elders about the dangers of food additives and the associated negative implications for their health. One sixty-five-year-old general informant explained, Good food is important. Our folks and grandparents had huge gardens and raised chickens and ducks right here in town They didn't use all those chemicals and preservatives." A third-generation sixty-three-year-old general informant acknowledged that heredity played a role in her diabetic condition but viewed a good diet and good food as important to her health. She stated, "I have diabetes. I think it is hereditary, but diet is important. Good food is important. I buy all my chickens and ducks from a Polish woman who raises them herself. She doesn't give them any chemicals." A second-generation sixty-four-year-old male general informant explained, "I really think my good health is due to the foods we grew when we were kids. We had our own cow, grew our own vegetables. My mother canned all her own foods; everything was our own." His wife added, "Let's face it, everything we get now [food] has chemicals in it. We didn't use any chemical fertilizer like they do now." Eating foods that were organically grown and preserved without additives were care practices that elderly Polish Americans viewed as important in maintain their health and the health of their families. The preparation and eating of tradition foods such as *pierogi* (fried filled noodle), *paczki* (deep fried, filled doughnuts) and *kielbasa i kapusta* (sauerkraut with pork sausage) were still viewed as important care practices to insure the survival of their cultural lifeways. However, all informants recognized that these traditional Polish foods were no longer considered healthy because of the fats and large number of calories they contain. They have limited the preparation and eating of those foods to traditional holidays in order to protect their health.

All eight elderly informants had health insurance and reported that they could afford to utilize local physicians and the one local hospital. Only the oldest informant, and eighty-four-year-old widow, reported she had problems paying for her prescription medicines. She said, "I have Medicare and Blue Shield, I pay both myself. I have to spend eighty dollars a month on medication...my kids help me with money because I just have my social security." Her family demonstrated the traditional care practice of providing financial assistance for elderly relative in order to maintain their health.

Theme 6

Elderly Polish American expressed care for their families and neighbors through the organization, support, and participation in church activities. In this community a Catholic-Polish society was formed more than 100 years ago to establish a local parish. The first church was a wooden structure built by the first-generation Polish Americans.[50] It was dedicated in 1874, and the pastor of the Polish parish in 1974 told the story of how a handful of settlers formed the first church with"...faith, hard work, and cooperation extending over three generations."[51]

The local church has served this Polish community not only as a place of religious worship but also as a center for social activities and a place to practice Polish traditions. One third-generation sixty-three-year-old female key informant stated:

> *The church is the center of our Polish activities. I go to church every week with my husband. Every Wednesday during Lent we have Polish literature [readings], we sing Polish songs. We have two Polish priests...they both speak Polish...that is very important.*

The same informant described a meeting of the local Polish cultural group. Her comment demonstrated the use of the church as a site for social gatherings:

> *Our Polish culture group meets once a month. We start at 9:00 a.m. on a Sunday with a Polish mass. At noon we have* Paczki *(Polish doughnuts) and coffee. At night we meet at a hall...you should have been there last night...we danced until 2:00 a.m. We raised money for Polish relief...for the children or nuns or maybe to send some local college students to a Polish university. My sister and I wore our Polish costumes.*

A third-generation sixty-one-year-old key informant descried her support and affection for the parish even though her family has moved out of the old neighborhood:

> *We still go to the same church. We are part of the parish family there. In this neighborhood the church is mostly Dutch. We moved out here from the south end [the Polish neighborhood], and we are the only Polish family on the road. We tried the parish out here, but they didn't welcome us, that is why we went back to the old parish.*

The same informant described the importance of the Polish parish in the lives of elderly Polish Americans.:

> *The south end [the Polish neighborhood] has been let down. We need a high rise for the elderly in the neighborhood. Where did they put the last one? Right behind the jail. Who wants to liver there?...Old people want to stay in the bosom of their families, close to the church.*

One second-generation eighty-four-year-old female general informant explained the support that people in the neighborhood give the church. "The people here really care about the church, they help keep it up and are generous...We have special collections for flowers at Easter and Christmas. People really contribute, we get almost $1,000 for flower at Easter." The elderly woman's fifty-one-year-old daughter explained how the church has provided for seniors:

> *We have almost 400 people in the senior citizens group...We have a senior meal site at the church, and have lots of activities...at Christmas time we give a big party for them at parish hall, and they will have a big dance and a meal.*

The neighborhood parish served the elderly as a setting for many social activities which often involved the practice of Polish traditions. Elderly Polish Americans expressed care for their families and neighbors through the support, organization, and participation in these activities that were often related to religious holidays. They viewed these activities as essential caring ways that assist them and others in supporting their health and well being and the survival of their culture and lifeways.

Theme 7

Elderly Polish Americans revealed some diversity in their views of the professional health care system especially nursing and nursing care. A third-generation female informant stated,

> *Right up until the 1940s and 1950s, older Polish American people went to the hospital as a last resort: it was seen as a place to die...I'm sixty-four and as kids we didn't go to the doctor much.*

All eight informants in this study reported that they now utilized the local hospital and other professional health care services and recognized their value in treating illnesses and in providing maternity care. Even though the professional services were viewed as beneficial, they were utilized with some reservation and reluctance. One third-generation sixty-five-year-old general informant explained, "I'm healthy and I was only ever in the hospital to have babies...I would go there if I needed to. We [she and her husband] both would go, but I hope we don't have to." A third-generation fifty-eight-year-old key informant explained her doubts about the medications a cardiologist had prescribed for her husband, "He takes sixty-five pills a day for his heart condition. Too many for his own good. He goes to a psychiatrist because he worries about his health, but it doesn't help much."

All informant valued professional health care but five informants expressed some reluctance about using the services. Keeping busy and active and not thinking about or worrying about one's health were believed to be as beneficial to their health and well being as professional care. Leininger defined a folk health system as, "traditional or local indigenous health care of cure practices that have special meanings and uses to heal or assist people which are generally offered in familiar home or community environmental contexts with their local practitioners."[52] Polish American elders in this study utilized the professional health care system but also valued their own folk health beliefs and used folk care practices to maintain their health.

There was diversity in the views elderly Polish American informants held about nurses and nursing care. Six of the eight informants had been hospitalized at some time and offered views on nursing care in that setting. Four (one key and three general) informants reported that they had good nursing care in the hospital, but two third-generation female key informants who were sisters and interviewed together (fifty-eight and sixty-three-years-old) felt nurses did not care as much as they used to. One was a Licensed Practical Nurse who had not worked as a nurse in over twenty years. Her sister remarked, "The nurses don't care as much as they used to. Years ago if a nurse wasn't a caring nurse, the hospital didn't keep them." The informant who was an LPN offered her views on nursing:

The LPNs were more caring the RNs. The RNs had the cap and wouldn't do the dirty work. A nurse shouldn't be afraid to get her hands dirty to give care...a caring nurse is friendly and has feeling for a person, a caring nurse lives to take care of people.

A third-generation sixty-one-year-old key informant discussed her experience with nurses, "I've never not had a caring nurse. The patient brings it on himself, if you complain, you suffer. You must be considerate; everyone is a human being, even a nurse." This informant though that a considerate attitude on the part of the patient was essential for nurses to encounter so they could render good care.

Several informants had utilized home health care nursing services. They valued this care because it was provided in their own homes or in the homes of their children rather than in a hospital setting. A second-generation eighty-four-year-old general informant explained how she was able to care for her sister in her home:

My sister has been with me about two months and has just about recovered from her mastectomy. She just lives a few blocks away. She left the hospital quite soon after her surgery and then she came to stay with me so I could take care of her. We had a home health care nurse to help us. She really cared and even came over one night when I called, just to reassure my sister. She was glad to come even though nothing was really wrong. My sister is almost better now, so she will be going home.

Discussion

The above qualitative research themes help the nurse to gain an understanding and meaning of the Polish culture in their environmental and historic contexts. They will now be discussed in relation to Leininger's Culture Care Theory Predictions. Culture care was found to be essential to preserve the health of Polish American elders and the survival of their lifeways.[53] *The major and dominant care constructs from this study were: giving to others and sacrificing, helping others, being there (staying close to Polish family and friends-solidarity), reciprocating, and visiting.* These care constructs were embedded in the world view and social structure features within the context of the Polish American culture. Care was continually reciprocated between Polish American elders and their Polish family members. Elders felt secure in the readiness of their families to give care and this feeling of security was an essential part of their health. Elderly Polish Americans cared for their family members by spending time with or being there for their children and grandchildren. All generations of family members were involved in many social activities at the local Polish church. Family members reciprocated care for each other by organizing, supporting, and participating in church activities. These care practices were related to their cultural values. Health for all key and general informants meant being comfortable and secure, working hard, keeping active, and eating the right foods. This is supportive of Leininger's definition of health which refers to health being culturally defined, valued, and practiced.[53] The expressions and practices of kinship, and cultural beliefs and values were the major influences on the care patterns of elderly Polish Americans which lead to their health. This is in accord with Leininger's theory about cultural and social structure dimensions influencing care and then the health of individuals, families, and cultural groups.[55]

Elderly Polish American care practices such as observing and practicing Polish customers, searching for their Polish roots, the efforts made to use and preserve the polish language, visiting with relatives in Poland, and sending food, medicine, and money to Poland were based on their cultural values and beliefs. This is congruent with Leininger's prediction that care was culturally constituted in every culture.[56]

Even though professional health care services were viewed as beneficial, they were utilized with some reluctance by Polish American elders. Often fold care practices such as keeping busy and active were viewed to be as beneficial to their health as professional care practices and were tried before consulting health professionals These findings regarding care and health are consistent with the finding reported by Leininger from several transcultural nursing studies with Mid-Western Polish Americans in the past decade.[57]

There was some *diversity* in the views elderly Polish Americans held about nurses and nursing care. Four informants reported they had good nursing care in the hospital setting but the two youngest informants reported that the nurses, "didn't care like they used to." Cultures are dynamic and changing, and the diversity in the views Polish Americans held about nursing care is an area to be considered for further study.

Culturally Congruent Care

In the theory of Culture Care Diversity and Universality, Leininger predicted that for care to be therapeutic and satisfying and to lead to health, it must fit the client's cultural beliefs, values, and lifeways.[58] The data from this study demonstrated that care constructs derived from and embedded in the world view, social structural factors, and cultural values influenced the care of elderly Polish Americans. Leininger has predicted three modes to guide nursing decisions and actions in order to provide culturally congruent nursing care: 1) culture care maintenance or preservation, 2) culture care accommodation or negotiation, and 3) culture care restructuring or repatterning. Nurses can use these modes to design care that is based on the views of care and health held by the elderly in the Polish American culture.[59,60]

Culture care preservation refers to care that preserves cultural values and lifeways and is beneficial to clients.[61] The Roman Catholic Church was important in the daily lives of the Polish American elderly, and their Polish cultural activities were closely tied to the neighborhood parish. Culture care was preserved among elderly Polish Americans who continued to organize and attend benefits for Polish relief through their local Polish culture club and the local Catholic church. These activities promoted and preserved the care pattern of caring for others in the Polish American culture that elders identify as an essential part of their lifeways.

Elderly Polish Americans continue to care for their immediate family members as well as for relatives in Poland. Culture care preservation was sustained and promoted for Polish American elders by the family structure that was organized to provide care for close relatives, and by the extended family structure that was organized to provide care for relatives in Poland. It has been a reciprocal care structure that was intergenerational, and international in nature. Polish American elders reciprocated care with other elderly family members. Knowledge of traditions and history were passed from the older generation to their children and grandchildren in turn provided physical care and social and financial support for elders. Polish American elders expressed care by visiting relatives in Poland and arranging for Polish relatives to visit the United States. Polish American elders also expressed care by sending money and material goods to Poland. Polish relatives reciprocated by the transmission of knowledge of contemporary Polish culture to their American kin. Elderly Polish Americans believed this infusion of current knowledge of Polish culture contributed to the survival of their cultural lifeways in the United States and positively influenced their health.

Nurses should strive to preserve the care pattern of promoting and maintaining cultural values and lifeways that are closely tied to the Roman Catholic Church through the neighborhood Polish American parish. The second care pattern to be preserved is that of family care that was reciprocally practiced intergenerationally and intergenerationally, both on a local and international level. These care patterns contributed to the major care theme of caring for others that has emerged from the emic data of this study. The care practices of giving to others, caring for others, or doing for others may be difficult for Anglo-American nurses to understand because many nurses value primarily self-care practices to maintain healthy lifeways. Nurses should make every attempt to preserve this Polish American care pattern of *caring for others*, that elderly Polish Americans have viewed as essential to their health and to the survival of their cultural lifeways.

Culture care accommodation refers to care activities that reflect ways to adapt health care services to benefit people.[62] Home health care services and institutions can modify services to accommodate family involvement in the care of elderly relatives. Polish American families can be supported by community nursing services if they wish to care for elderly family members at home. Polish American elders in this study preferred to receive health services in outpatient settings or in their own homes rather than being admitted to hospitals. As one third-generation key informant explained to the researcher, "Old people want to stay in their own homes in the bosom of their family, close to the church."

The traditional Polish American care practices of keeping busy and active can be modified to fit elderly Polish Americans health care needs. Exercise programs offered by the local hospital may be able to be offered at the local senior center at the Polish American parish. Exercise and activity programs can be designed an supervised by nurses and other health care professionals to meet professional health care goals for elders and at the same time accommodate the traditional care practices of keeping busy and active. The neighborhood setting would be congruent with the elderly Polish Americans desire to avoid going to the hospital to receive care services unless absolutely necessary.

Dietary information could be offered by dietitians and nurses at the local senior center. Diets that professionals consider therapeutic could be modified to allow for traditional Polish foods that are fried and have a high calorie count on special religious holidays that are celebrated by Polish American elders. The care practice of eating food that is naturally grown and prepared could easily be accommodated in most therapeutic diets.

Culture care repatterning refers to altering health or life patterns that are meaningful to them while still respecting their cultural values.[63] This may be difficult for nurses who do not understand the Polish American culture. If placement of an elder in a nursing home is necessary, both the elderly person and the family will need support as they experience this new pattern of care. Even though the Polish American elderly in this study acknowledged that nursing home care for themselves was a possibility, they viewed it as only as a last resort because they preferred to receive at home or in the homes of their families. If nursing home care becomes necessary, they will be the first generation of Polish American elders not cared for in the homes of their families. It is important for nurses to recognize and help elders and families to understand that care in a nursing home does not indicate an abandonment of elders by their families, but rather a repatterning in the way their families provide care for their elderly family members. However, nurses need to continue to try to accommodate the traditional care pattern of family care in the elders, own homes if at all possible.

Conclusion

This study was conceptualized within Leininger's Culture Care theory which served as a valuable theoretical framework to study the elders' lifeways by exploring their world view and social structure within the context of the Polish American culture. The ethnonursing method was used to systematically document and gain greater understanding of the Polish American elder's daily experiences related to care and health. In this study, the dominant care construct of Polish American elders was caring for others which substantiated the findings from other Polish American transcultural research.[64] Other care meanings and expressions already discussed were also similar to Leininger's previous findings with the Polish American culture.[65] It is the hope of the author that the findings from this study will assist nurses in providing culturally congruent care.

References

1. Leininger, M. M. "Leininger's Theory of Nursing: Cultural Care Diversity and Universality," *Nursing Science Quarterly*, v. 1(4), 152-160. 1988.
2. Leininger, M. M. "Ethnonursing: A Research Method With Enablers To Study The Theory Of Culture Care," *Culture Care Diversity and Universality: A Theory of Nursing*, M. Leininger, ed., 73-118, New York, NY: National League for Nursing Press. 1991b.
3. U.S. Department of Commerce. Statistical Abstracts of the United States (109th Edition). Washington, DC: Bureau of the Census. 1989.
4. Leininger, M. M. "Ethnomethods: The Philosophic and Epistemic Bases to Explicate Transcultural Nursing Knowledge," *Journal of Transcultural Nursing*. v. 1(2), 40-51.
5. Leininger, 1991b, op.cit.
6. Leininger, 1990, op. cit., p. 43.
7. Leininger, 1991a, op. cit., p. 47.
8. Leininger, 1991a, op. cit., p. 48.
9. Leininger, 1991a, op. cit., p. 49.
10. Leininger, 1988, op. cit., p. 153.
11. Leininger, 1988, op. cit., p. 154.
12. Leininger, 1988, op. cit.
13. Leininger, 1991a, op. cit.
14. Leininger, 1988, op. cit.
15. Leininger, 1991a, op. cit.
16. Leininger, 1988, op. cit.
17. Leininger, 1991a, op. cit.
18. Leininger, 1991a, op. cit., pp. 44, 45.

19. Bukowczyk, J. J. *And My Children Did Not Know Me: A History of the Polish-Americans*, Indianapolis: Indiana University Press, p. x. 1986.

20. U.S. Department of Commerce, op. cit.

21. Wytrwal, J. A. *America's Polish heritage: A social history of the Poles in America*, Detroit: Endurance Press, 1961.

22. Ibid.

23. Buckowczyk, op. cit.

24. Anderson, J. M. and Smith, I. A. (eds.). "Poles," The Peoples of Michigan Series, Volume 2: *Ethnic Groups in Michigan, Michigan Ethnic Heritage Studies Center and University of Michigan Ethnic Studies Program*, Ann Arbor, University of Michigan, pp. 218-221. 1983.

25. Wytrwal, op. cit.

26. Graff, G. *The People of Michigan: A History and Selected Bibliography of the Races and Nationalities who Settled our State*, Occasional Paper No. 1, Lansing, Michigan: Department of Education Bureau of Library Services, 1970.

27. Allison, M. "100 Years of Polish Heritage: St. Stan's has Left Indelible Mark on City," Bay City Times, 1974 (February 9).

28. U.S. Department of Commerce, op. cit.

29. Leininger, M. M. Basic Cultural Concepts for Nurses and Other Health Personnel to Understand About Culture, Class Handout, Detroit: Wayne State University, College of Nursing, 1989.

30. Bukowczyk, op. cit.

31. Wytrwal, op. cit.

32. Buckowczyk, op. cit.

33. Thomas, W. I., and Znaniecki, F. *The Polish Peasant in Europe and America* (rev. ed.), Chicago: University of Illinois Press, 1984.

34. Ibid., p. 248.

35. Wytrwal, op. cit.

36. Bukowczyk, op. cit.

37. Ibid., p. 76.

38. Obedinski, E. E. "Ethnic to Status Group: A Study of Polish Americans in Buffalo," Dissertation Abstracts International, v. 29(2A), 686, 1968.

39. Wrobel, P. *Our Way: Family, Parish, and Neighborhood in a Polish-American Community*, South Bend: Notre Dame Press, 1979.

40. Rempusheski, V. F. "Caring For Self and Others: Second Generation Polish American Elders in an Ethnic Club," *Journal of Cross-Cultural Gerontology*, v. 3, 223-271. 1986.

41. Ibid., p. 259.

42. Leininger, M. M. "Selected Culture Care findings of Diverse Cultures Using Culture Care Theory and Ethnomethods," *Culture Care Diversity and Universality: A Theory of Nursing*, M. Leininger, ed., 345-372, New York, NY: National League for Nursing Press. 1991c.

43. Ibid., p. 363.

44. Stasiak, D. B. (Speaker) & Leininger, M. M. (Speaker). *Cultural Care Assessment of American-Polish Informant*, videocassette, Livonia, MI: Madonna University. 1991.

45. Leininger, 1989, op. cit.

46. Bigelow, B. "Marital Assimilation of Polish-Catholic Americans: A Case Study in Syracuse, NY, 1940-1970," *The Professional Geographer*, v. 32(4), 431-438. 1980.

47. Arndt, L. E. *The Bay County Story: From Footpaths to Freeways*, Detroit: Harlo Printing Co. 1982.

48. Leininger, 1988, op. cit., p. 156.

49. Leininger, 1988, op. cit., p. 56.

50. Arndt, op. cit.

51. Allison, op. cit.

52. Leininger, 1988, op. cit., p. 156.

53. Leininger M. M. "The Theory of Culture Care Diversity and Universality," *Culture Care Diversity and Universality: A Theory of Nursing*, M. Leininger, ed., 5-68, New York, NY: National League for Nursing Press. 1991a.

54. Leininger, 1991a, op. cit., p. 48.

55. Leininger, 1991a, op. cit., p. 43.

56. Leininger, 1991a, op. cit., p. 23.

57. Leininger, 1991c, op. cit., p. 363.

58. Leininger, 1988, op. cit.

59. Ibid.

60. Leininger, 1991a, op. cit.

61. Ibid.

62. Ibid.

63. Ibid.

64. Leininger, 1991c, op. cit., p. 363.

65. Leininger, 1991c, op. cit.

Chapter 19

Lithuanian Americans and Culture Care

Rauda Gelazis, PhD, CTN, RN.

Lithuanian Americans in the United States constitute a culturally distinct group of people which has not been extensively studied to date, in nursing or in other fields. The many recent changes in Lithuania, culminating in its dramatic struggle for independence from Soviet domination and oppression, have placed Lithuania and the other Baltic countries into the forefront throughout the world as a country of great interest. Accordingly, nurses are aware of the country, its struggles and needs, but few have substantive knowledge of Lithuanian culture. Transcultural nursing knowledge is essential in order for nurses to understand the people as a basis to learn about their nursing care needs and especially to develop professional nursing care that will provide culturally congruent care to Lithuanian Americans.

During the last four decades Leininger has developed and done research in transcultural nursing to establish a knowledge base for nurse teachers and practitioners for the specialty field. Her culture care theory emphasizes understanding the cultural dimensions of human care. To achieve this goal the worldview, ethnohistory, social structure, language, cultural values, and care systems need to be studied to discover ways to provide care. The major theoretical premise of Leininger's theory of culture care is that knowledge and understanding of a people's culture care beliefs, practices, and values are essential to develop sound professional nursing care that is culturally congruent.[1] The theory predicts that nursing care that fits the client's lifeways will be more satisfying, effective, and lead to well-being.[2] Moreover, a lack of culturally congruent care can lead to cultural conflicts, noncompliance, and additional stress for clients. As nurses become more aware of the importance of transcultural nursing in a world in which many peoples are struggling for cultural independence and survival, it is important to understand the many diverse cultures who need quality nursing care practices.

In this chapter the author presents some transcultural nursing insights and knowledge about Lithuanian Americans with practical applications for nursing care. This specific, culturally congruent care knowledge is based upon the author's research findings using Leininger's culture care theory with Lithuanian American people, and from the author's lifelong personal experience with the Lithuanian culture.

Theoretical Framework

With the theory of Cultural Care Diversity and Universality, cultural perspectives of care are central to nursing.[3] The theorist postulates that if culture care values, expressions, and forms of care are known, the health or well-being of individuals or groups will be evident.[4] The goal of the theory is to provide culturally congruent nursing care or care that fits with the client's culture and lifeways.[5] In order to achieve this goal, Leininger describes three dominant modes to guide nursing care: culture care maintenance or preservation, culture care accommodation or negotiation, and culture care repatterning or restructuring.[6] These modalities give full consideration to the client's lifeways while at the same time providing professional information to clients to make choices and decisions of what professional ideas and practices will be viewed most helpful to them.

Leininger has identified care as essential to the growth, well-being, and survival of human beings. In order to understand fully the patterns of culture care, the professional nurse needs to closely study the social structure, language uses, symbols, and meanings about care of a given culture, for it is human care that makes a difference in well-being. However, values and beliefs about care are usually covert and embedded in the worldview and social structure of a particular culture. The Sunrise Model as developed by Leininger, helped the researcher focus on the various aspects of worldview, cultural, social structure, and health system dimensions that influence care and health in the various cultural contexts identified.[7] These diverse social structure factors were investigated by the author with Lithuanian Americans in a Midwestern metropolitan area in the United States.[8] The author used ethnonursing research method in order to tease out and make known care phenomena for nursing care practices largely from the people's emic perspective using the tenets and premises of the theory of Culture Care Diversity and Universality looking for similarities and differences among the people.[9] The ethnonursing method is designed to focus specifically upon learning from the people about actual and potential nursing phenomena through eyes, ears, and experiences.[10] The author used ethnonursing research method to study Lithuanian Americans in order to obtain data and to understand the peoples' views and beliefs about care and ways that these influenced health or well-being. The recommendations for culturally congruent, professional nursing care are based on this research. Since no previous nursing studies of Lithuanian Americans were found in a literature review, this research stands as an important first nursing care study with the culture.

Ethnohistory of Lithuanian Americans

A brief ethnohistory of the Lithuanian Americans' homeland on the Baltic Sea will be presented, followed by a focus on Lithuanian Americans in the United States.

Ethnohistory helps to set the context to explain and even predict some of the findings about Lithuanian Americans and their care expressions and needs. Lithuanian Americans are a relatively small culture in the United States when compared with other major cultures such as African Americans, Hispanic Americans, and European Americans. This culture has been highly influenced over several generations by the dominant culture of the Anglo-Americans in the United States. Lithuanian Americans have been able to deal with most conflicting intercultural values in a positive manner.

Lithuania—Baltic Sea Homeland

Lithuania, at present, is 25,200 square miles in area (about the size of West Virginia) with a population of 3,723,000, and a density of 108 persons per square mile.[11,12] The capital of Lithuania is Vilnius. Lithuania has a seaport, Klaipeda, on the Baltic Sea. Lithuania is bounded on the north by Latvia, Belarus on the East, Poland on the South, and the Baltic Sea on the West. In the past the economy was based on agriculture. The people are predominantly of the Roman Catholic religion.

Lithuanians, along with Latvians, are the only remaining remnants of the family of Baltic people who have inhabited the shores of the Baltic Sea for over 4,000 years. The other Baltic tribes of Old Prussians and Yatvingians became extinct during the later part of the Middle Ages through wars with the Teutonic knights and through assimilation into the Germanic tribes. Lithuanian prehistory goes back to 1500 B.C. when Lithuanians were already living in their present homeland. They were called "Aestians" (the Honorables) and were pagan nature worshippers.[13] Their earlier religious beliefs included worship of the sun and other natural phenomena. Artifacts symbolizing the sun god have been recovered, such as amber which came to represent the healing properties of the sun.[14] Evidence of goddess worship has also been found in the artifacts of these peoples.[15] In the Mesolithic and Neolithic eras the Aestians lived as tribes until the fifth century A.D., when a loose federation was formed headed by a pagan high priest. In the thirteenth century (1251) the tribes were united under Mindaugas, who defeated the Mongols. Mindaugas and many Lithuanians were baptized into Christianity and gradually became Roman Catholics. Roman Catholicism has been the dominant religion of the people since the thirteenth century.[16] Lithuania was a powerful nation for several centuries and spread over northeastern Europe. In the sixteenth century Lithuania joined with Poland and later declined in power. During the seventeenth and eighteenth centuries Lithuania was under Polish or Russian rule. Because of its key position on the Baltic Sea, various countries tried to gain power over Lithuania. In the nineteenth century the Russians attempted to eradicate the Lithuanian language and culture by forbidding the teaching of the language and banning printed matter in the language. By the end of this century, the serfdom which the Lithuanians experienced under the Russians ended. Lithuanians held tenaciously to their own language, and national leaders emerged to promote Lithuanian identity and language.

Lithuania became an independent state in 1918, but it was forcibly annexed by the Union of Soviet Socialist Republics in 1940. During the time of independence Lithuania, though still largely an agrarian country, had begun to make strides toward modernization and industrialization.[17] When the Communists took over, all private ownership was eliminated and all farming and industry were taken over under the direct rule of the communist government.[18] In 1941, hundreds of thousands of Lithuanians were deported in cattle cars to Soviet prison camps in Siberia.[19] The deportations to Siberia and political oppression continued for almost fifty years.[20]

The Lithuanian language is one of the oldest Indo-European languages.[21] It is part of the ancient European language family called the Indo-European languages.[22] The prehistoric Indo-Europeans left no written records such as did their Egyptian and Mesopotamian contemporaries.[23] The Indo-European language discovery came from clues during the opening of trade with India around 1585. At that time an Italian merchant named Filippo Sassetti discovered that Hindu scholars could speak and write an ancient language as venerable as Latin and Greek and he called this language Sanscruta (Sanskrit).[24] Scholars later studied this language and believed it to have the same roots as Latin and Greek. Sanskirt, or the Indo-Iranian branch of the Indo-European languages, and Lithuanian are both satem-languages, meaning that the primitive Indo-European K' has developed similarly in both languages.[25]

Lithuanians Come to the United States

After World War II Lithuanian emigration to the United States represented the attempts of thousands of Lithuanians to find freedom from political, religious, and economic oppression. Most post-World War II immigration occurred from 1940 to 1951, but there had been other migrations of Lithuanians to the United States in the latter part of the eighteenth and early nineteenth centuries. The famine of 1867–68 and land reforms in Lithuania had been responsible for earlier emigration to the United States. Those who came in the early nineteenth century came here to better their economic, political, and religious conditions, but many returned to their homeland after saving some money and rejoined families left in Lithuania. The choice of returning to their homeland had not been available to the Lithuanians in the United States until 1991, when Lithuania was recognized as an independent nation after the fall of the Soviet empire.[26]

Throughout the world there are approximately 800,000 Lithuanians in exile in various countries. There are about 650,000 Lithuanians in the United States, living mostly in industrial and metropolitan centers in the Eastern and Midwestern parts of the country. There are also Lithuanians in Brazil, Argentina, Uruguay, Canada, Australia, and Great Britain.[27] Today, over fifty years after the loss of independence and freedom, Lithuanians throughout the world struggle to maintain their language and culture and try to help Lithuanians in their homeland resist the influences of a Soviet communist regime.[28]

In Lithuania there was a pattern of Russification of the Lithuanian language while the country was under Soviet rule.[29,30] In the West, there are influences from the countries where Lithuanians settled after escaping.[31] In the United States, for example, there is now a generation of Lithuanians who have had to be bilingual almost from birth and for whom the Lithuanian language has never been their sole language. Under such conditions, the Lithuanian language becomes difficult to maintain and expression becomes somewhat stylized and awkward due to the fact that speakers use translation in their thought processes.[32]

In recent years Lithuania regained its freedom.[33] Under the Soviet Union's policy of glasnost, or openness (1988–1989) Lithuania began to push for freedom. On March 11, 1990 the Act of the Restoration of the Lithuanian State was signed, declaring independence from the Soviet Union.[34,35] In 1991, with the dissolution of the Soviet regime, the United States and many other countries have recognized Lithuania as an independent, sovereign nation. Today Lithuania is striving to become economically stable and is developing economic ties with Europe, the United States and other nations.[36]

Lithuania Americans living in the United States today consist of Lithuanians and their families who came to America after World War II, in the period of 1949 to 1951, as well as Lithuanians who came to the United States before World War I, and the descendants of the Lithuanian immigrants in the late nineteenth century.[37] They supported the movement for freedom in their homeland in any way they could over the years. Since the declaration of independence by Lithuania, support and assistance for their homeland continues.

Review of Literature on Lithuanian Americans

A review of literature on Lithuanian Americans revealed few research studies about this cultural group. The few existing studies of the culture discuss that the Lithuanian people value their religion, family, hard work, frugality, hospitality, and possess a strong regard for its culture, traditions, and particularly the Lithuanian language.[38,39,40,41] Lithuania has a very old culture and has withstood centuries of invasions and attempts at annihilating its people and identity.[42] Lithuanian scholars and anthropologists such as Gimbutas have studied various aspects of the culture, such as its myths.[43] Its ancient culture was once matriarchal and even to this day women are highly regarded in the culture.[44] To date, no nursing or ethnonursing studies have been published about this culture. This author has done research about Lithuanian Americans and the findings are consistent with the few studies mentioned here.[45]

Several, more recent ethnographies of Lithuanian Americans focus on the ethnic identity of the people in different parts of the United States. Baskauskas studied an urban enclave of Lithuanian refugees in Los Angeles.[46] She noted that even though Lithuanians participate in American economic, educational, and political systems, they also pursue their other major cultural and social objectives. Lithuanian American refugees viewed their culture as equal to, if not better than the surrounding one and had no desire to exchange it for the other. They have established stable and important social relations with others outside their group. Baskauskas noted that Lithuanians were among those selected to immigrate after World War II due to a seeming behavioral similarity to the population already present in America, but that the expected acculturation/assimilation did not seem to occur. Baskauskas postulated that post World War II Lithuanians who came here were refugees, rather than immigrants who left their homeland by choice. Refugees who had been displaced by the war and could not return to their homeland due to the Soviet Communist occupation may constitute a group differing from immigrant groups. Her study was done in the early 1970s before the interest that African Americans generated in finding their cultural roots. In the 1980s there has been a considerable change in attitudes toward cultural differences and cultural and ethnic pride in one's cultural heritage that has to some extent replaced the attempt of cultural groups to quickly become part of the melting pot.

Gedmintas in 1979 studied the ethnic identity among Lithuanian Americans in an urban industrial setting; Binghamton, New York.[47] Gedmintas concluded that ethnicity and ethnic identification, far from being all or nothing categories, vary according to social conditions. He noted that ethnicity, or ethnic interaction, may fade in importance in comparison to ethnicity at other levels, but the potential for ethnicity is maintained through the retention of ethnic identify as part of the individual's basic social identify. Gedmintas also found that although Lithuanian ethnicity has been declining (among third generation Lithuanian Americans) "Eastern European" ethnicity had gained in comparative importance. In other words, ethnicity as a social phenomenon had not disappeared among the Binghamton Lithuanians, but rather it had shifted in emphasis.

This author also noted that the Lithuanian Americans who were included in her study also held strongly to a Lithuanian identity. The population studied was in another urban center of the United States, and the study was considerably later than the Baskauskas and Gedmintas studies, but some of the findings hold true. The author found, for example, that Lithuanian identity was very important to Lithuanian Americans of various age groups and generations. Furthermore, during the study, Lithuania regained its independence from the Soviets, and there was an impetus for a renewed interest and pride in being Lithuanian.

Research Findings Related to Worldview, Social Structure, and Other Dimensions

The author conducted research with Lithuanian Americans and used Leininger's theory of Culture Care and the Sunrise Model[48] as guides to study the theory. The theory and model helped guide the author's research with both key and general informants who were first and second generation Lithuanian Americans. All social structure dimensions were studied with Lithuanian American informants in their native and in the English languages. Ethnonursing research methods were used to conduct qualitative research with Lithuanian Americans in an urban Midwestern area. The data were analyzed according to Leininger's four-phase analysis, wherein the data are studied for patterns, and eventually themes pertinent to the study emerge. An interview guide based on the social structure features of the theory and the Sunrise Model was used with both key and general informants. Observation and participation in various events in the Lithuanian American community also added important data to the study. The cultural values which were identified from the informant data and observations were the following: 1) family closeness; 2) deep religious beliefs and convictions (Roman Catholic); 3) education; 4) hard work *(darbštumas)* and industriousness; 5) conscientiousness *(saziningumas)*; 6) thriftiness and good use of material resources; 7) endurance and perseverance, in spite of hardships; 8) charity to others and hospitality *(vaišingumas)*; and 9) pride and emphasis on a continuation of their language and culture despite previous long-term attempts to oppress or annihilate the language and many social structure features. Each of these cultural values will be discussed in relation to culture care.

Kinship Factors

The value of family closeness and kinship was very evident.[49] Lithuanian American informants spoke of the importance of family in their lives. Frequently, family ties were maintained over time and distance. Since many informants had relatives in Lithuania where, until recent years, travel and communication were restricted by the Soviets, the difficulty in maintaining ties were a source of worry and concern. Many informants had for decades sent whatever material help they could to their relatives in Lithuania. This forced separation from loved ones was described as painful by informants. Informants spoke of being close to extended family members such as grandparents, aunts, uncles, and cousins. Informants frequently visit with relatives and described getting support through them. Divorce is not very common and informants placed value on intact family structures. Some informants linked strong family and kinship ties with strong religious beliefs and practices.

Care patterns and meanings related to kinship patterns for Lithuanian Americans were evident in the finding that care is expressed and intertwined with daily lifeways and expressed in interactions with family and friends. Care meant presence, and this was evident in the family interactions. For example, fathers described staying home when children became ill in order to give support through their presence. Persons also described that they showed care to each other in the family "in the everyday small things that you do for each other that you show care for one another." Care is also shown by listening and sharing with one another. Most Lithuanian Americans interviewed, and in participant observations, indicated that care in terms of family was very important to them.

Many said that it was support from relatives and friends that added to their ability to persevere despite difficulties such as illness. Informants who had been ill felt that Lithuanian friends visited frequently and let them know in other small ways that they cared. Being charitable to others was also a value expressed by informants. For example, many had helped their relatives in Lithuania.

Religious Factors

The majority of Lithuanian Americans are Roman Catholic. Informants described their strong faith as the reason they could endure years of hardship, especially informants who lived through World War II and who had to start their lives in American after escaping the Communist regime. Informants with prison experiences under communist or Nazi regimes talked of faith and a hope for the future as important to maintaining themselves in a state of well-being during their imprisonment. This is consistent with the writings of Franklin which the author describes survival in deplorable conditions of a concentration camp and emphasizes the key to survival is the meaning one gives to an experience.[50] Other informants pointed with pride at the attempts of Lithuanians to retain their religious beliefs despite mistreatment and punishment under an atheistic government in Lithuania for fifty years. *The Chronicles of the Church in Lithuania* were described as the written account of the peoples' persecution and suffering for their religious beliefs. Participant-observation of the Lithuanian American community revealed that much of the community's activities centered around the two Catholic parishes in the area studies. Many cultural events, for example, were at the parish auditorium. The Lithuanian elementary and high schools were both held in parish buildings. Religious life is also closely tied to cultural preservation, language, and education as well as other aspects of Lithuanian American life, such as politics and welfare organizations.

Religious values and beliefs permeate the daily lives of Lithuanian Americans and are the basis for care expressions. Informants described charity to others and "helping in terms of need" as part of the care patterns they experienced. For example, informants described attending a prayer group with a friend with a chronic physical illness. Hospitality, which is a hallmark of caring in Lithuanian Americans is viewed as an important way to show care to friends and strangers. Even persons of modest means make a great effort to share whatever they possibly can with guests and visitors. Also, the Lithuanian community has several organizations whose purpose is to help those in need. Lithuanians are known for their hospitality *(vaišingumas)* and take pride in this. Lithuanians in America as well as in Lithuania were noted to very hospitable toward guests. Informants remarked that as students they had traveled to other cities and had been cared for by Lithuanians who hardly knew them. Persons who have visited Lithuania all commented on the warmth and sincerity of the people and how visitors were always received with feasts of food and drink. Friends and relatives had saved and pooled their resources for weeks in order to receive people hospitably. It is considered poor manners to refuse food and drink and guests are encouraged numerous times to partake of what is offered. Some, jokingly told of times when they were new in American and had at first politely declined to eat, waiting to be asked a third or fourth time, only to find out that Americans usually only offered once. This made them think that this was a sign of non-caring until they realized that this was the usual custom in America.

Educational Factors

Education was described as important to informants, both younger and older. Older informants described sacrificing in order to be sure that their children could attend college. Younger informants shared their pride in completing college and working productively in various professions. Many informants pointed out that the sciences and technology were often selected for study because these were viewed as important fields. Material wealth was not emphasized, though informants were pleased that their lives were comfortable. Many of the older informants described coming to America decades ago with very little and being successful in a new world through considerable effort and hard work.

Care is evident in the many sacrifices that families make in order for children to be well educated. Parents with young children spoke of supervising children's homework and participating in school activities. Older parents spoke with pride about the educational successes of their children and described many sacrifices they had made to make sure the children received the best education possible. In turn, children expressed considerable respect and gratitude to their parents. Thus the caring was reciprocated, that is, from parents to children and children to parents. For example, most adult children do everything possible to care for elderly parents at home. Nursing homes are seen as a last resort. If nursing home care is required, attempts are made to have placement in Lithuanian-based nursing care facilities.

Economic Factors

The value of hard work *(darbštumas)*, industriousness and being conscientious *(saziningumas)* in any work that is done was noted by the informants. Many informants also noted that this value had changed greatly in Lithuania under the Communist regime. Under the communist system it was noted that people no longer had any incentive to work since all of the farms were put into collective farms and all industry was put under the Soviet government. Some of the informants who had visited Lithuania, or who had visitors from Lithuania, had noted the different view toward work. As one informant, who had recently emigrated, noted, "If you work hard here in America, you have something to show for it, but if you work hard there (Lithuania under Soviet rule) you still had nothing." Now that Lithuania has regained its independence, hope was expressed that many of the older values would eventually return to the people.

Lithuanian Americans also described themselves as thrifty and used material resources well. For example, many informants had small vegetable gardens or had fruit trees and canned these products. Some informants sewed or had family members who sewed in order to save money on clothing. Particularly the older informants described being able to endure and persevere through severe hardships.

Care is linked to economic factors in that persons expressed care economically when possible. Relatives in the homeland were sent money, food, and clothing when possible. In Soviet ruled Lithuania, for example, severe restrictions were placed on what could be sent by mail. Lithuanian Americans circumvented the restrictions by obtaining visas to visit relatives and would come to Lithuania loaded down with clothing, money, and other gifts for relatives. Recently, because Lithuania is independent, travel as well as sending packages have opened up, and Lithuanian Americans continue to demonstrate their care by sending and taking considerable material goods to Lithuania.

Cultural Values and Lifeways

Another value mentioned by all informants was pride in their culture and language. Younger informants described their participation in various dance and folk-ensembles and expressed the fact that they felt enriched by experiences with these groups. Older informants in particular expressed concern about passing on the language and traditions of the Lithuanian culture. The informants were also politically aware, particularly regarding the changing situation in Lithuania and the Baltics and other Soviet republics. When Lithuania regained its freedom, Lithuanian Americans rejoiced despite knowing that many future hardships would be faced.

Lithuanian Americans demonstrate care by showing continuing respect and value by their heritage to the point where considerable time and effort is placed on activities and organizations that serve to continue Lithuanian-ness *(lietuvybe)*. For example, families described participating in Lithuanian Saturday school, Lithuanian youth religious groups, Lithuanian scouts, parish choir, and Lithuanian sports groups, folk dance and song ensembles. These activities are done during weekend or evening hours after a full work or school schedule. Much appreciation was noted on the part of children, as they grew older, for the opportunities that these activities provided so that not only the Lithuanian heritage was perpetuated, but participants noticed that their world was widened by these additional activities. Many Lithuanian organizations and gatherings occurred in various cities in America as well as other countries. For example, parish choir members of various ages participated in Rome in the celebration of the anniversary of Lithuania's Christianity. This occasion put them in contact with other European people and cultures. Others spoke of traveling to South America with dance and singing groups or to Australia for Lithuanian scouting jamborees.

Political Factors

Lithuanian Americans of various ages expressed an interest in the political life of their homeland as well as of America. Young people in particular spoke of the importance and need to go outside the political sphere of Lithuanian American communities and enter the politics and influence of America. During the time of the study Lithuania was pressing for its independence from the Soviet Union. Lithuanian Americans throughout the country actively demonstrated, wrote and phoned their representatives in Washington, D.C. in order to get the United States to recognize Lithuania as independent. The author participated in a demonstration in Washington, D.C. as part of her participant observation and noted that considerable unity and organization was evident in the demonstration. For example, bus-loads of people met on the given date in front of the Lincoln Memorial. The feelings expressed by the demonstrators also included elements of political humor in the various placards carried by demonstrators. Examples of such humorous elements were phrases to the President such as "Mr. President, Lithuania doesn't grow broccoli" (the demonstration occurred shortly after the President had taken a firm stand against broccoli, but was seen as not taking a supportive stand toward freeing of the Baltics), or "Read my lips, Soviets, get out of Lithuania!" Lithuanians tended to use subtle humor and humorous approaches to deal with oppressive situations.

Caring was expressed in this sphere by Lithuanian Americans, in so far as many organizations exist in the Lithuanian American community to be sure that the needs of the people are met. Care is seen as both individual and in organized caring community effort through Lithuanian organizations. An example was the Lithuanian Golden Agers Club, which made sure that information about all available resources for the elderly was given to and understood by members so that the proper agencies would be turned to when needed.

Culture Care Meanings

The dominant meanings of care for Lithuanian Americans were the following: 1) care as presence of "being there" for someone else; 2) care as helping in times of need; 3) care as concern for or watching over another *(prieziura)*; 4) care as worrying about *(rupestis)* another; 5) care as hospitality toward others; 6) sharing with others (other-care); 7) flexibility to adapt; 8) cooperation with others; 9) praying with others; and 10) using subtle humor. The research showed that care meanings for Lithuanian Americans were embedded or part of daily lifeways and patterns. Care was part of the structure of the Lithuanian American community, for many organizations existing in the Lithuanian American community provided aspects of care to the people. Care was frequently described as being an integral part of everyday life and expressed in daily life patterns between family and friends in the little things that are said and done in family interactions. Care meanings and patterns were closely linked to Lithuanian American cultural values as highlighted earlier.

Among the important care meanings for Lithuanian Americans was care as presence or being there. For example, informants said that they valued visits from friends when ill and that at times fathers would take time off from work to be at home with ill children. Presence was seen as an important care expression in family celebrations and important family events, from baptism to funerals. Care as presence meant making the extra effort to be with another in times of need.

Care as helping others in time of need was another major finding. Informants described the Lithuanian American community as a caring community. Help in need was provided both by individuals and through organizations. For example, food was brought to the family during acute or long-term illnesses. Spiritual support at such times was evident through visits not only from the parish priest, but from friends and neighbors who visit regularly for prayer and reflection. Organizations, such as the Golden Agers Club, also provide help to members when needed in concrete ways, from providing transportation for medical care to providing information and needed material support.

Frequently care was identified as a watching over or concern for *(prieziura)*. This concept connotes a care that is broad in scope and includes various aspects of care for a person. It refers to assessing what is needed and providing for the need as possible. For example, an informant described care as "an attitude...it's from the soul; an orientation."

Another term frequently used for care was worry about or concern about another *(rupestis)*. Along with the concerned attitude is working toward providing the needed element of care. One informant described this as "Care is an on-going thing...it's taking care of someone, making it your first priority, also a responsibility."

Care meant sharing with others and was related to the high value placed on hospitality. Informants often described times of sharing with others despite lack of material wealth. Great value was placed on giving of oneself in terms of time or listening to another's problems. Important to this process is doing "little things" for someone else to show care, such as staying with young children so that a young mother can have a few hours to herself. One informant described this kind of caring as "an attitude...it's from the soul...it's an on-going thing like when you notice something is needed, you take care of it." Persons are graciously and hospitably received by Lithuanians, even of modest means, because the emphasis is placed on the attitude of caring about others and not on the lavishness of the hospitality offered a guest.

Care as lived in a community of Lithuanian Americans was clearly supported by descriptions of closeness felt by the members of the community. For example, even younger informants, frequently stated that they felt understood and accepted and a special closeness for other Lithuanian Americans. Young Lithuanian Americans met frequently and interacted with each other from various parts of America and even other parts of the world, because their involvement in various Lithuanian American organizations made such contacts possible. Informants saw care as cooperation with others with flexibility to meet survival conditions, especially in a new country and culture. Many of the older informants, for example, had to take any job they could find when they first came to America, despite their previous educational preparation or profession. For example, professional musicians, teachers, professors, etc., worked in factories in America. To survive one had to maintain a cooperative and flexible caring posture and attitude. Humor was seen as vital to other survival adaptation processes, especially in situations where direct confrontation was not seen as a productive or desirable end. Humor helped to buffer difficult situations and frequently was subtle in nature. Subtle humor could be used as part of caring forms of communication in difficult situations.

Transcultural Nursing Actions and Decisions Using the Three Modes for Culturally Congruent Care for Lithuanian Americans

Culturally congruent professional nursing care for Lithuanian American clients should reflect the nurse's knowledge of the clients' values and lifeways. Several nursing care actions and decision guides may be drawn from knowledge of culture as well as care meanings and values. Much of nursing care will involve the model of culture care preservation and/or maintenance.

Culture Care Preservation

Since Lithuanian Americans place value on education, and to some extent on science and technology, most Lithuanian Americans were aware of current medical and some nursing practices. The nurse needs to make certain that medications and other instructions are well understood. Because family is highly valued, for example, elderly clients may be living with family members. The nurse needs to include significant family members in caring for the client and in giving home-going instructions. Elderly clients will be likely to follow instructions from professionals very closely. This tendency may relate to the value and respect given to education and educated persons. In teaching Lithuanian Americans it is important to get feedback from them about what they heard and correct any misunderstandings. Informants, in describing how they followed instructions from physicians, have remarked that even the physician was surprised that instructions were followed so closely. Lithuanian Americans take pride in preserving their language and are likely to use Lithuanian when speaking to each other. This preference should be respected. Remembering that the people have been oppressed for years should help the professional nurse understand the reasons for the strong desire to preserve their language and culture. English is spoken by most Lithuanian-Americans and language is not generally a problem unless the client is elderly or recently from Lithuania. Spiritual beliefs are important to the people and should be incorporated into their care.

Because presence means caring for Lithuanian Americans it is important for the nurse to spend time with them. While technical care may be important, presence is highly valued and many informants spoke of listening as an important aspect of care. Therefore professional nurses should make a point of listening to the client and family members. Lithuanian Americans also value flexibility and several informants remarked that they preferred to have nurses who were able to adapt procedures or who were not rigidly holding to the rules of the institution.

Lithuanian Americans use few folk remedies and adhere to prescribed Western medical treatments and medications. Some informants spoke of using herbs and teas at times, such as chamomile tea for colds and linden blossom tea for fever. The nurse does need to assess each client in order to determine what, if any, such remedies are used and be sure that no effects are present which may counteract the medications prescribed.

Culture Care Accommodation

Culture care accommodation or negotiation would be used by nurses as well. Primarily this mode may involve accommodating family members and including them in the nursing care when possible. For example, in the case of hospitalized clients, family members may come long distances to be with the client. The nurse needs to accommodate the nursing care to their presence by extending visiting hours and giving family members a role in their care. Lithuanian Americans try to respect rules and regulations and may hesitate to ask for any special treatment, therefore, the nurse will frequently need to be astute enough to anticipate the needs of the client and family.

Culture Care Restructuring

Culture care restructuring and repatterning, referring to changing lifeways by repatterning expression would not be beneficial with this cultural group. Should any changes need to be made in lifestyle or pattern, the nurse needs to assess how such changes would be received by the client and plan for the changes together with the client and family. For example, if a client needed to change dietary habits because of high cholesterol level, the nurse needs to take a diet history. Since many of the traditional Lithuanian foods may be high in fat and cholesterol, the nurse may need to plan with the client and his/her spouse and family how the modifications in diet would be possible and still include some favorite dishes. Many Lithuanian American informants mentioned that as part of maintaining well-being, physical health and exercise were important. In the case of repatterning some aspects of their lives for the sake of health, most clients could be cooperative with changes, provided that the nurse is considerate of their preferences and culture care values, needs, and beliefs.

Summary Reflections

The theory of culture care was most valuable to study and document lifeways of Lithuanian Americans undergoing many changes in the United States. The theory of Culture Care Diversity and Universality and the Sunrise Model served as the basis for gaining an understanding of this culture and for making culture care guidelines to support the health and well-being of the people.

This chapter focused on Lithuanian Americans and their cultural values, as well as care meanings and values which were shared with the author in doing postmasters and doctoral research with this cultural group. An ethnohistory of Lithuanian Americans helped to explain some of their cultural lifeways and beliefs. Leininger's theory of culture care and ethnonursing qualitative research method were the basis of explicating the guides for culturally congruent care of the Lithuanian American. Culturally congruent care may include any or all three modes of professional actions. All three, culture care preservation, accommodation, and repatterning were considered, and specific recommendations were made for each mode. The professional nurse can use the above information to provide culturally congruent care for Lithuanian Americans in his/her nursing practice.

References

1. Leininger, M., "Leininger's Theory of Cultural Care Diversity and Universality," *Nursing Science Quarterly*, v. 1, no. 4, 1988, pp. 152–160.
2. Leininger, M., *Culture Care Diversity and Universality: A Theory of Nursing*, New York: National League for Nursing Press, 1991.
3. Leininger, op. cit., 1988, p. 155.
4. Ibid., p. 156.
5. Ibid., p. 155.
6. Leininger, op. cit., 1991, pp. 42–44.
7. Leininger, op. cit., 1988, p. 156.
8. Gelazis, R., "The Effects of Political Oppression on a Culture: A Study of the Lithuanian American," Presentation at the fourteenth Transcultural Nursing Society Conference, Edmonton, Alberta, Canada, 1988.,
9. Leininger, op. cit., 1991, p. 75.
10. Ibid., p. 79.
11. Urbonas, J., "Lithuanians," J. M. Anderson and I. A. Smith, eds., *Ethnic Groups in Michigan*, v. 2, Detroit: Ethnic Heritage Center, Ethnic Press, 1983.
12. LIETUVA: Journal From the Republic of Lithuania, v. 1, 1991, p. 10.
13. Sabaliauskas, A., *Mes Baltai*, Kaunas, Lithuania: Šviesa, 1986.
14. Gimbutas, M., "The Ancient Religion of the Balts," *Lituanus*, v. 4, 1985, pp. 97–109.
15. Gimbutas, M., *The Language of the Goddess*, San Francisco: Harper and Row Publishers, 1989.
16. Gerutis, A., ed., *Lithuania 700 Years*, New York: Manyland Books, 1969.
17. Šapoka, A., *Lietuvos Istorija*, Kaunas, Lithuania: Švietimo Ministerijos Knygu Leidinio Komisija, 1939.
18. Sruogiene, V. D., *Lietuvos Istorija*, Chicago: Terra, 1950.
19. Prunskis, J., *Lietuviai Sibire*, Chicago: Lithuanian Library Press, Inc., 1981.
20. Urbonas, op. cit.
21. Skardzius, P., "The Lithuanian Language in the Indo-European Family of Languages," 1 and 2, *Lithuanian Bulletin*, v. 5, nos. 9–10; 11, 1947, pp. 3–4.
22. Fraenkel, G., *Languages of the World*, Boston: Gin & Co., 1967.
23. Thieme, P., "The Indo-European Language," *Scientific American*, v. 199, no. 4, 1958, pp. 63–74.
24. Ibid., p. 65.
25. Klimas, A., "Lithuanian and Sanskrit," *Lithuanian Bulletin*, v. 5, no. 9–10, 1947, pp. 78–79.
26. Krickus, R. J., "Hostages in their Homeland," *Commonweal*, v. 80, February 15, 1980, pp. 75–80.

27. Senn, A., *The Lithuanian Language*, Chicago: Publications of the Lithuanian Cultural Institute, 1942.

28. Krickus, op. cit.

29. Šilbajoris, R., "City and Country in Recent Soviet Lithuanian and Russian Prose," *Journal of Baltic Studies*, v. 16, no. 2, 1985, pp. 118–127.

30. Mickunas, A., "Kad Tik Ne Zmogus: Filosofija Dabarties Lietuvoje," *Metmenys*, v. 51, 1986, pp. 145–162.

31. Bilaišyte, Z., "Ieškant Prasmes: Kalba, Istorinis Palikimas ir Tikrove," *Metmenys*, 1986, pp. 3–20.

32. Ibid., p. 5.

33. Ramonis, V., *Baltic States vs. the Russian Empire: 1000 Years of Struggle for Freedom*, Lemont, Illinois: Baltech Publishing, 1991.

34. Zumbakis, S. P., ed., *Lithuanian Independence: The Re-Establishment of the Rule of Law*, Chicago: Ethnic Community Services, 1990.

35. Ramonis, op. cit.

36. Ramonis, op. cit.

37. Urbonas, op. cit.

38. Alilunas, L. J., *Lithuanian in the United States: Selected Studies*, San Francisco: R. & E. Research Associates, Inc., 1978.

39. Budreckis, A. M., *Eastern Lithuania: A Collection of Historical and Ethnographic Studies*, Chicago: Morkunas Printing Press, 1985.

40. Dunduliene, P., *Lietuviu Etnografija*, Vilnius, Lithuania: Mokslas, 1982.

41. Bindokiene, D. B., *Lietuviu Paprociai ir Tradicijos Išeivijoje*, Chicago: Lithuanian World Community, Inc., 1989.

42. Gerutis, op. cit.

43. Gimbutiene, M., "Baltu Mitologija," *Mokslas ir Gyvenimas*, v. 1, January, 1989, pp. 37–38.

44. Bindokiene, op. cit.

45. Gelazis, op. cit.

46. Baskauskas, L., *An Urban Enclave: Lithuanian Refugees in Los Angeles*, New York: AMS Press, Inc., 1985.

47. Gedmintas, A., *Dynamics of Ethnic Identity Among Lithuanian-Americans in an Urban Industrial Setting*, Dissertation, Binghamton State University of New York, 1979.

48. Leininger, op. cit., 1991.

49. Ibid.

50. Frankl, V. E., *The Will to Meaning*, New York: New American Library, 1969.

Chapter 20
Transcultural Nursing Care
of American Gypsies

Annette Bodnar, MSN, RN, and Madeleine Leininger, PhD, LHD, DS, FAAN, CTN, RN.

The Gypsy worldview and part of their strategy for dealing with the outside world is to use an elaborate moral code of their own based on complex rules of purity and impurity. This code is used to relate to each other as a group as well as to maintain the boundary between themselves and outsiders.

Sutherland, 1986, p. xiii

Based on the authors' past experiences with Gypsies and the authors' desire to study the culture further from a theoretical transcultural perspective, this quote fascinated the authors. Nurses have frequently encountered or heard about Gypsies in their communities, but few have taken seriously the importance of understanding this large worldwide minority culture. Indeed, there is a paucity of nursing articles and research studies focused on the Gypsies, a large, growing, and fascinating culture. Gypsies have been the culture neglected by nurses and other health personnel who want to understand and provide culture-specific care. Some nurses view Gypsies as strange, uncooperative, and bizarre in their behavior. They know that Gypsies roam the world, occasionally become ill, and come to a hospital. When Gypsies enter the hospital, nurses fear the Gypsies will steal and so nurses often position themselves to watch the Gypsies day and night, and all valuables and personal possessions are put into locked places. These are traditional images, fears, myths, and actions which show a general lack of understanding about Gypsies.

Since transcultural nursing is the field of research and practice committed to discovering known and unknown cultures, the authors saw the need to explicate Gypsy care values, beliefs, and lifeways. The purpose of this chapter is to present the research and literature findings from a study of United States Gypsies focusing on their values, beliefs, and lifeways with respect to culture care meanings and expressions of culture care in order to improve nursing care to this largely neglected and unknown culture. The domain of inquiry was focused on the culture care beliefs, values, and practices of

American Gypsies with emphasis on their care expressions and meanings as they contribute to their health and well-being. Their study was conceptualized and investigated within Leininger's theory of Culture Care Diversity and Universality. Since no specific nursing research studies focused on Gypsy culture care and health, this transcultural nursing study was long overdue. The goal was to explicate ethnonursing raw data from the Gypsies worldview, social structure features, ethnohistory, and folk-professional health care systems. A synthesis of extant anthropological research insights from available literature sources was also reflected upon to confirm or refute research findings from this investigation. The intent was to increase nurses' understanding of Gypsy culture and to lessen the mystical ideas, myths, and general misunderstanding about Gypsy culture so that nurses can provide culturally competent and congruent nursing care.

Theoretical Perspective

Leininger's Culture Care Theory was the most appropriate theory to use to study the Gypsies because it is a transcultural nursing theory which provides a holistic and comprehensive theoretical framework to examine systematically different dimensions of the culture within a nursing perspective.[1] The theory was developed to be used in any culture or subculture to discover emic or etic inductively-based, grounded data that provide the epistemics and ontologic dimensions of nursing knowledge. The theory focused upon the major dimensions of culture care related to the worldview, social structure, ethnohistory, environmental context, and other factors predicted to influence human care and in turn the health and well-being of the people. The Sunrise Model served as an extremely valuable guide to explicate the diverse and similar Gypsy lifeways of the informants in relation to the tenets of the Culture Care Theory.[2] Due to space limitations and since Leininger's theory of culture care has been fully presented in several of her publications, the theory is not repeated here and the reader is referred to these definitive publications.[3,4,5,6,7]

In this study Leininger's general theoretical assumptions and definitions were used, but with the following specific theoretical premises for this investigation:

1. The American Gypsy cultural forms, meanings, expressions, and patterns of human care are embedded in their emic and etic worldview, social structure, ethnohistory, language, environmental context, cultural values, and in folk (generic) culture care practices which influence their caring modes and health status.

2. Gypsy generic (folk) and professional views related to culture care reveal identifiable differences and similarities that are essential to guide professional nursing practices for meaningful and beneficial care to Gypsies.

3. Culture-specific cultural values and care patterns grounded in the Gypsy cultural lifeways provide the epistemic and ontologic knowledge base for creative nursing actions or decisions.[8]

Research Method

The research method for this study was a mini-ethnonursing investigation focused primarily upon American Gypsies from three community areas in the United States, i.e., Northwest, Midwest, and central Atlantic, and studied different time periods (1970 and 1980s). The research data were collected mainly by one researcher, Leininger, using the mini-ethnonursing research method.[9] The other researcher, Bodnar, extensively studied Gypsy literature. Some observations and interviews were made in 1987 of European Gypsies living in two Gypsy communities. These data were, however, only for comparative reflections and are not the focus of this study.

In keeping with the ethnonursing research method designed for Leininger's Culture Care theory, three key and seven general informants in each American Gypsy area were studied with a total of nine key and twenty general participants. In addition, several in-depth participant-observations were made in their living context and in hospitals where Gypsies had been admitted. Leininger's Stranger-Friend Observation-Participant Model was a major and valuable guide to enter into and remain for study visits with the Gypsies.[10,11] All informant interviews and observations were made on the Gypsy home turf. The researcher conducted interviews in a very informal, naturalistic, open, and spontaneous way to allay suspicion and to build trust with the Gypsies. Initially, the Gypsies were not willing to talk to an outsider about their beliefs and lifeways, and so it took several "warm-up" sessions to gain entry to the Gypsy world. Since the Gypsies were initially very suspicious, guarded, and hesitant of the research, and so it took time for the researcher to move from a "distrusted stranger" to a "semi-friend" as depicted in the Stranger-Friend Model.[12] Approximately two to four group sessions were held with the key and general informants in each community. Gradually, the informants seemed pleased the *Gadje* (outsider) researcher was genuinely interested in them and envisioned some benefits in being understood by outsiders. The researcher visited with them in their mobile homes, "dropping in to have a chat." The Gypsies gradually decided the researcher was a safe *Gadje* to talk to. It took, however, considerable patience, presence, and time to move from a distrusted researcher to a *Gadje* friend. Adult males, females, and children were observed in their natural and familiar environments and while ill in the hospital. Only verbal consent was given as the Gypsies said it was "better than any written *Gadje* document." The time span varied in each area from three to six months.

Since the ethnonursing qualitative paradigm method has been fully described in other works by Leininger, it will not be repeated here.[13,14] Most importantly, and from the beginning, as the researcher studied the American Gypsy lifeways and culture care phenomena, the qualitative criteria of confirmability, credibility, meanings-in-context, and recurrency were systematically examined.[15,16,17,18] It was very difficult to meet the saturation criterion because the Gypsy informants were suspicious of repeated inquiries on ideas they had already shared with the researcher in "good faith." As frequently found with the ethnonursing qualitative research method, it was not until the second visit that the Gypsies began to share ideas with the researcher about their emic (insider's) lifeways and struggles, and how they differed from the etic (outsider or non-Gypsy) ways. The key and general informants liked the researcher's ways of discussing ideas in a group context rather than with one informant as this kept the research process open to all interested Gypsies. In the hospital the Gypsies were more willing to visit with the researcher in order to derive resources and to manipulate nursing staff to understanding Gypsy clients. In Europe the researcher found Gypsies were more eager to talk about their frustrating problems with "government harassers" or the *Gadje* (outsiders) than were the American Gypsies. As the data were collected, in keeping with the ethnonursing method, all data were coded, classified, and interpreted daily after each session in order to make final synthesized formulations. No tape recordings were acceptable to take with the Gypsies in America and Europe, nor were they necessary. The ethnonursing emic and etic raw data were studied by the researcher after each visit to grasp their full meanings and to avoid loss of recall. Areas of ambiguity were checked directly with the people. In the presentation of the social structure factors and other areas below, the authors combined the research literature with the research findings obtained in this investigation.

Ethnohistorical and Worldview

Understanding ethnohistorical factors and the worldview of nomadic Gypsies becomes extremely important for nurses to grasp their cultural lifeways. Ethnohistorical data from the literature and informants revealed that the Gypsies trace their origins from India and emigrated to Europe as wandering nomadic tribes. The term "Gypsy" is believed to have come from Egypt proper and Egyptus minor before arriving in Europe. Linguistic evidence related this fact to the discovery in 1763 that the Gypsy language in Hungary was similar to the Indian language Sanskrit.[19] It remains unclear whether the Gypsies left India as a single tribe or a collection of several tribes, or whether the emigration took place as a single mass exodus or over a long period of time.[20] It is known that the emigration proceeded westward using routes of classical travelers who faced persecution and loss of possessions along the way.[21] The earliest groups entered

Balkan Europe in the early fourteenth century and by the next century were dispersed in Western Europe. They were reported in Poland, England, and Sweden by the sixteenth century and in Russia by the eighteenth century.[22] The Gypsies were banished and exiled to North and South American from England to rid the country of the so-called "dangerous class." There is evidence the Gypsies lived in the Colonial United States of America, specifically in the Virginia area.[23]

Gypsies were initially met with curiosity and interest, but since their lifestyle was so different from mainstream society, they experienced harassment and persecution and were exiled from several places. Because the Gypsies did not become hunters or farmers as other nomadic travelers, they remained outside the society wherever they lived. Their occupations included fortune-telling, coppersmithing, tinkering, mechanics, and horse dealing, but some were involved in a variety of other occupations such as being musicians and magicians.[24] Their philosophy and worldview were to do a little of everything to survive and to make a living somehow from the natural environmental resources wherever they temporarily lived.[25]

Because of the long history of persecution which the Gypsies faced, social and cultural bonds were forged to sustain their lifeways. According to Denham, "by turning inward and rejecting the outside world they became a self-perpetuating system which renewed itself with each new generation."[26] Some scholars feel that this self-preservation may be the single element which helped maintain the Gypsies as a distinct culture. Today there are Gypsies throughout the world on all continents. Population estimates in various countries are India, 35,000,000; Hungary, 800,000; the Soviet Union, 250,000; France, 300,000; the United Kingdom, 70,000; and Italy, 85,000.[27] Current Gypsy population estimates in the United States are difficult to make because their cultural identity is not recorded on the census and Gypsies do not record their births. Gypsies are usually classified as "white" on the census. Sway estimates that there are approximately one million Gypsies living in the United States with the largest concentrations in major urban areas such as Los Angeles, New York, Chicago, Boston, Atlanta, Houston, Seattle, Portland, and San Francisco. Sway, referring to the Gypsies, states, "Probably half live in urban and half rural areas such as Virginia, California, Georgia, Utah, Minnesota, Texas, and Idaho."[28] These ethnodemographic literature facts supported many statements made by the Gypsies to the researcher. The authors realized the worldwide distribution of Gypsies and that they are a major part of not only American life, but life in many places in the world.

Leininger identified worldview as the way a culture tends to look out on their world and the universe.[29] The American Gypsies as a culture tend to view the world as a dichotomy between their world and a non-Gypsy one. Gypsies are highly conscious of their way of life and their desire to maintain a cultural identity different from the

Gadje (non-Gypsy) lifeways for cultural survival. According to Kornblum and Lichter, "the world of the Gadje is a corrupt one, in which human exploitation is the rule, and the misery the Gypsies have experienced is attributed to the Gadje society."[30] Despite many pressures for Gypsies to become a part of the dominant American culture in an integrated way, the Gypsies have resisted. Their worldview is a strong force to sustain their cultural identity and self-esteem. Kornblum and Lichter state "the Gypsy world view stress values of individual and group survival above all others."[31] They further identify three themes in Gypsy thought namely: 1) the outside society is corrupt and in turn, should be exploited whenever possible; 2) status pretensions of group members and outsiders should be deflated; and 3) loyalty to the Gypsy family must be maintained at all costs.[32] It is these beliefs and values that undergrid their social structure and way of living in the world. Leininger's study of the Gypsies in American and European hospital and community contexts has identified similar key major cultural values namely: 1) practicing a nomadic way of life; 2) maintaining strong kin and Gypsy ties; 3) distrusting Gadje; 4) practicing frugality; 5) keeping strong in-group cultural values and ties; 6) relying on folk caring lifeways; and 7) valuing temporality in time and space; and 8) maintaining a sacred and profane moral code.[33,34]

From the Gypsies' viewpoint, they like to be "familiar strangers" to outsiders. And since most Gypsies in their businesses depend on non-Gypsy customers, they need a degree of familiarity with others to earn a livelihood.[35] But their status as strangers often protects them. They contend that if government people know less about them, then they will be less harassed or restricted.[36,37]

As a people, they have never had a country of their own, but they have had their own language, lifeways, cultural values and beliefs. The fact that they have lived in the United States for many generations and are still not routinely cited in most history books reflects their minority status in the majority Anglo-American cultures. Many Gypsies tend to maintain only enough of a link with the outsiders to meet primarily their economic and cultural needs. According to Gropper, no Gypsy group makes its living from other Gypsies.[38]

Sutherland, who conducted an in-depth anthropological study of the Gypsies, identified that Gypsies are aware that they live in a society that despises them, and so they have erected their own boundaries against the *Gadje*.[39] They tend to demonstrate a sense of moral superiority and voice contempt of the *Gadje*. Denham discussed that within the Gypsy cultural boundary, control takes the form of physical, psychological, and cultural isolation, and these boundary controlling methods may be subtle or deliberate and reflect cultural ethnocentrism.[40] Sway cited Gypsies as extremely ethnocentric.[41] Their belief in taboo codes of *marime*, which refers to the outsider as soiled or unclean, prevents interaction with *Gadje* and is an additional force that limits becoming acculturated into the American lifeways. Sway states, "To interact with *Gadje* in any way other than business is to invite hostility and suspicion of the entire group."[42] This worldview of the Gypsy reflects a clear distinction with moral codes of the sacred and profane, or between the Gypsy and non-Gypsy worlds. Their efforts to strive toward individual and group survival are by perceiving the outside world as evil and the source of Gypsy problems. These ethnohistorical and worldview research factors are important to understanding the Gypsy's ethnohistory and general life experiences.

Language and Education

The Gypsies refer to themselves as *Rom*, "the people," or "we, the *Rom*" to distinguish themselves from the Gadje or non-Gypsies. They speak *Romanes* (the Gypsy language), *Romani*, or *Romaney*, a Sanskrit based language. It is an unwritten language though it has been published by non-Gypsy scholars. According to Denham, the language is one of the single most important elements that contributes to their cultural isolation from others.[43] Because *Romanes* is not a written language, no documents or records have been preserved by the Gypsies. Moreover, the *Rom* speak *Romanes* among each other, but they rarely speak the language in front of *Gadje*. The *Rom* also generally understand enough *Gadje* to function in business or an economic deal. Denham states that "ninety-five percent of Gypsies are illiterate."[44] They do not use the *Gadje* language to record births, participate in the census, or to record deaths. From these factors, one can identify the strong in-group cultural values and the use of language to protect themselves.

Educational Factors

The *Rom* generally do not like to send their children to American public schools as they do not believe it is necessary. In Europe, Leininger found that most children went to school in order to abide by the strict city and rural laws.[45] In America, young Gypsy boys attend early school and by ten years they are brought into the adult world roles and lifeways. American Gypsy parents fear that if their children attend public school, they will be influenced and corrupted by other *Gadje* children. And since they do not honor most *Gadje* laws and customs, they feel no concern regarding laws requiring their children to attend school. At eight to eleven years of age young American Gypsy children are fully incorporated into adult activities.[46] The girls learn fortune-telling, art projects, and domestic homework; boys become familiar with auto repair, tarmacking, furnace repair, and part-time masculine Gypsy activities. Sway believes their learning is not for the basic value of education but that they may be adept in dealing with and manipulating the welfare system and for other gains.[47] Sutherland relates her experiences as a principal in a Gypsy school established in San Francisco by

California's Children's Hospital. She found that the *Rom* were in total control of the school and utilized it to discuss the *kumpanias*, or the social-political issues.[48]

Some unsuccessful attempts to develop Gypsy schools have been reported in the literature. Denham reported about a Gypsy alternative school project in Seattle, Washington and that it took two and one-half years for the teacher to gain acceptance and trust with the *Rom*.[49] Leininger reported similar findings in the Northwestern and Midwestern Gypsy areas.[50] Sway reported a high rate of absenteeism among Gypsy students in schools and noted they frequently fail to succeed.[51] Further studies are needed worldwide to identify the extent of Gypsy educational practices and school health care needs of Gypsy children.

Religious Factors

Since the *Rom* believe from a religious perspective that they should remain a separate people, their religion helps them to maintain an insider-outsider boundary.[52] Gypsies tend to accept the dominant religion in the area in which they live.[53] They maintain a deep belief in the supernatural powers and have incorporated much of the philosophy of religion into their daily lives. Their adoption of a popular religion is another method to avoid persecution. Their temporary religious "conversion" is often superficial compared with religions such as the Muslims, Roman Catholics, Greek Orthodox, and Protestants.[54] Leininger found their traditional beliefs in the three American Gypsy areas of supernatural powers, magic, and their moral "pure and impure" codes sustained their decisions and served as a blueprint for daily living.[55,56]

Sway identified many similarities between Gypsy religion and Judaism. She found that they rejected the notion of Christ as the Son of God, they circumcised their sons, and they had a dictum against killing man or animal.[57] The men usually left religious duties to the women.[58] Some Gypsies continue to celebrate the usual Christian holidays of Christmas, Easter, and the Orthodox holidays which follow the Greek Orthodox calendar. Sutherland in her study on health and illness practices among the *Rom* of California identified the following ritual feast days that they celebrated, namely, Saints John, George, Anne, and Nicholas.[59]

Gypsies believe in ghosts and miracles.[60] While they do not recognize the devil, the use of curses is a common intervention when punishing members who have committed crimes. Much of their interpretation of religion is deeply embedded within their own traditional cultural rituals. For example, when a Gypsy death occurs, an extensive ritualistic process is initiated. Through an elaborate communication system, relatives from many places in the country come to be with the dying or dead. For three days all Gypsies must grieve by remaining in the presence of the dead. During this time, they may not bathe, shave, wear jewelry, or change clothes. After three days the funeral is held and it is followed by a *pomana* (death feast) in which they feast on food prepared in units of three, i.e., three chickens and three pots of potatoes. Additional feasts are held at three, six, and nine month intervals. Close relatives generally wear their mourning clothes for a full year after the death of a loved one.[61] It is believed that after a one year period, the deceased soul enters heaven. Religion, as part of the social structure factors, is clearly interpreted and practiced within the values, beliefs, rituals, and symbols of their culture. The caring concepts of *being with* and *giving presence* to *Rom* members are of great importance.

Economic and Technical Factors

Sway identified a variety of cultural and economic factors that have enabled the Gypsies to survive over time and in different geographic areas, especially because they are flexible and ready to travel and survive.[62] They tend to use and often exploit the natural resources of others. They avoid age or sex typing in the division of labor so that they can pursue more activities and occupations. Traditionally, they have a winter and summer economy. In the summer they tend to engage in farm work as hired helpers, as carnival workers, or in semi-skilled activities. Other activities include blacktopping driveways and auto repair. Fortune-telling is a common source of income in both seasons and is considered women's work.[63,64]

Women are trained in the art of fortune-telling. They practice fortune-telling at fairs, flea markets, or some practice out of their *ofisia* (store front for fortune-telling). The *ofisia* is usually on a main street where customers come in for a reading. In some cases the Gypsy's family lives in the rear of the *ofisia*. A reading fee may range from $10.00 to $25.00 per session.[65] Local laws on fortune-telling vary in the United States, and in some cities fortune-telling is illegal; in other cities a licensing fee is required.[66,67]

The *bujo* is a type of confidence game called "switch-the-bag" practiced in fortune-tellers in which a *Gadje* is swindled out of large sums of money.[68] This type of larceny is not considered a crime because it is directed only at the *Gadje*. Sutherland discusses that Gypsy female occupations such as extracting money, fortune-telling, selling flowers, and even begging requires skill in observing and in evaluating personalities to be successful.[69] Because fortune-telling is a skill which becomes better with experience, older women are considered to be very talented and are valued by their kin. Women also make paper flowers and sell them as a side business.

Traditionally, Gypsy men have engaged in a variety of skilled trades such as coppersmithing. Today this skill is no longer in demand and the men are involved in auto repair, farm work, repairing their houses, and a variety of other tasks where they live. Some men work as used car dealers or animal trainers, specifically those involved in the carnival life. In addition, some men are entertainers and musicians.[70,71] Young boys from age nine to eleven are included in these activities and are actively socialized into the work group.[72]

Finally, a recently recognized "occupation" frequently cited in the literature is the participation of Gypsies in the public welfare system.[73] To most individuals this would not be considered an occupation, but it is recognized as such by the Gypsies. They are held to exploit this system to its fullest and take pride in such endeavors.[74] Because the *Rom* have large extended families and often live under the same roof, it is easy to identify several children for welfare as belonging to different kin-related families. Sway believes that both children and the elderly contribute to the economic stability of their kinship groups.[75] Sometimes the Gypsies are able to confuse or connive case workers to give them what they need through welfare systems, such as getting funds through Aid to Dependent Children (ADC), Old Age Security (OAS), and Social Security Supplemental Income (SSSI).[76] Gypsies depend on their ability not only to observe outsiders, but to read personalities and develop sufficient rapport with welfare workers in amazing ways. They are skilled and comfortable in begging, cajoling, threatening, or using loud and seemingly irrational behavior with strangers.[77,78] Gypsies take pride in the amounts that they can obtain from welfare or outside sources. They pass on their strategies and effective techniques to other Gypsies and serve as role models to the young.

An overwhelming value is that the Gypsy does not work for the *Gadje*, rather he tends to use them for whatever gains can be made such as extracting income at the expense of the *Gadje*. Generally, Gypsies do not work for each other, but they may engage in work or group partnerships. Some modern Gypsies in the United States live in stationary homes and some are in modern mobile travel buses.[79,80] In early days, however, they traveled in wagon caravans drawn by horses.[81] Leininger discovered that most Gypsies in northern Europe lived in new, expensive, large, and beautifully equipped modern mobile homes.[82] The Gypsies park these motor homes on unused land sites (sometimes on the edge of garbage sites) and remain there until their time limit as squatters expires. Then the Gypsies move to another place and repeat a similar living process.[83,84]

During the research in northern Europe, the informants said their mobile homes were "almost paid for." The homes were furnished with modern appliances and furniture. Bright colored flowers were in each window of these modern mobile homes. These families also had cars and phones and television sets in the homes.[85] In contrast, the American Gypsies did not live in such lavish mobile homes in the early 1970s, but there have been more modern ones in recent years.[86] Because of large extended Gypsy families, there were about eight mobile homes in one United States geographic area so they could be readily contacted and remain interdependent for protection.

Most American Gypsy homes had furnishings that could be quickly and conveniently moved. Inside the home the Gypsies had very few magazines, books, or newspapers. In general, the Gypsies with sedentary homes tended to have more material possessions than Gypsies living in large mobile homes or buses.

Kinship and Marriage

Each Gypsy has four loyalties and identities, namely his *natsia* (nation, tribe, or Rom group), *kumpania* (Rom traveling together), *vista* (kin), and the extended family. The *natsia*, nation or tribe, is their identity group. The basic unit of the Gypsy nation is the extended family. Gypsy tribes are divided on the basis of settlement patterns. The sedentary ones are referred to as *sinte*; the traveling ones are referred to as *nomads*.[87,88] Each tribe is also often identified with the occupation most frequently practiced by the people. In the United States the four most common tribes are *Hovara* (the money people), *Macvaya* (the traders), *Kalderasa* (the coppersmiths), and *Churara* (the people of the knife). The two largest tribes in the United States are the *Kalderasa* and the *Macvaya*.[89] Even though cultural variation and dialect differences exist among the Gypsy tribes, there are no known systems for classifying them.[90]

The *kumpania* is a group of extended families who travel or reside together. They may not always be from the same nation, but they occupy a particular geographical territory or residence area. The *kumpania* generally maintain economic control of their territory. Newcomers into an area are expected to get permission to work and reside in a designated area. Each *kumpania* has a leader, generally the most respected member, who is the spokesperson to deal with *Gadje* on their turf.[91] This leader has authority over business matters and migrations and controls the Gypsy *kris* (tribunal). Each *kumpania* is composed of a number of *vistas*, or patrilineal extended families, in which the *vistas* average from twenty to two hundred in a *kumpania*, and men inherit their father's *vista*.[92] The *kumpania* tends to be more of a cross-section of various kin groups.[93]

Gypsies tend to marry young and practice arranged marriages. The groom's father selects a *bori* (daughter-in-law) with the *xanamik* (marriage arranger) and pays a *daro* (money). Sway and Leininger found that the bride prices in the United States range from $5,000 to $30,000.[94,95] The marriage festivities last three days after which the bride and groom consummate the marriage. After marriage, the newly married couple live in the groom's paternal household until they have several children of their own and the family is satisfied with their adult behavior and skills. A new nuclear household is established but remains only semi-independent. The *bori* must prove herself to her new family and is expected to perform services with few demands in return.[96] Marriage is generally not for love but for the most practical and best economic and social situation of the *kumpania*. The duties of the new bride are to care for her in-laws and produce grandchildren.[97,98,99] After the couple have several children, they usually establish their own residence.

Birth is considered a time of *marime* (pollution or unclean period) for the mother for six weeks after the birth of the infant. Generally, babies are born at home, but recently more hospital births have occurred. Children are believed to bring good luck. Because of the social structure and cultural values, Leininger found that the children were usually cared for by many different people including extended family members and by clan Gypsies living in the residential area.[100,101] Children are expected to respond and respect "multiple parents." Most adults cared for, protected, and expressed love to their children. For newly married couples, the birth of the first child changed the position of the *bori* to mother-of-the-child.

Children are, indeed, a major focus of Gypsy culture. Child-rearing is the responsibility of everyone in the family unit.[102] The children under age two are tended by grandparents or unmarried older children. Infant care is permissive and protective. Children are weaned and toilet trained in a gradual fashion as these activities are not considered important processes.[103] Children are regarded as miniature adults, and teenagers do not experience an adolescent period as traditionally practiced in the non-Gypsy world. Gypsy children begin a professional adult-like socialization at ten years and they remain with their own sex to learn the skills of the adults. This helps them to learn their occupational roles and maintains a desired sex role image. Bonds, in the past, found there had been limited juvenile delinquency among the Gypsies regardless of the environment in which they lived.[104] Today, with some Gypsy children attending public schools, there are more signs of juvenile social offenders, but still juvenile delinquency seems to be less than with non-Gypsy adolescents.[105,106]

The primary cultural taboo recognized by the Gypsy culture which influences nursing care practices is the concept of *marime*. *Marime* refers to a state of being polluted or soiled and of being considered profane or non-sacred. It is a broad concept and carries the idea of upsetting the harmony of the universe.[107] During menses, pregnancy, or some illnesses, a Gypsy can be *marime*. Certain foods or animals such as cats and birds are *marime*. During periods of *marime*, rituals of separation are practiced to protect the well-being of the Gypsies. A person can be found *marime* by the legal Gypsy leaders for selected infractions, such as violations of sexual conduct codes, or not following Gypsy rules of food preparation, clothes washing, or cleaning. Elaborate rituals generally occur to cleanse oneself of this state. Several American Gypsies told Leininger that "anything above the waist is sacred and below the waist is *marime* or polluted."[108] They were concerned that health professionals did not understand this important concept of *marime* and that health personnel violated their well-being and health when they were hospitalized. Leininger found in her research that nurses and other health personnel were unaware of this concept and its nursing implications.[109] The *marime* not only protects their perceived well-being, but the unity and strength of the Gypsy group. *Gadje* interactions with them could cause an unfavorable state of *marime*, and Gypsies need to guard against and watch nurses and physicians who violate their *marime*.

The focus of the family was to maintain the economic stability of the *vista* and *kumpania*. All decisions and activities of the two groups were conducted with the goal of economic and social stability. As consequence, isolation from the *Gadje* was maintained. Marriage outside the tribe was often considered serious and the person was generally expelled. Decision-making in the extended family was by the older dominant male. Because age was highly respected, an older dominant female was included in selected family decisions. Leininger found that in this elaborate kinship system caring was protective group care, watching over, and respecting Gypsy cultural values, beliefs, and moral code—all extremely important caring ways to maintain Gypsy health or well-being.[110,111] Thus the caring values of group protection, watching over, guarding against, alleviating harassment, and maintaining some suspicious behavior were important in Gypsy lifeways. These care values were embedded in the kinship, religious, political, and economic areas and must be explicated in nursing research.

Political and Legal Factors

Gypsy culture has its own system of justice. They do not honor, respect, or follow most of the laws of the *Gadje*, but rather have their own process called the *kris*, or court tribunal.[112] This is a decision-making body, rooted in the *kumpania*, that deals with problems and crime, and interfaces with the non-Gypsy world. Persons who betray the group are subject to judgments and punishments including permanent banishment from the tribe or clan. Banishment from the tribe is a very serious aspect of Gypsy life which impacts on many aspects of the kinship, social relationships, and cultural practices of the Gypsies.

The *kris* is a judicial body of two to five adult males who are selected on the basis of their reputation, wealth, and status. Decisions made by the *kris* are public and generally accepted by the group.[113] The *kris* can declare a member to be *marime* (soiled, taboo, or polluted) and considered to be outcast for a designated period of time. During this punishment time, other members of the *kumpania* may not interact with him or her. The types of infractions dealt with by the *kris* include marriage to a non-Gypsy; criminal cases such as murder, wife beating, adultery, or becoming too familiar with the *Gadje*.[114]

Sway holds that the major function of the *kris* is social control over the Gypsy community, and most Gypsies follow Gypsy laws and practices.[115] Those who do not follow the Gypsy code of conduct will be excommunicated and severely punished. The *kris* serves to reinforce a specific and definitive code of behavior among the Gypsy community. McLaughlin reports on a situation in Chicago where a young Gypsy man had attempted to establish a Gypsy school.[116] The *kris* determined that this was an intrusion into the Gypsy community. The man was shot by an unknown assailant, his home was burglarized, and his two sons were framed and spent time in jail. This exemplifies the extent of power in decisions of the *kris* and its enforcement.[117] The *kris* appears to maintain strong power and cohesiveness of the Gypsy community. While the *kumpanias* have leaders who preside over the *kris*, the practice of having Gypsy chiefs or kings is more a myth than reality. Leininger found that the dominant care values related to protective community care prevailed and were embedded in many aspects of the political and legal system, and that the *kris* was a highly functional means to protect the Gypsies from *Gadje*, especially "government harassers."[118,119]

Specific Nursing and Health Care Research

To date there has been limited nursing and health research on Gypsies in America, Europe, and other countries. Early nursing research studies by Leininger and Mandell revealed that Gypsies seldom used professional health services in the United States unless their folk (or generic) care system failed.[120,121] Gypsies used professional health care from a crisis-oriented perspective. Still today many Gypsies are not comfortable in entering the professional "stranger-*Gadje*" health system as it is perceived to cause potentially more harm than good. Gypsies, therefore, seek health care only when they have an acute and unresolved condition or for emergency major surgical and medical needs.[122]

In Leininger's early ethnonursing research study of Gypsies in the northwest, she found that when a Gypsy came to the hospital for major surgery, many members of the extended family accompanied the client.[123] These clan and family members expected to remain with the sick client and stay by their bedside day and night. This posed serious problems for the nursing staff and hospital administrators whose hospital norms were to have only one or two relatives per client visit with a client. Leininger recalls that as a transcultural nurse, she often was called to handle these cultural problems." After much explaining and negotiating with hospital room administrators, a large ward room was obtained to accommodate the Gypsy kin and clan members (often twelve to fifteen). The Gypsies were willing to pay for a large room and they had the money. A large ward was especially demanded when the queen or king Gypsy was admitted, as they had great status and prestige with their clan. Clan members were expected to watch over, protect, and give presence, and perform caring and curing rituals. The Gypsies also requested permission to use their electric cooker in the hospital room in order to make soup and warm beverages for their *vista* members. They also wanted to perform their religious rituals of lighting candles in the room and to chant their prayers aloud without interference from the nursing or medical staff. Candle burning was important to protect the Gypsy person if she (he) died. If the candle was burning, the soul would be favorably received in heaven. Burning a candle in the room created problems for the staff as the client would probably need oxygen after surgery. The problem was handled by turning off the oxygen (which was not needed all the time) and wheeling the tank from the room at certain agreed upon times. This greatly pleased and reassured the Gypsy clan members and especially the client. The Gypsies also wanted to sprinkle a small amount of dirt on the bed because of their belief in earthly blessing as a healing and caring mode. This was another professional nursing taboo, mainly related to cleanliness and keeping the environment clean. The nurses placed a small amount of dirt under the draw sheet, which satisfied the clan. Many of the above Gypsy's wishes were respected with creative transcultural nursing practices. This ethnonursing research action study was a major learning experience for the staff nurses and other health professionals. It helped to demonstrate creative ways to provide culture-specific care and client satisfactions. The Gypsies were exceedingly pleased with the transcultural nursing services, and this hospital became known as a good one and one that other Gypsies should use because they were treated well by the *Gadje*.[124]

Anderson and Tighe reported that the Gypsies generally have a distrust of the mainstream medical system and sometimes deliberately provide unreliable data or misinformation to health personnel.[125] They found follow-up nursing and medical care to be poor and inadequate. To the Gypsies medicine and medical help were for curing and not preventing. In situations where cures did not occur, a variety of responses from the Gypsies occurred including frustration, mistrust, and lack of continuation in health care.

Thomas, et al. reported a high incidence of Gypsies with hypertension, diabetes, vascular disease, coronary artery disease, hyperlipidemia, obesity, and tobacco use. These factors relate to the lifestyles, dietary habits and practices of the Gypsies.[126] Wenzel et al. present a case study of a young Gypsy child admitted to a pediatric intensive care unit who subsequently died from pneumonia.[127] Recognition of the kinship structure, allowing the families to practice selected rituals, honoring the Gypsy practice of allowing many family visitors to maintain a vigil, respecting the cultural practices or taboos of the tribe and using folk remedies were strongly recommended. These considerations were extremely important for nurses to promote Gypsy well-being and health. Thomas described ways in which health care workers can respect the cultural practices of Gypsies by becoming more knowledgeable of their specific lifeways and beliefs.[128]

There has been limited research about cultural folk cures except *marime* rituals related to cultural folk cures. Wood, a Gypsy from Britain, has written a text about generic folk care remedies. He stated, "Nowadays most Gypsies go to the chemists for their medicines, and you can no longer be sure the old cures will help you.[129] Leininger found American and European Gypsies relied heavily on folk care and cure modes with limited use of profession services and medications.[130,131] Gypsies were using onions, vegetables, and herbal teas for their sore throats, warts, fever, diarrhea, toothaches, and broken bones. They were very skeptical about and distrusted commercial medicines.

In a recent extensive study based on fifteen years of anthropological field work with the *Rom* of California, Sutherland provided an exhaustive list of the generic or folk remedies utilized by the Gypsies. Among them she discussed cures for high blood pressure, baldness, flu, epileptic fits, and infection of a baby's navel. She stated, "For itching, make a paste of pork lard and apply to itching area."[132] She further discussed comments made by Gypsies who assisted her in her field work such as "Publish the remedies because the young kids don't know what's good for them."[133] The Gypsies expressed fear that their grandchildren were turning more to American medicine and would lose their knowledge of herbs and plants.[134]

Because Gypsies have generally remained isolated and outside the mainstream health care system, few health care providers, especially nurses, have studied specific health practices in relation to acculturation. Acculturation or assimilation into the dominant society has, however, been limited because of the Gypsy philosophy of remaining isolated and distinct from *Gadje*. Hence their own health care programs remain more traditional and satisfying to them. Some Gypsy adolescents are being influenced by their *Gadje* peers to "try" other kinds of medicines and street drugs, but many have remained resilient to acculturation pressures to be part of the dominant cultures.

Analysis of Data and Cultural Care Findings

Analysis of the data for this mini-ethnonursing study of the American Gypsies was done by using Leininger's Phases of Ethnonursing Analysis for Qualitative Data. All data were collected and analyzed using the four sequential phases.[135] Phase One: Documenting the Raw Field Data included documenting all emic and etic field observations, participatory experiences, and interviews with key and general informants from the three different Gypsy groups (a total of nine key and twenty general group informants). Phase Two: Identifying and Categorizing Components entailed studying, coding, and identifying emic and etic descriptive components for similarities and differences among the Gypsies studied in the United States. In Phase Three: Search for Pattern and Contextual Features data were abstracted from Phases One and Two to identify recurrent patterns of similarities and differences among the Gypsies, and to consider these findings in relation to the domain of inquiry, theoretical premises, and research questions. Phase Four: Major Themes and Research Findings was focused on an explication and formulation of findings abstracted and verified from the previous three phases. Synthesis and interpretation of the data into meaningful Gypsy themes identifying specific findings in relation to the theory of Culture Care were done. Data from the three previous phases were carefully rechecked to confirm and substantiate findings and conclusions. All data for this qualitative ethnonursing study were studied from the first day of data collection continuing until the end. The data were studied in-depth in relation to each qualitative criteria, namely: credibility, confirmability, meaning-in-context, recurrent patterning, saturation, and transferability. Due to space limitations, the reader is referred to the definitions of each criterion and their uses in ethnonursing studies.[136]

Major Research Findings Bearing on Gypsy Culture Care

Several of the findings from this study have already been integrated into the above sections on the social structure with related research and literature on the subject. This integrated and related form of reporting qualitative findings brings ideas together in a meaningful contextual way. The worldview, social structure, ethnohistorical, and folk-professional narrative sections were areas to incorporate some of the findings. Hence these areas will not be reported again. Instead, additional major research findings specifically focused on the Culture Care theory, the questions, and other interesting care and health findings from the study will be presented.

With respect to three questions studied, a major finding was that the Gypsy culture care meanings, expressions, and patterns were clearly embedded and confirmed in the worldview, ethnohistory, political, legal, religious, kinship, and cultural values. Culture care findings were evident in the ethnohistorical, religious, kinship, social ties and especially the cultural values and worldview, and in relation to special language uses. These factors were extremely important to discover and confirm the dominant cultural values and care aspects. Education and technology were not significant factors with Gypsies. Generic or folk health practices were being used more than professional practices as the Gypsies distrusted and were skeptical about most professional health services. All nine key and fifteen of the general informants confirmed their views about the generic and professional health systems with this familiar refrain, "We rely on our own medicine, care and treatments because we cannot trust the *Gadjes*. We just don't know what they will do to us." Several key informants made statements similar to the following, "We only go to the hospital when we are acutely ill and cannot manage our health concerns in the hospital. It is too dangerous and uncertain to go to a *Gadje* hospital." Still another key informant and two general informants expressed concern that *Gadje* nurses and physicians do not understand them and their needs. They were very concerned about how professionals deal with *marime*. They also identified that their nomadic lifeway of moving from one location to another (except for two groups that had been sedentary) made using professional health systems impossible.

Findings revealed that the Gypsies disliked giving hospitals and health professionals information about their people as they felt the information was misused and could be used negatively against them. All key informants and general informants said it was too risky to give one's identity to professionals unless acutely ill or in serious crises, and then only in limited amounts. The Gypsy key informants reconfirmed that the Anglo-Americans and other health personnel revealed by their behaviors that they generally distrusted Gypsies. Several informants said "They locked up everything like we were stealing the place when we came into the hospital." Meanings-in-context were important to understand their comments and how they were treated, especially in the hospital. None had received any community or home (public health) care. They thought it was an interesting idea as they lived in community areas.

From the analysis of the data, four major themes were identified: 1) there is a marked dichotomy between the Gypsy and non-Gypsy *(Gadje)* world that greatly limits caring expressions, practices, and survival; 2) the sacred (spiritual and religious world) is valued; whereas the profane world of the *Gadje* is to be questioned and devalued; 3) the Gypsy worldview, social structure (especially kinship, religion, and economics) provide moral guidance of ways to interact with and protect Gypsy caring and relationships with *non-Gadje*; 4) specific cultural values and care means were evident to protect and maintain Gypsy lifeways.

From these themes the specific major cultural values and the care meanings and actions of the Gypsies were identified and are presented in Figure 20.1. These findings are extremely important to guide nurses decisions and actions and were confirmed from recurrent patterning and credibility criteria. These findings substantiate the research questions and theoretical premises of the Culture Care Theory.

Use of Leininger's Three Modes of Decision and Action

In the analysis, the three major decision and action modes from Leininger's Culture Care Theory were studied. They authors drew especially upon the findings of the informants' Gypsy worldview, ethnohistory, social structure, and folk-professional values and practices to identify nursing care actions and decisions as the goal of the theory. The nurse, in caring for the client, needs to understand and use ethnohistory, cultural values, and their health practices for specific care actions and decisions to attain culturally congruent nursing care. The three care modalities are discussed next in relation to the findings and as guidelines for the nurse to give care.

1. Culture Care Preservation and Maintenance Modes

In providing culture care preservation and maintenance, the strong kinship, political, and religious beliefs gave Gypsies security, protection, and identity as caring modes and especially for their cultural identity. These dimensions should be actively preserved by the nurse and would contribute to congruent nursing care that is satisfying and beneficial. The nurse would especially need to be attentive to *Rom* ways, the social structure features related to the *vista*, *kumpania*, *kris*, and other societal features that have linguistic and cultural meanings and provide Gypsies with group protection, especially in the hospital context.

Culture care preservation would need to be considered by not forcing the Gypsies into professional health care ways and a system which they distrust. Instead, offering them ways to make their hospitalization congruent and beneficial to their folk ways and values would be important. Expectations related to cultural rituals, spiritual care, and group kin presence would need to be maintained while in the hospital or in home care. The use of other-care by family, clan members, and others in their world would be very important.[137] The use of self-care practices of focusing on the individual, self-administered care, and independence of the Gypsy client would be limitedly used as these are counter to their cultural values.

Culture care preservation of *marime* should be used in certain nursing situations. For example, if a Gypsy woman delivered her baby in the hospital, the nurse should allow her to practice ritualistic cleansing. The nurses should not encourage the father to visit during this "polluted time" and nurses would respect and preserve the foods and use of safe Gypsy herbal medicines. Maintaining kin and Gypsy *vista* decisions would be imperative. For example, a young couple who still resides in the in-laws' house may defer decisions regarding their hospitalized child to the eldest male in the family. This may be strange to the Anglo-American, European, Australian and other nurses, but it has meaning to the kin as it provides protective group care. It is also a means for the kin to watch over and guard against *Gadje* decisions and influences that are distrusted or viewed as harmful as other-care protection.

The nurse must also realize and respect that Gypsies may not want to be acculturated into the dominant *Gadje* culture. If so, the nurse should not force, harass, or make them feel they have to adopt the dominant or another minority lifeway. This may be difficult for some nurses who have long held that Gypsies have to change some day and be like us. Cultural identity may need to be preserved with some of their benefits difficult for nurses to understand fully. When the Gypsies gain more confidence in *Gadjes*, they may then want to adopt some aspects of professional health practices. Confidence and trust may best be realized by nurses working with them directly in the home communities before the clients have to enter the hospital. Short term relationships will need to be considered rather than the usual longer term public health visits due to Gypsy mobility patterns. Working in one's familiar environment is a fundamental transcultural nursing principle that needs to be respected with cultures even amid some risks at times.

Figure 20.1

American (USA) Gypsy Dominant Cultural Values, Care Meanings, and Actions

Dominant Cultural Values	Dominant Care Meanings and Actions
1. Nomadic way of life	1. Protective in-group care
2. Distrust *Gadje*	2. Watch over and guard against *Gadje*
3. Strong kin and group solidarity	3. Facilitate and use of folk rituals and foods
4. Sacred and profane meanings	4. Respect Gypsy values, beliefs, and lifeways (especially *marime*)
5. Rely on generic (folk) care/cure	5. Maintain suspiciousness for well-being
6. Use of environmental resources	6. Give Gypsy presence when ill

2. Culture Care Accommodation and Negotiation

Culture care accommodation and negotiation will be major modes of nursing care as the nurse works with Gypsies. The nurse will need to accommodate extended families and *vista* members visiting hospitalized members, with several visitors coming and going during the hospital stay. The Gypsy client values culture care as presence, spiritual healing, and folk rituals. Bending the visiting rules may need to be practiced to accommodate the needs of the Gypsy client and the *vista*. It would be wise to have the client's room near the end of a hallway to accommodate several extended family or *vista* visitors. This would also prevent disruption and concern by *Gadje* clients. Culture care accommodation as an action and decision mode has already been discussed earlier in this chapter from Leininger's 1972 Gypsy research. From such care, the quality of transcultural nursing services as "good *Gadje* care" can be spread by word of mouth to other Gypsy groups in the region. The use of ritual prayer candles when death is imminent, accommodating the use of soups and other foods that Gypsies like when they are ill, and for clan members to be in the client's room would also need to be considered. This kind of culture-specific and congruent nursing care can greatly relieve the Gypsies' distrust of *Gadje* nurses.

3. Culture Care Repatterning and Restructuring

This refers to those caring methods used to help an individual or group make some major or modified structural changes related to unhealthy or non-beneficial care practices. This mode would be very difficult to achieve because of the Gypsies' suspicion, distrust, and fears of *Gadje* harassment. If trust were first established by nurses through culture care maintenance of some care practices as well as by accommodation modes, repatterning would be possible in some areas. For example, Gypsies have a high incidence of coronary artery disease, hypertension, obesity, and tobacco use. Planning with and getting them to understand how to repattern their lifeways related to these health hazards would need to be considered, as Gypsies value long life and want to see their children become adults and have children. Changes regarding diet, exercise, medication, and use of professional treatments with explicit use of the six care values in Figure 20.1 would be important in helping repattern these threats to health. Culture care repatterning must always be made with the client using creative thinking for beneficial outcomes. Active participation of the client and his (her) group would be very important with community perspectives. Individualistic care in repatterning could be attained. Most importantly, the nurse should have clients be active participants in planning, implementing, and appraising professional nursing care with respect to their emic care needs and lifeways to regain health and to build confidence and trust. Throughout any nursing action or decision using repatterning or accommodation strategies, the nurse needs to be knowledgeable about the worldview, social structure, past and present history, and the kinds of problems Gypsies have encountered in the *Gadje* world. The nurse needs to keep foremost in mind the cultural values and care meanings and actions as presented in Figure 20.1 as they serve as a cognitive map for actions and decisions. Working with the Gypsy extended family and *vista* within their environmental context would also need to be considered, especially in home care and to practice other-care rather than self-care.

While there are additional care practices that could be discussed, these will remain for the nurse to consider as she (he) works with Gypsies in the United States or elsewhere in the world within their specific environmental and cultural context. Cultural variation among Gypsies must be kept in mind in different countries as political, economic, and other factors influence their lifeways and values. For Gypsies who tend to get into trouble, one might hope nurses who understand legal processes could counsel them to avoid some major local problems with legal officials, schools, and community *Gadje*.

Concluding Statements

The ethnonursing study of the American Gypsies using Leininger's Culture Care Theory with the Sunrise Model was presented to enlighten nurses about a culture limitedly known and understood among health personnel.[138,139] The Gypsy culture has been a neglected culture. It is a culture with a long history in many countries in the world. The lack of interest and research on Gypsies appears related to negative views, prejudices, and distrust of the cultural group by nurses and other health personnel, along with negative stereotyped cultural myths. Findings from this study and from the literature of the Gypsy ethnohistory and research studies by anthropologists and sociologists such as Sutherland, Gropper, Sway, and Tomasevic are also helpful to understand these people. This chapter should serve as a springboard for future studies of Gypsies worldwide to discover culture care similarities (universals) or diversities using Leininger's theory of culture care. The culture, however, is not an easy one to study due to marked distrust and suspicious attitudes of the Gypsies toward non-Gypsies over a long period in the United States and elsewhere. Leininger's Stranger-Friend Enabler was a valuable guide to assess distrust and to move with the Gypsies during the study.[140] Transcultural nurses must continue to study difficult, neglected, and unknown cultures as we continue to build transcultural nursing knowledge to guide nurses in our present and rapidly changing immigrant and multicultural world. From this study, the reader should appreciate the tenacity of the Gypsies with their human spirit, their power to uphold what they value, and their ability to preserve and maintain that which they treasure most in their culture. While the Gypsy culture may well be a culture that nurses cannot readily or drastically change, it is a culture that nurses are challenged to respect and understand as a Gypsy human right.

Footnote: This slightly revised article was originally published in the *Journal of Transcultural Nursing*, v. 4, no. 1, Summer, 1992, pp. 17–29.

References

1. Leininger, M., *Culture Care Diversity and Universality: A Theory of Nursing*, New York: National League for Nursing Press, 1991a.
2. Ibid.
3. Leininger, M., *Transcultural Nursing: Concepts, Theories, and Practices*, New York: John Wiley and Sons, 1978.
4. Leininger, M., *Care: The Essence of Nursing and Health*, Thorofare, New Jersey: Charles B. Slack, Inc., 1984. (Reprinted by Wayne State University Press, 1988).
5. Leininger, M., "Leininger's Theory of Nursing: Culture Care Diversity and Universality," *Nursing Science Quarterly*, v. 2, no. 4, 1988, pp. 11–20.
6. Leininger, op. cit., 1991a.
7. Leininger, M., "Ethnonursing: A Research Method with Enablers to Study the Theory of Culture Care," *Culture Care Diversity and Universality: A Theory of Nursing*, M. Leininger, ed., New York: National League of Nursing Press, 1991b, pp. 69–118.
8. Leininger, op. cit., 1991a.

9. Leininger, op. cit., 1991b.

10. Leininger, op. cit., 1991a.

11. Leininger, op. cit., 1991b.

12. Leininger, op. cit., 1991a, p. 82.

13. Leininger, M., *Qualitative Research Methods in Nursing*, Orlando: Grune and Stratton, 1985.

14. Leininger, op. cit., 1991b.

15. Leininger, op. cit., 1985.

16. Leininger, op. cit., 1991a.

17. Leininger, op. cit., 1991b.

18. Lincoln, Y. and G. Guba, *Naturalistic Inquiry*, Beverly Hills: Sage, 1985.

19. Gropper, R., *Gypsies in the City*, Newark, New Jersey: The Darwin Press, 1975.

20. Ibid.

21. Denham, D., *Gypsies in Social Space*, California: Ragusan Press, 1981.

22. Ibid.

23. Sway, M., *Familiar Strangers*, Urbana: University of Illinois Press, 1988.

24. Sutherland, A., *Gypsies: The Hidden Americans*, Prospect Heights, Illinois: The Waveland Press, Inc., 1986.

25. Sutherland, A., *Gypsies: The Hidden Americans*, London: Tavistock Publications, 1975.

26. Denham, op. cit., 1988

27. Tomasevic, N., *Gypsies of the World*, London: Flint River Press, 1988.

28. Sway, op. cit.

29. Leininger, op. cit., 1978.

30. Kornblum, W. and P. Lichter, "Urban Gypsies and the Culture of Poverty," *Urban Life and Culture*, v. 1, no. 3, 1972, p. 239–253.

31. Ibid.

32. Ibid.

33. Leininger, M., Study of Gypsies in Large Hospital Context and Their Care Needs, Seattle: University of Washington, (unpublished manuscript), 1972.

34. Leininger, M., "Mini-Ethnonursing Comparative Study of Selected Gypsies in America and Europe," Detroit: Wayne State University, (unpublished manuscript), 1987.

35. Sway, op. cit., 1988.

36. Leininger, op. cit., 1972.

37. Sway, op. cit.,1988.

38. Gropper, op. cit., 1975.

39. Sutherland, op. cit., 1975.

40. Denham, op. cit., 1981.
41. Sway, op. cit., 1988
42. Ibid.
43. Denham, op. cit., 1981.
44. Ibid.
45. Leininger, op. cit., 1972.
46. Cotten, R., "Gypsy child care." Urban Nomads. New York: Transactions of Us New York Academy of Sciences, Series II 29: No. 50-5056, 1968.
47. Sway, op. cit., 1988.
48. Sutherland, op. cit., 1995.
49. Denham, op. cit., 1981.
50. Leininger, op. cit., 1972.
51. Sway, op. cit., 1988.
52. Ibid.
53. Gropper, op. cit., 1975.
54. Council of Europe. *Gypsies and Travellers Sociocultural Data*, Strasbourg: Council of European Publications Section, 1987.
55. Leininger, op. cit., 1972.
56. Leininger, op. cit., 1987.
57. Sway, op. cit., 1988.
58. Gropper, op. cit., 1975.
59. Sutherland, A., "Health and Illness Among the Rom of California," *Journal of Gypsy Lore Society*, v. 5, no. 2, 1992, pp. 19–59.
60. Council of Europe, op. cit., 1987.
61. McLaughlin, J., *Gypsy Lifestyles*, Boston: Lexington Books, 1980.
62. Sway, op. cit., 1988.
63. Leininger, op. cit., 1972.
64. Leininger, op. cit., 1987.
65. Sway, op. cit., 1988.
66. Leininger, op. cit., 1972.
67. Leininger, op. cit., 1987.
68. Sutherland, op. cit., 1986.
69. Ibid.
70. Leininger, op. cit., 1972.
71. Leininger, op. cit., 1987.
72. McLaughlin, op. cit., 1980.
73. Sutherland, op. cit., 1986.

74. Thomas, J., M. Dovcette, D. Thomas, and J. Stoechle, "Disease, Lifestyle, and Consanguinity in 58 American Gypsies," *The Lancet*, v. 8555, no. 2, 1987, pp. 377–379.

75. Sway, op. cit., 1988.

76. McLaughlin, op. cit., 1980.

77. Leininger, op. cit., 1972.

78. Leininger, op. cit., 1987.

79. Leininger, op. cit., 1972.

80. Leininger, op. cit., 1987.

81. Leininger, op. cit., 1972.

82. Leininger, op. cit., 1987.

83. Leininger, op. cit., 1972.

84. Leininger, op. cit., 1987.

85. Ibid.

86. Ibid.

87. Gropper, R., "Urban Nomads: The Gypsies of New York City," *Transactions of New York Academy of Sciences—Series II*, v. 29, no. 2, 1967, pp. 1050–1056.

88. Sutherland, op. cit., 1986.

89. Gropper, op. cit., 1967.

90. McLaughlin, op. cit.

91. Sway, op. cit., 1988.

92. Ibid.

93. Sutherland, op. cit., 1986.

94. Sway, op. cit.

95. Leininger, op. cit., 1987.

96. Gropper, op. cit., 1975.

97. Sutherland, op. cit., 1986.

98. Leininger, op. cit., 1972.

99. Leininger, op. cit., 1987.

100. Leininger, op. cit., 1972.

101. Leininger, op. cit., 1987.

102. Sway, op. cit., 1988.

103. Cotten, op. cit., 1968.

104. Bonds, A., "Romany Rye of Philadelphia," *American Anthropologist*, v. 44, 1942, pp. 257–274.

105. Leininger, op. cit., 1972.

106. Leininger, op. cit., 1987.

107. Gropper, op. cit., 1975.

108. Leininger, op. cit., 1987.

109. Leininger, op. cit., 1972.

110. Ibid.

111. Leininger, op. cit., 1987.

112. McLaughlin, op. cit., 1980.

113. Ibid.

114. Sutherland, op. cit., 1986.

115. Sway, op. cit., 1988.

116. McLaughlin, op. cit.

117. Ibid.

118. Leininger, op. cit., 1972.

119. Leininger, op. cit., 1987.

120. Leininger, op. cit., 1972.

121. Mandell, F., "Gypsies: 'Culture and Child Care'," *Pediatrics*, v. 54, no. 5, 1974, pp. 603–607.

122. Leininger, op. cit., 1987.

123. Leininger, op. cit., 1972.

124. Ibid.

125. Anderson, G. and B. Tighe, "Gypsy Culture and Health Care," *American Journal of Nursing*, v. 73, no. 2, 1973, pp. 282–286.

126. Thomas, Dovcette, Thomas, and Stoechle, op. cit., 1987.

127. Wenzel, R., M. Dean, and M. Rogers, "Gypsies and Acute Medical Interventions," *Pediatrics*, v. 72, no. 5, 1983, pp. 731–735.

128. Thomas, Dovcette, Thomas, and Stoechle, op. cit., 1987.

129. Wood, M., *In the Life if a Romany Gypsy*, London: Routledge and Kegan Paul, 1973.

130. Leininger, op. cit., 1972.

131. Leininger, op. cit., 1987.

132. Sutherland, op. cit., 1992.

133. Ibid.

134. Ibid.

135. Leininger, op. cit., 1991a.

136. Leininger, op. cit., 1991b.

137. Leininger, op. cit., 1991a.

138. Leininger, op. cit., 1988.

139. Leininger, op. cit., 1991b.

140. Leininger, op. cit., 1991a.

Chapter 21
Jewish Americans and Culture
Madeleine Leininger, PhD, LHD, DS, FAAN, CTN, RN.

The Jewish people, their religion, and related culture care beliefs, values, and lifeways remain limitedly understood by many nurses and other health personnel. The long cultural history of the Jewish people, with their migrations into different places in the world for freedom, to practice their religion, and to preserve their family lifeways, is important for nurses to understand in order to facilitate culturally congruent care. In this chapter, Jewish American culture will be investigated using Leininger's Culture Care theory and the Sunrise Model to highlight culture-specific nursing care practices appropriate to Jewish clients. Although the major emphasis will be on Jewish Americans in the United States, many ideas presented have relevance to Jewish people in other places in the world.

Ethnohistory
Understanding the Jewish culture begins with a brief account of their ethnohistory. The term Jewish primarily identified a person of religious beliefs and identifiable cultural practices that generally characterize the people. Since the sixth century B.C., the term "Jew" was given to members of the tribe of Judah. It refers to the descendants of Abraham, the first of the three Patriarchs and the founder of the Jewish nation.[1,2] The term "Jew" is not identical in meaning to "Israeli," for the latter refers to a person of political citizenship of the state of Israel without regard to religion.[3]

Since the beginning of time many Jewish people have been singled out and persecuted for their religious rituals, beliefs, and practices. For example, in 210 B.C. the king of Syria was upset by the Jews' strange monotheistic beliefs and their tendency to remain separate from others. Other rulers wanted the Jewish people to stop infant circumcisions and begin eating pork.[4] Although the Jewish people were often threatened by others, they maintained their religious beliefs, rituals, and prayers to help them survive spiritually. They have continued to observe their holy days, maintain social group solidarity, and retain cultural beliefs or preserving their health and well-being. Moreover, the Jewish people in Europe and many in America created a degree of autonomy by developing and establishing their own educational institutions, social welfare programs, and support systems. They even developed languages while in exile. And since the Hebrew language was sacred and reserved for prayer and special interpretation of scripture, the Yiddish language which combined Hebrew with German, was developed.

Since the mid 1600s Jewish migrations from different places in the world continue to grow, especially to the United States of America. By the 1800s the German Jews migrated in large groups to America which led to the homogeneity of American Jews.[5] Many of these German Jews began to build elite Jewish retailing businesses in the United States with the people bound by their Jewish cultural ties and interests. For example, in the late 1800s, nearly ninety percent of all wholesale clothing firms in the United States were owned by Jews.[6] Most of these immigrants settled in New York and others in Philadelphia and Chicago, and these cities represented fifty-eight percent of the Jewish population. The Jewish network of providing supportive culture care among their groups was noteworthy and contributed to maintaining their survival and well-being. Some theorists hold that the Jewish people became more at home in the United States and became more aware of their strong cultural ties than Jewish people living in other places in the world.[7] Indeed the importance of the United States as a center for Jews and their Jewish cultural life increased markedly with the impact of the Nazi genocide of the Jewish people.[8] Jewish persecution has also been experienced not only with the Nazi persecution, but also by Jews in Communist regimes such as the past Soviet Union had the second biggest Jewish settlement in the world. Jewish people have shared these tragic life experiences, especially the Nazi Holocaust, as they established themselves in different places in the world.

During the post-World War years the Jewish people maintained their strong convictions and religious practices. Many preserved their dress, beards, and earlocks as they dispersed across the United States. In addition, the Jewish people have held their reverence for learning and diverse intellectual pursuits. They have taken positions in academic institutions and in many scholarly fields and public endeavors. Jewish people became leaders in religious studies, music, fine arts, and the motion picture, and entertainment industries in the United States.

Jewish membership has grown in numbers in the United States and worldwide. Their influences have been often identified with legislation to support the underprivileged, defending their own civil liberties and civil rights, nurturing their Jewish kin ties worldwide, and promoting international trade policies. The ethnohistory of the Jewish people reflects many struggles to survive, grow, and maintain their cultural identity and place in the world. The nursing student will find readings about the past and present Jewish culture history to be of much interest.

Worldview

Continuing with the use of the Sunrise Model to examine Jewish lifeways and care, the worldview becomes essential. The author holds that every culture has a worldview or a way of looking upon the world or the universe. The Jewish worldview is frequently viewed as one of suffering and surviving in different places in the world. The long history of persecution and discrimination and the need to retain Jewish religious values, beliefs, and practices are often expressed when one talked with Jewish informants. The strength of their cultural identity and not yielding to dominant culture's way of living has been manifest over time. Most children of Jewish parents tend to retain a strong sense of cultural pride and ethnocentrism about their valued lifeways. The Jewish people find their worldview keeps them closely united, ethnocentric, and cautious of movements or leaders who may cause them to suffer or lose their cultural identity. Most importantly, their worldview is reflected in their beliefs of four ways to become and remain Jewish. They are: 1) being born of a Jewish mother, 2) marrying a Jew and accepting Jewish norms and lifeways, 3) converting to Judaism, and 4) being fully integrated into a primary Jewish group with sustained loyalties and retention of cultural norms.

Education and Religion

Since Jewish religion and education are closely interwoven, they will be discussed together. Religion, with its complex dimensions, is central to the Jewish people. Judaism is a monotheistic religion based on the interpretation of the laws of God as found in the Torah and explained in the Talmud. Jewish laws prescribe the lifeways of people in their activities, diet, education, and ceremonial activities throughout the life cycle. There are three major religious groups within Judaism: Orthodox, Conservative, and Reform. There is also a fundamentalist sect called Hasidism. The history and ethnogeographic aspects of these three groups are generally held to be that Orthodox Jews originated in Israel, Conservative Jews began in Eastern Europe, and Reform Jews started in Germany, Hungary, France, and England around 1830.[9] The Orthodox Jews are the strictest group and firmly uphold religious values and practices. The Reform Jews are more flexible. Conservative Judaism falls between Orthodox and Reform in upholding religious values and lifeways. In the United States, Reform Judaism is more evident in membership with approximately seventy percent of all Jews. Conservative Judaism constitutes twenty-nine percent and Orthodox Judaism about ten percent of Jews in the United States.[10]

In recent years attendance at religious services in the synagogue in the United States has been slightly decreasing and home rituals have become more evident. There are usually five religious rituals with the home services: 1) lighting Sabbath candles Friday evening, 2) having or attending Seder or Passover, 3) eating kosher meat, 4) using separate dishes for meat and dairy foods, and 5) lighting Chanukah candles. Having the children participate in these home ceremonies and keeping them instructed in the tenets of the religion are important in home services. Jewish boys have always been expected to be educated from an early age in the same tradition as their fathers. Maintaining intellectual pursuits, valuing education, and being charitable are important features of Jewish lifeways, especially for the enculturation of males.

Judaism is largely based on observance of the Torah laws as given to Moses by God on Mount Sinai. The purpose of the Torah is to teach the Jewish people to act, think, and feel within the Jewish laws. Klein holds that classical Judaism has no word for "religion;" the closest counterpart in Jewish vocabulary is "Torah."[11] The Torah supports the belief that all aspects of living, including worship, business affairs, use of leisure time, and maintaining rites of passage such as the *bar mitzvah*, are important. Marriage and death are part of the mandate that Jewish people are to serve God in everything.

Religious beliefs and the education of Jewish people support the sanctity of life and related cultural values as ways of living. Jewish people hold that their bodies are God's; one's body is on loan from God and must be returned to God at death. The Jewish people are, therefore, observant of the Talmud and must keep themselves in a good state of health by caring for themselves and others. They are duty bound to exercise, get sleep, eat well, avoid drugs and alcohol abuse, and not commit suicide. Moreover they are obligated to help others to prevent illness, injury, disabilities, and death.[12] Another important belief is that the body God has given them is good and should be a source of holiness and pleasure as long as enjoyment is within God's rules.

The Jewish people observe a number of holy days such as Rosh Hashanah (the Jewish New Year); Yom Kippur (Day of Atonement); Chanukah (the Festival of Lights); Passover; Shavuot (the Festival of the Giving of the Torah); and Purim. These holy days and a few others are for Jewish clients to observe, especially with regard to surgical or medical procedures. For example, surgery and medical treatments should not be performed on holy days or on the Sabbath unless there is an emergency need.

The Jewish Sabbath, which begins at sundown Friday and lasts until dark on Saturday, is the holiest day. It is a day of rest which signifies that God rested after creating the world, and so Jewish people are expected to rest on the Sabbath day. Orthodox and Reform Jewish people may avoid using modern technologies in the home. Some Orthodox Jewish people might not travel except on foot or relinquish using the phone, elevator, car, or electric bed. They may not want to handle business or money matters on the Sabbath and holy days. These values need to be given full consideration as culture care accommodation in nursing care practices.

The importance of attaining holiness is not only by one's intellect but also to have energy to perform God's expectations. For example, eating has a divine dimension as the Jewish people observe dietary kosher laws and not eating pork or predatory fowl, nor mixing meat and dairy products during the same meal or from the same dish. Moreover only fish with fins and scales are allowed, and shellfish are prohibited. Preserving the proper dietary laws is important to attain holiness and to maintain their culture lifeways. The term kosher is often misunderstood by non-Jewish people who view it as a type of food. However, it means that all animals must be ritually slaughtered to be kosher, i.e., properly handled and preserved. According to Jewish law, there is a prohibition against ingesting blood such as raw meat or bloody substances, but this does not apply to receiving blood transfusions.

The synagogue is the place for prayer and it is an integral part of the prayer services to study the Torah. The synagogue is the center for religious study and the formal education of children and adults. The rabbi is active in many activities in the synagogue. Judaism is not embodied in the synagogue, but in the Torah. The rabbi and other males often wear a small black cap or *kippa* and sometimes a prayer shawl or *tallith*. Today most Jewish men and women sit together in prayer services in the synagogue.

In the Jewish culture there are other special religious services that need to be understood by nurses. The *bris* is a traditional birth ritual in which the male child to be circumcised by a religious leader or *mohel* shortly after birth. This ritual varies today in how it is observed and who performs the ritual, i.e., a rabbi, or sometimes one finds a pediatrician involved in the bris. The bris is actually a religious celebration of birth and the naming of the child. It is common practice to name the child after a recently deceased relative.

When the Jewish young enter adulthood, there are two other religious events. For males, this event is called *bar mitzvah* and for the females *bat mitzvah*.[13] These are both important occasions with big celebrations for young males and females. These ceremonies mark the induction of the individual into full adulthood with their spiritual role expectations. For young males, their spiritual role responsibility includes mastery of scripture reading. Many families and friends help young males and females celebrate these events as the young adults take on their new status and role responsibilities in Jewish culture.

Unquestionably, education is greatly valued and expected for Jewish people throughout the life cycle. Intellectual achievement is highly respected and viewed as important. Education is expected of all Jewish people, for it leads to spiritual growth as well as to economic, social, and cultural well-being on success. Jewish men are expected to be well educated and in recent decades, Jewish women are likewise expected to pursue advanced education and to move into special employment and community leadership roles. Education is strongly valued because it can transform and protect the individual. It also gives Jewish people a strong appreciation for their cultural heritage. Indeed, a well educated Jewish person has opportunities and benefits that have served them well in the United States. In general, the Jewish people have always valued education which comes largely from their religious beliefs and expectations. Jewish parents continue to set high educational standards for themselves and their children.

From the above religious and educational dimensions, the nurse can see some important considerations to understand and to use in providing culturally congruent care. Unquestionably, the nurse needs to practice culture care preservation with Jewish clients in preserving their holy days, the Sabbath, and ritual life cycle activities. Culture care accommodations may also be needed to provide their expected foods and for other nursing care needs of Jewish clients.

General Cultural Values

Based on the author's use of the Culture Care theory and research findings of Jewish Americans and from research from other sources over several decades, several dominant cultural core values have been identified.[14] These findings are based upon the ethnonursing qualitative research method with many key and general informants over time. Some intergenerational variations are evident among the three different Jewish groups. However, these cultural core values remained evident with Reform and Conservative Jewish informants. The dominant core Jewish cultural values to guide nursing practices were the following:

1. Maintaining respect for Jewish religious beliefs and practices.
2. Maintaining the spiritual centrality of family with patriarchal respect and the importance of mother caring values in sickness and well-being.
3. Supporting education and intellectual achievements.
4. Maintaining intergenerational continuity of the Jewish heritage.
5. Being generous and charitable with contributions to the arts, music, and community services.
6. Achieving financial and educational success.
7. Being persistent and persuasive.
8. Enjoying art, music, and religious rites.

These core values can be viewed as important "holding care values" as the nurse works with Jewish clients to plan and provide culturally congruent care. At all times, individual and family variations may exist among the different Jewish people who differ in relation to their geographic and environmental contexts. The above cultural core values remained with the informants and were confirmed as important to providing quality nursing care practices.

Kinship and the Generic (Folk) and Professional Health Care Systems

The family remains the core of the Jewish lifeways buttressed by religious beliefs and cultural values. The Jewish family is often viewed as more closely united than many non-Jewish families. Family closeness, unity, and the stability of the family is regulated to some extent by the Jewish religious laws and intergenerational values. For example, one is expected to honor one's father and mother and to care for one another in the family. The family values and the relationship between a husband and wife are based on the importance of mutual aid, harmony, peace, and good will. However, if dissension and conflict occur between a husband and wife with fighting and anger, the marriage can be dissolved, but it must be done according to the Jewish religious laws to be valid.[15,16]

In recent work the cultural anthropologist Harland discusses in Haviland's book that the original Jewish descent groups who immigrated to New York from Eastern Europe were known as family circles.[17] These family circles included all the living descendants with their spouses of an ancestral pair. They were linked by male and females to establish ambilineal descent (or different group) membership so as to avoid problems of divided loyalties and interests.[18] Each family circle had a name, usually the surname of a male ancestor, and they met regularly throughout the year. This was an innovative way to be organized in order to maintain family solidarity and mutual aid to one another. The Jewish family, however, has traditionally recognized patrilineal descent. They remain pleased and excited for the first child to be a male. The first male child is recognized as establishing *primogeniture* or acknowledgment of intergenerational Jewish male descent.[19,20]

A Jewish marriage is an elaborate festivity which unites two families. In the wedding ceremony, a glass is broken (*kheysa*) to symbolize the fragility of marriage. Many gifts are given to the couple and there is much interaction between the Jewish families and friends at the wedding ceremony. The married couple is expected to keep the marriage together forever and divorce is not encouraged.

The Jewish woman remains very important in the Jewish family, especially as a caring or nurturant person to the nuclear family.[21] She is the cornerstone of the family's spirituality and to maintain optimal health or well-being through her caring activities and rituals. Any person born of a Jewish mother or converted to Judaism is revered as a Jew. It is the Jewish mother who remains close to the children. She is eager to offer chicken soup to a Jewish sick person and to be an active listener and advisor to them. The father and mother are usually active to bring the family together on the Sabbath and on all special holy days as well as on other special family occasions to increase family unity and well-being. It should be noted that Jewish women teach caring ways to other women and they are also formally educated. Many women maintain key leadership roles in Jewish organizations and in community activities doing charitable deeds and helping in contemporary local, national, and international activities.

In the Torah it is said that Jews should be fruitful and multiply, and so most parents have at least two children. In the past, contraception and abortion were seldom permitted unless the woman's health was threatened. Traditionally Judaism did not endorse abortion on demand, but today some liberal Jews permit abortion if it is not used as a means of birth control. With a rabbi's permission artificial insemination may be done. Judaism holds that the fetus is a human being and has full sanctity of life. Efforts are, therefore, made to preserve infant life as a high priority at birth and throughout the life cycle. The parents and grandparents are usually very thrilled to have a child, and much attention is given to the newborn. While the family uses wine as part of their religious and family rituals, it must be used in moderation. A good Jewish person is not drunken. Jewish people have had a low incidence of alcoholism, which is largely held to be related to strong family caring modes and religious beliefs to control and regulate behavior.[22]

Technology

The use of technology as a part of the American way of living is becoming more acceptable to Jews than in earlier days. Today, Jewish families are using some of the latest technologies for their homes, but especially to support their health or well-being. Often, Orthodox Jews are reluctant to use the modern technologies. The nurse would have to use cultural assessment data to determine the use of technologies in client care, especially on the Sabbath and holy days.

Providing Congruent and Acceptable Nursing Care

In this last section, some major nursing care considerations are presented in order for the nurse to plan and take action with the Jewish clients in providing culture-specific care. Some generic (folk) and professional services related to providing congruent nursing care using Leininger's three modes of action and discussions will also be discussed.

Jewish people tend to rely on both generic (their home remedies) and professional health knowledge. This is in keeping with Jewish intellectual, scientific, and humanistic interests. In the past, these generic home remedies had been relied upon considerably while experiencing many unfavorable living conditions, discrimination practices, and other conditions. Today there is less reliance on generic care, however, the mother's care is often based on generic folk care, and held to be highly efficacious. In the author's research many of the folk care practices were evident and used. The women also recalled "old" folk practices such as the "evil eye", cupping for chest colds, and the use of amulets as objects to protect the person, but some of these were not used today. The charm or amulet symbolizing the "hand of God" is frequently worn by a Jewish person for good luck and protection. In addition, many mothers were relying on their "good home remedies" for colds, i.e., chicken soup, and other home practices as primary care practices for their children or adult friends.

The Jewish dietary religious laws prohibit eating milk and meat at the same meal, which can be viewed as part of generic religious and traditional practices. Eating unleavened bread (*matzah*), vegetables, herbs, and fruits is also a generic health promoting mode, as is drinking small amounts of wine. Most foods and how they are prepared and consumed are of symbolic religious significance, and so the nurse needs to be aware of these religious values and preserve than to maintain the well-being of clients. The dietary practices and the Jewish mother's caring patterns and techniques are very important to integrate into nursing practices. The nurse needs to respect these generic practices and their care meanings. Food symbols such as eating of *matzah* at Passover symbolizes the time the Jews were forbidden to eat leavened bread, and the wine is a symbol of joy and gladness when they fled Egypt in the olden days.

From my research with the Jewish people the following care meanings and action modes were identified with twenty-four key and thirty-six general informants and are discussed in relation to the three theoretical modes of care.[23] The culture care meanings and action modes to be incorporated into nursing care were as follows:

1. Expressing one's feelings and views openly.
2. Getting direct and the best help possible.
3. Accepting shared sufferings.
4. Supporting maternal nurturance, i.e., overfeeding, permissiveness, and overprotection.
5. Giving and helping others in need as social justice (*tsdokeh*).
6. Performing life cycle (birth, marriage, and death) rituals.
7. Being attentive to others.
8. Caring for one's own people (Jews).
9. Teaching Jewish values to family and others.

These care meanings and action modes are considered in light of cultural findings related to the worldview, ethnohistory, social structure factors, and other ideas already discussed about the Jewish cultural values. The culture care meanings and action modes are derived from these different factors and provide a means for culture-specific and competent care to Jewish clients. The nurse uses this knowledge as she (he) gives creative individualized or group care to members of the three Jewish groups. Culturalogic assessment remains extremely important to discover individual care variability in relation to the Orthodox, Conservative, or Reformed Jewish client. The care is tailor-made to fit the three care modes of the Culture Care theory.

In considering Leininger's theory with the three major care modes, it was evident that culture care preservation and accommodation would need to be emphasized most often with Jewish clients unless they have greatly modified their lifeways or changing religious beliefs. Religious and family life values would be especially important to preserve in order to help Jewish clients recover from an illness, or to help them regain and maintain their health or well-being. If these care values are maintained, one can reasonably predict client care satisfaction and beneficial nursing outcomes.

The nurse, however, needs to be attentive to the Torah laws which guide Jewish health and well-being and should use culture care accommodation. The latter is essential with accommodations being made for 1) dietary practices in the methods of food preparation by not mixing meat and dairy dishes; 2) nursing practices on the Sabbath and major holy days; 3) maintaining, respecting, and accommodating modesty and especially the dignity of the body; 4) respecting the sanctity of the life of the newborn and of Jews of all ages, and 5) generic or folk home remedies that are held to be beneficial as well as using modern professional modes of care as requested by clients and according to their needs.

In addition, the sensitive and knowledgeable nurse prepared in transcultural nursing would keep alert to the importance of letting Jewish clients talk and express their ideas openly as one listens and assesses their needs. At times, some Jewish clients can be very demanding, assertive, and persuasive in regard to "their needs." The latter has been especially annoying to some nurses in the hospital and in relation to pain. Jewish clients tend to be highly sensitive to cultural and psychophysiological pain. Some nurses complain about the Jewish clients' assertive and demanding behavior in regard to pain and other expectations, and they may avoid helping them. When Jewish clients are shunned or avoided, they often feel discriminated and resent non-caring responses. It is well to deal directly with clients' requests and views, but at times it is necessary to set limits as indicated by factors such as the nurse helping many other clients in the hospital unit and being unable to remain with the Jewish client for long periods of time. The nurse will also observe that female family members tend to be over-attentive to their sick family member with their affection, nurturant attitudes, feeding the client, performing home care rituals, and seemingly intruding into the nurse's professional role. It would be wise to have the Jewish mother assist with or to participate in the nursing care rather than exclude, shun, or avoid her.

In general, the culture care values of being attentive to, providing frequent nurse presence, offering nurturant expressions, and providing care directly are important care values to guide nurses in all care activities. The Jewish client will expect good care and will complain if it is not given. Good care tends to be determined largely by how evident the above care values are with nurses. Recurrent nursing problems frequently expressed by nurses in caring for Jewish clients are their demands for attention, their limited tolerance for pain, and to be sure nurses follow medical regimes. While it would be well to practice culture care accommodation acts, it is also important to consider culture care negotiations or repatterning the client's ways for improved health such as repatterning for overuse of drugs, medications, or injections. With those different care modes, the Jewish client can learn other ways to handle perceived and actual pain for improved health. For example, the client, or often a family member, may vocally demand that pain medication be given every one to two hours after surgery. The nurse may need to negotiate a plan for expanding the time unless there is evidence of a lot of real pain. Sometimes the nurse can redirect or repattern demands for pain relief by reexamining past shared Jewish sufferings and ways the Jewish people overcame sufferings in the past and through current religious beliefs. Other creative strategies can be used when one understands the culture and religious beliefs and values which are so closely linked with their psychophysical and sociocultural expectations. Sometimes ritualized decisions and timed actions are beneficial in repatterning nursing care. The nurse must be aware that not all clients in the post-surgery recovery room should be treated alike due to cultural variability, and the Jewish client is a "case in point" to consider.

Another area of nursing care for Jewish clients that requires knowledge of *emic* Jewish understandings and development of creative strategies is providing competent nursing care to the dying client. The care to the dying Jewish client is of major importance and will briefly be highlighted because it is significant to providing culturally congruent nursing practices that can lead to client and family satisfactions. A number of literature sources and research studies such as Lamm, Sohier, Leininger, and Boyle and Andrews.[24,25,26,27] Cultural variabilities with Jewish individuals and families and the three Jewish groups are, of course, given full consideration with dying clients. One of the important points to remember is that the family is expected to remain with the dying client. By doing so, they are showing respect for the client. There is also a spiritual obligation to watch over the person as he passes from this world into another. Prayers are recited by Jewish family members seeking the blessing of the "True Judge" at the time of death. Many Jewish clients prefer to die in their homes. The nurse should respect this request as much as possible. In so doing, it facilitates family rituals and obligations to the dying member in their familiar environmental context. Moreover, in the hospital, the family is often concerned with how to care for the client properly while she (he) is dying in this strange setting. If nurses and physicians do not understand Jewish generic care to the dying family member and are absorbed in professional activities and treatment expectations, they miss the opportunity to give culturally-based care. Since death is inevitable, current medical and nursing practices should not be curtailed unless indicated by the family. Usually no new medicine and care practices that artificially and extensively prolong life are initiated. Euthanasia is prohibited and viewed as murder. Comfort care and alleviation of pain are essential to the dying client.

After death, an autopsy and donation of body organs may be permitted, but only for particularly good reasons. The decision is made in consultation with the family, physician, and rabbi. Only essential organs remain and these organs or body tissues must be returned for burial, as the whole body must be buried. Cremation is generally not acceptable for it is not in keeping with Jewish laws. The body is to be washed and buried in a simple coffin within twenty-four hours. For the next seven days there is intense mourning (*sitting shiva*), followed by an eleven month morning period with daily prayer (*kaddish*). *Kaddish* is also said on the anniversary of the death.[28]

Summary nursing care points to be considered with the death of the Jewish client are the following: 1) the body is ritually washed (*taharah*) by the family or members or sometimes the nurse in the hospital. If the person is in the funeral home, the *chevra kadisha* and Ritual Burial Society will do the ritual washing; 2) the eyes and mouth are usually closed by family members or friends and a sheet is placed over the face; and 3) a candle is often placed near the head and sometimes around the deceased person. If the Jewish client is Orthodox, there is often the custom of placing the body on the floor and positioning it so that the feet face the doorway. Non-Orthodox Jewish families will not usually expect the body to be placed on the floor. The family, relatives, and friends may ask forgiveness of the deceased for any harm or discomfort they may have caused during the client's lifetime. At that time many psalms are recited by family and relatives. They will need to have a quiet place to pray and the nurse should be sensitive to and accommodate this anticipated need. The rabbi is usually called, and he will usually notify the *chevra kadisha* (burial society). The latter will typically take care of the body with the funeral director. From the time of death until burial, the deceased is with a watcher (*shomer*) who is generally a family member or personal friend. This person recites from the Book of Psalms. All deceased are buried in the same type of garment whether wealthy or poor. The shrouds are of muslin, cotton, or linen and symbolize simplicity, dignity, and purity. The deceased are wrapped in a prayer shawl (*tallith*) with one of the fringes cut. Gifts and flowers are generally discouraged, but money donations can be sent to charity or Jewish organizations and are appreciated. The Jews value charity because it can protect them from spiritual death and charity is in keeping with social justice goals. The burial of the Jewish person always takes place soon after death, in accordance with Torah laws. A mourning period exists for several months and one will find the relatives, especially immediate family who espouse traditional Jewish values, often wearing black or dark clothing.

From the above cultural values of the Jewish people, the nurse realizes how important transcultural nursing knowledge is to guide the nurse to provide culture-specific care or care that is congruent to the client's cultural values, social structure, worldview and care meanings. It is through these culturally-based practices that the nurse becomes a truly professional, culturally-based care provider helpful to the client and Jewish groups. This kind of nursing care helps the client recover from illnesses or die with dignity according to the Jewish lifeways. Jewish clients are especially cognizant of their religious and other values and expect nurses and other health care providers to incorporate the culture care into practices. If done, the nurse will find many traditional professional nursing practices will be transformed to meaningful culture care practices in which the nurse can serve the people. Currently, such transcultural nursing knowledge and skills are just beginning to be used in nursing in culture-specific ways. Care to Jewish clients can help the nurse gain understanding of the importance of Jewish cultural values and practices to realize the beneficial outcomes of nursing care practices. Most importantly, the nurse who understands the Jewish client will find nursing care to be less difficult and more effective when one knows the *why* of cultural patterning along with cultural nursing skills.

In this chapter a number of important nursing care knowledge areas have been presented to guide nurses to give culture-specific and congruent nursing care to Jewish clients. The research findings from the theory of Culture Care (using the components of the Sunrise Model) were used as the knowledge base to understand clients and to develop culture-specific nursing care. Literature on the Jewish culture is valuable to increase the nurse's understanding of the culture, however, the nurse must bring these ideas into a nursing perspective and develop creative practices. Doing a culturalogic assessment remains critical to ascertain individual and group variations with the three existing Jewish religious groups.

References

1. Green, J., "Death with Dignity: Judaism," *Nursing Times*, v. 85, no. 3, 1989, pp. 64–65.
2. Samuel, R., *A History of Israel: The Birth and Development of Today's Jewish State*, London: Steinmatzky, 1989, pp. 1–30.
3. Tweddell, C. and L. Kimball, *Introduction to the Peoples and Cultures of Asia*, Englewood Cliffs, New Jersey: Prentice-Hall, Inc., 1985, pp. 88–89.
4. Samuel, op. cit.

5. Goren, A., *The American Jews: Dimensions of Ethnicity*, Cambridge: The Belknap Press of Harvard University Press, 1982.

6. Ibid.

7. Ibid., p. 89.

8. Sklare, M., *America's Jews*, New York: Random House, Inc., 1971.

9. Ibid.

10. Dorff, E., "Judaism and Health," *Health Values*, v. 12, no. 3., 1988, pp. 32–36.

11. Klein, I., *A Guide to Jewish Religious Practice*, New York: KTAV Publishing House, Inc., 1979.

12. Dorff, op. cit.

13. Ibid.

14. Leininger, M., "Selected Culture Care Findings of Diverse Cultures Using Culture Care Theory and Ethnomethods," *Culture Care Diversity and Universality: A Theory of Nursing*, M. Leininger, ed., New York: National League for Nursing, 1991, pp. 345–366.

15. Donin, H. H., *To Be a Jew*, New York: Basic Books, 1972.

16. Greenberg, S., *A Jewish Philosophy and Pattern of Life*, New York: Jewish Theological Seminary of America, 1981.

17. Haviland, W., *Cultural Anthropology*, San Diego: Harcourt Brace, Jovanovich College Publishers, 1992, p. 271.

18. Ibid.

19. Finkelstein, L., *The Jews: Their Religion and Culture*, New York: Schocken Books, 1971.

20. Goldsmith, E. S., and M. Scult, eds., *Dynamic Judaism: The Essential Writings of Mordeau M. Kaplan*, New York: Schocken Books, 1985.

21. Schlesinger, B., *The Jewish Family: A Survey and Annotated Bibliography*, Toronto: University of Toronto Press, 1971.

22. Leininger, op. cit., p. 366.

23. Ibid.

24. Lamm, M., *The Jewish Way in Death and Mourning*, New York: Jonathan David Publishers, 1969.

25. Sohier, R., "Gaining Awareness of Cultural Differences: A Case Example," *Transcultural Nursing: Concepts, Theories, and Practices*, M. Leininger, ed., New York: John Wiley and Sons, 1978, pp. 433–450.

26. Leininger, op. cit., p. 366.

27. Boyle, I. and M. Andrews, *Transcultural Concepts in Nursing Care*, Boston: Scott, Foresman, Little, Brown, College Division, 1989, pp. 405–409.

28. Ibid.

Chapter 22
Navajo Child Health Beliefs and Rearing Practices Within a Transcultural Nursing Framework: Literature Review

Suzanne Phillips, Ed.D, ARNP, RN and Sandra Lobar, PhD,ARNP, RN

Leininger defines transcultural nursing as a "subfield of nursing which focuses upon a comparative study and analysis of different cultures and subcultures in the world with respect to their caring behavior; nursing care; and health-illness values, beliefs, and patterns of behavior with the goal of developing a scientific and humanistic body of knowledge in order to provide culture-specific and culture-universal nursing care practices."[1] One goal of transcultural nurses is, according to Leininger, to "identify, test and understand a body of transcultural nursing knowledge and practices."[2] Non-native American nurses who work with a Native American population such as the Navajo Indian tribe, are frequently unaware of the significance of beliefs and traditions within everyday life practices. Since childbearing and child-rearing are important life events in Navajo society, tribal beliefs, traditions, and practices impact on parenting. Non-Native American nurses' ignorance of the Navajo view of their world can lead to misunderstandings and frustrations on both sides. Therefore, a nurse's ability to acknowledge and sustain Navajo caring within their cultural context facilitates successful interactions between Navajo families and the health care system. A thorough review of the literature establishes a parameter which can be used as a basis for further assessment of the family's belief system.

The Navajo are the largest of the Native American tribes with an estimated population in 1985 at over 171,000.[3] Most of the population resides on the 25,000 square mile reservation which lies within the states of Arizona, New Mexico, and Utah. The reservation is an area of semiarid desert, mesas, and canyons on the southern portion of a plateau which ranges in elevation from 3,000 to 10,000 feet. The climate is temperate in summer and cold in winter with wide day-night temperature variations. Families are widely scattered throughout the reservation. Many Navajos still live in small cabins or in a traditional hogan—a one-room, windowless, mud and log hut—

several miles from their nearest neighbors. Water may need to be hauled long distances. Larger groups have settled around old mission, government situations, and tribal headquarters.[4] An increasing number of Navajo are now living and working in cities and towns near or within the reservation. Because of their isolation, the Navajo have retained much of their traditional culture and language. Even so, the social structure of the tribe is changing. Sheepherding is still a major form of livelihood, but it is rapidly giving way to industrial development and tourism. The pickup truck has replaced the horse-drawn wagon as the chief means of transportation. Traveling long distances from home is still difficult because of washed-out or sand-covered dirt roads.[5]

Caring Behaviors

Caring, according to Leininger, refers to "actions directed toward assisting, supporting, or enabling another individual (or group) with evident or anticipated needs to ameliorate or improve a human condition or lifeway."[6] Navajo society has undergone changes and adaptations over the years. Many traditional beliefs about childcare are no longer practiced or practiced partially by the younger Navajo population. Boyle and Andrews note that cultural norms within a group can conflict with one another and behavior is not always clear.[7] Choice is a major factor. Personal forces such as temperament, education, experience, maturity, and motivation influence participation. The culturally sensitive pediatric nurse should assess each family as an individual within the context of tribal themes which underlie the cultural group.

Tribal Themes

Traditional social institutions play an important role in the daily lives of Navajos. A network of kinships and relationships centered in people form the basis for certain themes which prevail throughout Navajo society.[8] Three tribal themes described by Downs are matriarchy, the inviolability of the individual, and the prestige of age. These themes influence child-rearing practices among the Navajo.

The first tribal theme of matriarchy expresses the importance of the female. In daily life the important social units are those centering around a core of women — grandmother, mother, daughter, sisters, and their sons and brothers. Husbands and sons-in-law play a more peripheral role. Children consider themselves part of the descent group of their mother. The relationship between brother and sister is important and often overrides the relationship between husband and wife. A mother's sibling's children play almost as important a role in her life as do her own children, and the children of a sister are more significant than the children of a brother. Since children tend to remain with their mother in dissolved marriages, the mother may have children from several marriages living with her. The Navajo family unit refers not only to the nuclear family, but also to other relatives as well—mother, aunts, sisters, and their female descendants. These individuals of the extended family make up a clan. Shared maternal responsibilities foster the extended attachment relationships.[9] The nurse should be aware that although the Navajo child may be isolated on the reservation in a geographical way, he or she is rarely isolated from meaningful and supportive social relationships within the clan.

A second tribal theme is the inviolability of the individual. Despite close familial ties, Navajos remain highly individualistic people. Their primary social premise is that no person has the right to speak for or direct the actions of another. This theme may have implications in disciplining Navajo children and in obtaining a child's health history from a parent or other relative.

The third tribal theme is the prestige of age, particularly age coupled with a life of hard work and many children and grandchildren. Within the nuclear family there is a clear deference to age. A man with many descendants, although poor, will be listened to with respect. Therefore, the birth of a child is welcomed by the Navajo clan and considered an asset to the family.

Health-Illness Values and Beliefs

Leininger discussed the worldview which referred to "the way people tend to look upon the world or universe to form a picture or value stance about their life or world about them."[10] The prevailing worldview held by a specific cultural group is the basis for their ideas or theories about health and illness causation. Native Americans usually demonstrate a holistic worldview. Within this holistic paradigm, the personified force of nature is kept in balance or harmony. Nature is composed of many things, including human life, which is seen as part of the general order of the cosmos.[11] In traditional Navajo culture, illness occurs when a person falls out of harmony with the forces of nature. Rituals restore the harmony which has been disrupted, so that the body can heal itself. Disease can occur from a multitude of sources—infections from enemies or animals, natural phenomena such as wind or lightning, witchcraft, evil spirits, improper behavior, breaking taboos, or neglect at ceremonies. The healing process can be broken down into several categories: recognition of disease, diagnosis, symptomatic treatment, etiology, cure, and prevention.[12]

A specific hierarchy of practitioners, summarized by Crockett, exists to carry out the above functions.[13] The highest person in the hierarchy is the Singer or Chanter, the high priest of the Navajo religion. He cures illness or restores harmony. He does not treat or relieve symptoms, and his important skill is learned by years of apprenticeship. Below the Singer is the Diagnostician, who diagnoses the cause of the illness, and prescribes the proper Sing. His abilities come from a mystical source.

He uses techniques such as stargazing or hand-trembling to diagnose and receives compensation for his services. The lowest practitioner in the hierarchy is the Herbalist, who gives symptomatic relief until a ceremonial cure is arranged. Whatever relieves pain is resorted to whether it is a Navajo Herbalist, a Hopi medicine man, a Christian faith healer, or a non-Native American physician. If the non-Native American physician is young, he or she has even less status.

Patterns of Behavior and Child Rearing Phases

The need for the nurse to make a systematic and detailed assessment of the life patterns of an individual or cultural group with reference to health maintenance behavior has been emphasized by Leininger.[14] Recurring life patterns, such as child-rearing practices, should be identified within the family's natural and familiar setting. Child-rearing practices among the Navajo are closely tied to traditional and religious beliefs. Ceremonies (also known as Blessingways) and taboos play an important part in their daily lives. Awareness and understanding of these practices can increase the nurses effectiveness in working with Navajo families.

Arthur has identified four phases of child-rearing practices among the traditional Navajo population.[15] These phases are prebirth, pre-cradleboard, cradleboard, and post-cradleboard.

Pre-Birth Phase

During the prebirth phase the mother is given recognition of the pregnancy by ceremonies, taboos, and herbal medicine. A primiparous mother is given special attention. Recognition by the extended family and community helps the mother accept the pregnancy as a reality, an important task noted by Rubin for a positive and successful pregnancy.[16]

Navajo women concurred that pregnancy is a well state, not an illness.[17] Consequently, traditional Navajo prenatal beliefs and practices regarding exercise and activity have a good physiological basis for maintaining a healthy fetus and can be supported by the nurse. The pregnant woman is encouraged to exercise regularly and to go about her chores, as this routine keeps her calm and happy. Heavy work, such as carrying and lifting heavy loads, chopping wood, and making jerking, twisting motions, is to be avoided since this may cause a premature delivery or kill the unborn child. The pregnant woman is also advised not to ride horseback or to do heavy lifting in the first and last months of pregnancy. The woman is encouraged to work and to walk regularly so that the baby does not grow too big and cause a difficult delivery.[18]

A long-standing Navajo belief is that the fetus has no mind of its own but is very much alive through the umbilical cord. Consequently whatever affects the mother influences the unborn child as well.[19] Since the baby is a welcome addition to the family, precautions must be taken to give the child a favorable start in life. Ceremonies and taboos ensure health, prosperity, and the general well-being of mother and baby. They protect both mother and child from harm and place them "in tune" with the Holy People who watch over the Navajo. Ceremonies are therapeutic to the mother since they result in a good attitude, less anxiety about the pregnancy and also a protection against the breaking of taboos.[20] The midwife, grandmother, and Navajo practitioners are extremely important to the pregnant mother since they are well versed in traditions, taboos, and the ceremonial procedures which can influence the child's later talents and tendencies.[21]

Conduct of the parents is important to the unborn child. Not only the mother, but also the father can influence the fetus.[22] The father's participation in the ceremonies and practicing of taboos involves him prenatally with his child and enhances the attachment process. Many taboos are described in the literature. For instance, knots tied by the mother or father should not be left tied, or the fetus will be tangled in the umbilical cord. If the ceremony of dry painting or body painting is witnessed by the parents, the child will have severe illness during his life. If a pot is broken by the pregnant mother, the infant's soft spots will not close at the proper time, or he will stutter. This affliction can be averted by breaking another pot over the infant's head after he is born so that the pieces fall beneath him in a pile.[23] As Satz noted, pregnancy is a state of the living and the fetus should not be exposed to the realm of the dead.[24] Neither parent should attend a funeral or go through a graveyard, otherwise the child may have nightmares. If either parent kills, skins, or sees a dead coyote, snake, or cat, the child will become sick.

Newcomb noted that baby clothes were not made until the infant was about two weeks old, a tradition probably reflective of the high infant mortality of years ago.[25] It is the traditional Navajo belief that the infant would die before it could wear the new clothes. Even today, one of the authors found in her experience with the Navajo that the family will frequently delay buying baby clothes or making other provision for the baby until after birth. A non-Native American nurse may misinterpret the lack of physical preparation for infant as disinterest on the part of the Navajo family.

Pre-Cradleboard Phase

At the pre-cradleboard stage, a hogan is designated or built for an impending traditional birth. The Navajo religious practitioner or grandmother ties a red sash belt (for a girl) or buckskin rope (for a boy) to a log or ceiling rope to give the mother support during the delivery. A traditional midwife, a close female relative, and the Navajo practitioner may also be present to assist and to perform rituals. The newborn is gently shaken and massaged to stimulate breathing.[26] After birth the child is washed in a basket of yucca suds, dried, and then placed in a mattress made out of the pulped bark of wild rose bushes. The baby is covered with soft buckskin and wrapped in a sheep pelt. Wild rose bush pulp is placed on the genital area. The pulp is very soft, has a pleasant natural smell, is highly absorbent, prevents odors, and is nonirritating— an excellent diaper! When it becomes soiled by the infant, the pulp is disposed of or washed and replaced.[27] The infant's head is turned toward the hogan fire since in the Navajo religion the fire is a symbol of life and is sacred.[28]

The placenta is placed in the ashes of the hogan fire or else buried. Because the placenta is the "life tube" of the baby, the ashes are a safe spot since fire combats evil spirits. Proper disposal of the placenta and cord ties the child to the land. The cord is disposed of by burying it in the proximity of the home. Where the cord is buried determines in which vocation the parents want the child to excel. For instance, the cord is buried in the stockyard so that a boy will become a good stockman, or by a loom so that a girl will become an artistic weaver.[29]

Traditionally the baby is given to the mother or placed in a temporary cradle near here within a few hours after birth. This physical closeness continues until weaning and support the attachment process.[30] During the first four days of life the baby is attended by the midwife or grandmother. The mother is allowed to rest and to recover from the delivery with the help of the extended family, a support practice which enables the mother to accomplish more easily the physiological restoration and psychosocial postpartum tasks described by Gruis.[31]

Infant feeding has religious significance for the traditional family. The midwife or grandmother may brew an emetic from juniper bark which causes the baby to rid itself of mucus. A ceremonial food of corn pollen and boiled water is then fed to the baby. Corn pollen is used because of its religious significance, enduring nature, reproductive attributes, nutrient qualities, and beauty. With the traditional Navajo mother, breast-feeding is not begun until the mother's milk comes in.[32] However, many Navajo mothers now breast-feed soon after birth.[33] After four days the mother assumes care, and a permanent cradleboard and infant name is planned.[34] Breast-feeding is on a demand schedule, which is supported by current infant-feeding recommendations.[35] The baby is put to breast when hungry and nurses until satiated. Although infant formulas have now become more popular, traditional Navajos feel that breast-fed babies are healthier. A bottle-fed infant becomes too detached from the mother, and cow's milk infuses the child with faculties of animals.[36] Formulas for infant feeding during the first year of life are now widely available and more commonly used on the reservation. The Woman/ Infant/Child Program, a federally funded supplemental feeding and educational program, has made an impact on the nutritional status of the Navajo infant and child.[37] When formula is used, ready-to-feed rather than concentrated or powdered formulas are encouraged in certain areas because of the lack of refrigeration, good sanitation, and safe water sources in the hogans.

Today, most Navajo mothers deliver in the hospital, which can increase anxiety due to isolation from family and other significant persons. Hospital rules need to be flexible to allow for family support. The father or another significant person should be allowed to attend the delivery and the mother should be encouraged to breast-feed. Hospital stays should be as short as possible to allow the mother to return to her family. Since the placenta and cord are usually not disposed of in the traditional Navajo way in the hospital, a traditional Navajo feels this contributes to the child's losing his personal identity and eventually leaving Navajo society.[38] If the Navajo family desires to maintain tradition in a hospital setting, the nurse can make arrangements to allow the family to dispose of the placenta and cord in the proper way.

Chisholm found that Navajo infants are significantly less reactive and irritable both at birth and during the first year of life when compared with Anglo-American infants.[39] Although Chisholm did not rule out genetic influences, he speculated that a behavioral self-election may be caused by prenatal environmental factors, such as the lower blood pressures observed in pregnant Navajo women. After birth, maternal-infant interactions and familial socialization play more significant roles in observed behavioral differences. An infant is rubbed, pressed, and shaped by the traditional mother. This practice is to help "stiffen" the legs and make him or her "beautiful".[40] The tactile stimulation and attention the infant receives during that time further encourages attachment and optimal development.[41]

During the first month the child is given a Navajo name. Many times children are given the name of a long-lived person or grandparent, so that they too will live to an old age. The Navajo name protects the child and keeps him or her in tune with the Holy People. This name is kept secret until the proper ceremony. During their lives children are frequently given other names deliberately by inspiration, or just by general usage. The Navajo child may have a Navajo name, a kinship name, a nickname, and a European name, which is very confusing to outsiders and personnel in medical records. Infants may not be named until after their first laugh or when they begin to notice their surroundings.[42]

Making a fuss over a young child causes the family to become very uncomfortable. A stranger, by his or her attention, may "witch" a child, with the result that the child stutters or is unable to talk in the future. Other taboos have been noted in the literature. If a child's hair is cut before he talks, he will stutter or have difficulty with speech. If a mirror is held up to a baby, he will go blind. If the baby is given things a stranger really likes, he may die.

Some taboos show good insight into meeting the child's emotional and physical needs. Babies should not be hit in the mouth, or they will be stubborn. An infant should not be teased or hurt, or the teaser will become "bad". A baby's head should not be allowed to stay to one side on the cradleboard, or the baby will have a wide head.[43]

Cradleboard Phase

During the cradleboard phase the baby's first laugh is celebrated. The first laugh indicates that the child has developed a maturity and self-identify. The celebration causes the child to be generous, kind, and happy. A sheep is killed, a feast is given, and small amounts of salt are distributed to the relatives.[44] A nurse who elicits the infant's first laugh may be expected to give a gift to the child or even given the honor of underwriting the feast.

During this phase the child is placed in a permanent cradleboard. The traditional Navajo will use two cradleboards. The first has a face cover and is discarded as soon as the child is well assured of survival. To the Navajo the second cradleboard has both traditional and religious significance. Songs and prayers are chanted before journeying to the forest to obtain wood for making the board. The wood is selected by the father or grandfather, and it must be tall and straight—not struck by lightning or broken.[45]

The cradleboard serves as a protection for the baby and a convenience for the mother. It is like the womb—movement is restricted, support is present, and temperature changes are minimized. This child is placed in the board in an upright position after eating, which helps digestion and reduces reflux and regurgitation. The cradleboard provides warmth and security to the child and minimizes the traumatic changes that take place after birth. A cradleboard also helps to promote communication between the child and other persons since it brings an infant to the same eye level as the adults. The propped position of the cradleboard acts as a safety device since it protects the baby from being stepped on by scuffling siblings or inattentive adults. A canopy over the board guards the infant's eyes against the sun and protects against head injury if accidentally dropped. Swaddling protects against animal attacks. The board may actually promote walking since the baby's balance and vision are already on the same plane. Chisholm found that the cradleboard does not delay motor skill development.[46] When the child begins creeping, the board can be used as a temporary restraint if adults are not present to protect an infant from the fire. Generally, the cradleboard decreases conflicts and reduces frustrations between the child and the busy mother.[47]

In past years, hip dysplasias may have been exacerbated by the cradleboard practice. However, Rabin, Barnett, Arnold, Freiberger, and Brooks[48] found that hip dysplasias have decreased since the use of modern diapers. They concluded that the cradleboard used with disposable or cloth diapers tightly binds the hips in a slightly abducted position, the basis for treating hip dysplasia. If further treatment is needed, the cradleboard can be modified to accommodate splints, casts, or braces.

Language skills are acquired by the child through someone's constant talking to him, giving him words to imitate, repeating kinship terms, and praising him for repeated sounds. Maximum attention is given to the child when she learns to walk. Everyone takes turns leading the child around.[49]

Immunization deficiencies are no longer a major problem, but health clinic appointments may be missed because of transportation difficulties and lack of education regarding the importance of preventive care. Pediatric clinic personnel frequently should adjust immunization schedules to give maximum protection for a child.

Post-Cradleboard Phase

The main characteristics of the post-cradleboard phase are weaning, toilet training, and disciplining. The grandmother is often entrusted with the child-rearing of young grandchildren. Her influence greatly impacts the sensitive early developmental years; Navajo tradition and language are well ingrained from generation to generation and fully in place by the time the child attends school. If a grandmother is not available, a sister or other relative may care for the child while the mother resumes work or school.[50] This familial accommodation to the new child allows for less radical maternal role changes. The maternal-infant attachment remains strong, but the Navajo mother is also allowed to pursue individual interests with support of the extended family.

Weaning is introduced with a new pregnancy. If the mother is not pregnant, weaning is late and more gradual.[51] A disadvantage of late weaning is the prevalence of baby bottle mouth or dental caries in the primary teeth from milk or juice in the nap or bed bottle. Anticipatory guidance on weaning and nutrition is an important part of well-child care in the Navajo population. Solids are encouraged in the traditional Navajo culture from the time the baby can sit. The child is offered any food that he can safely handle, such as bread dipped in broth or coffee, canned tomatoes, fruit, rice, cereal, soft cookies, and squash. He is weaned to a cup or bowl with weak, sweetened liquids and encouraged to take squash, potatoes, and softened meat from a spoon.[52] In past years Newcomb found that some infants were fed salt since the Navajo creation myth indicates that infants fed this substance grew rapidly.[53]

The most frequent traditional foods in the children's diet are potatoes, meat, bread, and cereal. Native dishes frequently involved the use of corn. Alford and Nance found that Navajo children's diets in isolated areas are frequently low in calories, borderline in protein, and deficient in Vitamin A and Vitamin C.[54] Obesity was occasionally seen by one of the authors in well-child clinics because the child is allowed the breast or bottle and high caloric foods "if he wants it," again an indication of the inviolability of the individual. Growth charts need to be monitored to detect early overfeeding and to begin nutritional education using Navajo staple foods as a foundation for counseling.[55]

The Navajo have a relaxed attitude toward toilet training. Controlled bowel movements are not expected until the child is old enough to direct his or her own movements. Training is demonstrated and taught through modeling, and mother is quite patient, even with "accidents." Children may be half-clothed, which facilitates changes. The Navajos believe that forcing toilet training will cause the child to be fearful.[56]

The Navajos belief in the inviolability of the individual also plays a large part in their attitude toward discipline. A characteristic pattern is light discipline by persuasion, ridicule, or shame, in contrast to the corporal punishment commonly seen in Anglo-American culture. Children are "herded" rather than led. An adult or older child tends to interpose and to divert the young child to another activity rather than to punish. Children's wishes are usually honored unless they are absolutely impossible. Adults may even rearrange their plans to accommodate the child.[57] The child is allowed to explore and is responsible for her own actions. If a toddler is warned against touching a hot stove, she is responsible for that behavior, not the parents.[58] Navajo children do not ordinarily ask permission to do certain things—they eat when they are hungry and sleep when they are tired. To the outsider the child may appear "spoiled."[59] But again, this behavior is a reflection of the Navajo belief that no one has the right to impose his will on another person.

The traditional Navajo also makes skillful use of terror to enforce proper behavior and to instill dependence on the family. From infancy onward the child is exposed to frightening experiences from which he is then extricated by his mother or older siblings. These experiences suggest to the infant mind that safety exists solely with the family. Older children will tell stories of evil beings to younger toddlers and will produce more fear. Adults in turn tell fearful stories to older children. The ideas that one can feel safe only with one's close relatives and that one should turn to them for comfort and protection are reinforced.[60]

The Navajo father is required to provide for his children, teach them properly, and serve as a role model. If the father is absent, the mother's brother may assume some obligations toward her children. There are some differences in the behavior of children toward their mother and father. Children will usually approach their mother directly to ask a favor or for help. Girls are reluctant to approach their father and tend to use the mother as an intermediary. Fathers and sons have a more direct relationship.

Between siblings, age is a great determiner of authority and attitude. The elder will assume authority over the care for the younger siblings throughout life.[61]

Children are required to assume responsibilities, such as herding, as soon as they are able. Skills are developed as part of childhood play. Children grow up with animals and show little fear of them. Their lives are ones of experimental learning arranged to provide them with opportunities to develop skills and confidence. By the time children are three, they are allowed to participate in herding activities by "helping"—they may actually hinder the operation, but they are not discouraged. At six to seven years of age, they may accompany the herder to the range, and may take over full herding responsibility at eight to ten years of age.

Toys are few and shared by all. Girls have dolls and they boys' most prized possessions are usually their ropes. The skill in rope handling carries much prestige. Riding is learned early. At about twelve years of age, an adult (such as the father or uncle) will take the boy for a ride, evaluate his behavior on a horse, and if he passes the test, he is considered an adult. Thereafter he is expected to cope with the adult dangers of life.[62]

The first menstrual period of a girl is announced by a four-day ceremony or *kinaalda*, a pubertal ceremony.[63] The Navajo believe that during this period of her life, the girl is particularly sensitive to influences that will affect her later life. She is a plastic mold that can be easily injured and needs to be properly shaped, and she is the center of continuous ceremonial songs, prayers, and purification rites by her relatives during this time.[64]

Generally, the Navajo children are taught a positive self-concept by being allowed to succeed at tasks at their age level. Although there is evidence that they demonstrate poor self-concept in the outside world, in their own they are highly competitive and think highly of themselves. To call attention to oneself is "showy," and the reluctance to do so may result in poor academic performance. There is also a cultural prohibition, which is encouraged in the children at an early age, against overt expression of anger and aggression. Self-discipline and independence strivings are always rewarded and emphasized in all childhood training.[65]

Nursing Care

Cultural care preservation or maintenance, according to Leininger, refers to "those assistive, supportive, or enabling professional actions and decisions that help clients of a particular culture to preserve or maintain a state of health or to recover from illness and to face death."[66] Brandt discussed the Navajo child's concept of health and reactions to hospitalization.[67] The family's concept of health impacts on their decision concerning their choice of health care providers, whether it be a traditional health agent, a non-Navajo health agent, or a combination thereof. A pathophysiological explanation which excludes a holistic health care approach may cause the family to retreat from the health care regimen.

The nursing process can assist the nurse to understand the Navajo world. Through assessment of the cultural aspects of the family's lifestyle, health beliefs, and practices, the nurse can better facilitate shared decision-making while providing holistic care. Culturally sensitive interventions are relevant to the clients' needs and can reduce stress and conflict with nurse-family interactions.[68] As the process moves from assessment (e.g., what are the Navajo family's working beliefs, traditions, practices?) through evaluation (have those beliefs, traditions, and practices been violated or maintained?), the nurse can validate his or her helpfulness while caring for the Navajo child.[69] Active listening to elicit pre-existing beliefs allows the nurse to incorporate those beliefs into health service contacts and education.[70]

Navajo children as patients are usually shy and fearful of strangers. Older children may be stoic and noncomplaining. They are not prone to look at caregivers directly, they generally have little eye contact (a sign of respect), and do not say "thank you" or "please." During conversations, there may be brief silences after each speaker's words to show respect and to reflect on what was said.[71] The Navajo tend not to use touch for communicating comfort as much as other cultures do. Older children may be more comfortable with physical closeness rather than with frequent touching from a caregiver.

Visits by relatives are expected by the family and ill child and are comforting to them. The grandmother is especially important, and her permission may be needed for hospitalization or other procedures. In kinship terms, several persons may be designated as "mother" or "grandmother" which is confusing to the nurse, although perfectly understandable to the child.[72] Family members should be supported and encouraged in their childcare activities to decrease anxiety of both the child and the relatives.

Room and privacy should be allowed for a Sing if that is requested. Rituals such as sprinkling cornmeal on an ill child or allowing the possession of a curative item will reduce anxiety and unnecessary conflicts with the family. The cornmeal should be saved and not discarded without family permission. Medicines given to a child by a Navajo health practitioner during a ceremony should be cleared with the physician to avoid unfavorable reactions, but this is rarely a problem.[73]

Problems with medication scheduling may occur because Navajos do not have the same time sense that Anglo-Americans do. Indian time is casual and relative. Meals are eaten at different intervals and pills may be taken all at once rather than throughout the day.[74] Careful explanations are needed to prevent misunderstandings by parents. Problems can also arise in translations of medical terminology, as certain concepts are difficult to translate from one language to another. A Navajo health care worker can decrease translation difficulties during counseling and should have good insight into potential difficulties for carrying out therapeutic actions.

Death is seen as a part of life, and children are not shielded from it. However, after the traditional mourning period of four days, an excessive display of emotion is not looked on favorably, and there is a fear of the power of the dead person.[75]

The Navajo people have a rich heritage which has sustained itself remarkably well through the centuries. Knowledge of that heritage is the first step in establishing a therapeutic relationship. Nurses have a responsibility to individualize care based on an assessment of each family within the greater context of the Navajo belief system. A thorough review of the literature is one avenue that the nurse can use to establish a knowledge base for providing culture-specific care.

References

1. Leininger, M., *Transcultural Nursing: Concepts, Theories, and Practices*, New York: John Wiley & Sons, 1978.
2. Ibid, p. 8.
3. U.S. Department of Health and Human Services. *Indian Health Service Chart Series Book*, Rockville, Maryland: Public Health Service, Program Statistics Branch, 1986.
4. Downs, J. F., *The Navajo*, New York: Holt, Rinehart & Winston, 1972.
5. Chisholm, J. S., *Navajo Infancy*, New York: Aldine, 1983.
6. Leininger, M., "Leininger's Theory of Nursing: Cultural Diversity and Universality," *Nursing Science Quarterly*, v. 1, no. 4, 1988, pp. 152–160.
7. Boyle, J. S., and M. M. Andrews, *Transcultural Concepts in Nursing Care*, Boston: Scott, Foresman, 1989.
8. Downs, op. cit.
9. Satz, K. J., "Integrating Navajo Tradition into Maternal-Child Nursing," *Image*, v. 1, no. 3, 1982, pp. 89–92.
10. Leininger, op. cit., 1988, p. 156.
11. Boyle and Andrews, op. cit.
12. Porvaznik, W., "Traditional Navajo Medicine," *General Practitioner*, v. 36, no. 4, 1967, pp. 179–182.
13. Crockett, D. C., "Medicine Among the American Indians," *HSMHA Health Reports*, v. 86, no. 5, 1971, pp. 399–401.
14. Leininger, op. cit., 1978.
15. Arthur, B. J., *Traditional Navajo Childrearing Pattern: A Survey of the Traditional Childrearing Practices Among Elderly Navajo Parents*, Unpublished master's thesis, University of Utah, Salt Lake City, 1976.
16. Rubin, R., "Maternal Tasks in Pregnancy," *Maternal Child Nursing*, v. 4, no. 3, 1975, pp. 145–153.
17. Olds, S. B., M. L. London, and P. A. Ladewige, *Maternal Newborn Nursing*, 3rd ed., Menlo Park, California: Addison-Wesley, 1988.
18. Arthur, op. cit.
19. Wyman, L. C., *Navajo Eschatology*, Albuquerque: University of New Mexico Bulletin, 1942.
20. Arthur, op. cit.
21. Newcomb, F. J., *Navajo Omens and Taboos*, Santa Fe: Rydal Press, 1940.
22. Satz, op. cit.
23. Evans, P. C., and J. Fike, "The Navajo Way: As related to Pregnancy, Childbearing, and Childrearing," *Arizona Medicine*, v. 32, no. 2, 1975, pp. 97–99.

24. Satz, op. cit.
25. Newcomb, op. cit.
26. Satz, op. cit.
27. Arthur, op. cit.
28. Kluckhohn, C., and D. C. Leighton, *The Navajo, rev. ed.*, Cambridge: Harvard University Press, 1974.
29. Arthur, op. cit.
30. Kennell, J., and M. Klaus, *Maternal-Infant Bonding*, St. Louis: C. V. Mosby, 1976.
31. Gruis, M., "Beyond Maternity, Postpartum Concerns of Mothers," *Maternal Child Nursing*, v. 2, no. 3, 1977, pp. 182–188.
32. Arthur, op. cit.
33. Satz, op. cit.
34. Arthur, op. cit.
35. Lawrence, R., *Breastfeeding: A Guide for the Medical Profession, 2nd ed.*, St. Louis, C. V. Mosby, 1985.
36. Leighton, D. C., and C. Kluckhohn, *Children of the People*, Cambridge: Harvard University Press, 1948.
37. Duzan, J. V., J. P. Carter, and R. V. Zwagg, "Protein and Caloric Malnutrition Among Navajo Indian Pre-School Children—A Follow-Up," *American Journal of Clinical Nutrition*, v. 29, no. 6, 1976, pp. 657–662.
38. Arthur, op. cit.
39. Chisholm, op. cit.
40. Wyman, op. cit.
41. Kennell and Klaus, op. cit.
42. Kluckhohn and Leighton, op. cit.
43. Evans and Fike, op. cit.
44. Arthur, op. cit.
45. Ibid.
46. Chisholm, op. cit.
47. Arthur, op. cit.
48. Rabin, D. L., C. R. Barnett, W. D. Arnold, R. H. Freiberger, and G. Brooks, "Untreated Congenital Hip Dysplasia: A Study of the Epidemiology, Natural History, and Social Aspects of the Disease in the Navajo Population," *American Journal of Public Health*, v. 55, 1965, pp. 3–15.
49. Kluckhohn and Leighton, op. cit.
50. Satz, op. cit.
51. Arthur, op. cit.

52. Kluckhohn and Leighton, op. cit.

53. Newcomb, op. cit.

54. Alford, B., and E. B. Nance, "Customary Foods in the Navajo Diet," *Journal of the American Dietetic Association*, v. 69, no. 5, 1976, pp. 538–539.

55. Mandelbaum, J. L., "The Foodsquare: Helping People of Different Cultures Understand Balanced Diets," *Pediatric Nursing*, v. 9, no. 1, 1983, pp. 20–21.

56. Arthur, op. cit.

57. Downs, op. cit.

58. Satz, op. cit.

59. Primeaux, M., "Caring for the American Indian Patient," *American Journal of Nursing*, v. 77, no. 1, 1977, pp. 91–94.

60. Downs, op. cit.

61. Ibid.

62. Ibid.

63. Frisbie, C., *Kinaalda*, Middletown, Connecticut: Wesleyan University Press, 1967.

64. Downs, op. cit.

65. Primeaux, op. cit.

66. Leininger, op. cit., 1988, p. 156.

67. Brandt, P. A., "Two Different Worlds...the Navajo Child's Interactions Within the Health Care System," *Transcultural Nursing: Concepts, Theories, and Practices*, M. Leininger, ed., New York: John Wiley & Sons, 1978, pp. 251–266.

68. Boyle and Andrews, op. cit.

69. Mott, S. R., N. F. Fazekas, and S. J. Rowen, *Nursing Care of Children and Families*, Menlo Park, California: Addison-Wesley, 1985.

70. Maheady, D. C., "Cultural Assessment of Children," *Maternal-Child Nursing*, v. 11, no. 2, 1986, p. 128.

71. Kniep-Hardy, M., and M. Burkhardt, "Nursing the Navajo," *American Journal of Nursing*, v. 77, no. 1, 1977, pp. 95–96.

72. Ibid.

73. Primeaux, op. cit.

74. Ibid.

75. Miller, S. I., and L. Schoenfeld, "Grief in the Navajo: Psychodynamics and Cultural," *International Journal of Social Psychiatry*, v. 19, 1973, pp. 187–191.

Chapter 23
Transcultural Nursing and Child-Rearing of the Muckleshoots

Beverly Horn, PhD, MSN, CTN, RN

Child-rearing, a transcultural phenomenon, is influenced by a multitude of factors in every culture with behavioral expressions varying considerably from culture to culture. Minturn and Lambert found in six cultures that training in aggression, dependency, obedience, responsibility, achievement, sociability, social control mechanisms, and conscience development was present but varied from one cultural setting to the next.[1] Whiting and Child's classic study demonstrated that parents everywhere have similar problems to solve in rearing children.[2] First, they content that child training everywhere seems to be concerned with problems which arise from universal characteristics of the human infant and from universal characteristics of adult culture which are incompatible with the continuation of infantile behavior. Second, they concluded that the universal tasks of child training also differ considerable from society to society.[3] Minturn and Lambert suggested that, on the basis of their findings, differences in living patterns and economic activities account for most of the between-culture differences on the mean factor scores they analyzed.[4]

The purpose of this chapter is a description of child-rearing among the Muckleshoot, a North American Indian group from the Pacific Northwest. Specifically, I will: 1) briefly describe the cultural background of the Muckleshoot; 2) identify and explain ethnonursing care components of Muckleshoot women as they pertain to child-rearing; and, 3) show how Leininger's conceptual model for studying transcultural nursing was used to obtain data. These data could be used by nurses to provide meaningful and culturally congruent care to Muckleshoot parents and children.

The author's original study in 1972 was an ethnonursing and ethnoscience study to generate transcultural nursing knowledge. This study focused on how a particular group of Native American Indian women perceived the meaning of care in a caring relationship. The study also looked at the phenomenon of care perceived as helping. The research also focused on how the women saw differences in roles of various health care providers, and whom they perceived were most helpful and caring to them during pregnancy. The researcher identified transcultural nursing care components and formulated hypotheses to advance the body of evolving scientific and humanistic transcultural nursing knowledge. The investigator elicited many beliefs and values about child-rearing and caring from the emic, or Muckleshoot's inside views, about care and care values. Child-rearing practices were observed by participating in weekly well-child clinics on the Indian reservation for a period of approximately three years. Some of the material presented in this chapter reflects field documentation of what was observed and heard during clinic days on the reservation. This study was an early example of the use of the ethnonursing research method and Leininger's theory of Cultural Care. Both the method and theory were also used by Leininger in her earlier study of the Gadsup of the Eastern Highlands of New Guinea.

Social and Cultural Background

The Muckleshoot Indians are a North American tribe who live on a reservation approximately thirty-five miles southeast of Seattle, Washington. The Muckleshoot Reservation was established by executive order of the President of the United States, January 19, 1867.[5, 6] The Muckleshoot belong to the Nisqually dialectic group of the coastal division of the Salishan linguistic family. They are thought to be combination of at least three separate groups that were placed on a former military installation called Muckleshoot. The reservation was then named Muckleshoot and the persons living there called Muckleshoot.

Understanding the history of the culture is important, especially their cultural contact with outsiders and the influence of their contact on their health and well-being. It appears that the children of this Native American group were greatly influenced by the cultural history of Northwest Coast Indians. At the time of treaty-making, attacks were made by Whites on settlements of this group of Native Americans. The Native Americans retaliated but always returned any children they captured to the White settlement. The Whites, in counter-retaliation, slaughtered many, Native Americans, including all Native American children.[7] This disregard of Whites for their children has never been forgotten by the Muckleshoot. Perceptions expressed by many mothers included the notion that influential Whites, including health care persons, continue to have the power to take their children away.

Prior to the arrival of Europeans on the North American continent, the richest people in North America were the Native Americans of the Northwest Coast. These Native Americans were among the few fishing, hunting, and gathering societies-in the world that produced materials beyond what was needed for subsistence. The most important element for their way of life was the salmon.[8, 9, 10] Salmon provided a strong economic based for trade, as well as a year-round staple food. Religious and ceremonial life of Coastal Indians generally focused on the salmon as their greatest blessing. Today the salmon remains a powerful symbol and continues to be central to religious and ceremonial life. Other sources of food such as shellfish, game, berries, and edible roots were abundantly available in season. A mild climate permitted food to be available year round and thus starvation was a rarity. Nature provided abundantly for other material needs as well. The giant western red cedar was versatile and used for home building, canoes, clothing, basketry and cooking implements. Cradleboards, made of indigenous materials were used in the past and present by Muckleshoot women, and were artistically and beautifully designed. A rather leisurely existence enabled the Northwest Coast Indians to develop elaborate art forms such as sculpture and dancing.

Dwellings of the past were multifamily plank homes. Family groups had separate areas in the dwelling, but families shared resources. Child-rearing was not confined to the nuclear family but was shared in by many adults and older children. The extended family provided a ready resource for information, caring modes, and assistance in health related situations.

The Muckleshoot Indians originated from the Coast Salish, whose social organization involved a network of relationships in which an upper and a lower class existed. Class status was dependent in part on birth, but also maintained by the wealthy. The Muckleshoot Indians demonstrated their status through the potlatch which indicated they had amassed an abundance of goods, and could give them away. The naming ceremony was associated with the potlatch. Child-rearing techniques, which included important values associated with the drive to attain high status was part of the enculturation process. Knowledge of good behavior was thought to belong to good families, i.e., those of high status. The naming ceremony occurred at about the time of adolescence. A second name was given to the child as well as titles that proclaimed the position of that person in the group. Thus the potlatch was inextricably involved in preparation of children for the adult role.

At the time of treaty-making, the Muckleshoot people were ceded 3,440 acres, but much of the land was eventually sold to the White population and only 990 acres were owned by Native Americans of this tribe at the time of this study.[11, 12] Less than a quarter of an acre of land was now owned corporately by the tribe.[13] Approximately 278 members of the Muckleshoot tribe live on the reservation, about 60 members lived in two adjacent counties, and approximately 25 members lived away from the immediate area of the reservation. Tribal land borders the White River, which flows down from Mount Ranier, and is near the River. The latter flows through the nearby town of Auburn, Washington. The Stuck River, a tributary of the Puyallup River, is also on reservation land. Land owned by tribal members assumes a checkerboard configuration. A major highway divides the reservation, and much of the land adjacent to the main highway was sold to White persons in the past.

Tribal members distinguish among themselves between those that have property on the main highway and those that do not. Those that live near the main highway perceive themselves to be better than others in the sense that they can encourage their children to socialize in school and not be afraid to "talk up" to White children. One of the informants who lived near the highway discussed seeing a doctor during pregnancy and talking to him with these comments:

> *I think it depends on the type of person and how they've been raised. Like my parents never kept us away from people, and since we've been small we've always been out to meet people, and the people who have been on the reservation make the mistake of not doing this with their children. They are backwards and shy and they don't know how to meet different people. I think that there's a lot of difference in people.*[14]

On the other hand, persons who live further back from the highway project a low self-image. Until quite recently, governmental agencies and private groups have encouraged them to leave the reservation. There was a feeling expressed by some local residents that anyone of worth had probably left the reservation.

Geographical closeness of some reservation land to the small town of Auburn, Washington was less than a few hundred feet away. Differences in life-style between the White inhabitants of Auburn and the Native American Muckleshoot was striking. These differences were best exemplified by a street and road parallel to one another and separated only by a high steel cyclone fence. The paved street ended at a modern shopping center. On the other side of the fence was the dirt road which was tortuous and deeply rutted from the rains throughout much of the year. Alongside this road was property owned by reservation members. The homes were small rundown shacks with virtually no plumbing. A recent survey estimated that approximately ninety percent of the reservation housing was considered substandard.[15]

The Muckleshoot today are an acculturated group in several respects. First, they have had a close association with other bands and tribes of the Puget Sound area, as well as the Yakima Indians on the east side of the Cascade Range. Significant cultural exchange occurred, and continues today. Second, the proximity of the reservation to predominantly White metropolitan centers has led to continuing acculturation. Third, the mass media have affected persons of all age levels, but especially the young. The introduction of television in the 1950s, and increasingly sophisticated technology of the present have had a profound acculturative impact.

In the midst of cultural diversity, the Muckleshoot maintained many of the important cultural values of Native American life which they treasure and will not relinquish. In this study the following cultural values were elicited from interviews with Muckleshoot women, or were observed as persons interacted with one another.

There was and is recognition and appreciation of cultural diversity and rejection of a competitive stance when personal gain is the only goal. There is recognition of the interdependence of human beings with all other parts of creation and attribution of a spiritual quality to everything in the universe. Also valued are tribal sharing; intuitive as well as analytical thinking; and, a sensitivity to others that will avoid embarrassment or loss of face.[16, 17, 18] Adherence to these cultural values were observed in the child-rearing practices of the Muckleshoot people.

Cultural conflict occurred for the Muckleshoot when a choice between their own cultural values and the White middle-class value system was necessary. Cultural conflict was accentuated by maintenance of a separate identity. Native Americans were frequently rejected by the dominant group, i.e. White Americans because of a different value system, and maintenance of a separate cultural identity. A reaction to rejection by others is often manifested through alienation patterns. Behaviors related to alienation may include alcoholism, truancy, school dropout, withdrawn behavior and suicide. These behaviors were observed in some of the Muckleshoot children and adolescents.

Specific Child-Rearing Practices

Interviews with Muckleshoot women about their perceptions of health and care during pregnancy began with an open-ended question, "Tell me about your experiences with pregnancy." Responses to this question became cues for further exploration of issues identified by each woman. In a series of follow-up interviews each woman arranged and classified transcribed information from the first interview, adding and deleting data as she deemed appropriate. Examples and illustrations of child-rearing practices were fully explored with each informant.

A puzzling phenomenon occurred to the investigator. In the first or second interview each woman would briefly comment on pregnancy and use this as a point of departure to talk extensively of her own childhood. Understanding how the informant's childhood experiences related to discussion of pregnancy and health researcher. Informants clarified for the investigator that their childhood was related to who they are now, and their identity was determined by the extended family and their community — who their grandparents and parents were, as well as their aunts and uncles, cousins, brothers and sisters. Each woman's experience with pregnancy was embedded in intricate relationships with ancestors, family and community. Further, experiences which the researcher perceived as potentially negative, such as moving frequently from one relative's home to another, were perceived as positive experiences. Moving was only perceived as negative when it meant having to leave the reservation and live in White homes. The strength of the extended family was frequently discussed. An example was Judy, a sixteen-year-old girl who was removed from her biological parents' home at the age of sixteen months. She stated:

> *Mom adopted me. She's my second cousin. I have really had good care. She took me to the doctor all the time. I couldn't walk and I always had to wear special shoes. I couldn't sit up and she took me to the doctor. She's been good to me.* [19]

Following the birth of Judy's baby, her twenty-five-year-old cousin, Lois, stopped in during one of the interviews. Before Lois arrived, Judy said she had been thinking of giving her baby to Lois because Lois wanted a baby very much. When Lois came, she held the baby and fed her, and said "I really want a baby." Judy pointed to Lois and herself and said, "This is our baby." Judy pointed out that they have a baby every year in their extended family. The bassinet for Judy's baby was from Lois' home, where a baby was born the previous year.

Another example of the extended family's importance in child-rearing was given by Rosalie. Rosalie, an eighteen-year-old, lived with her husband and five-year-old son in her parents' home. Two other sisters and their families lived there also. Rosalie's mother had fifteen children and most of them lived nearby. Often, children from other families were staying in this home for a day or two while their parents were away. Every Sunday the entire family gathered at the parents' home and the Sunday the investigator visited there were fifty-eight people present. Child-rearing is a main topic of conversation gatherings and there is much support given to children and child-rearing needs.

Several women stated they believed that obvious preparation for a new baby could cause the death of the baby. These mothers experienced conflict when baby clothes were on sale, or they were given things such as clothes and furniture before the baby was born. After the baby's birth, however, there was active and extensive preparation for the new baby by the entire extended family. Mothers used all of the accoutrements for baby care available such as disposable diapers and disposable moistened baby wipes.

Muckleshoot mothers were concerned about the ill effects of the spirits of their ancestors on newborn babies. Ancestral spirits were believed to be around the home and land where the baby lived. Candles were burned and bells rung to keep the harmful spirits away. Shaker beliefs became evident in Northwest USA in the ninetheenth century. It is a combination of native American religion and Christian beliefs. Many Muckleshoot are active with the Shaker beliefs and ceremonies. They often altars in their homes with crosses, candles, and bells. The use of these religious symbols and others is thought to be very effective in preventing harm to babies from their ancestors.

Mothers frequently discussed feeding of babies and children. All expressed considerable nutritional knowledge and could identify foods that should be included and excluded from the pregnant woman's diet, to have a healthy outcome. Breast-feeding was encouraged by a licensed practical nurse who lived on the reservation, and many of her relatives and friends breast-fed their infants. Although breast-feeding was once the only way a baby was fed, it was abandoned in recent years because of the availability of prepared formula. In the past, infant feeding was on demand. One woman was told by the nurse in the hospital to try to keep her baby on a schedule. Her grandmother told her to feed the baby whenever it seemed hungry, and she chose to follow her grandmother's advice. Weaning takes place leisurely. Breast-feeding is usually ended between six months and one year of age. Many babies remain on bottles from two to five years of age.

Solid foods, such as cereal, were introduced as early as three or four weeks. The older child's breakfast often consists of cold cereal and milk. Meals for the rest of the day usually are not scheduled even though most mothers cook an evening meal. There is usually food available for children to eat whenever they are hungry. Parents and children consumed foods of moderate to low nutritional value such as, soft drinks, potato chips, candy and sweet rolls. Vitamin supplements were provided through the well-child clinic for mothers who attended.

Discipline of the Muckleshoot children was not harsh, rather it involved a great deal of coaxing and cajoling. Preschool children enjoyed a high degree of freedom with few restrictions and could explore, play, mess up the house, go into the to nearby family homes. When the child's behavior appeared dangerous, a parent or older child would restrain him or her, or frequently divert attention to something else. Physical punishment such as spanking was not observed. There is violence in the adult population, in contrast to the lack of harshness displayed toward children.

Children are taught that it is inappropriate to make direct requests to adults. One mother was taking her three: year-old to his grandmother's and said, "Don't ask Grandma for pop. She will give you some." Children are also told not to ask questions of adults, as adults will tell them what they need to know. In school, not asking questions is often misinterpreted as a child being dull. During the interviews with Muckleshoot women about their interactions with health care persons, a frequent statement was: "Indian women won't ask questions." Further exploration of the idea indicated that the women believed health care providers would tell you what you needed to know. Questioning what was said was an insult because it implied the health care providers did not adequately explain themselves.

Application of Leininger's Conceptual Model

Leininger's early conceptual model was used to study and analyze the findings under her mentorship.[20, 21] A small number of care examples of Muckleshoot child-rearing were studied in-depth. To elicit the Muckleshoot women's views of pregnancy and child-rearing, the ethnoscience care model and Spradley's ethnographic model were used. The ethnographic steps were: 1) a specific statement which included presentation of informants' own verbal expressions relative to the domain under study; 2) a general statement which organized terms and expression into taxonomically related categories; 3) an abstract statement which revealed formal patterns of meanings underlying a domain; and, 4) a correlational statement, which specified the relationship of the domain to other aspects of informants' lives.[22] Categorizing ethnonursing care material was accomplished in several ways. The verbatim specific statements were organized by each informant through card sorting into abstract categories of beliefs, knowledge and rules about health and care during pregnancy and child-rearing.

The verbally stated cognitions of informants expressed as beliefs, knowledge and rules fit quite nicely into the categories of ethnonursing care components of Leininger's model. The statements about expectations of health care persons during pregnancy seemed to cut across many aspects of life. A correlational statement showed how this occurred with each domain studied (see Table 1 in Appendix).

In the study, cognition, in the broadest sense, referred to how subjects knew their world, including the meanings and significance subjects attached to specific or general phenomena in their worldviews. Since cognitions referred to how informants knew their world; the beliefs, knowledge, and rules of behavior were included within the construct of cognitions and Leininger's conceptual model. Other definitions used were:

Beliefs: Statements which the informant holds as true, but which may or may not be based on empirical evidence; thus, the strength of belief does not depend on its degree of correspondence with objective fact or its lack of contradiction with other beliefs the informant may hold.

Knowledge: The informant's understanding of the subject under discussion, which has been gained through learning experiences, and which can be verified largely by empirical evidence, thus corresponding more closely to objective facts.

Rules: Cultural expectations which influence persons to behave in a particular manner and which may be either prescriptive of proscriptive.

Table 1 in the Appendix gives of the categories of the relationship of ethnonursing care components to cognitions. Perceptual data not included in this presentation certainly give deeper meanings to the theory of cognitions, but are not presented here because of space limitations. Cognitions are presented to reveal the direct and known experiences of informants,

Transcultural nursing components of ethnonursing care were identified and classified using Leininger's framework. This framework was applied to the ethnographic statements developed through the use of Spradley's ethnographic model. This resulted in nine ethnographic statements. Two of the ethnographic statements of interest that related to child-rearing and ethnonursing care included: 1) classification according to persons from whom health care services were sought; and 2) classification according to kinds of health care needed, i.e., health promotional, or restorative care.

Classification of Data According to Persons from Whom Health Care Was Sought

In research with the Muckleshoot people over a lengthy period of time, the researcher was impressed by the amount of health care rendered by family and community members. Nuclear and extended family members were an integral part of childcare. In most settings, health and illness were frequently discussed, and the researcher, who was also a nurse, was approached in her professional capacity only after a lengthy period of time during which trust was developed. Family members were identified by relational ties that existed with one another rather than legal relationships only. Thus decisions about health and illness depended upon the consensus of a large number of persons who had close ties with each other. Further studies are needed on how persons in a variety of settings, rural and urban, use relatives and/or friends for health knowledge and health care. Categories of ethnonursing care components might have the following classifications:

1. Health care services rendered by kin groups only.
2. Health care services rendered by professional and paraprofessional groups only.
3. Health care services for which both kin groups and professional and paraprofessional services would be appropriate.

Analysis of data in this study fitted into these three features well. Further exploration of data will provide clues for more accurate health planning in the future. In fact, as the features of the categories are specified, propositions could be developed for theoretical testing.

Classification of Data According to Kinds of Health Care Needed

Components of nursing care were also classified according to clients' perceptions about health care needed, both for health promotion and health restoration. A domain elicited from informants included their perceptions about the process of pregnancy and infant care as being regular or irregular. Health promotional care was seen when pregnancy and infant care were considered regular, and restorative care fitted into the irregular category. The researcher's definition of regular and irregular differed at times from that informants. An example was nausea and vomiting of the pregnant woman. In some instances the nausea and vomiting described seemed quite serious and would have been classified as irregular by the researcher but in fact was classified as regular by informants.

Informants identified certain features of pregnancy and infant care as regular and for which health care was obtained from relatives. An example of this was infant feeding. Trust in grandmothers, mothers, and aunts, beliefs about infants feedings, in terms of what to feed and when to feed, was greater than in professional health care persons. There were other features perceived to occur in a regular pregnancy or in infant care for which professional health care services would be sought, if available. For example, trust in the physician's or nurse's judgment about normal progress in pregnancy during prenatal care and normal infant development at the well-child clinic was very high.

The characteristics of an irregular pregnancy and irregular aspects of childcare indicated to informants the need for professional care. Irregular characteristics of pregnancy included excessive bleeding, excessive fluid retention and/or convulsions. Irregular characteristics of infants and children included high fevers, convulsions and what is often termed the "failure to thrive" syndrome. The severity of all of the irregular aspects was clear.

These and other data obtained in this study provide a basis for development of further areas to study and contribute to the body of transcultural nursing knowledge. The following statements are not true hypotheses but state relationships of health care to pregnancy and child-rearing and were derived from the analysis of cognitions of the Muckleshoot women. These statements concern caring and caring interpersonal relationships that can apply to a wide variety of health care situations besides pregnancy and child-rearing. They are:

1. If nursing care plans are derived from knowledge of the growth and developmental process of children that Native American persons are most concerned about, there will be better utilization of health care services.
2. If nursing care plans for Native American children and parents take into consideration crises of daily living that affect both groups, there will be increased utilization of the plans.
3. If nursing care plans for the neonatal and postneonatal period incorporate members of the extended family in health care, there will be better utilization of professional health care persons during this period.
4. If nursing care plans focus on the neonatal and postneonatal periods for child-rearing, there will be decreased morbidity and mortality rates for Native Americans this critical period of life.
5. If the health-illness continuum as perceived by a specific group is incorporated into nursing care plans, there will be increased utilization of professional health care persons.

Summary

From this investigation, some child-rearing practices among the Muckleshoot were similar to the dominant Anglo American middle class, but still major differences existed. The Muckleshoot were slowly renewing pride in their cultural heritage and were beginning to transmit their traditional Native American knowledge to their children in a more public manner, without fear of retaliation from the Anglo society. Care as related to child-rearing was focused to a great extent on the family except when a very serious illness occurred. The children were frequently seen in the "Well-Child Clinic" with acute illnesses. Some of the informants associated poor use of available health care services with prejudice and alienation experienced in the past.

Use of Leininger's transcultural model to generate transcultural nursing knowledge related to child-rearing was helpful. The identification of ethnocare and ethnohealth cognitions provided important information for health care providers concerned about culturally congruent care. The Muckleshoot women's perception of health care during pregnancy is essential knowledge requirements for nurses. Identifying the beliefs, values and practices of the Muckleshoot in relation to child-rearing and care is essential to understanding and giving quality transcultural nursing care to the Muckleshoot *now* and *in* the future. Valuable new insights about child-rearing and care were identified from this study and can now be used to provide culturally congruent care.

Addendum

The investigator is currently working with the Muckleshoot in establishing baseline data for improvement of health care. There is little specific data about Muckleshoot health and they would like to know whether their issues are the same or different from those published about other tribes in the United States.[23, 24, 25] Health care services have improved considerably on this reservation since 1972. The original clinic building was expanded in size and operates a clinic five days per week with physicians and nurse practitioners in attendance. Recently, another building supporting mental health, substance abuse care and parenting education, was dedicated. A sense of cultural pride is clearly evident and many tribal members have moved back to the reservation from urban areas. Problems continue to exist due to poor and overcrowded housing, poverty, and challenges of the present day related to the environment. Logging and fishing, once the major sources of employment, no longer exist. Health concerns continue to be those that existed previously as well as AIDS, high infant mortality rate due to Sudden Infant Death Syndrome, and an adult mortality rate that is at least a decade behind Anglo American Western rates. Nevertheless, a sense of optimism not perceived by the investigator twenty years ago currently exists amidst tribal members. The strength of persons to tolerate ravages left by colonialism is impressive and bodes well for the future of this small but resilient group of Native Americans.

*Footnote: This is a slightly revised version of the chapter as originally published in the first edition of *Transcultural Nursing: Concepts, Theories and Practice,* New York: John Wiley and Sons. 1978. The author was one of the first nurses prepared in an individualized Ph.D. program focused on transcultural nursing, studying under Dr. Leininger in the early 1970s. She did this study in early 1970's and is in 1994-95 continuing to study the people for changes in lifeways, caring and health.

Ethnonursing Care Components & Cognitions

Table 1

Categories of Ethnonursing Care Components	Cognitions		
	Beliefs	Knowledge	Rules
Coping Assistance	Indian women need help from someone in learning to care for their babies (and children). Older brothers and sisters know how to care for younger ones in the family. Mothers and fathers care for their children better than anyone else. Real parents love their children even if they're taken away.	The persons who help most in baby care are my mother and sisters. Older brothers and sisters know more than younger ones. Children get taken away from parents when they're not well cared for.	Learning baby care by yourself is what you have to do (unless your mother and sisters help you). If children are to live, mothers should take good care of them.
Succorance Acts	Indian people help each other out.	Sometimes Indian people aren't able to help.	Relatives who know what is happening are the ones to go to for help first; if they can't help, they will know who can.
Surveillance Measures	If what is happening to you is normal, you don't have to have health care.	Some preventive measures are important.	If you are treated poorly (when you go for health care), try to find someone who will treat you well.
Health Instructive Acts	Indian people want to know what is happening to them. Health-care persons should know what I need to know. A nurse has knowledge about what mothers should know.	There are certain things we need to know, but no one ever tells us. Indian women (people) won't ask questions.	Find out what you want to know by listening to your sisters and family. Find out what you need to know from books.
Health Maintenance	Families, especially mothers, care for their children when they're young, and at other times, as during pregnancy. Health-care persons are there for when things are not normal (you are sick).	Health maintenance care is available for children at clinic. If you bring your child to clinic when he or she is sick, they will check to see if he is okay otherwise and has shots, etc.	Bring the child to the clinic when he is sick.

References

1. Minturn, Leigh and Lambert, William W. *Mothers of Six Cultures*, New York: John Wiley & Sons, Inc., 1964.
2. Whiting, John W. M., and Child, Irvin L. *Child Training and Personality,* New Haven: Yale University Press, 1953, p. 63.
3. Ibid. p. 64.
4. Minturn, op cit.
5. *Muckleshoot Tribal Constitution,* Adopted 1934, from Muckleshoot Archives, Muckleshoot Indian Reservation, Washington, 1934.
6. Reaugh, Catherine E. "Muckleshoot, Port Gamble, Puyallup, and Tulalip: Four Puget Sounds Communities Today." Unpublished senior thesis, Seattle: University of Washington, 1979.
7. Wickersham, James, "The Indian Side of the Puget Sound Indian War, 1855-1856, Pro and Con—An Address-Prepared and Delivered Before the State Historical Society, October 2, 1893," from the files of the Secretary's Office of The Washington State Historical Society, Tacoma: Washington.
8. Drucker, Phillip. *Indians of the Northwest Coast,* Garden City, New York: The Natural History Press, 1955.
9. McFeat, Tom. *Indians of the North Pacific Coast.* Seattle: The University of Washington Press, 1955.
10. Smith, Marian W. *The Pusallup-NisquallY*, Columbia University Contriubtions to Anthropology, No. 32. New York: Columbia University Press, 1940.
11. *Auburn Globe News,* May 14, 1972.
12. Ibid., February 27, 1972.
13. Ibid.
14. Horn, Beverly M. "An Ethnoscientific Study to Determine Social and Cultural Factors Affecting Native American Indian Women During Pregnancy," Unpublished doctoral dissertation, Seattle: The University of Washington, 1975.
15. *Seattle Post Intelligencer,* April 1, 1973.
16. *Are You Listening Neighbor?* Report of Task Force on Indian Affairs in the State of Washington, Olympia: State of Washington Printing, 1972 .
17. Cahn, E.S., ed. *Our Brothers Keeper: The Indian in White America.* Citizens' Advocate Center, New York: World Publishing Company, 1969.
18. McNickel, D'Arcy. "The Sociocultural Setting of Indian Life," *American Journal of Psvchiatrs,* v. 125, no.2, August l, 1968, pp. 219-223.
19. Horn, op cit.

20. Leininger, Madeleine. "Toward Conceptualization and Studying Transcultural Nursing Practice," *Transcultural Nursing: Concests, Theories and Practice,* New York: John Wiley and Sons, 1978, pp. 75-84.

21. Leininger, op cit.

22. Spradley, James P. "A Cognitive Analysis of Tramp Behavior," paper read at the English International Congress of Anthropological Sciences, Tokyo and Kyoto, 1968. (Mimeographed)

23. Blum, Robert W., Harmon, Brian, Harris, Linda, Bergelsen, Lois, Resnick, Michael. "American Indian-Alaska Native Youth Health," *Journal of the American Medical Association,* vol. 267, no. 12, March 25, 1992, pp. 1637-1644.

24. Irwin, Kathleen, Oberle, Mark W., Kimball, Ernest H. "Teen Pregnancy Among Washington's Native Americans," *Washinqton Public Health,* Winter, 1990, pp.14 -15.

25. Koepsell, Thomas D., Hildebrandt, Kristine M., Shultz, Linda, Pearson, David, Wagner, Edward. "Findings of a Health Survey on a Western American Indian Reservation" *Washington Public Health,* Winter, 1991, pp. 26-27.

Chapter 24
Japanese Americans and Culture Care

Madeleine Leininger, PhD, LHD, FAAN, CTN, RN

In the past two decades, Japanese lifeways, values, and business activities have become of great interest to people worldwide. One of the reasons for such heightened interest in the Japanese is because of their active business ventures, marketing, and tourist activities in many countries. Indeed, Japan has had a very active growth and expansion period which is one of the most significant in the world. Japan's gross national product has expanded about 10 percent annually from the mid 1950s that by the late 1960s was the third largest economic power in the world and is one of the top today.[1,2,3] Japan has become a big business culture with modern cars, railroads, planes, and a host of microtechnologies. It has one of the most rapid and modern transit systems in the world. Japan is a culture that has established strong international trade practices and increased its scientific material products. Most significantly, it has one of the highest literacy rates in the world and publishes more books annually than most countries. Grossberg states that "Japan is one of the world's most creative and innovative societies, and that is no small collateral with which to face in the future."[4]

Amid these highly successful developments, one will find lifestyle variations in rural and urban communities and in different countries where the Japanese live. Their lifestyles vary from their traditional values and beliefs to that of modern Western practices. Today, the Japanese are living or temporarily working in many countries, but many still retain some traditional practices because of their coherence and meaning to themselves and their extended families in their homeland. Some of these traditional Japanese cultural values are seen in their communal activities, their strong cultural living and working patterns, and their cultural pride related to their long and distinguished cultural history. It has been some of their strong cultural values and living modes that have sustained and advanced the Japanese people into a modern period of rapid economic development and growth. Such cultural values, developments, and changes are of particular interest to health care professionals, but especially to professional nurses as they interact with Japanese people living in many places in the world.

In the United States there are over 716,331 Japanese living in the country and approximately 50,000 Japanese who are yearly tourists in the country.[5] Many Japanese Americans live on the West Coast of the United States and in Hawaii. Accordingly, American nurses are aware of many Japanese people in the community and know about their increased numbers in the United States. More and more nurses are seeking to learn about the Japanese people with their specific values, beliefs, and lifeways in order to provide quality—based nursing care to Japanese clients and their families.

In this chapter emphasis is given to the Japanese Americans who were born in Japan and migrated to the United States to live and work. This focus has been chosen because of the author's work with Japanese Americans in the United States and because of many requests from nurses to learn more about this growing culture. The author has also spent time in Japan on several occasions since the early 1960's and studied the Japanese culture and is keenly aware of nurse's questions about Japanese living in other lands. The author, therefore, will briefly highlight Japanese ethnohistory, worldview, social structure, cultural values, environmental factors, and other factors influencing nursing care practices. Emphasis is given to the use of the theory of Culture Care with the Sunrise Model and especially the importance of understanding cultural variability among Japanese in the United States and elsewhere. Ways to provide culturally competent nursing care are discussed with the three predicted modes of action or decision. As with other cultures presented in this book, the reader is encouraged to read more about the culture under study and their care needs.

Ethnohistory and the People

The ethnohistory of the Japanese people in their homeland is exceedingly fascinating with thousands of years of evolutionary development. Japan's history can be briefly divided into four periods, known to Japanese and social science scholars as the primitive period, ancient period, middle ages, and modern periods.[6] The primitive period was the beginning period in which the people were involved largely in rice cultivation and with internal warfare that united many small territories within the country. The ancient times covered approximately the 4th to 12th centuries, with the people united into a single nation under an emperor — this was the time of interaction with the Chinese and the rise of the nobility. The Middle Ages, from the 12th to the 19th century, was characterized by warriors who were used by the nobility to regulate or control the people. If the warrior was outstanding in the view of the emperor, he became a shogun. The feudal system prevailed in the 17th century with many warring groups which led to a period of isolation, during which the country developed its educational, industrial, and socioeconomic institutions.

Very little by the West was known about Japan until the middle of the 19th century when the American Commodore Perry went to Japan and influenced Japan entering the modern period.[7] There were many periods and dynasties that rose and fell over the long history of Japan and shaped Japanese lifeways. The Meiji period led to the end of isolation, and trade was established with selected other countries. Japan captured the most desirable features from other countries, especially military influences of Britain and German, and Japan was soon at war with China, Korea, Russia, and finally, in World War II, with the United States. These brief glimpses of the ethnohistory of Japan have great implications for understanding the past and current cultural values and lifeways of the people.

Anthropologically, it is held that the Japanese are mainly of Asian ancestry with a mixture of Malay origin. They apparently came from different areas of the Asian continent and from the South Pacific to inhabit the islands more than 10,000 years ago.[8, 9] There is archeological evidence that early paleolithic man inhabited the islands as early as 200,000 years ago. Among the early islanders were the Ainus. Some ancestors still live in Tokkaido today with only 16,000 Ainus remaining, and according to Hane, the Japanese language appears related to Polynesian and Altaic languages.[10]

Japan consists of four major islands and nearly 4,000 smaller islands with a total size of about California. Most of the 125 million Japanese people live on a small portion of the land, as two-thirds of the land is uninhabitable. Japan is the fifth most densely populated country in the world, with 721 people per square mile compared to 56.6 in the United States.[11] Thus the Japanese people who immigrated to the United States or to any place in the world have been used to living in small and compact geographic areas. This factor has influenced their goal to live in harmony with their neighbors and to form self-sufficient communities with similar cultural values as well as to explore other places to live in the world.

Thousands of Japanese male immigrants began coming to the United States beginning in 1885 from Japan and Hawaii, but by 1908 to 1913 it was limited due to Gentleman's Agreement.[12] In 1924, the American immigration curtailed Asian immigration. Many of the first immigrants were young men with a rural agricultural orientation who took on farming, but others worked in gardening, landscaping, and small businesses, e.g. fruit, fish, and vegetable markets. With the exclusion law of 1924, the Japanese male immigrants had a difficult time getting a spouse, which led to many single elderly men in the United States in the early immigration days.

It should be noted that the Japanese Americans are one of the few cultures to identify themselves within the generation born. These generational groups are distinguishable by age, language, experiences, and values. They are the following: *Issei* are the first generation living in the United States; *Nisei* are the second generation;

Sansei are the third generation, and *Yonsei* are the fourth generation.[13] These different groups help to understand intergenerational family cultural values, beliefs, and patterns of behavior and are often referred to by Japanese in common communication exchanges. The *Issei* upheld strong family traditional values and practices and could endure hardships; whereas the *Sansei* and *Yonsei* have adopted many nontraditional values, particularly American and other Western views. The anti-Japanese law of 1913 prohibited *Issei* from owning land in America which was difficult for them to accept. The *Nisei* generation, who were strong in education and obedience, maintained a hard work ethic, and they were not forced to attend segregated schools as were Indian, Chinese, and other immigrants from Southeast Asia

Japanese Americans were evacuated from their homes and placed in government relocation centers during World War II. This caused many serious problems with the tragic disruption of family interdependency and the loss of Japanese businesses, farms, and homes. The relocation camps were declared unconstitutional in 1945. In 1991, President Bush proclaimed forgiveness to the Japanese relocates, and offered financial recompense for the harm and related problems caused. World War II and the relocation camps led to much distrust between Americans and Japanese for many years. It has taken nearly fifty years to heal partially the distrust between the two nations, and at times factors arise which reactivate degrees of distrust. *Nokkei* was often used to refer to all Japanese Americans.

During the past two decades, there has been a large influx of Japanese tourists, students, and many businessmen into the United States, but especially into Hawaii. The Japanese have actively-bought land, hotels, industries, large homes, and established car and other businesses in the country. Some Americans are frightened by these activities and some feel threatened by aggressive overseas Japanese interests, buying power, and trade agreements. However, most Americans value the Japanese people and are learning about their traditional and changing cultural lifeways, group entrepreneurship, and successful rising transnational marketing.

Dominant Cultural Values

Although more Japanese Americans have been coming to America since World War II, there are signs of intergenerational variability and degrees of acculturation. My research of the Japanese over the last two decades revealed signs, however, that many Japanese value their traditional lifeways and retaining these values in their thinking, business and daily living activities.[14] From my observations and direct participant experiences with the Japanese, there were cultural variations among the Japanese male and key informants such as the following dominant cultural core values: 1) duty and obligation to kin and work group; 2) honor and national pride; 3) patriarchal obligations with respect; 4) systematic group work goals; 5) ambitiousness with achievements; 6) honor and pride toward elders; 7) politeness, self-restraint and control, patience, and forbearance (*gaman*); 8) non-assertiveness in interaction (*entyo*); 9) group compliance; 10) high educational standards; and 11) futuristic expansion plans worldwide.[15] These cultural core values are important to understand Japanese Americans.

World View

Japanese Americans view the world with harmony and relative congruence between one's internal and external environments, which essentially means being attentive to harmony factors within and outside oneself. The Japanese worldview includes collective group harmony by being attentive to kin and work group lifeways rather than becoming preoccupied with individual concerns. While serving as a transcultural nurse consultant in a Midwestern industrial car plant, it was interesting that the employees from Japan were often misunderstood because of their collective group management philosophy and mode of operation. In contrast, Euro-American employees focused on individual needs, achievements, and rights, and found the Japanese collective group work values and group consensus difficult to accept because of their strong focus on individual behavior. Such differences in cultural values often pose similar problems for Japanese nurses working with Euro-American nurses. In addition, Japanese American's worldview supports group interdependence, family support and protection, and group performance. As the Japanese continue to travel world wide as tourists or land seekers, one finds their worldview is being expanded from a small village to a worldwide perspective.

Technology and Economics

Since technology and economics are closely related in the Japanese culture, they will be discussed together. Technology and economics are of great importance to Japanese in their homeland and overseas. Japan and the United States are two of the strongest cultures in the world giving high relevance to the development, use, and marketing of technologies for economic growth. Since World War II, the Japanese have been leaders in developing, refining, and perfecting a wide variety of technologies, and then exporting them worldwide. Many Japanese technological products are found in homes, businesses, and in other public places such as many kinds of electronic equipment, radios, television, cameras. In addition, automobiles, buses, trains, and a vast array of micro computer products are manufactured in Japan and sold worldwide. The Japanese have been very successful in marketing their technologies and in stimulating worldwide competition with high-technologies offering some of the most reasonable, efficient, and compact products. Lower costs and maintaining quality products with new innovations have been important Japanese production goals for local and world markets. The Japanese continue today to be active international exporters and are known for small and efficient cars and large technologic products such as cars, cameras, and audiovisuals.

Japanese American clients in hospitals or clinics expect the latest, best, and most efficient machines, instruments, and other technologies to be used for surgery and human caring. Most Japanese clients are also able to pay for such modern technologies and modern treatments. Hence high technologies have great economic gains for the Japanese. The technologies are diversified and have become an integral part of thew social structure and cultural values of the Japanese.

Kinship, Social, and Political Factors

The traditional extended family structure has been strong in the past, but has been weakening with more evidence of nuclear families today. It is, however, important to assess the Japanese family and kinship structure, patterns, and ways that kin ties are patterned and expressed as caring modalities. In the past, the oldest son was important, and the father was the head of the household who arranged marriages and occupations for his children. The oldest son and his wife usually lived in the father's family home. With the birth of a son, the daughter-in-law attained recognition and was expected with the son to care for the elderly parents. The husband with his patriarchal rule continues to be the dominant bread winner in the family, with the wife expected to care for the children and husband.

Currently only a few marriages are arranged in the traditional ways, but one often finds that most brides and grooms are of the same cultural heritage because of values, descent benefits, property, and inheritances.

Japanese living in America are seeing many diverse American patterns of parent roles and models, and so some changes are occurring in marriage and family-parent role responsibilities. It is still evident, however, that newly wed Japanese couples value remaining close together and patterning their lifeways to support some traditional parental values and norms. Divorce is not seen as good for the children, but it may occur. In general, Japanese parents highly cherish and desire children. They tend to treat their small children with indulgence, much attention, and leeway for their actions. They use limited physical punishment with children. Moreover, the first born male (primogeniture) child is still valued in Japan and in America with special ritual acknowledgments and favoritism to male children and adults.

Japanese women remain the principal caregivers in the home. They are nurturing women who look after, anticipate, and protect the needs of children, the husband, and close kin. The Japanese American mother today usually bears two children. The mother, may work outside the home as long as she cares for the children with surveillance, affection, protection, and active attention to their needs. These mothers are usually employed outside the home, but make arrangements for child care. They are often seen shopping for their sons and daughters, and being concerned about the children's needs. The concept of *amaeru*, which means to depend upon and presume upon another's benevolence, is often observed in child-rearing practices between mother and child.[16] Doi holds that this practice of amaeru, or learning to be dependent upon another's goodness and kindness, especially from females, is related to neuroses with Japanese.[17]

Japanese women in America are finding many freedoms. Several Japanese women interviewed told about their freedom to be employed and have husbands begin to help with child care responsibilities like Americans. Hane recently gave a summary of the status of women in Japan. He contends that while the legal rights of women have been strengthened, their political, social, and economic conditions have not improved measurable in Japan.[18] Male supremacy still prevails in Japanese offices and women are struggling to get executive male positions. Temporary work status and the responsibilities of raising children in the home are keeping Japanese women from executive roles, university positions, and other positions outside the home. While legal social reforms in Japan have been passed to give women equal status, there are still no legal ways to eliminate disciminatory practices. In America in 1984 more than half the married Japanese American women held jobs. [19] However, several Japanese men the author interviewed would like their wives to be content in the home with the children so that men can retain their executive positions and work for long hours at their offices. It is also important to realize that Japanese men seek and attend some of the best colleges. Japanese women have only recently begun to pursue graduate studies. The husband's commitment is to his company and the collective Japanese group work is important. Such work should not be handicapped by his wife. Japanese men work very hard and long hours and sometimes suffer from mental exhaustion. The wives told me that their husbands are often so tired that on Sunday they are not interested in social activities. Indeed, male success in their work is of high priority both in the United States and in Japan.

Education

Traditionally and today, Japanese value education greatly and will assist their offspring in getting the best education possible. Japan has a very high literacy rate and excellent standards of education. Education is a Japanese lifeway which is highly esteemed throughout one's life. Education of the child begins with preschool, with entrance exams for admission that continue throughout the years. Students study diligently to prepare for rigorous higher education entrance examinations in Japan. If they perform well in the tests, they can enter outstanding colleges. Test-taking is, however, very stressful to most Japanese students because they want to excel, get high grades, and be admitted to good schools.[20] Male students are especially high achievers in order to get future positions desired by their family and corporate groups.

The concept of *saving face* remains important to Japanese in education, kinship, and testing. Saving face is somewhat comparable to Anglo-Americans trying to maintain their reputation or good image. Nevertheless, many Americans have difficulty understanding the importance of the Japanese concept of saving face. Since Americans emphasize the individual, the idea that the Japanese group and family are more important seems strange. The Japanese student is concerned about saving their self-esteem with their family, work group, or the company where employed. They tend to be more other-directed than self-focused. Japanese are quite concerned for their group or family members and do not want to cause them embarrassment or shame. Saving face, therefore, becomes an important caring cultural expression for Japanese, whether they live in Japan or in the United States. Saving face is not, however, a mental illness, psychotic or neurotic condition. It is also possible that a Japanese individual may take his life in order to save face because of great shame brought to one's family and group. Thus the concept of saving face needs to be kept in mind for transcultural nurse clinicians, managers, teachers, and others working with Japanese people.

Political and Legal Systems

The current political system in Japan is parliamentary (Diet) with a prime minister and independent supreme court. The party functions as conservative liberal democratic systems in both houses of parliament. The emperor inherited political status since World War II with the allied occupation. The Japanese legal system and politics are kept separate so that fair hearings are maintained. Judges are appointed not elected on the basis of their educational preparation and expertise rather than political selected influences. While in America, the Japanese citizens follow the American political process in government affairs, but they remain influenced in their thinking and actions by their traditional political values and practices. It is evident that in the last decade, young Japanese Americans are becoming more relaxed and seem less interested in formal traditional political ritual behavior, but they still cherish the cultural values of honor, politeness, and justice for harmonious living and coherence among Japanese and others. These adults are beginning to study and value some aspects of the democratic process and modes of functioning in the United States. Young Japanese Americans dislike, however, getting caught up in major political and legal hassles.

In Japan, political reforms are occurring, with efforts aimed at democratization by reducing the power of the emperor and making the executive branch more responsible to the people. They are advocating that adults become more responsible for democratic activities and with political parades. But changes are slowly occurring including the support for women's political and legal rights and more employment opportunities for women. Most American Japanese in the United States and in other countries keep in close contact with their homeland and especially government and organizational changes. Several informants told me they want to maintain their "homeland political practices" and Japanese interest groups in order to maintain the strength of their cultural heritage within a democratic system.

Religious and Philosophic Orientations

Traditionally, Shintoism, Buddhism, and Confucianism have had a significant influence on Japanese culture, and today the temples and shrines are being used for healing purposes. Each religion or philosophic orientation has contributed in different ways to the thinking living, and healing of Japanese people. Efforts to live in harmonious relationships with each other and to remain well in their geographic areas or communities has been important Shintoism is one of the early forms of Japanese religion which developed from local legends, rituals, and myths and provided guidelines for living for many years. Many of the shrines in Japan are Shinto, and are where newborn children are registered and presented approximately one month after birth. The Shinto shrines are also where the people come for special ceremonies when the child is three, five and seven years of age.

In the sixth century Confucianism came with Buddhism from China. Confucianism emphasizes the promotion of harmony in the social and natural order and to follow many ethical rules of behavior. Buddhism seeks the truth brought the two extremes of asceticism and self-indulgence. It teaches how to attain *nirvana* through meditation and relaxing the mind and body in order to see life as it really is. Nonviolence is important as well as privacy, quietness and self-control.

Buddhism teaches that death is inevitable and is a part of all living things, for humans inevitably disintegrate and come to an end. People are instructed by Buddha not to make big plans for living without full awareness of death. In Buddhistic thinking the person accepts death with confidence and strength and does not fight it. Today there are very few Buddhist and Shinto priests in Japan and elsewhere and those available often take secular positions to survive.

Roman Catholicism and the Protestant faiths have been in Japan in recent decades and have experienced more growth the past two decades. Today there are a host of new religious sects which draw from Buddhism, Shintoism, and Christianity. Traditional

Japanese religion's formal ritual seems to be waning. However, in my recent visit to Japan in 1990, I found there were many Japanese praying at the Buddhist temple or at a Shinto shrine especially for healing needs or to deal with trouble. Bus tours with elderly were noted going to temples and shrines that specialize in healing older people or to bring harmony into their lives.

In the United States there are only a few temples or shrines for Japanese Americans. I found that many Japanese in America tend to use Christian churches more because of their interest in what they call the "newer Christian religions, while some Japanese continue to rely on their traditional religion. Many older Japanese Americans told me that they wanted to return to their native country to die with traditional Buddhistic ceremonies, or with afterlife Christian beliefs. In general, traditional religion does not seem to play a major role with Japanese, particularly with those Japanese living in America. However, the philosophic and religious values of practicing nonviolent and maintaining peace and harmony are important.

Generic and Professional Health Care Systems

In Japan both generic and professional health systems are found. Most of the traditional generic and folk practices came originally from China. They gradually became a part of the Japanese culture until the Meiji Restoration when the country was no longer isolated from other people in the world. After this time Japanese men studied abroad, which led to the introduction of many Western ideas and especially the German model of professional medicine.[22] Western medicines and treatment modes were brought to Japan and some are used in the country. However, generic home remedies are used especially when Western practices fail or have limited meanings and therapeutic effectiveness.

The generic folk system includes Chinese *Kampo* medicine which has been used since the sixth century. Kampo is a holistic approach of all body systems and includes the use of the therapeutic folk practices of acupuncture, herbal medicines, moxibustion, and spiritual exercises.[23] Kampo provides an answer to a familiar traditional way to receive care and treatment, but its strengths also complement the weakness of Western biomedicine.

Generic home care practices are found in some Japanese hospitals especially as the family members provide client care. Still today, family members continue to care for clients after they are hospitalized. There are many home remedies which mothers use as primary care or as prevention modes. The ginger, sake, and egg are used for a cold and the herbal teas are a "cure-all" for many conditions. Headaches are treated with sesame oil and ginger oil rubbed on the head. Finger massage and exercise are valued to prevent illness and maintain wellness. The yin-yang (hot-cold) theory is important in Japanese care, especially during pregnancy and with medical and surgical conditions. Acupuncture is increasingly being used in Japan and is often sought by Japanese in America where available.

For the Japanese there has never been a split between the body and the mind. When illness occurs, it is often expressed in somatic complaints, depression or stress.[24] The healing approach is to restore harmony, order, and control through caring ways in one's environmental context.[25, 26] Harmony is highly valued as a healing mode. Appropriate cultural and social behavior are required in order to regain harmony and alleviate stress. Today Japanese men in America and in their homeland may seek places to rest, primarily hotels, to restore their harmony and health. Several informants said they will stay in a quiet place for several days in order to relieve themselves to present-day stresses and to regain their coherence with life. They like hotels with no external distractions such as radios or television programs.

Japanese clients who are hospitalized seek physicians who have excellent expertise in surgery and in medical treatments. Clients like to be introduced to physicians and to choose them rather than vice versa, for then they know they will get proper attention and services.[27] Medications are requested mainly to help tie clients regain harmony and well-being. The goal or form of therapy is usually to facilitate a repatterning of life or to reintegrate oneself into one's social group in meaningful ways. Most importantly, transcultural health professionals and especially psychiatric nurses need to be aware that to verbalize negative feelings about family members in psychotherapy will usually lead to unsuccessful therapy. It is not appropriate to express negative feelings about the family or to dichotomize or manipulate the mind and body. Instead, harmony of mind and body need to be restored through the sociocultural harmonization and ritual activities that facilitate coherence in Japanese values.[28] Ohnuki-Tierney states that the average length of stay in Japanese hospitals in 1977 was 42.9 days, which contrasts with eight days in the United States, and was the longest in the world.[29]

Japanese have national health insurance, and employers are required to provide insurance for their employees and to pay ten percent of the medical costs. Physician's fees are low as they are set by the government. Christopher states:[30]

> *The Japanese tend to visit doctors more often than Americans do. And preventive medicine is more widely practiced in Japan. School children get mandatory medical and dental checkups, and as a result of vaccinations and inoculations administered at school or through neighborhood organizations Japanese of every age are better protected against disease than the citizens of most other countries.*

The professional health care system in Japan is based on a holistic approach which local physicians and nurses use in care to clients. Only recently are nurses prepared in baccalaureate degree nursing programs and adopting both Western and traditional nursing skills. The Japanese nurse must remain attentive to family practices and the hospital as learned in the home. Physicians are well educated and do major and minor surgeries. According to Lock:[31]

> *Patients are socialized, as are their physicians, to think holistically about their bodies, to focus on somatic rather than psychological levels of explanation and to expect the family, place of work, and other social units to participate actively in health care except for the actual diagnosis and specialized treatment of diseases. The Japanese public is also, for the most part, extremely well versed in a scientific approach to the body. Pluralism in the organization of medical care and in medical practice is the norm in Japan but despite the great diversity apparent in hospitals and clinics, there are nevertheless, certain striking and dominant features which can be discerned in a variety of clinical settings and which form the basis for uniquely Japanese approaches to health care.*

Culture Care Meanings and Action Modes with the Theory of Culture Care

From the above ethnohistory worldview, social structure, and health system features, nursing care considerations can be identified from the theory of Culture Care. By now, the reader has entered the emic world of Japanese whether in the United States or in other places to consider ways to provide culturally congruent and specific care to clients for their well-being and health. The nursing care is derived from the many factors presented thus far in this chapter especially from the Japanese worldview, social structure, and dominant cultural values stated previously.

From the use of the Culture Care theory while studying twenty key and thirty-five general Japanese American informants, several culture care meanings and action modes were identified as important common or universal features to guide nursing care practices.[32] They are the following: 1) respect for family, authority, and corporate groups; 2) obligations to kin and work groups; 3) concern for group with protection; 4) prolonged nurturance to care for others over time; 5) control of emotions and actions to save face and prevent shame; 6) looking to others for affection (amaeru); 7) indulgence from caregivers; 8) endurance and forbearance to support pain and stress (keeping restrained in expression); 9) respect for and attention to physical complaints; 10) personal cleanliness; 11) use of folk therapies (kampo medicine); and 12) quietness and passivity.[33] Many similar patterns were observed with informants while staying in Japan but with some intergenerational variations. These care values need to be considered as the heart of nursing with Japanese families or individuals.

In planning or providing care, the nurse would first do a culturalogic assessment and consider the cultural context. After the nurse reflected upon general ideas about the Japanese culture, worldview, ethnohistory, social structure, and general culture values as presented in this chapter, the nurse would design care plans and actions with the client and family. The client's identified specific care needs would be given full consideration with the theoretical three modes of action.

The three modes of action and decision derived from the above ideas presented in this chapter would be important in the care of the Japanese American client and will be discussed next.

Culture care preservation and maintenance should reflect respect for the client and ways to provide peace and harmony. These care modes would be especially important for the Issei or elderly Japanese American client. For example, the nurse would be attentive to the Japanese elderly's needs by showing respect for and honoring their ideas regarding care the believe is essential. Respect as care tends to be a dominant and essential care construct for all Japanese clients, and especially the Japanese family and kin. Family members need to be included as participants in care to their elderly. For example, the daughter might be expected to bathe her mother or to provide personal hygiene. The nurse would let the daughter fulfill her obligations to her mother by accepting the family member's anticipated need. Honor and respect must also be maintained and preserved to those in authority as well as those who know home remedies and foods held best for their family. The term *oya-koko* is often used to refer to "caring for parents" which may be used by family members in talking to the nurse.

Another area to provide culture care presentation and maintenance is to be attentive to ways of saving face or to prevent unnecessary shame or embarrassment. Reducing the Japanese client's self-esteem or confidence should be avoided, especially in conversations with them or in casual discussions in the hallways. The nurse would especially watch so that one does not confront the Japanese client directly or blame them in front of family members or work groups. Japanese tend to feel like they are always indebted to their family and work group, so saving face is very important.

Culture care presentation would also be considered with foods the client desired in order to regain health, harmony, and to prevent illnesses. The Japanese client's preference for fish, steamed vegetables, fresh fruit, rice, and herbal teas would be given full consideration by the nursing and dietary staff. Maintaining Japanese exercises and daily life activities in a quiet environment would likewise be important. Recognizing and preserving *gaman* as efforts by the client to be patient, persevere, or to show self control would need to be maintained as well as the concept of *amearu*.

Most importantly, the nurse would need to plan for ways to preserve and maintain Japanese health in a peaceful environmental context so that healing can occur. Rest as healing is extremely important for Japanese clients to regain their health and harmony with those in one's environment. Work stresses in America and Japan are clearly apparent today. Thus many Japanese in executive positions may request a private room if hospitalized. Finding a quiet place in the hospital is quite a challenge as our American hospitals tend to be noisy and busy places. Loud speakers, many treatment activities, and limited time to rest without interruptions from staff or physicians are difficult to find.

Culture care accommodation/negotiation.

Accommodations need to be made by the nurse for family involvement. This means letting family members participate in care with the client in nursing care practices. Family members may want to give direct care to their kin and make decisions about their care except where professional nursing actions or decisions are critical. For example, family members may want to be responsible for feeding and exercising their kin. They may want to use home remedies such as herbal tea massage. Some folk therapies *kampo* and spiritual therapies may be requested by healers. Combining professional nursing care with generic care practices should be considered, but assessed for potential therapeutic outcomes. At all times, the nurse remains open to discussing folk (generic) remedies and other care practices with the client to observe their limitations or benefits. If some folk practices seem deleterious to the client, the nurse has an ethical responsibility to share her professional ideas with the client and family.

The nurse will be expected to assess Japanese pain and stress expressions. Often Japanese clients may be restrained and endure considerable pain. Sometimes they may request medications if under stress to save face or to deal with stressful demands in the work place. Somatic complaints may be anticipated as one expressive pain pattern. Clients' needs would be considered and discussed with them trying to blend their ideas with professional practices. Japanese clients may avoid a lot of pain medications due to fear of drug addition. The nurse would give attention to physical complaints but would avoid talking about physical or mind-body (somatic) expressions as separate entities. Instead, the nurse would maintain a holistic or total care viewpoint respecting the total person functioning within one's particular lifestyle and environmental context.

In providing culturally congruent care for the Japanese client in the United States or elsewhere, it would be important to use culture care accommodation so that the Japanese client can use traditional (*kampo*) or alternative care services. Supportive care from kin and employment groups may be important as well as assessing and respecting their group suggestions. Some male corporate work groups like to provide special foods to their sick group member. The concept of *amaeru*, or looking to others for affection and offering help is very important in regaining and maintaining the client's health because it expresses group and family care which is more other-care directed than self-care focused. Personal cleanliness is also valued and should be given to the client in quiet and proper ways.

Culture care repatterning/restructuring.

This area would be difficult to know until one first assessed the client and identified what the nurse and client thought important to repattern in nursing care. For example, I recall a Japanese American pregnant woman who wanted to adopt some professional maternal-child care practices. I worked directly with her in a co-participatory way to determine what specific changes in care she desired to alter or repattern. The areas the client wanted me to help her change from her traditional Japanese ways were the following: 1) to avoid using the traditional Japanese abdominal binder after birth (this had been used by her mother and kin for years); 2) to have her "shy husband" and mother-in-law remain in the delivery room with her, but not to have them directly help with the physical delivery of the baby or assist with labor pushes. It was especially taboo for Japanese men to be involved with the actual delivery and it was also counter to men's ideas of self-esteem and gender role activities; 3) be more physically active after delivery rather than staying in bed. (The usual Japanese traditional stay is three weeks.) These were major areas which the client wanted to change, and so we developed nursing care plans to repattern these care needs. With the repatterning, the mother-in-law and husband became more involved, but only in certain activities. The extended Japanese family members had to be reeducated about the shorter stay of the mother in the hospital in order to allay their fears and to reduce the mother's somatic complaints. The mother had to be reassured along with other female kin about not using the abdominal binder. In general, this was a client-family nurse repatterning plan which had favorable outcomes. The client was extremely pleased with nursing care. This is an example of creative transcultural nursing with culture care repatterning. It led to culturally congruent and specific care that fit with the client's and the family's expectations of good nursing care.

In this chapter, the reader has been presented with an overview of important cultural information about the Japanese worldview, ethnohistory, religion, kinship, economic, cultural values, and care meanings and actions as well as education, technology, and political-legal factors influencing care expressions and needs of Japanese clients Japan, but primarily in America. Such information needs to be used with Japanese clients with the theory and the three modes of action or decision making. The theory of Culture Care with the Sunrise Model can be a highly valuable guide to the nurse to assess, plan with, and providing nursing care to the Japanese client. Entering the world of the Japanese client requires knowledge of the culture and consideration of action modes with the individual, family, or group. The extent of acculturation and intergenerational value changes also must be considered. Variations in culture care will always need to be considered according to the extent of acculturation along with the environmental contextual factors. Such nursing care practices can prevent cultural imposition by the nurse and avoid major cultural clashes or other unfavorable consequences between the Japanese client and the nursing staff. Recently an undergraduate nursing student completed a field study project with a Japanese American family. She said,

> *This transcultural nursing experience was extremely valuable to me. I had such great difficulty caring for the Japanese patient until I studied transcultural nursing. I had been using Euro-American professional practices and this did not know the client's world. Through the guided mentorship experience, I learned the meaning of culture specific and congruent care. I also learned how to use your theory to guide my work and to provide creative transcultural nursing care. Now I have an entirely new way to practice nursing with Japanese clients and with people of different cultures due to transcultural nursing knowledge and practices.*

References

1. Farley, H.P. *Japanese Culture.* Honolulu: University of Hawaii Press, 1984.
2. Hane, M. *Modern Japan. A Historical Survey,* Boulder: Westview Press, 1986, pp. 6-30.
3. Norbeck E. *Changing Japan,* New York: Holt, Rinehart and Winston, 1965.
4. Grossberg, K. *Japan Today,* Philadelphia: Institute for the Study of Human Issues, 1981, p. 8.
5. U.S. Department of Commerce, Bureau of Census, 1981.
6. Nakamura, O. *Nippon: The land and its people.* Japan: Nippon Steel Corporation, 1984.
7. Ibid.
8. Op. cit, Norbeck E., 1965.
9. Op. cit, Hane, M., 1986.
10. Ibid p. 6.
11. Ibid p. 368.
12. Kitano, H. *Japanese Americans: The evolution of a subculture,* 2nd ed. Englewood Cliffs, New Jersey: Prentice-Hall, Inc., 1976.
13. Hashizume, N. and J. Takano, "Nursing care of Japanese Amencan patient." *Ethnic Nursing Care: A Multicultural Approach*, M. S. Orque, B. Bloch, and L. S. A. Monrroy eds., St. Louis: C.V. Mosby, 1983, pp. 219-243.
14. Leininger, M. *Culture Care Diversity and Universality: A Theory of Nursing,* New York: National League for Nursing Press, 1991.
15. Leininger, M. "Nursing Care of a Patient from Another Culture: A Japanese American Patient." *Transcultural Nursing Concepts, Principles, and Practices,* M. Leininger ed. New York; John Wiley & Sons, 1978, pp. 335-350.
16. Doi, L. "Amaeru: A key concept for understanding Japanese personality structure." *Japanese Culture,* Smith, R. ed. Chicago: Aldine Publishing Co., 1961, p. 132.
17. Ibid., p. 86.
18. Op. cit., Hane 1986.
19. Ibid., pp. 391-392.
20. Leininger, M. "Nursing Care of a Patient from Another Culture: A Japanese American Patient." *Nursing Clinics of North America,* 1967, v. 2, pp. 747-762.
21. Emiko, Ohnuki-Tierney. *Illness and Culture in Contemporary Japan An Anthropological View,* New York: Cambridge Press, 1984.
22. Long, S. "Health care providers: Technology, policy, and professional dominance." *Health Illness and Medical Care in Japan: Cultural and Social Dimensions*, E. Norbeck and M. Lock eds., Honolulu: University of Hawaii Press, 1987, pp. 66-88.
23. Op. cit., Emiko, 1984, pp. 91-122, 219-223.

24. Lock, M. "Japanese Responses to Social Change—Making the Strange Familiar in Cross-cultural Medicine." *Westem Journal of Medicine,* 1983, pp. 829-834.

25. Leininger, M. Ethnocare of Japanese Americans in an Urban Context., unpublished study, Detroit, Wayne State University, 1990.

26. Op. cit., Leininger, 1991, pp 337-350.

27. Op. cit., Emiko, 1984.

28. Ibid.

29. Ibid.

30. Christopher, R. *The Japanese Mind.* New York: Fawcett Columbine, 1983, p. 237.

31. Lock, M. 'The impact of Chinese medical model on Japan." *Social Science and Medicine,* v. 21, No. 8, 1985, p. 945.

32. Leininger, M. "Theory of Culture Care Diversity and Universality," *Culture Care Diversity and Universality: A Theory of Nursing,* M. Leininger ed., *New* York: National League for Nursing Press, 1991, pp. 5-73.

33. Ibid., p. 358.

Chapter 25
Southeast and Eastern Asians and Culture Care (Chinese, Korean, and Vietnamese)
Madeleine Leininger, PhD, LHD, DS, FAAN, CTN, RN.

If you are planning for a year, sow rice;
If you are planning for a decade, plant trees;
If you are planning for a lifetime, educate people.

A nursing student who had recently completed a transcultural nursing program was eager to use her expertise with a staff nurse who had not been prepared in the field. The staff nurse was having difficulty caring for a client and his family from Vietnam. The student effectively addressed Mr. Yu and helped to care for him in culture-specific ways. The nursing student discussed the needs of the Vietnamese client and told the staff nurse that "It is always important not to lump all Asians together as being alike because there are differences among these people." The student's comment was an important one, for there are many different Asian cultures that are different and need to be understood. There are Asians from China, Japan, Korea, Cambodia, Laos, Vietnam, Burma, Thailand, Malaysia, Indonesia, Singapore, Philippines, India, Pakistan, and Sri Lanka. Each has different historical, cultural, sociopolitical, economic, and geographic roots, but they also share some common characteristics as part of the Southeast Asian culture.

In this chapter the focus will be on three major Asian cultures, i.e., the Chinese, Koreans, and Vietnamese to show culture care similarities and differences. However, in other chapters, the Japanese and Philippine cultures have been presented and other Asian cultures remain important to be studied by students with a transcultural nursing view. The theory of Culture Care Diversities and Universalities is the conceptual and theoretical framework to examine the worldview, social structure, and other features of these cultures in relation to considerations for developing culturally-based nursing care. Each of the three cultures has a very long history covering thousands of years.

However, space will permit a discussion of only a few highlights of each culture. The student however, is encouraged to read further on the unique historical and social structure features of each culture and others in the Asian region from anthropological and transcultural nursing literature.

Ethnohistorical and Geographic Dimensions

During the past two decades Asian Americans have been one of the fastest growing populations in the United States and in other countries in the world such as in Canada and Australia. In the United States the Asian population has doubled since 1980, is reaching over seven million, and is predicted to reach approximately ten million by the year 2000.[1,2] This fast increase in the United States has largely been related to different waves of refugees and immigrants arriving after troops withdrew from Vietnam in 1975. It is also related to the United States Immigration and Nationality Act Amendments of 1965 which facilitate immigrants to leave their homeland and come to a new world away from intense political tensions and economic conditions.

With the rapid growth of Asians in North America have come misunderstandings about diverse groups and a tendency to perceive all Asian immigrants as alike without an awareness of their unique origins, history, cultural values, and other differences. Specific beliefs, norms, and practices of Asians based on their political, kinship, and religious foundations cannot be overlooked by health personnel as such factors influence health care outcomes. As Asian immigrants came to Canada and the United States, they encountered many obstacles and prejudices due to their physical appearance, language, and "strange" or different lifeways. For example, the early Chinese immigrants to the United States were excluded from many jobs except to build railroads from the Pacific to the Atlantic coast and to do menial tasks such as laundry, restaurant work, and street cleaning. There was marked distrust of these early immigrants due to prejudices and negative views. Many Asian immigrants and refugees were victimized, experienced hostility, and were exploited as cheap laborers, especially the early waves of Asians who came to America. However, the immigrants maintained their self-esteem and survival by living together in geographic areas within urban and rural areas. "Chinatowns" were an early cultural adaptation for survival, cultural identity, and social needs. A number of Chinatowns exist today in the urban areas of the United States, Canada, and Australia. They are viewed as areas to learn about Asian cultural values, material items, and to enjoy Chinese food, art, and festivities.

In learning about Asians, it is well to keep in mind that there are Asians from the northern, southern, southeastern, and western regions of their vast geographic territory. Some of them migrated over different time periods to the United States, Canada, Australia, and to other countries.

For example, since the early part of the twentieth century, there have been Chinese who immigrated to the United States from the east. Around 1975, there were many Vietnamese refugees who came to other countries to escape highly unfavorable political and economic conditions. The Vietnamese, Laotians, and Cambodians were refugees who came in successive waves to the United States. As these Asians entered new countries, they usually looked for relatives or Asians who had come at an earlier time for it gave them security, property, language use, livelihood, social ties, and often survival.

The earlier immigrant laws with national origin quotas such as the Chinese Exclusion Act of 1943 in the United States excluded Asians, but this law was abolished in 1965 and led to new waves of Asian immigrants into the country. The early Chinese immigrants were mainly laborers and farmers from rural villages, but subsequent groups were largely professionals and skilled workers. Historically these different migrations reflected changing circumstances due to war, persecution, and other problems in the homeland. For example, the Vietnamese, Laotian, and Cambodian refugees came under some of the most difficult situations due to a devastating war in their homeland. Many arrived acutely ill, starved, and persecuted to a new and strange land. Let us look next at the general geo-historical facts of the Chinese, Koreans, and Vietnamese.

Geo-Historical Glimpse of The People's Republic of China

The People's Republic of China (PRC) is the homeland for over one billion Chinese. China is located in the eastern part of Asia bound by the Pacific Ocean in the East, the Arctic Ocean on the North, the former Soviet Union and Middle Eastern countries to the West, and India, Vietnam, Thailand, Malaysia, and the Indian Ocean to the South (cf. figure 26.1). There are many different provinces in the People's Republic of China, possessing different languages and dialects along with variations in material cultural items and of some differences in cultural values, beliefs, and lifeways. China is one of the oldest living civilizations in the world with a history going back over 5,000 years. Its cultural art, dynasties, and general lifeways have spread over the Asian region, and in more recent centuries, into other lands.

With over one billion Chinese from The People's Republic of China, Hong Kong, Taiwan, and other Asian areas, they represent nearly one quarter of the world's population.[3] Interestingly, it was not until the late 1840s that the Chinese began to leave mainland China due to economic depressions, civil wars, and famine.

The gold rush in California attracted many Chinese to the United States but they failed to find gold. These early immigrants to North America made significant contributions to the host countries as farm laborers and by helping to build the transcontinental railroad

Figure 26.1

East and Southeast Asia

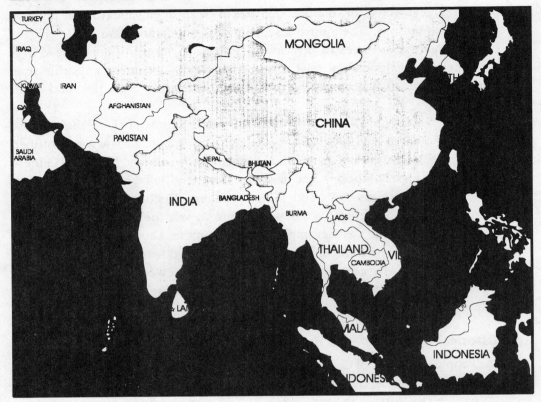

across the United States. Unfortunately hostility toward the Chinese increased, and this led to the Chinese Exclusion Act of 1882 that ultimately prohibited Chinese from coming to the United States. This Act was not repealed until 1943, after China gradually became an ally. In the meantime, racial violence and discrimination occurred, as well as loss of property and lives. The 1965 United States immigration law led to the second major wave of immigrants (called San Yi Man) to the United States composed mainly of professionals who lived in cities, settling mainly in California and New York.[4,5] The immigrants spoke Cantonese and Mandarin, which most Americans did not understand. By 1979 United States relations with China had improved and there were major increases in the numbers of Chinese coming to the United States and Canada.

Geo-Historical Glimpse of the Koreans

Korea is a peninsula located in eastern Asia, extending southward from the Asian mainland (Manchuria) for six hundred miles. Because of Korea's location, it has been a land bridge between Japan and China. Its location has also led to attacks from outsiders and foreign domination and exploitation by Japan, Manchuria, and China. In fact, Japan in its imperialistic expansion, annexed and colonized Korea in 1910 for thirty-five years. The Koreans fiercely retained their cultural values and practices and were finally liberated from Japan in 1945. However, at the end of World War II, United Nations troops (mainly composed of United States nationals) occupied South Korea and Soviet troops occupied North Korea. Then came the Korean War (1950–1953) which was one of the fiercest and most destructive wars in human history. Millions of Koreans were killed, the country was almost destroyed, and many Koreans became homeless and refugees.[6] Amazingly, Koreans, due to their strong cultural pride and determination, rebuilt their country. South Korea is today one of the strongest and most influential countries in the region with a booming economy. Korean history attests to Koreans' cultural endurance, strength, and determination to live and maintain their cultural identity against many odds. It also attests to their cultural solidarity and willingness to defend some of their important traditional cultural values.

Since the 1965 Immigration and Nationality Amendments Acts, many Koreans have come to the United States for education and employment opportunities.[7] Korean immigration is about 30,000 per year, and they are becoming one of the fastest growing cultural minorities in the United States.[8] The largest number of recent Korean immigrants came to Los Angeles, California, Chicago, Illinois, and New York. Once they mastered English and Anglo-American lifeways, they have been dispersed geographically seeking graduate education and to establish their own businesses in many urban and suburban areas.[9] Because of their noteworthy achievements and a proliferation of small business in Latino and African American communities in the United States, they have recently become targets of conflict and hostility.[10]

Geo-Historical Glimpse of the Vietnamese

Vietnam is bordered by Laos, Thailand, Cambodia, and the Gulf of Siam (cf. figure 26.1). Vietnam has 1,200 miles of coastline, with the northern part mountainous, the central area with coastal plains and high mountains, and the southern part a flat, agricultural area formed by the MeKong Delta.

The Vietnamese are held to be from southern China and from Indonesia's Red River Delta. There are cultural minorities in Vietnam, such as the Chinese, many mountain tribes (called Montagnards by the French), Chams in the lowlands of southern Vietnam, and Cambodians or Khmers, and other smaller groups in the country, e.g., Pakistanis, French, Malaysians, and Indians. Most of the latter groups left Vietnam in 1975.[11,12]

The history of Vietnam is one of struggles to survive repeated foreign domination during its approximately 2,000 years of unrecorded identity. Vietnam was ruled by China for about 1,000 years, and then came a time of Vietnamese independence. Later the French conquered Vietnam and colonized it from 1883 to 1954. The French greatly influenced the Vietnamese culture, and French was a second language. While there were some positive changes and influences, the Vietnamese suffered severe hardships under the imposition of French cultural modes of rule and control, which the Vietnamese resisted. After World War II, the Vietnamese defeated the French, and the country was divided into two separate states along the 17th parallel: North Vietnam, with its Communist government in Hanoi; and South Vietnam, with a non-Communist government based in Saigon. This led in 1956 to curtailment of fighting, national elections, and division of the country.

But the hostilities did not cease between the North and South. The United States assisted the South Vietnamese government, and the Soviet Union and China supported North Vietnam. The full scale Vietnam War of the 1960s finally ended in 1975 when the South Vietnamese government fell and the Communist regime took over.[13] An estimated two million Vietnamese were killed and over 58,000 Americans died in the war. As a consequence, thousands of Vietnamese fled the country as "boat people" seeking refuge in the United States, Canada, and other countries. Many died in boats, many were wounded and killed, others were placed in camps, and still others died of starvation. Many were subjected to robbery, disease, extortion, rape, and other atrocities during the war period. It was a horrible disgrace to humanity.

In 1975 over 200,000 first wave refugees came to the United States and France.[14] The refugees were dispersed throughout the United States by state and local governments with the idea of limiting ethnic enclaves. However, the Vietnamese sought to find their relatives and establish Vietnamese communities like other Asians who had come to the United States and other countries previously. The author served as a transcultural nurse consultant to many displaced Vietnamese in Maine, Texas, the Midwest, California, and Washington during the first and second waves. Clearly, these Vietnamese refugees wanted to be with their families, to have Vietnamese foods, and to reestablish their cultural identity. As refugees, they were experiencing deep cultural pain which was not always understood by social workers and other health personnel who did not know their cultural values and earlier lifeways. The second wave of Vietnamese were often relatives or friends of the first wave. The third wave occurred between 1978 and 1980 bringing many "boat and land people" from Vietnam who were forced to leave the country because they were being persecuted. The refugees' crude, small, and unsafe boats were attacked by pirates, and many refugees lost their lives. Moreover, many boat people were over exposed to harsh weather and had no food or water, which led to serious illnesses and death. Some Vietnamese refugees were held in Thailand, Malaysia, and Philippines in prison-like centers, and others made it to the United States. Some Americans were very compassionate, but there were also those who resented the Vietnamese due to cultural differences, communication problems, a perceived dependence on United States welfare, and competition for jobs.

Since 1975 over one million Southeast Asian refugees have come to the United States. Many of the Vietnamese refugees resettled into farm and fruit lands, and other have in recent years moved into urban areas. The relatives of refugees in the United States are not eligible for resettlement in the country under the Refugee Act of 1980. About 62% of Southeast Asians are from Vietnam, 21% from Laos, and 17% from Cambodia. Approximately 40% of Southeast Asian emigrants reside today in California, Texas, and Washington State.[15] Over half of the Hmong living in California, especially in Fresno, where the author served as a consultant with nurses who are working with the Vietnamese. Many immigrants are young, school-age children and young adults seeking a new life in the United States.

Worldview, Social Structure Commonalties, and Diversities with the Three Cultures

In keeping with the Culture Care Theory and use of the Sunrise Model, the nurse focuses on worldview, social structure, and related factors to assess their influence on human care, health, and well-being. Only the most universal features of the diversities and commonalties of the three cultures will be highlighted: Chinese (PRC), Korean, and Vietnamese.

Worldview and Philosophies of the Cultures

The worldview of Asians is embedded in the philosophy, religion, and cultural values of the Chinese, Koreans, and Vietnamese. These dimensions are extremely important to understand the people for they are powerful guides for the people's thinking, actions, and general lifeways. The three cultures have shared some common traditional philosophies, religious beliefs and cultural values over extensive time periods. They are Confucianism, Taoism, and Buddhism, the distinct features of which will be briefly highlighted.

Confucianism: A Philosophy

Confucianism is viewed as a philosophy of humanity and a guide to living. Confucius lived from 551 to 479 B.C. He believed in "proper" human relationships in order to provide social order and harmony. Cultivating individual virtues was held by Confucius to be of prime importance of any society. He believed in promoting and restoring ethical governments so individuals could regulate their behavior to good outcomes. Confucius believed in "five virtues" which were: *Li* (proper conduct), *Yi*, (righteousness or morality), *Ren,* or *Yen*, (benevolence and humanism), *Zhi* or Chih (wisdom or understanding), and Xin (trustworthiness).[16] These five virtues supported individual virtues through study and self-discipline so that the person would contribute favorably to public life. Confucius' philosophy was not a religious doctrine, but rather supported human potentials of being virtuous and wise. Most importantly, Confucianism emphasized filial piety in which individuals owed their parents and ancestors obedience and loyalty and should anticipate their parents' needs and wishes. Filial piety also included reverence for ancestors whose spirits needed to be appeased and held in reverence.

Taoism: "The Way"

Taoism first originated between 280 and 240 B.C. Its founder or originator is unclear but is thought to be Lao Tzu.[17] Taoism is a philosophy and a worldview that promoted inner strength, spontaneity, selflessness, balance, and harmony with nature and human beings. Taoism teaches that man should "hold fast to the submissive" to overcome the strong.[18] It is different from Confucianism in that one must transcend human culture or society and give emphasis to "The Way" or "The Path," which is toward an ultimate reality as eternal. With Taoism, one would, therefore, avoid worldly affairs since all is relative and there is no way to make valid judgments in the world. Practices related to meditation and asceticism discipline thinking in the pursuit of a long life with good health. Taoism includes the yang (creative and dominating focus represented by the male and heaven) and yin (the recessive, receptive, hidden, and submissive background force represented by the female and earth).[19] Yang and yin forces are important in all interactions and for good care practices and health. The Taoist believer follows the cyclical nature of life and never overdoes anything. Most importantly, a Taoist tries to understand "The Way" so that harmonious living, happiness, and well-being will occur and be maintained through life.

Buddhism

Buddhism was founded by Siddhartha Gautama between 560 and 480 B.C. in India long after Confucianism and Taoism. It spread to China and greatly influenced the people's lives. This is a religion with a doctrine that is viewed as a "Middle Path" to avoid self-torture and pleasure in order to reach a "good life."

Buddhism promotes the "good life" doctrine by following the "four noble truths": 1) All life is suffering; 2) Suffering is caused by desire or attachment to the world; 3) Suffering can be extinguished and attachment to all things (including the self) can be overcome by eliminating desire; 4) To eliminate desire one must live a virtuous life by following the eight-fold paths of: right views, right thoughts, right speech, right conduct, right livelihood, right effort, right mindfulness, and right meditation.[20] Buddhism holds that an attachment to reality produces suffering and leads to an endless cycle of rebirths. This cycle follows the law of *karma* which identifies that an individual's fate in this world is determined by what one did in the previous existence. Hence, the only way to escape the cycle of birth, aging, sickness, and death is to be enlightened by *dharma*, or the Buddha doctrine. One must be released from the cycle of life and death or be reincarnated by reaching a state of complete redemption or *nirvana*, where suffering is transcended and one's soul merges with cosmic unity as the true reality.[21,22] These beliefs were incorporated with Chinese beliefs in filial piety and practical ways of living. Buddhism spread from India to China and to Korea, Thailand, and Japan with common value influences and practices in daily living.

The Chinese, Koreans, and Vietnamese also believe in ancestor worship, which is a link between the world of people and the spirit world. Ancestor spirit is essentially a respect for one's departed ancestors who helps one with their fortunes or misfortunes. They recognize that their ancestor's spirit lives on and that the ancestors have needs the same as the living which must be honored and addressed. The moral and ethical worth and the good deeds of the departed ancestors lives on as a guide to daily living. There is a mutual interaction and interdependence between living and dead that leads to a close and positive relationship. As Hsu states "the worst imaginable plight for any Chinese is, while living, to be without known parents and relatives, and when dead, to be without living descendants."[23]

Today, in China, Korea, and Vietnam, polytheism is found which support many gods and supernatural beings. But there are also other religious orientations today that have come into their worlds namely, Christianity, Islam, neo-Confucianism, Taoism, and Buddhism. In China Catholicism has been actively suppressed for centuries, but there are Catholics and other Christians who are today practicing their religious beliefs. Their practices occur "underground" or covertly to prevent a public view. In Vietnam Catholicism was strong until 1975 when the French Catholics left. In Korea the missionaries promoted modern education and a Western work ethic as they did in Vietnam. The Koreans encouraged Christianity and to emigrate to the America. It is estimated that 60–70% of Korean Americans in the United States are affiliated with Christian churches, which remain important to them since the end of the nineteenth century. Yu states that "Wherever there are Koreans, there are churches, a pattern that clearly differentiates Koreans from other Asian immigrant groups."[24]

It is important to know that Korea was one of the early cultures to value shamanism and spirit worship which came from the ancient tribal social structure especially in the rival areas. The Koreans believed in many spirits with different functions for health, well-being, and fortune or misfortune. Animism or the belief that all forms of life and things in the universe meant their existence by anima or soul. Shamans serve between the spirit world and people world to prevent, diagnose, and treat illnesses. Sometimes they brought good luck and facilitated one's passage from this world to the next. Some traditionally and some contemporary-oriented Koreans often accommodate both sets of values and use them in different life and health contexts.

Education

The Chinese, Koreans, and Vietnamese greatly value education. They respect, honor, and value their teachers as authority persons with wisdom and societal contributions. From an early age children are taught a respect for learning and to acquire knowledge, wisdom, and the love of learning. Parents and extended social groups assume early responsibility, especially to see that children go to school and get a "good education." Parents sacrifice and actively support their children to get a sound education. The children, in turn, fulfill their responsibility and obligation to care for their parents and family members through the life cycle. If a child or adult excels in school, this brings honor and a great tribute to the parents and extended family. Education enhances the family's social status, economic benefits, occupational success, and general well-being of families and individuals. Education is a lifetime and intergenerational value, hence the proverb at the opening of this chapter.

Kinship and Family Structure

Kinship ties and the family are basic to the three cultures even though the family structure has changed somewhat in recent years. Traditionally, and still today, the families of the three cultures are patriarchal. They trace their descent through the paternal descent lines with patrilinial ownership of property. Confucian and Buddistic teachings give support to the extended family, husband, wife, and unmarried children, and often son's wives and children as well as to the ancestors. The extended family shows close interdependence of roles and activities within the patriarchal family structure.

The family structure derives support from the Confucian doctrine of filial piety that recognizes the "three obediences" of woman to obey her father as a daughter, her husband as a wife, and her eldest son as a widow.[25,26] Each family member has a designated form of address with honorific kinship terms. The form of address indicates one's relative position and role within the family structure with respect to gender, age, generation, authority, and reverence, i.e., the highest level with paternal grandparents and youngest with son. These Eastern values, beliefs, and practices can be found among the Chinese, Koreans, Thais, Malaysians, Taiwanese, and Vietnamese often with selected contemporary Western values and beliefs they have accepted.

In the three cultures under discussion a deep sense of duty, responsibility, and obligation to each other is evident, but especially to promote honor and respect to the extended family members and the family name. Children are expected to obey their parents and not bring dishonor to the family. Accordingly, childrearing practices are focused on developing children who are obedient, respect parents, and serve their extended family. Mothers and female kin are the primary caretakers in the family and are responsible for disciplining the children. The mothers develop close physical and sociocultural bonds with their children. They seldom let infants cry for long periods of time.[27,28] Infants are fed on demand and weaned around two years old. The father and male kin assume an indirect protective caring role, but are not direct caregivers providing nurturant caring responsibilities to the children. Asian children seldom receive physical punishment and seem to get immediate gratification of their needs. Asian children seem spoiled to Americans. Asian families want to enculturate their children to have a strong cultural identity, respect elders, and to have their cultural values and lifeways conform to traditional Chinese values. Children are usually directly supervised at home and at school by adults and extended kin. In China since the early 1980s only one child per family is permitted, but this is not the rule with Koreans and Vietnamese nor Taiwanese.

In general, the extended family is viewed as the single strongest unit and it is from the family that one gains honor, self-esteem, and support. The success or disgrace of one member is felt by all family members. Parents often sacrifice to provide for their children, especially for the best education possible. They will often work extra hours and make many sacrifices for their children. Children are much desired and receive parental affection and respect. They are highly valued as security for old age, for the children are expected to return care to elder parents in advanced years. Caring for the elderly and all family members is an expected norm, and to not care for parents would be viewed as ungrateful and disgraceful. The Koreans often have a daughter cut and sell her hair to provide something special for an aging parent or grandparent.

Technology and Economics

During recent decades technology has become of great interest to the citizens of the People's Republic of China, and even more so to the Koreans. Today in Seoul, South Korea with 6.5 million people, one finds automobiles and modern trains and planes. There are many signs that high technology is of great importance in a rapidly growing country that is being modernized. South Korea today has modern skyscrapers, television aerials, theaters, sport centers, churches and many more Western high-technology materials. Tweddell and Kimball state that the gross national product of

South Korea's thirty-six million people was about sixty million in 1976 and represented one of the most rapidly expanding economies of the world.[29] North Korea and Vietnam are growing in technology and economics, but do not compare with South Korea in the use and dependency on technologies. It should be noted that in the Vietnamese villages in the Red River Delta, there are from 1,500 to 10,000 persons, and there are markets, temples, and pagodas in the city and rural areas. The low valley is surrounded by farmland and fruit trees, which are Vietnam's main source of currency. Rice remains a staple food in all three cultures, but especially with the Vietnamese. In general, technology has become of great importance to Koreans and is of steadily increasing importance in China, North Korea, and Vietnam and Taiwan.

Political Dimensions

All three cultures have complex political systems with different political structures and varying political ideologies. Communism, totalitarianism, and central authority continue to dominate in the People's Republic of China and North Korea. South Korea and Vietnam are undergoing changes in establishing different political systems. South Korea in 1993 experienced its first national democratic voting process. Politics, religion, and philosophies greatly influence political decisions and actions in the three cultures.

Asian Health and Illness Beliefs with Care-Cure Aspects

Throughout the long history of Asian culture, distinctive health and illness beliefs were developed. While there is considerably variation among the Koreans, Chinese, and Vietnamese, there are some commonalties or universal features even among all Southeast cultures. This section will identify a few of the many interesting Eastern traditional folk care, health, and illness features along with acculturation changes and contrasts with Western professional nursing and health care practices.

In caring for Asians, the nurse remains in a strategic position to observe, listen to, and understand traditional folk (generic) practices and areas of cultural conflict with professional providers while trying to provide culturally congruent care that is satisfying and beneficial to clients. One of the most important areas for the nurse to observe and understand are the *yin* and *yang* forces that guide health care decisions and actions for Koreans, Chinese, and Vietnamese. To restate, the *yin* is believed to be the negative, dark, cold, and feminine principle; whereas the *yang* is the positive, bright, warm, and masculine force. The *yin* and *yang* forces ideally should be kept in balance in nursing care practices and in other health restoration activities. If there is an imbalance, illness, disease, and catastrophes will occur and wellness will not be evident. The three Asian cultures believe that the *yin* and *yang* forces influence all aspects of illness, wellness, and maintaining a good life.

Another important Asian health care value is to remain in harmony (or *ho*) with nature, spirits, people, and social institutions in order to be well and functioning. Being in harmony means to show filial piety and to be loyal, sincere, and benevolent to others. It means avoiding strong emotions and negativism. In keeping with Taoist philosophy or "The Way," one maintains a "middle position" and avoids all extreme aspects of living by practicing moderation. For example, one does not overeat, become too angry, or possess too much. One does not overdo in activities, but regulates the amount and duration. The Buddhist particularly believe in doing good deeds by being compassionate as it enables people to reach a higher state of being or *nirvana*, and to remain well and happy. Such philosophical ideas, principles, and cosmic beliefs guide Asian health caring modes and human relationships and need to be incorporated into nursing care practices. The Eastern philosophy of focusing on the total being or a holistic view of humans must also be maintained rather than focusing on body parts, symptoms, or diseases. Disharmony also causes illnesses and disabilities, and so one strives to avoid illness and disabilities by living a "proper life." One tries to remain healthy and prosperous by keeping in harmony with the universal order, worldview, and value the Eastern philosophy of living and serving others.

As the nurse applies the hot-cold theory to illness and wellness conditions, one is aware that Asians often view "bad winds" that enter the body as the cause of respiratory problems such as coughing, as well as muscle pain, headaches, airborne infections such as measles, diarrhea, and also cancer.[30,31] These "wind illnesses" disturb holistic health and can lead to death. "Bad winds" are prevalent beliefs with Vietnamese, especially during childbirth and surgery as the body is open and vulnerable to "winds." Thus the nurse must prevent drafts and cold air that can lead to wind illnesses and to imbalances in hot and cold forces that make one ill.

The hot and cold (yin-yang) theory is also important in dietary intake as it can lead to imbalances, illnesses, and death. Asians believe foods have hot and cold properties and need to be considered to maintain health. Cold foods such as vegetables, fruits, bean sprouts, cold juices, rice water, and seaweed must be understood in relation to hot foods such as chicken, fried foods, beef, pork, ginger, spices, coffee, alcohol, and eggplant. During the last trimester of pregnancy, which is a "hot period" for the woman, there are strict food taboos such as avoiding hot foods such as shellfish, lamb, rabbit, or taking iron pills. After delivery of the infant and for about one month, women eat hot foods such as chicken, beef, pork, and some salty foods, but they are not to eat cold foods, such as raw vegetables, fruits, and cold juices. This maintains the hot-cold balance before and after delivery.

Still another example of a "hot" condition is ear infection, which should be treated with cold foods such as fruit; but a cold disease such as cancer, would need hot foods, for example chicken soup, for proper treatment. It is also interesting that body illnesses correspond to *yin* and *yang* principles. The liver, heart, lungs, spleen, and kidneys are considered to be *yin*, or cold; whereas the gallbladder, stomach, and small and large intestines are *yang*, or hot. The *yin* and *yang* forces are viewed as complementary to each other and essential components to function together in order to maintain a health state of balance.

Special foods for the Koreans, Vietnamese, and Chinese are used to maintain wellness and to prevent and cure certain illnesses. For example, roasted rice paper with shrimp sauce or vermicelli is taken by Vietnamese to cure flu. Red chili peppers are eaten to prevent worms. And even though betel nuts stain the teeth, the Vietnamese chew areca and betel nuts to "refresh the heart" and to prevent other illnesses.

Because of lactose intolerance and the fact that milk is expensive and not popular with Asians, especially the Vietnamese, the nurse needs to work with the people to prevent rickets and osteomalacia. Asians like tofu (soybean curd) and different kinds of pork soups. Koreans and Vietnamese often have hypertension because they use food preservatives, such as soy, fish, and oyster sauce and monosodium glutamate which are high in sodium. Moreover, Asians like to ferment pickles and beans and to salt fish which are also high in sodium. Hence the nurse needs to consider ways to use culture care repatterning in order to alter hypertension so that the Asians can maintain wellness.

There are other factors that contribute to imbalances in well-being and disharmony in one's life, such as jealousy, anger, excessive worry, fears, hate, and being overjoyed which the nurse needs to understand. These expressions can lead to an imbalance and to illnesses or being unable to function properly in society. Vietnamese and Koreans are especially sensitive to being humiliated by others and will avoid contacts that potentially lead to humiliation. Asians are discouraged from showing strong emotions, especially anger and indignation, as it disrupts peace, harmony, and well-being. It is believed one must hide such feelings, or refrain from saying anything in anger that one might later regret. Family feelings that are disruptive and anger are kept within oneself or within the family circle. They are also to be handled within the family context rather than by outsiders such as mental health or professional specialists unless acculturated to their perspective. Asians are taught from early childhood how to suppress feelings, save face, and to maintain harmonious relationships in their extended families.

Such emotional constraints and family regulations are in sharp contrast to Western philosophies and psychotherapy which usually advocate open self-expression, assertiveness, and confrontational acts. They differ from Freudian views of catharsis or to get things off one's mind by talking to others, especially therapists. Western mental health nurses using or advocating open catharsis would probably encounter resistance and would observe cultural clashes and difficulty doing individualized catharsis therapies. More and more Western health personnel are learning about Asian holistic health values such as self-restraint and family involvement. With our Western expressions of open violence, killing, and hatred towards others along with encouraging expressive modalities, we need to learn from the ancient philosophers of China, and other Eastern schools of thought and their therapies. Discovering how Eastern philosophers and therapists restrain strong emotions, promote self-control, respect for others, and regulate behavior within families seems valuable ways to consider in our Western culture. Moreover, many Western therapies, such as Freud's theory of catharsis, are generally at odds with Taoism and Buddhism, and with the hot-cold theory of Southeast and East Asians.

From a transcultural nursing perspective and with the use of the author's Culture Care Theory and the three modes of action and decision, culture care maintenance is essential to help Asians maintain peaceful and harmonious values in their daily life. The nurse would also use culture care accommodation with Asian beliefs and values that help them to control their anger and negative feelings rather than to express them openly or excessively. Culture care preservation would be used to support the ways Asians honor their parents, value age, gender, and intergenerational differences to provide culturally congruent care. Being aware of ways to accommodate Asians to "save face" or to not embarrass their family members are important in practicing culture-specific care. Respect for elders as filial piety toward parents and grandparents, and to preserve educational and occupational achievements that bring honor and success to the family and extended kin would also be part of providing culturally congruent care. The nurse, however, must be aware that as Asians live in other countries such as the United States, Canada, or Australia, their submissive, passive, or non-assertive ways will be in conflict with dominant values such as assertiveness and confrontation. Moreover, these Asian values can limit them from getting some positions and maintaining self-esteem. Such cultural value differences are especially critical to be considered for submissive Asians who are entering Western work places and educational systems. Other factors influencing changing the cultural values identified above would be to avoid racism, disgrace, and victimization of Asians. Western cultures could benefit from Asian values of non-violence and harmony.

Culture-Specific Diagnostic, Treatment and Healing Modes

There are a variety of common diagnostic and treatment methods for Chinese, Koreans, and Vietnamese who rely on traditional folk (generic) care and health practices. These cultures have common features, but also slight variances in emphasis, types of treatments, and care-cure modes. Muecke, a nurse anthropologist and transcultural nurse specialist with Southeast Asian refugees, has conducted research and found that the best healers and diagnosticians are ones who look, listen, inquire, and feel the pulse.[32] Feeling the pulse is held as the best method to assess the client's condition. This belief and practice contrasts with Western medical practices in which the physician relies on extensive laboratory tests, client histories, and other means to diagnose a disease or explain symptoms of specific diseases or illnesses. Taking a pulse gives Asian therapists good clues about health or illness. Moreover, taking blood samples may be disapproved of by Asians, especially Koreans, who believe the blood belongs to the kin and that others should not have access to their blood.[33]

The use of herbs to prevent and treat illnesses has been an important contribution of Asian cultures, especially the Chinese, for nearly 4,000 years. Many Chinese herbs have been efficacious and are usually found to be based on sound pharmacological principles. Herbs are natural products and can often be used over time with limited negative or toxic effects. Most of the Chinese herbs are in dried forms, but are often used at home in boiling water. Herbal tea is one of the most common treatments used by the three cultures to treat a wide variety of hot-cold imbalances. For many Asians, our Western medicines are viewed as "too strong" and "too hot" when compared to Asian herbal and other treatment modes. Western medicines are often chemical substances, and some Asians fear them. It is common for Asian clients to stop taking Western pills or prescribed medications such as antibiotics because they are viewed as too powerful and hot. Moreover, if Asians do not see quick relief of symptoms, they may stop taking the medications. Asians also realize that Western medicine is mainly focused on diseases and symptoms rather than ways to prevent illnesses and to maintain holistic health with hot-cold balances. Asians are continuing to use their folk home remedies, but many are trying to understand and use professional medications and treatment regimes. They often contend that their traditional herbs and treatments are more effective than Western ones. In general, Asians tend to value caring modalities by nurses who listen, use silence and reflection, and know something about where the client came from with their current life interests, historical origins, and cultural values and beliefs.

Asian therapists traditionally have used different treatment approaches for different Asian conditions. Dermabrasion, massage, acupressure, and acupuncture, and moxibustion are some common native or emic therapies which have been used for centuries. Dermabrasion refers to abrading the skin in areas such as the chest (over the ribs), spine, neck and face. This treatment is to heal respiratory conditions (including coughing), fever, muscle soreness, headaches, sore throat, and related somatic concerns. The most frequent form of dermabrasion is coining of *cao gio* (scratch wind) in which tiger balm is first used followed by gently rubbing the area with the edge of a coin or spoon in order to release the "toxic wind." Health professionals may be alarmed to discover this treatment with its resulting blue or black bruises. They often view such bruises as physical abuse of children or adults. There is, however, generally no reason to be alarmed, as this folk practice usually causes no serious harm and is often used by Asian mothers. Other dermabrasive methods are occasionally used in the home such as cupping (pressure massage), pinching the skin, applying heat and using steam on the body surfaces. These treatments have long be viewed as effective and therapeutic by Asians.

Spiritual methods of healing by meditation chants, prayers, and special healing rituals are used when ghosts, evil spirits, or demons are believed to cause illness, especially related to disabilities, epilepsy, and other conditions.[34] Shamans, priests, spiritualists, and exorcists may be sought for traditional caring and folk healing purposes. These treatments are viewed as home care modes and may not be known or discussed with Western health personnel.

Many Asians, but especially Vietnamese, use rituals to prevent illnesses and restore the holistic balance of wellness. For example, Vietnamese mothers perform rituals at a Buddhist shrine of the goddess Quang Am to protect their children and to bring about an easy childbirth. When sick, they pray to their ancestors for good health and to keep them well. Christian prayers are also used today by Vietnamese and Koreans to protect and health themselves or others. They also use positive caring means to attain health, such as looking at pictures of healthy families and children, which they contend leads to healthy outcomes. They also help or serve others as important caring modes to reflect good works and gain heaven (Christian belief) or to gain the Buddhistic *nirvana* state.

Mental illness among the Vietnamese is believed to be caused by "bad spirits," malicious intent, or bad luck. If the person has offended a deity or used moral indiscretion, this can lead to mental illness. Mental illness brings disgrace to the family and is usually kept from the public.[35] Hence, Vietnamese may avoid going to mental health clinics or talking about these matters. Asians may present their mental concerns as physical problems, to Western therapists or care providers, as it is more acceptable, but behind these problems are often cultural and social concerns.

Vietnamese refugees (boat people) experienced severe trauma and physical torture when leaving their homelands, which may lead to sleep disturbances and signs of depression and anxiety. Mollica et al. identified this as post-traumatic stress.[36] The occurrence of depression among Vietnamese refugees was very high in the United States and Canada.[37] Nightmares and sleep disturbances with signs of depression and anxiety are still noted in these refugees. Hence nurses need to be aware of these earlier traumatic experiences as they do not disappear quickly. Many Asians will continue to relive them at different times because of their traumatic features. In addition, the *yin* and *yang* theory needs to be kept in mind to facilitate healing with folk home remedies, cultural healing rituals, and professional practices. The blending of folk and professional practices remains essential to achieve the goal of providing culturally congruent nursing care and maintaining holistic health. Most assuredly, to achieve this goal requires knowledge of the culture and of the diverse life experiences that refugees and immigrants experience as they come to a different country.

Language Diversity and Communication

The Asian languages include three major Chinese dialects, Mandarin, Shanhainese, and Cantonese, plus Hokkien but there are a great variety of Southeast Asian dialects and languages which makes communication for non-Asian nurses and other health providers quite difficult. Asians tend to use proper forms of address and especially family names. They rarely use slang and get confused with English hospital terms, such as "tied up," "turkey," "pulling my leg," "cool person," "place on third floor," etc. In communicating with Asians, the family name comes first, followed by the given name, which is the opposite for Americans and other Westerners. The title of Mr. or Mrs. is important in addressing the Asian client. Siblings are often referred to as older or younger sister, and older or younger brother, rather than by a specific name. Kinship terms are often used as a mark of respect. In general, Southeast Asian cultures prefer to be formal and in referring to health personnel they use Ms., Mr., or Dr. Asians view persons in authority as having status and power and deserving of respect. Hence, clients may not question the nurse or physician, for they are expected to respect and obey those in authority. The nurse, however, needs to let the client know that questions and viewpoints are important and are not disrespectful, but indicate a desire to learn and understand others.

It is also important to realize that Asian communication is largely context-bound. This means that the receiver must be aware of the speaker's intent within a physical and cultural frame of reference or setting in which one received the information. Reference to the speaker's verbal message is not as important as the non-verbal expressions, gestures, setting, and any nuances or shaded meanings. In other words, it is the speaker's intent in a situation, rather than the words said, that are important. Asians are a high-context culture; whereas Anglo-Americans are a low-context cultures. The latter relies heavily on lots of verbal or written words to receivers than on non-verbal communication of high context cultures.[38,39]

Some additional information for nurses to consider in their care to clients can be summarized as follows:

1. Do not assume that a "yes-yes" response means affirmative stance with Asians. It may mean the opposite. A "yes-yes" may mean that the listener accepted what she thought the speaker wanted to hear. The Asian client may not agree, but yet may show respect with a "yes-yes" or affirmative head nodding. The nurse needs to pick up cues and context to know the recipient's views and how the message is being received. Koreans "read the eyes" (*nun-chi*) by which they can assess another's attitudes and the message.

2. Asian eye contact and facial expressions are important in communication, but differ from Western use and interpretations. Generally, Asians do not like direct and sustained eye-to-eye focus with strangers for it is often viewed as a sign of disrespect, impoliteness, hostility, and may even have sexual connotations. Casual smiling with direct eye contact with strangers is inappropriate. Smiling (or blushing) may be viewed as an expression of apology for some inappropriate action or offense. It may also be acknowledgment of a mistake or for a fault committed. The one who smiles may be masking true emotions (pain or discomfort) to avoid conflict.

3. Use of gestures and non-verbal communication modes needs to be carefully considered, as it often has different meanings. For example, the American gesture to "come forth" while pointing a finger with hand raised and palm inward is often viewed as a hostile and aggressive animal-like expression: it is demeaning. The practice of crossing the index and middle fingers for "good luck" may be viewed as an obscene gesture with sexual connotations. Waving good-bye may mean "come here," particularly to a child.

4. Use of silence and meditation are extremely important with Asians. They value silence and meditation as they are expressions of concentration and spiritualism. Silence serves to help the client consider whether one agrees with the speaker ideas and suggestions. North and South American nurses and other health professionals often have difficulty remaining silent to listen and think before speaking or to not speak at all.

5. Asians expect physical distance in speaking to others which is greater than the American (United States) "12 inches of comfort." Likewise, physical touch, especially between genders, is avoided in public. However, people of the same sex may touch and hold hands in public. Hand shaking is often gender prescribed as well as done in different ways.

These above points are important to consider to provide culture-specific and congruent care. One must, however, know that there are subtle variations among Chinese, Koreans, and Vietnamese due to the extent of acculturation, trust relationships, and with their specific traditional values and lifeways.

Specific Transcultural Nursing Care Research-Based Meanings and Action Modes

Leininger's research findings from studying Vietnamese, Chinese and Korean in the United States from 1984 to 1988 revealed the following culture care meanings and action modes by using the theory of Culture Care Diversity and Universality.[40]

A. **Vietnamese American Culture Care Meanings and Action Modes to Provide Culturally Congruent Care:**
   1. Use of harmony and balance in caring according to the philosophy and teachings of Confucianism, Taoism, and Buddhism especially for traditional Asians.
   2. Respect for elderly, family ties (filial piety) and cultural taboos.
   3. Use of natural (generic) folk care practices and treatments, using the hot-cold theory and native foods for healing.
   4. Creative use of family-centered caring values, beliefs, and practices.
   5. Enabling others to perform daily functions for those who need help (other-care) through good deeds for *nirvana*.
   6. Use of spirituality in caring, drawing upon spirits, God, and ancestors.
   7. Use of touching as healing.
   8. Focus on prevention and maintaining health and well-being through caring.

B. **Chinese American Culture Care Meanings and Action Modes to Provide Culturally Congruent Care:**[41]
   1. *Serving others* rather than self-care practices.
   2. Use of harmony with nature, family, and environmental context.
   3. Compliance as respect for elders and those in authority.
   4. Obedience to elders in authority, and filial piety.
   5. Use of surveillance and silence as caring modes to care for those near or at a distance.
   6. Valuing and depending on generic (folk) medicines, treatment, and healing modes as meditation, reflection, and silence.
   7. Valuing group or communal assistance to others.
   8. Working hard to achieve good deeds to others in society.

C. **Korean Culture Care Meanings and Action Modes**
   1. Deference to elders and authority.
   2. Use quietness, be calm and gentle.
   3. Respect family values and lifeways.
   4. Use generic folk healers and ways.
   5. Use spiritual philosophy and ethics.
   6. Show love for humanity (*hongik ingan*).

Throughout this chapter some universal (or common) values, beliefs, and lifeways of East Asian Koreans, Chinese, and Vietnamese have been identified and discussed. From the worldview, social structure, ethnohistory, and the folk and professional practices, the nurse can now thoughtfully and creatively use the three modes of culture care and systematically assess their value. The three modes are: 1) culture care maintenance/preservation; 2) culture care accommodation/ negotiation; and 3) culture care restructuring/repatterning.[42] The goal is to provide culturally congruent care which leads to health and well-being. Conducting a thoughtful and sensitive culturalogical assessment is one of the most important bases to facilitate culturally congruent and competent care. Some suggested common guidelines for the three cultures that flow from the material presented are the following:

1. **Culture Care Preservation and Maintenance:**
   a. By the use of herbs as healing modalities and other generic folk practices.
   b. With support of cultural rituals, prayers, meditation, and medications that foster healing and well-being through spiritual care..
   c. With child-rearing practices that have proven beneficial to Asians over time.
   d. With acceptance of somatic complaints as expressions of the need for care, understanding, and assistance with illnesses and daily sociocultural concerns.
   e. With respect for parents, elders, and deceased ancestors as family-centered ways of supporting unity, honor, and filial love.
   f. With obedience to and compliance with parents as respect and honor.
   g. With focus on family care rather than individual or self-care.
   h. With use of hot and cold (*yin-yang*) foods and treatments that are safe and without harmful effects to the client's condition.
   i. With their interest in prevention and health maintenance rather than focusing on diseases and symptoms.
2. **Culture Care Accommodation/Negotiation may be needed in these areas especially if living outside their native Asian homeland.**
   a. Accommodation of folk with professional practices that will most benefit the client and family.
   b. Accommodation of philosophical worldviews from Confucianism, Buddhism, and Taoism, especially related to harmony, peace, and family unity and spiritual care.
   c. Accommodation and negotiation in dealing with *yin-yang* forces as Asians receive non-traditional or Western treatments and care practices.
   d. Accommodation and provision for hot-cold foods in professional systems as hospital and clinic, and sharing professional information that may be useful to Asians.
   e. Accommodation with the use of silence, meditation periods, and to be an active listener as care giver in teaching and clinical practices.
   f. Accommodation in the use of common language Asian expressions by health professionals to build trust and understanding.

g. Negotiate use of some folk treatments with professional practices for beneficial outcomes to clients.

h. Accommodation to communication modes presented in this chapter.

3. **Potential Areas for Repatterning and Restructuring to Attain Culturally Congruent Care:**

a. Repattern Western individualism to family-centered Asian culture-care values.

b. Repattern selected traditional Asian health problems such as food concerns related to hypertension and high sodium intake to that of low sodium intake to decrease hypertension and related systemic health problems.

c. Repattern traditional use of medications so that the dosage fits the client's body weight, expectations, and folk consideration and desired uses.

d. Restructure community lifeways in a co-participant way so that Asian immigrants can participate in the Western community lifeways without undue prejudices, stresses, and embarrassment to the people.

e. Repattern health care systems to include desired cultural practices that lead to Asian health and well being and avoid undue cultural imposition practices.

f. Restructure and redesign research and care practices to incorporate Asian health care values and beneficial health practices.

g. Restructure Western mental health practices to incorporate Asian spiritual beliefs and values into nursing therapies.

In this chapter commonalties and diversities of the Chinese, Korean, and Vietnamese cultures have been discussed with a focus on ways to increase nurses' and other health professionals' knowledge of the Southeast Asian people. The Theory of Culture Care Diversity and Universality was used as a guide to provide culturally congruent nursing care. These selected Asian cultures are important to understand as they are a growing population worldwide. It is imperative that knowledge of these cultures and many others in Southeast Asia be studied in transcultural nursing and especially their long historical cultural history and health care values to provide culture-specific care. Unquestionably, nurses with transcultural nursing knowledge and skills will be in the best position to provide congruent, responsible, and sensitive care to traditionally or non-traditionally Asian clients, their families, and other societal members.

References

1. Bouvier, L. F. and A. J. Agresta, "The Fastest Growing Minority," *American Demographics*, v. 7, 1985, pp. 31–33,46.

2. "Asians in America: 1990 Census," *Asian Week*, San Francisco: Great Printing House, August, 1991.

3. Brigham Young University, *Culturegram*, Provo, Utah: Brigham Young University, David M. Kennedy Center for International Studies, Publication Services, 1986.

4. Doerner, W., "Asians: To American with Skills," *Time*, July, 1985, p. 5.

5. Takaki, R., *Strangers from a Different Shore: A History of Asian Americans*, Boston: Little, Brown, 1989.

6. Ibid.

7. Ibid.

8. Yu, E-Y., "Korean Communities in America: Past, Present, and Future," *Ameriasian Journal*, v. 10, 1983, pp. 23–51.

9. Ibid.

10. Siao, G. W-T., "L. A. Koreans, Blacks Try to Work Out Differences," *Asian Week*, August 10, 1990, pp. 14–15.

11. Rutledge, P. *The Vietnamese in America*, Minneapolis: Lerner Publication Co., 1987.

12. Te, H. D., *The Indochinese and Their Cultures*, San Diego: San Diego State University, Multifunctional Resource Center, 1989.

13. Ibid.

14. Rutledge, op. cit.

15. Chan, S. "Families with Asian Roots," *Developing Cross-Cultural Competence: A Guide for Working with Young Children and Their Families*, E. W. Lynch and M. J. Hansen, eds., Baltimore: Paul H. Brooks Publishing Co., 1992, pp. 181–242.

16. Major, J. S., *The Land and People of China*, New York: J. B. Lippincott, 1989.

17. Lau, D. C., *Lao Tzu-Tao Te Ching*, Middlesex, England: Penguin, 1963.

18. Ibid., p. 26.

19. Leung, E. K. "Cultural and Acculturational Commonalties and Diversities among Asian Americans: Identification and Programming Considerations," *Schools and the Culturally Diverse Exceptional Student: Promising Practices and Future Directions*, A. A. Ortez and B. A. Ramirez, eds., Reston, Virginia: Council for Exceptional Children, 1988, pp. 86–95.

20. Gaer, J., *How the Great Religions Began*, New York: American Library, 1958.

21. Major, op. cit.

22. Te, op. cit.

23. Hsu, F. L. K., *Americans and Chinese: Passages to Differences*, Honolulu: University of

Hawaii Press, 1981.

24. Yu, op. cit.

25. Louie, K. B., "Providing Health Care to Chinese Clients," *Topics in Clinical Nursing*, v. 7, no. 3, 1985, pp. 18–25.

26. Chan, op. cit.

27. Ibid.

28. Suzuki, B., "The Asian American Family," *Parenting in a Multicultural Society*, M. D. Fantini and R. Cardenas, eds., New York: Longman, 1980, pp. 74–99.

29. Tweddell, C and L. Kimball, *Introduction to the Peoples and Cultures of Asia*, New Jersey: Prentice Hall, 1987, p. 260.

30. Muecke, M. A., "Caring for the Southeast Asian Refugee," *American Journal of Public Health*, v. 73, 1983a, p. 222.

31. Lee, R. V., "Understanding Southeast Asian Mothers-to-Be," *Childbirth Educator (American Baby)*, v. 8, 1989, pp. 5–8.

32. Muecke, M. A., "In Search of Healers—Southeast Asian Refugees in the American Health Care System," *Western Journal of Medicine*, v. 139, 1983b, p. 224.

33. Leininger, M., *Field Study with Asians in Urban Context*, unpublished research report, Detroit, 1986.

34. Chan, S. "Parents of Exceptional Asian Children," *Exceptional Asian Children and Youth*, M. K. Kitano and P. C. Chinn, eds., Reston, Virginia: Council for Exceptional Children, 1986, pp. 36–53.

35. Calhoun, M. A., "Providing Health Care to Vietnamese in America," *Home Healthcare Nurse*, v. 4, no. 5, 1986, pp. 14–22.

36. Mollica, R. and K. Lavelle, "Southeast and Asian Refugees," *Clinical Guidelines in Cross-Cultural Health*, L. Comas-Diaz and E. H. Griffith, eds., New York: John Wiley and Sons, 1988, pp. 262–302.

37. Muecke, op. cit., 1983a.

38. Hall, E., *Beyond Culture*, Garden City, New York: Anchor, 1976.

39. Wenger, A. F., "Transcultural Nursing and Health Care Issues in Urban and Rural Contexts," *Journal of Transcultural Nursing*, v. 3, no. 2, Winter, 1992, pp. 4–10.

40. Leininger, M., *Culture Care Diversity and Universality: A Theory of Nursing*, New York: National League for Nursing Press, 1991, pp. 360–361.

41. Ibid.

42. Ibid.

Chapter 26
Gadsup of New Guinea: Child-Rearing, Ethnocare, Ethnohealth, and Ethnonursing*

*Madeleine Leininger, PhD, LHD, DS, FAAN, RN, CTN***

    In the early 1960s I lived with and studied the Gadsup of the Eastern Highlands of New Guinea, who lived thousands of miles from the West Coast of the United States. As a single woman, I wanted to study a culture that was assumed to be very different from the American ways in order to do an anthropological field study, gain new insights about the people, and seek ways to establish knowledge and practices essential to the new area of transcultural nursing. I was eager to learn about non-Western people who had no contact with our world to discover their lifeways, caring modes, and other features about their culture. And since I was developing my theory of Culture Care, I wanted to examine the theory systematically in a non-Western culture to see if the major tenets of the theory could be upheld.

    After completing nearly four years of a rigorous doctoral program of study at the University of Washington in Seattle, I was ready to do ethnographic and ethnonursing field research. The ethnonursing method was entirely new to nursing and I needed to use the method to explicate knowledge about the culture care and health of the Gadsup. Moreover, I had recently discovered the concepts of emic (insider's viewpoints) and etic (outsider viewpoints) and wondered how these concepts could be used to discover generic and professional care knowledge. I also was curious about care practices, illnesses, and wellness with Gadsup of New Guinea. The concepts of ethnocare and ethnohealth were new ideas that I had coined to study transcultural nursing phenomena.[1] It was also clear to me that diverse knowledge of cultures was essential to change nursing education from a unicultural viewpoint to a multicultural stance. This knowledge would be critical to establishing transcultural nursing education and practices and to changing nursing's focus in the future.

    The idea of comparative life cycle practices between cultures in the world was an entirely new idea in nursing. I wondered about Gadsup child-rearing practices and how children were enculturated and developed throughout the life cycle. The influence of social structure factors such as religion, kinship, economics, politics, and cultural values on the life cycle was of great interest. Anthropologists had greatly stimulated me to think anew from a transcultural comparative perspective to discover cultural differences and similarities. And since I had to meet anthropological research degree requirements for the Ph.D. in nursing, I had to do a good ethnographic investigation. Thus I wanted to achieve research goals from both nursing and anthropology, including systematically examining my theory with the ethnonursing research method. It was a full and exciting agenda when I departed for New Guinea early in 1960. It was, indeed, a land and culture unknown to anthropologists with limited contacts with Western people.

Before leaving the University of Washington, several questions and thoughts came to me: Would it be safe for me to live alone as a single female with strange people? Could I work in a very different culture over an extended period of time and make sense out of the people's lifeways? What would I eat and where would I live in the village? Since there had been no outside women who had lived alone in the village without a spouse, would the people permit me to live under those conditions? With no mentor to confer with while in the field and no nearby Western neighbors to come to my aid if needed, I knew I was alone. When Margaret Mead was a visiting professor at the University of Cincinnati from 1955-59, she told me that she had always had some Americans who lived with and helped her while she was doing field work in a northern village in New Guinea. Naturally my family was concerned about my living alone in a strange land with no phones, postal service, or other modern communication modes and conveniences. I had already been informed by the Papua New Guinea government that I needed to get a gun to protect myself from "headhunters." Government official told me, "the Gadsup were fierce headhunters in the past and these people could kill you." Such ideas were of concern, but I had sufficient tough rural life experiences, had functioned as a psychiatric nurse clinician and leader and accepted such challenges.[2]

In this chapter, some of my direct experiences and observations are shared with a focus on the life cycle experiences of the Gadsup. This focus was important to the development of transcultural nursing as a new approach in nursing and away from the traditional medical disease model prevalent in nursing in 1960s. I wondered how the Gadsup prevented illnesses, maintained wellness, and how the people lived from birth to old age. In addition, I will present how I entered and lived with the villagers for nearly tow years as a beginning transcultural nurse researcher and theorist.

Entering and Living with Gadsup

My entry into the Gadsup land was initially a cultural shock as everything was so different from my lifetime experiences in the United States. I was an Irish and

German American who had lived in rural American for sixteen years and in a large urban American community for about twenty years. The Gadsup country, people, and lifeways were shockingly different to me except for the rural features. I could not initially communicate with and respond appropriately to the people as I did not know their language, and the language had not been recorded. The people, their lifeways, and environment were very different and difficult to understand. Through time, I learned from the people much which I can share with the readers.

The Gadsup were small, dark-skinned people with very dark brown eyes. The average height of the women was about five feet four inches, of the men about five feet and seven inches. The women and young children stayed close together in the village while the young men strayed away from the village. The Gadsup lived in bamboo huts with no electricity, modern appliances such as refrigerators, stoves or other modern conveniences. There were no clocks or watches in the village, and so no one lived by the clock or kept rigid time schedules. This was very strange for me to adjust to having come from a time-centered culture. The Gadsup water supply was carried in bamboo tubes from a mountain stream about two miles from the village and was used without boiling. There were no modern indoor toilets and only external "toilet holes" in the village were used. There was no exchange of money, but instead garden and forest products were exchanged under certain rules and conditions.

This culture had limited outside contacts, and so there were no professional health personnel such as nurses, dentists, physicians, pharmacists, or social workers. There were no formal schools with professional teachers. There were, however, native or indigenous folk caregivers and folk curers who provided for the health care needs of the people in the two villages. There were no Western people or Australians living in or near the villages. The Gadsup were quite isolated from the outside world in the 1960s and only knew their village neighbors as traditional friends or enemies. These factors and others made me realize that the Gadsup had a way of living and valuing that was very different from mine.

I began my research by focusing on the Gadsup's daily lifeways of the villagers. The men went into the forest area for hunting and to their garden areas; the women went to the gardens each day. I soon identified particular beliefs, taboos, values, and practices of the Gadsup, but I initially could not understand the meanings. Their lifeways were like a puzzle that I had to put together and make sense out of every day. Initially, I tried to interpret their strange actions and practices, but with limited success. Gradually, the pieces of the cultural puzzle began to come together, but not until we came to know and trust each other, which took several months. I came to know the unusual lifeways over an extended period of time. Living directly in the two villages over time was valuable to see the totality of the Gadsup lifeways.

Initially I was an object of curiosity to the Gadsups, as the majority of the people in the two villages had never seen a white woman. The people followed me wherever I went and they observed everything I did or tried to do! This behavior was strange to me, as I had never had twenty to thirty people watching or trailing me each day and evening. My life was not private but open to all the Gadsup. There was no way of being completely private in my bamboo hut for even at night the people peered through the lattices of the bamboo hut to watch me. I discovered that my feeling about the lack of privacy and my American values of independence, privacy and autonomy were clearly different from those of the Gadsup, who valued openness and shared community living. The people were not only curious about me as a white woman, but they wondered about my skin and hair. They would touch my skin and stare at my light brown hair. Some stood at a distance and watched my general behavior and my efforts to communicate with them, especially during the first six months in each village. When I came to the first village, they were curious about the contents of my two overnight suitcases, in which I had brought my essentials for two years. They stared at my tennis shoes and the skirts and blouses I wore each day. My attire contrasted with the Gadsup, who wore no shoes; women wore grass skirts and men wore shorts or laplaps. The Gadsup often asked me what tribe I came from. Later, the Gadsup told be they first saw me as a ghost because my skin was white, and because I came from a place unknown to them. I learned to be sensitive to their actions, my own initial survival was at stake because my behavior and theirs had limited meanings at first.

Since the Gadsup language had not been recorded or published, I had to learn and record their common language expressions. The language was tonal and I found it very difficult. At first, I used Melanesian pidgin (a lingua franca, or limited conversational language), but found only two or three men in the village who could use this language. I used nonverbal communication for nearly two months until I learned language expressions of the people. Thus, for the first few months, the Gadsup were difficult to understand due to my unfamiliarity with their cultural lifeways, values, language, foods, and physical and general cultural environment. Gradually, I learned firsthand from the people by daily and nightly interaction with them. I participated in practically everything they did, and they were with me almost constantly during my sixteen months in the two Gadsup villages (about eight months in each village). Living in two Gadsup villages was another adjustment as the two villages were different. There were traditional enemies and they had feuds and wars with each other in earlier years. I had to learn about how the Gadsup got along with their clans, subclans and lineages and their social ways of living together or apart at times.

After about three months the villagers became more comfortable with me and I with them. They began to share ideas and became protective of me, telling me what to do or avoid. Protective caring and surveillance caring became evident as modes of caring for "true friends." In time, I became their "trusted true friend" and they did not want me to leave the village. When the time came for me to leave each village, the villagers openly mourned and grieved for me. I could not promise them I would be back because I did not know if this would be possible. However, in 1978 I returned an visited them in both villages, which were about fifteen miles apart. At this time, the villagers told me about many happenings in each village and were glad to see me return to them. While it was a joyful reunion, it was also sad, as several key informants and Gadsup friends had died. It was evident that after an absence of fifteen years, they had not forgotten me, and I was pleased to see them and to hear what had happened during my absence. I had remained their trusted true friend who had learned much from them, and they had become dear to me.[3]

The above experiences were actual happenings, and other nurses might have similar experiences in strange or unknown cultures. Learning about such different cultures, and living directly in the people's native villages required courage, patience, flexibility, sensitivity, a caring attitude and a strong commitment to learn from strangers in strange places. It also required some hardships, discomforts, and major adjustments to study and live a different lifestyle with limited technologies and Western conveniences. To understand the Gadsup lifeways and the use of my theory with the Sunrise Model was important. A ethnographic and ethnonursing account is necessary and will be discussed next.

Ethnograpy and Social Structure of the Gadsup

The Gadsup live in the Eastern Highlands of New Guinea, which is about six degrees south of the equator and in a tropical environment. The island of New Guinea is shaped like a large bird with its tail and feet toward Australia and the bird's head looking to Indonesia and the Pacific Ocean to the east. The island is about 1,500 miles long and 500 miles wide. It is marked with high mountain ranges of nearly 12,000 feet above sea level and with many valleys and rivers. There are also large, open grassland areas between the mountainous ranges. The Gadsup frequently walked for miles across these grassland and mountainous areas to visit their kinsmen in other villages or to explore new areas for tribal or political reasons. Young boys and men often walked ten miles or more to explore new areas for tribal or political reasons to explore their land, hunt, get fruits and vegetables or to meet other friendly "tribal brothers". In 1961, no cars were owned by the Gadsup people and only a few cars were owned by Europeans or Australians living and working on selected plantations.

The Gadsup built their huts on the top of low mountain ridges to protect themselves from their enemies and to prevent their huts from being washed away by torrential rains during the wet season. The county is quite picturesque with the high mountains in the distance, beautiful lush green trees, tall grasses, and native wild flowers, such as bright red poinsettias, in their villages. The grassland valleys, round huts sitting on the ridges of the mountains, and no electricity poles or modern modes of transportation make one realize that this county is very different from our industrialized Western rural and urban communities.

There are two main season each year, namely, a wet season from December to April, and a dry season from May to November. The average rainfall for the area is about 85 inches per year. During the wet season hard rains frequently washed away the crudely built Gadsup roads, walking paths, and man-made bridges. Small streams rise and drain into the nearby valleys to produce a tall grass called kunai. In the dry season the people enjoy warm and sunny days with temperatures of 80 to 90 degrees Fahrenheit in the daytime, but dropping to 68 to 75 degrees Fahrenheit at night. In the rainy season there was a 15 to 20 degree temperature difference from the dry season. The temperature in the rainy season sometimes dropped to 57 degrees at night. Such marked changes in temperature often lead to infant respiratory conditions and occasionally death for infants and older Gadsups.

Each Gadsup village plaza was comprised of 20 to 40 small dwelling huts which were made of native bamboo. The roofs of the huts were covered with a tall grass called kunai. Gadsup huts had two or three partitioned rooms, with either a raised or ground floor fireplace to cook native foods, roast nuts, and to keep occupants warm during the wet season. Smoke often filled the room when the door was closed, as there were no windows in the huts. During the dry season the foods were cooked outside the hut and the indoor fireplace was seldom used.

The Gadsup in the early 1960s were hunters and gatherers, and so their daily life was spent producing, gathering, and distributing foods to maintain daily subsistence life. They lived on a subsistence economy, in that what they raise, they used each day with limited accumulation or storage of foods. They had no way to refrigerate or store large amounts of foods. Food producing and gathering was central to their lifeway. Food was used not only for their physical needs, but also for social political, and religious ceremonial purposes. Gardening was the daily activity for the women and young girls, and the men participated by clearing and building new gardens. Wild birds and animals were sought in the forest by young Gadsup boys and men. The men were also involved in a great variety of political meetings, doing "walk-abouts" to their neighboring villages, and conducting ceremonial life cycle activities and village rituals. Garden and forest products were the main exchanges between social groups within and outside the village. Coffee and tea raising were new developments when I arrived in the early 1960s and these products were sold to Australians. The people used this small irregular income to buy small amounts of rice, canned goods, and other material items that were available at a small-town store about five to ten miles from each village. The little stores were recent developments in the Eastern Highlands of New Guinea since the mid 1950s.

The kinship ties of the Gadsup were complex with many kinship terms to guide social and cultural relationships. The important kinship themes for nurses and other health personnel who might work with them are:

1. Gadsup adults carefully regulate their behavior according to whether the individual or group was close or distant kin, and to what social or clan group they belonged.

2. Male and female behavior had different expectations and were closely related to kinship expectations, roles, and decisions.

3. Care and health practices were embedded in their kinship behaviors, responsibilities, and expectations.

4. Kinship ties strongly organized the Gadsup lifeways and greatly influenced care and health practices.

Of great importance was the fact that if a child or adult became ill or needed to maintain wellness, the Gadsup individual had naturalistic built-in care providers from the extended family (often twenty to forty people), the lineage (often thirty to eighty people), clans and subclans (hundreds of people), and finally the tribal group, which was the largest cultural group one could belong to and from which to expect support and care.

This unique culturally based social and caring system had different role expectations within different aspects of the extended kinship structure and sharply contrasts with the Anglo-American small and limited nuclear family structure with approximately 2.5 family members. If one pauses to think about the Gadsup culture care structure, the Gadsup children have a unique, powerful, and effective natural care system to receive care from their extended kinsmen and tribal groups. There were also choices for the children to get help from both men and women, but of different kinds of care. The Gadsup often told me, "We are all one big family;" "We come from one source; and "We belong to each other." Indeed, their daily behavior supported these statements throughout the year and life cycle. When family feuds occurred, different methods were used to reconcile the difference among the kinspersons. Aggressive or violent acts were regulated by kinship, clan and tribal rules. The assurance of culture care continuity was a regulatory cultural norm and contributed to their state of well-being, and to their ability to function without a lot of physical or mental illnesses.

The roles of the kinspersons were guided by the particular cultural context and gender roles which they knew well. For example, there were appropriate times and places to give foods, conduct lifecycle ceremonies, provide direct care to others, help the sick or dying, protect villagers from strangers, and give advice to their kinsperson. Gadsup children learned at an early age to know these proper modes of conduct and rules of behavior. The Gadsup kinship structure, with its caring expressions, was a powerful influence on the health and well-being of the people throughout the life cycle.

The political system was complex, because kinship was closely related to influencing others along gender lines and with other village politics and political behavior. Political groups varied in size and function according to the clans, lineages, subclans, and tribes. The men maintained an active public role in all political affairs such as conducting village gift (largely food) exchanges, ritual life cycle ceremonies from birth to death, pig festivals, daily political debates in the village, religious activities, and affairs with outside strangers or traditional enemies. These political roles took much of the men's daily activities in the village, but they always had time to hunt, which was usually a political and social activity among males. The Gadsup women influenced the political thinking and actions of men in a variety of subtle ways, but also by their occasional loud pronouncements in the village plaza. The men listened to the women and often heeded their concerns.

With *respect to religion*, the Gadsup believed in *ancestor worship,* which meant that they worship their deceased kinsperson. The Gadsup believed that after a kinsman died, the life spirit or essence lived on, and this life spirit became an ethical and moral guide to govern the daily actions and judgments of the people. The people frequently talked about their ancestors, their moral values and how they lived a good life. These moral values were usually positive and they guided the young children and adults in many of their daily actions and thinking. The adults taught the children about their ancestors and how they lived according to "the good Gadsup values of brotherly caring and lifeways". The children were rewarded or sanctioned according to whether their acts were like those of their ancestors. Thus their ancestral religion was meaningful and a powerful moral and ethical guide for al villagers.

In the early 1960s a Western Lutheran group came to one of the Gadsup villages. The Gadsup struggled to understand the beliefs of this Christian group such as faith, God, heaven, and hell. These concepts and the associated beliefs were very strange to the Gadsup, as they did not fit with their ancestral beliefs. They told me these ideas were strange, impersonal, and frightening to them.

Infant to Adult Phases with Values, Beliefs, and Practices[4]

There are few cultures today having a sharp or dichotomy between the roles and activities of men and women than the Gadsup. Male and female Gadsup secrets pervaded their beliefs throughout the entire life span, and strongly in the early 1960s. Sex role activities clearly organized men and women's social, economic, political and religious activities. The villagers taught their children the appropriate male and female behaviors early in life which were respected and maintained.

The Gadsup had many male and female beliefs and secrets about conception, birth, growth, marriage, and death. These beliefs were kept within each gender group, and it was taboo (or forbidden) to discuss sex secrets with members of the opposite gender. For example, the men had traditional beliefs and secrets about their sacred bamboo flutes, which had religious and sociocultural significance. Men were not permitted to talk about their bamboo flutes to the women and if they did, it could lead to unfavorable consequences such as sickness, death, or village feuds. Likewise, women had their secrets about child and adult care and ways to deal with men's behavior and the male sacred flutes. The women believed that the men had originally taken these sacred flutes from the women. The flutes symbolized fertility, sexual power, social relatedness, and procreation. The men wanted the flutes to get some female sexual power. It was interesting to discover these beliefs, as there had been a traditional emphasis in the anthropological literature that only males had power, and especially sexual power. But I found the Gadsup women had sexual power which men had traditionally envied and used with their symbolic sacred flutes. Female menstruation, childbirth, child-rearing, and marriage were sources of sexual knowledge which the women kept away from the men in the village. The importance of gender secrets and male-female ceremonies were closely related to the daily patterns of Gadsup living, eating, playing, and in all sociopolitical activities. In 1978 I found that the Gadsup gender secrets were not as strictly guarded as in the past. Nonetheless, these secrets and other values, beliefs and practices were a powerful influence on the Gadsup infant to adulthood phases which will be discussed sequentially.

Pregnancy through Childbirth Phase

While living in the two Gadsup villages, I carefully observed and documented the pre-natal, natal and post-natal activities of the women. Perhaps most striking was the tremendous physical strength and the role expectations of young, middle-aged and older women. The Gadsup women were short (5'4") and muscular in body build. They were physically strong largely because of their rigorous physical activities such as daily gardening, cleaning the village plaza, walking great distances to their gardens, carrying infants and garden tools or firewood on their backs, and doing daily family or clan chores. During pregnancy, the women maintained a physically active daily work schedule. There were no complaints or signs of morning sickness in either village. There was no pampering of women during pregnancy, for pregnancy was a normal and a highly desired life experience for women. Young girls were expected to get married, become pregnant and raise healthy children. These were the hallmarks of becoming a respected Gadsup woman. There were no unmarried girls in the village beyond the age of nineteen years. Indeed, a girl becomes a woman only when she is married and gives birth to her first child. Marriage and child-bearing lead to a highly desired social status and recognition for women. Likewise, boys become men only if they are married and have at least one child. Marriage and having the first child make Gadsup complete human beings and socially recognized by all Gadsup in the lineage, clan and tribe.

Gadsup married women viewed pregnancy not only as highly desired, but also as a symbolic expression of maintaining the continuity of Gadsup people. It reaffirmed a woman's fertility, her femininity, and her social role in the village. Gadsup women try to have four living children per husband, and most women had four or five children. The women held that through their long history, they were the "real culture carriers", as they had the power to bear children, while men did not have this sexual power. Female and male secret sexual legends and beliefs confirmed these beliefs and action patterns. Gadsup men, however, held that they determined the viability and healthy status of the child by their semen and strong male physical condition. Thus a comparative and complementary gender status prevailed between males and females with their sexual abilities. It was of interest that the number of children per couple remained fairly constant by the genealogies over three generations.

Gadsup males and females were married between the ages of seventeen and twenty one years. There were very few divorces. A boy who was unmarried by eighteen years was an extremely restless male who often asked adult villagers to help find a good wife. The first child was born usually within the first two years after marriage which was a happy occasion. The succeeding children were born two or three years apart, which the women said they regulated by using of indigenous plants as contraceptives. The Gadsup confirm their manhood and womanhood statuses by marriage and children. They loved children, and the first child was especially warmly welcomed as this established adult status.

A married girl who did not bear a child early in marriage faced the possibility of divorce or separation, which was viewed as most unfortunate. When a Gadsup female knew she was pregnant, she happily told her mother and close kinswomen. A small informal female gathering occurred to rejoice that the girl would soon be a woman and that she would be a desired Gadsup in the village with a child. During the course of my research a few young girls were anxious and afraid of becoming pregnant. These girls were counseled by the older and experienced Gadsup women about their concerns. Some counseling occurred before pregnancy, but only a few weeks before, by the use of personal accounts or legends by older women who functioned like lay midwives. Then the woman knew she was pregnant she told her female kinswomen, but not her husband or any males. This was to be kept as a surprise to males to protect the unborn infant from male magical harm.

While Gadsup males believed they influenced whether the child would be strong and healthy, the women believed they had the strongest procreation abilities and powers to assure a viable infant in utero and after the infant was born. It was the woman's belief that she determined the sex of the child and whether the child would survive during pregnancy, and the first year of life. The males believed that their semen takes hold after the first year of life and makes the child a strong Gadsup person, and that in utero and early infancy the female sexual powers prevail.

During pregnancy, women often crave rare foods, and so the Gadsup spouse and his kinsmen are expected to get special foods for the pregnant wife by walking great distances for them. Foods craved by pregnant women were usually fresh fruits, nuts, bird meat, taro and greens, all foods they seldom have in their daily diets. There were no accounts of the Gadsup men experience pregnancy symptoms or food cravings while their spouse was pregnant. Foods which normally are associated with males were taboo during wife's pregnancy. These foods are special male foods used for ceremonial and political gatherings, and pregnant women are not to eat these foods, such as eel and forest meats, when pregnant. It is believed that if the woman eats these foods she would become deathly sick and the child would probably die, as these are male power foods and far too strong for women. Instead, nurturing foods such as sweet potatoes, taro, greens, fresh fruits, and nuts are to be eaten for a healthy child. Women who had eaten male taboo foods were identified as becoming very sick and their children were physically handicapped. The pregnancy period emphasized the woman's procreative and fertility abilities, and foods were eaten to make a healthy and active baby in utero and shortly after birth.

Of the twenty Gadsup women studies in-depth, none complained of morning sickness during her pregnancy. A pregnant woman went to her garden to work each day until a few hours before she delivered her child. The daily work schedule of the pregnant woman included routine garden labor, cooking, and child care. The pregnant woman occasionally paused to relax and feed a child while into the garden, but worked hard each day for about ten hours. Of the twenty pregnant women in both villages (one-half were primparous and one-half multiparous) none had swollen extremities, signs of toxemia, or unusual pre-natal problems during the pregnancy. These women were in good physical health and seemed relaxed about pregnancy which seemed to contribute to a healthy and normal pregnancy. Moreover, I would hold that their lifelong strenuous physical activities (since approximately the age of four years) put them in good physical and mental condition for pregnancy and delivery. In addition, their positive attitude about pregnancy and wanting children supported their pregnancy and influenced favorably the birth of a healthy infant.

As the day of delivery approached, the expectant mother continued to work hard in her garden, planting seeds, pulling weeds by hand, digging and cleaning vegetables. She stooped over and dug plants or sat on the ground to do her garden work. She only paused for short rest periods to care for or feed children. During pregnancy, the wife is expected to provide daily foods for the family and to help around the village from early in the morning until late at night. Interestingly, she does these activities to maintain her female role and village status. Gadsup males do not assume any female roles or helping activities before, during or after the birth of the child.

The pregnant woman may talk to lay midwives about her expectations and pregnancy signs while they work in the gardens or while they prepare food in the woman's hut or village place. Pregnancy guidance is largely based on traditional beliefs and stories of women in the village and how to have a well child. There is much pride in sharing these secrets with young girls during the last phase of their pregnancy.

The following incident was fairly typical of Gadsup childbirth practices. Anu was a twenty-year-old mother ready to give birth to her second child. Her first female child, Annurunu, was three years old and her husband was twenty two years of age. It was about 10 p.m. when Anu's mother knocked on my door and told me, "We go now to the forest." Anu was having regular uterine contractions about fifteen minutes apart. On this night, there were earthquake tremors of about 4.5 in intensity and it was the dry season with the night temperature at 68 degrees Fahrenheit. Anu's mother, her grandmothers, father's sister, and myself left the village for the forest pregnancy hut on a bright moonlit night. We walked up and down mountainous terrain for about three miles until we reached the delivery hut located in a densely forested area. It took about one hour to walk the three miles with Anu and her maternal kinswomen. I had expected that Anu would probably deliver along the way as her labor pains became closer together, stronger, and more regularized. We stopped only twice along the way to rest briefly and to look at the moon. There was limited talk among the women as we walked fairly vigorously to the delivery hut.

After arriving at the hut, the three Gadsup kinswomen (like lay midwives) quickly moved to prepare the area for Anu's delivery. Anu sat outside the delivery hut as the women swept the dirt floor inside and started a fire to heat some water which they had carried in bamboo tubes to the hut. Then Anu came inside (about ten minutes later) and knelt on a pandarnnus mat on the floor. She was told to grasp a wooden post which was fixed in the center of the hut. She used the pole to help her bear down with each labor contraction. The midwives showed Anu how to use her arms in a crossed position over her abdomen to bear down on the abdomen and facilitate the labor contractions. Soon the child's head appeared (within ten to fifteen minutes) and the midwives guided the infant gently from the vaginal orifice.

A large seven-pound male infant was born and showed immediately to the mother. The placenta was soon delivered by the skilled lay midwives. The infant and the placenta were smoothly delivered without complications such as excessive bleeding or great pains. (There were no delivery complications with any of the seven deliveries I witnessed.) The actual delivery took about twenty minutes. Joy was expressed by the women in their quiet ways with the infant. Anu seemed very happy to have a second child, especially her first male child. And since the Gadsup love and are overjoyed to have children, the delivery was a big event. Immediately after birth, Anu laid on a big pandanus mat with the infant in her arms and across her abdomen. The mother and midwives held the infant closely to their bare skins. Women in the hut cleaned the floor while one woman stayed close to Anu. The women gave Anu a herbal (non-alcoholic) drink about twenty minutes after the delivery. Anu did not show signs of being exhausted or ill. Instead, she appeared relieved and pleased with a well child. Anu's husband and his kinsmen were not allowed to be present during the delivery. If males were present, this could bring unfortunate ill effects to the child and mother, and show the secrets of the women. This point has significant nursing implications and contrasts with American and European nursing practices in which fathers are taught to bond with the infant immediately after birth. For the Gadsup, such bonding or attachment practices would be a cultural taboo as they are not congruent with their cultural values. American nurses would need to be aware of and respect such cultural differences and provide for culture care accommodation rather than forcing parents to bond with the infant. Transcultural nurses support culturally congruent care as postulated with my theory, and shown in the next section with in-depth life cycle processes, and would not impose bonding practices.

Post-Natal Ethnocare Behaviors and Practices

After the infant is born and the placenta is delivered, the Gadsup midwife uses a bamboo knife to cut the cord. Before cutting the cord, she sterilizes the knife by moving the tip of the knife over an open fire to heat and clean the knife. The women told me this aseptic technique had been used for years by the Gadsup women. Then the mother's sister buried the placenta under a tree near the delivery hut to symbolize the perpetuation of women's fertility and women's procreative abilities. The placenta must not be buried in a garden as the woman's blood is so powerful it would contaminate the food and make males and children ill. The cultural taboo principle would be that female fertility blood can produce illness and death in males as it is powerful and does not belong in men's bodies. Hence, female blood must not get into garden plants at any time. This was a major reason why the delivery huts are always built a far distance from the village.

After the placenta was buried, the kinswomen and the new mother carried her infant in their new net bag and walked back to the village (this was approximately one hour after the delivery of the infant). With Anu and the baby, we walked up and down rugged, mountainous terrain resting only occasionally to check the infant upon my request. Needless to say, I was impressed with the strength of the mother to walk such a great distance so soon after delivery of the infant. This practice was not unique to Anu as I found it was common with other mothers studied.

When the mother and infant return to the village, the husband, father and other males did not come near the woman (even though they were extremely eager to see the newborn child). It was a cultural taboo to have males close to a woman who had just delivered as she is "full of blood that could be harmful to men and kill them." Several Gadsup men gave me this interpretation or explanation as well as the women. The father of the child and male kinsmen live with their fathers away from the hut, usually in a nearby hamlet.

It is culturally desired that the mother and infant establish a close relationship with bare skin contact (no cloth between infant and mother) as she feeds and cares for the infant. The mother holds the infant against her breast and body as she sits and does daily household tasks. The infant might also lay in her lap as she works in preparing taro and sweet potatoes for a family meal. Gadsup infants are breast-fed for two to three years. There is no cow's milk or infant-feeding bottles. The mothers told me they would not like to use "such things" (bottles) as they enjoy breast-feeding their infants. Some wet mothers feed other infants in the village when the need arose because of the absence, illness, or death of the mother. The mother does a fair amount of touching and holding the infant, but she seldom coos or gives a lot of facial communication to the infant as found with American mothers. The mother and her close kinswomen and young girls in the village provided the primary care to the newborn infant. More skin contact than direct facial action can be observed between female care providers after the child is born and for several months. Touching and being nurturing were major caring modes to help the infant grow and survive. The midwives or maternal kinswomen continued to remain close to the mother to provide protection, surveillance, direct help, and other care expectations. While the mother is able to provide for her own care and that of the infant, she expects to have her kinswomen provide "other care" acts for her and not be involved in self care activities.

One could observe the mother holding the infant while sitting on a pandanus mat outside her hut and working. Her legs are often crossed as she sits on the pandanus mat, and she puts the infant across her legs while doing sedentary activities. The mother never leaves the infant alone or out of sight until after the third or fourth week. She breast feeds the baby as often as she believes the infant needs her milk, and especially when the infant cries or is restless. The breast is viewed by the mother as a consoling to the infant but also the key source of nutrients. While the mother is nursing her newborn infant, a two-or-three-year-old child may want the mother's breast, and so she permits him to have it, and a few minutes later he runs away. This tends to allay and meet the child's needs and to prevent sibling tensions. After three months, breast-feeding occurs less and new supplemental foods are gradually given to the infant.

When the newborn female infant returns to the village, she is immediately wrapped in a grass skirt; whereas the male child receives no clothing until about the age of five. Early childhood phases of development were known by the way girls and boys are dressed.

The Gadsup people believe it is extremely important for the infant and small child to relate to his immediate physical and cultural environment. When the mother and her infant sit outside the hut, women in the village come to see, hold, and talk to the child and mother. Several women hold the small child close to their bare-skinned bodies and use touch to stimulate the child. Thus human care with the child touching the bare body of women is important. Small male children observe and touch infants, however, males over seven or nine years are not encouraged to touch the child for fear of sickness to themselves and the infant. This is because older boys (over seven years) are held to have female blood in them, and until they undergo male initiation rites.

In the village context small pigs or dogs are permitted to come close to the infant, and are seldom chased away. The Gadsup believe these animals are part of their natural environment, and that it is most important for small children to see and hear these animals as part of their environment. The mother gives an environmental test to the child by placing the infant on a pandanus mat on the ground to see if the child becomes ill. This test lets the child have a feel of Gadsup land that he (she) is to live on and share with others. At the same time, the mother assesses the potential wellness or illness state of the child If the child is strong, he (she) will survive the test on the ground; if frail, he (she) will become ill and not survive the rigors of the Gadsup environment.

Small Child Phase. After the child is growing well (beyond the sixth month), the wife's kinsmen present the child to the biological father, his male kinsmen and to her kinspeople. Recently, the time has been shortened, but it symbolizes the child's entry and presentation to all the Gadsup villagers and the parents' kinsfolk. It is anticipated with pleasure and celebrated with a big village ceremony. In the process of presenting the child to the father and to all the Gadsup kinsmen, there is very little physical touching of the child. Instead, the villagers make statements of praise, such as "He is like us, Gadsup;" "He is good and strong;" "He is our brother," and so on. Again, only female relatives touch and hold the child to insure the child's health an well-being.

After the new child is presented to all the villagers in a formalized and ritualized ceremony, cooked food is shared with all the villagers. It is the mother's first presentation of the child to all kinsmen and villagers. The mother's kinswomen and children obtain the food from her garden, and the husband gets the food from the forest areas to give to their close kinsmen. Bundles of food such as bananas, sugar cane, taro, pit-pit, sweet potatoes and occasionally some fruits from the Markham Valley are offered. At this special occasion, it is the fathers' oldest brother (social father) who makes a speech indicating the child comes from their blood lineage and the food is a give to their people (relatives). The small piles of food are formally presented to the husband's kinsmen and to the wife's kinsmen. This ceremony signifies an appreciation for and recognition of the status of the kinspeople and of their contribution to the Gadsup culture and of their lineages. During this ceremony the wife and newborn child sit near the piles of food (often in the center of the village). The mother shows the child to the kinspeople as they casually come to view the child (mostly women admirers as the men are afraid to get close to the mother and child). This ceremony signifies that the child is now an integral part of the village and has a relationship with all Gadsup and especially kinsfolk. The child is, therefore, first a cultural being belonging to a large extended social network of family, the lineage and community. This child ceremony contrasts with our American emphasis and beliefs that American children belong to their parents and not the larger community or social group.

During the village presentation of the infant the mother's father's brother holds the child and offers a small taste of garden or forest foods. A male child is given a taste of male foods such as sugar cane and forest meat as "his" foods; a female is given food such as sweet potatoes. When the father's brother presents the food to the child, he says, "I give you these foods so that you will taste them and then want them. You will work hard to get these foods as you grow in our place." This symbolic ritual ceremony has economic and sociocultural significance as it imprints upon the Gadsup villagers their sex roles, the division of labor for males and females, and their sociocultural roles.

During the first year of life the child's most intensive relationship is with the mother and her extended kinsmen. The infant sleeps with the mother and she stays close to the child as she works in her garden or near the hut. The villagers show interest in the infant by stimulating him (her) to respond to them as they hold and nurture the small child. The child learns to respond to diverse kinspersons and their expectations. The child relates to all other children in the village, and is often cared for by female girls aged seven to twelve years. On the basis of Western theories one might expect that there would be a lot of sibling jealousy and rivalry with the young child, but this is not the case. This is due to the belief that a child belongs to the villagers, and all villagers share in caring for or about the new member in their cultural world. The child, too, learns that all the Gadsup are interested in the child becoming a responsible and good person in the village.

During the early child-rearing period, the mother breast-feeds the infant whenever the child expresses the need for food or cries. There is no rigid time to feed the child, whether on the breast or soft foods. At night, the child sleeps with the mother, cuddled under her arms or on one side of her bare-skinned body. The husband sleeps in another hut away from the mother and child for about six to eight months after the child is born. The infant becomes attached to women's voices, touches, and other care modes, and there is no bonding of the child to his biological or socio-legal father because of cultural taboos.

When the child begins to walk (about ten months to one year), the mother lets the child explore the village area, and the female kinspersons provide surveillance as good childcare. Surveillance means to watch and protect the child from external harm in the environment. Young female sibling provide most of surveillance and protective caring to the child along with the mother and her kinswomen in the village. Surveillance as caring was done as women watch the infant explore his social, cultural, humane and physical environment. When the mother works in the garden (usually three months after delivery), the infant is hung in a handmade pandanus net bag on a nearby garden fence. The child sleeps in the pandanus bag until he awakens or needs to be fed. When the mother is in her hut, she places the infant on a pandanus mat or hangs him in the net bag on an internal house post. Small children are free to run about in the garden, home or village, and learn what areas are safe to explore.

Gadsup infants and children do not cry often, but when they do, female siblings come to them. Mothers tend to let children cry until they have finished whatever task they are doing. Mothers believe it is important to let children cry and not be overly responsive to the, or feed them every time they cry. And since Gadsup mothers are extremely busy, hard-working, and responsible for their village roles, the child must fit his rhythm of life to the daily role activities of the mother. Nonetheless, the child is never unduly neglected, ignored or abused. Disciplining of the child fits with cultural values, norms, and taboos, and is seldom too harsh or inappropriate.

The Gadsup stages of development are different from what most Americans or Westerners learn in child development courses. The stages do not precisely fit Piaget's or Erikson's stages of development. From a nearly two year period of daily observations in both villages, with interviews, and first-hand participant experiences by this investigator, the following stages were identified. The first stage of child development is called the "tiny baby" stage. During the tiny baby stage, the infant must be cared for through surveillance and protective care acts of the mother and other females. The dominant care behaviors to insure a healthy child were surveillance, nurturance, protection, stimulation and the use of prevention to avoid illness and death. These kinds of care especially from females were essential for infant survival, growth, and remaining well.

The tiny baby needed protection from sorcery, damp or cold weather, and from strangers who might cause illness by their careless acts or words. Older mothers gave young mothers advice on ways they must be surveillant to protect the vulnerable child. Many nurturant acts such as holding, encouraging activity, and breast-feeding were ways to help the infant grow. The child was exposed early to many different sounds, people and animals in the village environment. A comparative analysis revealed only slight differences in the infant and early child care patterns in the two villages because Gadsup women married into the village from and outside Gadsup clan. Thus the Gadsup child-rearing care practices and values were similar, but the techniques and expressions of caring showed some slight cultural differences. For example, in one village the infant was fed solid foods two months after birth; whereas in the other village the infant was four- to five-months-old being given solid foods. In both villages the mothers premasticated banana or sweet potato to feed the infant along with breast milk.[5] I observed that infants who received solid foods two to three months after birth grew more rapidly, cried less and were more content than infants who were given solid foods after five or six months. There were no signs of allergy or difficulty with the infant taking premasticated foods. In both Gadsup villages infants were breast-fed frequently for six months, and less frequently after one or two years of age. The techniques of feeding the infant solid food showed slight variation as some mothers would use their fingers to feed the infant, whereas others would let the child pick up the food and eat is by themselves. Very small infants (during the first three months) received the premasticated food from the mother as she placed it in the child's mouth.

The Gadsup mothers valued breast milk highly as the best and most essential infant food. Cows milk was never used or brought into the villages. A religious group brought goats into the village, but the people would not milk the goats or eat the meat. To the Gadsup the goats were a nuisance, and they called them "Seventh Day Pigs" to reflect the fact that the Seventh Day Adventists brought the goats into the village. With the Gadsup women breast-feeding their infants, there was no contamination of milk, and breast milk was readily available to the child for food and as a comfort measure.

Although pinworms existed in the village, only a few children were ill due to these pinworms. The mothers were more concerned about cultural factors that might cause illnesses to small children, such as sorcery and harm from outsiders, rather than biological factors. Early infant mortality and morbidity were low, largely due to the excellent female caregiving using the care values of protection, nurturance and surveillance and culturally valuing and wanting to keep children well. In addition, the young girls (ages eight to fourteen years) and older kinswomen were also attentive care providers for infants and young children. Older females and males who could no longer work in their gardens or go to the forest took care of young children and enjoyed care role responsibilities. Thus, the mothers, young girls, and maternal kinswomen were the primary caregivers of small infants and children in the two villages, and were known and valued for their caring ways that kept infants alive and well.

Gadsup children remained well unless a respiratory or sorcery condition occurred. If the child became ill, the mother and her kinsmen used folk remedies and folk-care methods to care for the child. There were no professional health services in the villages. If the infant became acutely ill and died, the mothers and maternal kinsmen were often viewed as inadequate caregivers or protectors. During the nearly two years in the two villages, I saw only one infant die in each village, and this was due to a very chilly rainy season. If a child died, the Gadsup were deeply saddened and greatly mourned this loss. The genealogical history of fifteen and thirty general informants revealed that fewer than three infants died in each village per year, and there were twenty to twenty-five births per year in each village.

During the nearly two year stay in each Gadsup village in the early 1970s, there was an Australian public health nurse who came to a distant patrol post to weigh and advise mothers, but most Gadsup women did not use or value this service. Since the nurse did not understand the Gadsup life-cycle of care, her advice was noncongruent and was seldom used or valued. These one day clinics were poorly attended by Gadsup mothers as they viewed them as potential sorcerer places. It was a high risk to take an infant or sick child outside the village to a potential sorcery place, as this would be a source or precipitating illnesses or death of vulnerable child. Although government officers encouraged the Gadsup to use these clinics, infants and children's mothers would take only the strongest child to this place, and with great reluctance. If the mother's attended, they were very tense and feared something would happen to the children while at the clinic. I observed that the mothers stood away from the nurse and were very reluctant to give their children to the nurse to be examined and weighed.

The nurse spoke only Pidgin English; most of the mothers could not speak this language and so they were frightened. If the nurse had spoken the Gadsup language, she could have greatly alleviated some of the mothers' fears. The nurse was not aware of the Gadsup child-rearing cultural beliefs, values and practices and did not realize that as a stranger, she was a potential source for sorcery and could cause more harm than good. Hence, this professional service was of limited help to the Gadsup mothers in both villages.

In the second stage of development Gadsup mothers encouraged "the small child" to walk and not crawl during the first two years of life, and so Gadsup children often learned how to walk by ten months without crawling. It was fascinating to watch Gadsup mothers and other caretakers encourage children to stand and walk as early as possible so the children could walk to the gardens with them. Male children were especially encouraged to explore their village environment at an early age and not to remain inside the huts. This exploration was always within the Gadsup land for small children. Children were warned not to leave their village by themselves until after the age of five or six years. If the child left the village, he(she) was always accompanied by an adult kinsperson as the child was vulnerable to sorcery and possible dangers by potential enemies of the Gadsup. Thus, prevention of illnesses was achieved by limiting the child's territorial areas of exploration. There was less emphasis in both villages on teaching the child to talk. Several informants told me that their children will learn Gadsup naturally, and that they will talk as they begin to experience village troubles. Children begin to focus on learning the Gadsup language around two years.

Little and Young Girl-boy Phases. After the tiny infant phase (from birth to one year), and the small child phase (from about one to three years), the other phases of development with their names are the following: the *little girl and boy phase* (about three to six years); the *companion phase* (about ten to fourteen years); the *exploring and courting phase* (about fourteen to twenty years); the *becoming a man or woman phase* (after marriage and having one child); and the *becoming recognized as a Gadsup man or woman phase*. Since the Gadsup have no Western calendars, the ages of the villagers had to be estimated from special events, observations, genealogies, and views of key informants. Due to space constraints these remaining phases will be briefly highlights with their major characteristics realizing that tiny infant and small child phase had already been presented.

The little girl and boy phase covered about three to six years of age and was characterized by the girl beginning to work closely with her mother and maternal kinsperson in the gardens and in all female village activities. Likewise, the little boy phase began when he followed his father and male kinspersons into the nearby forest or grassland areas and learned male interests and activities. During this time, the small boy was never completely separated from his mother and maternal kinswomen as the Gadsup believe that small children of both sexes need their mother's breast milk for nurturance and protection along with other maternal caring acts. The father and male villagers were always excited and eager to have the little boy with them in the forest and while hunting. They would show him how to hunt birds and mammals with handmade bows and arrows, and how to know the secrets of the male world including the natural forest and other male friends. Some sacred male objects were introduced to the boy. The little girl was socialized early and continuously into a female work role and was taught by the village women how to share female role responsibilities. In the garden and in the villages the little girl would help collect food, firewood, and watch infants. The little boy activities were directed towards exploring the village and with limited emphasis on male work roles.

During the next *phase* known as *young girl and boy* (roughly six to ten years), the girls assumed a heavier work role than in the previous phase. The little boys remained free to roam about the village with or without male kinsmen. During the little boy phase, the boys spent most of their day playing with other young and older boys, interacting with villagers, and going to the forest with adult men. I discovered that young boys in this phase learn how to be highly innovative as they are free to explore and express themselves in the Gadsup physical, social and general ecological environment. Young boys made creative and new toys such as seed popguns, clay animals, and hunting devices. In contrast, the young girls did not have free time to explore and create. Instead, they worked almost a full day with female kinswomen, with virtually no time to play. Their task was to focus on child care-taking and adult women's work roles. They were told to be responsible good women who knew how to work and care for children.

Companion Phase. During the companion phase (about ten to fourteen years), the girls had "pals" and kept together, whereas the boys had companionship groups (often four to six in a group). The companion boy's group activities included going far into the deep forest area to hung birds and cassowaries. Gadsup boys would sit and visit together, wash themselves in the small stream, and have "walkabouts" to nearby villages. This phase was highly exploratory and an exciting time for the boys to develop social friendship ties. The girls had small pal groups (two or three) who would walk together to the gardens and work close to each other and small children in the village. Girls of this age would talk, laugh, and enjoy each other while working together. It was common to observe boys and girls putting their arms around the neck or waist of companions of the same sex as they walked around the village, garden or forest. While some might be tempted to call them "homosexuals" in Western terms, they were not. There was no sexual play, intercourse, or intense sexual affection expressed. These companion groups often reaffirmed that this phase meant good friendship and not sexual activities. Boys and girls developed strong social relationships, learned about sex roles, and had fun walking about together. They also learned about cultural activities of adults within and outside the village area, and discovered lifeways of other Gadsup villages and their ecological setting.

Courting Phase. The courting phase (ten to eighteen years) was characterized by young boys making themselves attractive to girls as potential spouses. It was fascinating to observe young boys (still not called men) during this phase go to the stream to wash themselves (without soap, as none existed in the village), wash laplaps or go to a trade store for new laplaps or trouser-like apparel. They would also look within and outside the village for young girls whom they thought would be good wives and mothers, and would have brief talks with them. The boys sang courting songs to the girls. If a boy saw a girl he would like to court, he would toss a pebble at her. The girl would respond by looking to see who tossed the pebble, and then she would decide if she wanted see him. This was an emotionally exciting experience with boys taking active steps to find and court girls to be their wives. Interestingly, the girls were not active pursuers of young boys but waited for boys to seek them out. The girl, however, had to decide if she wanted to know and be courted by the boy with the intent that he should be a future husband. The young girls were the decision makers and were in control of who they courted and who they wanted to be with or with whom to make Gadsup love. If the girl agreed to see the boy, the boy would sing love songs outside her hut, and if acceptable, a love tryst would probably occur in which they would hug each other or occasionally sleep with one another. Premarital sexual intercourse was a cultural taboo and not sanctioned. Active courting was, however, acceptable. The girls and boys enjoyed this phase and were often found together in their groups talking about good wives (or husbands) they would value as spouses. Giggling, making themselves look attractive, and making brief "tough and go" encounters characterized this phase. It was a phase that helped the young girls and boys develop gender identity, responsibilities and confidence in themselves. There was limited interference from married spouses or biological parents unless they broke cultural norms by "stealing married women or men." The later was a serious cultural taboo and violation. This phase led to spouse selection and to the next phase of getting married, which all young boys and girls desired.

Becoming a Man or Woman Phase. The phase of becoming a man or woman referred to the person who was married and had a child. Gadsup could not be called a man or woman unless they were married and had an offspring. Great pride and excitement were evident in both villages as young boys and girls decided on their marriage partners. For the boys, it meant achieving new status in the village as a man.

Becoming a man meant having a number of desired rights, responsibilities, privileges, and cultural acceptance as an adult. For the young girl, it meant she achieved new rights and responsibilities as a wife and mother. For both boys and girls, it legitimized their full adult status as Gadsup. The girl knew it meant that when she got married, she would be leaving her village to live with her husband's village (called neolocal residence). Married women lost much of the earlier protection, surveillance, and nurturant support of their mothers and maternal kinsfolk. It was, therefore, common to see young girls and later brides, cry before and during the wedding ceremony as they would lose their close kin ties. As the boy became groomsman, he was very happy, especially at the marriage ceremony because he no longer needed to search for a wife. Courting periods were often long in order to find a good wife, especially due to a shortage of girls in both villages. The marriage ceremony symbolized uniting people from different villages, as the bride usually came from village other than the groom's, There was also an exchange of foods and material services. Divorce was rare in the two villages in the early 1960s, but in 1978 divorce was becoming more common, with women wanting to divorce more often than the men.

Becoming Recognized as a Gadsup Adult. The last phase of becoming recognized as a Gadsup man or woman meant that the married couple were now married and would soon have offspring to legitimize their status. The couple knew they were to serve as "true and good Gadsup" embodying Gadsup ideals and values. They were to reflect the right ways of living and respect adults and their ancestors who served as moral and ethical guides to proper living. The married couple regulated their behaviors in order to get and retain cultural approval, recognition, and sanctions by the villagers and extended lineages. Gadsup who behaved properly were often chosen for special village roles. Some males were chosen as village orators, leaders, and "big men." Women, were recognized and respected as "good women", who had healthy looking children, pigs, and cultivated gardens. This life cycle of becoming a man or women as only fully recognized and sanctioned by the villagers when the couple had a child. If they did not have a child, they were not called "man" or "woman" and did not have full rights and privileges. The first child was, therefore, a joyous occasion and legitimized full adult social and cultural status as Gadsup. It was a life cycle phase greatly desired by young adults.

Culture Care nursing Implications With Leininger's Theory

The above life cycle data generated and analyzed by the use of the ethnonursing and ethnography research methods had many nursing care implications. From the author's theory of Cultural Care, it was predicted that cultural patterns, expressions, structural forms, and meanings would be discovered by studying the components of the Sunrise Model and systematically examining the tenets of the theory directly with the people. Many new insights and specific findings were forthcoming from the author's study of the two villages over nearly a two year period. The following dominant care meanings and daily action patterns were important discoveries.

1. Caring meant nurturance, which referred to the ability help people grow, live and survive throughout the life cycle.
2. Care meant surveillance, which referred to watching attentively small children and others who were vulnerable in order to protect their well-being, health, and to prevent accidents, disabilities, or untimely death.
3. Care meant protection, which referred to different ways to guard against harmful acts or thoughts by others, and especially to heed cultural taboos.
4. Care meant prevention of illness or harm to others, which referred to being attentive to culturally prescribed norms, taboos, values, and living the right way to remain healthy or well.
5. Care meant touching, which referred to the importance of using one's hands or body to heal, console, or make others become well or secure.

These major care values were recurrent findings in both Gadsup villages, and they were frequently observed and confirmed by the people in their language and their general lifeways. Besides the above definition of Gadsup care, there were many additional findings that came from key and general informants about each care construct and their lifeways which will be highlighted below.

Care as nurturance was known to the Gadsup as how the people helped others to grow and to be strong and well. By being attentive to the total needs of children, adolescents, and the elderly, care as nurturance was especially valued to help infants and children survive. Gadsup women had a major responsibility to provide nurturance by periodically assessing the child's growth, eating patterns, and helping the young to become good Gadsup adults. Nurturant expressions and patterns were observed as the Gadsup gave good food to the child each day; told children not to break cultural taboos; encouraged children to handle new roles or difficult tasks; and following moral codes of what the ancestors had lived by to be healthy and "good" Gadsup. Gadsup women took active steps to monitor the nurturant status of infants and children as they ate, played and slept, and in other daily activities. The women often talked about what was needed to keep children and adults healthy throughout the life cycle and of ways to have strong and healthy Gadsup. Women displayed more nurturant acts than men. These nurturant acts and patterns of living would need to be preserved and maintained as important parts of nursing care of the Gadsup in order for them to remain well and healthy.

The *second and third* dominant Gadsup care *constructs of surveillance and protection* were documented, and are closely related concepts. Surveillance as care meant actively watching over those who might be vulnerable to external harm, or harm from outsiders such as sorcerers, strangers, bad food, environmental conditions, and bad influences. Surveillance was closely linked with protective care. The Gadsup believe that if you gave good surveillance to Gadsup "brothers or sister," you would be protecting them, and ensuring their well-being, safety, and health. The Gadsup adult men and women stressed surveillance and protection of young children and the necessity of protecting them from harm such as poisonous snakes, sorcerers, and many potential physical accidents or natural disasters. External sociocultural factors were of more concern to Gadsups than internal mental factors or emotional forces because cultural forces were more powerful and, if neglected, could lead to serious illnesses and even death. The Gadsup watched where their children went, and warned them of dangers if they strayed too far from the village. Such surveillance was important as children are believed to be highly vulnerable to external malevolent forces that can lead to illness and death, especially from sorcery or by witchcraft practices. Surveillance as caring also meant being a good parent and protecting children, the lineage, or clan. Older women who did not go to the garden each day were often providers of surveillant care for the young and others who need to be watched. Protecting children from cassowaries that came into the village was important as these animal could claw a child to death. Children needed to be protect from deadly snakes that could kill children (and adults) in a few minutes. Unquestionably, the care value of surveillance was important, and thus professional nurse would need to preserve and maintain these protective and surveillant activities to care for Gadsup. A non-caring nurse in these areas could lead Gadsup to sickness and death. Care as protection was very closely related to surveillance but was a separate concept. Cultural protective care measures would also need to be maintained and preserved as an action mode of the nurse.

The *fourth dominant care concept* to maintain *well-being and health was prevention with counseling.* Preventive behaviors as a caring modality were observed in many daily life activities and from the cultural history of the people over time. Gadsup were dependent upon ways to prevent sociocultural illnesses and harm from within or outside the village. They practiced preventive care by giving specific advice to adults and children to prevent many causes of illness, and adults warned children not to break their cultural taboos. They taught them to prevent illnesses by properly handling fecal materials, nail and hair clippings, and other human products to prevent sorcerers or sorceresses from doing harm to individuals or the whole village. Gadsup women in both villages talked about ancestral spirits and the need not to displease their ancestors by breaking cultural rules or showing disrespect to them. If a child or adolescent was too aggressive, ancestral admonitions were recited to prevent deviant behaviors. Counseling at different times helped to modify any deviant person's behavior, and ultimately contribute to his(her) well-being. Hence, prevention, like surveillance and protection as caring modalities and values, prevented illness and promoted well-being and health. Preventive measures would need to be maintained and preserved in Gadsup land. In addition, the nurse would need to consider ways to do *culture care repatterning or restructuring* when deviant behavior occurred to ensure the health and well-being of an individual or the village.

The *fifth care value of touching* was less dominate, yet evident on different occasions through the life cycle, especially during infancy and young adulthood. Mothers touched children's genitalia and kissed infants and children. Touching was used with children if they got upset or angry. Both maternal and paternal kinspersons would firmly hold or shake a child by the arm if the child acted badly. Male Gadsup did not touch women in public, but only in private. Touching with body hugs among Gadsup kins was frequently observed, but touching strangers was done cautiously. Touching strangers was done to discover if one like them or could trust them. Some adult Gadsup's fights were violent and led to fractured limbs, cuts, and bruises for both sexes. Domestic quarrels were usually related to major conflicts about women's infidelity, stealing garden foods and pigs, and harming children. Bodily touching and hitting of an aggressive nature was observed and reported with domestic night fights. Non-violent body hugs among men (and seldom among women) were observed in political greetings.

Nurses working with the Gadsup would need to consider the above Gadsup care concepts to provide culturally congruent care. In addition, the following general cultural values would need to be understood to give further meaning to the care practices and expressions. The major Gadsup cultural values identified by the researcher and confirmed by the villagers were: 1) *respecting sex role differences*; 2) *acknowledging strong kinship ties among extended family and lineage members*; 3) *valuing the concept of "brotherhood" and egalitarianism*; 4) *valuing land, women children, and pigs*; and 5) *giving birth to healthy children and keeping children well*. To implement these values, the nurse would first need to be cognizant of marked differences in sex roles and functions of men and women. All Gadsup activities were sex-linked and reinforced by the people's political, religious, kinship, and cultural values. For example, if the nurse were a strong feminist and wanted to promote equal sex right, (she) he would encounter serious cultural conflicts and stresses with the Gadsup. Such ideas and practices would be culturally incongruent and lead to serious village problems. If a Western nurse attempted to change women's roles in infant and child care practices, this could seriously jeopardize Gadsup women's lifeways. The nurse would need to maintain sex role differences as women and men remain well in their respective functioning roles. A Western nurse might also be tempted to make Gadsup women more politically active in the village and in ceremonial activities. This would be difficult to do because women are already politically active in this home or domestic area. There are beneficial outcomes from both sexes in their respective male and female political and power roles. *Women have domestic political power*, whereas *men* have more *direct and overt public power to influence decisions and actions*. The researcher documented several times how the women's domestic power were frequently used by men in public decisions.

If a Western female nurse were functioning with the Gadsup, she would need to realize that she might be viewed as a sorceress. Knowing how to handle sorceress beliefs or comments would be important. A nurse might want to convince the people that she was not a sorceress. However, this would not be effective as the people must observe one in action to see if one's acts and ideas reflect harmful or helpful behaviors.

Another dominant cultural value that would influence transcultural nursing care practices is that kinship ties amount the Gadsup extended families, lineages, clans, subclans, and tribes are strong and important. Gadsup kinship ties designate the social relationship among and between groups inside and outside the village. These kinship ties determine who are the "real" Gadsup and the fictive kinspeople. Kinship and sex roles influence who care for whom throughout the life cycle. For example, Gadsup females provide much of the nurturant and surveillant care behaviors to infants and adults. In contrast, the male kin provide a lot of protective care especially to children and vulnerable people. Gadsup men are also the external curing specialists, whereas females give far more attention to caring.[6] Gadsup women, such as the mother's and father's sisters, and their female kin are important lay midwives to provide prenatal, natal, and postnatal care to mothers and newborn infants. These Gadsup lay midwives were quite competent in deliveries, and they practice care as surveillance and nurturance. Outsiders who are not viewed as "Gadsup brothers" would not be assured of receiving care or cure. The concept of the Gadsup "brother" and its linkage to clans, subclans and lineages would need to be understood to provide beneficial nursing care.

The cultural value of respecting Gadsup land, women, children, and pigs was important. *Land, women, children and pigs are valued as cultural symbols* of the Gadsup and signify Gadsup continually throughout their long history. Land and women have been fought for in many past feuds and wars. Gadsup want and love healthy children to perpetuate their culture.[7] One women said, "Without children and healthy ones, no people would exist in the future." The women took pride in having healthy children, and they admonished women who had ill or weak children. Children represented the future life and preservation of the Gadsup. Some domestic fights occurred over pigs, land, and women while the researcher lived in the villages, and were usually resolved by political discussions.

Another dominant cultural value was for the Gadsup to *treat each other as "brothers" who are equal in social and cultural relationships*. The Gadsup frequently state they are "brothers," which reaffirms their bonds of unity and solidarity. The concept of "brother" generates feelings of warmth, respect, belonging, and nurturance among Gadsup. It is a highly desired and favorable concept of treating others as a "brother" was often noted in warm, supportive and helpful relationships.

In the Gadsup culture, I discovered Gadsup patterns of care and cure with differential of carers and curers. Male curers often came from *non-Gadsup* villages to cure acutely ill villagers. These outside curers had an ethical responsibility to assist another Gadsup tribal brother. In return the curers usually received gifts of food, material goods, or reciprocal services. In the village *female carers* were responsible for assisting others by listening, counseling, or providing direct caring services to those who were well or sick. Adult female carers were highly effective in ways to help men, women, and children avoid illnesses, recover from all kinds of cultural sicknesses, and maintain patterns of wellness. The Gadsup female carers were expected to perform these roles to please their ancestral spirits and thus perpetuate the Gadsups over time. Maintaining cultural taboos and values were a powerful means to keep Gadsup well so that they could perform their expected daily role activities. The ethical norm to prevent harm to others, especially in the Gadsup village, was viewed as another means to prevent illness and destructive behaviors. The caring sensitivity of female carers was noteworthy as well as the skills of outside Gadsup carers.

To provide *culture specific nursing care*, *cultural care maintenance and preservation* would be a dominant theme for the nurse to use in light of the above cultural care values and practices.[8,9] The nurse would need to preserve the generic patterns of surveillance, nurturance, prevention, illnesses and many other positive and beneficial caring modalities of Gadsup health and well-being. Caring practices of prevention and counseling without breaking cultural taboos would be essential for Gadsup well-being. The nurse might use *culture care accommodation* to change care practices that might further enhance their well-being such as the use of new medications and selected professional treatments for illnesses. The Gadsup mode of cleaning wounds with limited clean water could be changed to prevent infections. The author also found some of their folk practices for healing open wounds was not effective and could be improved by culture care *accommodation or negotiation strategies*. Cultural care *repatterning and restructuring* would not be considered unless the people wanted to change some practices that were dysfunctional or harmful to their health. There were very few of these practices. Unquestionably, the nurse would need to give much though to social structure factors and cultural values before repatterning or restructuring Gadsup health care practices because many of their ethnocare and ethnohealth practices were functional for them and the people were generally healthy. With recent cultural contacts with Western health systems, I found the Gadsup traditional folk system was being threatened, and the quality of care was less positive when I visited them in 1978 and 1992. It was unfortunate to see the impact of Western cultures on Gadsup generic care and daily lifeways.

Still another consideration to care for the Gadsup people *would be to blend folk care rituals with professional practices.* Gadsup ritual behaviors such as the festival for the birth of a new baby were especially beneficial and satisfying to the Gadsup, and they had positive health benefits. The symbolic food rituals for helping the infant grow were essential to protect and nurture the infant through kinship support. The cultural ritual of putting small amounts of white ashes on the head of a newborn infant to protect him from evil spirits could also be linked with professional personal hygiene. Pregnant mothers had cultural taboo rituals such as not leaving the home village unless accompanied by other women. The men had many protective care rituals that protected them and other villagers. Thus, one would note a *community caring culture* and *rituals of importance to the people.* A caring community was evident to provide a healthy environment for children, adults, and the aged.

Finally, to provide effective care to the Gadsup, professional nurses and other health providers would need to know how to *use the local native foods* and understand their value in health maintenance practices. I found the majority of the Gadsup in both villages were quite healthy except for intestinal parasites. Western medical treatments with care accommodation modes would be needed to eradicate this condition. Their native foods were different from many Western foods with many healthy foods such as greens, sweet potatoes, bananas, passion fruit, taro, and seasonal nuts. The Gadsup have lived for hundreds of years on these native nutritious foods with many grown in their local gardens and forests. There were no canned foods, no butter, and no table salt. There was also very little meat except of occasional wild game. With no nearby lakes or large rivers, fish was not available. One may wonder how these people survive without meat and fish in their diet, but they did and were quite healthy. There were no signs of hypertension, obesity, diabetes, cardiovascular disease or psychoses in the early 1960s, and limited evidence in 1978 or 1992.

Another interesting discovery was the absence of animal milk or any milk product except for infants taking breast milk for twelve to twenty months. Gadsup never expressed a desire for milk. I later discovered the Gadsup had a lactose intolerance which was a rather new discovery in the early 1960s. In general, food was closely linked with many cultural ceremonies and rituals which would need to be understood by the nurse. Eating cultural foods with the people, reinforced a trusting relationship with strangers and helped to gain new insights about foods and their uses.

In this chapter I presented an overview of my first field research observations and experiences with the Gadsup people of the Eastern Highlands of New Guinea mainly in early 1960s. It was one of my richest learning and discovery experiences. As a researcher, I learned much from the Gadsup as they became my teachers and friends for nearly two years. I discovered how greatly different their world was from mine. It was an important and fascinating experience to life directly with the people in their village to observe and learn daily about their cultural beliefs, values, and practices related to ethnocare, ethnohealth, and ethnonursing. After I became their trusted friend and then they shared many detailed ideas and their "cultural secrets" with me. They gave me protective care after they knew and trusted me as their friend. Our friendship grew in a caring way. Mutual respect was evident as we acknowledged different life experiences and values. And although I was initially told these were "head hunters" by the New Guinea Australian officers when I first came into the country, I found that this was not really accurate and I never saw them in this way. Remaining sensitive and open to learn the Gadsup's lifeways, I learned much from them and became their trusted friend and researcher. It was a special privilege and opportunity to live with and study the Gadsup.

My theory of Cultural Care differences and similarities could be substantiated as it led to the discovery, meanings, expressions of health or well being. Using a theory with ethnographic and ethnonursing research methods was invaluable to make detailed and creative discovered with a full interpretation of Gadsup lifeways. This transcultural nursing and anthropological research study was a major breakthrough to advance knowledge in both disciplines, but each having a slight different focus and goal. It was the first transcultural ethnonursing qualitative research study in nursing.

Addendum

In 1992 I returned to the Eastern Highlands of Papua New Guinea to obtain a longitudinal perspective regarding cultural changes over three decades.[10] Readers are encouraged to read this research article which show the multiple social structure forces influencing the Gadsup life of today and their current ethnocare needs with changes (or the lack of them) over three decades (1962-1992).

---

*This is an edited and expanded version from the 1978 Transcultural Nursing book for life cycle care practices. It is written in first person to capture the lived experiences of the author as observed and recorded.

References

1. Leininger, M. "Caring Phenomenon: *The Essence and central Focus of Nursing*," American Nurses' Foundation, Nursing Research Report, v. 12, no. 1, February 1977, pp. 2 & 14.

2. Leininger, M. Ecological Behavior Variability: Cognitive Images and Sociocultural Expressions in Two Gadsup Villages, unpublished doctoral dissertation, Seattle University of Washington, 1966.

3. Leininger, M. "The Culture Concept and Its Relevance to Nursing," *The Challenge of Nursing: A Book of Readings,* M. Auld and L. Birum, eds., St. Louis: C. V. Mosby, 1973, pp. 39-46.

4. Leininger, M. Transcultural Nursing and a Proposed Conceptual Framework, Transcultural Nursing Care of Infants and Children, *Proceedings of the First National Transcultural Nursing Conference,* M. Leininger, ed., Salt Lake city: University of Utah, College of Nursing, 1977, pp. 1-18.

5. Leininger, M. Some Cross-Cultural Universal and Non-Universal Functions, Beliefs, and Practices of Food Dimensions of Nutrition, *Proceedings of the Colorado Dietetic Association Conference,* J. Dupont, ed., Fort Collins: Colorado Associated Universities Press, 1970, pp. 153-179.

6. Leininger, M. "Ethnoscience: A New and Promising Research Approach for the Health Sciences Image," (Sigma Theta Tau Magazine), v. 3., no. 1 1969, pp. 2-8.

7. Leininger, M. "Gadsup of New Guinea: and Early Child-Caring Behaviors with Nursing Care Implications," *Transcultural Nursing: Concepts, Theories and Practices,* New York: John Wiley & Co., 1978.

8. Leininger, M. "Transcultural Care Diversity and Universality: A theory of Nursing," Seattle: University of Washington, 1960 (unpublished paper).

9. Leininger, M. "Leininger's Theory of Cultural Care Diversity and Universality," *Nursing Science Quarterly,* v. 1, no. 4, 1988, pp. 152-160.

10. Leininger, M. "Gadsup of Papua New Guinea Revisited: A Three Decade View." *Journal of Transcultural Nursing.* Vol. 5, No. 1, Summer 1993, pp. 21-31.

Chapter 27
Culturally-Based Health-Illness Patterns in South Africa and Humanistic Nursing Care Practices

Grace Mashaba, DLH/ET/Phil, RN

Knowing and respecting the culture of one's patients is a major factor in providing effective health care in any country including South Africa. This country is not culturally homogeneous as some people would like to think. By virtue of its multiracial and tribal differences South Africa has cultural diversity in spite of many generations of the Westernizing influence of whites. Health care personnel need to consider the possibility of their indifference to distinct cultural values being a barrier to healthy communication, understanding and mutual acceptance between the health care provider and the recipient of care. Such indifference amounts to lack of caring, which can leave the patient wounded inwardly even in the middle of the best nurses and the best technology. Barker, a medical practitioner for many years at Charles Johnson Hospital, Nqutu, sounds this warning:

We should cease from scorning those who pass our hospitals to the care of the traditional medicine man, or seeing this movement as necessarily retrogressive. It is nothing of the kind, but rather a barometer of our failure to satisfy that part of a sick man's consciousness which he reserves for himself.[1]

The purpose of this paper is to present, explain, and introduce the reader to those aspects of traditional cultural practices of Africans of South Africa that pertain to health and illness in order to highlight humanistic nursing care practices based on transcultural nursing theory with the view to enhancing health care to people in South Africa. This is especially important for nurses in South Africa, but also for nurses coming to this country desirous to understand and work with the people with a transcultural nursing perspective.

South Africa refers to the area that lies south of the Limpopo River. This includes the Republic of South Africa and its independent and self-governing states of Transkei, Ciskei, KwaZulu, Venda, Gazankulu, Bophuthatswana, Lebowa, Qwaqwa, and Kangwane, as well as the countries which were previously British protectorates and are therefore outside the borders of the Republic. These are Swaziland, Lesotho, and Botswana. There continues to be a marked intermingling of populations of these countries. Swazis, Basothos, and Batswanas cross their borders in order to seek work primarily in the mining industry in the Republic of South Africa. Health and nursing services of the Republic must, of necessity, serve all these cultures.

South African major cultures are: Indigenous Africans (who can be further subdivided into Sotho, Tswana, Shona, Zulu, Xhosa, Venda, Swazi, and others); Coloreds (who are a culture that developed from marriages between Anglo-caucasians and Africans); Anglo-caucasians, or Anglo-Europeans who immigrated from European countries; and Asians who came from the Middle and Far East. Although Anglo-Europeans are the political majority, Africans are the numerical majority. The total population of the Republic of South Africa in 1989 was thirty million. Africans were twenty-one million; Coloreds, three million; Anglo-Europeans four million, and Asians less than a million.[2]

If the country's goal of health for all by the year 2000 is to be realized, nurses have to make an effort to reach the numerical majority by getting to know the traditions, beliefs, and values to meet the health care needs of the Africans as the majority who are the recipients of care. This should enhance the quality of nursing care and curb the incidence of ill health especially in the light of Gumede's statement that "...over eighty percent of African patients visit the traditional healer before coming to the doctor and to the hospital."[3]

The Cultural Background of Africans

From the eighteenth century, when British and Dutch missionaries and settlers came to Africa, there has been an ongoing movement to Westernize the indigenous people who were found inhabiting the continent. To date cultures are mixed, but the more dominant culture of South Africans is the Western type. However, health-illness beliefs and values are held to varying degrees within and between the cultural groups. In light of this reality, nurses need to assess the extent to which the health practice and behavior of patients conforms to the Western model.

Spector maintains that values exist on a continuum and a person can possess value characteristics of both a consistent heritage (traditional) and an inconsistent heritage (acculturated).[4] African values, beliefs, and practices have a tight grip on their practitioners, more than appears on the surface. Gumede maintains that his informant, a teacher, said it is a disgrace for a teacher, a graduate, or a nurse to say that he or she *once* used traditional medicinal practices such as *ukuncinda* (to lick); *ukubhema* (to inhale medicine like snuff); and *ukugcaba* (to be incised and have medicine rubbed into the incisions). These treatments are, however, practice by affluent Africans as well as by the less affluent to achieve their ends on a regular basis.[5] Further, Gumede gives many examples to illustrate that neither living in the rural areas nor in the urban area of the city of Johannesburg shakes the African's belief in witchcraft as "one of those things which belong to the childhood of our race."[6] Gqomfa, a senior professional psychiatric nurse speaking at a National Convention on Holistic Health and Healing testifies:

> *Customs, rites, rituals, and ancestral spirits make up a culture whose complexities are bewildering to the Western orientated person: yet these traditions have been carried on from generation to generation without the benefit of the written word. I, as a Xhosa tribesman in my own right, have attended and assisted at rites and rituals never for a moment doubting their importance within the Xhosa cosmology.[7]*

As a way of removing the cutting edge from the competition between African traditional doctors and Western medical practitioners in South Africa, there are rumblings of a movement to have dialogue with traditional healers and to even bring them within the fold of health services. A bold positive step in this direction has been taken through passing the KwaZulu Act No. 6 of 1981, providing for the practice of African medicinemen, herbalists, and midwives. Gumede studied, presented and explained a list of the *inyanga's* (traditional herbalist) pharmaceutical medicines or healing modes,[8] which was an improvement on earlier, similar work by Bryant.[9]

The above statements support the fact that nurses need to know and understand the established cultural lifeways and values of their patients regardless of their color and creed so as to reach patients and win their confidence and cooperation in a genuine and competent way to meet their health problems or concerns.

The African Tradition of Health, Illness and Healing

Literature shows that the worldview of African nations across the continent have much in common. Diversity is limited largely to the use of different terminology because of differences in languages. According to Ngubane, it is possible for a Zulu traditional medical practitioner to operate in a Sotho, Xhosa, Shona, and Thonga Society.[10] This is reflected in the works of Kenyatta,[11] Krige,[12] Lienhardt[13] Bryant[14] Vilakazi[15] Kuper[16,] and Gumede.[17]

Health-Illness States

In the African lifestyle there are ceremonies, customs, and rituals for every stage of human development, from birth to death at an old age, which, if observed, bring about a normal steady state of individuals and families. Traditionally for an African, health and healthy living is interwoven with religion which is a way of life and of daily living. It is not confined to worship on one particular day. Africans believe in the existence of God or a supreme being, but each nation gives Him a different name. Zulus call Him *Mvelinggangi*, Sothos, *Modimo*, Xhosas, *Tixo*, Shonas, *Mwari*, and Tsongas, *Tilo*.[18] Traditionally this supreme being is not approached directly through individual prayers. He is approached through the ancestors or spirits of dead relatives (*amadlozi* or *abaphansi*).

A bond exists between the living and the ancestral spirits in that the latter not only safeguard the living and make them successful in their undertakings, but they also intercede for the living people to the unseen God. When a relative dies, a beast is slaughtered and a ceremony is made to bring back the spirit of the dead relative from the grave to the family house, so that this spirit can be with other ancestral spirits and look after the living family members. Regular sacrifices must be made to the ancestors so as to retain the well-being, health, and welfare of the family.[19]

When misfortune or illness strikes in the family, an illness is not responding to treatments, or a newly wed bride does not conceive, it is interpreted to mean that the ancestors are angry. The head of the family or the afflicted person then slaughters a goat, brews beer, and pleads with ancestors (*ukushweleza*). In response the ancestors reverse the situation or problem.

At times the ancestors decide to pay a visible visit to the family and so they become a particular kind of harmless snake that enters the house. Family members do not chase or kill such a snake, because it is symbolically a visitation by ancestors. A story is told of a woman who once found and kept a puff adder in her clay pot for weeks believing that it was the ancestors. Ancestors also communicate messages to the living members through dreams. Therefore, being in harmony with ancestors and keeping the ancestors appeased promotes health and prosperity. For this reason nurses are often faced by a patient who fails to improve after being hospitalized for weeks and requests to go home. The patient may or may not explain the reason for this request to the nurse and other health personnel. Members of the family or the patient become convinced that his or her illness is due to the anger of the ancestors (*ulaka lwabaphansi*). A sacrifice is needed to appease them. At times leaving the hospital against medical advice is due to the realization that one's illness cannot be cured by the white man's medicine and caring modes because it is the disease of the African people (*ukufa kwabantu*). It can be cured and cared for only by traditional healers.

There are also cultural belief practices and taboos that are observed, and if maintained lead to a state of health and protection against evil forces. Some customs are no longer kept and several taboos have been abandoned as superstition. For some people failure to observe these culturally based taboos affects the whole person, physically, psychologically, and in sociocultural relationships. Some of the customs that are still observed are paying *ilobolo*, or paying bride money or giving cattle to the parents of the girl that one intends to marry. Burial of the dead and mourning in a traditional way, and circumcision of boys carried out in the mountains accompanied by a certain ceremony are often customs that can be identified in African lifeways. In the process of circumcision, occasionally some of the boys develop an infection and come to the hospital.[20]

Most importantly, to retain a healthy state Africans must try and maintain a balance with their environmental surroundings and between people. People often go to the extent of using medicine to maintain this balance. It is alleged that using such medicine not only ensures protection against evil spells, but it also ensures a positive reaction and relationships with other people. Employers and authorities do favors or even promote one even if one does not deserve promotion. When an individual is the accused in a court case, such medicines are used to help the person win the case, even if this individual is actually guilty. If the individual uses very strong medicine for maintaining balance, this can adversely affect other people with whom one associates and they can fall ill due to such influences. This is called *ukweleka ngesithunzi*, meaning to overpower or overshadow other people. For this reason people who live together are strengthened at the same time to keep this balance among them.[21] Transcultural nurses functioning in South Africa would need to understand these indigenous beliefs and practices to be effective and practice what Leininger refers to as culturally congruent care.[22]

Traditional Cure of Illnesses

Apart from accidents and animal bites, diseases are believed to take one of the following forms. There are those diseases which are natural such as flu, diarrhea, and others. These are cured by herbs, most of which are commonly known by most people and can be found in one's surroundings. There also are indigenous or culture-specific diseases or illnesses which are caused by the anger of the ancestors. There is also a group of illnesses that is related to witchcraft. Witchcraft practices can bring about illness through eating food or drinking a beverage with medicine that has been deliberately added to the food to harm the victim. Pulmonary tuberculosis is one such illness. It is called *idliso* because the victim ingested poisonous food. At times a person falls acutely ill due to "walking over medicine" that has been deliberately put in the path, with the intention to harm this person. This is called *umego*, meaning jumped over medicine. There are times when an evil spell is cast to make one ill.

Witches also magically use lightning to kill people. Some illnesses are caused by dreaming, seeing or being sent a familiar which can be a snake, baboon, river dwarf, owl, tiger, or another animal. Witches or night sorcerers use charms to cast a spell on the above-named animals. Thereafter, the animal is under the sorcerer's control and carries out his instructions entirely. Victims of these familiars get very ill.[23] At other times people are possessed by wandering evil spirits or spirits of the ancestors, which leads to serious illness. It is believed that most of the above-stated diseases and illnesses cannot be cured by Western medical practitioners. However, some illnesses like *umego* that can lead to cellulitis of the leg, *idliso* known as pulmonary tuberculosis, and other illnesses often get cured through Western treatments and medications if used by the people.

It is a popular practice to go to a diviner or diagnostician (*isangoma*) to find out who bewitched the sick person. This is done regardless of whether the sick person dies, recovers or remains chronically ill. In most instances of witchcraft-induced illnesses when the patient is acutely ill, wastes away, or can be mentally deranged, medical tests and investigations will show nothing abnormal. At times it could only be an elevated temperature. Knowledge about the African patients' traditional beliefs and practices is essential to understanding African behavior which seems strange or baffling.

The healer (*inyanga*) uses one or more of the following methods to heal the afflicted person. Use is made of emetics (*ukuhlanza*); enemas (*ukuchatha*); inhaling medicine (*ukubhema*); steaming (*ukugguma*); licking medicine (*ukukhotha* or *ukuncinda*); making small razor incisions on different parts of the body and rubbing in medicine (*ukugcaba*); and chewing a root or bark, then spraying this in the air from the mouth (*ukukhwifa*).[24] With the advent of Christianity there came a new breed of healers called African spiritual healers. They heal using the same means as traditional healers, such as emetics, enemas, and steaming. Instead of using medicine they use candles and water. Spiritual healers take ordinary water, pray for it to have medicinal properties, then give it to patients. Patients are instructed to either drink it, wash with it, or use it for steaming, enemas, and so on. They communicate with ancestors but give them the name of *izidalwa* or *izithunywa*. Spiritual healers have prophetic powers and pray to God and to Jesus Christ. "Saved Christians" refer to this phenomenon as spiritualism in order to differentiate the works of spiritual healers from the miracles of God and the Holy Spirit.

These brief accounts should help the transcultural nurse to realize the importance of knowing, interpreting, and understanding African values, beliefs, and lifeways. The nurse should not impose these practices on every African patient because some Africans have accepted the Islamic religion and others are committed, saved, and born-again Christians. Many people in these groups have tried to distance themselves completely from the *inyanga-sangoma* syndrome, for they use methods within their religion to fight magic spells and evil spirits. There are also some people in South Africa who have become indifferent to traditional practices. However, today most Africans essentially hold a firm belief in magico-religious aspects of their traditional culture along with Western practices.

Looking to the Future

The future South Africa will be a fundamentally different society from what it is today. This means that nurses need to be prepared and open–minded to cultivate an atmosphere of mutual respect and trust between themselves and their patients. In support of this Gumede maintains that "As we learn more about other people's cultures, and values, as our understanding and our humility grow, as our prejudices erode...(we can) have much to learn from each other."[25]

Trying to relate to patients in terms of identifying and respecting their culture is not meant to create stereotypes or to divide people. On the contrary, it purports to enable the nurse to forge links across people of different cultures. In fact, according to Leininger, "Nurses will have to learn about their own cultural background and how their cultural values facilitate or serve as barriers in helping people of different cultural orientations."[26]

This statement serves to clarify and explain the intention of this presentation lest we fall into the trap described by Nakagawa who warns, "Too often we are drawn to the colorful or exotic aspects of cultural manifestations and inadvertently lead students to strengthening rather than reducing stereotyping.[27]

It must also be remembered that culture is not static. On the whole, South African people align themselves with more than one culture and can be described as culturally multi-faceted. The nurse needs to capitalize on commonalities while being mindful of diversities.[28]

Humanistic Nursing Practices

The foregoing information should enable culture-sensitive nurses to evolve nursing care plans and nursing practices that promote culturally congruent care. During the assessment phase of the nursing process nurses can accumulate facts and information that lead not only to a nursing assessment, but also to understanding of patient's fears and anxiety about particular health problems. A patient may dream of a baboon and thereafter wake up with a severe headache. When talking to the patient the nurse will discover that the patient is anxious and worried more about the dream than the headache. In other words, in his opinion being a victim of a familiar requires, alongside taking headache pills, a traditional healer's treatment to remove the evil spell. A patient may refuse surgical removal of a tumor if this tumor is perceived to be the result of the anger of the ancestors and surgical removal therefore amounts to defying or disregarding the ancestors.

Knowledge of African health-illness cultural practices should help nurses understand and interpret culture-specific terms accurately. In this way proper communication can be fostered even with a traditionally oriented African patient. If the patient reports that his swollen painful leg is due to *umego*, the nurse will understand this to mean that the patient "jumped over medicine." Another patient may explain the cause of his chest pains as being *idliso*, meaning that he ate poisoned food or drink. This implies that in addition to assisting the patient to recover from tuberculosis chest pains, the nurse has to deal with the patient's cultural belief which may cause this patient to abandon hospital care and go for traditional healing.

At the stage of nursing assessment, patients' responses can be analyzed using Leininger's Acculturation Health Care Assessment Enabler for Cultural Patterns in Traditional and Non-Traditional Lifeways. This Enabler provides criteria that are rated on a scale of 1 (mainly traditional) to 5 (mainly non-traditional).[29] Such ratings will show the position of the particular patient on the traditional and non-traditional continuum. Nurses can then make decisions on nursing action using Leininger's Culture Care theoretical model. This model focuses on culture care preservation and maintenance, culture care accommodation, and negotiation and culture care repatterning and restructuring.[30]

There are aspects of this culture that could be preserved and maintained by the nurse in the process of giving nursing care. The African belief in a supreme being could be strengthened. In daily contact with the patient the nurse can discuss how this supreme being is the creator, giver and taker of life, and that this being is actually superior to all forms of magic and to any force. Strong reliance on this being should enable the patient to be resilient to the influence of evil forces and magic spells. As this reliance grows, patients will become less likely to yield to the notion that their fate is in the hands or at the mercy of witches and ancestors. Guidance and support can be given to patients to talk or relate regularly to this supreme being in order to build a stronger person-to-God relationship.

Kinship ties can be preserved and maintained through involvement of the family in care practices. The family support and cooperation that is evident in making decisions about traditional healing practices can be employed by nurses. Nurses can get information from relatives to either support or refute the patient's statements. Relatives can be consulted especially if the patient is unable to answer questions properly. They can be involved in a decision to give consent for a surgical operation when the patient is hesitant. Members of the family can be asked to take on roles to facilitate recovery of their sick relative. They can remind and assist the patient to take pills or treatment, watch for signs of bleeding, assist with ambulation or assist the patient with exercises for a limb to return to its normal functioning. Nurses may identify other aspects that can be maintained to the advantage of therapeutic and humanistic caring processes.

With respect to accommodation and negotiation, an example of patient's reliance on herbs can be used. Nurses must try to become familiar with medicinal herbs that are commonly used by African people. Gumede's list of herbs will give guidance and explain the pharmacological action of these herbs as well as their side effects.[31] Patients using these herbs are usually not aware of other actions and effects of herbs apart from what the traditional healer prescribes. The nurse can establish the nature, action, and effect of medicinal herbs that a patient insists on using. Based on the nurse's knowledge of the medicine, discretion can be used to accommodate continued use of the medicine while the patient is undergoing hospital care. This should be the case if the medicinal herb will not interfere with prescribed care. On the contrary if the herb will, for instance, cause vomiting when the patient is supposed to rest the gastro-intestinal tract, depress appetite when the patient needs to have regular meals and a nourishing diet, or cause mental alertness when the patient must relax and sleep, the nurse should negotiate with the patient for suspension of use of the herb, at least, pending the outcome of hospital care.

Traditional healers could be allowed to visit their patients while these patients are hospitalized. This opportunity could be used by nurses to secure the cooperation of the healers and promote holistic well-being. The nurse can negotiate for a compromise on the traditional healer's part for suspending and omitting some of the healer's prescriptions using the principle discussed in the previous paragraph. The traditional healers could also be encouraged to refer to nurses those patients that appear to be problematic. If the traditional healer is taught about healthy habits like eating a balanced diet, cleanliness of people, houses, and the environment, the traditional healer can also be persuaded to sell these ideas and habits to patients.

African patients could be trained and educated to perform minor skin incisions (*ukugcaba*) and circumcisions through hygienic means, in order to reduce the risk of infection and to do these common home practices properly. The nurse could negotiate with physicians, if necessary, to have these surgical operations done by health personnel or under their supervision. Patient education as part of nursing care plans could be a means of repatterning and restructuring aspects of traditional culture like caring modes. In the case of pulmonary tuberculosis, alleged to be *idliso*, patients can be assisted to focus attention on what causes the illness instead of consulting the *isangoma* to establish who is responsible for inflicting the disease. Other patients with a similar diagnosis can be used as a reference and support group.

The idea of maintaining balance in the traditional sense could be repatterned around the prevention of spreading an infectious disease to other members of the family. Nurses could impress upon patients that the microbes that caused the disease from which the patients are suffering should be prevented through immunization and/or certain precautions from spreading to other people and disturbing balance. Susceptibility to diseases caused by microorganisms can be structured and patterned around the idea of susceptibility to magic and evil spells. Patients can be made to understand that poor nourishment, lack of fresh air, dirt, and uncleanliness all raise the level of susceptibility not only to microorganisms but also possibly to evil spirits and magic spells. In this way nurses can carry on providing culturally acceptable care. In evaluating nursing care, the nurses could consult and involve the patient and relatives so as to get their opinion on the effectiveness of care given.

Africans, like members of other cultures, are proud of their cultural identity. There are practices and beliefs which may need to be considered rather than dismissed as myths or superstition seeing that traditional healing as part of African culture should be protected.[32] For the African these are real because they have been handed down by their foreparents or ancestors, and they are firmly held to be important and efficacious. Nurses should not ridicule these beliefs, because doing so may antagonize and repel the patient. This will defeat the goal of quality nursing care and health for all. Respect of other people's culture has implications also for non-clinical nursing areas. Nurse administrators and nurse educators should serve as role models by resisting the tendency to be ethnocentric in their dealings with colleagues and students. The nurse administrator has to recognize culturally-determined situational variations in role expectations of the staff. Through staff development the nurse administrator may have to assist a colleague resolve the conflict between the passive traditional role of a woman and the assertive professional role of a patient's advocate. The professional nurse needs to take the initiative in negotiating, restructuring and repatterning activities discussed earlier in order to help patients take responsibility for their own health.[33]

The nurse educator who has African students in her class should be careful of sole reliance on unicultural educational practices. Students will probably imitate the nurse educator and adopt unicultural approaches in caring for patients. The educator needs to be flexible and knowledgeable to support culturally congruent systems and practices known in the student's environment and culture. There will be organizations and social groups in the community with which students can establish contact for mutual education and information towards enabling more and more people to be health conscious within and outside of their culture.

Clinical nurse researchers need to discover and confirm the existence of adherence by patients to their traditional lifeways and also establish credibility of the African subjective experiences. In view of the fact that South Africans are in a state of cultural transition and that transcultural nursing research focuses on subjective and objective experiential humanistic inquiry, research studies can generate new or traditional knowledge about South Africans in terms of who they are, what they do, and why. It should be helpful to do a cultural analysis of different people of all cultures, rather than taking for granted that all people in the country share the same beliefs about health, illness, and healing. Transcultural nursing is essential and meaningful today in South Africa as the people continue to assess and use the best of indigenous traditional and rich cultural heritage with that of different Western cultural groups. Professional nurses need to maintain an open discovery attitude using transcultural nursing theories and knowledge to develop creative ways to practice nursing. This will enable them to take health and care as near as possible to those people who need it most.

This paper was written in 1991 before the National Election in April, 1994. The traditional health-illness conditions and care practices are still an integral part of the culture with some Western practices.

References

1. Barker, A., "The Social Fabric," *The Leech*, v. 44, no. 2, 1974, p. 32.
2. *South African Statistics*, Pretoria: Central Statistical Service, 1990, pp. 1–4.
3. Gumede, M. M., *Traditional Healers*, Johannesburg: Skotaville, 1990.
4. Spector, R., *Cultural Diversity in Health and Illness*, Norwalk: Appleton-Century-Crofts, 1985.
5. Gumede, op. cit.
6. Ibid.
7. Gqomfa, J., "Tradition and Transition," *Odyssey*, v. 12, no. 4, 1987, p. 29.
8. Gumede, op. cit.
9. Bryant, A. T., *Zulu Medicine and Medicine Men*, Cape Town: C. Struik, 1970.
10. Ngubane, H., *Body and Mind in Zulu Medicine*, London: Academic Press, 1977.
11. Kenyatta, J., *Facing Mount Kenya*, New York: Vintage Books, 1965.
12. Krige, E. J., *The Social System of the Zulus*, Pietermaritzburg: Shuter and Shooter, 1957.
13. Lienhardt, G., *Divinity and Experience: The Religion of the Dinka*, Oxford: The Clarendon Press, 1970.
14. Bryant, op. cit.
15. Vilakazi, A., *Zulu Transformation*, Pietermaritzburg: University of Natal Press, 1962.
16. Kuper, H., *An African Aristocracy*, London: Oxford University Press, 1969.
17. Gumede, op. cit.
18. Ibid.

19. Ibid.
20. Funani, S. L., *Circumcision among the Ama-Xhosa*, Johannesburg: Skotaville, 1990, p. 37.
21. Ngubane, op. cit.
22. Leininger, M., *Culture Care Diversity and Universality: A Theory of Nursing*, New York: National League for Nursing, 1991, pp. 5–68.
23. Gumede, op. cit.
24. Ngubane, op. cit.
25. Gumede, op. cit.
26. Leininger, M., *Transcultural Nursing for Tomorrow's Nurse*, (unpublished paper) Detroit: Wayne State University, 1986.
27. Nakagawa, M., "Multicultural Education," *Transcultural Nursing Newsletter*, v. 1, no. 1, 1991, p. 2.
28. Leininger, M., op. cit., 1991.
29. Leininger, M., "Leininger's Acculturation Health Care Assessment Tool for Cultural Patterns in Traditional and Non-Traditional Lifeways," *Journal of Transcultural Nursing*, v. 2, no. 2, 1991, p. 40.
30. Leininger, M., "Leininger's Theory of Nursing: Cultural Diversity and Universality," *Nursing Science Quarterly*, v. 1, no. 4, 1988, pp. 152–160.
31. Gumede, op. cit.
32. *Traditional Healers in Health Care in South Africa: A Proposal*, Johannesburg: The Center for Health Policy, 1991, p. 1.
33. Leininger, op. cit.

Section IV:

Teaching Transcultural Nursing

Chapter 28
Teaching Transcultural Nursing in Undergraduate and Graduate Programs

Madeleine Leininger, PhD, LHD, DS, FAAN, CTN, RN.

Nursing as a profession and discipline is changing to new ways of knowing, new ways of understanding, and new ways of helping people. Some of the most significant changes in nursing are related to learning, teaching, and applying transcultural nursing knowledge. Discovering, understanding, and using transcultural nursing knowledge in people care is leading to new ways of practicing nursing. Comparative knowledge of differences and similarities among individuals, groups, and institutions is challenging nurses to expand their worldview and to value human diversities and similarities. The globalization of transcultural nursing knowledge and practices remains one of the most essential and important challenges for the twenty-first century. It is these thoughts that lead to the purpose of this chapter, namely to identify developments, content, and trends in the teaching of transcultural nursing in undergraduate and graduate programs. For it is through the dynamic teaching and learning process that a new era in nursing will occur, one which has the potential to transform nursing education and practices as we enter the twenty-first century.

Transforming Nursing Through Teaching Transcultural Nursing

Since the advent of transcultural nursing, nursing has gradually been expanding its perspectives to a wider conceptualization of nursing and incorporating knowledge about different cultures in the world.[1] This has largely occurred through educational processes and with curricular changes in undergraduate and graduate nursing programs. A new generation of nurses are learning about transcultural nursing, expanding their worldviews and gaining knowledge about diverse cultures.[2,3] This has been encouraging to witness and is a major achievement in some schools of nursing. There are, however, some schools of nursing that have only recently begun to incorporate transcultural nursing knowledge and to develop culture care competencies. Actually much work remains in the United States and in other countries to integrate transcultural nursing into all aspects of undergraduate and graduate nursing programs. For the goal of transcultural nurse educators is to establish transcultural nursing as the major and arching framework of all aspects of nursing education and practice. This has been the author's dream since initiating the field in the mid 1950s and there are some signs that in the mid twenty-first century this goal will be realized in most schools of nursing.

The transformation of nursing through the educational process has been directed toward using a *comparative global philosophy* and practice of nursing in which nurses are cognizant that they are living and functioning in diverse transcultural communities. Nurses need to remain sensitive and knowledgeable about many cultures with different ways to provide nursing education and practice. This philosophy promotes active and open learning about many different cultures in the world and to reexamine past and current teachings that may be largely ethnocentric and unicultural. Shifting nursing educators from a unicultural to a multicultural perspective has been difficult because of many factors, but especially with the lack of faculty preparation in transcultural nursing. Nonetheless some significant strides have been made by a core of dedicated and persistent transcultural nurses. Much work remains to change and educate resistive faculty by expanding their worldview through transcultural nursing knowledge and reflective cultural experiences.[4,5] Both general and culture specific experiences are important to help nursing educators and curricular specialists to transform nursing curricula to a transcultural focus. *Transcultural nursing knowledge is one of the richest and most powerful knowledge in nursing.* Nurses will want to become knowledgeable and clinically skilled in this area to support new directions in nursing.

The major question for nursing educators worldwide is how best to educate nearly five million nurses in the world so that they will be effective in responding to and providing culturally congruent care. This significant question must be considered if nurses are to function and be successful in a growing and intense multicultural nursing world. For some nurses, this idea will be an exciting challenge as they await leaders and teaching experts to help them. For other nurses, this idea may be viewed as impossible and minimal effort will be made to make transcultural nursing an integral part of nursing education and practice. It is encouraging to see some nurse leaders committed to transcultural nursing and they are stimulating faculty and students to join them. But time is drawing near for hundreds of nursing faculty to become fully aware of and to value transcultural nursing as imperative in order to function in a growing multicultural nursing practice world.

Reasons for Shifting to Transcultural Nursing with New Curricular Perspectives

There are several reasons why nursing education and practice needs to shift to transcultural nursing which will require nurses to do some major rethinking, planning, and establish action plans if nursing is to be relevant in the intense multicultural world of the twenty-first century. Some reasons have been identified earlier in this book, however, a few major ideas need to be highlighted here so that faculty can realize why nursing education must become transculturally grounded and taught in schools of nursing.

One of the most important reasons for transcultural nursing education and concomitant practices is that the world has become intensely multicultural and will be more so in the future. Consumers of health services expect their care and treatment modes to reflect transcultural care knowledge, sensitivities, and competencies.[6] This has become increasingly apparent in nursing care services but also in nursing education as clients and nursing students expect that they will be understood and responded to in meaningful and helpful ways. Understanding cultural differences and similarities has become an imperative for quality of nursing education and practice. For without cultural understandings and culture care competencies, nursing education will fail as will health care services. Nursing educators need to conceptualize transcultural nursing curricula with different teaching approaches to accommodate cultural variabilities among students and consumers and still remain alert to the commonalties. Transcultural nursing has a critical mandate to fulfill nursing's role as a meaningful global profession. Nurses are expected to respond to societal health care needs and also to function today with global comparative nursing perspectives and action modes. Nursing schools can only fulfill these imperative expectations if they become transculturally based in nursing education and practice.

A second reason for shifting nursing education to a transcultural nursing focus is that most communities and human service institutions are changing to meet population shifts in which immigrants, refugees, and other cultures continue to move around the world. In the earlier days, immigrants tended to live and work in homogeneous communities for an extended period of time, but today there is more of a constant movement of immigrants and others in short spans of time. As a consequence, health personnel encounter clients of many different cultures and they are experienced to know about their client's cultural background and needs in order to provide culturally congruent health care services. Likewise, nursing students today, are entering nursing schools from many different cultures and they need to be understood and cared about as nursing students. It is this "new age" of transculturalism and this "new age" of functioning that calls for nursing faculty and administrators to understand and function thoughtfully with people of many different cultures. Transculturalism is essential to survive and thrive in this new age culture. For without this shift to transculturalism in nursing education and service, one can predict many unfavorable and unfortunate outcomes that could lead to a host of teaching problems, but especially to angry and dissatisfied students and clients. Transcultural nurses were the first to carve the new pathway to transculturalism. They remain in a unique position to use their knowledge and skills to help other faculty, administrators, and students shift their focus and practice goals to transcultural nursing.

As faculty move forward to prepare a new generation of transculturally educated nurses, they must first find ways to educate themselves in order to be effective teachers, mentors, and role models. It is essential to educate faculty about the nature, scope, goals, theories, practices, and desired outcomes of transcultural nursing. Such knowledge is essential to insure teaching competencies and to develop transcultural nursing undergraduate and graduate courses. It is also important to insure that faculty can mentor students in clinical settings and field areas as students study and care for clients of diverse cultures. Nursing courses in universities, colleges, and institutes need to increase their transcultural offerings to many nursing faculty who still today have limited knowledge and skills in transcultural nursing. For if faculty are not educated about transcultural nursing, students will not be able to serve people appropriately and responsibly. As faculty learn about different cultures in their local and regional communities, this will stimulate their thinking to value the new age transcultural nursing curricula and concomitant learning practices. Helping faculty to become immersed in cultures and to use this knowledge and experience often brings about dramatic changes in faculty ways of teaching and doing research. Moreover, learning about "the other" cultures from a skilled transcultural mentor can lead faculty to new understandings and ways of caring for people, students, and friends.

Currently, the popular faculty talk is "to be culturally sensitive and competent" with students and clients. But this popular cliché requires faculty to learn about different cultures locally and worldwide. Transcultural learning can be a most rewarding experience for faculty as they develop new skills and knowledge. *Faculty need to learn how to prevent cultural imposition practices, reduce ethnocentrism, and prevent serious cultural conflicts and clashes.* Faculty also need to learn how to mentor students with new or different cultural ways. Only then can faculty from different cultures become valuable in teaching and practicing transcultural nursing or in any nursing.

Currently fewer than twenty percent of faculty are prepared in transcultural nursing in the United States and even fewer in other countries.[7] Fewer than two percent of doctoral nursing students in the United States are prepared in transcultural nursing, which has led to serious problems when these students began to function in nursing after graduating.[8] Still today only forty percent of baccalaureate nursing students and about seventeen percent of master degree nurses have had substantive courses in transcultural nursing or programs focused on transcultural nursing. There are, however, faculty proclaiming that they are teaching transcultural nursing, but many of these faculty have had no graduate preparation in transcultural nursing. Many of these faculty have told the author that they teach "common sense" about cultures, from their home or personal experiences. As a consequence, one may find students exposed to inaccurate and questionable content and lacking substantive knowledge and skills to guide their thinking and actions appropriately. The author contends that deans and faculty of schools of nursing are morally and ethically responsible for educating students in transcultural nursing and being culturally competent to hold faculty positions in schools of nursing.[9]

Student demand for faculty who are knowledgeable and competent to teach and mentor students in transcultural nursing is markedly increasing. Students are keenly aware of the multicultural world in which they live and that they must develop competency skills with clients, families, and cultural groups. These nursing students value faculty who can help them understand different cultures and also to demonstrate strategies for helping clients. Students also value nursing faculty who can adapt their teaching to different cultural strategies, models, and approaches to learning about transcultural nursing. Many of these teaching approaches and strategies have been developed and used by transcultural nursing faculty during the past three decades.[10,11,12,13,14]

Fortunately, nursing faculty now have access to a body of transcultural nursing literature and to role models to help advance their knowledge and perfect their skills. Faculty have opportunities to become immersed in different cultures in their home communities, health centers, and in many other places to learn and teach transcultural nursing. Multiple opportunities remain for nursing faculty to learn about cultural groups throughout the life cycle.

As faculty and students *learn together* about people of different cultures with a focus on human caring and health, much excitement often occurs with many new faculty insights. Nursing faculty and students can also draw upon knowledge from the humanities, liberal arts, and social sciences as they learn about different cultures, environments, and material and nonmaterial aspects of cultures. For example, knowledge from anthropology about the material and nonmaterial features of diverse cultures can challenge nursing faculty and students to discover together the meaning and importance of culture care beliefs and practices. Different practices in a culture and different caring patterns and expressions are some of the new learning aspects for nurses. In this process, transcultural nursing faculty have a responsibility to facilitate the faculty in learning about culture care and health and to deal with faculty resistance and prejudices. Nursing faculty have been encouraged to extend their thinking beyond the biophysical and mental health dimensions of human beings and to discover the influences of culture on care and health. Without the cultural focus in nursing, teaching has major gaps in providing an understanding of people. Nursing faculty can be invited into courses and seminars taught by transcultural nurses to provide insights and important ideas for curricular development, research, teaching, and clinical field experiences.

A current urgent need in nursing is the *recruitment of graduate-prepared transcultural nursing faculty in schools of nursing*. Currently, there are far too few faculty to meet diverse student and the diverse health care needs of consumers. Rigorous and persistent recruitment efforts are needed in schools of nursing to fulfill teaching, research, consultation, and student guidance in clinical settings. Transcultural nursing faculty will continue to be in high demand worldwide as teaching and curricular changes shift to multiculturalism. Far more funds and human resources are much needed for transcultural nursing faculty and nurse clinicians to meet the current and future crisis in transcultural nursing education and practice. Without faculty well-prepared in transcultural nursing schools of nursing and students will be greatly deprived of what they need most to teach and function with people of diverse cultures. Moreover, the quality of the nursing curricula as well as research studies and community services will be noticeably deficient. But first let us look further at some current issues and the state of transcultural nursing education.

The Current State, and Issues of, and Approaches to Transcultural Nursing Education

In 1966 the author developed and taught the first class in transcultural nursing at the University of Colorado. Since then, a slow development of transcultural nursing education has occurred in schools within and outside the United States. The concept of *teaching at a distance began with transcultural nursing telelecture* series within the United States and in the Pacific Islands in 1967. Although this was an intriguing early mode of teaching, it had limitations. Entering the people's world and environments physically facilitated seeing and understanding the peoples' culture on a remote island.

Student-faculty lectures and discussion on transcultural nursing with individuals, families, and community groups remain the dominant teaching and learning approach. Students worked closely with clients and families in hospital or community contexts over several weeks to learn about transcultural nursing while in the diverse nursing clinical fields, but they do so with guidance from transcultural nursing faculty. Students identify their concerns and difficulties working with cultural strangers. Community nursing faculty have been especially eager to learn about transcultural nursing in order to be effective with Native Americans, Mexican Americans, Vietnamese and African Americans in the United States. Until recent years, these faculty and students in community health nursing were more aware of cultural differences than faculty in medical-surgical and psychiatric nursing.

Today a few transcultural nursing specialists are available in some hospitals and community agencies serving as role models and consultants to teach other nurses about cultural variabilities. Both transcultural nurse specialists and generalists frequently provide in-service education on transcultural nursing in health care settings. These transcultural nurse specialists are much needed, but there are far too few of them. One is fortunate today to have one or two transcultural nurses in general hospitals or in university teaching centers where they are expected to cover all clinical units, work with noncompliant clients, and help health personnel deal with their problems serving the culturally different. Hence, there is a critical need for many more transcultural nurses in clinical client care settings, health research centers and teaching.

To meet this urgent demand for graduate-prepared transcultural nurses in education and service, many innovative plans and active strategies are needed. Transcultural nursing workshops, conferences, and special courses are needed to prepare faculty, clinical staff, and other health personnel in health care situations. Some nurses travel great distances and spend time and money to take intensive short-term undergraduate and graduate transcultural nursing courses in order to learn transcultural nursing concepts from experts. For example, since 1978 nurses have come from many different countries and states to take the author's short-term graduate courses in transcultural nursing. These courses have been extremely valuable as nurses learn about the diverse cultures when they live and work with cultural groups in Australia, the Republic of South Africa, Botswana, several Pacific Islands, Asia, Finland, the United States, Netherlands, Canada, and Europe. Nurses who have enrolled in these graduate courses in transcultural nursing have been expected to be leaders and experts upon completion of the course, when they return to their homeland. The demand for transcultural nursing knowledge and skills is extremely great in most places, as nurses recognize that they must provide effective and competent nursing care to clients who are increasingly multicultural. Far more education programs are needed to meet the critical shortage of transcultural nurses worldwide.

Another teaching and learning approach is to have an exchange program with nurses from different countries participating and learning from each other. With this approach *prior preparation of students is needed and transcultural nursing faculty to direct and arrange the experiences*. In order to insure positive learning outcomes, students must be prepared in advance by learning the basic concepts, principles, theories, and practices in transcultural nursing before sent to another country. Currently, some transcultural nurse faculty are going with students to different countries, and there have been some unfavorable outcomes. These unfavorable learning outcomes are evident when students had no transcultural nursing courses and had unqualified faculty to guide their experiences.

Another means to stimulate students and registered nurses to learn about and teach transcultural nursing has been the certification and recertification of nurses in transcultural nursing. Through oral and written examinations and a portfolio of experiences, nurses with basic and advanced transcultural experiences and education are being certified to practice transcultural nursing in safe and knowledgeable ways. To date, approximately seventy nurses have been certified and recertified to teach and practice transcultural nursing. Transcultural nurse specialists' and leaders' interest in certification has been most encouraging. Graduate preparation in transcultural nursing and direct experiences with clients have been essential to insure success with the examinations and to establish their competencies as transcultural nurse specialists, generalists, and consultants. Currently, many of these certified nurses are functioning in diverse clinical (hospital and health agency) nursing practice settings and in schools of nursing. These nurses are skilled at demonstrating ways to prevent culture care problems related to cultural clashes, cultural imposition practices, prejudices, and a host of other cultural problems or issues. Well-prepared certified transcultural nurses are making major differences in the quality of nursing care and are providing entirely different ways to practice, teach, and do research in nursing.

Transcultural nurse practitioners must continue to function in clinical and educational settings to teach and guide other nurses in ways to provide culturally sensitive and competent nursing care. These nurses are demonstrating ways to use transcultural nursing concepts, principles, theories, and research findings in clinical practices. Several have initiated transcultural research projects in health settings, schools of nursing, and in private and public community interdisciplinary organizations. Some of their work has been reported in the *Journal of Transcultural Nursing* since 1989 and in other publications. For example, a transcultural nurse specialist is functioning with a private American agency to study women's health care in the United States and overseas. Another is working in communities with new immigrants and refugees. Several are working in community agencies and acute care units or in foreign countries. Some transcultural clinical nurse specialists are working in urban and rural community agencies to assist teenage mothers with neonatal and related pregnancy problems. The demand for transcultural nurse practitioners in primary and tertiary clinical settings continues to grow within the United States and overseas. Opportunities in the field for transcultural nurses are unlimited and largely untapped. Transcultural nurses, however, are expected to identify and carve out their teaching, clinical practices, and research niches because of the lack of firmly established positions in several settings. They must also establish their role, title, economic value, and areas of functioning.

Incorporating Transcultural Nursing in Nursing Education Programs

Incorporating transcultural nursing into undergraduate and graduate programs remains a major challenge in most schools of nursing because of an overloaded curriculum and the reluctance or resistance of faculty to change curricula into a transcultural nursing one. Transcultural nurses have had to be astute strategists, diplomats, organizers, and politicians to get transcultural concepts, principles, themes, and research-based knowledge into most nursing curricula in the United States and in other countries. Accommodating or facilitating the inclusion of transcultural nursing ideas is usually difficult, as faculty tend to hold fast to their traditional areas of content and are generally afraid to include what is often unknown or vaguely known to them. During the past three decades, the author has found that nursing faculty who are reluctant to incorporate transcultural nursing into the curricula are fearful that new courses or content will replace what they currently teach. Still today, faculty may have limited knowledge about transcultural nursing as they have never taken a course or read the literature on the subject. Hence, they fear or resist incorporating transcultural nursing ideas. There are some faculty who may say, "I've been teaching it [transcultural nursing] for years. It's all in my courses I teach." However, students and faculty in transcultural nursing find that virtually no theory and content are taught, nor are their provisions for clinical transcultural nursing experiences. Some instructors today talk about "cultural diversity" but often with no substantive content about culture and transcultural nursing phenomena related to care and health. There are also faculty who are not interested in incorporating anything new unless it has been proven statistically or has measurable outcomes into nursing curricula. There are also nurses who teach anthropological and sociological concepts about culture, but fail to transform ideas into transcultural nursing. Such faculty problems and concerns have been major barriers to making transcultural nursing a reality in nursing curricula. However, with State Board Examinations questions on transcultural nursing now being included in national examinations, faculty are scurrying to incorporate transcultural ideas into nursing curricula. Fortunately, transcultural nurses seldom give up in their curricular efforts as they value and are committed to including transcultural nursing in nursing programs.

To be an effective transcultural nurse educator, one has to assess the political and organizational cultural climate of the faculty and institution before launching new courses and programs of study. Political alignments of faculty along clinical lines such as pediatrics, medical-surgical, community, and other traditional areas of nursing may be evident. Helping faculty to see the relevance and value of transcultural nursing to their traditional teaching and practice areas takes time, patience, and often much education by transcultural nurses. The philosophy of the school, time factors, the readiness of faculty, and the dean's attitude can make a great difference in getting transcultural content into nursing curricula. Often the transcultural expert "at home" may not be recognized in order to disguise other faculty members' lack of knowledge and resistance. Hence, outside consultants with less knowledge and skills are often brought into the school. Nonetheless, diverse approaches and strategies are important to try to get transcultural nursing courses and programs into nursing curricula. These approaches and strategies will be identified and briefly discussed next.

The first approach to incorporate transcultural nursing content is often to introduce into existing courses within different curricular areas specific definitions of concepts and principles with examples of transcultural nursing practices and principles. With this *concept-principle incorporation approach*, undergraduate and graduate courses are often more acceptable to faculty and faculty seem less fearful of changes. Dispersing transcultural nursing concepts and principles into several courses has advantages, however, deep concerns remain about who teaches what and the faculty's knowledge of and skills in transcultural nursing. Some nurses say, "It is better than nothing in the curriculum," but there is no certainty that faculty are qualified to teach the concepts and principles unless they have been prepared in the field. Students are the first to voice their views when faculty fail to know the subject matter, especially about cultures. Building in-depth the concepts or constructs in several courses is problematic with the concept of the integration approach. It is also difficult to evaluate the student learning outcomes because of the usual absence of substantive content and the absence of transcultural faculty to assess what was taught and the outcomes. If a transcultural nursing faculty member is teaching transcultural concepts across all units one generally finds they are taught with progression of depth and scope. Students are usually very pleased to have transcultural nursing concepts, principles, and theories taught in their programs, and they usually want more content. But students are critical of faculty who show signs of prejudice, social slurs, and other problems. They are also skeptical of unprepared faculty who base their teaching on mainly personal experiences, selected cultural encounters, or tours.

The second approach to curricular work and the teaching of transcultural nursing is to *teach modules or specified culture care units*. With this approach, transcultural nursing faculty are usually responsible for teaching whole units or modules of instruction in undergraduate or graduate programs on transcultural nursing. For example, a unit of instruction might be "Transcultural Nursing Care of Mexican

Americans with Hypertension." This module is usually part of another course such as physiological nursing. The modular teaching approach requires that transcultural nursing faculty have specific objectives, content, learning activities, and plans to teach and evaluate the content as well as to assist other faculty in reinforcing the ideas in their teaching and clinical supervision of students. This approach is often a step before moving to a full course, tract, or program in transcultural nursing. The module or unit approach lends itself to laboratory learning of generalized constructs or concepts. Some faculty and students view this as a compromise with fragmented units or as "a teaser" for more to learn in transcultural nursing. The module and unit approach often does not offer enough contrast to enable students to grasp fully the meaning and complexity of transcultural nursing care and health. The approach, however, can stimulate student learning about transcultural nursing and is being used in a number of undergraduate and graduate schools of nursing in the United States.

The third teaching and curricular approach is to offer *organized and substantive courses, often three–five semester credits on transcultural nursing in undergraduate and graduate programs.* This approach has been the most successful and has insured that students will be able to learn about cultures and humanistic caring. Courses on transcultural nursing should be comprehensive and taught by qualified transcultural nurses. A great variety of approaches can be used with one or two course offerings. Most faculty begin with definitions of concepts, principles, and demonstrate the need for transcultural nursing. They soon focus on specific cultures and subcultures, identifying the culture care needs of clients within a theoretical perspective. Specific concepts and principles are linked closely to the specific and general culture care needs of clients. Transcultural nursing faculty and students like and want this approach because they get in-depth content and diverse field experiences and have time to assimilate the ideas into meaningful perspectives. At least one course should be taught early in the program and one later by faculty prepared in transcultural nursing.

A basic transcultural nursing course should be required for all undergraduates and at least one advanced course for graduate students to acquire essential knowledge to provide culturally competent and responsible care. These courses need to have field or clinical experiences with transcultural faculty providing clinical guidance. The undergraduate course often becomes a foundation for graduate preparation in transcultural nursing. Students are exceedingly pleased with a full course as they are given time to relate the ideas to practice. Many positive comments can be heard such as, "It is exactly what I needed to care for African Americans and others in my clinical practices as I am working in an urban area with 87% African Americans," "This course has transformed my entire view of professional nursing and competencies as I see a whole new and different world in which to practice," and "As a graduate student, I actually had to relearn what

I learned earlier as it did not fit the care to these clients." Most students contend they had to learn nursing anew when they learned about culture care dimensions as they are so essential to nursing. The courses expand the student's thinking into a holistic view of people care especially influenced by Leininger's Culture Care Theory and advanced care concepts. Transcultural nursing faculty who are responsible for the courses are usually happy and excited to see students learn about transcultural nursing. Exhibit 1 in the Appendix gives some sample course content domains for faculty to consider.

The fourth teaching and curricular approach is to offer *a major program or substantive track in transcultural nursing with a series of courses and related learning experiences*. In the early 1970s the author launched the first programs and tracks in transcultural nursing in master (M.S.N.) and doctoral (Ph.D.) programs. A series of courses, including both classroom and clinical field experiences, continue to be offered as part of the program or track approach to transcultural nursing (see the Appendix for examples of graduate transcultural nursing content domains). Specialized preparation in transcultural nursing is now available in graduate programs in the United States. These programs lead to clinical specialization, advanced practitioner roles, and beginning teachers, and new leader roles in transcultural nursing.[15] Graduate transcultural specialization is comprehensive, complex, analytical, and has in-depth transcultural content with opportunities to learn about several cultures. A theoretical and practice focus is emphasized related to culture care, health, environmental context, and other related nursing dimensions. Transcultural undergraduate and graduate field experiences are now an expected requirement to make teaching content come alive and help the student develop clinical skills. These field or clinical experiences are with individuals, families and specific cultures in different communities, hospitals, or alternative care centers.

Transcultural nursing students find graduate programs are highly stimulating and essential to developing their cultural competencies through seminars and guided field studies. Graduate student specialists in transcultural nursing are prepared to work effectively and competently with clients of several cultures and to continue learning about other cultures in the future. Many graduates have been active leaders in advancing and changing nursing from a unicultural to a multicultural perspective and in introducing different practices of transcultural nursing into nursing and multidisciplinary practices. Most encouraging is the trend of some students to pursue doctoral study after B.S.N. or M.S.N. programs. The Ph.D. programs generally focus on transcultural nursing research, teaching, practice, and consultation. In contrast, the master's transcultural nursing program major varies from forty to fifty semester credits with sequenced courses in theory, research, and clinical findings in nursing practices. There is critical need for more graduate programs in transcultural nursing to meet worldwide needs in nursing.

Since many faculty wonder what could be offered in graduate programs, and example from the transcultural nursing program offered at Wayne State University for several years will be highlighted next. The purpose of the Master of Science in Nursing degree in transcultural nursing provides students with in-depth culture care knowledge and skills for working with individuals, families, and groups of various cultural backgrounds who reflect diverse values, beliefs, and lifeways. A variety of teaching approaches are used during the three to four semester programs; thirty-seven semester credits are required. Classroom and field experience enable students to become competent culture care practitioners, clinical specialists, consultants, and teachers in transcultural nursing. Graduates of the program are able to function as transcultural nurse specialist with specific cultures and to teach, conduct research, and serve as beginning consultants in the field. Wayne State University remains one of the major institutions in the world providing opportunities for students in master's, doctoral, and post-doctoral studies in transcultural nursing. All doctoral and post-doctoral courses and experiences are tailored to meet students' interests and goals in the field.

Some sample graduate course titles at Wayne State University are the following: Nursing and Health Care Environments; Transcultural Health throughout the Life Cycle; Transcultural Nursing: Theory, Research, and Practice; Field Practices in Transcultural Nursing; Culture Care Seminar; Transcultural Nursing Seminar; Qualitative Research Methods in Nursing; Transcultural Nursing Ethics and others. Often anthropological courses and other social sciences and humanities courses are recommended to expand student learning and to study related work in students' interest areas. The following courses from anthropology are often selected: Urban Anthropology; Gender: Cross Culturally; Anthropological Theory; Language and Culture; Magic, Illness and Health Conditions; Medical Anthropology; Ethnography of Four Urban Cultures; Area Ethnographies; and Physical Anthropology.

In masters programs in transcultural nursing students learn in-depth about three of four cultures and conduct an independent field study or thesis using a specific theoretical research method. Doctoral students focus in-depth on nursing theories and research methods and study a specific cultural area with an original study of a transcultural domain of inquiry for their dissertation. Creative and original dissertations in transcultural nursing are expected (see in the Appendix a sample list of Ph.D. research studies in transcultural nursing). Graduate seminars are planned so that they build upon, reinforce, expand and deepen student learning. Students present and defend their theoretical and research domains with faculty and seminar participants. Graduate students generally have innovative field research studies that generate new knowledge in transcultural nursing. These students have opportunities to be clinical and community consultants under clinical mentorship with transcultural nursing faculty.

A fifth teaching and curricular approach to advance transcultural nursing is *establishing and maintaining transcultural care institutes and/or centers*. With the rapidly growing demand for transcultural nursing education and practitioners worldwide, institutes and centers in transcultural nursing are greatly needed. The author has been a proponent of these institutes or centers for two decades, but funds for them have not been found in the United States. It is envisioned that transcultural nursing faculty experts in theory, research, and clinical work will teach and conduct research and scholarly forums on transcultural nursing in these institutes. Some interdisciplinary colleagues, such as anthropologists and sociologists, would also participate in the advanced seminars, research projects, and scholarly activities related to transcultural nursing. Regional centers or institutes need to be funded soon by private or public funds with scholarships and financial aid to meet the critical shortage of transcultural nurses and ultimately to improve health care to people of diverse cultures. Highly motivated graduate transcultural nursing students are already requesting these institutes or centers and also need fellowship monies to study with transcultural nurse experts.

Suggested Topic Domains for Undergraduate and Graduate Curricula

Since many faculty and students often inquire about general topic domains related to undergraduate and graduate transcultural nursing education, the author offers some suggestions in Exhibit 3. These content domains will vary with the institutional philosophy and with cultural areas and interests of faculty and students. Moreover, the scope, depth, and special foci will vary in undergraduate and graduate curricula, in particular with respect to the cultures in different geographic regions. Knowledge of common health and care needs of cultures in light of their ethnohistorical backgrounds, environment and cultural values are important considerations in the development of national, regional, or local curricula. For example, there may be large population groups of cultural immigrants such as Vietnamese, Cubans, Native Americans, Hutterites, or others in regional area that would need to be considered by the faculty. In Miami, Florida there are many Haitians, Puerto Ricans, and other Hispanic speaking groups that would be the foci of study and could be a regional area for transcultural nursing. Each school of nursing will vary with their goals, and with cultures living in their geographic area as well as with faculty experts in transcultural nursing for undergraduate and graduate curricula. The goal is to meet local and area needs, but also to expose students to different cultures worldwide.

Transcultural Nursing: A Creative Teaching and Learning Process

One of the exciting features of transcultural nursing is that teaching and learning about culture care and health in relation to nursing is a highly creative and stimulating experience. Transcultural nursing faculty are expected to open-minded, curious, and creative in teaching and working with students. Helping students and faculty learn together from cultural informants and from diverse life experiences about transcultural phenomena is important. This approach fits the principle and philosophy that transcultural nursing is largely based upon open emic discoveries largely derived from learning about cultures locally and worldwide. Transcultural nursing faculty generally use an inductive process as they learn from people of different or similar cultures with a focus on emic and etic comparative discoveries. Gaining comparative and in-depth insights about cultures with respect to care, health (or well-being), and environmental context are central to transcultural nursing. Establishing and maintaining a cultural ethos of *learning from and about others* in an active and listening manner is essential. Helping students to see "the whole picture" of people lifeways, rather than "bits and pieces" is used in teaching and guiding transcultural students. A gestaltic experiential approach helps students grasp a holistic and comprehensive picture of clients of diverse and similar cultures. Leininger's Culture Care Theory with the use of the Sunrise Model has been a great facilitator to help students look at the multiple factors influencing the care and health of individuals and groups. In addition, the transcultural nursing faculty maintain a strong caring and learning ethos to enable students to discover phenomena with sensitivity, openness, and special insight. There is great latitude to be innovative in teaching transcultural nursing and to draw upon faculty research experiences, the literature, and the growing body of transcultural nursing research. Maintaining a relaxed and open inquiry attitude while valuing the students, the clients, and the cultural context are important.

During the past several decades the author has formulated the following premises and beliefs related to teaching transcultural nursing in undergraduate and graduate programs:

1. Faculty and students need to be *co-participants in the learning and teaching process* to discover transcultural nursing phenomenon. While faculty members assume the major responsibility of facilitating transcultural learning, guiding the student's with specific observations and reflections related to life experiences is important.

2. Students and faculty bring *their cultural or personal heritage and experiences in the teaching-learning context and process* which includes their values, beliefs, and lifeways. Cultural heritage factors have special meanings, symbols, and insights which faculty and students need to discover and understand.

3. Nursing students need to study enculturation and socialization aspects of the culture of nursing, the health professions, and often the culture in the community in which one lives, studies, and serves people. Understanding other cultures and different nursing practices greatly increases one's insights about oneself and transcultural nursing patterns, values, and lifeways.

4. Student learning is generally effective when students are active participants and willing to get involved or *become immersed in a culture* as they study transcultural nursing phenomena. Comparative cultural reflections of one's own cultural experiences and others greatly expands student learning and an appreciation for differences and similarities among cultures. *Holding knowledge is imperative to practice.*

5. Transcultural nursing faculty are expected to help students reduce unfavorable or marked ethnocentrism, cultural biases, cultural imposition practices, and many other cultural expressions that tend to limit students' full potential to become a competent, effective, and responsible transcultural nurse.

6. Teaching transcultural nursing is *a mode of being with students in a caring relationship directed toward discovering experiences together.*

7. Discovering culture care *differences and similarities* between students and faculty, and between others in the culture of nursing is essential for intellectual and professional growth. Accordingly faculty are expected to be culture care facilitators to explicate comparative cultural care learning.

8. Selected and *diverse immersion in community field experiences* under qualified faculty mentorship is one of the richest and most powerful means to learn transcultural nursing and the culture care needs of cultures.

9. *Discovering, experiencing, documenting, and analyzing* one's own cultural values, beliefs, and patterned lifeways and those of cultural groups are essential to transcultural nursing and to make appropriate and beneficial nursing actions and decisions for clients.

10. Transcultural nursing theories are essential to guide students' critical thinking and to discover new or different patterns of culture care that can lead to health or well-being through the use of culture-specific or universal nursing care practices.

11. The theory of Culture Care with the use of the Sunrise Model serve as valuable holistic guides to provide comprehensive biophysical, social, political, spiritual, environmental, ethnohistorical, and language expressions of individuals, families, groups, cultures, and societies.

12. Transcultural nursing instruction is a humbling and gestaltic growth experience involving *learning from others* and also *risk-taking* and to using largely unknown ways to help people.

In teaching and doing research in transcultural nursing, a great variety of different methods and approaches are used today, such as the following: 1) oral and written life histories; 2) films, videotapes, and other audiovisual materials; 3) narratives, epics, and storytelling modes of student and client experiences; 4) direct immersion in cultures as lived experiences for short and long periods of time; 5) gestaltic lifestyle experiences; 6) use of reflection or meditation experiences; 7) hermeneutic phenomenology experiences; 8) cultural care interactional and value-focused incidents; and 8) short- and long-term ethnonursing experiences. These teaching methods, approaches, and material resources are but a few of many different teaching modes that can be used today to discover and facilitate students and learning about cultures with their care and health needs in different environmental contexts.

The author holds that students should have *at least one substantive transcultural nursing course with a mini-field experience before launching a major research study or being expected to function in a complex transcultural nursing position.* Students with preparation in transcultural nursing have demonstrated a reduction in experiencing culture shock, misinterpreting what they see, hear, or experience, avoiding legal problems, or in grossly misinterpreting people and situations. The courses and experiences help students identify whether they are racially biased, have prejudices about cultures, or have unfavorable motives to work in transcultural nursing. Most importantly, students learn much about themselves and other cultures through class discussions and field experiences.

Sometimes students without educational preparation have considerable problems when they work with cultures for which they have no transcultural knowledge. This is especially evident when students go into unfamiliar communities or overseas for cultural experiences. Sometimes students have to return because of serious intercultural and personal problems. Unfortunately, there is an erroneous and dangerous myth held by some faculty that students do not need to be prepared in advance before going overseas or to strange cultures. Instead, it is believed they can rely on "common sense," survive and do what is right professionally and personally. Some faculty even believe that whatever is communicated and experienced between students and the client (verbally or non-verbally) can be accurately understood and interpreted without culturally based holding knowledge and skills. The importance of *transcultural knowledge is essential for student learning and to survive and thrive in local and transnational cultural contexts.* Holding knowledge about the life cycle expectations offers student's a vital means to reflect upon what one sees, hears, and experiences, and to avoid cultural ignorance. Placing students in foreign lands for experiences without adequate preparation has led to serious problems, legal difficulties, and sometimes death. Some nursing students have returned home in culture shock, disappointed, angry, and are terribly disinterested in other cultures when they fail to understand cultures. This point is especially true with students who experience great differences between the student's culture and another culture. Hence, students should possess some prior transcultural knowledge before moving into strange or unknown cultures in order to understand people cues, survive and gain new insights.

There is also another myth that nursing students prepared in anthropology can function as transcultural nurses. Anthropology and nursing are two different disciplines. Nursing is a discipline and practice profession focused on humanistic care, health, and environmental context; whereas anthropology is a discipline that focuses on specific cultures over time and place. Unquestionably, knowledge of anthropology is most helpful in understanding cultures, but it falls short in understanding nursing care, health, illness, and nursing contextual phenomena. This becomes evident when non-nurse anthropologists teach and guide nursing students in the classroom, and clinical and field areas. There exists also the myth that transcultural nursing and cross-cultural nursing are one and the same.[17] This myth also needs to be changed when nurses realize that transcultural nursing has been deliberately chosen and developed by the author in the early 1960s and since then by others focusing explicitly on transcultural nursing phenomena. In contrast, cross-cultural nursing has generally focused primarily on anthropological knowledge for advancing the discipline of anthropology using different theoretical, research foci and goals.

Critical Issues and Problems Facing Transcultural Nurse Educators

In this last section some of the most critical issues and problems facing transcultural nurse educators and curriculum specialists will be identified. The following can be used for faculty awareness and discussion, as a means to alleviate, resolve, or prevent some of the current problems. The most critical issues are the following:

1. Employing faculty who are unprepared to teach transcultural nursing because of the assumptions that a) anyone can teach about cultures, b) if a nurse is of a culture she (he) knows that culture, and c) a teacher is a teacher regardless of one's cultural background and values.
2. Working with faculty and students who have strong cultural biases, racist attitudes, or who are frightened or refuse to work with certain cultures.
3. Teaching students from stranger cultures who do not value Western teaching modes such as open and direct questioning, confrontation questions, and having assertive teaching expectations or rigid requirements.
4. Working with faculty and students whose values and beliefs about certain cultures are counter-cultural and leads to moral distress and ethical dilemmas for them.
5. The misuse and overemphasis of cultural diversity as transcultural nursing, failing to emphasize cultural similarities. Most faculty do not realize that cultural diversity is only one aspect of, not the totality of transcultural nursing.

6. Problems of matching faculty and students of the same cultural background, which greatly limits transcultural learning opportunities, e.g., African American students with African American faculty, etc.

7. The tendency of faculty to teach transcultural nursing as "traits" of cultures or to use cookbook characteristics of cultures for cultural stereotyping assessment such as found with Mosley's mini-cultural assessment publication.[18] This can lead to narrow, limited, and inaccurate ideas to guide nurses' thinking about cultures and health care.

8. Misusing or remaining dependent upon translators in client care, teaching, and research rather than learning to speak the native language.

9. Using ethnonursing data, client family stories, field journal notes, and other cultural information for classroom teaching when permission was not granted by the informants.

10. Conceptual problems in shifting students from a narrow and fragmented medical and nursing perspective to a broad holistic cultural view and other ways of knowing people.

11. Overuse and dependency on tape recordings with cultural informants or clients for teaching and research purposes rather than using direct talk experiences, field journal data, naturalistic modes of inquiry, and appropriate qualitative discovery methods.

12. Devaluing or demeaning the importance and therapeutic benefits of folk (generic) care practices of clients and giving far too much emphasis to scientific or professional facts or experiences.

13. Using culture-bound, biased, and inappropriate instruments and scales in nursing research and for teaching purposes that limit understanding people and specific cultures. Looking for measurable outcomes and missing non-measurable qualities and ways of knowing cultures.

14. Lack of identification of academic ethical issues related to student-faculty cultural imposition, clashes, and related problems that limit student sharing and learning.

15. Conducting overseas exchange programs with faculty and students who have had no advance preparation for the experience.

16. Lack of local and national funds in nursing to study transcultural nursing phenomena or to change nursing curricula from a unicultural to multicultural focus as well as lack of funds for institutes and centers.

17. Lack of research funds to support mainly qualitative paradigmatic studies in transcultural nursing in order to discover emic and etic culture care and health knowledge.

18. Inappropriate use of nursing diagnoses and misdiagnoses of cultural expressions that fail to meet emic cultural values and lifeways of the people.

19. Lack of administrative support from deans and others for transcultural nursing faculty, teaching, research, and curriculum development.

20. Failure to use transcultural nursing research and publications to advance transcultural knowledge.

The above critical issues can be used in faculty awareness discussions and to stimulate ways to overcome these problems in schools of nursing and clinical settings.

In this chapter several trends of and reasons for the importance of transcultural nursing education have been presented. The general and important thesis is to prepare nurses in transcultural nursing in order to meet critical, worldwide needs of caring for clients of diverse or similar cultures. The goal is to prepare culturally competent and responsible nurses. Several trends and critical issues were identified so that excellence in teaching transcultural nursing will be supported. The author contends *that all nurses need to be prepared in transcultural nursing in order to survive and develop quality nursing care practices.* Time is urgent and limited to prepare nurses in transcultural nursing because of worldwide multicultural needs and conditions impacting on quality health care services. Several suggested objectives and content domains for undergraduate and graduate nursing education and curricula were offered along with teaching methods and approaches. In the last section some critical issues and ethical dilemmas were identified for faculty discussion and consideration to advance transcultural nursing education. The author leaves the reader with the idea to consider in relation to *transcultural nursing education: the most significant development and challenge for nursing in the twenty-first century will be educating nearly five million nurses in the world to become culturally competent and effective to serve the culturally neglected, oppressed, or misunderstood people in the world. Nursing will hopefully meet this challenge in the immediate future.*

References

1. Leininger, M., Transcultural Nursing: Concepts, Theories, and Practices, New York: John Wiley and Sons, 1978.
2. Leininger, M., "A New Generation of Nurses Discover Transcultural Nursing," Nursing and Health Care, v. 8, no. 5, May, 1987, p. 3.
3. Leininger, M., "Transcultural Nursing: An Essential Knowledge Field for Today," The Canadian Nurse, v. 30, no. 11, December 1984, pp. 41–45.
4. Leininger, M., "Cultural Dimensions in the Baccalaureate Nursing Curriculum," Cultural Dimensions in the Baccalaureate Nursing Curriculum, New York: National League for Nursing Press, 1977, pp. 85–107.
5. Leininger, op. cit., 1978.
6. Leininger, M., Teaching Transcultural Care Theory, Principles, and Concepts in Schools of Nursing, unpublished manuscript, 1992.
7. Leininger, M., Survey of Nursing Programs with Transcultural Faculty, Courses, and Programs, unpublished survey, 1994.
8. Ibid.
9. Leininger, M., "Report and Recommendations for the First National Conference on Teaching Transcultural Nursing," Journal of Transcultural Nursing, v. 4, no. 11, Summer, 1993, pp. 41–42.
10. Andrews, M., "Educational Preparation for International Nursing," Journal of Professional Nursing, v. 4, no. 6, 1988, pp. 430–433.
11. Leininger, op. cit., 1978.
12. Carpio, B. and B. Majumdar, "Experiential Learning: An Approach to Transcultural Education for Nursing," Journal of Transcultural Nursing, v. 4, no. 2, 1993, pp. 32–33.
13. DeSantis, L., "Developing Faculty Expertise in Culturally Focused Care and Research," Journal of Professional Nursing, v. 7, no. 5, 1991, pp.
14. Leininger, M., op. cit., 1978.
15. Leininger, M., "The Significance of Transcultural Concepts in Nursing," Journal of Transcultural Nursing, v. 2, no. 1, 1990 pp. 52–59.
16. Leininger, M., "Transcultural Nurse Specialists and Generalists: New Practitioners in Nursing," Journal of Transcultural Nursing, v. 1, no. 1, Summer, 1989, pp. 33–46.
17. Leininger, M., "Strange Myths and Inaccurate Facts in Transcultural Nursing," Journal of Transcultural Nursing, v. 4, no. 2, Winter, 1992, pp. 39–40.
18. Geissler, C. M., Pocket Guide to Cultural Assessments, St. Louis: Mosby Year Book, Inc., 1993.

Exhibit 1

Sample Transcultural Undergraduate Nursing Course (BSN)

Title: Transcultural Nursing: Concepts, Principles, Theories, Research
                      and Practices
Credits: 3 Semester Credits
Placement: Early in Undergraduate Program
Instructors: Faculty with Graduate Preparation in Transcultural Nursing

Course Description

This is an introductory undergraduate course focused on transcultural nursing with care as the central phenomenon to promote health and well-being. This course is designed to help students learn about culture care beliefs, values and practices of specific cultures and subcultures. In addition, the student learns how to assess the culture care differences of and similarities among cultures to provide culturally congruent and competent nursing care. The student learns how to use a nursing theory to discover and guide nursing care practices and living contexts. Specific transcultural nursing concepts, principles and strategies are learned to facilitate nursing decisions and actions. Contemporary transcultural nursing conditions, gender problems and diverse issues are identified to assist students in conceptualizing and working through problem areas related to culture care nursing practices in diverse environmental contexts.

Course Objectives

Upon completion of the course, students will be able to:
1. Identify reasons for the development and importance of transcultural nursing in improving people care from diverse cultures.
2. Discuss the major historical developments, achievements and leaders that shaped the field of transcultural nursing.
3. Use major transcultural nursing constructs and principles to assess client needs and guide transcultural nursing practices.

4. Discuss the importance of the theory of Culture Care Diversity and Universality as a major theory to provide culturally congruent, sensitive, and responsible care throughout the life cycle.
5. Compare generic (folk) and professional health care and illness beliefs, values and practices among clients and health personnel of diverse cultures with gender and social structure factors.
6. Examine tendencies for cultural and gender biases, ethnocentrism, cultural blindness and imposition practices.
7. Demonstrate ways to provide culturally congruent and competent nursing care from infancy through old age.
8. Discuss the importance of culture care research and health in diverse environmental contexts for people well-being and to prevent illness.

Teaching-Learning Methods or Experiences

A great variety of teaching learning methods can be used for this course, such as the following:

A. Direct observations
B. Participation and interaction accounts
C. Reflective analysis and discussion of daily cultural life events
D. Use of client-student encounters or situations
E. Use of cultural and transcultural nursing films
F. Open discussion on cultural heritage and life experiences
G. Transcultural games, skits and lifecycle events
H. Use of student experiential accounts
I. Storytelling and narratives related to particular cultures
J. Lecture-discussion exchanges between faculty and students
K. Panel presentations on specific cultures or subcultures
L. Use of poems, paintings, drawings related to culture care and health
M. Use of biographies of cultural representatives
N. Use of ethnonursing field journal data

All students are expected to know how to do culturalogical holistic care and health assessments. In addition, students prepare a 15-16 (double-spaced) term paper on a specific culture. This paper should reflect a focused emphasis on transcultural nursing care theory, principles and concepts and ways to provide culturally congruent care.

Content Domains with Diverse Teaching Methods and Strategies

I. Introduction to transcultural nursing: Cultural diversities and similarities.
   A. Student's knowledge and views of transcultural nursing.
   B. Orientational definition of transcultural nursing.

C. Purposes and goals of transcultural nursing.

D. World forces and influencing the need for transcultural nursing.

E. Philosophical and practical knowledge in developing the field.

II. Discovering the historical factors that lead to establishing transcultural nursing (focus on Leininger's Three Eras of transcultural nursing — see references).

    A. Early and later developments in transcultural nursing

    B. Leaders and their specific contributions

    C. Barriers and facilitators in developing the field

III. Discussion of major concepts, definitions and expressions of transcultural nursing using many examples and life events from different cultures.

1.	Human care/caring	10.	Culture pain
2.	Culture, culture values and culture beliefs	11.	Cultural diversity
3.	Culture care	12.	Culture similarities
4.	Health and well-being	13.	Culture conflicts
5.	Ethnocentrism	14.	Culture context
6.	Cultural imposition	15.	Cultural sensitivity
7.	Emic and etic	16.	Cultural backlash
8.	Culture shock	17.	Uni- and multiculturalism
9.	Culture clashes	18.	Other concepts

IV. Understanding the importance of language, culture context, culture history and lifeways of specific cultures in community context with a transcultural nursing focus.

V. Identifying lifecycle processes and their meanings (use examples)

    A. Assimilation

    B. Enculturalism

    C. Socialization

    D. Acculturation

    E. Gender role and age expectations

VI. Discovering the culture of nursing, the culture of the hospitals, the culture of medicine and other cultures in health systems.

VII. Identifying American culture values, beliefs and lifeways and contrasts with other world cultures (comparative analysis).

VIII. Discovering the meaning and relevance of the theory of Culture Care Diversity and Universality with the Sunrise Model to assess clients and guide nursing actions and decision.

    A. Discussion of the Culture Care Diversity and Universality Theory: Major purposes and uses

    B. Meaning of worldview

    C. Use of social structure factors which includes economic, kinship structure, religion and spirituality, philosophy of life, legal views, education, specific cultural values and beliefs, and technologies.

    D. Meaning of environmental context(s)

    E. Importance of language and communication modes

    F. Importance of ethnohistorical factors

    G. Relevance of generic and professional care practices

    H.   Use of Leininger's three modes of nursing actions and decision to provide culturally congruent nursing care
        1.   Culture care preservation and maintenance
        2.   Culture care accommodation and negotiations
        3.   Culture care repatterning and restructuring
        4.   Indicators of culturally competent and congruent nursing care

IX. Learning how to do culturological health care assessments using the culture care theory and Sunrise Model (students gain considerable knowledge and skills in this area taking different roles in a culture as client, family or as nurse).

X. Discussion of the use of research findings from the literature on specific cultures.

XI. Exploring and discovery of comparative lifecycle beliefs, values, lifeways with gender and age considerations in at least two cultures with focus on human caring and health.
    A.   Prenatal through early infancy
    B.   Early childhood era
    C.   Adolescent period
    D.   Middlescence
    E.   Early and advanced years

XII. Discovering special transcultural conditions, meanings, and problems with cultures such as African, Mexican, Arabs, Polish, Native Americans, and Asian-Japanese-Chinese.
    A.   Expressions of cultural pain in diverse cultures
    B.   Expressions of grief and dying in different cultures
    C.   Chronic and acute illness and disabilities in diverse cultures
    D.   Ethical, moral and spiritual dilemmas in transcultural nursing
    E.   Healing, caring and curing practices

XIII. Discovering the meaning and realities of transcultural mental health and care needs.
    A.   Cultural interpretations of normal and deviant behaviors
    B.   Culture-bound conditions and healing modes
    C.   Misdiagnoses and misconceptions of mental health and illness
    D.   Role of mental health healers, carers and cureres

XIV. Discovering transcultural nursing as a meaningful and important career
    A.   Career opportunities in transcultural nursing in different countries
    B.   Transcultural care and specialist functions and roles
    C.   Economic, political, and interprofessional issues

XV. Demonstration of ways to make appropriate transcultural nursing decisions, actions and judgements. Evaluation of the different transcultural nursing actions and decisions. This is an important session to let students demonstrate their skills and practices in transcultural nursing within different clinical, community and classroom contexts.

References

See extensive references cited in the appendix of this book for this course.

Exhibit 2
Sample Transcultural
Graduate Nursing Course

Title: Advanced Transcultural Nursing
Credits: 3-4 Graduate Semester Credits
Placement: Early in Master Nursing Degree Program
Instructors: Faculty with Graduate (MSN or PhD) or post-baccalaureate degree
                with preparation in Transcultural Nursing

Course Description

   This graduate course is focused on the philosophy, historical leaders, theories, research and practices related to transcultural nursing as a formal area of study and practice. The course is focused on the trends, issues and developments of transcultural nursing as a specialty and general area of study and practice. Theoretical perspectives, anthropological concepts and diverse research methods are discussed with the goal of improving the quality of care to people of diverse cultures. Ethnonursing, ethnography and other qualitative research methods are considered to generate and analyze transcultural care phenomena. Cultural differences and similarities in care health beliefs, values and practices of Western and non-Western cultures with an emphasis on emic and etic factors are used to reaffirm, establish or discover new knowledge in the field. Leininger's theory of Culture Care is examined along with selected other theories and research studies generated from the theories. Future directions of transcultural nursing are discussed with worldwide perspectives of different cultures and subcultures.

Course Objectives — Upon completion of the course, the student will be able to:

1. Analyze philosophical, historical and cultural trends and issues influencing the development and evolution of the field of transcultural nursing and its impact on many areas in nursing.
2. Analyze different emic and etic cultural beliefs, values and practices of Western and non-Western cultures using anthropological, clinical and specific transcultural nursing concepts, theories and research relevant to different cultures.

3. Discuss the use of major transcultural nursing concepts, principles, theories and research findings as substantive and advanced transcultural nursing clinical community knowledge to advance and improve nursing care throughout the life cycle.

4. Analyze the meanings and expressions of diverse and similar cultures of nursing.

5. Demonstrate the use of Leininger's theory of Culture Care Diversity and Universality to advance transcultural nursing knowledge and practices in Western and non-Western cultures with use of research findings from the theory.

6. Analyze folk (generic) and professional care practices of selected cultures, supporting ways to provide culturally sensitive and congruent nursing care.

7. Demonstrate the uses of culturological health care assessments in transcultural nursing practices in clinical and community services or in nursing education.

8. Discuss the rationale and use of selected qualitative or quantitative research methods to study transcultural nursing phenomena in different cultures or subcultures.

9. Discuss critical issues, trends and problems related to contemporary transcultural nursing and ways to resolve these issues or problems to advance nursing worldwide.

10. Analyze state-of-the-art and transcultural nursing knowledge in education, research, consultation and in rural and urban clinical contexts.

11. Analyze the ethical and moral issues in transcultural nursing in relation to nursing practices in the care of people of different cultures or subcultures.

12. Demonstrate the use of literature and research findings in transcultural nursing education, curricular work and other areas of nursing.

Suggested Content Domains:

1. Historical, philosophical, epistemological and cultural factors that influenced the development of the field of transcultural nursing as a legitimate and specialty area of study and practice in nursing.

2. Current issues, trends and problems that have facilitated or impeded the development of transcultural nursing in the country and worldwide.

3. Leaders and followers in the globalization of transcultural nursing: their achievements and contributions under diverse conditions.

4. The past, current and future relationship of anthropology and related fields to transcultural nursing: commonalties and differences.

5. The culture(s) and tribes of nursing in a specific country.

6. Conceptual models, theoretical formulations and domains of inquiry that have been used to study transcultural nursing phenomena worldwide and throughout the life cycle.

7. Theories related to the study of transcultural nursing, especially use of Leininger's theory of Cultural Care Diversity and Universality.

8. Generic folk and professional nursing emic and etic knowledge as essential to advance transcultural nursing practices.

9. Culturalolgical care assessments and the use of data for individual, family and community culture care to provide culturally congruent, competent and beneficial care practices.

10. The roles of the transcultural nurse specialist and generalist in nursing education, consultation and administration.

11. Use of qualitative and quantitative comparative research methods to study transcultural nursing phenomena in relation to care, health, illness, well-being, environmental context and other nursing dimensions.

12. Ethical, moral and legal issues related to transcultural nursing research, practice and the problems with using the NANDA nursing diagnosis in diverse cultures.

13. Globalization of nursing education and administration to meet multicultural health and nursing care needs of people worldwide.

14. Trends, issues, and problems in nursing education, administration and consultation to prepare nurses in providing culture-specific and culturally congruent nursing care to people in diverse environmental contexts.

15. Intra- and interprofessional cultural clashes with different health care values and practices and ways to resolve them.

16. Future directions, issues, and challenges to establish transcultural nursing as the arching framework for all areas of nursing, nationally and transnationally by the year 2020.

17. Strengths and limitations of research studies, theories and instruments that are culture-bond, biased or inappropriate for credible transcultural knowledge.

Teaching Methods

The course is taught as a graduate seminar. Each student is expected to 1) be an active, informed participant; 2) assume the role of seminar leader for one or two topic domains; 3) read widely and critically on topics; 4) meet general course objectives; 5) demonstrate creative thinking and work.

Student Learning and Evaluation Areas:

1. **Demonstrating Active Seminar Participation:** Student uses literature in the field to advance ideas, ask scholarly questions, uses theories appropriately and demonstrates creative ideas and research suggestions.

2. **Demonstrates Skill in Oral Presentation:** Student presents in seminar on an area of particular interest in transcultural nursing. The student presents domain of the inquiry, literature and research methods to study the domain with theoretical interests and a specific research design. The student discusses ideas to advance transcultural nursing knowledge and improve client care.

3. **Completes Term Paper:** The student is expected to develop a scholarly term paper that will demonstrate in-depth knowledge and the creative study of a specific domain of transcultural nursing. The term paper will give evidence of scholarly and critical thinking in the domain, use of literature, use of a theory and use of research plans to study the phenomenon or domain of inquiry. The student's creative thinking, theoretical and research perspectives are important as well as cultural sensitivity.

References for Course (see Appendix A)

Exhibit 3
Suggested Undergraduate and Graduate <u>Common</u> Transcultural Nursing Knowledge Domains

These content domains below are suggested for teaching transcultural nursing in undergraduate and graduate programs. The scope and depth of content will vary with the philosophy and curricula of the programs, the students' needs, faculty expertise, and the cultures in the area, region, or transnationally. These content domains can be considerably expanded and used in creative ways for teaching transcultural nursing and to plan for specific learning experiences.

1. Discussion of the definition, nature, scope and meaning of transcultural nursing, culture care and culturally sensitive, competent, and responsible care.
2. Examination of the rationale, goals and importance of transcultural nursing locally, nationally and worldwide.
3. Discussion of the evolutionary phases of transcultural nursing as developed and implemented by transcultural nurse leaders.
4. Discussion of the evolutionary phases of transcultural nursing as developed and implemented by transcultural nurse leaders.
5. Discussion of reality dimensions of transcultural nursing to improve people care, advance knowledge and transform nursing education and practice, including relations to anthropology, nurse specialty areas, and other areas relevant to transcultural nursing and health care.
6. Analysis of the progress, challenges, and major barriers to establishing transcultural nursing as a global area of study and practice.
7. Discussion of the conceptual ideas and meanings of care, caring and culture care as central to the transcultural nursing field based on research studies bearing on transcultural nursing.
8. Reflections on the conceptualizations of health, well-being, illness, diseases, oncology and environmental context in relation to transcultural nursing.
9. Discussion of the meaning and clinical/community uses of care concepts, constructs and principles developed for study in transcultural nursing, e.g., worldview, culture care, health, well-being, bioculturism, ethnocentrism, cultural imposition, cultural clashes, cultural conflict and shock, cultural context, cultural

blindness, cultural pain, cultural taboos, culture care, health variations, cultural change, cultural diversities and similarities, culture care values and norms, cultural authenticity, care patterns and expressions, health and well-being patterns and expressions, enculturation, assimilation, rights of passage, culture-bound conditions, prejudice, discrimination and racism.

10. Discussion of the meanings and importance of generic (folk) and professional care, and *emic* and *etic* perspectives to establish and advance transcultural nursing knowledge and practices.

11. Discussion of the cultures of nursing, hospitals and other health disciplines and their impact on nursing care practice decisions, discipline and development of transcultural nursing and health practices.

12. Examination of the theories pertinent to advance transcultural nursing, especially Leininger's theory of Culture Care Diversity and Universality with the use of the Sunrise Model as a central and specific transcultural nursing theory. Discussion of other relevant theories useful to advance the study of transcultural nursing and human care.

13. Discussion of the principles and guidelines for a culturological holistic care assessment providing examples and real experiences of students, researchers and transcultural nurse practitioners.

14. Discussion of the biocultural, biogenetic, social, and ecological dimensions of transcultural health care in diverse environmental contexts.

15. Examples of the meaning of providing culturally sensitive, responsible and competent care; popular meanings and misuses by nurses; and uses of concepts to improve people care.

16. Discussion of comparative birth to death life cycle phenomenon in relation to transcultural practices and use with Leininger's three models: 1) Culture care preservation and maintenance; 2) Culture care accommodation and negotiation; and 3) culture care repatterning and restructuring.

17. Critical examination of past and current transcultural research studies and uses to improve people care, includes diverse research methods such as ethnonursing qualitative methods and quantitative methods, plus diverse strategies in research.

18. Discussion of the ethical and moral dimensions of transcultural nursing in client care, research and educational processes drawing upon research studies and philosophic stances.

19. Discussion of transcultural nursing and international consultation, exchanges and collaborative practices with issues and trends.

20. Discussion of future directions and issues in transcultural nursing, including the globalization and particularization of transcultural nursing in different places in the world with projected benefits.

21. Critique of transcultural nursing progress and related research literature related to diverse cultures as means to improve the well-being and health of people, or to help people face death or disabilities.

22. Discussion of the meanings and experience of transcultural nursing to the student in educational and clinical contexts.

Exhibit 4
Sample of Dissertation Studies Focused on Transcultural Nursing

The following dissertations studies focused on transcultural nursing research and theory and were completed under the dissertation guidance of Professor Madeleine Leininger, PhD, RN, CTN, LHD, FAAN, at Wayne State University, College of Nursing, Detroit, Michigan. They are offered as examples of doctoral research investigations in transcultural nursing.

1994

Joan MacNeil, PhD, *Culture Care: Meanings, Patterns, and Expressions for Baganda Women as AIDS Caregivers within Leininger's Theory*
Marjorie Morgan, PhD, *African American Neonatal Care in Northern and Southern Contexts using Leininger's Culture Care Theory*
Rauda Gelazis, PhD, *Lithuanian Care Meanings and Experiences with Humor Using Leininger's Cultural Care Theory*

1993

Julianna Finn, PhD, Professional Nurse and Generic Caregiving of childbirthing Women Conceptualized with Leininger's Theory of Cultural Care and Using the Phenomenological Method
Antonia Villarruel, PhD, *Mexican American Cultural Meanings, Expressions, Self-Care, and Dependent Care Actions Associated with Experiences of Pain*

1991

Zenaida Spangler, PhD, *Nursing Care Values and Practices of Philippine American and Anglo-American Nurses*

1990

Cynthia Cameron, PhD, *An Ethnonursing Study of Health Status of Elderly Anglo Canadian Wives Providing Extended Caregiving to Their Disabled Husbands*
Theresa Thompson, PhD, *A Qualitative Investigation of Rehabilitation Nursing Care in an Inpatient Rehabilitation Unit Using Leininger's Theory*
Janet Rosenbaum, PhD, *Cultural Care, Culture Health, and Grief Phenomena Related to Older Greek Canadian Widows with Leininger's Theory of Culture Care*

1989

Linda Luna, PhD, *Care and Cultural Context of Lebanese Muslims in an Urban US Community within Leininger's Cultural Care Theory*

1988

Marie Gates, PhD, *Care and Care Meanings, Experiences, and Orientations of Persons Dying in Hospital and Hospital Settings*
Anna Frances Wenger, PhD, *The Phenomenon of Care of the Older Order Amish: A High Context Culture*

APPENDIX A
References to Support Transcultural Nursing Education and Research

BOOKS

Agar, M.H. (1980). *The professional stranger: An informal introduction to ethnography.* New York: Academic Press.

Amoss, P.T. & Harrell, S. (1981). *Other ways of growing old: An anthropological perspective.* Stanford, CA: Stanford University Press.

Archer, D. & Gartner, R. (1984). *Violence and crime in cross-cultural perspective.* New Haven: Yale University Press.

Becerra, R.M. & Shaw, D. (1984). *The elderly Hispanic: A research and reference guide.* Lanham, MD: University Press of America.

Boyle, J. & Andrews, M. (1995). *Transcultural concepts in nursing care.* Hagerstown, MD, T. B. Lippincott Co.

Brink, P. (1984). *Transcultural nursing: A book of readings.* Englewood Cliffs, NJ: Prentice Hall.

Brown, J. & Kerns, V. (1985). *In her prime: A new view of middle aged women.* MA: Bergen & Garvey Publishers, Inc.

Bryant, C.A. (1985). *The cultural feast: An introduction to food and society.* St. Paul, MN: West.

Caddy, D. (1972). *Culture, disease, and healing: Studies in medical anthropology.* New York, NY: MacMillan.

Carson, V.B. (1989). *Spiritual dimensions of nursing practice.* Philadelphia, PA: W.B. Saunders.

Carnegie, M.E. (1987). *The path We tread: Blacks in nursing 1954-1984.* Philadelphia, PA: J.B. Lippincott.

Comas-Diaz, L. & Griffith, E.E.H. (1988). *Clinical guidelines in cross-cultural mental health.* New York, NY: J. Wiley & Sons.

Dobson, S. (1991). *Transcultural nursing.* London: Acutari Press.

Kolenda, P. (1988). *Cultural constructions of women.* New York, NY: Sheffield Publishing Co.

Langness, L. L. & Frank G.

Langness, L.L. & Frank G. (1987). *Lives: An anthropological approach to biography.* Novato, CA: Chandler & Sharp Publishers, Inc.

Lawless, E.J. (1988). *God's peculiar people.* Lexington, KY: University of Kentucky Press.

Lefcowitz, E. (1990). *The United States immigration history timeline.* New York, NY: Terra Firma Press.

Leininger, M. (1995). *Transcultural Nursing: Concepts, Theories, Research, and Practices.* New York and Columbus: McGraw Hill and Greyden Press.

Leininger, M. (1994). *Nursing and Anthropology: Two Worlds to Blend.* Columbus, OH: Greyden Press (originally published in 1970, New York, NY: John Wiley & Sons).

Leininger, M. (1994). *Transcultural nursing: Concepts, theories, and practices.* Columbus, OH: Greyden Press (originally published in 1974, New York, NY: John Wiley & Sons).

Leininger, M. (1979). *Transcultural nursing-1979.* New York, NY: Masson Publishing Co. This book contains the following proceedings of three National Transcultural Nursing Conferences: 1) Transcultural nursing care of infants and children, 2) Transcultural nursing care of the adolescent and middle years, and, 3) Transcultural nursing care of the elderly.

Leininger, M. (1985). *Qualitative research methods in nursing.* Orlando, FL: Grune & Stratton, Inc. (First book by nurse researchers).

Leininger, M. (1988). *Care: The essence of nursing and health.* Detroit, MI: Wayne State University Press. (First published by Slack Inc., 1984).

Leininger, M. (1988) *Care: Discovery and uses in clinical community nursing.* Detroit, MI: Wayne State University Press.

Leininger, M. (1988). Care: *An essential human need.* Detroit, MI: Wayne State University Press. (First published by Slack Inc., 1981).

Leininger, M. (1990). *Ethical and moral dimensions of care.* Detroit, MI: Wayne State University Press.

Leininger, M. (1991). *Culture care diversity and universality: A theory of nursing.* New York, NY: National League for Nursing Press.

Leininger, M. (1994). *Transcultural nursing: Concepts, theories, and practices* (2nd Ed). New York, NY: National League for Nursing Press.

Lincoln, Y. & Guba, E. (1985). *Naturalistic inquiry.* Newbury Park, CA: Sage Publications.

MacElroy, A. & Townsend, P. (1988). *Medical anthropology* (2nd. Ed.). Boulder, CO: Westview Press.

Mead, M. (1956). *Understanding cultural patterns.* Nursing Outlook 4, 260-262. Meyer, C.E. (1985). *American folk medicine.* Glenwood, IL: Meyerbooks.

Moore, et.al.. (1990). *The biocultural basis of health* (2nd Ed.). St. Louis, MO: C.V. Mosby.

Meyer, C.E. (1985). *American folk medicine.* Glenwood, IL: Meyerbooks.

Norbeck E. & Lock M. (1987). *Health, illness, and medical care in Japan.* Honolulu, HI: University of Hawaii Press.

Oswalt W. (1986). *Life cycles and lifeways: An introduction to cultural anthropology.* Palo Alto, CA: Mayfield Publishing Co.

Pederson, P. (1986). *Counseling across cultures.* Honolulu, HI: University of Hawaii Press.

Rosenthal, M. (1987). *Health care in the People's Republic of China.* Boulder, CO: Westview Press.

Spector, R. (1991). *Cultural diversity in health and illness (3rd Ed.).* Norwalk, CT: Appleton & Lange.

Spector, R. (1993). *Culture, ethnicity, and nursing.* In Potter, P.A. & Perry, A.G. (Eds.) Fundamentals of nursing (3rd Ed.). St. Louis, MO: Mosby Yearbook pp. 95-116.

Spradley, J.P. (1970). *You owe yourself a drink.* Boston, MA: Little, Brown, & Co.

Spradley, J. (1979). *The ethnographic interview.* New York, NY: Holt, Rinehardt, & Winston.

Spradley, J. (1980). *Participant observation.* New York, NY: Holt, Rinehardt, & Winston.

Stewart, E. & Bennett, M. (1991). *American cultural patterns* (rev. ed.). Yarmouth, ME: Intercultural Press, Inc.

Strange, H., Teitelbaum, M., & Contributors (1987). *Aging and cultural diversity.* South Hadley, MA: Bergin & Garvey.

Tweddell, C. & Kimball, L.A. (1985). *Introduction to the people's and cultures of Asia.* Englewood Cliffs, NJ: Prentice Hall.

VanGennep, A. (1960). *The rites of passage.* (Translated by M.B. Vizedom & G.L. Caffee). Chicago, IL: University of Chicago Press. (Originally published in 1909).

Whiting, B. (1963). *Six cultures.* New York NY: John Wiley & Sons.

Whiting, B. & Edwards, C. (1988). *Children of different worlds: The formation of social behavior.* Cambridge, MA: Harvard University Press.

Williams, T. (1990). *Cultural anthropology.* Englewood Cliffs, NJ: Prentice Hall.

Wolf, A. (1988). *Nurse's work: The sacred and the profane.* Philadelphia, PA: University of Pennsylvania Press.

Worsley, P.W. (1984). *The three worlds: Culture and world development.* Chicago, IL: University of Chicago Press.

Zambrana, R.E. (1982). New York, NY: Fordham University.

CHAPTERS AND ARTICLES

NOTE: *The Journal of Transcultural Nursing,* M. Leininger, Editor, is the official refereed publication of the Transcultural Nursing Society. It is a major source to learn about transcultural nursing phenomena.

Bernal, H. & Woman, R. (1993). Influences on the cultural self-efficacy of community health nurses. *Journal of Transcultural Nursing, 4*(2), 24-31.

Bodner, A. and Leininger, M. (1992). Transcultural nursing care values, beliefs, and practices of American (USA) gypsies, *Journal of Transcultural Nursing 4*(1), 17-28.

Brink, P. & Saunders, J. (1976). Cultural shock: Theoretical and applied. In P. Brink (Ed.) *Transcultural Nursing: A Book of Readings.* Englewood Cliffs, NJ: Prentice Hall.

Burkhardt, M.A. (1993). Characteristics of spirituality in the lives of women in a rural Appalachian community. *Journal of Transcultural Nursing 4*(2), 12- 18.

Cabral, H. et.al. (1990). Foreign born and United States born black women: Differences in health behaviors and birth outcomes. *The American Journal of Public Health,* 80, 70-72.

Carpio, B.A. & Majumdar, B. (1993). Experiential learning: An approach to transcultural education for nursing. *Journal of Transcultural Nursing 4*(2), 4- 11.

Chmielarczyk V. (1991). Transcultural nursing: Providing culturally congruent care to the Hausa of Northwest Africa, *Journal of Transcultural Nursing 3*(1), 15-20.

Chrisman, N. (1990). Cultural shock in the operating room: Cultural analysis in transcultural nursing. *Journal of Transcultural Nursing 1*(2), 33-39.

Conway, F.J. & Carmona, P.E. (1989). Cultural complexity: The hidden stressors. *Journal of Advanced Medical Surgical Nursing, 1*(4), 65-72.

DeSantis, L. & Thomas, J. (1990). The immigrant Haitian mother: Transcultural nursing perspective on preventive health care for children. *Journal of Transcultural Nursing,* 2(1), 2-15

Duffy, S., Bonino, K., Gallup, L. and Pontseele, R. (1994). The community baby shower as a transcultural nursing intervention, *Journal of Transcultural Nursing, 5*(2), 38-41.

Eliason, M.J. (1993). Cultural diversity in nursing care: The lesbian, gay, or bisexual client, *Journal of Transcultural Nursing,* 5(1), 14-20.

Field, L. (1991). Response to published article: Nursing diagnosis, *Journal of Transcultural Nursing, 3*(1), 325-30.

Finn, J. (1993). A transcultural nurse's adventures in Costa Rica: Using Leininger's Sunrise Model for transcultural nursing discoveries. *Journal of Transcultural Nursing,* 2(2), 18- 23.

Finn, J. (1994). Culture care of Euro American women during childbirth: Applying Leininger's theory for transcultural nursing discoveries, *Journal of Transcultural Nursing, 5*(2), 25- 37.

Foreman, J.T. (1985). Susto and the health needs for the Cuban refugee population: Symptoms of depression and withdrawal from moral social activity. *Topics in clinical nursing,* 70), 40- 47.

Friede, A., et.al. (1988). Transmission of hepatitis B virus from adopted Asian children to their American families. *American Journal of Public Health,* 78, 26-30.

Frye, B.A. (1990). The Cambodian refugee patient: Providing culturally sensitive rehabilitation nursing care. *Rehabilitation Nursing,* 15(3), 156-158.

Gates, M. (1991). Transcultural comparison of hospital as caring environments for dying patients. *Journal of Transcultural Nursing,* 2(2), 3- 15.

Giger J. and Davidhizar, R. (1995) *Transcultural Nursing* second ed. St. Louis, MO., Mosby Co.

Glittenberg, J.E. *To the Mountain and Back: The Mysteries of Guatemalan Highland Family Life,* Prospect Heights, IL., Waveland Press 1994.

Glittenberg, J.E. (1974). Adapting health care to a cultural setting. *American Journal of Nursing, 74,* 12, 2218-2221.

Hilger, M. (1960). Field guide to ethnological study of child life. *Human Relations Area Files: Behavior Science Field Guides,* New Haven, CT.

Hobus, R. (1990). Living in two worlds: A Lakota transcultural nursing experience. *Journal of Transcultural Nursing, 2*(1), 33-36.

Honigmann, J. (1954). *Culture and personality.* New York NY: Harper & Row Publishers.

Horn, B. (1990). Cultural concepts and postpartal care. *Journal of Transcultural Nursing, 2*(1), 48-51.

Huttlinger, K. & Wiebe, P. (1989). Transcultural nursing care: Achieving understanding in a practice setting. *Journal of Transcultural Nursing, 1*(1), 17-21

Huttlinger, K.W. and Tanner, D. (1994). The Peyote way: Implications for culture care theory, *Journal of Transcultural Nursing, 5*(2), 5-11.

Kalnins, Z. (1992). Nursing in Latvia from the perspective of oppressed theory, *Journal of Transcultural Nursing, 4*(1), 11-16.

Kavanaugh, K. (1993). Transcultural nursing: Facing the challenges of advocacy and diversity/universality, *Journal of Transcultural Nursing, 5*(1), 4- 13.

Kelley, J. & Frisch, N. (1990). Use of selected nursing diagnoses: A transcultural comparison between Mexican and American nurses, *Journal of Transcultural Nursing, 2*(1), 2- 15.

Kendall, K. (1992). Maternal and child care in an Iranian village. *Journal of Transcultural Nursing, 4*(1), 29-36.

Kirkpatrick, S. & Cobb, A. (1990). Health beliefs related to diarrhea in Haitian children: Building transcultural nursing knowledge. *Journal of Transcultural Nursing, 1*(2), 2-12.

Lawson, L.V. (1990). Culturally sensitive support for grieving parents. *American Journal of Maternal Child Rearing, 15*(2), 76-79.

Leininger, M. (1967). Nursing care of a patient from another culture: A Japanese-American patient. *Nursing Clinics of North America, 2,* Philadelphia: W.B. Saunders, 747-762.

Leininger, M. (1967). The culture concept and it's relevance to nursing. *The Journal of Nursing Education, 6*(2), 27-39.

Leininger, M. (1968). Cultural differences among staff members and the impact on patient care **Minnesota League of Nursing Bulletin, 16**(5), 5-9.

Leininger, M. (1969). Ethnoscience: A new and promising research approach for the health sciences. Image: *The Journal of Nursing Scholarship, 3*(1), 2-8.

Leininger, M. (1970). Some cross cultural universal and non-universal functios, beliefs, and practices of food. Dimensions of Nutrition. *Proceedings of the Colorado Dietetic Association Conference.* Fort Collins, CO Colorado Associated Universities Press

Leininger, M. (1971). Anthropological approach to adaptation: Case studies from nursing *Theoretical Issues in Professional Nursing.* New York: Appleton-Century-Crofts

Leininger, M. (1973). An open health care system model. *Nursing Outlook, 21*(3), 171-175

Leininger, M. (1973). Anthropological issues related to community mental health programs in the United States. *Community Mental Health Journal.* Ann Arbor, MI: 7(1), 50-62.

Leininger, M. (1973). Nursing in the context of social and cultural systems. *Concepts Basic to Nursing.* New York NY: McGraw Hill Book Co., 35-45

Leininger, M. (1973). Witchcraft practices and psychocultural therapy with urban United States families. *Human Organization, 32*(1), 73-83.

Leininger, M. (1973). Becoming aware of health practitioners and cultural imposition. *American Nurses' Association 48th Annual Convention Proceedings, 9- 15.*

Leininger, M. (1974). Humanism, health, and cultural values. In M. Leininger (Ed.) *Health Care Issues,* Philadelphia: F.A. Davis, 37-60.

Leininger, M. (1974). Transcultural nursing presents an exciting challenge. *The American Nurse, 5*(5), 4.

Leininger, M. (1976). Cultural interfaces, communication, and health implications. *An Adventure in Transcultural Communication and Health Proceedings of Continuing Education Interdisciplinary Health Professional Workshop* in 1974. Honolulu, HI: University of Hawaii Press.

Leininger, M. (1976). Transcultural nursing: A promising subfield of study for nurse educators and practitioners. *Current Practice in Family Centered Community Nursing.* St. Louis, MO: C.V. Mosby Co.

Leininger, M. (1976). Two strange health tribes: The Gnisrun and Enicidem in the *United States Human Organization, 35*(3), 253-261. (See updated chapter in this book.)

Leininger, M. (1977). Cultural diversities of health and nursing care. In H. Dietz (Ed) *Nursing Clinics of North America.* Philadelphia, W. B . Saunders, Co. 5- 18.

Leininger, M. (1977). Culture and transcultural nursing: Meaning and significance for nurses in *Cultural Dimensions in Nursing Curriculum, (Proceedings of NLN Workshop)* New York, NY: National League for Nursing Press.

Leininger, M. (1981). Transcultural nursing: It's progress and it's future. *Nursing and Health Care, 2*(7), 365-371.

Leininger, M. (1983). Cultural care: An essential goal for nursing and health care. *The American Association of Nephrology Nurses and Technicians (AANNT) Journal, 10*(5), August, 11-17.

Leininger, M. (1984). Transcultural nursing: An overview. *Nursing Outlook, 32*(2), 72-73

Leininger, M. (1986). Care facilitation and resistance factors in the culture of nursing. In Z Wolf (Ed.), *Clinical Care in Nursing.* Maryland Aspen Publications.

Leininger, M. (1988). Leininger's theory of nursing: Culture care diversity and universality *Nursing Science Quarterly, 2*(4), 152-160

Leininger, M. (1989). Transcultural nurse specialists and generalists: New practitioners in nursing. *Journal of Transcultural Nursing, 1*(1), 4-16.

Leininger, M. (1989). Transcultural nurse specialists: Imperative in today's world *Nursing and Health Care, 10*(5), 250-256.

Leininger, M. (1989). Transcultural nursing: Quo wadis (Where goeth the field.). *Journal of Transcultural Nursing, 1*(1), 33-45.

Leininger, M. (1990). Ethnomethods: The philosophic and epistemic bases to explicate transcultural nursing knowledge. *Journal of Transcultural Nursing, 1*(2), 40-51.

Leininger, M. (1990). Issues, questions, and concerns related to the nursing diagnosis cultural movement from a transcultural nursing perspective. *Journal of Transcultural Nursing, 2*(1), 23-32.

Leininger, M. (1990). The significance of cultural concepts in nursing. *Journal of Transcultural Nursing, 2*(1), 52-59.

Leininger, M. (1991). Becoming aware of types of health practitioners and cultural imposition *Journal of Transcultural Nursing 2*(2), 32-39.

Leininger, M. (1991). Culture care of the Gadsup Akuna of the Eastern Highlands of New Guinea. In M. Leininger (Ed.) *Culture Care Diversity and Universality: A Theory of Nursing.* New York, NY: National League for Nursing Press, 231-280.

Leininger, M. (1991). The transcultural nurse specialist: Imperative in today's world. *Perspectives in Family and Community Health, 17,* 137-144.

Leininger, M. (1991). Transcultural care principles, human rights, and ethical considerations *Journal of Transcultural Nursing, 3*(1), 21-24.

Leininger, M. (1991). *Transcultural nursing.* Pride, Kaiser Permanente Publication, Van Nuys, CA: Communication Plus.

Leininger, M. (1992). Current issues, problems, and trends to advance qualitative paradigmatic research methods for the future. *Qualitative Health Research, 2*(4), 392-414.

Leininger, M. (1992). Reflection: The need for transcultural nursing. *Second Opinion,* April 1992, 83-85.

Leininger, M. (1993), Gadsup of Papua New Guinea revisited: A three decades view, *Journal of Transcultural Nursing 5*(1), 21-30.

Leininger, M. (1993). Evaluation criteria and critique of qualitative research studies. In J. Morse (Ed.) *Qualitative nursing research: A contemporary dialogue,* Newbury Park, CA Sage Publications, 392-414

Leininger, M. (1993). Towards conceptualization of transcultural health care systems: Concepts and a model. *Journal of Transcultural Nursing, 4*(2), 32-40. (Originally published in 1976 in M. Leininger (Ed.) Health Care Dimensions. Philadelphia, PA: F. A. Davis Publishers.

Leininger, M. (1993). "Quality of Life from a transcultural nursing perspective." *Nursing Science Quarterly, 7*(1), pp. 22-28.

Leininger, M. (1994). "Transcultural nursing education: A worldwide imperative." *Nursing and Health Care, 15*(5), May 1994, pp. 254-257.

Leininger, M. (1994). "The Tribes of Nursing in the USA Culture of Nursing." *The Journal of Transcultural Nursing, 6*(1), pp. 18-23.

Leininger, M. (1994). "Time to celebrate and reflect on progress with transcultural nursing." *Journal of Transcultural Nursing, 6*(1), pp. 2-4.

Leininger, M. (1994). "Are nurses prepared to function worldwide?" *Journal of Transcultural Nursing 5*(2), pp. 2-5.

Leininger, M. (1994). "Nursing's agenda of health care reform: Regressive or advanced discipline status." *Nursing Science Quarterly, 7*(2), pp. 93-94.

Leininger, M. (1994). "Teaching and learning transcultural nursing." In Mashaba, G. and Brink, H. (Eds.), *Nursing Education: An International Perspective.* Juta and Co., Ltd., Kenwyn, South Africa.

Luna, L. (1989). Transcultural nursing care of Arab Muslims. *Journal of Transcultural Nursing, 1*(1), 22-26.

Luna, L. (1994). Care and cultural context of Lebanese Muslim immigrants with Leininger's theory, *Journal of Transcultural Nursing, 5*(2), 12-20.

Masipa, A. (1991). Transcultural nursing in South Africa: Prospects for the 1900s. *Journal of Transcultural Nursing, 3*(1), 34.

McKenna, M. (1989). Twice in need of care: A transcultural nursing analysis of elderly Mexican Americans. *Journal of Transcultural Nursing, 1*(1), 46-52.

Morgan, M. (1992). Pregnancy and childbirth beliefs and practices of American Hare Krishna devotees within transcultural nursing, *Journal of Transcultural Nursing, 4*(1), 5- 10.

Muecke, M. and Srisuphan, W. (1990). From women in white to scholarship: The new nurse leaders in Thailand, *Journal of Transcultural Nursing, 1*(2), 21-32

Oneha, M.V. & Magyarry, D.L. (1992). Transcultural nursing considerations of child abuse/maltreatment in American Somoa and Federated States Micronesia. *Journal of Transcultural Nursing, 4*(2), 11 - 17.

Osborne, O.H. (1969). Anthropology and nursing: Some common traditions and interests. *Nursing Research, 18*(3), 251-255.

Pasquale, E.A. The evil eye phenomenon: It's implications for community health nursing. *Home Health Care Nurse, 2*(30), 19-21.

Phillips, S. & Lobar, S. (1990). Literature summary of some Navajo child health beliefs and rearing practices within a transcultural nursing framework. *Journal of Transcultural Nursing, 1*(2), 13-20.

Pickwell, S. (1989). The incorporation of family care for Southeast Asian refugees in a community based mental health facility. *Archives of Psychiatric Nursing, 3*(3), 173- 177.

Presswalla, J.L. (1994). Insights into Eastern health care: Some transcultural nursing perspectives, *Journal of Transcultural Nursing, 5*(2), 21-24.

Ray, M. (1988). The development of a classification system of institutional caring. In M. Leininger (Ed.), Care: *The essence of nursing and health*. Detroit, MI: Wayne State University Press, 93- 112.

Ray, M. (1989). Political and economic visions. *Journal of Transcultural Nursing, 1*(1), 17-21.

Reeb, R.M. (1992). Granny midwives in Mississippi: A mini ethnonursing study, *Journal of Transcultural Nursing, 4*(2), 18-27.

Reinert, B.R. (1986). The health care beliefs and values of Mexican Americans. *Home Health Care Nurse, 4*(5), 23, 26, 27.

Rosenbaum, J. (1990). Cultural care of older Greek Canadian widows within Leininger's theory of Culture Care. *Journal of Transcultural Nursing, 2*(1), 3747.

Ross, J.E. (1989). Providing health care for Southeast Asian refugees. *Journal of the New York State Nurses' Association, 20*(2).

Sevcovic, L. (1973). Health care for mothers and children in an Indian culture. In *Family Centered Community Nursing*. St. Louis, MO: C.V. Mosby & Co.

Smith, D.L. (1971). *Aspects of the ethnoscience approach to the study of values and needs as perceived by the North American Indian woman in relation to prenatal care*. (Unpublished Master's thesis, University of Washington, Seattle.)

Sobralske, M.C. (1895). Perceptions of health: Navajo Indians, *Topic in Clinical Nursing, 7*(3), 32-39

Sohier, R. (1976). Gaining awareness of cultural differences: A case example. In M. Leininger did.) *Transcultural health care issues and conditions*. Philadelphia, PA: F.A. Davis Co.

Spangler, Z. (1992). Transcultural nursing care values and caregiving practices of Philippine American nurses, *Journal of Transcultural Nursing, 4*(2), 28-37.

Tripp-Reimer, T. (1989). Cross cultural perspectives on patient teaching. *Nursing Clinics of North America, 24*(3), 613-619.

Valente, S.M. (1989). Overcoming cultural barriers. *California Nurses, 85*(8), 4-5.

Villarruel, A.M. & Ortis de Montellano, B. (1992). Culture and pain: A Meso-American perspective, *Advances in Nursing Science, 15*(1), 21-32.

Wallace, G. (1979). Spiritual care: A reality in nursing education and practice. *The Nurses Lamp, 21*(2), 1-4.

Wenger, A.F. & Wenger, M. (1988). Community and family care patterns of the Old Order Amish. In M. Leininger (Ed.) *Care: Discovery and Use in Clinical Community Nursing.* Detroit, MI: Wayne State University Press.

Wenger, A.F. (1991). Role in context in culture specific care. In L. Chinn (Ed.) *Anthology of Caring.* New York, NY: National League for Nursing Press, 95-110.

Wenger, A.F. (1992). Transcultural nursing and health care issues in urban and rural contexts. *Journal Of Transcultural Nursing, 4*(2), 4-10

Wuest, J. (1991). Harmonizing: A North American Indian approach to management for middle ear disease with transcultural nursing implications, *Journal of Transcultural Nursing, 3*(1), 5-14.

Zborowski, M. & Horzog, E. (1952). *Life is with people.* New York NY: International University Press.

Zborowski, M. (1952). Cultural components in response to pain. *Journal of Social Issues, 8*(4), 16-30.

CLASSIC CULTURE AREA WORKS OF ANTHROPOLOGISTS & SOCIAL SCIENTISTS

Adair, J. & Deuschle, K.W. (1970). *The People's Health.* New York, NY: Appleton Century Crofts.

Arsensberg, C. (1968). *The Irish Countrymen.* Garden City, NJ: The Natural History Press

Benet, S. (1974). *Abkhasians: The long living people of the Caucasus.* New York, NY: Holt, Rinehardt, & Winston.

Benedict, R. (1956). *The chrysanthemum and the sword.* Boston, MA: Boston Press.

Benedict, R. (1934). *Patterns of culture.* Boston, MA: Boston Press.

Clark M. (1970). *Health in the Mexican American culture.* Berkeley, CA: University of California Press.

Friedl, E. (1962). *Vasilika: A village in modern Greece.* New York, NY: Holt, Rinehardt, & Winston.

Gans, H.V. (1962). *The urban villagers: Group and class in the life of Italian Americans.* New York, NY: The Free Press.

Goodman, M.E. (1970). *The culture of childhood.* New York, NY: Teachers College Press.

Gorer, G. & Rickman, J. (1949). *The people of Great Russia: A psychological study.* London Cresset Press.

Hsu, F.L.K. (1953). *Americans and Chinese: Two ways of life.* New York, NY: H. Schuman.

Kiev, A. (1968). *Curanderismo: Mexican American folk psychiatry.* New York, NY: The Free Press.

Leacock, E.B. (1971). *The culture of poverty: A critique.* New York, NY: Simon & Schuster

Leininger, M. (1964). A Gadsup village experiences it's first election. *The Journal of Polynesian Society, 73*(2), 29-34.

Leininger, M. (1978). The Gadsup of New Guinea and early child caring behaviors with nursing care implications. In M. Leininger (Ed) Transcultural nursing: *Concepts, theories and practices.* New York, NY: John Wiley and Sons, 375-398.

Lewis, O. (1961). *The children of Sanchez.* New York, NY: Holt, Rinehardt, & Winston

Lewis, O. (1962). The culture of poverty. *Scientific American, 215*(4), 19-25.

Linton, R. (1936). *The study of man.* New York, NY Appleton Century.

Lowie, R.H. (1945). The German people: *A social portrait to 1914.* New York, NY: Farar & Rinehardt.

Maclachan, J.M. (1958). Cultural factors in health and disease. In E. Gartly Faco (Ed.) *Patients, Physicians, and Illness.* Illinois: Glenco Press

Mead, M. (1929). *Coming of age in Samoa.* New York, NY: New American Library.

Mead, M. (1935). *Sex temperament in three primitive societies.* New York, NY: New American Library.

Mead, M. (1956). *New lives for old.* New York, NY: Morrow.

Minturn, L. & Lambert, W.W. (1964). *Mothers of six cultures.* New York, NY: John Wiley & Sons.

Obeyesekere, G. (1963). Pregnancy cravings in relation to social structure and personality in a Sinhalese village, *American Anthropologist, 65,* 323-341.

Oliver, D. (1989). *The Pacific Islands* (3rd Ed.). Honolulu, HI: University of Hawaii Press.

Paul, B.D. (1955). *Health, culture, and community: Case studied of public reactions to health programs.* New York NY: Russell Sage Foundation.

Read, K.E. (1965). *The high valley.* New York, NY: Charles Scribner's Sons.

Redfield, R. (1955). *The little community.* Chicago, IL: University of Chicago Press.

Rebel, A.J. (1960). Concepts of disease in Mexican American culture. *American Anthropologist 62,* 795-814.

Snow, L.F. (1993). *Walkin' over medicine.* Boulder, CO: Westview Press.

Spicer, E.H. (1952). *Human problems in technological change: A case book.* New York, NY Russell Sage Foundation.

Spiro, M. (1963). *Children of the Kibbutz.* New York, NY: Schocken Press.

Stack C. (1975). All our kin: *Strategies for survival in a black community.* New York, NY Harper & Row.

Strutevant, W.C. (1964). Studies in ethnoscience. *American Anthropologist, 66*(2), 99- 131

Thomas, W.L. & Znaniecki, F. (1918). *The Polish peasant in Europe and America.* Chicago, IL: University of Chicago Press.

Wallace, A.F. (1970). *Culture and personality.* New York, NY: Random House.

Whiting, B. (1963). *Six cultures: Studies of child rearing.* New York, NY: John Wiley & SON

Whiting, J.W. & Child, I.L. (1953). *Child training and personality.* New Haven, CT: Yale University Press.

SELECTED TRANSCULTURAL NURSING AUDIO-VISUALS

Leininger, M., M. Andrews, M. McFarland (1994) *Transcultural Nursing. Transforming the Profession,* Madonna University Audio-Visual Department, Livonia, MI, (34 min. color).

Leininger, M. Gaut, and M. MacDonald (1994) *Human Caring.* Produced by Madonna University Audio-Visual Department, Livonia, MI (38 min. color).

Bloch, C. & Bloch, C. (1993). *Transcultural Nursing Video.* Produced by Education and Consulting Services, Los Angeles County and University of California Medical Center .

Leininger, M. (1992). *Transcultural Nursing* (with A. Kulwicki & K. Edmunds), recorded for Madonna Magazine, Livonia, MI: Madonna University.

Leininger, M. (1990). Leininger's *Theory of Cultural Care: Diversity and Universality,* produced by Madonna University Audio Visual Department, Livonia, MI (50 minutes, color).

Leininger, M. & Stasiak, D. (1990). *Cultural Assessment of American Polish Informant,* produced by Madonna University Audio Visual Department, Livonia, MI (50 minutes, color).

Leininger, M. (1989). With ABC Studio, Oakland California, under Dr. David Wallace, *Leininger's Culture Care Theory, Portraits of Excellence of Theorist,* Produced, Oakland, CA (45 minutes, color).

Leininger, M. (1984). *Care: The essence of nursing and health,* St. Louis University, St. Louis, MO: Educational Satellite (40 minutes, color).*

Leininger, M. (1984). *Transcultural Nursing,* St. Louis University, St. Louis, MO: Educational Satellite (30 minutes, color).*

Leininger, M. (1983). *Arab Americans: Cultural Care,* Wayne State University, Detroit, MI: (35 minutes, color).*

Leininger, M. (1983). *Philippine Americans: Culture Care,* Wayne State University, Detroit, MI: (40 minutes, color).*

Leininger, M. (1983). *Polish Americans: Cultural Care,* Wayne State University, Detroit, MI: (45 minutes, color).*

* available only from author; others available from *Transcultural Nursing Socioety, office,* Madonna University, Livonia, Michigan.

APPENDIX B

Leininger Publications on Transcultural Care and Health Care

Books

Leininger, M. and Hoping, C. (1960). *Basic Psychiatric Concepts in Nursing,* Philadelphia, PA: Lippencott Co. (Published in 11 languages); (Major text in schools of nursing in the United States and overseas).

Leininger, M. (1994). *Nursing and anthropology: Two worlds to blend.* Columbus, OH: Greyden Press (originally published in 1970, New York NY: John Wiley & Sons).

Leininger, M. (1973). *Contemporary issues in mental health nursing.* Boston, MA: Little, Brown, and Co.

Leininger, M. (1974). *Health care issues. First ed. Health Care Dimensions.* Philadelphia, PA: F.A. Davis Co.

Leininger, M. (1975). *Barriers and facilitators of quality health care, Health Care Dimensions.* Philadelphia, PA: F.A. Davis Co.

Leininger, M. (1976). *Transcultural health care issues and conditions. Health Care Dimensions.* Philadelphia, PA: F.A. Davis Co. (American Journal of Nursing, Book of the Year Award).

Leininger, M. (1978). *Transcultural Nursing: Concepts, Theories, and Practices,* New York, NY: John Wiley and Sons. (First textbook on transcultural nursing).

Leininger, M. (1977). *Transcultural nursing care of infants and children.* Salt Lake City, Utah.

Leininger, M. (1977). *Transcultural nursing care of the elderly.* Salt Lake City, Utah.

Leininger, M. (1979). *Transcultural nursing care of the adolescent and middle age adult.* Salt Lake City, Utah.

Leininger, M. (1979) *Cultural change ethics and nursing care implications.* Salt Lake City, Utah.

Leininger, M. (1979). *Transcultural nursing–1979.* New York, NY: Masson Publishing Co.

Leininger, M. (1984). *Reference sources for transcultural health and nursing.* Thorofare, NJ: Charles B. Slack, Inc.

Leininger, M. (1985). *Qualitative research methods in nursing.* New York, NY: Grune and Stratton, Inc. (First comprehensive text on qualitative nursing research methods.)

Leininger, M. (1988). *Care: An essential human need.* Detroit, MI: Wayne State University Press. (Originally published in 1981, C. Slack Inc.)

Leininger, M. (1988). *Care: The essence of nursing and health.* Detroit, MI: Wayne State University Press. (Originally published in 1984, C. Slack, Inc.)

Leininger, M. (1988). *Care: Discovery and uses in clinical community nursing.* Detroit, MI: Wayne State University Press.

Leininger, M. (1988-1990). *Human care and health series.* Detroit, MI: Wayne State University Press.

Leininger, M. and Watson, J. (1990). *The caring imperative in nursing education.* New York, NY: National League for Nursing Press.

Leininger, M. (1990). *Ethical and moral dimensions of care.* Detroit, MI: Wayne State University Press.

Leininger, M. and Gaut, D. (1991). *Caring: The compassionate healer.* New York, NY: National League for Nursing Press.

Leininger, M. (1991). *Cultural care diversity and universality: A theory of nursing.* New York, NY: National League for Nursing Press.

Leininger, M. (1995). *Transcultural nursing concepts, theories, research and practices.* Second edition, New York and Columbus: McGraw Hill Co. and Greyden Press.

Leininger, M. (in progress). *The Gadsup of New Guinea: Lifestyles, health, and caring modes.*

Chapters (Past Eight Years)

Leininger, M. (1985). 1) Nature, Rationale, And Importance Of Qualitative Research Methods In Nursing; 2) Ethnography and ethnonursing: Models and Modes of Qualitative Data Analysis; 3) Life Health-Care History: Purpose, Methods, and Techniques; 4) Southern Rural Black and White American Lifeways on Care and Health Phenomena; 5) Ethnoscience Methods and Compenential Analysis. In M. Leininger (Ed) *Qualitative Research Methods in Nursing,* New York, NY Grune and Stratton.

Leininger, M. (1989). Transcultural nursing: Developments and issues. In McCloskey J. and Grace, H.K. (Eds.) *Current Issues in Nursing,* Boston, MA: Blackwell Scientific Publication, 940-995.

Leininger, M. (1986). Care facilitation and resistance factors in the culture of nursing. In Wolf, Z. (Ed.), *Clinical Care in Nursing,* Maryland Aspen Publications.

Leininger, M. (1986). Importance and significant uses of ethnomethods: Ethnography and ethnonursing research. In Calhoun, M. (Ed), *Research Methods in Nursing,* London: Cambridge University Press.

Leininger, M. (1986). Introductory comments-Chapter 9 On Nature of Science and Nursing. In Nicoll, L.H. (Ed.), *Perspectives of Nursing Theory,* Boston, MA: Little Brown and Co.

Leininger, M. (1986). Strategy for theory development: Ethnomethodology. In Briggs, C. (Ed.), *Proceedings of the Second Annual Nursing Science Colloquium,* Boston, MA: Boston University School of Nursing, 149-171.

Leininger, M. (1986). Transcultural nursing theory. In Marriner, A. (Ed.), *Nursing Theorists and Their Work,* St. Louis, MO: C.V. Mosby, 144-160.

Leininger, M. (1987). Importance and uses of ethnomethods: Ethnography and ethnonursing research. In Calhoun, M. (Ed.), *Current Research in Nursing* Cambridge: Cambridge University Press.

Leininger, M. (1987). Current doctoral education: A culture of mediocrity or excellence. In McCloskey, J. and Grace, H. (Eds.), *Current Issues in Nursing,* Boston, MA: Black well Publishers.

Leininger, M. (1988). Cultural care theory and nursing administration. In Henry, M. (Ed.), *Nursing Administration: Theory and Research,* Boston, MA: Blackwell Publishers

Leininger, M.. Transcultural nursing: Imperative for tomorrow's nurses. In McCloskey, J and Grace, H. (Eds.), *Nursing Issues,* St. Louis, MO: C.V. Mosby, Third Edition.

Leininger, M.. Culture care theory. In Marriner, A. (Ed.), *Nursing Theorists and Their Work,* St. Louis, MO: C.V. Mosby, Second Edition.

Leininger, M. (1988). *Chapter in Making Choices Taking Chances: Nurse Leaders Tell Their Stories.* Schoor, T. and Simmermann, A. (Eds.), St. Louis, MO: C.V. Mosby, 188-192

Leininger, M. (1992). *Current issues in using anthropology in nursing education and services* CONNA of 1988, Medical Anthropology

Leininger, M. (1989). Transcultural nursing: A worldwide necessity to advance nursing knowledge and practice. In McCloskey, J and Grace, H. (Eds.), *Nursing Issues,* St. Louis, MO: C.V. Mosby, Third Edition

Leininger, M. (1989). Historic and epistemologic dimensions of care and caring with futuristic directions. *In Knowledge About Care and Caring: State of the Art and Future Developments.* Proceedings of Wingspread Conference. Stevenson, J. and Reimer, T. (Eds.), American Academy of Nursing of American Nurses Association, Kansas City, MO 19-31.

Leininger, M. (1989). Issues and trends in the discovery and uses of care in nursing. In Leininger, M. (Ed.), *Care: Discovery and Clinical Community* Use, Detroit, MI: Wayne State University Press, 11-29.

Leininger, M. (1989). History, issues, and trends in the discovery and uses with Philippine and Greek Americans. In Care: Discovery and Uses in Clinical Community Nursing. Detroit, MI: Wayne State University Press, 26.

Leininger, M. (1990). The phenomenon of caring: Importance, research, questions, and theoretical considerations. In Ismeurt, R., Arnold, E., and Carson, V. (Eds.), *Readings: Concepts Fundamental to Nursing.* Springhouse, PA, 5-11.

Leininger, M. (1991). The theory of culture care diversity and universality. In *Culture Care Diversity and Universality: A Theory of Nursing,* New York, NY: National League for Nursing, 5-72.

Leininger, M. (1991). Ethnonursing: A research method with enablers to study the theory of culture care. *In Culture Care Diversity and Universality: A Theory of Nursing*, New York, NY: National League for Nursing, 73-118.

Leininger, M. (1991). Culture care of the Gadsup Akuna and the Eastern Highlands of New Guinea. In *Culture Care Diversity and Universality: A Theory of Nursing*, New York, NY: National League for Nursing, 231-280.

Leininger, M. (1991). Selected culture care findings of diverse cultures using culture care theory and ethnonmethods. In *Culture Care Diversity and Universality: A Theory of Nursing*, New York, NY: National League for Nursing, 345-372.

Leininger, M. (1991). Culture care theory and uses in nursing administration. In *Culture Care Diversity and Universality: A Theory of Nursing*, New York, NY: National League for Nursing, 373-390.

Leininger, M. (1991). Looking to the future of nursing and the relevancy of culture care theory In *Culture Care Diversity and Universality: A Theory of Nursing*, New York, NY National League for Nursing, 391-418.

Leininger, M. (1992). Reflections on Nightingale with a focus on human care theory and leadership. In *J.B. Lippincott's 200 Year Anniversary edition of Nightingale's Notes on Nursing*, PA: J.B. Lippincott.

Leininger, M. (1992). Leininger's three windows on culture care theory, transcultural nursing certification, and transcultural nursing: Field study and practice. In Miller-Keane *Encyclopedia and Dictionary of Medical Surgical Nursing and Allied Health* (5th Edition). Philadelphia, PA: W.B. Saunders and Co.

Leininger, M. (1992). Psychiatric nursing and transculturalism: Quo vadis. In N. Kerr (Ed), *Perspectives in Psychiatric Care*.

Leininger, M. (1992). Transcultural mental health nursing assessment of children and adolescents In P. West and C. Sieloff Evans (Eds.), *Psychiatric and Mental Health Nursing with Children and Adolescents*. Aspen Publications, 53-58.

Leininger, M. (1992). Reflections on WCHEN and the Research Critique. In J. Kearns (Ed.) WCHEN *Anniversary Book*, Boulder, CO: Western Institute of Nursing.

Leininger, M. (1992). Theory of culture care and uses in clinical and community contexts. In M. Parker (Ed.), *Theories on Nursing*, New York, NY: National League for Nursing, 345- 372.

Reynolds, C. and Leininger, M. (1992). *Leininger's cultural care theory.* In C. McQuiston and A. Webb (Serial Eds.) *Notes on Nursing Series*, Newbury Park, CA: Sage Publications.

Leininger, M. (1992). Current issues, problems, and trends to advance qualitative paradigmatic research methods for the future. In *Qualitative Health Research*, Newbury Park, CA: Sage Publications, vol. 2, no. 4, 392-415.

Leininger, M. (1993). Culture care theory: The comparative global theory to advance human care nursing knowledge and practice. In D. Gaut, *A Global Agenda for Caring*. New York, NY: National League for Nursing, 3- 18.

Recent Refereed Journal Articles: 1991-1994

Leininger, M. (1991). Nursing theories to differentiating nursing practice. *In American Academy of Nursing,* Kansas City, ANA Press.

Leininger, M., at. al. (1991). Nursing theories essential to guide nursing practices. *Nursing Outlook*.

Leininger, M. (1991). Transcultural nursing: The study and practice field. *Imprint, National Student Nurses Association.*

Leininger, M. (1991). Becoming aware of types of health practitioners and cultural imposition. In *Journal of Transcultural Nursing,* Memphis, TN: University of Tennessee Press, 2(2), 32-39.

Leininger, M. (1991). Transcultural care principles, human rights and ethical considerations. In *Journal of Transcultural Nursing,* Memphis, TN: University of Tennessee Press, 3(3), 21 -24.

Leininger, M. (1991). The transcultural nurse specialist: Imperative in today's world. In K. Saucier, *Perspectives in Family and Community Health,* St. Louis, MO: Mosby Book Co., 17, 137-144.

Leininger, M. (1991). Transcultural nursing. In *Pride,* Kaiser Permanent publication, Chicago, IL: The Park Ridge Center.

Leininger, M.. A day in the life of a transcultural nurse. In M. Martin (Ed.), *Second Opinion,* Chicago, IL: W.B. Saunders, Co.

Leininger, M. (1991). Three windows: Culture care theory; Transcultural nursing certification; and Transcultural nursing: Field study and practice, (5th Edition). In Miller-Keane *Encyclopedia and Dictionary of Medical Surgical Nursing and Allied Health* (5th Edition). Philadelphia, PA: W.B. Saunders and Co.

Leininger, M. (1991). Transcultural mental health nursing assessment of children and adolescents. In *Psychiatric and Mental Health Nursing with Children and Adolescents.* Aspen Publications, 53-58.

Leininger, M. (1992). Psychiatric nursing and transculturalism: Quo Vadis. In N. Kerr (Ed.), *Perspectives in Psychiatric Care.*

Leininger, M. (1992). Reflections on Nightingale with a focus on human care theory and leadership. In *J.B. Lippincott's 200 Year Anniversary edition of Nightingale's Notes on Nursing,* PA: J.B. Lippincott.

Leininger, M. (1992). Transcultural nursing care values, beliefs, and practices of American (USA) Gypsies. *Journal of Transcultural Nursing,* Dearborn, MI: Desktoppers USA, 4(1), 17-28.

Leininger, M. (1993). Toward conceptualization of transcultural health care systems: Concepts and a model. *Journal of Transcultural Nursing, 4*(2). (Originally published in 1976).

Leininger, M. Transcultural Nursing and Education: A Worldwide Imperative. *Nursing and Health Care,* May, 1994. vol. 15:5 pp. 254-257

Leininger, M. (1994) Nursing's Agenda of Health Care Reform: Regressive or Advanced-Discipline Status. *Nursing Science Quarterly,* Special Feature Summer 7:2 p. 93-94

Leininger, M. *Transcultural Nursing: Concepts, Theory, Research, and Practice,* (Second Edition) New York: McGraw, Hill and Columbus: Greyden Press, 1994. (30 Chapters, 400 pages)

Leininger, M. (1993) Quality of Life From a Transcultural Nursing Perspective. *Nursing Science Quarterly*. 7:1 Spring p. 22, pp. 22-28

Section V:

Future of Transcultural Nursing

Chapter 29
Transcultural Nursing: Quo Vadis (Where Goeth the Field?)*

Madeleine Leininger, PhD, LHD, FAAN, CTN, RN

Transculturalism expands one's thinking, the human spirit, knowledge and practice of people in the world.

Madeleine Leininger

It is encouraging to know that new lines of inquiry and different pathways of education and practice can successfully lead to new directions in a profession or discipline. All too frequently, strongly entrenched professional values, norms, and practices can seriously limit the full development of a field. Creative leaders with innovative ideas and strategies are essential to establish new areas of study and practice, or to institute some different directions in a profession.

During the past thirty years a cadre of creative leaders and enthusiastic followers have successfully established and developed the field of transcultural nursing as a formal area of study and practice in nursing.[1,2] It has been a major breakthrough in nursing knowledge and in establishing new directions. Transcultural nursing has opened the doors to nurses in discovering fresh perspectives about human care and different ways to serve people. As the founder and central leader in establishing this new field, it has been one of the most exciting and promising developments in nursing. It has given new hope for many nurses who realized that our world is multicultural and that a new knowledge base is essential to help nurses understand and care for people of different cultures.

To establish such a different pathway of knowledge and practice required thoughtful planning and strategies in order to redirect nurses' thinking to different normative values and practices. When the field was initiated in the mid 1950s nurse educators were deeply concerned about their professional identity and ways to meet the physical, technical, and psychological needs of patients. The thought of developing transcultural nursing knowledge and of preparing nurses to practice transcultural nursing was an enigma and a strange line to pursue in nursing. How to get nurses interested in cultural factors in client care was difficult when nurses were so wed to biomedical concepts and practices and Western ideologies. The culture of nursing was deeply steeped in Western medical beliefs and practices with limited awareness of non-Western cultures and of diverse health care beliefs and practices.

A tremendous challenge was before the early leaders, namely to develop knowledge and skills to care for clients from Western and non-Western cultures. It was clear that our world of nursing would be different in a relatively short period of time and especially by the end of this century when nurses would be functioning in a highly multicultural nursing and client world. Nursing curricula and clinical practices worldwide had to change markedly from a largely unicultural dominant perspective to a multicultural one, but too few nurses were cognizant of this reality and some were too busy dealing with medical technologies.

With a changing world and especially needed for nursing, I predicted that a transcultural nursing focus could greatly revolutionize nursing. It would require, however, that nursing education become multicultural and that clinical practices accommodate the diverse cultural needs of clients.[3,4] It would also require strong and persistent leadership to make such changes over time. The idea of "quo vadis" (or where goeth) transcultural nursing and the health care field and what would be the long-range impact upon nursing and the health care field would be important. Nursing education, research, and practice would have to change quite drastically to incorporate the largely unknown cultural dimensions of human care services. Thus, "quo vadis" had meaning and relevance to those making transcultural nursing a reality for the future.

Where would the field go? Could nurses shift their thinking from Western unicultural ideologies based largely on biomedical beliefs to a worldwide cultural perspective? Who would be the followers? Would nurses be willing to discover a new body of knowledge and develop skills to meet the culture-specific needs of individuals, families, and groups? Would professional nurses and new students be willing to think about different ways of knowing and helping people? The idea of valuing the potential power, relevance, and importance of culture care to promote wellness and healing would be a radically different way of thinking and acting. How could one promote multiculturalism in a largely unicultural world? The time had come for transcultural nursing to be established and developed as an area of formal study and practice in nursing to meet the future needs of clients from a multicultural world. This new and different area of knowledge and practice became the real challenge of brave, bold, and venturesome nurses in the first era of transcultural nursing from 1955 to 1975.

Three decades later the field of transcultural nursing had been well established as an essential, legitimate, and significant area of formal study and practice in nursing.[5,6,7,8] Today a new generation of nurses are being exposed to, and prepared in the field of transcultural nursing. They are changing their nursing care practices to accommodate clients' cultural needs. Transcultural concepts, principles, theories, and findings are being used to provide a different kind of nursing care than was found in the pre-1950s days. Today, more nurses are aware that culture can play a significant role in gaining client cooperation, helping clients, and in understanding the lifeways of clients. Transcultural nursing is making a difference in the way individuals, families, groups, and cultures recover from illness, face disabilities, or handle daily life problems. Concepts such as transcultural shock, cultural clashes, ethnocentrism, cultural imposition practices, and cultural value conflicts have been incorporated into nursing curricula and practice. Some nurses also know how to do culturalogical holistic health care assessments and provide culturally sensitive, skilled, and congruent care.[9,10,11,12] No longer are all clients or families treated totally alike without thought to their culture, but differential cultural care is tailored to fit the client's cultural values and can be found in settings where transcultural nursing is a major focus. Using different cultural beliefs and values in providing client care has led to more therapeutic and humanistic nursing care practices. In general, the concept of culture-specific care has greatly sharpened nurses intellectual skills and nursing care practice.[13,14,15]

Another major breakthrough is that nurses are becoming comfortable to use the cultural care theory rather than mainly biophysical and psychologically derived nursing theories. The author's theory of Culture Care Diversity and Universality has become a major and meaningful theory for nurses who are studying culture care and want to improve client care.[16,17,18] This theory has greatly expanded nurses' thinking in considering cultural values, social structure, and other factors influencing care and health. It has also helped nurse researchers and clinicians to see the broad meaning of truly holistic health care from a culturally based world in which clients live, become ill, or die. The Culture Care Theory and the findings from the theory have provided an epistemological base for nursing knowledge and support for transcultural nursing knowledge and practices.

In 1986 there were approximately 800 nurses in the United States who had been prepared in formal graduate programs of study in transcultural nursing and several with a human care focus.[19,20] To date the author has offered transcultural nursing courses and workshops to approximately 10,000 nurses.[21] There are now transcultural nurse generalists and specialists who are prepared to serve people of different cultural backgrounds, beliefs, and values. This is remarkable, realizing the fact that prior to 1950, there were no nurses formally prepared in transcultural nursing courses or programs, as they did not exist. Nurses are also actively conducting transcultural nursing research and using the findings in client care. Most recently, transcultural nurses are being certified as transcultural nurse specialists or generalists by the Transcultural Nursing Society, reflecting that these nurses have knowledge and skills to provide safe, responsible, and meaningful care to people of different cultures. Such progress has been made by a relatively small number of dedicated leaders and followers in transcultural nursing who recognize the need for and are committed to transcultural nursing as a legitimate and essential area of education and practice.

With this overview of transcultural nursing, some specific developments within three major historical eras will be highlighted next. The following eras will help the reader understand and appreciate both the struggles and progress when a new area of study and practice comes into existence:

1. The Era of Establishing the Field of Transcultural Nursing (1955–1975)
2. The Era of Program and Research Expansion (1975–1983)
3. The Era of Establishing Transcultural Nursing Worldwide (1983 into the twenty-first century).

The First Era: Establishing the Field of Transcultural Nursing (1955–1975)

Although nurses had worked with clients of different cultures within one's own society and some in foreign cultures, for many years, there were no formal courses or programs to understand people of diverse and complex cultures. Unquestionably, many nurses experienced transcultural shock and intercultural tensions and conflicts in giving care as well as communicating with health personnel of different cultures. Since the days of Florence Nightingale there had been no culture-specific or transcultural nursing knowledge base to guide nursing decision and actions or to understand "different" behaviors to give quality-based nursing care. Transcultural nursing education and practices were clearly needed locally, nationally, and worldwide. I recognized this need and took leadership to develop the field of transcultural nursing.

Anthropology was the major discipline which focused on the comparative study of human cultures in different geographic locations in the world. Nurses and the nursing profession needed anthropological insights in order to help nurses develop transcultural nursing knowledge. There were some anthropological theories and research findings that could serve as a beginning knowledge base to stimulate nurse's thinking, but these ideas had to be transformed into transcultural nursing.[22,23] I held that if nurses were knowledgeable about several specific cultures, they could begin to conceptualize the relationship of nursing to anthropology and develop specific transcultural nursing concepts, principles, theories, and research findings. Transcultural nurse scholars, theorists, researchers, and practitioners were greatly needed to achieve this goal.

It was a challenge for nurses to conceptualize a body of nursing knowledge different from traditionally established nursing knowledge. Many nurses in the 1950s were so deeply steeped in studying medical disease symptoms, treatments, and diagnostic conditions that they found it quite difficult to consider new ideas or broad and complex concepts such as culture and care to develop transcultural nursing knowledge.

It was also a major challenge to launch transcultural nursing as a field of study, as most nurses had never taken courses in anthropology or considered how such knowledge could be used in nursing. The relationship between nursing and anthropology was largely unknown and unexplored in the 1950s. Nursing and anthropology were two strange and different worlds, but with some commonalities.[24] Gradually as I encouraged nurses to become educated in anthropology, they became fascinated with this discipline, but some nurses became more committed this field than to nursing. There were nurses, however, who remained committed to and were active in developing a body of transcultural nursing knowledge.

In the early part of this era (1955–1970), it was imperative to develop transcultural nursing knowledge with specific concepts, principles, and potential practices. Undergraduate and graduate courses were needed to educate a new generation of nurses to see the value and importance of transcultural nursing.[25] Establishing graduate courses in transcultural nursing was most essential to generate a sound knowledge base with theory and research. This was difficult not only because most nurses had limited preparation in anthropology and in theories and ways to study culture care phenomena. In addition, some nurses were wholesale borrowers of knowledge from anthropology rather than developing knowledge specific and relevant to transcultural nursing. Much time and energy was given to the idea of transcultural nursing theories and research methods for the new field and discipline of nursing. Graduate transcultural nursing became a major and first priority to prepare nurses to transform nursing through transcultural nursing knowledge.[26,27] Nurses were encouraged to take social science and humanities courses to expand their worldview and its relationship to transcultural nursing. Graduate prepared nurses were held to be the leaders for transcultural nursing.

Undergraduate courses and units of instruction were gradually developed and taught as more graduate faculty were prepared in transcultural nursing. The first baccalaureate and graduate courses in transcultural nursing were developed and taught by the author at the University of Colorado (1965–69), later at the University of Washington (1969–74), and the University of Utah (1974–80). Many of these transcultural nursing courses, educational programs, and workshops became prototypes for other schools of nursing. Undergraduate and graduate students began to value and use transcultural nursing ideas in courses and in nursing practice with a few clinically prepared mentors. These nursing students had difficulty using transcultural ideas because most faculty were unfamiliar with and unprepared in transcultural nursing.

In the first era of transcultural nursing, the author deliberately wanted nurses well prepared in transcultural nursing through masters and doctoral programs because culture care, and anthropology were very complex ideas to master. These nurses were expected to serve as role models and leaders in transcultural nursing education, research, and practice. Community health and maternal-child health nurses were first to take graduate transcultural nursing courses, for many saw the need to understand cultural factors in nursing care with others. In contrast, medical-surgical and psychiatric nurses were the last to pursue study in the new field, mainly because they were so involved in Western mental diseases and psychoanalytic thought that they had difficulty valuing transcultural nursing and anthropologic perspectives. Medical-surgical nurses gradually recognized the need for transcultural nursing with resistive and uncooperative patients of "strange" cultures who did not readily comply with their nursing activities.[28,29]

With the author's early position that care was the essence and the distinct and unifying feature of nursing, ethnocare studies of Western and non-Western cultures were done in the early 1960s. The first ethnocare or transcultural study was with the Gadsup of the eastern highlands of New Guinea using the ethnonursing qualitative research method.[30] Ideas related to the Culture Care Diversity and Universality theory were used by the author and later by several graduate students pursuing transcultural nursing.[31,32] Culture care was one of the early theories in nursing having been conceptualized in the late 1950s and undergoing further refinements in succeeding years. By 1975 the theory (with the Sunrise Model) and care became of general interest to many nurses as they began to study Western and non-Western cultures. Gradually, other nurses were contributing to transcultural nursing knowledge through the use of qualitative ethnoresearch methods. Ethnocare, ethnohealth, and other ethnonursing phenomena were being described, documented, and explained by nurses in several cultures with ethnography and ethnonursing research methods. As an early leader in the use of qualitative research methods in the early 1960s, this idea gradually was valued by other nurses by the 1980s.[33]

Contrary to Tripp-Reimer and Dougherty's views, transcultural nurses have made significant and noteworthy contributions to advance nursing knowledge about comparative care, health, and holistic cultural perspectives of several cultures.[34] These authors seemed more committed to anthropology than to transcultural nursing and failed to understand or provide an accurate account of the many important findings from transcultural nursing research during the past three decades. Moreover, their absence from transcultural nursing conferences seemed to limit their awareness of the significant role that transcultural nurses had played in the evolution of nursing, especially to advance qualitative research methods and culture-specific care practices. It is of interest that although the first nursing book focused on qualitative research methods in nursing, it was not published until 1985. Transcultural nurses had been using qualitative methods (especially ethnography and ethnonursing) since the early 1960s.[35] There was evidence that Tripp-Reimer and Dougherty were wed to the quantitative paradigm as they reviewed the work and failed to recognize the great importance of qualitative research studies as equally valuable as quantitative studies.

In early era teaching and promoting qualitative research methods in nursing schools was most difficult because most nurse researchers in the 1960s to 1980s were so strongly committed to the quantitative paradigm grounded in logical positivism, empiricism, linear thinking, statistics, and measurable outcomes. In fact, practically all graduate nursing programs emphasized quantitative methods as the only valid and reliable "scientific" means to do research and get valid knowledge. There were virtually no nursing faculty prepared in qualitative methods except for a few prepared in anthropology and sociology. Several transcultural nurses forged the pathway to demonstrate the use of qualitative methods from the early 1960s and encourage nurses to discover the many unknowns about care, health, and environmental context as the major phenomena of the discipline of nursing.[36,37] Transcultural nurses in early era and still today face great difficulties to get qualitative research grants approved and funded through federal, state, or provincial governments in many countries because only quantitative studies with statistical formulas and measurable precise outcomes are valued. Such factors and others greatly curtailed research in transcultural nursing. In the future of nursing, transcultural nurses must, however, be recognized for their creativity, tenacity, and perseverance in studying transcultural phenomena with virtually no research monies because they did not want to succumb to studying cultural care phenomena with methods appropriate to the quantitative paradigm.

In early era transcultural nurse researchers were the first nurses to use the concepts of *emic* (insider's or local perspectives) and *etic* (outsiders' views) about care, health, and lifeways of individuals, families, and cultures. With emic studies there is an emphasis on the meanings and lived experiences of people in difference cultures. Today, emic and etic are being widely used in nursing along with the use of other qualitative research methods and modes of data analysis that have been largely promoted by transcultural nurses.

From the theoretical work and research findings of transcultural nurses in the first era (1955–1975), a number of articles, books, and conference proceedings were published. These publications became the first transcultural sources for the book,

Nursing and Anthropology: Two Worlds to Blend, written in the mid 1960s and published in 1970. This became the first major book to show the relationship between the two disciplines of nursing and anthropology and to identify the differences and similarities between the two fields.[38] It was also written to encourage interdisciplinary collaboration between nurses and anthropologists. In 1978, the book, *Transcultural Nursing: Concepts, Theories, and Practices*, became the first comprehensive textbook on transcultural nursing to become used in many countries.[39] Other articles and several books were published by nurses in subsequent years.[40,41,42,43] In 1968, the author spearheaded establishing the Committee on Nursing and Anthropology within the American Anthropological Association. The organization encouraged interdisciplinary sharing of theoretical and research work between nurses and anthropologists.

In 1974 the Transcultural Nursing Society was established, but was preceded by an earlier conference in Hawaii focused on transcultural communication in 1972. The Transcultural Nursing Society became the official organization to support the academic, clinical interests, and work of transcultural nurses. Since 1974, annual meetings have been held to share nurses' thinking and research with other nurses; proceedings and refereed publications from the society became a valuable literature resource for the members and many other nurses and health professionals. In fact, these publications were the key reference sources for teaching, research, and practice in transcultural nursing.

In sum, the first historical period (which covered two decades) was significant because it laid the foundation for establishing the field of transcultural nursing with a human care focus. It was the period in which theory, research, and education were all emphasized in order to establish a sound base for transcultural nursing. It was the era in which transcultural nursing concepts, theories, principles, and research findings became known to nurses, other health professionals, and the public. Most assuredly, it was the most difficult period because the idea of transcultural nursing based on culture care was very strange and different from most nurses to conceptualize let alone envision ways to practice in this new field. Nurses had to learn about cultures, anthropological ideas, and think what would constitute comparative care and health knowledge. Even the idea of establishing transcultural nursing as a legitimate and essential area of formal study and practice was an enigma to many nurses. Envisioning transcultural nursing and health care into the twenty-first century was a very futuristic idea and almost impossible to consider in the mid 1950s. The evolving theory of Culture Care Diversity and Universality was also strange to most nurses who did not value theories and were not prepared in theory development in the early 1960s. But by 1975 culture care concepts, theories, and practices had become of interest to nurses, especially those who had taken courses in transcultural nursing theory construction and research methods. Slowly, some faculty in schools of nursing realized the importance of transcultural nursing as they worked with students and faculty of diverse cultures. By 1975 there were very few nurses in clinical nursing who were prepared in transcultural nursing and who understood and valued transcultural nursing as an area of practice, or to be incorporated in people care modes.

Initially, nursing organizations such as the ANA and NLN showed very limited interest in preparing nurses through formal programs of study in transcultural nursing until the late 1970s. The author tried to establish a transcultural nursing council within the ANA in the early 1970s, but there was limited interest and the idea of cultural differences was feared as leading to discrimination practices. In this era, initially no federal funds for transcultural nursing programs or research were available. Nursing funds were given to nurses conducting studies of nursing tasks within the quantitative paradigm. Nurse leaders were busy establishing clinical nursing programs and dealing with daily hospital activities and medical dominance problems of the day. Persistence in goals and enthusiasm for their work, helped transcultural nurse leaders to establish the field as a vital area of study and practice in nursing.

The Second Era: Program and Research Expansion (1975–1983)

From 1975 onward there was a growing and heightened interest in transcultural nursing with more nurses ready to learn about transcultural nursing and use the concepts, theories, and research findings with specific cultures. By 1979 more nurses were realizing the need for transcultural nursing because they were experiencing great difficulty working with clients of different cultural values and lifestyles. Caring for people who were from markedly different cultures than their own was now a "big problem." Nurses were reading about transcultural nursing courses in the United States and believed such knowledge would help them in clinical areas. Some nurses were going to work in Saudi Arabia, India, Africa, or to other unknown places and believed a quick course or workshop would help them. There were some nurses who said they were bored with functioning in the traditional four medical areas of medical-surgical, pediatric, psychiatric-mental health, and orthopedic nursing. These nurses wanted to try something new and futuristic in nursing. As these nurses read about transcultural nursing, they became interested in this area and many continued to pursue transcultural nursing.

During the second era there were more prepared transcultural nurses who were active researchers. They enjoyed field research and the discovery of new insights from cultures which they had studied especially in the United States. The study of folk health care practices and their contrast with professional nursing practices was of much interest to transcultural nurses. Folk and professional studies by Aamodt,[44]

Boyle,[45] Glittenberg,[46] Horn,[47] Leininger,[48,49,50] Ray,[51] and many other transcultural nurses were bringing much new knowledge to nursing. Anthropologists such as Chrisman[52] became active contributors to make anthropology relevant to nursing. In fact, most anthropologists were very interested and supportive of the transcultural nursing movement and helped to facilitate ongoing work in the field of transcultural nursing.

As the field grew, some minority nurses in the United States wanted to control and establish ethnic teaching programs about "their culture." Since most of these nurses had no advance preparation in transcultural nursing nor anthropology to teach or to do research, this became a major problem. While some nurses had knowledge of their own culture, still many showed signs of cultural blindness with limited in-depth knowledge about their own culture and diverse cultures, cultural theories, and historical factors influencing the nature and direction of transcultural nursing. Some deans and faculty of schools of nursing made false assumptions that any minority nurse was prepared to teach transcultural nursing because they were from a particular culture. These factors and others limited progress in establishing transcultural nursing as a subdiscipline. In the 1970s minority recruitment programs for nurses in the United States were only for the four specified federal government groups, i.e., African, Asian, Hispanic, and Native American. Many additional underrepresented cultures were grossly overlooked and received no attention with human resources in education, research, and practice.

As more students sought preparation in transcultural nursing, the need for well prepared, more qualified transcultural nursing faculty was clearly evident by 1980.[53,54] Young nursing students were eager to learn how to care for clients they had never known before, or to understand their lifeways and needs. By this time there were more students pursuing masters and doctoral degrees in transcultural nursing in the United States, and they wanted faculty to help with their research. The supply of qualified faculty seriously failed to meet the demand.

In the clinical areas transcultural nurse specialists and generalists were beginning to work with cultural groups, especially with refugees and immigrants from South East Asia, Hispanics, Cubans, and others. By 1982 requests for workshops, courses, and in-service programs in transcultural nursing had markedly increased. A few nurse clinicians in maternal-child and community nursing had obtained master's degrees in transcultural nursing and were working with families of diverse cultures. Transcultural nurse consultants were being sought to work with nursing staff in hospitals and clinics in the United States and in other countries where nurses were struggling with multicultural care problems. Unquestionably, the need for transcultural nurse specialists and generalists were clearly evident by 1982, but there were insufficient numbers of master's prepared transcultural nurses to meet the demand for culturally responsible care. By this time physicians and pharmacists were interested in transcultural phenomena and were requesting transcultural nurse specialists to teach their students about cultures, uncooperative cultural clients, and ways to help them.

In the second era the initiation of doctoral programs in transcultural nursing with a theoretical and research focus at the University of Washington (Seattle, 1973), University of Utah (Salt Lake City, 1978), and Wayne State University (1982) helped to ease the critical shortage of transcultural nurses in a variety of roles. The University of Miami, University of Arizona, and Universities of California (Los Angeles and San Francisco) later launched graduate programs on mental health and culture, international exchanges, and general culture and nursing courses or programs.

By 1980 approximately twenty percent of the schools of nursing accredited by the National league for Nursing in the United States had begun to incorporate cultural concepts and principles into undergraduate programs and twelve percent of the graduate (master's degree) nursing programs.[55] Less than one percent of the doctoral degree nursing programs had something to offer on transcultural nursing. So, while some progress had been made to incorporate transcultural nursing into undergraduate and graduate programs in the United States, far more work was needed to make the content an integral part of all areas of nursing.

In Canada and Australia a number of nurses became greatly interested in transcultural nursing through workshops, conferences, and publications largely sponsored by the Transcultural Nursing Society. Several nurses came to the United States to study with transcultural nurse leaders and learn ways to develop similar programs (educational or clinical) congruent with their homelands' cultures. Many of these nurses readily recognized the importance of transcultural nursing because of the marked increase in multiculturalism in their countries and their desire to improve client care through transcultural nursing education. In addition, a few nurses from Brazil, China, Japan, Korea, Sweden, Denmark, and the Netherlands came to the United States to study transcultural nursing and returned to initiate transcultural nursing in their nursing curricula. Making transcultural nursing fit the societal expectations of different cultures in their countries became quite a challenge rather than to impose a foreign pattern on the country. Such work required graduate prepared faculty in transcultural nursing to work closely with the host community. Faculty were needed who could teach transcultural nursing, be flexible and creative in their thinking to meet diverse cultural imperatives across all areas of nursing, and to integrate concepts and experiences in meaningful ways. This was almost an impossible challenge, but efforts were made in this direction.

During the second era, nurses began to write about transcultural nursing and culture care problems and patterns. The ideas of culture and care are central to transcultural nursing and became popular topics to write about. A few journals published articles on transcultural nursing, some about culture and nursing, and others about anthropology and nursing. There was a lack of journal reviewers prepared in transcultural nursing, so some published articles were not transcultural nursing but the use of anthropological ideas in nursing without any theoretical or general nursing perspective. Thus, considerable variability existed with the quality of the publications. It was difficult to get scholarly articles published in some journals.

The need for transcultural nursing experts and mentors in research, teaching, and consultation came about by 1978. Several non-nurse theorists and faculty from the social sciences were employed by schools of nursing to meet student research guidance needs. Transcultural research was largely focused on descriptive concerns such as cultural value conflicts, cultural biases, and the failure to respond to individual, family, and community needs. A number of important research studies focused on the cultural care, life span experiences, and health conditions of particular cultures such as Mexican, African, Philippine, Greek, and other cultures in particular communities. Nurses had expanded their viewpoints to include the idea of identifiable cultures in different communities. This was most encouraging to observe and have documented.

By 1982 requests for transcultural nursing specialists as consultants within and outside the United States were made by nurses to help with cultural diversity conflicts, stresses, and strains among clients, nurses, and hospital staff. Because of the increased complexity of being a transcultural consultant, the Transcultural Nursing Society recommended that these consultants be prepared minimally through doctoral and master's degree programs. Assessing cultural factors such as political, economic, religious, educational, kinship, and technological aspects that impacted upon culture care problems or human conditions was a major skill required in consultation.

During the second era there was a marked increase in requests for workshops and conferences on transcultural nursing for schools of nursing, hospitals, and health agencies. Several concerned how to do culturalogic assessments and apply transcultural nursing principles, concepts, and the culture care theory. Some institutions wanted a quick recipe or quick fix approach to handle complex problems that were related to discrimination, racial problems, and ethnocentrism among health personnel. One day workshops or conferences posed problems, as it was virtually impossible to prepare participants in transcultural nursing with such limited background about cultures and transcultural perspectives. Emergency telephone calls were also provided to some agencies and schools. Transcultural nurse specialists and generalists were beginning to be recognized and employed by hospitals, health agencies, and educational institutions to handle such growing problems, but demand far exceeded the supply. Nonetheless, these specialists were able to help many nurses apply transcultural concepts and principles in direct client care through direct counseling and role modeling. Several transcultural specialists had to serve the whole institution such as a hospital or agency because of the critical need for and shortage of these specialists. Although transcultural nurses were much in demand, there were limited salaried positions for them so they had to negotiate for positions and acceptable salary. The economic crunch in hospitals and health agencies in the early 1980s made it difficult to establish new positions for transcultural nurse specialists or generalists. Many administrators and staff nurses were pleased to see how effective these nurses were in dealing with transcultural care conflicts between clients and staff, increasing client satisfaction, and reducing noncompliance and anger expressions between nurses and clients. Transcultural nurses also were instrumental to reduce actual or potential legal suits when cultural lifeways and values were violated or not recognized in nursing care. These legal suits, related to client and nurse defense, are predicted to markedly increase in the future due to major conflicts about cultural values, beliefs, human rights, lifeways, and rights of cultures. Institutional studies such as Ray's have been valuable to learn about potential legal problems and the consequences of bureaucratic structures to provide culturally congruent care practices.[56] Unquestionably, transcultural nursing knowledge was clearly needed to help nurses to understand the culturally different and to prevent violation of human ethical rights.

In sum, the second era in transcultural nursing reflected considerable growth and progress in establishing nursing education, research, practice, and consultation, especially in the United States and with variability in other countries. Transcultural concepts, principles, theories, and research findings were being studied. The expertise of transcultural nurse specialists and generalists became evident in hospitals, health agencies, and community-based alternative services. The transcultural nurse was now visible and much in demand as she (he) offered an entirely new kind of service to people.

The Third Era: Establishing Transcultural Nursing Worldwide (1983 and into the Twenty-First Century)

The third major era in transcultural nursing has been focused on making transcultural nursing a global agenda and imperative. Nurses worldwide need to be prepared in transcultural nursing to function effectively in diverse areas of nursing. Since the mid 1980s more nurses have been traveling and working in different countries and interacting with people of many different cultures. These nurses need very much to learn about cultural differences and how to communicate and work effectively in transcultural situations. Nurses are realizing they need to learn an almost entirely new body of knowledge and to develop new kinds of skills as they enter and function in nursing as a transcultural professional. Encouragingly, for transcultural nurses competence is the key to success in their future profession endeavors. This awareness characterizes the third era in transcultural nursing.

In 1988 the Transcultural Nursing Society held its first annual meeting in Canada, and in 1989 in the Netherlands. These conferences attracted nurses within the country but also worldwide. The sessions led to a rich exchange of ideas, values, and transcultural experiences. Transcultural nurse leaders continued to expand their linkages with nurses worldwide in diverse educational, clinical, and research programs. Transcultural nurses are now working or doing consultation in many places in the world such as China, Japan, Korea, Africa, Pacific Islands, Australia, South America, and Europe. In each encounter people have an opportunity to learn about the nature, goals, and achievements in transcultural nursing from experts. Indeed, these transcultural nursing experts continue to help with transcultural curricular changes and with research projects that are tailor-made to a particular country. They have been involved in developing transnational nursing policies with some cultural groups since 1984 in order to facilitate communication, education, and clinical exchanges. Some transcultural exchange programs for nurses have been developed and are successful, but much more work is needed in this area due to major political, economic, and cultural changes in different countries. Many changes have occurred in Eastern Europe, the Middle East, Asia, Latin America, and Africa. These changes are challenging transcultural nurses to be dynamic and accommodate major changes.

Another achievement in the third era was establishing the *Journal of Transcultural Nursing*. While the journal had been planned for more than a decade, it took considerable time and effort to establish because it was a very different kind of publication. The *Journal of Transcultural Nursing* is the official publication of the Transcultural Nursing Society. The purpose of this publication is to share scholarly work among transcultural nurse generalists and specialists, and for other nurses who meet specific criteria related to advancing knowledge in transcultural nursing. Authors are encouraged to share their teaching, research, and clinical practices in the journal. Many theoretical and research-based articles are presented, especially qualitative studies. In fact, this is the major journal that has supported and encouraged qualitative articles in order to establish the epistemic and ontological basis of nursing. The journal has been well received as a highly scholarly and relevant publication. It is the first journal to focus explicitly on transcultural nursing.

The third era is being directed toward the goals of making transcultural nursing better known worldwide and to help nurses develop and participate in transcultural nursing education, research, and consultation programs in accord with their interest and expertise. It is the era of reaching out to nurses every place in the world to help develop a body of transcultural nursing knowledge and skills that will be the new focus of nursing by the year 2020. The founder's goal that all nurses will someday be prepared and skilled in transcultural nursing remains paramount. This goal is gradually being realized, but considerably more work lies ahead for its full realization. It is an era in which nurses in other countries are beginning to exchange ideas more frequently and with greater enthusiasm than ever in the past.

Future Trends and Challenges in Transcultural Nursing

In looking into the future with the "quo vadis" theme, several predictions of the author and founder of the field will be briefly stated.

First, transcultural nursing will markedly increase worldwide by the end of this century, and nurses will be expected to be knowledgeable about transcultural knowledge and competent to provide culturally congruent and responsible care. By 2020, transcultural nursing will be expected professionally of all nurses and will be the arching framework of nursing. *Nursing will be called transcultural nursing in philosophy and goals by the year 2030!*

Second, clients from different cultures will expect (and some will demand) that their cultural values, beliefs, and lifeways be recognized, respected, and acted upon by nurses and other health personnel who have been prepared in transcultural nursing. The nursing profession will be forced to value fully the early groundwork of transcultural nursing leaders, who were visionary to establish transcultural nursing as an essential area of study and practice in the mid 1950s. The author's concepts of culture-specific care and culturally congruent care will be used universally in nursing education and practice.

Third, certification in transcultural nursing will be required of nurses by the year 2020 in order to protect people so they can receive safe and culturally congruent care. Certification will be valued by consumers and will gradually be recognized in education and clinical settings. Moreover, a master's degree in transcultural nursing will be essential to insure certification and competencies.

Fourth, the concept of human care will continue to be valued and expressed as the distinct, central, and meaningful phenomenon to explain the essence of transcultural nursing. Both universal and diverse care concepts will have been identified largely through the use of the author's theory of Culture Care and ethnonursing research methods to study cultures. The theory is already being viewed as the most comprehensive, holistic, and relevant theory to be used worldwide.[57] Many valuable comparative studies will be established through this theory as well as an assessment guide. Transcultural care skills will be a powerful guide for effective nursing actions and decisions in all areas of nursing education and administration. Transcultural knowledge will diffuse into all practice areas of nursing and to other health professions.

Fifth, nursing research methods that are now largely quantitatively based will be changed to qualitative. The criteria of credibility, confirmability, meaning-in-context, recurrency, and transferability will be used worldwide.[58] Transcultural nursing research will be greatly valued by the year 2020, but many nurse researchers will see the need to be well prepared in qualitative research methods so that they can get the source of culturally-based nursing care with a comparative perspective. Unfortunately, there will not be sufficient numbers of well prepared qualitative faculty and mentors until nearly 2030, and this will limit programs in the field. Quantitative paradigm research will also continue but will not be as fruitful in knowledge generation.

Sixth, many transcultural ethical and moral issues will become evident as nurses conduct transcultural studies with different cultures. To date, limited attention has been given to ethical issues because so few nurses are knowledgeable of what constitutes the ethical issues of a specific culture with respect to culture care and health values, beliefs, and lifeways.

Seventh, there will be a major shift in nursing curricula and in ways of teaching and doing research due to the impact of transcultural nursing education, learning philosophy, and research findings. The need for transcultural nursing curricula with new teaching learning models, and the use of research funding will be extremely important. Transcultural nursing will revolutionize nursing education and practice with changes in teaching, curricula, and research. Most importantly culturally-grounded nursing education theories will be essential to serve students and clients.

Eighth, transcultural health problems related to violence, terrorism, drug abuse, and other serious human conditions will increase. Many new theories and research approaches will be developed by 2010. Anthropological and other comparative social, psychological, and humanistic aspects of cultures will markedly increase by the turn of the century, and will provide rich multidisciplinary participation in research, education, and human services. Competition among disciplines in transcultural health care will occur by the year 2010.

Ninth, transcultural nursing education and research centers and institutes will be in demand by the year 2000. These centers and institutes will be needed to meet scholarly needs of graduate students and for generating some entirely new knowledge of transcultural diversities and universalities. Transcultural comparative research regarding nursing and health care will markedly increase. Private and public funding will be needed to support these institutes, for the public will want better care to clients of diverse cultures. These centers or institutes should have outstanding transcultural nursing scholars and clinicians. They will be rich centers for learning about transcultural human care, health, research, and related phenomena. This is a dream the founder has long hoped for by the year 2000, but it will not occur until the year 2010.

Tenth, transcultural nursing policies will guide quality care practices in education, administration, research, and practice. These policies will need to be established at a national and transnational level to protect vulnerable cultures whose values and ethical models may differ greatly. Both culture-specific and some universal cultural health policies will be established. Transcultural nursing administration will grow and be a major area of study in the future.

Eleventh, legal actions and judgments of diverse cultures related to care, health, and environmental context (the three major areas of nursing) will grow and be led by transcultural nurse experts. A cadre of transcultural nurses will have entered the legal profession to protect the culturally vulnerable citizens of different cultures and to handle transcultural legal cases that will increase worldwide. This trend will again make transcultural nursing a required area for study for all nursing in the twenty-first century.

Twelfth, the shortage of expert transcultural nursing leaders, teachers, researchers, clinicians, and administrators will remain critical until the year 2020. It will greatly influence the forward thrust of nurses and the profession. It will be, however, the new nursing title and arching framework of all areas of nursing education, research, practice, and administration.

These major trends seem inevitable but will require much knowledgeable leadership grounded in transcultural knowledge and intercultural skills. In fact, the future of transcultural nursing will rest largely on culturally competent transcultural nurses in action. With the marked increase in transculturalism, nursing will and has come of age in the public and in many worldwide areas with world travel, high technology, diverse electronic devices, and satellite modes of communication, a new and exciting era will have occurred in the nursing profession and in academia.

*This is a revised and shortened version of the original paper presented earlier at the Transcultural Nursing Society Conference in the mid 1980s and published in *The Journal of Transcultural Nursing*, v. 1, no. 1, Summer, 1989, pp. 33–46. Because of many requests for this article, this version has been made available.

References

1. Leininger, M., *Nursing and Anthropology: Two Worlds to Blend*, New York: John Wiley and Sons, 1970.

2. Leininger, M., *Transcultural Nursing: Concepts, Theories, and Practices*, New York: John Wiley and Sons, 1978.

3. Leininger, M., "Toward Conceptualization of Transcultural Health Care Systems: Concepts and a Model," *Transcultural Health Care Issues and Conditions*, Philadelphia: FA Davis Company, 1976, pp. 3–23.

4. Leininger, M. ed., *Transcultural Nursing*, New York: Masson International Press, 1979.

5. Leininger, op. cit., 1970.

6. Leininger, op. cit., 1978.

7. Leininger, M., "Transcultural Nursing: Its Progress and Its Future," *Nursing and Health Care*, v. 2, 1981a, pp. 365–371.

8. Leininger, M., "Transcultural Nursing: Developments and Issues," *Current Issues in Nursing*, J. McCloskey ed., Boston: Blackwell Publishers, 1985a.

9. Leininger, op. cit., 1978.

10. Leininger, M., "Transcultural Nursing: An Essential Knowledge and Practice Field for Today," *The Canadian Nurse*, v. 80, no. 11, 1984, pp. 41–45.

11. Leininger, M., "Transcultural Nursing: A Different Way to Help People," *Handbook of Cross-Cultural Counseling and Therapy*, P. Peterson ed., Norwalk, Connecticut: Greenwood Press, 1985b, pp. 107–115.

12. Leininger, M., "Transcultural Nursing: A New Focus for Nursing," *Anthropologia Medica*, Italy, 1987, pp. 3–10.

13. Leininger, M., *Caring: An Essential Human Need*, Detroit: Wayne State University, 1981b.

14. Leininger, M., *Care: The Essence of Nursing and Health*, Detroit: Wayne State University, 1988.

15. Leininger, M., "The Transcultural Nursing Specialist: Imperative in Today's World," *Nursing and Health Care*, v. 10, no. 5, 1989, pp. 250–258.

16. Leininger, op. cit., 1978.

17. Leininger, op. cit., 1984.

18. Leininger, M., "Transcultural Care Diversity and Universality: A Theory of Nursing," *Nursing and Health Care*, v. 6, 1985c, pp. 209–272.

19. Leininger, op. cit., 1984.

20. Leininger, op. cit., 1989.

21. Ibid.

22. Leininger, op. cit., 1970.
23. Leininger, op. cit., 1978.
24. Leininger, op. cit., 1970.
25. Leininger, op. cit., 1978.
26. Leininger, op. cit., 1970.
27. Leininger, op. cit., 1976.
28. Leininger, op. cit., 1978.
29. Leininger, op. cit., 1979.
30. Leininger, M., *Qualitative Research Methods in Nursing*, Orlando: Grune and Stratton, 1985d.
31. Leininger, op. cit., 1978.
32. Leininger, op. cit., 1979.
33. Leininger, M., "Importance and Uses of Ethnomethods, Ethnography, and Ethnonursing Research," *Recent Advances in Nursing Series Research Methodology*, M. Cahoon ed., London: Churchill-Livingston, 1986.
34. Tripp-Reimer, T. and M. Dougherty, "Cross-Cultural Nursing Research," *Annual Review of Nursing Research*, v. 3, H. Werley and J. Fitzpatrick eds., New York: Springer, 1985.
35. Leininger, op. cit., 1985d.
36. Ibid.
37. Leininger, op. cit., 1986.
38. Leininger, op. cit., 1970.
39. Leininger, op. cit., 1978.
40. Aamodt, A., S. Grassl-Herwhe, F. Farrell, and J. Hutter, "The Child's View of Chemically Induced Alopecia," *Care: The Essence of Nursing and Health*, M. Leininger ed., Detroit: Wayne State University Press, 1988, pp 217-233.
41. Boyle, J., "Illness Experiences and the Role of Women in Guatemala," *Proceedings of Eighth Annual Transcultural Nursing Conference*, 1983, pp. 1–19.
42. Glittenberg, J., "An Ethnographic Approach to the Problem of Health Assessment and Program Planning: Project Genesis," *Developing, Teaching and Practicing Transcultural Nursing*, Salt Lake City: University of Utah, 1981.
43. Horn, B., "Transcultural Nursing and Childbearing of the Muckleshoot People," *Transcultural Nursing: Concepts, Theories, and Practices*, M. Leininger ed., New York: John Wiley and Sons, 1978, pp. 223–238.
44. Aamodt, op. cit., 1988.
45. Boyle, op. cit., 1983.
46. Glittenberg, op. cit., 1981.
47. Horn, op. cit., 1978.

48. Leininger, op. cit., 1978.

49. Leininger, op. cit., 1979.

50. Leininger, op. cit., 1985a.

51. Ray, M., *A Study of Caring Within an Institutional Culture*, (unpublished doctoral dissertation) Salt Lake City: University of Utah, 1981.

52. Chrisman, N., "Anthropology in Nursing: An Exploration of Adaptation," *Clinically Applied Anthropology*, Chrisman and Maretzk eds., Boston: D. Reidel, 1982, pp. 117–140.

53. Leininger, op. cit., 1979.

54. Leininger, op. cit., 1981a.

55. Leininger, M., *Survey of Schools of Nursing Offering Transcultural Nursing*, Salt Lake City: University of Utah, 1980.

56. Ray, op. cit., 1981.

57. Leininger, M., *Culture Care Diversity and Universality: A Theory of Nursing*, New York: National League for Nursing Press, 1991.

58. Ibid.

Chapter 30

The Future of Transcultural Nursing: The Global Perspective

Madeleine Leininger, PhD, LHD, DS, FAAN, CTN, RN.

Like an eagle spreading its wings and soaring upward and outward to unknown places, so nursing will be soaring to many places in the world in the twenty-first century to become transcultural nursing. The next century will be known as the *Era of Globalization*, in which nurses will fully realize that the profession must be viewed as one world with many diverse cultures linked together with some common professional interest, knowledge, and goals. Transcultural nurses and others prepared in transcultural nursing will be expected to give leadership to many nurses in order to serve people in culturally competent ways. The world will continue to be intensely multicultural and many health professionals will scurry to learn about different cultures and how to function in culturally responsible and effective ways. By the year 2020, the author *contends that all health care must be transculturally based, in order to serve people appropriately from many different cultures in the world*. But the reality will be that there will be far too few nurses prepared to function as effective practitioners, researchers, clinicians, and teachers in transcultural nursing. A major crisis will prevail as consumers of diverse cultures make demands of health professionals for meaningful and competent care in a changing multicultural world.

With the globalization of transcultural nursing in the next century, the nursing profession will gradually be transformed from the past largely unicultural, biomedical, and mind-body emphasis to a transcultural comparative multicultural caring and curing focus to prevent illness and disabilities and to maintain the health and well-being of people. This transformation will require considerably work with shared and cooperative interests among health professions. It will require a much broader perspective to understand the meaning and values of transculturalism and to make appropriate decisions. In contrast to other health professions, nursing will have had a head start in transculturalism with several decades of research, teaching, and practice. By the year 2020, many nurses will have realized the critical importance of transcultural nursing and will build upon existing knowledge and practices. The transformation process will require many changes in education and service. Nurses will, however, meet the challenge and provide culturally competent caring practices with some new teaching and research modes. Nurses will value this statement: to know, understand, and serve people holistically from a transcultural nursing perspective will be the most meaningful professional experience to nurses, but it will be even more meaningful to consumers as recipients of transcultural nursing practices.

Transforming nursing into transculturally based practice will require master and doctoral educational preparation with research and field experiences. Nurses will learn how to be effective primary, secondary, and tertiary advanced care practitioners in many different community-work contexts. Most of all nurses will be *facilitators* of care and establish different ways to function creatively in educational, hospital, and many new kinds of community settings. Graduate nursing education will be required of nurses by the year 2020 to meet consumer expectations and new ways of providing care in different communities. Identifying cultural patterns of clients and health centers for many different cultures will challenge nurses to use a wide range of selected knowledge from the health professions, humanities, and different disciplines. Nurses will, however, remain active learners from consumers to generate relevant care decisions and actions. Most importantly, nurses will develop creative strategies to advance health care to people of diverse cultures. Changing past policies and administrative practice in education and service, to transcultural ones will be one of the greatest challenges. In addition, there will be far more emphasis on multidisciplinary cooperation than competition among health disciplines to build new kinds of practice.

Nurses already prepared in transcultural nursing will be able to demonstrate comparative transcultural caring skills and strategies. Listening, reflecting, and planning with health disciplines and with consumers will be a dominant mode in the next century. Maintaining an open learning attitude and remaining alert to emic and etic cultural data will be important as well as demonstrating the values and benefits of transcultural caring practices with individuals, families, groups, and communities. Nurses will value learning from informants of different cultures living in different ecological environments. From the nurses' ongoing relationship with specific cultures, entirely new insights and ways to care for and with clients will be discovered contributing to the existing body of transcultural multidisciplinary knowledge.

General Changes in Nursing

The twentieth century will be an especially challenging era as nurses learn how to function in multifaceted organizational structures in different communities and institutions. Nurses will be challenged to practice effectively transcultural nursing in education, clinical settings, and consultation. Nurses will shift from largely illness treatment modes to that of wellness using creative caring maintenance health practices. Globalization of transcultural nursing with comparative knowledge in all areas of nursing will lead to many rewards in nursing. It will be a dream come true for many nurses who have been pioneers of transcultural nursing.

There will be major changes in all areas of nursing. The major changes will be from hospital to community nursing services with new alternative health care centers. Transforming nurses to use transcultural nursing perspectives and practices in community settings will be the major challenge. This will include knowing and understanding the cultural patterns, values, and lifeways of people of diverse environmental and community settings. Nurses will be expected to assess and use a holistic transcultural caring focus that promotes the health and well-being of people. Identifying and using specific caring factors influencing the client's or group's health and well-being within diverse ecological and community settings will be essential. Different communities will expect nurses and other health professionals to be knowledgeable about cultures and also the environments in which they live, work, functions, and enjoy leisure time. What constitutes illness prevention and health maintenance in different environments with different cultures and subcultures will be important. Past narrow and fragmented medical views of clients will be inadequate and limitedly used. Professional nurses of the future will, therefore, need to be highly knowledgeable about ways to use political, economic, kinship, religious (or spiritual) cultural values and education factors that influence health and well-being of clients in community contexts. Such knowledge will enable the nurse to make appropriate and meaningful decisions with consumers in preventing illnesses, disabilities, and other threats to people well-being.

By the year 2020 migrations of people from many different cultures and countries will increase ten-fold. It will be difficult to determine who represents a cultural minority or majority with such changing populations and frequent resettlement patterns. There will be major migration of people from Southeast Asia and the Pacific Islands to the United States and Canada. Nurses with limited knowledge of these cultures such as the Indonesians, Thais, Malaysians, Fijians, Ponapeans, Guamians, Marshalese, and other will be handicapped in their work. The increased number of Koreans, Chinese, Japanese, Thais, Indonesians, New Zealanders, Australians and others with their different languages will be especially difficult for many United States and Canada nurses to work with due to language and cultural differences. One can predict there will be fewer immigrants from Europe to the United States in the next century. Such population and migration shifts will make nurses realize the dynamic nature of cultures. It will also be difficult to maintain census tracts or demographic data as population shifts will be continuously and frequently changing. Nursing will need to adapt to such global changes wherever they work and live, but especially in relation to different cultural groups entering and leaving their countries or local communities.

Transcultural agencies will be established as information centers to help people become aware of cultural and population changes. There will be centers to assist people with language differences with general and basic information about specific cultures. Transcultural nursing data will be available as orientation data to help nurses adjust to cultural changes. Professional nurses will be expected to learn about and use general transcultural nursing concepts and principles as presented in this book in order to develop appropriate actions with clients. Most nurses will find such knowledge extremely helpful. Many nurses will be handicapped and frustrated in care practices due to language barriers and insufficient cultural knowledge and skills to assist people of different cultures.

Let us look further to other changes which can be predicted that will require nurses to be culturally sensitive, competent, and responsible to function in the next century. There will be many new micro and macro electronic devices that provide interpersonal communication modes with diverse cultures worldwide. Nurses and clients will be active users of these different electronic devices. Clients will, however, still expect presence and direct interaction time with nurses. The presence of the nurse will remain essential for transcultural caring and to support a nurse-client trusting relationship along with the use of electronic communication equipment in client homes, nursing centers, hospitals, clinics, and other kinds of health care settings. Most consumers will welcome modern electronic equipment, but there will be some cultures who will fear high-powered technologies as spirit intruders in communication, caring, and treatment. For clients who fear or question modern technologies, they may avoid them as magical and dangerous devices with negative consequences. It will be important for nurses to be alert to such cultural differences in response to modern technologies and the use of unfamiliar equipment. For without such cultural understanding, the client's recovery process may be thwarted with unfavorable consequences.

In the future, as nurses travel to many known or unknown countries to work and live, they will see cultural groups who live in marked poverty, while others live in wealth in their special environment. Seeing and experiencing the cultures of poverty and affluence in the same city will be difficult for some nurses to understand. Cultural shock and discontent by nurses will be a stimulus to help clients in poverty or to help the wealthy share resources with the poor. How to repattern different lifeways that will promote wellness and satisfaction will require knowledge of culture values and social structure. In many non-Western cultures, group care or group culture care will be more important than individual or self-care practices. Moreover in the United States, Canada, and Europe with an increase of age span, group care will also be important in health care. *Other-directed* group and family care will be far more important than self or individualized care to reach many elderly people.

Knowing how to do community cultural assessments will be essential in order to promote and maintain the well-being and health of people within different rural and urban communities. Culturalogical assessments of institutions will remain important to establish meaningful hospital policies and predict trends, but the focus on *communities with diverse cultures will be the major emphasis in assessments and care practices.* Cooperative working partnerships and sharing of community resources will require nurses to be open and creative political, social, and cultural entrepreneurs. Indeed, community nursing practices by the year 2020 will be remarkably different than today because of interagency and interdisciplinary cooperative plans and better use of physical and human resources. Transcultural nurses will be highly valued in helping to make community changes. These trends will also impact on physicians, social workers, physical and occupational therapists, pharmacists, and other health professionals as they struggle to learn about and change to view health care as a global phenomenon. Transcultural nurse specialists already prepared in formal academic programs will be much needed to help other nurses and colleagues to grasp this worldview of health care. Computer programs, textbooks, and articles from transcultural nursing and anthropology will be in high demand as well as short- and long-term educational programs.

Many ethical and moral problems will arise due to cultural value conflicts and clashes as nurses function in different world cultures. Transcultural ethicists will increase in numbers and lawyers will remain interested in ethical problems but be poorly prepared to deal with them in legal ways. Accordingly, many self-proclaimed pseudo and minority transcultural experts will become evident. These proclaimed experts with virtually no preparation in transculturalism will lead to many problems and should be avoided as consultants or negotiators. Clients and institutions will need to be protected from such pseudo-commercially oriented people. Only staff prepared in transcultural health care can assure competent and safe care to people of diverse cultures. Alternative health care clinics will markedly increase.

Undoubtedly with the rapid trend in transculturalism, there will be nonprofessional staff and academic personnel in health resource and education institutions. One can predict more medical anthropologists will have entered hospitals and communities. Some of these anthropologists can be helpful to assess cultures and to educate health personnel about cultures. They will probably be less helpful to assist with specific culture care and health needs of clients because of lack of professional health knowledge and skills. There will also be linguists and many electronic language computer experts eager to help health personnel with communication problems of clients and staff. In addition there will be many multidisciplinary colleagues trying to conduct research related to transcultural health care but who have limited understanding of cultural and health care phenomenon.

With the increased emphasis on transcultural skills in service community settings, nurse administrators will scramble to become prepared in transcultural nursing and to learn about culturally based management modes effective for cultures. Nurse administrators and service managers will be the least prepared for transcultural changes in the twenty-first century and they will experience a variety of staff-client clashes, racial conflicts, legal suits and other problems.

For several decades transcultural nursing experts will be few in number to meet consumer needs. Nursing service will be extremely important to facilitate quality care that is tailored to fit clients' cultural needs. These nurses will also be dependent upon the use of ethnonursing, ethnography, narratives, and oral and written life histories to guide nursing decisions and actions. Diverse qualitative methods will be much in demand in the next century. These methods will largely replace the use of traditional quantitative research methods that provide limited meaningful data to understand, humanistic and culturally-based nursing care.

Unfortunately the twenty-first century will not see a decrease in violence, crimes, and overt terrorist acts because of intercultural misunderstandings, biases, and racial accusations among different subcultures and major cultures. In fact, violence will increase in homes, hospitals, schools, workplaces and in other work places due to marked differences in people's cultural beliefs, values, and action modes. Transcultural care principles and practices with intergroup skills will be helpful to prevent acts of violence and cultural clashes. The current trend of relying on psychological and physical causes will be insufficient, for cultural and social factors will give new explanatory insights. Understanding the cultural lifeways of how families and groups value, believe, and experience life in their home and work place will be important to reduce violence.

In the future, worldwide media will be used extensively in many places as a powerful means to learn about cultural behavior and action modalities. Educational public media should become a major means to learn about diverse cultures but to also learn how to prevent serious conflicts, illnesses, or problems among cultures. Transcultural nurse specialists and generalists will need to be active media specialists to inform the public along with health anthropologists. The role of cultural factors as major influencers of illnesses, violence, health, and death will at least become recognized by the public. Far more intercultural stresses and conflicts will be discussed in the media in the next century than with the present day emphasis on biomedical diseases with dramatic surgeries and medications. Nurses prepared in transculturalism, anthropology, and in comparative cultural life expressions will be able to help clients, staff, and the public understand the importance of transcultural health care and ways to maintain health within culturally based perspectives.

By the year 2010 nurses will realize the critical need for transcultural nursing and will begin to draw upon all available knowledge, especially basic concepts, principles, and theories that have been developed by transcultural experts in the twentieth century.[1,2,3,4,5,6] This knowledge along with current research discoveries will help nurses learn different ways to care for clients. Granted some nurses will try to reinvent transcultural nursing by giving it another name or will try to ignore existing knowledge, but most nurses will reaffirm the significant work in the twentieth century and will build upon that knowledge base with added new discoveries. (The three transcultural nursing eras discussed in chapter twenty-nine should be reviewed to give an overview of the historical knowledge and research developments in transcultural nursing since the mid 1950s.)

More and more the theory of Culture Care Diversity and Universality will be used worldwide because it will be found to be practical, relevant, and the most specific and comprehensive theory to discover cultural data. The theoretical framework and the Sunrise Model will be extensively used for mini- and maxi-culturalogic studies and assessments of people. Likewise, the ethnonursing research method will be valued and used with the Culture Care Theory and with other theories to discover complex and yet overt data about cultures.

Several current nursing theories will become extinct because they will be proven to be inadequate to discover and explain cultural lifeways and other nursing phenomena related to human care, health, and environmental contexts—the major foci of nursing for the twenty-first century.

Some Specific Changes in Nursing Education and Practice

As transcultural nursing becomes the central and arching framework for all aspects of nursing, a number of major changes in nursing education and practice that are barely known today will occur. Providing culturally congruent, sensitive, and responsible care will have a high priority in most worldwide health care reforms in education and service settings.[7] Most importantly, transcultural nursing education will be viewed as essential to all areas of nursing and to have well-prepared faculty. The toughest change in nursing will be with nurses who have become so medicalized and focused on diseases, symptoms, and treatment modes, that they will neglect to consider the client's culture. Faculty thinking will need to shift to social structure, worldview, and environmental factors that influence clients' lifeways and health status. While nurses will use some medical science knowledge, they will need to place such knowledge within a holistic cultural perspective.

By the year 2020 nursing will be practiced in different ways. Nurses will no longer be studying and practicing in traditional areas such as medical-surgical, psychiatric, maternal-child, orthopedic, oncology, and nearly twenty other medically-based specialties. Instead, nurses will be using research-based knowledge and skills which are focused on new knowledge largely related to *life span and lifestyle* phenomenon. Culture care and health will be emphasized throughout the life span with in-depth focus on particular cultures such as Greeks, Native Americans, African Americans, Haitians, Hispanics and other cultures worldwide. *Comparative life cycle maintenance and illness prevention for children, middlescents, and adults will be major areas of focus.* Environmental and ecological community care, institutional culture care, rural-urban care, and along with a few specialty areas will be the other foci. Nurses prepared less than two decades ago will be outdated unless they have learned new knowledge and skills in new nursing areas. Most assuredly, nurses will be working with many immigrant and non-immigrant families, groups, and cultures in specific community contexts. Refugees, the homeless, the poor, the affluent, gays, lesbians, abused women, men, and children will all be part of the new profession of transcultural nursing. Keeping people well and preventing unfavorable life-threatening human and environmental conditions will be a major responsibility of professional nurses in the future. Nurses will see the tremendous value of using transcultural comparative and holistic knowledge as they work with people in their homes, communities, and work places. The impact of social structure and environmental factors on health care outcomes will be far more fully valued and understood than it is today.

Many nurse educators will be expected to change their teaching content and curricula approaches from mainly the biomedical, pathological, psychological, and physical science focus of the past century to emphases on holistic care and especially the influence of sociocultural and environmental factors. A "new transcultural comparative nursing curricula" will give emphasis to learning about complex and diverse cultures with respect to their life cycle patterns, nutritional needs, caring and health patterns, community values, folk and professional beliefs and values, and the ethnohistorical and social structure factors influence health and well-being. Teaching will mainly include different ways to *prevent illnesses, accidents, violence, and death within a cultural community context.* Transcultural nursing instruction will become highly innovative. Faculty will be challenged to use in-depth comparative knowledge of several cultures with creative teaching approaches. Faculty who are creative, flexible, and open-minded and have limited cultural biases will be desired teachers and researchers. Most importantly, faculty teaching transcultural nursing will develop many new kinds of learning experiences for students and design some entirely new ways of teaching and learning about cultural phenomena and transcultural care.

In the next century nurses will be deeply involved in ethical, moral, and legal issues as they work with clients of different cultures. Religious and spiritual beliefs, philosophy of life, and ethical values of different cultures will challenge nurses to understand *why* cultures have their unique or specific moral perspectives. Nurses will reflect upon their own moral and ethical beliefs and values in teaching and clinical mentoring. Comparative cultural ethical theories will be in great demand for master, doctoral, and post-doctoral nursing students and faculty. Transcultural academic and clinical ethics will be major areas of research. Unquestionably, legal cases will markedly increase and lead many nurses to take courses in law to protect themselves and to help them understand their work. There will be many lawyers, but few will be prepared in transcultural law. This will greatly thwart obtaining just and favorable legal decisions and outcomes for nurses and clients.

By the year 2030 transcultural nurse specialists and generalists will have a body of research knowledge and skills that can serve as foundational "holding knowledge" to help nurses function in different cultural areas of the world, such as the Middle East, Europe, Africa, Indonesia, Southeast Asia, South America, the Caribbean, North America, South America, and the Pacific Islands (Oceania). This holding knowledge will serve as a reflective base to respond appropriately to the people and to build new knowledge. Major cultural areas will be the focus of nursing curricula in the future rather than the past medical model symptom and disease categories and treatment areas. Nurse specialists will especially draw upon knowledge from fields such as anthropology, arts and humanities, ecology, space science, linguistics, communication, and history for dynamic curricular content and changes related to the major cultural areas in the world. Some schools will specialize in related cultural areas such as Africa and Southeast Asia.

Nurses will not be expected to know everything, nor to be skilled in every area. Instead, nurses will draw upon some transcultural or universal concepts, principles, and research-based knowledge that is relevant to the cultural and environmental context of peoples being cared for in different places in the world. The author's concepts of culture-specific and culturally congruent or relevant will guide nurses in achieving knowledge and competencies.[8] Already several transcultural nurse experts are using culture-specific models, particularly in their teaching and research. Transcultural specialists will be prepared in master, doctoral, and post-doctoral nursing programs in the future. As the author has predicted for some time, undergraduate nursing programs will largely disappear as nurses realize the need for graduate preparation to function in a complex and diverse cultural world. This is already becoming a reality in 1994. Transcultural nursing will remain essential and a worldwide imperative largely taught in graduate nursing programs.[9,10] Baccalaureate students today will use transcultural knowledge to assist in their practices but also for preparation for graduate studies. Nurses in graduate programs will demonstrate the usefulness of research and theory to understand how to give culturally competent care. Post-doctoral programs will become a necessity for nursing faculty and staff who have never had formal research and theory courses in transcultural nursing. In the United States this would be approximately 92% of nurses prepared in 57 doctoral programs in 1994 as most nurses have not had formal preparation in transcultural nursing.[11] The percentage would be even higher in other countries where there are very few transcultural nurse programs and faculty.

In the future transcultural nursing will be based upon what I call *partnership care* with active participation of nurses with clients. This means nurses will work closely with groups and individuals to discover, understand, and find meanings in the way people believe they can best keep well and function together in their particular culture or environment. The nurse will form a partnership with individuals or groups in a culture to work together over time. In so doing, they build trust and friendly relationships focused on understanding care modalities to support wellness or health. With partnership care, clients and the nurse discover together and identify ways to maintain health and to be helpful to the client over an extended period of time. The goal of the partnership care is to establish a quality of life that is culturally congruent taking into consideration the client's human conditions and desired healthy lifestyle. Partnership care involves mutual trust, learning, cooperative interests and action modes. It constitutes a culturally holistic approach to people care rather than a "band aid," "fix it," or short-term approach with specific disease and illness conditions.

Still another major area for transcultural nursing study and practice will be a focus on urban, suburban, and rural community care practices and needs. Urban-rural community areas will be essential to understand to prevent or reduce crime. Understanding differences and similarities between rural and urban living will be important as client's move between these two areas and to discover different modes of living. Understanding violence, prejudices, crime, conflicts, strains, and lifeways will require nurses to have a comprehensive knowledge of differences and similarities between rural and urban communities. This knowledge is important because many immigrants are coming into or leaving rural or peasant communities and suddenly living in a large urban area where crime and social ills exist. Discussions of ways to care for or with people will best occur with the concept of partnership care in rural and urban settings. Forced relocation or displacements of people due to wars and political and economic problems will also require considerable understanding by nurses to help these newcomers adapt to different communities.

Most importantly, community nurses with traditional unicultural practices will need to change to multicultural ways to help people in communities or with aggregate populations. The community as a culture will be the focus, with urban and rural community consideration. Nurses will be responsible for doing culture care assessments and for developing policies and practices that are culturally based. The concept of cultures in communities will provide new insights for nurses to guide their practices. The theory of culture care the use of the Sunrise Model can be a big help to nurses in identifying diverse cultures in a given community and how to discover outside influencers on specific cultures and the larger community. Political, economic, educational, technological, and other related social structure factors along with the ethnohistory will be essential to assess communities of diverse or similar cultures. Transcultural nurse specialists can be helpful to nurses who are shifting from the old to the new community partnership caring focus.

Some communities with dominant or multiple cultures will challenge nurses to know and understand their care values and beliefs within the culture context. For example, for Western nurses to assess and help people in India who live and function in relation to the Ganges River would be a challenge. In India the Ganges River is sacred, but it is also used for washing, burying the dead, and for drinking. Knowledge of the Hindu religion will be essential to understand this culture and to develop strategies for working effectively with the Hindus. Any sanitation measures related to improving physical health would need to be considered within their strong religious and cultural values and rituals. Still another example to challenge community based nursing is to understand communities of starving people in the world who are cut off from food supplies due to tribal wars or feuds, political conflicts, economic greed, or religious intolerance. Nurses will need transcultural knowledge related to cultural values, ethnohistorical factors, religious, economic, agricultural, and other social structure factors. Such transcultural knowledge dimensions will enable nurses to be effective in community and institutional decisions.

The above predictions by the author as well as writings by Naisbett,[12] Toffler,[13] and Theobald[14] will greatly influence health and nursing care practices in the future. Terrorism and other forms of violence will lead to critical emergency care given by nurses in disaster areas. The nurse will be expected to understand complex crises-oriented, transcultural political conflict situations. Major changes in the Republic of South Africa, the Middle East, and other places in the world make nurses realize the need for understanding people first in order to insure congruent care and well-being. Transcultural nurses will also help international business corporations as they also shift to a transcultural perspective in selling their products to cultural strangers. Most business executives will have limited cultural insights and skills. Some transcultural nurses will probably establish transcultural business nursing centers for overseas immigrants in order to facilitate their entrance into a new country. These transcultural centers will be focused in health maintenance and cultural conflict reduction.

Brief Glimpses of Transcultural Nursing Today and in the Future Worldwide

Since the author predicts that transcultural nursing will become the arching framework and practice for nursing in the twenty-first century, a few glimpses and predictions are in order about transcultural nursing today and in the future. Nurses will remain the largest profession, but they need to move quickly to become effective transcultural nurse practitioners, educators, researchers, and administrators. Globalization of transcultural nursing as a universal phenomenon should encourage all nurses to pursue advanced study in transcultural nursing in order to establish their practice and credibility in different places in the world. Without transcultural nursing knowledge, one can predict that cultural imposition with cultural conflicts will exist within or outside the nurse's work place. The nurse will also need to be aware of cultural backlash and other unfavorable features in transnational endeavors. The uncertainty of human resources and funds to make transcultural nursing a full reality will vary in each country. However, many countries are already moving toward using their human and financial resources to support transcultural nursing education and practices because of intense and multicultural problems. With these general trends, some specific predictions can be identified from the author's extensive travels and worldwide consultation with nursing leaders in different cultures over the past three decades. Leaders and trends in United States have already been presented in earlier chapters.

My first prediction is that Canada, with its strong multicultural society and its diverse native Canadians as first citizens in addition to a steady flow of immigrants throughout its long cultural history will soon initiate specific transcultural nursing educational (graduate) programs to meet nurses' many requests during the past two decades. It is most encouraging that many early Canadian nurse leaders such as Helen Glass, Helen Mussalem, May Yoshida, and Dorothy Froman have been multiculturally focused for many years. With recent Canadian nurses, Cynthia Cameron, Joan MacNeil, and Janet Rosenbaum, who have been prepared in transcultural nursing doctoral programs, they are providing a new kind of leadership but will need graduate transcultural nursing programs to support their endeavors. The Canadian Multicultural Act of 1987 and the work of other professional Canadian nurse leaders and non-nurses are supporting this climate, these goals, and the context for transcultural nursing.[15] Currently, a number of Canadian nurses come to the United States, especially to Wayne State University, to pursue transcultural nursing graduate study. Many of these Canadian nurses are active in transcultural nursing and organizational work. Canadian nurses will hopefully establish transcultural nursing courses and programs to meet their growing demands and needs for multicultural health and nursing practices.

Although transcultural nursing was established as a legitimate, formal area of study and practice in the early 1960s in the United States, some nursing leaders have been extremely slow to value and take steps to develop transcultural nursing education and practice programs. The author believes this has largely occurred because many nurses in the United States tend to be fearful of accusations of racism and discrimination and ideally want to treat everyone alike. Ethnocentrism is also evident among some American nurses. There is also competition among female minority and majority nurse leaders for status and to make claims for what is transcultural as their special idea and views. Political, social, and economic problems of nurse have also limited progress in supporting transcultural nursing in the United States. Only recently have major nursing organizations such as the AAN and the ANA begun to address the need for transcultural nursing and to consider the idea of developing nurses to provide culturally competent care. This latent response was preceded by the author's encouragement of such a focus in the early 1970s. There are also nurse leaders without any formal preparation in transcultural nursing who are attempting to be experts in the field which has limited progress and misled interested nurses.[16] But despite these hurdles the absence of federal funds to support transcultural education and research in transcultural nursing, the author and other colleagues have prepared nearly 10,000 in formal educational programs in transcultural nursing. In addition, a few graduate programs and courses have been established in key locations in the United States. It is the graduates of these programs who are the major leaders preparing other nurses in transcultural nursing and developing new programs where possible. Nursing students' interests remain extremely strong as are the demands by consumers within and outside the United States.

Still another concern is that there are the limited numbers of cultural minorities with graduate preparation neither in transcultural nursing or anthropology who are being placed in key national and local roles as experts in transcultural matters. With inadequately prepared nurses and "pseudo experts" functioning as "experts" in transcultural nursing, students and clinical staff often will be poorly mentored. Many more graduate transcultural nursing programs and courses are needed, as are actual and potential top leaders in nursing. This is urgent now because the United States has one of the largest numbers of immigrants each year. In addition, many immigrants and "minorities" continue to move around for positions or to establish their work. The increasing numbers of Southeast Asians, Japanese, Chinese, Koreans, Cubans, Muslims from Indonesia and the Middle East have made nurses acutely aware of the need for transcultural nursing knowledge and skills. This trend will continue in the United States, with many people coming from Latin America, Africa, Oceania, and Southeast Asia. Unquestionably, transcultural nurses prepared in graduate programs have largely shaped education and practice in the United States. This trend will continue, but many more transcultural nurses are needed to make transcultural nursing a full realization in the United States.

Since my first visit in Hawaii in the early 1950s, I have held that the Pacific Islands, especially Hawaii, were a natural and fertile place for transcultural nursing. In fact, the first transcultural nursing conference was held at the University of Hawaii in 1972. This conference was an overwhelming success because Hawaiians knew how to accommodate strangers and be gracious hostesses and hosts. Their cultural history for the past three centuries has reflected this trend with many explorers, traders, visitors, vacationers, and missionaries. Recently, Dr. Genevieve Kinney became the first native Polynesian transcultural nurse, and she continues to demonstrate outstanding leadership to establish transcultural nursing as the major focus of baccalaureate nursing education on the big island of Hawaii. Since the early 1970s, Hawaii and the Pacific Islands have been moving to make transcultural nursing education and practice a full reality.

Turning to Europe, one finds considerable emphasis is being directed toward the unification of European nurses to work together on future developments of common interest. Europe has had a long-standing tradition of dealing with diverse cultural lifeways. Different political ideologies, economic constraints, and a host of other factors have limited unification and establishing sound and substantive programs in transcultural nursing. Recently a spirit and thrust for unification with the 1992 conference with interest in transcultural education and practice has been observed.[17] While European nurse leaders have long recognized the need to deal with multicultural concerns of diverse cultures within and without their country, there has been limited progress in recognizing the need for formal transcultural nursing education and service programs. There are a few nursing groups and schools of nursing beginning to recognize and use transcultural nursing knowledge in their work. In a few places, anthropological concepts and theories are being taught, but, again, with limited conceptualization of transcultural nursing within a nursing perspective. Because of Europe's long and distinguished nursing history and strong traditional cultural values, one would predict it will take some time and fresh new leadership to establish formal transcultural nursing programs with explicit clinical practices in Europe. Some nurses are making claims of "doing" transcultural nursing (or some version of it) and cite their long colonial experiences in different cultures. However, the transcultural nursing theory and comparative nursing practices remain essentially a new area of formal study and practice yet to be developed in most of Europe.

With the collapse of communism in the late 1980s, many Eastern European countries are just beginning to experience and plan for a new beginning in nursing and health care. Most encouraging is that several nurses, such as Anita van Smitten, in Finland with post-RN education in transcultural nursing are establishing transcultural nursing courses and organizing their nursing programs to incorporate transcultural concepts, principles, and practices with support from United States transcultural nurse leaders.[18] In Russia, Dr. Gelina Perfilijeva is making outstanding strides to lay the foundation for transcultural nursing amid inevitable economic problems. Other nurses in Russia and Eastern Europe are also working to establish similar programs. In the Netherlands and Belgium a few nurses, such as Drs. Abu Saad and George Evers, have given support for transcultural nursing education, research, and practice since the author's first consultation and teaching visits in 1981. Far more specific and diverse graduate or advanced programs are greatly needed in the future to establish transcultural nursing firmly in this multicultural European world.

It is fortunate that in the Republic of South Africa, some doctorally prepared nurse leaders, such as Drs. Hilda Brink, Grace Mashaba, and Philda Nzimande, have been active supporters and leaders of transcultural nursing education, research, and clinical practice for a number of years. These leaders and others in the community have valued transcultural nursing programs and have been teaching and are doing transcultural nursing research in their institutions amid many incredible transcultural political and economic hurdles. These African nurses are to be highly commended for their persistent efforts to teach and do research in transcultural nursing. The first book on transnational or international education has recently been published.[19] With the election in 1994, one can anticipate many new and promising directions bearing on transcultural education and practice in South Africa.

In Papua New Guinea many nurse leaders have already made a firm commitment to transcultural nursing as the only and best approach to their future in nursing education, research, and practice.[20] They hold that all nursing practices must be transcultural nursing in their country. During my visit with the nurses in 1992 it was encouraging to hear nurses express their ideas and plans for transcultural nursing education. With 800 different cultures and 600 dialects in Papua New Guinea, transcultural nursing was held as the only way to provide culture care accommodation, preservation, and repatterning nursing practices. In 1992 nurses were already using the Culture Care Theory because it was the only theory that had relevance to their people. Indigenous nurses were seeking transcultural nursing education as the central focus for their new degree program at the University of Papua New Guinea in Port Moresby. It was encouraging to hear the president of the Papua New Guinea Nursing Association say at a major gathering:

"Transcultural nursing actually began in New Guinea when you [Dr. Leininger] first came to this country to study our people in the early 1960s. It will continue to be the focus of our professional work as it is essential to our people and for effective nursing practices."[21]

The enthusiasm and commitment of Papua New Guinea nurses for transcultural nursing education and practice were noteworthy. This country could well be an excellent example to demonstrate transcultural nursing in all areas of nursing. These nurses held transcultural nursing to be the essential and only promising goal for their nursing future. From the author's three decades of field visits and seeing what has been happening in the country, transcultural nursing seems a highly relevant and most encouraging and appropriate approach nursing focus.

Since the mid 1980s a core of Australian nurses have been active leaders in developing units of instruction and in teaching transcultural nursing. Nurse leaders such as Olga Kanitisaki, Dorothy Angel, Faith Jones, Carol Gaston, Sandra Paech, and Akram Omeri have been persistent, enthusiastic, and nurses committed to incorporating transcultural nursing into institutions of higher education and clinical practice. Some hospitals and health agencies in Sydney and Melbourne have established unique transcultural projects to care for clients from several different cultures. Similar plans are slowly unfolding in New Zealand, especially in relation to transcultural mental health programs and research projects. Hence, the future looks quite promising as nurses move forward in transcultural nursing with funds and government support for this important national goal of multiculturalism.

In Southeast Asia interest in transcultural nursing as a formal area of study and practice has only recently begun to be expressed by a few nurse leaders in Japan, Korea, Thailand, Taiwan, Indonesea, and China. Nurses in this part of the world are learning about transcultural nursing and humanistic caring. Several nurses have expressed their interests in incorporating transcultural concepts and principles with their transnational nursing interests and international visits. To date, only a few schools of nursing are drawing upon the body of knowledge and studying transcultural nursing.

In the Middle East, Dr. Linda Luna, the first American nurse prepared with a Ph.D. focus on transcultural nursing theory, research, and practice, has been conducting research and teaching transcultural nursing at King Faisal General Hospital and Research Center since 1988. She has been working with nurses coming from many different countries as employees in a large clinical, research, and teaching Arabic hospital. Her work with approximately eighty staff nurses, and multidisciplinary personnel from different countries challenges her transcultural skills daily. Dr. Barbara Brown, a former American nursing administrator at this same hospital, was an early advocate of transcultural nursing. She took administrative leadership to help encourage nurses to learn about the use of transcultural nursing concepts, principles and research findings in nursing. During the author's consultation visits and presentations in the Middle East, it was most encouraging to see the nurses' interest in transcultural nursing grow. To date, there are no formal graduate programs in transcultural nursing in the

Middle East, but plans for such education programs are beginning to unfold. In Jordan, under the leadership of Dr. Rowaida Al Ma'aitah, nurses are beginning to develop formal instruction in transcultural nursing. The school has recently established a few educational exchange programs and is conducting annual transnational conferences.

In South American and the Caribbean, the concept of transcultural nursing has been known to several nurses since the mid 1980s. Drs. Gloria Wright, Elouise Neves, Dulce Gualda, and Lucie Gonzales were early supporters of transcultural nursing theories and qualitative research methods. Drs. Jody Glittenberg and Joyceen Boyle were active transcultural nurse researchers in the Caribbean and have conducted some noteworthy transcultural nursing research studies. Dr. Glittenberg's recent book on her research reflects her keen sensitivity and great insight about "her people."[22] A few Brazilian nurses have studied transcultural nursing in the United States with the author and are give in leadership to this field in their homeland. In the future, considerable work is needed to establish courses and programs of study in transcultural nursing and clinical practice areas to meet the changing population in Latin American and Caribbean countries. Nurses working or studying in this part of the world will need to be fluent in the local languages but also draw upon cultural holding knowledge to guide them in their work.

Nursing in New Foundland, Iceland, Prince Edward Island, Alsaka, and other places in the Northern hemisphere is just beginning to draw upon transcultural nursing concepts, theories, and research findings. There are several nurse leaders who are promoting the importance of transcultural nurses and human caring as they work in these countries with immigrants from within and without this region.

There are other places in the world where transcultural nursing leaders and followers are learning about and taking steps to incorporate transcultural nursing into nursing education and research. The Journal of Transcultural Nursing, as the official Journal of the Transcultural Nursing Society, continues to help many nurses in the world learn about transcultural nursing research findings and educational content. It is always encouraging and rewarding to learn how nurses in many different countries have become almost self-educated because there have been no leaders and programs in transcultural nursing. Nurses' sincere and genuine interest in this area is highly commendable as are their future plans and goals to incorporate transcultural nursing into their traditional and current nursing curricula and clinical practices.

Transculturally, there is an urgent need to establish graduate programs, centers, and institutes in transcultural nursing to meet worldwide education and research demands. Currently, the major graduate programs or courses to prepare transcultural nurses (or similar variants) are at Wayne State University (Detroit), the University of Washington (Seattle), the University of Florida (Miami), Emory University (Atlanta), and the University of California (San Francisco and Los Angeles). Student requests worldwide for graduate programs in other countries remain constant. Present transcultural nurse experts tend to be in constant demand for consultation, teaching, clinical work and research and to conduct workshops. These experts are also in demand to redesign nursing curricula from a unicultural to multicultural perspective, to participate in interdisciplinary research projects and seminars, and serve as consultants in service, education, and research institutions. Many more leaders in transcultural nursing will be needed to meet the critical shortage and demand for transcultural specialists and generalists in all areas of nursing education and practice.

Strategic Planning: Essential for the Future of Transcultural Nursing

In the future, strategic planning for the twenty-first century is imperative so that transcultural nursing education, research, consultation, clinical services, and administrative leadership will continue to meet the global needs of clients, students, and staff nurses as well as those of general academic and health care institutions. Strategic planning has been initiated by Dr. Margaret Andrews former President of the Transcultural Nursing Society. In addition, some faculty in schools of nursing are doing strategic planning to meet short- and long-range goals in their region or country. The greatest and most urgent strategic planning is with schools of nursing to prepare faculty to teach a new generation of students in transcultural nursing. Graduate programs are needed as well as some institutes and centers for advanced study and research programs in this area. Transcultural nursing faculty are much needed to teach and mentor students as they learn from cultural groups and individuals in practically every place in the world. Most urgently needed are nurses with graduate (master and doctoral) preparation: 1) to mentor a growing number of graduate nursing students in education, research, and consultation; 2) to conduct sound, comparative transcultural nursing research studies; 3) to develop new transcultural nursing curricula and establish centers and institutes; 4) to obtain federal and private funds to advance transcultural nursing education, research, and practice models; 5) to help nursing students and faculty become clinically competent in the use of transcultural nursing concepts, principles, and competencies; 6) to design ways to incorporate folk emic knowledge appropriately with professional etic knowledge and skills; 7) to develop collaborative projects (research and educational exchanges) through the Transcultural Nursing Society and with other organizations; 8) to develop worldwide consultation outreach field service stations to help nurses practice transcultural nursing with research teams; 9) to encourage professional nursing organizations to incorporate transcultural nursing in their work; and 10) to develop interdisciplinary and multidisciplinary comparative research, education, and practice models worldwide.

Since 1988 the Transcultural Nursing Society has been certifying nurses in order to protect the public with safe, competent, and effective transcultural nursing care. In addition, some nurses have operated Information Hot Line Telephone Service for several years to assist clinical staff in dealing with intercultural client-staff problems. The demand for such telephone assistance has steadily increased, so that many calls are received daily not only to help nurses but also to prevent serious consequences for clients, and to avoid unnecessary and costly legal suits. Internet and other telephone and computer communication modes need to be greatly expanded worldwide. Such strategic communication modes would help many nurses in providing culturally responsible care. Another urgent strategy is to get funds to educate faculty, undergraduate and graduate students, and to develop some action-research community projects. To date, transcultural nurses have received very limited funds for their research and educational endeavors in the United States. Nurses remain concerned with similar needs to help them advance transcultural nursing education. These needs should get on the public agenda soon.

Still another concern is to help faculty learn about transcultural comparative ethics in all aspects of nursing. There are also a host of moral and ethical problems related to transcultural nursing that need to be studied, as presented in an early chapter in this book. Research on nursing diagnosis, cultural imposition, cultural conflicts, and negative consequences of care merit ethical and general study. An interdisciplinary and multidisciplinary focus with anthropologists, nurses, philosophers, ethicists, and others would also be stimulating and beneficial. Major ethical conflicts with nurses and clients of different cultural values await study by transcultural nursing researchers.

A final strategic plan is to work with nursing administrators in education and service to make transcultural nursing the prevailing focus of their education goals and management practices. Nursing administrators need preparation in transcultural nursing so that they can be more responsible, skilled and understanding of student and client needs. They also need to unlock human and financial resources for quality transcultural nursing education and service programs. Transculturally prepared nurse administrators could be most helpful by establishing policies and practices that are appropriate to specific institutional cultural contexts and policy practices.

In sum, there is a slow and steady transformation occurring in the health field as transcultural nursing education and practice come into full reality worldwide. Transcultural nursing research and education have been soundly established, but considerably more work needs to be done to actively apply available knowledge in practices and in different contexts. Helping nurses to develop competency skills in people care has a high priority as the movement continues to grow and expand.

Developing culturally competent and responsible nurse practitioners through formal education programs has been the missing dimension since the beginning of nursing. This deficit must be remedied soon to prevent major global problems, cultural conflicts and violence in nursing, health care and educational settings. The profession is being helped by transcultural nursing and human caring experts in teaching and research, but many more nurses are needed. Most assuredly, transcultural nursing has markedly expanded nurses' research, intellectual, professional, and clinical interests. Nurses are gaining a new or different appreciation for human diversity and similarities and developing a deeper understanding of their own and other cultural heritages, values, and lifeways with potential influence on people care and students. The World Health Organization's dictum of "Health Care for All" was promoted in the late 1970s. The author contends this goal can never be fully realized until nurses are knowledgeable and skilled in transcultural knowledge. For health care is culturally constituted and the critical factor to attain and maintain wellness or reasonable health is transcultural knowledge. When transcultural nursing becomes integrated into staff's and people's lifeways, only then will we see signs of "health care for all."

A small cadre of transcultural nurse leaders and followers have been incredibly persistent and creative leaders since the mid 1950s working to develop knowledge, teach students, and practice transcultural nursing. Their pioneering work has been a significant development in nursing in the twentieth century which will have even greater significance in the next century. Transcultural nursing has opened the door of hope for many immigrants, refugees, underrepresented cultures, the culturally oppressed, neglected, and unknown groups. Transcultural nursing has provided some of the most innovative ways of knowing, teaching, and practicing nursing. Its leaders have developed theories and research methods to guide many nurses into the path of transcultural nursing. A substantive body of transcultural nursing knowledge has been established to guide nurses to provide culturally congruent and meaningful care to people. Such developments are highly laudatory and significant. Transcultural nurses have taken leadership steps where many nurses have feared or neglected to tread. The impact of their work is evident in many nursing educational and service institutions. As more nurses are prepared in transcultural nursing, one can anticipate even greater benefits and a new ethos in nursing.

The founder's concluding thought for readers of this book is that the past thirty-five years have laid a sound foundation for transcultural nursing education, research, and practice. It is now urgent to launch worldwide transcultural nursing and health care programs. In the past it was an incredible challenge for transcultural nurse leaders to establish new pathways and goals in nursing. The next generation of nurses must carry this "Olympic Torch" to many lands and be persistent and committed to have the torch touch many nurses, consumers, and health care providers. When this occurs, nursing and other health professions will have attained a truly global and meaningful health care approach to human beings.

References

1. Leininger, M., Transcultural Nursing: Concepts, Theories, and Practices, New York: John Wiley and Sons, 1978. (Reprint, Columbus, Ohio: Greyden Press, 1994.)
2. Leininger, M., Nursing and Anthropology: Two Worlds to Blend, New York; John Wiley and Sons, 1970. (Reprint, Columbus, Ohio: Greyden Press, 1994.)
3. Leininger, op. cit., 1978.
4. Leininger, M., Culture Care Diversity and Universality: A Theory of Nursing, New York: National League for Nursing Press, 1991.
5. Boyle, J. and M. Andrews, Transcultural Concepts in Nursing Care, Glenview, Illinois: Scott, Foresman, 1989.
6. Dobson, S., Transcultural Nursing: A Contemporary Imperative, London: Scutari Press, 1991.
7. Leininger, op. cit., 1991
8. Leininger, M., "Transcultural Nursing Education: A Worldwide Imperative," Nursing and Health Care, v. 15, no. 5, May, 1994, pp. 254–257.
9. Leininger, M., "Transcultural Nursing: An Essential Knowledge and Practice Field for Today," The Canadian Nurse, v. 80, no. 11, 1984, pp. 41–45.
10. Leininger, op. cit., 1994.
11. Leininger, M., Transcultural Nursing in Graduate Programs in the United States, unpublished survey, Detroit: Wayne State University, 1993.
12. Naisbett, J., Megatrends, New York: Warner Books, Inc., 1982.
13. Toffler, A., The Third Wave, New York: Bantam Books, 1980.
14. Theobald, R., The Rapids of Change: Social Entrepreneurship in Turbulent Times, Indianapolis: Knowledge Systems, Inc., 1987.
15. *Multiculturalism Policy of Canada Act*, Ministry of Health, Ontario, Canada, 1987.
16. Leininger, M., "Rebuttal Excerpts on AAN Culturally Congruent Care Report," *Journal of Transcultural Nursing*, v. 1, no. 4, 1993, pp. 44–48.
17. *European Nursing Congress*, Amsterdam, The Netherlands, personal communication, October 10–14, 1992.
18. *Personal Visits in Finland*, 1987–1992.
19. Mashaba, T. and H. Brink, *Nursing Education: An International Perspective*, Ndabini Cape, South Africa: Juta and Co., Ltd., The Rustica Press, 1994.
20. Maiasa, S., *Introductory Comments to Dr. Leininger for the Papua New Guinea Nurses Association*, personal communication, July 1992, Port Moresby.
21. Ibid.
22. Glittenberg, J., *To the Mountain and Back: The Mysteries of Guatemalan Highland Family Life*, Prospect Heights, Illinois: Waveland Press, Inc., 1994.

Index